TELEVISION
PRODUCTION

TELEVISION PRODUCTION

RON WHITTAKER

Pepperdine University

Mayfield Publishing Company
Mountain View, California
London ● Toronto

Library of Congress Cataloging-in-Publication Data

Whittaker, Ron.
    Television production / Ron Whittaker.
       p. cm.
    Includes bibliographical references (p.   ) and index.
    ISBN 1-55934-020-7
    1. Television — Equipment and supplies. 2. Television — Production
and direction. I. title.
TK6650.W45 1992
791.45 — dc20   92-16005
                                             CIP

Manufactured in the United States of America

10 9 8 7 6 5 4 3 2 1

Mayfield Publishing Company
1240 Villa Street
Mountain View, California 94041

Sponsoring Editor, Lansing Hays; production editor, Sharon Montooth; copyeditor, Nicholas Murray; text designer, Jean Mailander; cover designer, Jeanne M. Schreiber; cover art, © Ken Fabrick, 1992; art coordinator, Robin Mouat; illustrators, Susan Breitbard, Carolla Iannone, and Joan Carol. The text was set in 10.5/12 Times Roman by Thompson Type and printed by Arcata Graphics.

Photo credits: The majority of the photos are by the author. Additional photos were provided by: *Aerospatiale;* Air Products and Chemicals, Inc.; *AKG;* Amway Corp.; Andrew Corporation (Bernard J. Surtz); Band ProFilm/Video Inc.; Boeing Corp.; Canon USA; Century Precision Optics; *Cinema Products;* CNN; Colortran; Conus Communications; Denny Mfg. Co., Inc.; *Dynatec;* Echolab Inc.; *EMC²;* Grass Valley Group; Griffolyn; Hitachi Denshi America, Ltd.; Hubbard Communications; Kurta Corporation, Phoenix (IS/ADB Graphics Tablet); Lowel-Light Mfg.; Lynx Video Ltd.; Micro-Trac Corp.; Miller Fluid Heads (USA) Inc.; NCR Corporation, Stakeholder Relations Div.; NEC America/Broadcast Equipment Div.; *Newstar;* Nikon Electronic Imaging; Nurad; Panasonic Broadcast (Division of Matsushita Electronic Corp. of America); Panasonic Industrial Company AV Systems; Panther Corp. of America; Pepperdine (University) Sports Information; Pioneer Electronics; Pixar; Porta-Pattern; Prime Ticket © Barbara White; Sharp Electronics Corp. Professional Products Div. (World globe graphic developed by Tom Rzoncer and Scott McNulty, Griffin Bascal Advertising); *Professional Video Services; Erik Rimer (Makeup);* Sony Corp. of America; Smith-Victor Corp.; Stata Vision (Ed. Tutle); Steadicam; Studio Eleven; Sure Brothers Inc.; Tekronix, Inc.; *Telex Communication;* Tiffen Corporation; Toshiba; Travellers; Truevision, Inc.; Union Carbide Corp.; Vinten Equipment Corp.; Westinghouse Corporate Video Services.

PREFACE

Working in commercial and non-commercial television production for more than 20 years gives you more than graying hair and an ability to draw on an interesting collection of personal "war stories" for the classroom. It enables you, among other things, to stand back and trace the directions of change.

When you do, you first have to acknowledge that some things actually haven't changed much since television started—the principles of good composition, lighting, writing and newsgathering, for example. But other things—especially the things related to technology—are changing at an almost dizzying pace. These changes are having a major impact on the entire television production and postproduction process.

Fears about being inadequately prepared to cope with this change are illustrated in a good-news, bad-news story. A highly successful broadcast professional was invited to speak to a group of graduating students. As with most visiting speakers, he was first fed, given a tour of the school's production facilities and introduced to faculty members. Later, while addressing the graduating students, he started out by saying, "First, I would like to congratulate all of you on four successful years in college." However, the room full of smiles quickly faded when he went on to say, "But, I regret to inform you that everything you've learned is now out of date."

While the truth of this is a bit exaggerated, we must admit that many of the things today's students confront on their first job—sophisticated single-camera, film-style production; random-access editing; audio and video workstations; satellite links; and a plethora of thorny legal and ethical issues—are simply not covered in most of today's production textbooks. The burden of adding this information then shifts to the already overburdened classroom instructor.

There are those in academia and in the television profession who say that the broadcast curriculum shouldn't actually be burdened with trying to teach skills. Corporate presidents and station managers sometimes advise students to "simply get a well-rounded, liberal education and let us take care of teaching you how to use the equipment." Considering the difficulty schools have in keeping up with the latest technology, this is tempting advice—except for one thing. When faced with an abundance of applicants for entry-level production positions, the people further down the corporate ladder, the ones who actually do the hiring, are generally in a position to demand much more. And they do. For example, they often request a résumé reel of production segments.

Résumé reels—the kind students typically develop while taking production courses—serve three purposes: (1) they constitute evidence beyond good intentions (no matter how enthusiastically stated by an applicant) and represent a kind of "proof of performance"; (2) they are an efficient way for employers to rather quickly identify good prospects from a torrent of applicants; and, finally, (3) they serve the interests of the production facility (and maintain the credibility of the person doing the hiring) by reducing expensive on-the-job training (not to mention the possibility of costly production mistakes that can take place during the on-the-job training process).

Although a well-rounded education is indispensable to personal and professional success, we also have to face the realities of an extremely competitive profession. The better students can be prepared to effectively make use of today's complex audio and video tools, the easier they will attain internships, employment and professional advancement.

This text is designed for junior college, college and university students who fall into two groups:

1. Those who desire to work in some phase of video production
2. Those who need a solid understanding of video production to assist them in such allied fields as advertising and public relations

This text does not assume the reader has had a basic course in studio production; it starts at the beginning and tries to quickly establish a broad-based understanding of the audio and video media. Technical material is included only when it is seen as important to an understanding of larger issues.

Although the order of the chapters is consistent with the approach of many production courses, the chapters may be covered in any sequence. Institutions that require prerequisite courses such as audio production or visual composition may want to skip over or simply quickly review related chapters. This will allow more time to develop such topics as composition; editing; or single-camera, film-style production. The instructor's manual that accompanies this text includes suggestions for changing the order of chapters, as well as going beyond the text material in each chapter.

Since being able to quickly and effectively communicate with proper terminology is an important part of today's rapidly changing field of video and audio production, this text includes an up-to-date and comprehensive glossary. In fact, as of this writing, the Glossary, with more than 1,500 production terms, far exceeds that of any other broadcasting text. (Besides making excellent fodder for matching quizzes, instructors know that a knowledge of the basic terms of the profession is often a good gauge of general production savvy.)

I would like to thank a number of people who helped in the preparation of this manuscript. First, my wife, Alana, who assisted in many ways, including acting as a model for numerous photos. Paul Long, President of Kappa Video of Burbank, California, provided suggestions on the editing chapters; Dr. Larry Bumgardner, professor of Communications at Pepperdine University, reviewed the chapter on legal and ethical issues; and Laura Hewitt, one of the most efficient student assistants I've worked with, helped hold my office together during much of the time the manuscript was in preparation. Reviewing the manuscript and offering helpful suggestions were Steven D. Anderson, Ph.D., Virginia Polytechnic Institute and State University, Bruce Mathews, The University of Tennessee Television Center, Franklin Miller, University of Iowa, Robert B. Musberger, University of Houston, Virginia Gregg, Moorhead State University; William J. Rugg, Northern Arizona University; Doree Steinmann, Cosumnes River College; Richard Worringham, Radford University; and Don Wylie, San Diego State University.

Finally, I owe a great debt to many professional colleagues over the years who worked with me at several radio and TV stations in the United States and Canada. They not only tolerated my frequently cloddish efforts at learning the various phases of audio and video production and presentation, but they were willing to freely pass on knowledge that they had gained during their many years of professional experience.

BRIEF CONTENTS

1   An Overview of the Production Process   1

2   How Television Works   15

3   Lenses and Their Effects   32

4   Video Cameras   57

5   Color   93

6   Lighting   113

7   Audio   159

8   Composition   211

9   Video Control and Effects   232

10   Video Recording   257

11   Sets and Graphics   284

12   Scripts and the Creative Sequence   317

13   Producing and Directing   341

14   Principles of Editing   364

15   Editing Techniques   393

16   ENG and Single-Camera, Film-Style Production   427

17   Multiple-Camera Field Production   447

18   On-Camera Concerns   474

19   Legal and Ethical Guidelines   496

20   Institutional and Private Video   516

CONTENTS

PREFACE   v

1

AN OVERVIEW OF THE PRODUCTION PROCESS   1

The Dimensions of Television Production   2
Broadcast and Non-Broadcast Production   2
Production Staffs — Large and Small   2
**Production Personnel and Their
Responsibilities   3**
Production Phases   5
The Preproduction Phase   5
Production Rehearsals   5
The Production Phase   5
The Postproduction Phase   6
The Complete Production Studio   7
The Control Room   8
The Master Control Area   11
Preparing for the Future   12
Summary   12
Key Terms   13

2

HOW TELEVISION WORKS   15

It's All an Illusion   16
International Systems of Television   17
The NTSC Television System   17
The PAL and SECAM Television Systems   17
Standards Conversion   18
High-Definition Television   19
Converting Wide-Screen Formats   20
Digital and Analog Technology   22
Analog Signals   22
Digital Signals   22
Sampling Signals   23

Manipulating Digital Signals for Special
Effects   23
Quantization   23
Monitoring Video Levels   24
The Waveform Monitor   25
Blanking and Sync Signals   26
The Synchronizing Signal   26
The Transmission Process   27
Transmitting the Television Signal   28
TV Monitors and Receivers   28
Video Losses   29
Loss of Detail   29
Safe Areas   29
SAFE ACTION AREA   29
SAFE TITLE AREA   29
Summary   30
Key Terms   31

3

LENSES AND THEIR EFFECTS   32

The Lens Housing   32
Lens Focal Length   33
Prime Lenses   34
Angle of View   34
The Zoom Lens   34
Motorized Zoom Lenses   37
The Zoom vs. the Dolly   39
Focal Length and Perspective   39
Geometric Distortion   39
Focal Length and the Speed of Objects   40
Super-Telephoto Lenses   40
What Is Normal Focal Length?   41
Supplementary Lenses   41
Image Stabilizers   42
Lens Mounts   43
C-Mount Lenses   43

Bayonet-Mount Lenses   43

Changing Lenses   43

Lens Aperture   43

F-Stops   44

Lens Speed   45

Supplementary Lenses and F-Stops   45

Lens Coatings   46

Cleaning Lenses   46

Condensation on the Lens   47

Depth of Field   47

Acceptable Sharpness   47

F-Stop and Depth of Field   47

Depth of Field and Focal Length   49

Division of Depth of Field   49

Focusing a Lens   50

Minimum Subject Distance   50

The Macro Lens Setting   50

Follow Focus   51

Auto-Focus Lenses   52

Back Focus   52

Lens Shades   52

Filters   53

Ultraviolet Filters   53

Colored Filters   53

Neutral Density Filters   53

Contrast Filters   53

Polarizing Filters   54

Special-Effect Filters   54

Camera Filter Wheels   54

Matte Boxes   55

Summary   55

Key Terms   56

4

VIDEO CAMERAS   57

The Camera Imaging Device   57

CCD Cameras   57

CCD Shutter Speeds   58

SHUTTER SPEEDS AND F-STOPS   59

STROBOSCOPIC EFFECTS WITH SHUTTER

SPEEDS   60

CCD Problems   61

Camera Tubes   61

Video Resolution   62

Determining Resolution   62

Vertical and Horizontal Resolution   62

Minimum Light Levels for Cameras   64

Light Multipliers   64

Camera Setup   64

Base Stations   65

Memory Cards   65

Video Level Considerations   65

Contrast Range   66

Overexposure   66

Clipped Whites   66

Tonal Compression   66

Controlling Excessive Contrast Ranges   67

Handling Spectral Highlights   68

Camera Underexposure   68

Camera Black Level Considerations   70

Setting the Pedestal Control   70

Using Chip Charts   70

Subjective Elements of Video Levels   71

The Camera Viewfinder   73

Viewfinder Status Indicators   73

Adjusting the Viewfinder Image   74

Checking Viewfinder Accuracy   74

Viewfinder Sharpness   74

Basic Camera Types   75

Studio Cameras   75

Portable Field Cameras   75

Convertible Cameras   77

Electronic Cinematography Cameras   77

HDTV Cameras   77

Camcorders   77

Camera Mounts   78

Body Mounts   79

Vehicle Mounts   80

Tripods   80

Tripod Dolly   80

Camera Pedestals   81

Crabs and Cranes   82

Camera Jibs   84

Pan Heads   84

Fluid Heads   84

Cam Heads   84

Friction Heads   85

Gear Heads   85

Camera Balance   86

Locking Down Cameras   86

Robotic Camera Systems   86

Script-Controlled Robotic Camera
Positioning   87

Prompting Devices   88

Hard Copy Prompters   89
Soft Copy Prompters   89
Considerations in Using Prompters   90
Summary   91
Key Terms   91

5
COLOR   93

Light   93
Color Temperature   94
Color Standards   94
Approximate Color Consistency   96
Simultaneous Contrast   96
Subtractive and Additive Color   97
Subtractive Color   97
Additive Color   99
The Color TV Camera   99
How the Camera Sees Color   100
One- and Two-Chip Cameras   101
A Little Algebra   101
White Balancing a Video Camera   101
Luminance and Chrominance Signals   102
TV Picture Tubes   102
LCD Color Displays   104
Recomposing the Color Image   104
Accurate Color Reproduction   105
Analysis of Color in the TV Process   105
Plotting Accurate Color   106
"Good" Color vs. "Real" Color   108
Tube Registration   108
Color Resolution   108
Color Compatibility   109
Color Effects   109
Summary   112
Key Terms   112

6
LIGHTING   113

The Evolution of TV Lighting   113
Light Coherence   114
Hard Light   114

Lighting Angles and Quality   115
Soft Light   116
Color Temperature   118
Sunlight's Varying Color Temperature   118
Related Technical Continuity Problems   119
Light Intensity   119
Typical Foot Candle Intensities   119
Light Meters   120
Reflected Light Meters   120
Incident Light Meters   120
Controlling Light Intensity   121
Incandescent Lights: Problems and Solutions   122
The Problem of Incandescence   123
The Solution   123
HMI Lights   124
Problem Light Sources   125
Standard Fluorescent Lamps   125
The Daylight Fluorescent   125
Warm-White Fluorescent   125
Color-Balanced Fluorescent   126
Other Discharge Lights   126
Mixed Light Sources   126
Using Color as a Prop   127
Lighting Instruments   127
The Fresnel Light   127
Barn Doors   128
Flags   128
Filter Frames   129
Safety Considerations   129
Scoops   129
Broads   129
Ellipsoidal Spots   129
The Key Light   131
The Rule of Simplicity   131
To the Right or to the Left?   132
The Key's Vertical Angle   132
Keys and Boom Mics   132
The Sun as a Key   133
The Fill Light   133
The Back Light   136
Background Lights   138
Lighting Ratios   139
Back-Light Intensity   140
Background Light Intensity   141
Subject-to-Background Distance   141
The Lighting Grid   143
Approaches to Lighting Multiple Subjects   144

News, Weather and Sports   145
Multiple-Purpose Lights   145
Approaches to Area Lighting   146
   Using a Stand-In   146
High-Key and Low-Key Lighting   147
**Single-Camera vs. Multiple-Camera
Lighting   147**
Following Source   148
Lighting Control Equipment   149
Creating a Lighting Plot   151
On-Location Lighting   151
Lighting Packages   151
Setting Up On-Location Lighting   151
Camera Lights   153
ENG and EFP Work   153
Camera Lights on Studio Cameras   154
Using Existing Light in ENG Work   154
Placement Problems   155
Setting Up Lights   155
Power Problems   156
The Art of Lighting   157
Summary   157
Key Terms   158

7

AUDIO   159

Audio Quality   159
Amplitude and Frequency   160
Amplitude   160
Frequency   161
   Timbre   161
The Amplitude-Frequency Relationship   162
Shaping Playback Response   163
Loudness-Perception Issues   164
Amplitude Control Devices   165
Audio Compressors   165
Audio Limiters   165
AGC Circuits   165
Audio Expanders   167
Peak Program and Loudness Meters   167
Needles vs. LEDs   168
Frequency Response and Audio Quality   169
Microphones as Transducers   169

Directional Characteristics of Microphones   169
Omnidirectional Mics   170
Bidirectional Mics   170
Unidirectional Mics   170
   Cardioid   170
   Supercardioid   171
   Hypercardioid and Ultradirectional   171
   Parabolic   171
Proximity Effects   171
Microphone Transducer Types   173
Ribbon Microphones   173
Dynamic Microphones   173
Condenser Microphones   175
Microphone Impedance   176
Balanced and Unbalanced Lines   176
Electrical Interference Problems   177
Application Design   177
Personal Microphones   177
   Placement of Personal Mics   177
Hand-Held Microphones   178
   Microphone Windscreens   178
   Positioning Hand-Held Mics   179
PZ Mics   179
Headset Mics   179
Contact Mics   179
Wireless Microphones   180
Types of Wireless Mics   180
Wireless Mic Applications   180
Transmitting-Range Considerations   180
Interference Problems   181
Wireless Mic Receiving Antennas   181
Using Off-Camera Mics   181
Room Acoustics   182
Hanging and Slung Microphones   183
Fishpoles   183
Microphone Booms   184
Hidden Microphones   184
Line Mics   184
Stereo   185
The Stereo Effect   185
Multitrack Stereo Recording   185
Recording Live Music in Stereo   187
Stereo Mics   187
The X-Y-Micing Technique   187
The M-S Micing Technique   188
Maintaining a Stereo Perspective   189
Concessions in Stereo Perspectives   189
Using Pan Pots   189
Holding Dialogue to "Center Stage"   189

Stereo in Sports Coverage 190
Guidelines for Stereo Placement 190
Stereo Playback 190
Surround-Sound Techniques 190
Quadraphonic Mics 191
Single and Double System Sound 191
Single System Recording 191
Double System Recording 191
Mic Connectors and Cords 191
Sources of Prerecorded Audio 192
Turntables 192
Cart Machines 192
Reel-to-Reel Tape Machines 193
Editing Reel-to-Reel Tapes 193
Compact Discs (CDs) 194
CD Defects 195
Automatic Error Correction 196
Programming CD Playback 196
Mini Disk (MD) 196
Digital Audio Tapes (DAT, RDAT) 196
DAT Time Code 197
Digital Compact Cassette (DCC) 198
The Audio Console 199
Audio Inputs 199
Audio Console Controls 199
Input Selector Switches 200
Level Control and Mixing 201
Control Room Monitors 201
Audition and Cue Channels 202
Master and Sub-Master Gain Controls 202
Master Gain Control 202
Sub-Masters 202
Background Music Levels 202
Audio Foldback 203
Lip Sync Presentations 203
Multiple-Microphone Setups in the Field 203
Using Audio From PA Systems 204
Music Synthesizers and MIDI Interfaces 204
Synthesized Music 204
MIDI 205
Tapeless Editing Systems 206
Editing Workstations 207
Audio Quality Considerations 207
Audio Head Problems 207
Head Clog 207
Magnetized and Misaligned Audio Heads 208
Summary 208
Key Terms 209

8
COMPOSITION 211

The Elements of Composition 211
Form vs. Content 211
The Best Work Is Invisible 212
A Director Directs Attention 212
Pictorial Composition 214
Rules vs. Guidelines 214
Clearly Delineate Your Objectives 214
Bit Rate and Boredom 215
Nice, but Not Essential 215
Depicting Emotional States 216
Make Sure Scenes Have Unity 216
Design the Scene Around a Single Center of Interest 216
Developing an Objective Eye 217
Using Selective Focus 217
A Basic Component of "the Film Look" 217
Using Lighting to Focus Attention 218
Shifting the Center of Interest 218
Shifting Attention With Sound 218
Observe Proper Subject Placement 219
Rule of Thirds 220
Handling Horizontal and Vertical Lines 220
Create a Pattern of Meaning 220
The Concrete and the Abstract 222
Including Multiple Levels of Meaning 223
Use Leading Lines 224
Frame Central Subject Matter 225
Use Perspective Control 225
Maintain Tonal Balance 226
Balance Mass 226
Use the Psychological Effects of Color and Tone 226
Avoid Mergers 227
Tonal Mergers 227
Dimensional Mergers 228
Border Mergers 228
Control the Number of Prime Objects 228
Balance Complexity and Order 229
Use the Direction of Movement 229
Summary 230
Key Terms 231

9

VIDEO CONTROL AND EFFECTS   232

Computer-Based Switching and Effects   233

Elements of Video Switching   234

The Program Bus   235
Mix/Effects Buses   236

Preview/Preset Monitors   237

Visual Effects   238

Supers, Faders and Dissolves   238
Multiple Mix/Effects Sources   240
Luminance Keys   241
Internal and External Key Sources   241
Downstream Keyers   242
Adjusting the Key Source   243
Altering Key Colors   243
Title Keys and Legibility   244
Chroma Key   244
    Chroma Key Blue   244
    Chroma Key Applications   245
    Chroma Key Problems   246
    TAKING THE SHADOW WITH THE ACTOR   246
    Panning, Tilting and Zooming With Chroma
    Key   246
Wipes — 5,000 Ways to Change a Picture   247
    Keying in Background Graphics   247
Auto-Key Tracking   249
Programming Visual Effects   249

Computer-Based Systems   250

Desktop Video   250
Amiga, Apple and IBM Desktop Video
Standards   250
Multitasking   252
Transmitting and Receiving Production Data by
Modem   253

Keeping Video Effects in Perspective   254

Routing and Master Control Switchers   254

Summary   255

Key Terms   256

10

VIDEO RECORDING   257

A Quick Look Back at the Technology   258

The Two-Inch Quad VTR Debuts   259

Helical Tape Machines Take Over   259

The Video Recording Process   260

The Time-Base Corrector Arrives   260

VTR/VCR Classifications   261

VTR Inputs and Outputs   261

VTR Inputs   261
VCR Outputs   261
Composite Video   261
Y/C Video Signals   262
Component Video Signals   262

Acquisition Formats   263

One-Inch Professional Standards   263

One-Inch Type-C   263

Three-Quarter Inch Videotape   264

Betamax   265

VHS   265

Eight mm Video   266
Compact-8   266

Prosumer Formats   267

S-VHS   267
Hi8   267

**Half-Inch, Broadcast-Quality Analog
Formats   268**

Betacam   268
The M Formats   269

Digital Video Recording   270

Videodisc   270
Digital Videotape Advantages   271
The D-1 Format   272
The D-2 Format   272
The D-3 Format   273
Computer Disk Video   274

Solid-State Recording   275

Volatile Memory   275
Non-Volatile Memory   276

Film vs. Electronic Recording   276

Relative Costs   276
The Advantages of Film   277
Technical Quality Compared   277
Coping with Brightness Ranges   278
Single-Camera, Multiple-Camera
Differences   278
Film vs. Videotape Equipment Costs   278

VCR Operations   279

Spot-Checking a Tape   279

Basic VCR Adjustments   280

The VCR Skew Control   280

The VCR Tracking Control   281

Common VCR Meters and Status Indicators   281

Maintaining Videotape   281

Summary   282

Key Terms   283

11

SETS AND GRAPHICS   284

Sets, Props and Staging   284

Five Types of Studio Sets   285

Neutral/Indeterminate Sets   285
The Studio Cyc   285
Curtains   287
Representational-Supportive Sets   287
Symbolic Sets   288
Realistic or Replica Sets   288
Fantasy Sets   290

Tonal Value Considerations   290

Basic Set Building Blocks   292

Softwall Flats   292
Hardwall Flats   292
Creating Your Own Surface Designs   292
Wallpaper and Contact Paper   294
Ready-Made Panoramic Scenes   294
Surface Problems   294
Joining Flats   294
Self-Supporting Set Pieces   295
Painted Canvas Drops   296
Seamless Paper   296
Polystyrene Set Pieces   297
Columns   297
The Floor as Part of the Set   298
Risers   299
Modular Scenery   300

Drawing Floor Plans for Sets   300

Toothpicks and Two-by-Fours   301

Television Graphics   302

The 4 × 3 Aspect Ratio   302
Safe Areas   302
The 16 × 9 Aspect Ratio   303
Coping With Vertical Graphics   303
Legibility of Written Material   304
Camera Cards   305
Thirty-Five-Millimeter Slides   305

Electronic Still Cameras   306
Electronic Still Store   308

Electronic Graphic Systems   309

Electronic Animation   311
Electronic Image Layering   312

Three-Dimensional Television   312

Vector-Based 3-D Modeling   312

Control of Electronic Graphic Systems   313

Keyboard, Mouse and Trackball Controls   313
Pull-Down Menus   313
Macro Control Sequences   314
Electronic Palettes   314
Touch-Screen Control   315
Voice Control   315

Summary   315

Key Terms   316

12

SCRIPTS AND THE CREATIVE SEQUENCE   317

Form and Content   317

Capturing and Holding Viewer Attention   318

Creating the Emotional Experience   318
Audience-Engaging Principles   319

Timing, Budgeting and Scheduling   319

The Range of Production Needs   319

The 15-Step Production Sequence   320

Identify the Goals of the Production   320
Analyze Your Target Audience   320
Review Similar Productions   321
Determine Value and Marketability   321
Develop a Treatment or Production Outline   322
Develop a Production Schedule   323
Commission Key Personnel   324
Select Locations   324
Decide on Talent, Costuming and Sets   324
Engage Remaining Production Personnel   324
Obtain Permits, Insurance and Clearances   325
Determine Supporting Production Elements   325
Start the Production Sequence   326
Begin the Editing Sequence   326
Do Postproduction Follow-up   326

Planning the Script   326

The Concrete-to-Abstract Continuum   327
Structuring the Script   328

Working Around Weaknesses in Interviews 328
Organizing and Writing an Interview-Based Production 329

Matching Production Techniques to Content 329

Pacing the Production 329

Basic Scriptwriting Guidelines 330

Guarding Against Information Overload 331

Video Protocol 332

Script Formats 334

News, Documentary and Commercial Scripts 334
Shot-by-Shot and Master-Scene Formats 334

Summary 339

Key Terms 339

13
PRODUCING AND DIRECTING 341

Costing-Out a Production 341

A Typical Institutional or Local Station Production 342

Renting vs. Buying Equipment 346

Approaches to Attributing Costs 347

Cost per Minute 349
Cost per Viewer 349
Cost per Measured Results 349

Directing Studio Productions 350

Directing Responsibilities 350
The Primary Job of the Director 350
Requisitioning Equipment and Facilities 350
Directing Strategies 353
The Need to Anticipate 356

Producing and Directing a News Show 356

The Network Approach 358
News Bureaus 358
Network News Services 358
Local Station Approaches to News 359

News Segments 359

The Four-Segment News Format 359
The Five-Segment News Format 360
Segment Rundown Sheets 360

The Newscaster's Role in Production 361

Newsroom Computer Systems 361

Quality Control 362

Summary 362

Key Terms 363

14
PRINCIPLES OF EDITING 364

The Roots of Video Editing 364

Initial Video Editing Problems 365
The Dawn of Linear Editing 366
Random-Access Editing 367
Videodisc-Based Editing 367
RAM-Based Editing 367
Dedicated and Software-Based Edit Controllers 367

Continuity Editing 368

Parallel Cutting 369
Continuity Editing in an ENG Story 369
Using Insert Shots and Cutaways 371
Insert Shots 371
Cutaways 371
Altering Expected Continuity 371
When Effect Precedes Cause 372
Causality 372

Relational Editing 373

Acceleration Editing 373

Compressing Time 374
Expanding Time 376

Thematic Editing 376

Editing Trends 377

Jump Cuts 377

Bridging Jumps in Action 377
Bridging Interview Edits 379
The 1-2-3 Formula 379
Shooting-Angle Considerations 381
Crossing the Line 381
Maintaining Consistent Eyelines 382

Technical Continuity Problems 382

Audio 382
Video 382

Music Continuity Considerations 383

Conforming Music to Video 383
Backtiming Music 383
Tapping Into Music Libraries 384

Seven Editing Guidelines 384

Cutting Between Moving Camera Shots   384
Cutting on Subject Movement   384
   Matching Action   385
   Cutting After Subtle Action   385
   Editor as Magician   385
Motivated Cuts   385
Editing to Accommodate the Medium   386
Determining the Length of Shots   387
   Accommodating Visual Complexity   388
   Varying Tempo   388
   Capturing and Holding Audience Interest   389
The Function of B-Roll Footage   389
   Reaction Shots   389
   Insert Shots   390
   Cutaway Shots   390
The Principle of Parsimony   391
Summary   391
Key Terms   392

15

EDITING TECHNIQUES   393

Control Track Editing   393
SMPTE/EBU Time Code   394
The Advantage of Replication   394
Time Code in Audio   395
Interlocking Multiple Machines   395
Breaking the Code   396
User Bits   397
Drop-Frame Time Code   397
Adding Time Code   399
Longitudinal Time Code   399
   Recording Longitudinal Time Code   400
Vertical Interval Time Code (VITC)   400
   Recording VITC Time Code   400
How Time Code Is Displayed   401
Logging Time Codes   403
On-Line and Off-Line Editing   403
Off-Line Editing   404
On-Line Editing   405
Logging Scenes   405
The Paper-and-Pencil Edit   406
Creating EDLs and News Scripts With Notebook Computers   407
Preparing the Final EDL   408
The Editing Process   408

Assemble Editing   409
Insert Editing   410
The Pre-Roll Phase   410
Defining an Edit   410
Editing News and Documentary Pieces   411
Preparing a Typical News Package   411
   The A-Roll Footage   411
   The B-Roll Footage   412
Linear Editing Procedures   415
   Initial Procedures for Full-Length Programs   415
Room Tone   417
Adding Cutaway and Insert Shots   418
Splitting Audio From Video   418
Adding Narration   419
Random-Access Editing   420
Digital Editing   421
Time Compression and Expansion   421
On-Line Considerations   422
Compensating for Off-Line Problems   422
   The Trace Capability   422
Preparing On-Line Materials   423
Taking the Off-Line EDL to the On-Line Phase   423
Audio Sweetening   424
Editors vs. Technicians   424
Summary   425
Key Terms   425

16

ENG AND SINGLE-CAMERA, FILM-STYLE PRODUCTION   427

Developments Leading to ENG   427
Implications of the ENG Revolution   428
The Impact of ENG Coverage on War   428
Reporting News vs. Making News   429
ENG-EFP Differences   429
Television News   430
Sources of Television News   430
Balancing News and Production Elements   431
Ten Factors in Newsworthiness   431
Packaging the News   433
Building National Credentials   434
If in Doubt, Check It Out   435

The Hazards of ENG Work   435
**The Development of Film-Style Production
Techniques   436**
  Film-Style Production Comes to Video   437
  The Master Shot Perspective   438
  Setups   438
  Shooting a Scene From a Dramatic
  Production   439
  Maintaining Interscene Relationships   443
  Working With Actors and Talent   443
  Controlling Script Revisions   444
  Inventing "Business"   444
  Plans B and C   444
  Creative Compromises   444
  Learning to Visualize   445
  Single-Camera vs. Multiple-Camera
  Production   445
Summary   445
Key Terms   446

17

MULTIPLE-CAMERA FIELD PRODUCTION   447

The Importance of Preproduction Planning   447
The On-Location Survey   448
  On-Location Survey Factors   450
The FAX Sheet   451
Selecting Camera Positions   453
On-Location Audio Concerns   453
Determining Lighting Needs   454
Production Communication   454
Permits, Clearances, Bonds and Insurance   455
The Equipment Inventory   456
Directing the Remote Production   456
Coaxial Cable   457
  Coaxial Cable Problems   457
Fiber Optics   457
  The Advantages of Fiber Optics   458
  Converting Audio and Video to Light   458
  Fiber Optic Cable Applications   459
Microwave Links   459
  Short-Hop Transmitters   460
  Microwave Characteristics   460
  Vans, Boats and Airplanes   461
Satellite Links   462

  Geosynchronous Satellites   462
  Ground Control Centers   462
  Satellite Transponders   462
  Satellite Consortiums   463
  C-Band   463
  Ku-Band   464
  Satellite Distribution of Network
  Programming   465
  SNG Satellite Links   466
  Flyaway Satellite Links   466
  Setting Up a Satellite Dish   467
Covering SNG Assignments   468
  B-Roll Satellite Footage   469
  Typical Field-Production Setups   469
Summary   472
Key Terms   473

18

ON-CAMERA CONCERNS   474

Announcing   474
  Scripted Narration   474
  Effective Announcing Traits   476
  Eliminating In-Studio Distractions   478
  Correcting Programs in Narration   478
  Considerations in Using Prompters   478
  Maintaining Optimum Eye Contact   479
  Recognizing Effective Voice
  Characteristics   479
  Restricting Hand and Head Gestures   480
Working With Actors   480
**Research on Effective On-Camera
Presentation   480**
Makeup   481
  Basic Makeup   481
  Corrective Makeup   483
  Character Makeup   483
  Makeup Basics   483
  Applying the Base   483
  Concealing and Emphasizing Features   486
  The Eyes   488
  The Lips   488
  Hands, Ears and Teeth   489
  Dark-Skinned People   489
  Children   490
  Removal of Makeup   490
  General Makeup Considerations   490

Wardrobe and Jewelry 490

Wardrobe Considerations 490

Jewelry 491

Considerations in Doing Live Stand-Ups 491

IFB Communication 492

Hand Signals 492

Summary 492

Key Terms 495

19

LEGAL AND ETHICAL GUIDELINES   496

Principles of Privacy 496

Private and Public Individuals 497

Intrusion on Seclusion 497

Conflicts in Constitutional Rights 497

The Roots of Invasion of Privacy 497

The Public's Right to Know 497

First Guideline for Intrusion 498

When the Camera Distorts the Truth 498

Offensiveness and Harrassment 499

Six Guidelines for Intrusion 499

Free and Restricted Access 500

Official Invitation 500

Press Passes 500

Civil Disobedience 501

Shield Laws 501

Confidentiality and the My Lai Massacre 501

The Two Sides of Shield Laws 502

Misrepresentation 502

Commercial Appropriation 502

The Boundaries of Commercial
Appropriation 502

Defamation, Libel and Slander 503

Defamation 503

Per Se and *Per Quod* Defamation 503

Guarding Against Trade Libel 504

Legal Defenses Against Defamation Suits 504

Truth 504

Consent 504

Privilege 505

False Light 505

Legal Pitfalls in Doing Docudramas 505

Honest Mistakes 506

Confronting Lawsuits 506

Handling Subpoenas 506

Issuing Corrective Statements 506

Staging 507

Unacceptable Staging 507

Questionable Staging 507

Acceptable Staging 508

When Authenticity Is an Issue 508

Using "Comparable Footage" 508

Dramatic License 508

Copyrighted Materials 509

Background Music 509

Public Domain Music 509

ASCAP and BMI Music Licenses 509

Securing Rights to Use Music 509

Music Libraries 510

Advantages of Original Music 510

Synthesized Music 510

Other Types of Published Works 511

**Electronically Altered Video and Audio
Materials 512**

Digitized Images 512

Sampling Audio Recordings 512

Talent Releases 512

Summary 513

Key Terms 515

20

INSTITUTIONAL AND PRIVATE VIDEO   516

The Scope of Institutional Video 516

The Scope of Private Video 517

Religious Programming 517

The History of Institutional Video 518

Institutional Video Applications 518

Institutional Video Today 520

Typical Organizational Approaches 520

The Field of Institutional Video 521

Areas of Proven Effectiveness 521

The Power of Immediate Feedback 522

The Power of Close-Ups 523

Medical Applications 523

Interrelating Diverse Elements 524

Problems in Overstatement 525

Altering Time 525

Animation 527

Portable Expertise 527

Videoconferencing 528

Replicative Advantages 529

Basic Program Formats   530

Holding Viewer Attention   531

The Future of Institutional Video   531

Private Television   532

Summary   535

Key Terms   536

Glossary   537

References   564

Index   574

TELEVISION PRODUCTION

An Overview
of the
Production
Process

Television is the most powerful and pervasive tool for mass communication yet devised. At its worst it is a narcotic that dulls our social consciousness, promotes superficial materialism and squanders our time. At its best television is arousing, stimulating, informative and inspiring. How this most-powerful-of-all communication media is used depends solely on the knowledge, skill and professional and moral predispositions of those working in the field.

Because of the influence of television, it is one of the so-called glamour professions. As a result, many people are attracted to the field, and this, in turn, makes most jobs in the profession highly competitive. Consequently, only highly motivated people equipped with superior knowledge and skills are apt to be successful.

Some people seem to be born with motivation (although, admittedly, developmental psychologists have a much more grandiloquent explanation). Skills and knowledge, however, must be learned. This text is designed to give you that professional advantage by explaining the most important concepts behind good television production—concepts that any video professional or serious student should know. The time taken to thoroughly familiarize yourself with this material will pay off by giving you a critical head start in the field. At the same time, the material is designed to keep you from making many common production mistakes, which should make it possible for you to advance more quickly and with fewer problems.

We can look at the production process in terms of the people, places and things that are involved. The people we'll introduce are the various production personnel, from the executive producer to stagehands; the places, the major production areas; and the things, the basic production equipment from the camera to the transmitter. We'll also look at the three phases of production: preproduction, production, and postproduction.

THE DIMENSIONS OF TELEVISION PRODUCTION

Television production refers to the complete process of creating television programs. It includes the preproduction, production and postproduction phases. Before we examine these, we need to recognize two basic types of production: broadcast and non-broadcast.

Broadcast and Non-Broadcast Production

Broadcast television, the kind you are probably most familiar with, is the kind that is produced by commercial TV stations and professional production companies. It is programming for a mass audience: dramas, situation comedies (Figure 1.1), news, documentaries, game shows—and, of course (with the possible exception of Public Broadcasting), omnipresent commercials.

Non-broadcast television is referred to as **institutional video,** and its audience is more specialized. Institutional video encompasses a wide range of areas including programming produced by educational institutions, corporations, medical facilities, religious groups and the government. This category also includes *camera of record* productions that range all the way from covert videotapes made by law enforcement officials to a family videotape made of your little brother's first haircut.

camera of record: Videotaping an event as it happens, generally without effects or production embellishments. Intended only as a "raw record" of the event.

Production Staffs—Large and Small

The videotape of your little brother's first haircut will probably have a production "staff" of one: you. Small educational, cable and industrial facilities typically have production crews of only a few individuals. In contrast, a major commercial production will require the specialized talents of several hundred people. Programs made by TV stations, moderately sized cable companies and video production facilities typically require between five and 20 people. This is the range we'll emphasize in this book.

FIGURE 1.1
In 1992, the average TV household in the United States had at least one TV set on for more than seven hours a day. The programming viewed during this time represents hundreds of thousands of hours of production time by thousands of people working in television. Situation comedies (sit-coms) have for some time been the most popular category of network programming. They are followed closely by feature films, football, suspense and mystery, general drama and informational programming.

By its nature this type of studio production must be a team effort. No one individual can do it alone. The production team must not only understand the concept of the production, but be committed to working closely together to achieve the production goals. If there is a lack of communication, or a desire in some personnel to "go their own way," not only will the production be compromised, but a breakdown of the entire production process can result.

What follows is a bit of a whirlwind tour of the complete production process. As in most quick tours, no one will expect you to grasp everything. But you should end up with a basic idea of the production process. Keep in mind that most of these things will be explained more fully in later chapters.

The following discussion also includes elements associated with large productions. Depending upon the project, many of these elements will be scaled down, combined or eliminated altogether in smaller productions. They are covered here so that a reasonably comprehensive view of the entire production process can be presented. (And we might as well start off by thinking big and then scale things down as needed.)

FIGURE 1.2
Most people think of television programs simply in terms of on-camera talent. However, for each person seen in front of the camera it may take 20 or more people working "behind the camera" to make their appearance possible. It is the creativity and expertise that takes place behind the camera that commonly underlies the show's success or failure.

director: Person in charge of coordinating production elements before and during a production. Typically, the director "calls the shots" during a production.

PRODUCTION PERSONNEL AND THEIR RESPONSIBILITIES

The person in charge of the entire production is the **producer**. He or she typically develops the program concept, lays out the budget for the production and coordinates advertising or financial support. From the beginning, this person is the team leader, the person who works with the writers, decides on the key talent, hires the director and guides the general direction of the production. Larger production facilities will have an **executive producer** who is in charge of several individual producers. This person is directly accountable to management for the progress of a series of projects.

One of the producer's first jobs on a major production is to hire a writer and commission a **script,** the written plan or "blueprint" for the production. TV **writers** range from those who create the scripts for 90-minute dramatic productions to staff members who write the material for short videotaped segments in newscasts. Besides spoken words, the writers may include descriptions of scenes and locales, music, video and audio effects, and descriptions of the actions of talent.

The principal talent for the production will normally be the next thing considered by a producer. **Talent** (an admittedly charitable term in some cases) includes actors, reporters, hosts, guests and off-camera narrators—anyone whose voice is heard or who appears on camera (Figure 1.2).

Next, the producer will probably hire a *director* (Figure 1.3). He or she will be in charge of working out preproduction details, coordinating the activities of the production staff and on-camera talent, working out camera and talent positions, selecting the camera shots during the production and overseeing postproduction work. In short, the director is responsible for transforming the script into the final TV production. Often in television the jobs of the producer and director are done by one person: a producer-director.

One or more **production assistants** may be hired to help the producer and director. During rehearsals production assistants keep notes on changes made by the producer or director and notify appropriate personnel. Some productions will have an **associate director** or AD. This person assists the director during the actual production doing such things as keeping track of time, seeing that camera shots and tape and film inserts are ready when needed, etc.

FIGURE 1.3
The director is responsible for transforming a TV script into a final product. The director's duties include working out preproduction details, coordinating the activities of the production staff and on-camera talent, working out camera and talent positions, selecting the camera shots during the production and overseeing postproduction work. Often the jobs of the producer and director are done by one person: a producer-director.

FIGURE 1.4

The video switcher is operated by the technical director, or TD. The switcher is used to select the various video sources and create video effects. This production switcher is similar to those found in small and medium-sized TV facilities.

Other production personnel include

technical director: Person responsible for technical aspects of a production. Typically, the individual who operates the video switcher.

- the *technical director,* who operates the video switcher (Figure 1.4) and coordinates camera shots for the director;
- the **lighting director,** who designs the lighting plan and sees that the lights are in place; and
- the **set designer** (Figure 1.5), who, in collaboration with the producer and director, designs the set and supervises its construction, painting and installation.

Next, there may be

- a **makeup person,** who, with the help of makeup, hair spray etc., sees that the talent either looks their best (or, depending upon the role, possibly makes them look their worst).

FIGURE 1.5

Set designers and art directors work in conjunction with a show's producer or director to design the settings used in TV productions. The most demanding live TV production to be produced on a regular basis is the annual Academy Awards ceremony. This production originates from Los Angeles and is viewed around the world.

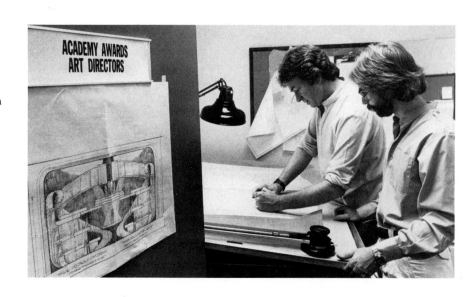

Larger productions will have

- a **wardrobe person,** who is responsible for seeing that the talent have clothes or costumes appropriate to the needs of the production;
- the *floor manager,* who supervises studio activities, relays the director's cues to the talent, handles cue cards and coordinates the work of stagehands;
- **stagehands,** who set up and move sets, props and equipment;
- the **audio technician,** who typically mixes and controls sound from microphones, recorded music and sound effects; and
- a **video engineer,** who adjusts the various video sources for the best quality (often this person also runs the **VTRs,** or videotape recorders).

The last two categories are

- **camera operators** (Figure 1.6), who find and compose the shots needed by the director, and
- **editors,** who, in a videotaped production, take the tapes and meld the segments together, adding music and video and audio effects.

PRODUCTION PHASES

The Preproduction Phase

The first (and most important) phase of production is **preproduction**. In this phase the basic concepts and approaches of the production are decided. In order for the program to be successful, the needs, interests and general background of the **target audience** must be considered. This is important for any type of program, from a light comedy intended for commercial television to a videotape for medical personnel explaining a new surgical technique.

Once key production members have been selected (including the director, set designer and lighting director), the next step in preproduction is to arrange a series of production meetings. Since all elements of the production are interrelated, things such as scenic design, lighting and audio must be carefully coordinated.

Production Rehearsals After all of these elements are taken care of, rehearsals can start. For a simple show this may only be a quick check of talent positions and major transitions so that cameras angles, audio and lighting can be checked before the show. However, a complex, fully scripted production may require many days of rehearsals. These generally start with a **dry rehearsal** where the talent sits around a table with key production personnel and reads through the script. Suggestions made at this time are passed on to the writer. A script often goes through several revisions before everyone is satisfied.

Next is *camera blocking*. The first phase of camera blocking often takes place in a **rehearsal hall** (any large empty room) without cameras, equipment or scenery. Once the basics are worked out, the production can move into the studio with a full complement of cameras, sets and mikes.

At this point a **dress rehearsal** can take place. Dress rehearsals represent the final opportunity for production personnel to solve remaining production problems.

The Production Phase

Productions can either be broadcast live or recorded on videotape. With the exception of news shows, sports remotes and some special event broadcasts,

FIGURE 1.6
It is the camera operator's responsibility to find and compose the shots needed by the director. Total familiarity with a camera's operating controls, an eye for good composition and a quick response time are essential.

floor manager: Individual responsible for all activities on the studio floor including relaying a director's signals to talent. Sometimes called a stage manager.

camera blocking: Working out and walking through camera and talent positions and movements prior to actual rehearsals.

FIGURE 1.7

As computer-controlled editing techniques and visual effects have become more sophisticated, editing has gone far beyond simply joining sequences together in a logical order. Today, the editing phase of production is a major focus for production creativity.

most productions are recorded on videotape for later broadcast or distribution. Recording the show often provides an opportunity to fix problems by either stopping the tape and redoing segments, or making changes during editing. Even so, because of the temptation to constantly redo segments that are "not quite perfect," some producers insist on the **live-on-tape** approach. All but the most glaring problems are covered in the best way possible as the show progresses — just as if it were being done live. Although some polish may be lost, the live-on-tape approach saves money and tends to keep everyone more alert.

The Postproduction Phase

strike: To take down, remove and store set pieces and props at the end of a production.

postproduction: Any production work done after all the main taping has been completed.

editing: The process of arranging in a predetermined sequence various segments from one or more tapes into a final edited version of a production.

All after-production tasks such as *striking* (taking down) sets and lights, handling final financial obligations and evaluating the effect of the program are part of the *postproduction* phase. Even though postproduction may actually include many after-the-production duties, most people associate postproduction with videotape editing. In its most basic sense *editing* refers to the process of rearranging and joining together the recorded video and audio segments of a production. However, as computer-controlled editing techniques and postproduction special effects have become more sophisticated, editing has gone far beyond this and is now a major focus for production creativity (Figure 1.7).

Complex TV productions are almost always assembled in postproduction because it is virtually impossible to coordinate live — with error-free, split-second timing — the myriad of shots, production decisions and video and audio effects that go into an intricate production. Editing offers the opportunity to rearrange program segments, alter camera shot sequences and try out a variety of audio and video options. Changes in the audio during the editing phase may include adding narration, sound effects and background sounds; filtering out noise; and rerecording dialogue that is unclear or requires modification. This audio postproduction phase is called **audio sweetening**.

THE COMPLETE PRODUCTION STUDIO

Production facilities vary widely, from one-camera basement facilities to the commercial networks with scores of studios and tens of thousands of square feet of space. Most studios fall somewhere in between with about 2,000 square feet of floor space.

Although more and more production is being done in the field, the TV studio is still the center of a large percentage of TV production. Even programming segments that originate outside the studio, called electronic field production (*EFP*) segments, are often introduced from a studio and then "rolled into" a studio production. The many short news segments that are done in the field that end up as part of the nightly newscasts are examples. This type of EFP production is called *ENG* for electronic news gathering.

TV studios are normally equipped with at least two cameras. Some cameras require operators, and some are **robotic cameras** that are remotely controlled. Cameras are mounted on *pan heads* that allow them to swivel left and right and up and down.

The director uses specific production terms to tell camera operators the moves needed. Although camera operation and the various parts of the camera will be covered in Chapter 4, as part of this introduction we'll quickly cover some basic camera moves. **Panning** refers to the left-to-right movement of the camera on the pan head. **Tilting** is the up and down movement. A studio camera is generally mounted on a *dolly* or pedestal that allows it to be rolled to different parts of the studio. When the entire camera is rolled toward or away from a scene, it is referred to as **dollying**. When the camera is rolled to the left or right on its dolly, it is referred to as **trucking**. A director may tell a camera operator, for example, to "truck left and then dolly in for a close shot."[1]

Since almost all studio cameras are equipped with **zoom lenses** that can optically alter the size of the image without moving the camera, the need for dollying is minimized. Although some zoom lenses operate with a mechanical crank, most are electrically controlled. After the size of the image is adjusted in the camera viewfinder with the **zoom control,** the lens must be focused with the **focusing knob** to make the image as sharp as possible.

Studio cameras are equipped with *tally lights* to indicate when they have been switched on-line, or are "on the air." These are normally red lights located above the lens (see Figure 1.8). One of the duties of floor directors is to listen for "stand by" cues from the director. These come over the private **production line** or *PL,* which is a party line communication system that links all the members of the production crew. When a camera is about to change, a floor director will raise an arm, and then, as the new camera is switched on-line, bring the arm down and point to the new camera. Ideally, the talent should be able to see this gesture out of the corner of his or her eye and be able to turn to the new camera just as its tally light comes on.

Studio cameras may also be equipped with prompting devices, called *camera prompters* or **teleprompters.**[2] Most use a half-silvered mirror over the camera lens that can display the video image of the script, and at the same time,

EFP (electronic field production): The process of using portable video equipment for doing on-location production.

ENG (electronic news gathering): The use of portable cameras and videotape machines (and often field-to-studio microwave links) to cover on-location television news stories.

pan head: The device that connects the camera to the mount or pedestal and allows the camera to be tilted vertically and to be panned horizontally.

dolly: To move the camera on its mount in a straight line directly toward or away from a subject. The term also refers to a wheel-based camera mount.

tally light: The red light on a video camera that indicates the camera is on the air or that videotape is rolling.

PL (private line; phone line; production line): Wired or wireless headset intercommunication link between production personnel.

camera prompter: A electrical device displaying the text for on-camera talent to read during a production.

---

1. Two other terms are occasionally used to describe camera movements: *arc* and *ped.* When a camera is **arced,** it is moved either forward or backward along a curved path — sort of a combination truck and dolly. The term **ped** stands for pedestal. A director may ask a cameraperson to "ped up" or "ped down," referring to the raising or lowering the camera on its pedestal mount.

2. Although widely used, the term *teleprompter* (TelePrompter) is actually a brand name for one of the first manufacturers of these prompting devices.

FIGURE 1.8

Video signals from studio cameras first go through a camera control unit, or CCU, where color balance and video levels are controlled by a technician. Sometimes a base station can be used to control all CCUs simultaneously. From the CCUs the signals go to video monitors, which display a high-quality image from each camera. In addition to studio cameras, there are a wide variety of other video sources normally available, including videocassette recorders and feeds from satellites and remote production units. Video signals from all of these sources go to the video switcher, where they are selected and switched on-line as needed. When a specific camera is punched up (selected) on the video switcher, the red tally light on top of that camera goes on. Audio is controlled with an audio board, or audio console. In addition to microphones, audio sources include CDs (compact discs), DATs (digital audio tapes) and audio cart (cartridge) machines.

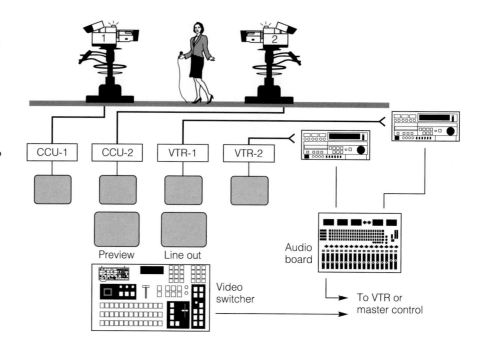

cyc; cyclorama: A large, curved, seamless background, generally white or light gray.

not obstruct the camera's view of the talent. Although some on-camera talent control their teleprompters themselves, in most studios a teleprompter operator is responsible for scrolling the script as it is read by the on-camera talent.

Studios are also equipped with a variety of **microphones.** They may be attached to the talent (a **personal microphone**); held by the talent; mounted on a desk or floor stand; or hung above the talent. In the latter case the mic[3] may be suspended with wires or attached to a **microphone boom,** where it can be easily moved as needed to follow the actions of the talent.

As the name suggests, the **set** in the studio provides the setting for the production. A set may be as simple as a *cyc* (for cyclorama), which is a large, gray, seamless muslin backdrop, or it may be as elaborate as a dramatic setting for a resplendent 18th-century drama. Somewhere in between are the basic news, weather, sports and interview sets (Figure 1.9).

Since television is a visual medium, it is dependent on light and lights. But in television production we are not simply talking about the presence or absence of light. Because light has such a great effect on how subject matter will be visually rendered, lighting, at its best, is considered an art form. A complex dramatic scene in a large production facility may require several hundred carefully placed lights.

The Control Room

Video signals from the studio cameras first go through a **camera control unit,** or **CCU.** (See Figure 1.8.) Here the **video levels** (the amplitude of the video signals) are controlled by the video engineer. This person may be located in an engineering section of the station or in the **control room** with the director and technical director. On the CCU there are a wide variety of controls that affect video quality, including video white level and black level adjustments, and

---

3. The term *mic* is now more commonly used for *microphone* than *mike,* even though *mikes* and *miking* seem to be less confusing phonetically than *mics* and *micing.*

FIGURE 1.9
Studio sets range all the way from an elaborate dramatic setting for a re-splendent 18th-century drama to a sim-ple muslin backdrop. The familiar news, weather, sports and interview sets we commonly see on TV lie some-where in between these extremes.

controls that alter the balance of colors in a picture. Sometimes several CCUs can be switched into a single *base station,* where a single set of controls can be used to adjust all the cameras at the same time.

From the CCU the video signal goes to a **video monitor** that displays a high-quality picture from the camera. The video signal also goes to the *video switcher,* where it will appear as one of several video sources that can be selected and switched on-line as needed. The **SEG**, or **special effects generator** (some-times called *DVE* for digital video effects unit), is the part of the video switcher that is responsible for many of the visual effects that we see in television produc-tion. Basic **visual effects** (also called **special effects**) include the fade, where video increasingly dims until it goes black (a **fade out**), or slowly appears out of black (a **fade up**); the dissolve, where one picture fades out while another simultaneously fades in; the super (for superimposition), where two pictures are simultaneously shown on the screen (resembling a double exposure in still pho-tography); the wipe, where a moving border progressively replaces one picture with another; the *key,* where solid text, graphics or a part of another video source appear over (while completely blocking out) the background image; and chroma key. In chroma key a specific color in the primary scene (generally a deep blue in some area of the background) is electronically removed, and an-other video image is inserted in its place. An example is the weather map and the associated graphics that are electronically inserted into the background be-hind a weatherperson. Today, we commonly see much more elaborate video effects than these; we see pictures twisted, rotated or spun around or even molded into a spinning ball or rotating cube. (See Figures 5.19A to 5.19F at the end of Chapter 5.)

Although the switcher is normally operated by the technical director under instructions from the director, sometimes directors will operate the switcher themselves. The technical director uses the switcher not only to **cut** (instanta-neously change) from one camera to another but to manipulate and control the wide variety of video sources that are typically a part of a sophisticated television production. These may include videotapes, non-studio cameras, electronically generated graphics, satellite feeds or still pictures.

base station: Central digital control sys-tem used for adjusting levels, color balance etc., of several studio cameras.

video switcher: An electronic switching and mixing device that controls multiple video sources.

DVE: Digital video effects. A device for electronically creating video effects. Often a component of a video switcher.

key: An electronic effect in which a video source is electronically inserted into back-ground video.

FIGURE 1.10

The control room is the central control center for a studio. The technical director operates the switcher to select and blend various video sources.

effects monitor: A video monitor where video effects are set up and checked before use.

line out monitor: A video monitor displaying the final video output intended for broadcast, recording or distribution.

audio board: Audio console. A basic desktop control center used to switch, mix and control audio levels for a variety of audio sources.

level: The strength or amplitude of an audio or video signal.

Some production facilities have an area called **telecine** where film and slide projectors are located. Here the images from 16mm films[4] and 35mm slides are converted into a video signal by projecting them into a video camera through a **film chain**. A bank of video monitors above the switcher displays the available video sources for the director and technical director (Figure 1.10). Most of these typically show **monochrome,** or black-and-white, pictures. But there are normally two or three monitors—often slightly larger—that display color pictures. One of these, an *effects monitor,* displays (and helps the technical director set up and adjust) visual effects before they are needed. The second, a preview monitor, shows a standby source of video, such as a satellite feed or a report from the field. Any video source can be switched up on the preview monitor so that it can be checked prior to being put on the air. Sometimes one monitor is used to display both effects and preview functions. The most important monitor, the *line out monitor,* displays the video being recorded or broadcast.

The audio that is picked up by microphones in the studio is routed into the *audio board* or **audio console** (Figure 1.11). This is where the audio engineer or technician, under command of the director, selects which mics and audio sources are to be heard. Recorded music, sound effects and the sound from videotapes, films and satellite feeds are just some of the audio sources that are routed into the audio board.

Audio engineers must not only switch on the various sources at the right time, but they are responsible for seeing that audio *levels* (amplitudes) are maintained at about zero dB, as measured by the VU meter (volume units meter) on the audio board. (See Figures 1.12A and 1.12B.)

The audio person is also responsible for maintaining an appropriate mix between audio sources. Among other things, this means that background music should not be so loud as to interfere with the intelligibility of speech.

---

4. Although 16mm is the primary film gauge used in television stations throughout the world, some of the larger TV stations are equipped with 35mm film projectors. Film chains capable of projecting Super-8 film are occasionally used by some stations. Whatever the gauge, film is almost always transferred to videotape before being broadcast.

FIGURE 1.11

An audio board such as this is suitable for a medium-sized production studio. Audio technicians must do more than just switch in the right audio at the right time. They must carefully balance the various audio sources and keep overall audio levels within a specific loudness range.

Although the audio board and audio engineer are often in the TV control room, there are advantages to housing them in a separate, acoustically isolated room called an **audio booth**. For one thing, TV control rooms are generally noisy, and if the audio engineer is in the same room, it may be difficult to concentrate on subtle distinctions between audio sources.

The Master Control Area

Programming intended for immediate broadcast is routed through the studio's control room to a **master control** area (Figure 1.13). This is the final switching point before the audio and video signals are sent to the television transmitter.

The **transmitter** consists of two parts: the large, rather complex electronic device that imposes the audio and video signals on an electromagnetic **carrier wave** (Figure 1.14), and the tower that radiates the resulting signal. In the United States these carrier wave frequencies will either be in the **VHF** range (Channels 2 to 13) or the **UHF** range (Channels 14 to 83). The power of the carrier wave is measured in watts. Depending upon the transmitter's power, the channel used and the terrain, the broadcast signal may cover up to a 75-mile radius.

In non-broadcast television the signals from the control room will either be videotaped for distribution or sent live to an audience by one of several means of direct, point-to-point electronic distribution.

In our attempt to give you a quick tour through the entire production process, we've covered a lot of ground. We've probably also introduced you to many new terms. Remember that most of what we have covered will be discussed in more detail in later chapters. Also, in case you forget the meaning of a term, you can quickly refresh your memory by turning to the Glossary at the end of the text.[5]

5. The Glossary contains more than 2,000 of the most commonly used terms in television production. It has been designed to go beyond text material and provide you with definitions of terms you will often encounter while reading professional and technical publications.

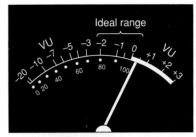

(a)

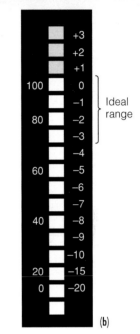

(b)

FIGURE 1.12
Although the VU meter shown in Figure 1.12A is the traditional means of monitoring audio levels, it has now been replaced in many types of equipment by all-electronic devices such as LED meters (Figure 1.12B). During a production, audio operators must see that maximum (peak) audio levels are kept within the ideal range illustrated. If levels are allowed to go significantly above zero dB, audio distortion may result.

FIGURE 1.13
Although a station can have several studio control rooms, it will have only one master control area. The master control area of a TV station is the final switching point before the audio and video signals are sent to the television transmitter. In addition to the video and audio outputs from control rooms, program sources directed to the master control area include videotape machines, field production units and satellite feeds.

FIGURE 1.14

A television transmitter electronically superimposes audio and video signals onto an electromagnetic carrier wave of an assigned frequency. In the United States these frequencies will either be in the VHF range (Channels 2 to 13) or the UHF range (Channels 14 to 83). Depending upon the transmitter's power, the channel used and the terrain, the broadcast signal may cover up to a 75-mile radius.

PREPARING FOR THE FUTURE

Production facilities differ greatly. Some of the equipment discussed in this text will not be available in many schools and small production facilities. Even so, it is important to understand the equipment and techniques that are common to a wide variety of production facilities. (It is amazing how you can suddenly be confronted with an internship or job opportunity where this knowledge will be important.)

The time taken to acquire a thorough understanding of the full range of techniques and tools of television production will pay off in many important ways—ways which often won't be evident to you until later in your career. Camera operators, writers, directors, producers and even on-camera talent find that having a solid understanding of the tools and techniques of the production process plays an indispensable role in professional success. Even so, there is also another side to this issue. Today, it is easy to become entranced with impressive technology and sophisticated production techniques. We should never lose sight of the fact that television, in essence, is only a medium of communication, albeit the world's most powerful and influential mass medium of communication to date. As essential as technology and sophisticated production techniques are, they should be considered only as essential tools for accomplishing a greater goal: the effective communication of ideas and information.

SUMMARY

Because television is a so-called glamour profession, many people are attracted to the field. This means most jobs in the profession are highly competitive. Consequently, only highly motivated people equipped with superior knowledge and skills are apt to be successful.

Television production refers to the complete process of creating television programs, including the preproduction, production and postproduction phases. Productions can either be broadcast live or recorded on videotape. Broadcast television is programming for a mass audience; it is the kind that is commonly produced by commercial TV stations and professional production companies. Non-broadcast television, referred to as institutional video, encompasses a wide range of areas including programming produced by educational institutions, corporations, medical facilities, religious groups and the government.

Although more and more production is being done in the field (on location), the TV studio is still the center of a large percentage of TV production. Programming segments that originate outside the studio are called electronic field production (EFP) segments. One type of EFP production is called ENG for electronic news gathering.

Camera operators must be familiar with four basic types of camera moves: panning (the left-to-right movement of the camera on the pan head), tilting (the up-and-down movement), dollying (when the entire camera is rolled directly toward or away from a scene) and trucking (when the camera is rolled to the left or right on its dolly or pedestal). Two other operator controls, zooming and focusing, refer to adjusting image size in the viewfinder and bringing the image into sharp focus.

Red tally lights on the top of cameras indicate when the cameras have been switched on-line, or are "on the air." Production personnel are linked by a communication system called a production line, or PL. Studio cameras may be equipped with talent-prompting devices called camera prompters.

Microphones may be attached to the talent (a personal microphone); held by the talent (a hand-held mic); mounted on a desk or floor stand; or hung above the talent. The audio picked up by microphones in the studio is routed into the audio board or audio console, where the audio engineer or technician selects and mixes the various audio sources. Audio technicians must not only switch on the various sources at the right time, but they are responsible for seeing that audio levels are maintained at about zero dB as measured by the VU meter on the audio board.

A studio set may be as simple as a cyc (a large, gray, seamless muslin backdrop), or it may be as elaborate as a dramatic setting for an 18th-century drama.

Video signals from studio cameras first go through a camera control unit, or CCU, where video levels can be controlled by a video engineer. Sometimes several CCUs can be switched into a base station, where a single set of controls can be used to adjust all the cameras at the same time. From the CCU the video signal goes to a video monitor in the control room that displays a high-quality picture from the camera. Other control room monitors include the effects monitor for setting up visual effects and the preview monitor, which shows a standby source of video, such as a satellite feed or a report from the field. The most important monitor, the line out monitor, displays the video being recorded or broadcast.

Programming intended for immediate broadcast is routed through the studio's control room to a master control area, which is the final switching point before the audio and video signals are sent to the television transmitter.

Many people are involved in creating major TV productions including the

producer	stagehand
executive producer	audio technician
set designer	production assistant
writer	video engineer
makeup person	associate director
wardrobe person	camera operator
talent	technical director
floor manager	lighting director
director	editor

The production areas we've introduced in this chapter include the

studio	master control area
telecine area	audio booth
video control room	transmitter

The basic production equipment introduced in this chapter includes the

switcher/SEG	video monitor
VTR	lights
audio board/console	film chain
PL (production line)	microphone
camera	

KEY TERMS

arc (camera movement)	audio technician
associate director	base station
audio board	camera blocking
audio booth	camera control unit (CCU)
audio console	camera of record
audio sweetening	camera operator

camera prompter
carrier wave
CCU
control room
cut
cyc
director
dolly
dollying
dress reheasal
dry rehearsal
DVE
editing
editor
effects monitor
EFP (electronic field production)
ENG (electronic news gathering)
executive producer
fade out
fade up
film chain
floor manager
focusing knob
institutional video
key
level
lighting director
line out monitor
live-on-tape
makeup person
master control
microphone
microphone boom
monochrome
pan head
panning
ped (camera movement)
personal microphone

PL
postproduction
preproduction
producer
production assistant
production line
rehearsal hall
robotic camera
script
set
set designer
special effects
special effects generator (SEG)
stagehand
strike
talent
tally light
target audience
technical director
telecine
teleprompter (prompter)
television production
tilting
transmitter
trucking
UHF
VHF
video engineer
video level
video monitor
video switcher
visual effects
VTR
wardrobe person
writer
zoom control
zoom lens

How Television Works $\;$ **2**

Most people take television for granted; they turn on their TV set and somehow, almost magically, their favorite programs appear. For most people all they need to know is how to turn their TV sets on and off, how to adjust the volume and how to operate the channel selector. For those that are a bit more technically minded there are the contrast and brightness controls, the color and hue controls and possibly, if they should ever need them, the vertical and horizontal controls.

But for you—an aspiring professional in a competitive field—things will not be this simple. In order to have control over the medium, you must thoroughly understand it, or at least understand the areas that can provide you with important creative controls.

Those who shun technical things sometimes say, "I don't have to understand how a car works in order to drive it, so why do I have to understand how TV works to operate a camera or be a director?" True, you may not have to understand cars if you are simply going to *drive* them, but you better understand them if you are going to *manufacture* them. In the same way, you don't have to understand the audio and video process to simply be able to watch TV; but you do need to understand it if you are going to produce effective TV programs. If we need further evidence, all we have to do is to examine the talents of successful directors—people like Mike Nichols and Stanley Kubrick in film. These directors have been able to introduce many innovative techniques because they thoroughly understood the tools of their medium. This knowledge also results in more predictable quality—an important professional attribute in a medium where "time is money." With these things in mind we will explore eight major areas in this chapter:

- How video works in terms of fields and frames
- World broadcast standards, including standards conversion

- The characteristics and advantages of high-definition television
- How light is transformed into a video signal
- Digital and analog signals
- The role of the waveform monitor in video production
- The quality limitations of video
- The television transmission process

IT'S ALL AN ILLUSION

Strictly speaking, there are no "moving pictures" in either motion pictures or television. It's an illusion. In the 1830s, it was discovered that a sequence of still pictures presented at a rate of about 16 or more per second would blend together, giving the impression of a continuous, uninterrupted image. Even more important, it was found that if the individual pictures varied slightly to show changes over time, the illusion of a continuous motion could be created.

According to perceptual psychologists, two processes are involved in this illusion. One is best illustrated by the groups of neon images in an electric sign that, when sequentially lit, give the impression of movement. An arrow can be made to appear to move, for example, if two or three separate arrows light up in the proper sequence. The illusion of motion induced by this type of sequence is referred to as the **phi phenomenon**.

This is closely linked to **persistence of vision,** which is responsible for fusing together the separate images into one, apparently continuous image. For example, between the times the individual frames (pictures) in a film are projected, the motion picture screen is completely black. (This interval is necessary so the projector can pull down and illuminate successive frames on the film.) But when the individual still pictures on the film are projected in a rapid sequence, our eyes retain each of the images for a fraction of a second and fill in the blank intervals between the pictures. When this visual fusion process is added to the illusion of motion created by the phi phenomenon, we end up with the illusion of motion in motion pictures and television.

Although early silent films projected images at 16 or 18 frames each second, when sound was introduced the rate was increased to 24 frames per second. The higher rate was necessary to achieve needed sound quality when an optical sound track was added to the film. Unlike broadcast television, which can have a frame rate of 25 or 30 per second, depending upon the country and broadcast standard, film enjoys a single, international standard of 24 frames per second.

Although a motion picture camera records complete pictures on each frame of film, a video camera breaks down each frame into hundreds of horizontal lines of brightness and color information. Figure 2.1 illustrates the individual lines that compose a complete TV frame. The lens of a TV camera focuses the image of a scene on an internal imaging device, and the image is electronically read out a line at a time in a top-to-bottom, left-to-right, motion. The electronic signal generated varies with differences in brightness in the original picture. (Chapter 5 will discuss how the camera "sees" color.)

The lines, however, are not scanned in sequence. To help persistence of vision and reduce flicker and brightness variations when the picture is reproduced, each complete television picture is divided into two, **interlaced** (interleaved) segments. The odd-numbered lines are scanned in the first pass of the electron beam. The beam then returns to the top of the frame and fills in the even-numbered lines (Figure 2.1). Each of the odd-even line passes is called a **field**. Each field is completed in 1/60 second.

field: One-half of a complete television picture or frame. In the U.S. system of television there are 60 fields transmitted per second. (See also *frame.*)

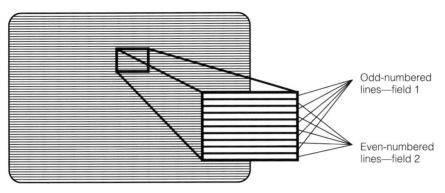

Odd-numbered
lines—field 1

Even-numbered
lines—field 2

Monochrome television screen

Once the even-numbered lines are added to the odd-numbered lines, a complete TV picture, or complete *frame,* is created. The basic system of television used in the United States and a number of other countries uses 525 lines in each frame. Since each field is completed in 1/60 second, this means that a complete TV picture is formed every 1/30 second (1/60 second plus 1/60 second equals 1/30 second).[1] (Figure 2.2 shows a close-up of the combined odd- and even-numbered lines on a black-and-white TV screen.) This process of scanning fields and frames applies to both how the picture is originally broken down inside a TV camera and how the picture is later recreated on a TV screen.

frame: A complete TV picture of 525 horizontal lines (in NTSC) composed of two scanned fields of 262.5 lines each. (See also *field.*)

NTSC standard: Normally refers to the 525-line, 60-field system of broadcast television, which combines chroma with luminance information into one composite signal.

INTERNATIONAL SYSTEMS OF TELEVISION

The NTSC Television System

In 1941, the Federal Communications Commission (FCC) officially adopted the monochrome standard advanced by the electronic industry's National Television Standards Committee (NTSC). This established the basic **NTSC standard** of 525 lines, 30 frames per second now used for broadcasting in the United States, Canada, South America, Japan and a number of other Asian countries. Because 30 frames consist of 60 fields, the NTSC system is often referred to as a 525-line, 60-field system. The majority of TV *receivers* being used in the world use the NTSC standard. Even so, 75 percent of the *countries* in the world use a version of the PAL or SECAM broadcast standards. Since television programs represent one of the top exports of the United States, a basic understanding of the different international broadcast TV standards is important.

The PAL and SECAM Television Systems

PAL-M, the broadcast standard used in Brazil, has 525 lines and 60 fields just as the NTSC system does. However, unlike NTSC, PAL (phase alternate line) systems have the ability to electronically reverse specific video information with each scanning line and, in the process, cancel certain types of interference. This

FIGURE 2.2
An extreme close-up of a small section of a black-and-white TV screen shows how a TV image is composed of horizontal lines of brightness information. The same concept is used with color TV screens, except that each line of information is further divided into red, blue and green dots of light. This is explained in Chapter 5.

1. Although the 1/30 and 1/60 second rates are commonly given in describing fields and frames, they only apply to one system of high-definition TV (HDTV) and black-and-white NTSC television. To be exact, the numbers for NTSC color television are 1/29.97 second for fields and 1/59.94 second for frames. We should also note that a few TV systems use a system of *progressive scanning,* which varies somewhat from the description presented here.

Hz (hertz): Cycles per second. A unit of frequency measurement for sound and electromagnetic waves named after Heinrich Hertz.

is a definite advantage in areas where there is poor TV reception or if there is static interference.

Since many countries use a 50 *Hz* (cycles per second) electrical system, it was logical for these counties to develop a system of television based on 50 fields and 25 frames. For related technical reasons these countries also decided on a 625-line system. Although the 100 additional lines make the picture look sharper and provide added picture detail, the slower 50-field rate means that a slight flicker can sometimes be noticed. **PAL-B, -G,** and **-H** are standards used in Continental Europe and some African and Middle Eastern countries. **PAL-N** is used in Argentina, Paraguay and Uruguay. **SECAM** (roughly translated as "sequential color and memory") is used in France, Eastern Europe, some Middle Eastern countries and many African nations. These systems are referred to as 625-line, 50-field systems.

It should be noted that the different world TV standards (there were some 14 standards at one point) were not based solely on 60-cycle, 50-cycle electrical power differences or the perceived technical superiority of one system over another. Some national leaders intentionally selected a TV system for their country that was incompatible with neighboring countries so they could isolate their people from "foreign" viewpoints. In some cases they also wanted to favor electronic equipment manufactured in specific countries.

STANDARDS CONVERSION

The incompatible television standards in use throughout the world create many problems. A videotape made in the United States, for example, cannot be played in England without first being converted to the 625-line PAL standard. A similar problem exists in using satellite TV signals from different countries.

standards converter: An electronic device for converting signals from one broadcast standard to another.

Originally, the only way to convert one standard to another was to photograph a TV monitor with a 16mm motion picture camera and use the film. This process, called **kinescope recording,** resulted in a significant loss of quality. With the recent introduction of digital *standards converters,* one world TV standard can be directly converted to another with only a moderate loss of quality. Because of the differences in the 25-per-second or 30-per-second frame rates, when conversions are made certain fields and frames have to be either scanned twice or dropped at periodic intervals (Figure 2.3). Three problems result.

Judder (Figure 2.4) is the result of NTSC being converted to a 25-frame-

FIGURE 2.3
When video is converted from NTSC's 60-fields-per-second to PAL's or SECAM's 50-fields-per-second standard, fields have to regularly be dropped. This is referred to as culling out frames. Frames have to be repeated when the 50-field PAL and SECAM systems are converted to NTSC. Figures 2.4 and 2.5 illustrate the problems this conversion process causes.

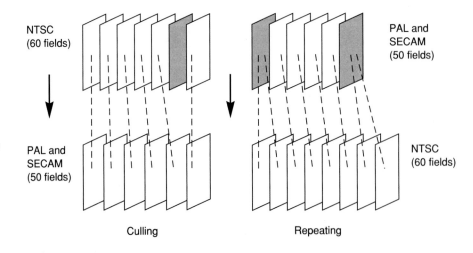

NTSC
(60 fields)

PAL and
SECAM
(50 fields)

PAL and
SECAM
(50 fields)

NTSC
(60 fields)

Culling   Repeating

per-second standard. This is noticeable with rapid camera or subject movements and is primarily the result of frames being dropped. **Ghosting** (Figure 2.5) is another problem. Since a standards converter has to periodically combine some NTSC frames before it can convert them to the slower 25-frame standard, occasionally you will see two images on the screen at the same time. This is particularly noticeable during a series of fast cuts in a NTSC production. Finally, due to the conversion process, color sometimes ends up looking muted or smeared.

Because of the quality loss in converting NTSC to PAL or SECAM and vice versa, many people looked forward to a single, worldwide standard — preferably one that was technically superior to all existing broadcast standards.

HIGH-DEFINITION TELEVISION

It was hoped that as the world moved to **high-definition television,** or *HDTV,*[2] nations could agree on a single, worldwide television standard. It appeared that this might be possible in the late 1980s when many countries initially agreed on a proposed 1,125-line, 60-field HDTV standard. However, after technical, political and economic concerns surfaced, the 200 national leaders attending a world conference on broadcasting in 1989 backed away from the initial agreement due to ". . . unresolvable differences in opinion." Now, the dream of a single, worldwide television standard has all but disappeared.

2. By late 1992 no final agreement had been reached in the United States on a broadcast or production standard for high-definition television. At that point the concept was being referred to in various ways, including HDTV, HD, and ATV (for Advanced Television). To add to the confusion, other countries were using their own designations. For the sake of simplicity, the first widely accepted designation, *HDTV,* is being used throughout this book. This refers, in general, to a high-resolution standard using a 16 × 9 aspect ratio.

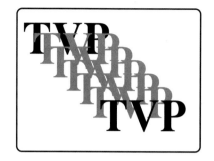

FIGURE 2.4
Converting 30-frames-per-second NTSC programming to the 25-frames-per-second standard used in the PAL and SECAM systems can result in problems. Judder, which is a kind of stroboscopic effect associated with movement, is illustrated here.

HDTV; HD (high-definition television): Any one of several systems of television that use more than 1,000 scanning lines and an aspect ratio greater than 4 × 3.

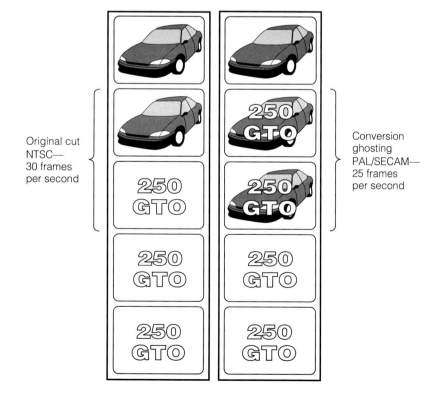

Original cut NTSC— 30 frames per second

Conversion ghosting PAL/SECAM— 25 frames per second

FIGURE 2.5
Ghosting is another problem resulting from converting NTSC video to the PAL or SECAM standards. Since a standards converter has to combine some NTSC frames before it can convert them to the slower 25-frame standard, occasionally you will see two images on the screen at the same time. This is particularly noticeable during a series of fast cuts.

FIGURE 2.6

This computer simulation of a section of a TV screen compares the detail possible with three TV standards: the 525-line NTSC system, the 625-line PAL and SECAM systems and the 1,125-line high-definition production standard. Note that the number of lines makes a considerable difference in the ability of the TV system to reproduce detail.

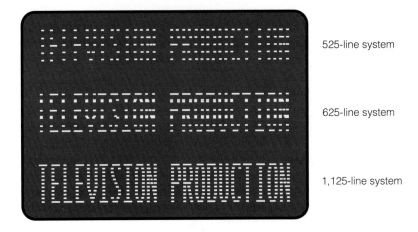

525-line system

625-line system

1,125-line system

In the early 1990s, two types of high-definition standards were being debated: a production standard and a broadcast standard. To take advantage of the high-definition process, many producers were recording programs in the 1,125-line, 60-field production standard that had originally been worked out between Japan, the United States and several other countries. Once a production is recorded in this system, it can be either transferred to film or converted to any one of several broadcast standards for over-the-air transmission.

How much better is an HDTV system? First, HDTV is able to reproduce a much greater range of colors and tones than standard, over-the-air broadcast systems. More importantly, HDTV can reproduce much more picture detail. Figure 2.6 is a computer simulation of a small section of a 525-line, a 625-line and a 1,126-line HDTV television display. You will note that as the number of lines increases, the TV system is able to reproduce much more detail. The picture detail in the better HDTV systems equals what is normally attainable by projected 35mm motion picture film.[3] Even so, since video and film are inherently different media, the question of their relative "quality"—a word that can mean many things to many people—has been a subject of active debate. As we will see, in broadcast television the difference between video and film is based more on the respective production approaches than on inherent quality differences between the media.

aspect ratio: The ratio of the width to the height of a video image; typically 4 × 3 or 16 × 9.

One other element to consider in television systems is the *aspect ratio,* or the numerical ratio of picture width to height. Instead of the **raster** (TV image) being three units high and four wide (4 × 3), as it is in NTSC, PAL and SECAM television, the aspect ratio of most HDTV systems is 16 × 9. This more naturally conforms to human vision and to wide-screen film formats. (See Figures 2.7 and 2.8A.)

CONVERTING WIDE-SCREEN FORMATS

The conversion of 16 × 9 HDTV images to the standard 4 × 3 aspect ratio is done in basically the same way as the conversion of wide-screen films to NTSC television. There are three approaches.

FIGURE 2.7

Squares can be used to illustrate the difference between the 4 × 3 and 16 × 9 aspect ratios. Figures 2.8A to 2.8D illustrate approaches to converting a 16 × 9 aspect ratio to a 4 × 3 image.

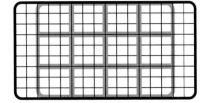

3. The word *projected* is important here. Although the resolution possible with a single still frame of normal 35mm film can far exceed present HDTV capabilities, there is normally a significant loss of clarity when film is projected. This is in part due to a lack of perfect vertical registration between successive film frames in the gate of the projector. Since there are no moving mechanical parts in the HDTV process, high-definition video does not have this problem.

- First, the sides of the picture can be cut off. This is shown in Figure 2.8B. If the original HDTV (or wide-screen film) is shot with the narrower 4 × 3 cutoff area in mind, this may not be a problem.

- Second, if the production is done without considering the standard broadcast aspect ratio, and important visual information appears at the extreme sides of many scenes, the entire production may have to be **panned-and-scanned**. This involves a technician reviewing every scene and programming a computer-controlled imaging device to electronically pan the 4 × 3 window back and forth over the larger, wide-screen format. In Figure 2.7 this would be like someone moving the 4 × 3 frame to the left and right over the larger 16 × 9 area so that it would favor the most important information at any one time.

- Finally, if the *full* HDTV frame contains important visual information (as in the case of written material extending to the edges of the screen) panning-and-scanning will not work. In this case a ***letterbox*** approach can be used (Figure 2.8C). But there is a problem. As you can see, this results in small blank areas at the top and bottom of the frame. Often, the letterbox approach is reserved for the opening titles and closing credits of a production with the remainder of the production being panned-and-scanned.

Since many directors feel that the pan-and-scan approach introduces pans that are artificial and not motivated by the action, they insist that the letterbox approach be used throughout the production. Originally, producers feared that audiences would object to the black areas at the top and bottom of the letterbox frame. However, today the letterbox format is commonly seen, and audiences apparently understand that this format represents the most accurate NTSC, PAL or SECAM rendition of a wide-screen production.

For short segments of a production, there is another way of handling the difference between the 16 × 9 and 4 × 3 aspect ratios. You have probably seen the opening or closing of a film on television horizontally "squeezed" to accommodate the titles and credits (Figure 2.8D). The effect is especially noticeable when people are a part of the scene — people who, as a result, suddenly become rather tall and thin. (This is not to say that the physique of some of us might not be improved by this process.) The narrowing effect is caused by the **anamorphic** lens on the film camera, which compresses the original wide-screen view onto a film frame that is essentially in the 4 × 3 ratio. Normally, of course, when this film is projected in a theater, the compressed image is stretched back to its original wide-screen ratio.

letterbox: Term used for one method of adapting a 16 × 9 aspect ratio to 4 × 3 that results in a black or patterned bar at the top and bottom of the 4 × 3 image. Since this technique does not involve altering original images or scenes in any way, it is considered the "most honest" form of conversion.

(a)

(b)

(c)

(d)

FIGURE 2.8

This series of drawings illustrate three approaches to converting a 16 × 9 aspect ratio to 4 × 3. Figure 2.8A shows an image in a full 16 × 9 aspect ratio. One way of converting the 16 × 9 image to 4 × 3 (Figure 2.8B) results in a loss of the edges of the image. In Figure 2.8C another approach to conversion is illustrated — shrinking the 16 × 9 image so that it all fits within the 4 × 3 space. However, this results in a dark area at the top and bottom of the frame. This type of conversion, called letterbox, is preferred by some directors because it preserves the full 16 × 9 image. Figure 2.8D illustrates the way the conversion process is typically handled in feature films: reproducing the 16 × 9 image with compressed horizontal dimensions. Note that the ball at the top of the frame, which was perfectly round in the original image, is now oval-shaped. This approach, which involves simply projecting the compressed wide-screen film image as it appears on the 35mm film, is often used during the titles and credits when a wide-screen feature film is shown on TV. The final approach to format conversion, pan-and-scan (not illustrated), could be likened to moving the 4 × 3 frame in Figure 2.7 to the left and right within the larger 16 × 9 area as necessary throughout a production. This approach is discussed in more detail in the text.

Digital and Analog Technology

Recent innovations in video, such as standards conversion and special effects, rely on developments in digital technology. Since digital electronics is now such an integral part of television, people preparing for the field should be familiar with its principles.

In explaining the difference between analog and digital the contrast between digital watches and a traditional, wall-mounted electric clock is often used. The electric clock—the kind that's plugged into an electrical outlet—has a continuously moving second hand. In contrast, the second hand on most battery-powered clocks and watches jumps from second to second. Note that in the first instance the information smoothly and continuously changes; in the other, the information jumps from value to value (second to second) in distinct increments.

Analog Signals

analog: As opposed to a digital signal, a signal that varies smoothly between certain ranges. An analog signal bears an exact, continuous relationship to the original information.

noise: Any background interference in video or audio signals. Typically manifested as hiss or hum on sound tracks, and as snow or graininess in video.

Analog audio and video signals vary smoothly and continuously from one value to another. Although that sounds like the most accurate way of representing data, a problem comes about when this type of (analog) data has to be amplified. Whenever an analog signal is amplified (a process that must be repeated over and over again in broadcast electronics) some amount of electronic *noise* is inevitably introduced into the signal. With audio, this takes the form of a subtle hiss or hum; in video, noise resembles a very subtle snow-pattern in the background of a picture.

Although limited reamplification with good equipment will not produce a discernible problem, if the analog signal has to be reamplified many times, problems can quickly multiply. Eventually the resulting noise and signal distortion will become quite objectionable. This becomes a major issue in copying analog audio- and videotapes. With each subsequent copy, or *generation,* the quality of an analog tape drops appreciably. After several generations (copies of copies), the quality may fall below minimum broadcast standards. All this was changed with the introduction of digital technology.

generation: Refers to the number of times a tape is copied. An original recording is the first generation; a copy of that copy is a second generation tape; and a copy of the second generation is the third generation, etc.

Digital Signals

digital: In contrast to the analog process, the encoding of electronic information in the form of discrete "on" or "off" pulses.

Digital electronics was introduced to broadcasting during the mid-1980s. By the early 1990s television equipment manufacturers had moved toward *digital* electronics in all phases of broadcasting, including audio- and videotape machines, cameras, switchers and editors. Although equipment designed to handle digital audio and video signals is technically complex, digital electronics does solve many of the problems of analog signals.

Since most audio and video starts out as an analog signal, the trick is to convert it as soon as possible to digital information. As illustrated in Figure 2.9, digital signals are based on assigning numbers to amplitude and frequency characteristics of an analog signal. The numbers correspond to the original attributes of the signal, and their values won't change, no matter how much the signal is amplified.

Specifically, digital signals consist of strings of **binary numbers,** which are simply strings of zeros and ones. As an example, a value of 3 is equal to the binary number 011. Note in Figure 2.9 that binary numbers are assigned to the amplitude of the signal at various points. If a mathematical reading can be obtained from the varying state of the analog signal thousands of times each second, the continuously changing analog signal can be turned into a long sequence of binary numbers. So, thousands of times each second an analog-to-digital converter checks on an analog signal and with each check translates the

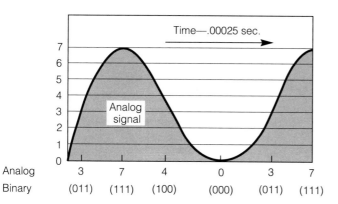

FIGURE 2.9
In the analog-to-digital (A/D) conversion process binary numbers are assigned to the amplitude and frequency characteristics of the analog signal. Thousands of times each second an analog-to-digital converter translates characteristics of the analog signal into binary numbers. Note in this figure that an amplitude of 3 equals 011, an amplitude of 7 equals 111, etc. Using this process, any analog signal can be converted into a string of computer-type numbers.

status of the signal into a binary number. The binary number simply reflects the voltage of the analog signal at any one moment in time.

Sampling Signals

The process of "checking on" the status of an analog signal and converting it into binary numbers is called **sampling**. This must be done thousands of times per second. In professional audio recording a **sampling rate** of 48,000 is used, which means that the audio recorder samples the value of analog signal 48,000 times each second.

Since the zeros and ones are simply equivalent to "on" or "off" electrical states, binary numbers are largely immune to signal interference, system noise and general distortion. However, since the numbering system is based on two instead of 10, many more numbers are needed to express numerical values. For this reason, **bit speed**, or the number of bits of information (zeros and ones) that can be transmitted per second, becomes a major concern. In order to handle digitized audio and video signals, digital equipment must be capable of handling massive amounts of data per second — far more than with analog signals.

Manipulating Digital Signals for Special Effects

Once in the form of numbers, digital information can be mathematically manipulated in many ways. For example, the signals can be expanded or compressed by simply multiplying or dividing the numbers. In audio this opens the door to manipulating time: segments can be shortened or lengthened. In the process the frequency or pitch of the audio signal can be corrected. In fact, it is possible to speed up an audiotape of a voice to almost twice the normal speed and not encounter a high-pitched "chipmunk" effect. If the original speech was clear and distinct, the speech will even remain reasonably intelligible. Digital manipulation of audio is often used to disguise a person's voice in order to hide their identity.

In video, the digital numbers can be mathematically manipulated to expand, shrink and reverse a picture. By linking the mathematical possibilities, a video picture can be made to rotate and spin, or to take the form of objects of various sizes and shapes.

Quantization

There is one other term that is bandied about in digital electronics: *quantization*. While sampling rate refers to the number of times per second that the analog signal is electronically plotted, **quantization** refers to the manner in which the

FIGURE 2.10
The more quantization levels in the analog-to-digital conversion process, the smoother transitions in loudness will be. At 16 quantizing levels, the level used by many audio systems today, loudness transitions become imperceptible.

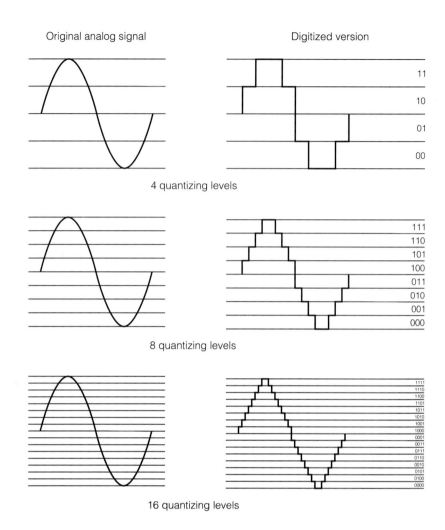

Original analog signal · Digitized version

4 quantizing levels

8 quantizing levels

16 quantizing levels

signal is digitized. Figure 2.10 illustrates three quantization systems, which contain four, eight and 16 quantizing levels, respectively. Note that the four-level sample shows a crude stairstep effect. We could say that the resolution of this sampling rate is quite low. In the analog-to-digital (A/D) converter, sound values must be moved up or down to the nearest "step" — since there can be no in-between state in digital electronics. As we move up to the 16-level quantization, the accuracy or resolution of the sound increases, but so do the demands on our numbering system. At this level, binary numbers have 65,536 possible combinations of ones and zeros! (Fortunately, we don't have to worry about handling such numbers; we have computers to do it for us.) Once we arrive at 16-level quantization, we've arrived at the resolution of today's compact disk and digital audiotape systems. At this point we can no longer hear the "stairstep" digital values; our ears perceive the sound as a seamless web of smoothly varying sounds.

MONITORING VIDEO LEVELS

waveform monitor: A type of oscilloscope or CRT that displays the amplitude of a video signal and its sync.

As we noted in the last chapter, we use the VU meter with audio signals to observe and maintain proper levels. Since video is more complex, a simple meter won't tell us enough. Instead we need a ***waveform monitor,*** which, among

FIGURE 2.11

The waveform monitor, which represents the primary piece of video monitoring equipment in production facilities, provides a graphical display of video levels. Although a waveform monitor makes it possible to carefully control luminance (black and white video) levels, it provides no information on the accuracy of colors. The latter can be determined by a vectorscope (Chapter 5).

other things, is able to graphically display and measure the white and black levels in video (Figure 2.11).

The Waveform Monitor

Although today's cameras and videotape equipment include much automatic circuitry, automatic controls cannot distinguish between good video and bad; all they can ensure is whether the video meets rudimentary technical specifications. In professional video work waveform monitors are often used as original scenes are being taped and later, during postproduction when the scenes are edited together. By passing (looping) a video signal through a waveform monitor, the characteristics of the video can be electronically graphed on the face of the waveform monitor screen (Figure 2.12). The dark areas of the video picture are represented near the zero point of the waveform monitor, and white areas appear near the top. A scale along the side of the waveform monitor is calibrated in units of amplitude called **IRE** (Institute of Radio Engineers) units.

Reference black is the darkest part of the picture. Such things as dull black paint and new blue jeans reflect about 3 percent of the light falling on them.

reference black: The darkest portion of the video picture, generally with a reflectance value of 3 percent.

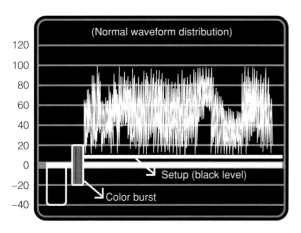

FIGURE 2.12

Just as the VU meter in audio is used to keep levels within specified limits, video levels must be kept within a limited range to ensure video quality. The blackest areas of a video picture should drop down to the 7.5 (setup) point on the waveform monitor, and the white areas should reach 100. Blanking pulses reside below the 7.5 point. The color burst signal indicates only the presence of a color signal; it reveals nothing about the accuracy of colors. The sync signal must be kept between minus 40 and the baseline, or zero point on the scale.

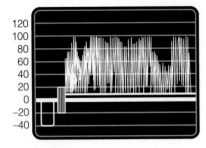

FIGURE 2.13

A normal video picture should have a reasonably even distribution of tones from TV black (represented in the top area of the picture) to TV white (the ice at the bottom of the picture). Although video cameras have circuitry that can automatically maintain this range, this circuitry can be fooled by non-standard subject matter. In this case the bright ice, which comprises a large part of the picture area, will result in darkened skin tones unless video levels are manually adjusted with the help of a waveform monitor.

reference white: The whitest portion of the video picture, generally with a reflectance value of 60 percent or above.

This reflectance value is considered "TV black." A waveform monitor should display this at the 7.5 point (Figure 2.12). ***Reference white*** is created by subject matter that reflects 70 percent to 90 percent of the light falling on its surface. Reference white, or "TV white," should come up to the 100 mark on the waveform monitor. Video that is more or less evenly distributed from 7.5 to 100 on a waveform monitor (Figures 2.13A and 2.13B) reproduces well.

BLANKING AND SYNC SIGNALS

In the process of scanning a video picture, there are "return trip" intervals when the electron beam has to return from the right side of the picture to start scanning another line, and from the bottom of one field in order to start scanning another field. These intervals can be likened to the times when we are writing in a piece of paper and our hand returns from the right side of a page after we finish a line. If we didn't lift our pen or pencil, we would draw a line through what we just wrote. Likewise, when we finish a page we must lift our pen or pencil and move it to the top of the next page. The same principle holds for "writing" lines and fields; the electron beam must be extinguished so it won't obliterate or blank out information.

Signals called **blanking pulses** blank out the electron beam during these phases of scanning. These are in a sense "blacker-than-black" signals that reside below the 7.5 point on the waveform monitor (Figure 2.12).

The Synchronizing Signal

sync: (synchronization) The basic synchronizing pulse in video. The crucial timing signal that keeps various pieces of video equipment electronically coordinated.

Some type of time-keeping signal must keep the rapidly moving electron beam of cameras in synchronization with other pieces of equipment that are reproducing the signal. In fact, unless every piece of equipment is at the same place in the scanning process at the same time, video chaos results. *Sync* (short for synchronization) pulses are the high-speed timing pulses that keep all video equipment in step during the process of scanning lines, fields and frames. These pulses dictate the precise points at which the electronic beam starts and stops while scanning each line, field and frame. A single source of sync from a master **sync generator** is used to supply common timing pulses for equipment within a facility.

Like the video and blanking levels, the amplitude of the sync signal must be maintained within certain limits. On a waveform monitor the bottom line in the sync should be at minus 40 (the very bottom of the waveform scale), and the top should extend to the baseline, or the zero point on the scale (Figure 2.12). Too much sync and the black level of the video is pushed too high; too little and the picture will roll and break up.

sync generator: An electronic device that generates the variety of timing pulses needed to keep the video equipment synchronized.

THE TRANSMISSION PROCESS

When the video signal is broadcast, the line-by-line read-out of the video signal is superimposed over a type of electromagnetic energy called an RF carrier wave. (RF refers to *radio frequency*. The first broadcast use of this range of electromagnetic energy was for radio.) Six million cycles (6 MHz) of RF energy is broadcast per second to carry the information in a NTSC television signal.

Figure 2.14 shows that about 4 MHz of the total 6 MHz is for the video signal, and only about 0.25 MHz is for the FM audio signal. The remaining area is reserved for a sideband (a necessary but non-utilitarian part of the complete signal) and for a **guardband** (safety area) separating the audio and video signals. If the video level is too high, this guardband will be overrun by video information. The result is that unpleasant buzz in the audio that you sometimes hear when bright subject matter is suddenly introduced into a broadcast video signal.

Color information in the form of a **color subcarrier** is interleaved within the basic *luminance* (black-and-white) video information. We'll discuss color in more detail in Chapter 5.

luminance: The black-and-white aspect of a television signal. Also called the Y signal.

Although the video signal uses amplitude modulation just as AM radio does (and is, therefore, subject to the same types of static interference), the audio part of the television signal is frequency modulated (FM). For this reason, television audio resists interference and is capable of virtually the same high audio quality that is associated with FM radio.

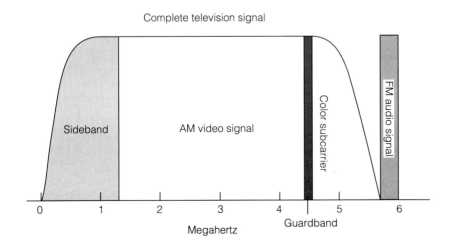

FIGURE 2.14
A complete TV signal, as broadcast, consists of an AM video signal, a sub-carrier for color information and an FM audio signal. Remaining areas include a sideband (a necessary but non-utilitarian part of the complete signal) and a guardband (safety area), which separates the audio and video signals. If the video level is too high, the guardband will be overrun by video information. The result is a loud, unpleasant buzz in the audio and a "tearing effect" around the white areas of the video.

FIGURE 2.15
Unlike AM radio transmissions, TV signals go primarily in a straight, line-of-sight fashion. For this reason TV stations often put their antennas 1,000 or more feet high—either on a mountaintop, a tall building or on a tall supporting tower. This array of antennas is located near San Francisco.

CATV: Community Antenna TV. A system of distributing TV signals over a geographic area via coaxial cable or fiber optics.

Transmitting the Television Signal

The process of putting the audio and video signals onto an RF carrier wave for broadcast is called **modulation**. Carrier waves used in broadcasting may be anywhere from a few thousand watts of power for a limited range, **low-power TV** station (LPTV) to several million watts of power for a powerful UHF television station. It should be noted that other things besides transmitter power affect the coverage area of a TV transmitter. The most important is frequency. All things being equal, the lower the frequency (Channels 2, 3, 4, for example), the less power is required to cover a specific area. The UHF frequencies (especially when you get up to Channel 30 and beyond) take much more power to cover an area. A station on Channel 2 with a power of 100,000 watts will typically have a greater coverage area than a TV station on Channel 45 with 500,000 watts of power.

Another important factor affects the area that a TV transmitter can cover. Unlike AM radio transmissions, TV signals go primarily in a straight, line-of-sight fashion. This means that obstructions between the TV transmitting **antenna** (the device that dispatches the RF energy) and a TV receiver can block, reflect or diminish the signal. Mountains and tall buildings are major problems. For this reason TV stations often put their antennas 1,000 or more feet high—either on a mountaintop, a tall building or on a tall supporting tower (Figure 2.15).

If obstructions such as tall buildings totally *blocked* the TV signals, we wouldn't have one of the major problems we do with TV reception. But these objects often *reflect* the RF energy. Multiple reflections often result, especially in a city with many tall buildings. Each of the reflected signals travels over a different path before it is received by a TV set. This is called **multipath reception**.

When a TV set receives RF energy that has been reflected from two or more objects, it has to cope with multiple signals. Even though RF energy travels at 186,000 miles per second, just as light does, these different paths result in timing differences. When two or more signals arrive at your TV set at different times, the result is "ghosts," or multiple video images. Reorienting the antenna on your TV set to favor the stronger signal will lessen the problem.

Community Antenna Television (*CATV*), commonly called cable television, can deliver a TV signal directly to your TV set, thus solving the multipath problem. Because they get their signals directly from satellites some 22,500 miles overhead, home satellite receivers also eliminate the ghosts associated with terrestrial transmissions.

TV MONITORS AND RECEIVERS

The **video monitors** associated with TV stations and production centers have no tuner and are wired directly to a source of video. Most don't have audio-processing circuitry. Monitors have the ability to underscan (reduce the size of) the video picture so that the full width of the picture is seen (Figure 2.16). Standard **TV receivers** (commonly just called TV sets) have a RF tuner that can tune in specific stations (and, in the process, separate the audio and video signals from the RF carrier wave).

There are a number of areas of quality loss associated with the standard broadcast transmission and reception process. Although these will not normally be apparent on video monitors within the production facility, they affect video on home receivers. If production personnel are not aware of these disparities, the results of their work may end up being disappointing.

FIGURE 2.16
Video monitors have the ability to underscan the video picture so that the full width of the picture is seen.

Safe
title
area

Safe
action
area

FIGURE 2.17
Because of overscanning, about 10 percent of the outside perimeter of a video
image is lost by the time the picture
reaches a home receiver. To keep subject matter from being lost, it should be
confined to the safe action area (sometimes called the essential area). Since
the area that is cut off is even greater
than 10 percent on some home receivers, a few technicians recommend
keeping really critical subject matter
within an "even safer" area: the safe
title area.

Video Losses

Loss of Detail   First, the transmission process results in a significant loss of detail. Today's studio cameras can resolve three to four times the
amount of detail that the typical home receiver can reproduce. This loss of detail
is due to both the 4 MHz bandwidth limitation on the broadcast signal and to
home reception problems. This loss may mean that important details in a picture
(including written information that is discernible on monitors in the TV control
room) may not be visible on a home viewer.

Safe Areas   Another significant problem results from overscanning
in the home receiver. Because of *overscanning* (a loss of video information at
the top, bottom and sides of the TV picture), about 10 percent of the outside
perimeter of the image as seen in a camera viewfinder is normally lost by the
time the picture is reproduced on the typical home receiver. Put another way,
only the inner 90 percent of the original video will be seen on home receivers.
Since the cut-off area is partially dependent on home receivers, the area affected
can be rather unpredictable. Therefore, two *safe areas* are sometimes suggested:
the safe title area and the safe action area. These areas, which are illustrated
in Figure 2.17, are often indicated in camera viewfinders and control room
monitors.

Safe Action Area   In order to be seen on the home receiver, all
important action must be confined to the inner 90 percent of the video frame,
the **safe action area**. Although a few home receivers may show action outside
the safe action area, this can't be relied upon. To be safe, it is important to
confine basic video information to the inner 90 percent of the frame. This area
is sometimes referred to as the *essential area*.

Safe Title Area   As the name suggests, titles and written material, to
be really safe, should be confined to an "even safer" area. Because the effect of
overscanning varies greatly, a few technicians feel that written material (or any

overscanning: A loss of some information
around the outer edges of a picture, typically as a result of the broadcast and reception process.

safe area: Essential area. The inner 80
percent to 90 percent of the video picture
not lost in the transmission process.

highly important material) should be confined to an even smaller area—the inner 80 percent of the frame. This is referred to as the **safe title area**. Fans of old movies have probably had the experience of watching a movie through to the closing credits in order to get the name of a particular actor or actress—only to find that the names are unreadable because they are cut off at the sides of the screen. In this post-television era, film personnel know (or at least they should know) about television's safe areas and shoot films accordingly.

With the basic information on the TV process established, we can now turn to specific components in the TV production process. In the next chapter we'll start with the video camera and, specifically, its most critical and versatile component, the lens.

SUMMARY

The illusion of motion in television and motion pictures is based on two perceptual phenomena: the phi phenomenon and persistence of vision. To achieve the illusion of motion, films are projected at a rate of 24 frames per second, and television pictures are presented at either 30 or 25 frames per second, depending upon the broadcast standard used. Whereas a motion picture camera creates complete pictures on a film, each of the images in a video camera is broken down into several hundred horizontal lines of luminance (black-and-white) and chrominance (color) information. The odd-numbered lines in a camera are scanned and then the even-numbered lines. Each set of (odd or even) lines is referred to as a field. Two fields equal a frame, or a complete television picture.

Three basic systems of television are used in the world: NTSC, PAL and SECAM. PAL is divided into several subsystems. Since these three basic international systems are incompatible, they must go through standards conversion (with some loss of technical quality) before programming made with one system can be viewed on another. Although the systems differ in several ways, the number of scanning lines and the field rate constitute the major differences.

High-definition television systems typically use a wider aspect ratio and many more scanning lines than NTSC, PAL or SECAM standards. Although a single, worldwide broadcast standard for HDTV has not been agreed upon, many production facilities have been using an HDTV system based on 1,125 lines and 60 fields with a 16×9 aspect ratio. HDTV and wide-screen films are normally converted to the normal 4×3 TV aspect ratio in three ways: by the letterbox technique, by panning-and-scanning or by simply cutting off the sides of the picture.

Since digital audio and video signals offer major advantages over analog signals, digital electronics has been rapidly replacing analog electronics in broadcasting. Digital signals consist of binary numbers that can be manipulated mathematically to create various audio and video effects.

A waveform monitor is used to adjust and monitor several important aspects of a video signal including black level, white level, blanking and sync. Audio and video signals are broadcast by a television transmitter on an RF carrier wave. Although the power of the transmitter is important to the broadcast coverage area, other factors like frequency (channel number) and antenna height are even more significant. Multipath reception, which causes ghosts in a TV picture, is caused by reflected RF signals.

There are several areas of loss associated with the video transmission process, including a loss of detail and a loss of the outermost edges of the picture. Although these losses will generally not be apparent on a control room monitor, they can be seen on a home TV receiver after the signal is broadcast.

KEY TERMS

analog
anamorphic
antenna
aspect ratio
binary numbers
bit speed
blanking pulse
CATV
color subcarrier
digital
field
frame
generation
ghosting
guardband
HDTV (high-definition television; HD; ATV)
Hz
interlaced
IRE
judder
kinescope recording
letterbox
low-power TV (LPTV)
luminance

modulation
multipath reception
noise
NTSC standard
overscanning
PAL-B, -G, -H, -M, -N standards
pan-and-scan
persistence of vision
phi phenomenon
quantization
raster
reference white
reference black
safe action area
safe area
safe title area
sampling
sampling rate
SECAM
standards converter
sync
sync generator
TV receiver
video monitor
waveform monitor

3 | Lenses and Their Effects

Not only are lenses the primary factor in establishing the clarity and quality of a video image, but they can provide a knowledgeable director or cameraperson with a wide range of creative controls. A high-quality zoom lens is also a major investment; in some cases it can cost more than the camera itself.

In this chapter we will look at five general topics: lens components; the differences between prime and zoom lenses; the apparent effect that lens focal length has on perspective, depth of field and the speed of objects; how lens f-stops not only control exposure but can be used to force attention to certain areas of a picture; and how filters and lens attachments can dramatically affect the appearance of subject matter.

THE LENS HOUSING

The housing of a lens (Figure 3.1) serves five functions:

- It securely holds the many glass elements within the lens in a precise position.

- It provides a smoothly controlled means through which the relationship between the lens elements can be altered in order to change focus or zoom setting.

- It houses the iris, which controls the amount of light passing through the lens.

- It includes the mount that affixes the lens to the camera and provides the electrical contacts that make possible the interactions between the lens and camera electronics.

- It (to varying degrees) seals out dust, dirt and dampness that can damage the lens.

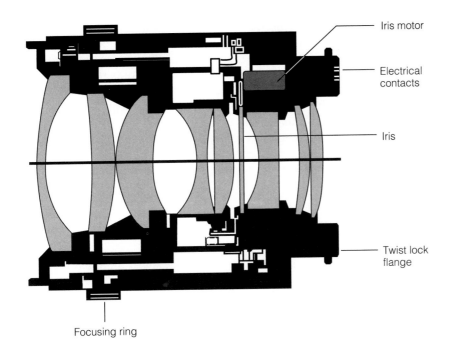

Iris motor

Electrical contacts

Iris

Twist lock flange

Focusing ring

FIGURE 3.1

This drawing illustrates the basic elements of a prime lens. Because of its high resolution and availability in focal lengths, which are either shorter or longer than those of standard zoom lenses, this type of lens can meet the most demanding needs of film and HDTV production.

LENS FOCAL LENGTH

Video cameras can use either prime (fixed focal length) or zoom (variable focal length) lenses. Before we can explore the differences between these two types of lenses, we need to look at focal length itself.

Focal length is defined as the distance from the optical center of the lens to the target (where the image is formed inside the camera) when the lens is focused at infinity. This distance, which is illustrated in Figure 3.2, is generally measured in millimeters. In the case of a **prime lens,** which has a fixed focal length, we can talk about a 12mm lens, a 25mm lens, a 100mm lens etc. **Zoom lenses,** which are also called *variable focal length lenses,* can be continuously adjusted over a wide range of focal lengths.

Taking a 25mm prime lens as an example, the distance between the center of the lens (its optical midpoint) and the image it creates on the camera target will be exactly 25 mm when the lens is focused at infinity. Any object in the far distance is considered to be at infinity. (The symbol ∞ is the universally accepted symbol for infinity.)

focal length: The distance from the optical center of the lens to the camera target when the lens is focused at infinity.

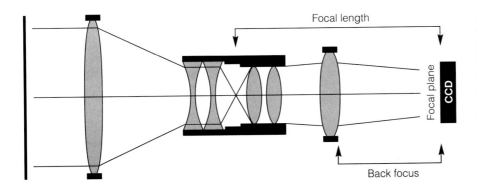

Focal length

Focal plane

CCD

Back focus

FIGURE 3.2

The most basic lens attribute, focal length, is defined as the distance from the optical center of the lens to the camera target. Although the effective focal length will change as the lens is zoomed, the critical back focus (the distance from the back of the lens to the target or CCD, or charge-coupled device, of the camera) will not.

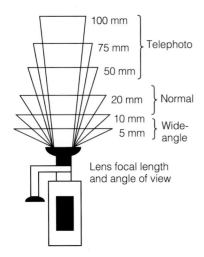

FIGURE 3.3
The focal length directly affects the angle of view of a lens. Note that as the focal length increases, the angle of view decreases. For cameras with ⅓-inch CCDs, the same effect would be achieved in each case with focal lengths slightly less than those shown. For cameras with ⅔-inch CCDs, lens focal lengths would be slightly greater for each angle represented.

When a prime lens is focused on objects closer than infinity, the distance between lens elements within the housing and the target must be increased to keep the image in focus. With prime lenses (and many zoom lenses), focusing is done by rotating a section of the lens. A focusing scale marked in feet or meters is generally apparent on the barrel of the lens. Many zoom lenses now use **internal focus,** where a small electric motor focuses the lens by altering the position of glass elements within the lens.

Because the lens-to-target distance can vary with some lenses as they are focused, a single reference point is needed for defining lens focal length. That standard reference point is infinity. Hence, the definition of focal length specifies the lens be set at infinity.

PRIME LENSES

Although most TV cameras use zoom lenses, prime lenses are often used on 35mm motion picture cameras and some of the high-quality video cameras associated with HDTV production. As we've noted, prime lenses have a set focal length, and this does not vary. To alter the camera's angle of view, you must change lenses.

Prime lenses have two main advantages. First, over time camera operators (or directors of photography) get to thoroughly know the attributes of a particular lens. Many have a film background where prime lenses are regularly used. If they want a specific effect, they immediately know what lens to use. Since zoom lenses have a varying focal length, the attributes are not as easy to get to know and predict. Second, there are prime lenses that go beyond the capabilities of zoom lenses. For example, prime lenses can be found that are capable of transmitting much more light in very low-light situations than a zoom lens. Prime lenses are also available in much shorter and much longer focal lengths than zoom lenses—which brings up another important concept: angle of view.

Angle of View

Although Figure 3.3 relates to a zoom lens, we can use it to illustrate the relationship between focal length and **angle of view,** or the coverage area of any type of lens. Note that the shorter the focal length, the wider the lens' angle of view; and conversely, the longer the focal length, the narrower the angle of view. When you double the focal length of a lens, you will double the size of an image created on the target; and, of course, the reverse is also true. Later, we'll discuss some of the ways focal length affects the appearance of subject matter.

THE ZOOM LENS

Unlike a prime lens, the focal length of a zoom lens can be varied. This is done by altering the relationship between certain glass elements within the lens as it is zoomed. Figure 3.4 is a simplified drawing illustrating the movement of the internal elements of a zoom lens from its wide-angle to telephoto settings. Figure 3.5, which is a cutaway photo of an actual zoom lens, more realistically depicts the complexity of such a lens.

The term **zoom ratio** is used to define the focal length range of a zoom lens. If the maximum range through which a particular lens can be zoomed is from 10 mm to 100 mm, it is said to have a 10-1 (ten-to-one) zoom ratio (10 × 10 = 100). Most professional zoom lenses have zoom ratios between 10-to-1 and 30-to-1. An example of the effect of a 30-1 zoom ratio is shown in Figures 3.6A

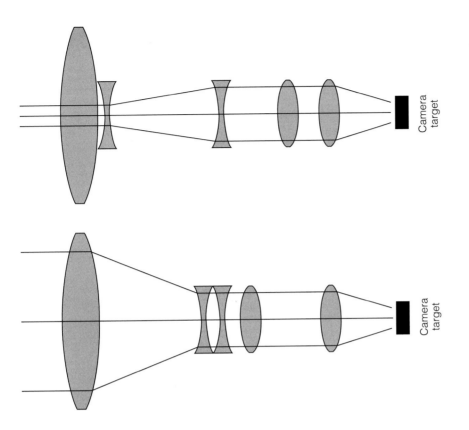

Camera target

Camera target

FIGURE 3.4
As you change the focal length of a zoom lens, the spacing between groups of internal glass elements is altered. In the top drawing the lens is zoomed in full (to its maximum focal length); in the bottom drawing the lens is in a wide-angle (minimum focal length) position. Note how the angle of view of the lens changes in each case. These drawings have been greatly simplified. Figure 3.5 shows the true complexity of a typical zoom lens.

and 3.6B. Some zoom lenses have ratios of 55-to-1. Lenses in this zoom range are typically larger than the video cameras, themselves. With a 55-to-1 zoom ratio, a video camera placed in the press box high in the stands above a football stadium could zoom out and get a wide shot of much of the field and then zoom in and get a close-up of a specific player.

Often in planning a production you will need more than just the zoom ratio

FIGURE 3.5
A zoom lens consists of scores of perfectly ground and polished lens elements. In the process of zooming and focusing a lens, groups of these elements are made to move precise distances in relation to each other. It was not until the development of the computer that the highly complex mathematical equations involved in the design of a zoom lens could be effectively handled.

FIGURE 3.6
Figure 3.6A shows the effect of a 30-to-1 zoom lens in the wide-angle position. When the lens is zoomed in fully, a portion of the picture that was hardly visible before now fills the frame (Figure 3.6B). Zoom, or variable-focal-length lenses, are available in ratios from 8-to-1 to 55-to-1.

(a)

(b)

of the lens. In order to see if the lens will fully cover the field of view you have in mind, you'll also need to know the lens' minimum focal length. Thus, another—and in many ways a much better—way of describing the characteristics of a zoom lens emerges. For this, another set of numbers is used. For example, a 10 × 12 (ten-by-twelve) zoom lens would have a minimum focal length of 12 mm and a maximum focal length of 120 mm (10 × 12 = 120).

Although zoom lenses are convenient because they save dollying (physically moving the camera), videographers[1] are careful to avoid zooms whenever a cut

---

1. The term *videographer* refers to a professional video cameraperson or someone who uses a video camera in a serious avocational pursuit.

would be clearer and faster. In fact, the constant use of zooms is one of the marks of an amateur.

Motorized Zoom Lenses

Instead of the handles or cranks that all zoom lenses previously required, today, most zoom lenses are controlled by small, variable-speed electric motors. These are referred to as **servo-controlled zooms**. On an electronic field production camera, the zoom is typically controlled with the forefingers by a rocker switch (Figure 3.7). On a studio camera the zoom control is generally mounted on the pan handle of the camera and controlled by the thumb (Figure 3.8). Zooms on professional cameras are variable speed; the further the zoom button is pushed, the faster the zoom action. In studio production a motorized zoom is generally preferable to a manual zoom because smoother zooms are possible.

There can be minor problems associated with motorized zooms. First, the zoom motor can sometimes be heard with the built-in microphone of a *camcorder* (the combination *cam*era and videotape re*corder* used in electronic field production). Second, unless the zoom lens includes a damping mechanism that

FIGURE 3.7
A rocker switch (in the center of the photo) controls the speed at which the lens on this ENG camera zooms in (to telephoto) or out (to wide-angle). To keep them smaller and lighter, the zoom lenses associated with ENG cameras have a lower zoom ratio than the lenses on studio or field cameras.

camcorder: An all-in-one *cam*era and re*corder* unit.

FIGURE 3.8
The zoom position of studio camera lenses is typically controlled with a rocker switch by moving the thumb to the left (to zoom out) or to right (to zoom in). Field cameras often use manual cranks to control zoom position because they are faster for covering sports events. Just above the zoom control is a shot box, which allows the operator to preset six zoom positions. These shots can later be called up simply by pushing one of the buttons.

Shot box

Zoom control

(a)

(b)

(c)

(d)

(e)

FIGURE 3.9

In studying this sequence of photos it is important to note that the distance between the subject and the background remains exactly the same in each photo. The only thing that changes is the camera-to-subject distance. Figure 3.9A was shot with a zoom lens in a wide-angle position; Figure 3.9B, with the lens in a semiwide-angle position; Figure 3.9C, with the lens at a normal focal length setting; Figure 3.9D, with the lens at a medium telephoto setting; and Figure 3.9E, with the lens set at an extreme telephoto position. In order to keep the woman approximately the same size in each photo, the camera-to-subject distance increased from just a few feet in Figure 3.9A to several hundred feet in Figure 3.9E. The difference in the apparent position of the background in each of these shots is technically due to the difference in camera position and not, as commonly assumed, due to the lens focal length.

takes affect at the end of the zoom range, an abrupt stop can result when the lens reaches either end of its travel.

Although servo-controlled zoom lenses can provide smooth zooms at varying speeds, manually controlled zoom effects are often desirable. Camera operators prefer them for covering fast-moving sporting events (generally, to quickly move to new shots when their camera is not on-line). They may also occasionally be used for doing a **snap zoom** (a very rapid and abrupt zoom to achieve a dramatic effect).

The Zoom vs. the Dolly

Unless you are zooming in on a flat object like a map, you will find that a zoom gives a much different effect than a dolly (where the camera is physically rolled toward or away from a subject). Although audiences have gotten used to zooms, they actually represent a slightly artificial effect, similar to optically enlarging a portion out of the middle of a still photo. In contrast, when a camera is dollied, it moves past objects and the effect is the same as if you walked toward or away from a subject. Although it is much more difficult to smoothly achieve, some videographers prefer the more natural effect of a dolly.

FOCAL LENGTH AND PERSPECTIVE

If you look at Figures 3.9A to 3.9E, you will see a progressive change in the background. It is important to note that the distance between the subject and the background in each photo remains exactly the same. Figure 3.9A was shot with a zoom lens in a wide-angle position; Figure 3.9B, with the lens in a semiwide-angle position; Figure 3.9C, with the lens at a normal focal length setting; Figure 3.9D, with the lens at a medium telephoto setting; and Figure 3.9E with the lens set at an extreme telephoto position. This effect is shown in a slightly different way in Figures 3.10A and 3.10B. Even though different focal length lenses were used in these photos, the dramatic difference in the apparent position of the background is, actually, due to the difference in the subject-to-camera distance and not the difference in lens focal length.[2]

Geometric Distortion

When you move in close to a subject and use a wide-angle lens to fill the screen, a type of **geometric distortion,** a bending of parallel lines, results. With a face this can be used to create an intentionally eerie effect — or it might be just plain unflattering, depending on whether the effect is accidental or done on purpose.

2. It is commonly believed — and even commonly stated in textbooks — that focal length affects both perspective and depth of field. Technically, neither is true. Although a technical discussion would lead us astray at this point, suffice it to say that it is camera-to-subject distance and not lens focal length that controls perspective. We'll deal with depth of field later in this chapter.

FIGURE 3.10
Although some people believe that "the camera can't lie," these two photos show what appears to be a dramatic difference in the apparent space between the objects. In actual fact, the distance between the objects in these photos does not change — only the camera-to-subject distance. When a wide-angle lens is used and the camera is moved in close (Figure 3.10A), the objects appear to be far apart; when the camera is backed up and a longer focal length lens is used to create the same image size, the distance between the objects appears to greatly decrease (Figure 3.10B).

(a)

(b)

(a)   (b)

FIGURE 3.11
When the camera is placed close to an object and tilted up, a wide-angle lens will also cause a convergence of vertical lines (Figure 3.11A). Note in Figure 3.11B that the problem is fixed when the camera backs up and a longer focal length is used.

When the camera is placed close to an object and tilted up (Figure 3.11A), a wide-angle lens will also cause a convergence of vertical lines. Note in Figure 3.11B that the problem is fixed when the camera backs up and a longer focal length is used.

Focal Length and the Speed of Objects

Very much related to perspective differences are the *apparent* changes in speed of objects moving toward or away from the lens. A long focal length lens (or a zoom lens used at its maximum focal length) will appear to slow down the speed of an object moving toward or away from the camera. (You might recall watching someone in the distance run when they seemed to be hardly moving.) Let's draw an example from a film that many people are familiar with. Throughout Mike Nichols' film *"The Graduate,"* camera distance (and lens focal length) was used to get across various ideas. An example at the end of the film was most striking. As Benjamin (Dustin Hoffman) was desperately running down the street toward the church in an effort to stop a wedding, the camera was moved a great distance back from the subject. A 500mm lens was then used to convey what the character was feeling: that even though he was running as fast as he could, it seemed as if he were hardly moving—that he would never make it to the church in time. Had a wide-angle lens been used (and the camera moved in close to Benjamin) his speed would have apparently increased greatly. He would then have passed the camera in only a couple of seconds, giving an impression of almost a superhuman speed, and the intended effect on the audience would have been completely lost.

Super-Telephoto Lenses

Super-long lenses, such as those used for getting spectacular close-ups of wild animals and birds in their natural habitat, are generally of a fixed focal length—sometimes 1,000 mm or more (Figure 3.12.) The angle of view of a 1,000mm prime lens when used on a typical video camera would be about 0.6 degree. Since these lenses are relatively poor at transmitting light, it is difficult to use them under low-light conditions. Shooting over such distances also means that things such as atmospheric haze and heat rising from the ground will distort the image. Despite their disadvantages, telephoto lenses are commonly relied upon to photograph things you can't (or sometimes don't want to) get close to.

What Is Normal Focal Length?

With varying lens focal lengths available to the videographer, the question arises as to what is a normal focal length (and, therefore, what is a normal angle of view). The answer is related to the viewing distance of the final image. The closer you are to TV screen, the wider the camera's field of view must be to be considered normal. Even so, a good general rule of thumb is supplied by still photographers. With a 35mm camera, a 50 to 55mm lens is considered normal because this represents the diagonal distance from one corner of the film to the other. The same applies to video. A normal focal length for the average viewer-to-TV-set distances (10 to 12 feet) would be equal to the distance from one corner of the camera's target area to the opposite corner. Thus, if the diagonal distance on the target of a CCD (charge-coupled device) camera is 1/2 inch, a 13mm prime lens or a zoom lens used at about 13 mm will provide a normal angle of view. For a 2/3-inch target size, a normal focal length will be about 17 mm. For a 1/3-inch CCD, the diagonal would be about 10 mm. Although what represents a normal perspective is not a significant issue on a small video screen, with large-screen video (4 feet by 3 feet or larger) differences in perspective become more noticeable.

SUPPLEMENTARY LENSES

You can modify the focal length of a lens (including the zoom ratio of a zoom lens) by using a **supplementary lens** (Figure 3.13). A positive supplementary lens will reduce the focal length of the lens and increase its angle of acceptance

FIGURE 3.12

Zoom lenses with range extenders or long, fixed-focal-length lenses allow close-ups of birds and animals in their natural habitat. The slightest camera movement is also greatly exaggerated with long focal lengths. Because of this, it is generally necessary to use tripods or steady camera supports.

FIGURE 3.13

The focal length of a lens can be modified (including the zoom ratio of a zoom lens) by adding a supplementary lens. A positive supplementary lens will reduce the focal length of the lens and increase its angle of acceptance (angle of view). Conversely, a negative supplementary lens — commonly called a range extender — increases the focal length and narrows the angle of view. On many zoom lenses, range extenders are located inside the lens and can be activated with a flip of a switch.

lens extender: An optical lens unit that increases the effective focal length of a zoom or fixed-focal-length lens. Some lens extenders are electrically flipped into position within the lens housing; others are manually placed over the front of or behind the lens.

(angle of view). Conversely, a negative supplementary lens — commonly called a *lens extender* or **range extender** — increases the focal length and narrows the angle of view. A 2× range extender can change a 100mm fixed-focal-length lens into a 200mm lens, or it can change a 12 to 120mm zoom lens into a 24 to 240mm zoom lens. Positive (wide-angle) supplementary lenses are attached to the front of a lens; negative lenses (range extenders) can go either in front or behind the lens. Many zoom lenses have built-in 2× range extenders that can be engaged with a flip of a switch.

IMAGE STABILIZERS

In video production, solid, steady shots look professional, whereas images that are constantly floating up and down and from one side to the other (generally accompanied by constant zooms and pans) are the mark of an amateur. For this reason, one of the things that separates the amateurs from the professionals in video production is the use of a tripod (to be discussed in the next chapter). However, there are times, such as when shooting from some type of "moving platform," when even a tripod won't provide a steady shot. Helicopter and boat shots are an example.

In 1962, a type of lens housing was created that can compensate for camera vibration and motion. The device uses a gyroscopically controlled damping mechanism that resists short, fast movements by allowing lens elements to "float" in the housing. Consequently, the vibration or general movement associated with moving vehicles can be eliminated, or at least minimized. (See Figure 3.14.) These devices are also quite useful in reducing the shakiness of hand-held cameras in news and documentary work.

A typical gyro-stabilized zoom lens weighs from 5 to 7 pounds and requires a 12- to 15-volt power source. After the lens stabilizer is turned on, a standby light will blink until the internal motor comes up to full speed and the unit is ready for use.

FIGURE 3.14
An image stabilizer is useful with cameras that are hand-held or mounted on a boats, cars or helicopters. These stabilizers cancel or greatly reduce vibration or general camera movement. A typical gyro-stabilized zoom lens weighs 5 to 7 pounds and requires a 12- to 15-volt power source.

LENS MOUNTS

Prime and special-purpose lenses require that one type of lens be replaced with another. Camera lenses can be removed by unscrewing them (in the case of C-mount lenses) or by turning a locking ring (in the case of the bayonet mounts).

C-Mount Lenses

Some field cameras use **C-mounts**. C-mounts are about 25 mm in diameter and are screwed into the camera body with about six turns. Because C-mount lenses are basic to 16mm motion picture work, a wide array of zoom and prime lenses are available in this mount.

Bayonet-Mount Lenses

Most video camera lenses use **bayonet mounts**. They are faster to attach than the C-mount because the lens can be removed by a partial turn of a locking ring. This mount typically incorporates multiple electrical contacts to control the iris, zoom position and, for some cameras, the auto-focus circuitry.

When replacing a bayonet-mount lens, you need to carefully line up the index tabs or alignment indicators on the lens mount with the corresponding indicators on the camera body. Unlike C-mounts, there has been little standardization in bayonet mounts. Occasionally a bayonet-mount lens will fit a camera and still not operate correctly. Consequently, a camera operator must always select the bayonet-mount lens that has been designed for a specific make and model of video camera.

In 1991, a standardized **VL bayonet mount** was introduced. With the adoption of this mount, a wide variety of lenses, including lenses designed for 35mm still cameras, can now be used with VL mount camcorders.

CHANGING LENSES

Whenever a lens is removed from a camera, there is a risk that specks of dust will find their way inside the camera and affect the internal optics. Therefore, lens changes should be done as quickly as possible and in relatively dust-free environments. Generally, specks of dust can be removed from the inside of a camera (or from a camera lens) with the help of a soft, clean camel's hair brush and light puffs of air.

LENS APERTURE

Like the pupil of an eye, which automatically adjusts to varying light levels, camera lenses have an *iris* that controls the amount of light that can go through the lens. Most of us know that under very low-light conditions the iris (pupil) of the eye opens up almost completely to allow in the maximum amount of light. In the bright sunlight the pupil contracts in an effort to avoid overloading the light-sensitive rods and cones in the back of our eyes.

iris: An adjustable diaphragm that controls the amount of light passing through a lens.

In the same way, the amount of light falling on the light-sensitive target of a TV camera must be carefully controlled with the aid of an iris in the middle of the lens (Figure 3.15). Too much light, and the picture will become overexposed or washed out; too little, and detail in the darker areas of the picture will be lost.

FIGURE 3.15
The iris of a lens serves the same function as the pupil in the eye: it controls the amount of light passing through the lens. The iris opening also affects depth of field.

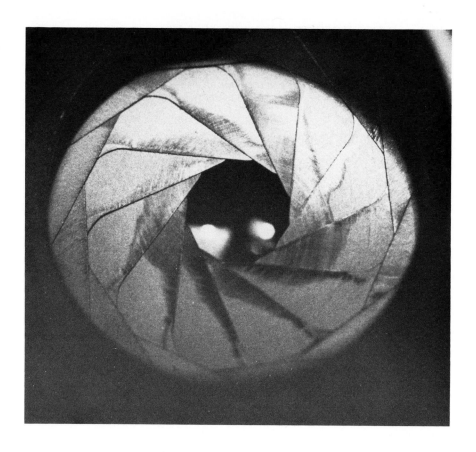

f-stop: A number indicating the amount of light passing through the lens and, consequently, the exposure level. The mathematical relationship between the focal length of a lens and the diameter of the lens opening.

F-Stops

Although an iris can be smoothly adjusted from a very small opening to the point of being wide open, certain specific points along this range have numerical designations. These calibrated points are called *f-stops*. (The terms **aperture** and **aperture setting** are also used to describe this opening.) Contrary to what you might assume, the smaller the f-stop number, the more light the lens transmits. The relationship between f-stops and light transmission may seem backward until you realize that f-stops do not represent amounts of light, but a ratio between lens focal length and the diameter of the iris opening. The following formula explains this relationship.

$$\text{f-stop} = \frac{\text{focal length of lens}}{\text{diameter of aperture}}$$

Example:

$$\text{f/8} = \frac{25 \text{ mm}}{3.1 \text{ mm}}$$

Note that the larger the ratio between focal length and iris diameter, the larger the f-stop number.[3]

3. Technically, f-stops represent the light transmitted by comparatively simple fixed-focal-length lenses. When zoom lenses were introduced with their dozen or more glass elements (each of which absorb and reflect a small amount of light), the simple focal length/lens aperture formula was found to be slightly inaccurate. The **t-stop** was then devised. The t-stop (*t* for transmission) is based, not on the ratio shown, but on the actual amount of light that a particular lens is transmitting at various stops. However, for the sake of simplicity, we'll use the more common designation of *f-stop* throughout the remainder of the text.

TABLE 3.1
Typical F-Stop Range

1.4	2.0	2.8	4.0	5.6	8	11	16
		← more light		less light →			

Table 3.1 shows a typical f-stop range for a camera lens.

Figure 3.16 shows the iris opening for each of these settings. Occasionally we see f-stops not shown here; examples would be f/1.2, f/1.8, f/3.5 and f/4.5. These are midpoint settings between whole f-stops. On some lenses they represent the maximum aperture of the lens.

Lens Speed

Lens speed is defined as the maximum amount of light a lens will transmit. This is equal to the lowest f-stop number on the lens. In Table 3.1, f/1.4 would be the speed of the lens represented. "Fast" (high-speed) lenses are expensive because they contain many glass elements and are difficult to design and build. These elements are necessary to cancel out various kinds of optical problems that result from inconsistent bending of light rays within a complex lens. At the other end of the f-stop scale, the iris of many lenses typically stops at f/16. Some prime lenses go beyond this to even smaller openings: f/22 or f/32.

When an iris setting is opened up one f-stop (from f/8 to f/5.6, for example), it represents a 100 percent increase in the light going through the lens. Conversely, if the lens is "stopped down" one stop (as from f/1.4 to f/2.0), the light is cut by 50 percent. Put another way, when you open up one stop you double the light; when you stop down one stop you halve the amount of light going through the lens. Once the f-stop range is understood, it will be obvious which way a lens iris should be adjusted to compensate for a picture that is either too light or too dark.

Video cameras with automatic exposure circuits use a small electric motor to automatically open or close the iris in response to varying light conditions. Automatic exposure can be an advantage in many circumstances where there is no time to manually set up the camera. But, as we will see later, there are situations where this automatic mode will not provide the best video.

Supplementary Lenses and F-Stops

Earlier we talked about the role of supplementary lenses and lens range extenders in multiplying focal length. Since f-stops are based on the relationship between focal length and lens aperture, when lens focal length is altered, f-stops are no longer accurate—regardless of what the scale on the lens says (Figure 3.17). When a lens is zoomed in, it may lose up to one full f-stop. To compensate, some zoom lenses internally change the iris setting as the lens is zoomed. We've noted that on most video cameras exposure can be automatically set and maintained with an **auto-iris** circuit. On studio cameras, this option is generally turned off, and the camera's iris is set remotely on the CCU to provide an optimum distribution from 7.5 to 100 on the waveform monitor. This optimum exposure and video level is illustrated in Figure 2.12 in the last chapter.

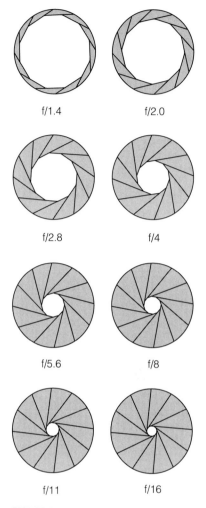

f/1.4 f/2.0

f/2.8 f/4

f/5.6 f/8

f/11 f/16

FIGURE 3.16
The size of the iris opening in a lens is given a number called an f-stop. All lenses set at a particular f-stop will transmit the same amount of light to the camera target. Contrary to what you might think, the larger the opening, the smaller the f-stop number will be.

lens speed: The f-stop that transmits the maximum amount of light for a specific lens. The smallest f-stop number.

FIGURE 3.17
F-stop numbers are clearly visible on the lenses of professional cameras. Video cameras with automatic exposure circuits use a small electric motor to automatically open or close the iris in response to varying light conditions. Although automatic exposure can be an advantage where there is no time to manually set up the camera, there are many situations where this automatic mode will not provide the best video. For this reason many videographers prefer to adjust the iris themselves while they are shooting.

LENS COATINGS

Some light is lost in a lens as a result of reflections from the surface of glass lens elements. To reduce this problem, the surfaces of elements are coated with a microthin, magnesium fluoride anti-reflection coating. The coating, which greatly reduces light loss, typically gives the glass elements a light blue appearance.

Lenses and lens coatings are easily scratched. It is easy for an object to come in contact with a camera lens — especially when it's being carried in a case. Once a lens is scratched, its sharpness is diminished, and image contrast is reduced. Since a scratched lens is quite costly — and sometimes even impossible — to repair, a lens cap should be used over the lens whenever it is not being used.

We should also note that lens coatings are particularly vulnerable to fingerprints. Because of the chemical composition of the oil in fingerprints, some lens coatings have been permanently damaged — the fingerprint being etched into the lens coating when it was allowed to stay on the lens for a long period of time.

CLEANING LENSES

FIGURE 3.18
Although small quantities of dust on a lens will not appreciably affect image quality, fingerprints or oily smudges will. To clean a lens, first remove any surface dirt by blowing it off with an ear syringe or by brushing it off with a soft, clean camel's hair brush. Then dampen a lens tissue with lens cleaner and very gently rub the lens in a circular motion while rolling the lens tissue slightly so that any dirt will not be rubbed over the lens surface. Because of the danger of scratching a lens during this process, lenses should only be cleaned when absolutely necessary.

Although small quantities of dust on a lens will not appreciably affect image quality, fingerprints or oily smudges are a different matter. To clean a lens, first remove any surface dirt by blowing it off with an ear syringe or by brushing it off with a soft, clean camel's hair brush. Dampen a lens tissue with lens cleaner and gently rub the lens in a circular motion. (It's important not to put the lens cleaner directly on the lens where it can seep behind lens elements.) While *very* gently rubbing, turn or roll the lens tissue slightly so that any dirt will not be rubbed over the lens surface (Figure 3.18).

Never clean a lens with silicon-treated lens tissues or the silicon-impregnated cloth commonly sold for cleaning eyeglasses. The residue may permanently discolor the coating. Each time a lens is cleaned there is a risk of tiny abrasive particles creating microscopic scratches in the lens coating. So, recalling the "if it's not broken, don't fix it" maxim, don't just routinely clean a lens. Wait until it is obvious that the lens needs cleaning.

Condensation on the Lens

Although studio cameras rarely have a problem with moisture condensing on the lens, portable cameras often do, especially when the camera is moved from a warm to a cool temperature. A change of 20 degrees, such as when the camera is taken from inside to outside on a cool day, is enough to fog up a lens. Even though moisture can be gently wiped off the lens, it may continue to fog up until the temperature of the lens equals the surrounding air. Suffice to say, if you need to move to an area where the temperature is significantly different, allow 30 minutes or so for the lens (and camera) to reach the surrounding temperature.

DEPTH OF FIELD

Now that we've covered focal length and f-stops, we can move on to a major area of creative control: depth of field.

Acceptable Sharpness

Depth of field is defined as the range along the lens's axis that is acceptably sharp. *Acceptably* is a key term here. Theoretically, if a camera is focused at a specific distance, only objects at that exact distance will be sharp, and objects in front of and behind that point will be blurry. But, what is theoretically sharp and what is acceptably sharp are different. An image doesn't just abruptly become unacceptably blurry at a certain point in front of and behind the point of focus. The transition from sharp to out of focus is gradual. In fact, our eyes cannot notice when images are only slightly blurry. It is only when the images go beyond a certain point that we realize the image is "out of focus."

depth of field: The range of distance in sharp focus along the lens axis.

What is acceptable also depends upon the medium. For NTSC television,[4] a much greater area will be seen as "acceptably sharp" than for HDTV, where we can much more readily recognize blur. For both NTSC and HDTV, the distance you are from the screen and the image size are also important factors; the larger the screen and the closer you are to it, the more you will tend to notice a lack of sharpness.

A normal viewing distance for NTSC television is considered seven times the height of the TV picture. So if the TV screen is 16 inches (a so-called 25-inch picture tube), the normal viewing distance would be 9 to 10 feet. HDTV, with its higher resolution, makes possible both larger screens and closer viewing distances — and the reproduction of several times the picture detail.

F-Stop and Depth of Field

For a particular image size on the target and for a specific lens-to-subject distance, depth of field depends upon only one thing: lens f-stop. The larger the f-stop number (the smaller the iris opening), the greater the depth of field will be. Therefore, the depth of field of a lens used at f/11 will be greater than when the same lens is used at f/5.6. (See Figures 3.19, 3.20A and 3.20B.)

---

4. Although the 625-line PAL and SECAM systems have slightly greater resolution than the NTSC system, for the purposes of this discussion they can be considered in the same category as NTSC.

FIGURE 3.19
Note in this figure that when a lens is opened up to a wide f-stop, depth of field is minimized; when the lens is stopped down to a small f-stop (bottom illustration), the depth is great. This effect is shown in another way in Figures 3.20A and 3.20B.

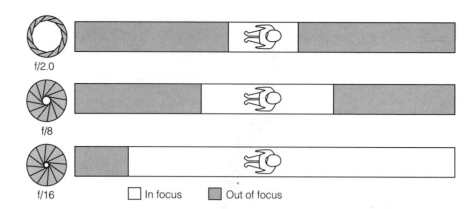

f/2.0

f/8

f/16   ☐ In focus   ■ Out of focus

The depth of field in a scene—especially when you are close to the subject—may be only a few inches when a lens is used at a wide f-stop (Figure 3.21). In such cases things both in front of and behind the point of focus will be blurry. This situation can represent either a major problem or a creative tool in effective composition. In the latter case it can force a viewer to concentrate on a specific area or object in a scene and not be distracted by others (Figure 3.22). Our eyes tend to avoid areas of a picture that are not clear, and they are drawn to areas that are sharply focused.

Since depth of field is minimal under low-light conditions (when lenses are opened to wide f-stops), focusing becomes quite critical. A sharply focused individual can lean forward slightly in a chair and go out of focus. A camera operator must be constantly alert to "touch up the focus" as needed.

For a particular point of focus, most lenses are the sharpest (have the highest resolution) when the iris is stopped down from one-third to one-half of their full f-stop range. Therefore, a lens with a maximum aperture of 1.8 would typically deliver the sharpest images when the iris was set somewhere between 2.8 to 5.6. Although this is not a consideration with the relatively low-resolution NTSC, PAL or SECAM video systems, optimum lens performance is a major consideration in HDTV.

FIGURE 3.20
The difference in sharpness of the boat in the background of these photos is the result of using two different f-stop settings. Figure 3.20A was shot at f/16; Figure 3.20B at f/4. Intentionally throwing the background out of focus in this way so that it will not be distracting is an important artistic control for videographers.

(a)   (b)

Depth of Field and Focal Length

It is widely believed that depth of field is also directly related to lens focal length. Although this appears to be the case, this assumption is actually based on differences in camera-to-subject distance and the resulting difference in target image size. For a specific lens-to-subject distance and comparable image size on the target, all lenses of similar optical design, regardless of focal length, will have the same depth of field when used at the same f-stop.

It is true that a zoom lens used at 10 mm *appears* to have a much greater depth of field than when the same lens is used at 100 mm. But the "condensed" 10 mm view simply hides the existing lack of sharpness through a reduced image size. This explanation is more than just academic; it explains, for example, why a subject (which seems perfectly sharp) can suddenly go completely out of focus when a camera is zoomed in. By zooming in you are magnifying the existing out-of-focus area until it becomes noticeable — and objectionable. Even if the central subject matter is initially in focus, you will notice that foreground and background areas will suddenly appear to go out of focus as you zoom in (Figure 3.23).

If a lens is used at a short focal length (zoomed back to a wide shot) and the iris is stopped down to a small opening (as it would be if you were shooting in bright sunlight), depth of field can extend over a large area: probably from just a few feet to infinity. This is a definite advantage when shooting fast-moving sporting events where the continuous adjustment of focus would be difficult. But remember, the out-of-focus areas are still there, and they may quickly be revealed when you zoom in.

Division of Depth of Field

You may notice in Figures 3.19 and 3.23 that the area of sharp focus does not extend equally in front of and behind the point of focus. The total area of acceptable sharpness extends one-third of the way in front of the point of focus and two-thirds of the way behind it.

FIGURE 3.21
Depth of field is minimal in extreme close-ups. Note in this photo that depth extends only 2 or 3 inches and that both the dog's nose and ears are out of focus. The limited depth is used to keep attention focused on the dog's eyes and away from the nose and ears.

FIGURE 3.22
By using selective focus, we are able to throw background and foreground objects out of focus and quickly direct viewer attention to the area of a picture we want to emphasize. In this photo the stands full of spectators in the background do not distract you from the expression of the coach at a decisive moment in a game.

FIGURE 3.23

This drawing illustrates why a zoom lens should be focused by first zooming in all the way. Note that at 20 mm (when the lens is zoomed out) the image looks fine; the depth of field of the lens keeps the woman in focus. However, when the lens is zoomed in to 70 mm for a close-up, the depth of field diminishes, and the woman appears to go out of focus. Actually, the image does not go out of focus when the lens is zoomed in; the process of zooming in optically enlarges the image and makes the already existing blur noticeable and, for the first time, objectionable. Note also in this drawing that depth of field is not evenly divided in front of and behind the point of focus. The in-focus area extends about one-third of the way in front of the point of focus and two-thirds of the way behind it.

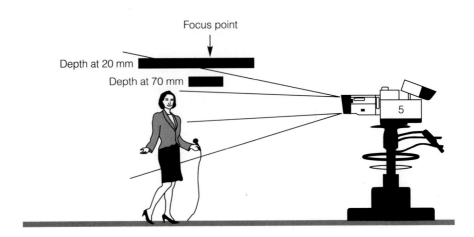

Not only does the depth of field increase as the iris closes and diminish as the iris opens up but the transition rate from sharpness to out of focus is also more gradual at small f-stops and more rapid at wide f-stops.

As an example, the depth of field of a lens focused at 4 feet, zoomed into 100 mm, and set at f/4 has a total depth of field of only 2 inches. This doesn't leave any room for a focusing error — or much room for the subject to move. If the same lens were opened up to f/1.4, the depth of field would, for all practical purposes, be zero.

FOCUSING A LENS

It might seem that focusing a lens is a simple process of just "getting things clear." True, but a few things complicate the issue.

First, from Figure 3.23 it should be apparent why a zoom lens must be focused after first zooming in on a close shot (using maximum focal length). Once focused, the lens can be zoomed back to whatever initial focal length is needed. If the scene contains a person, you will generally want to focus on the catchlight or gleam in one eye. There are two reasons: the person's eyes are the first place we will probably look in viewing a scene, and this small bright spot is easy to focus on.

Minimum Subject Distance

There is a limit to how close subject matter can come to the lens and still be kept in focus. A zoom lens will normally focus to 3 or 4 feet. Prime lenses of medium and short focal lengths can focus much closer.

macro: A lens focusing mode in which extreme close-ups are possible.

The Macro Lens Setting   Most zoom lenses have a *macro* setting that enables you to attain sharp focus on an object only a few inches in front of the lens (Figure 3.24). With some lenses the subject matter can even be at a "zero distance" — that is, actually touching the front element of the lens. To reach the macro position on most lenses, a button or lever on the barrel of the lens is pushed to allow the zoom adjustment to travel beyond its normal stopping point. However, when used in the macro mode this type of lens loses its zoom capability. Some zoom lenses have full-focus capability; these **full-focus lenses** can smoothly shift their focus from infinity through the full macro range without losing zooming capabilities.

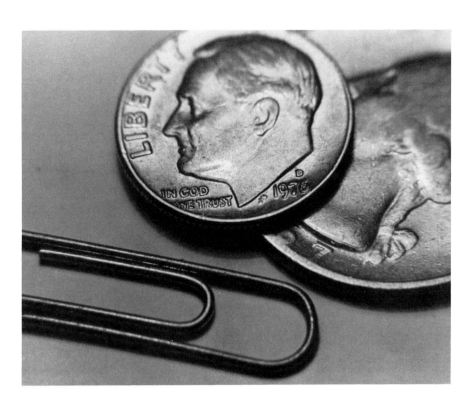

FIGURE 3.24
Most zoom lenses have a special macro setting that enables you to attain sharp focus on an object only a few inches in front of the lens. On some lenses the macro range has to be manually engaged by pushing a control on the lens. Some auto-focus lenses will smoothly and automatically bridge the normal to macro ranges.

Videographers often forget the many dramatic possibilities that the macro mode of a zoom lens offers. For example, a flower, stamp or a portion of a drawing or snapshot can be made to fill the TV screen. A tripod or camera mount is "a must" in using the macro setting. Since depth of field extends only a few millimeters at this super-close range, focus is extremely critical.

Follow Focus

In television we are often dealing with moving subjects. A person may quickly move outside the limits of depth of field unless the lens can be quickly refocused. Professionals know which way to turn the focus controls to keep a moving subject in focus. (Non-professionals generally end up throwing a slightly blurry image completely out of focus for a few seconds after they first turn the focus adjustment the wrong way.) The technique of ***follow focus*** is used to refocus the camera to accommodate subject movement.

follow focus: Shifting camera focus to accommodate subject movement.

When zoom or prime lenses are used in motion picture and HDTV work, an assistant cameraperson will use the footage scale on the lens to adjust focus as subjects move. This leaves the camera operator free to pan and tilt the camera as needed. In this case the scenes have to be carefully rehearsed and specific points marked on the floor or ground for the talent to "hit" as they move.[5] This approach means that focus can be smoothly changed by an assistant cameraperson as the talent moves and that a camera operator will not have to awkwardly "search for focus" to compensate for the change in camera-to-subject distance.

5. For talent this is referred to as "hitting your mark." At these points not only is camera focus information recorded but optimum audio and lighting are also generally dependent on the talent stopping on these marks.

Auto-Focus Lenses

Although **auto-focus lenses** (lenses that automatically focus) can be helpful in following moving subjects, you will regularly encounter problems unless you understand their limitations. There are five problem areas:

- Auto-focus devices generally assume that the area you want in sharp focus is in the center of the picture. This is often not the case, especially if you are trying for interesting and creative composition.
- Most auto-focus mechanisms can be fooled by reflections and by flat, monochrome areas with little or no detail.
- Many auto-focus devices have difficulty focusing on areas that contain closely spaced patterns such as vertical or horizontal stripes.
- Most auto-focus lenses have difficulty focusing when you shoot through glass, wire fences etc.
- Auto-focus devices can unexpectedly throw a scene completely out of focus when they are momentarily thrown off track and start searching for the proper focus.

Because of these problems, auto-focus devices have not been generally accepted by professional videographers. If this feature is present on a video camera, it is generally turned off and reserved for fast-breaking news stories in tight, crowded areas where constant refocusing would be a problem.

Back Focus

Back focus is the distance between the back of the lens and the camera target (refer to Figure 3.2). If the back focus of a zoom lens is adjusted properly, it should be possible to zoom in tight on a subject, focus and then zoom back and still have a sharp image. If the lens goes out of focus when it is zoomed out, the back focus is out of adjustment. This problem can develop, for example, if the camera is subjected to a severe jolt. With back focus we are dealing with an extremely precise setting. A lens on a high-definition camera used at 100 mm at f/2.8 has a whisker-width back focus tolerance of a mere 0.000028 mm. The procedure for adjusting back focus varies with cameras. It is a task best left to a technician.

LENS SHADES

FIGURE 3.25

In the same way that our eyes must be shaded from a strong light in order for us to see clearly, the camera lens should be protected from strong light hitting the lens from an oblique angle. A lens shade or lens hood serves this purpose. Even if a strong light striking the lens does not create obvious lens flare, it can reduce image contrast and degrade picture quality.

In the same way that our eyes must be shaded from a strong light in order for us to see clearly, the camera lens also has to be shielded from direct light. A **lens shade** or **lens hood** (Figure 3.25) is designed to protect the lens from offending glare and loss of contrast. Even if a strong light striking the lens does not create obvious **lens flare** (a bright spot on an image caused by bright light hitting the lens), it may reduce image contrast. Since most lens flare problems are apparent in the video viewfinder, the effect of a lens shade (or, in an emergency, a piece of dark paper taped to the barrel of the lens) can be readily seen.

When selecting (or hastily improvising) a lens shade, make sure that it extends as far as possible in front of the lens without becoming visible around the edges of the picture when the lens is at its wide-angle position. Many zoom lenses have built-in lens shades in the form of recessed lens mounts.

Square or rectangular lens shades (which roughly conform to the shape of the video image) do a slightly better job of shielding the lens from light than round shades do. However, their use is limited to internal focus-type lenses.

Otherwise, rotating the front of the lens (and the square lens hood) may result in corners of the image being cut off.

Lens shades are just one of many lens attachments.

FILTERS

Ultraviolet Filters

News photographers who have to cover stories under adverse conditions often use an **ultraviolet filter** (UV filter) over their camera lens to protect it from scratches. This is particularly important when the camera is used in adverse conditions, such as during wind storms, where the lens could be pitted by sand or where the presence of dirt would require the lens to be constantly cleaned. (UV filters can easily be replaced; lenses can't.) By screening out ultraviolet light, the filter may also slightly enhance color quality.

Colored Filters

General color correction in a video camera is done through the combination of optical and electronic camera adjustments. However, it is sometimes desirable to introduce a dominant color into a scene. Although small color shifts are generally introduced electronically, large color shifts (generally for special effects) are often done by using colored filters over the lens. (To have the intended effect, automatic color balance cannot be used once the filter is in place.) **Colored filters** consist of a transparent colored gel sandwiched between two optically ground (and sometimes coated) pieces of glass. They either fit into a circular holder that screws over the end of the camera lens similar to Figure 3.13, or are inserted into a filter wheel behind the camera lens. For example, a deep red filter could be used to simulate the lighting in a photographic darkroom[6] or the interior of a Word War II submarine during a battle. We'll cover the electronic aspects of color balance in Chapter 5.

Neutral Density Filters

As we've noted, we use the lens f-stop to control the amount of light passing through the lens. But since f-stop also affects depth of field, it is sometimes desirable to control light in another way. As an example, under bright light conditions you may want to keep a relatively wide f-stop opening to reduce depth of field so that you throw distracting objects in the background and foreground out of focus. Or, under extremely bright conditions (bright sunlight in white sand or snow, for example) even the minimum f-stop may still result in camera overexposure. There are two solutions: use a high shutter speed with CCD cameras, or use a neutral density filter.

A **neutral density** or **ND filter** is a gray filter that reduces the amount of light going through the lens without affecting color.

Contrast Filters

As we'll see in the next chapter, handling excessive brightness ranges is often a problem in video production, especially in on-location production. As explained

---

6. Interestingly, red filters haven't been used in normal photographic darkroom work for about 40 years, but since the public widely believes they are, producers apparently feel obliged to continue perpetrating the myth.

in Chapter 6, sometimes an excessive brightness range can be controlled by lighting. Sometimes, however, this is not an option. As the name suggests, **contrast filters** are used to alter scene contrast and bring them within range of the TV system. A **low-contrast filter** acts on the dark end of the gray scale and lightens the shadow areas; a **soft-contrast filter** maintains the dark areas while reducing highlight brightness. In each case the brightness range is reduced. Although these filters in some ways slightly degrade image quality, they can be helpful in video production when other methods of controlling the brightness range can't be used.

Polarizing Filters

polarizing filter: A filter (often adjustable) that reduces or eliminates reflections from glass, water and shiny surfaces. Also used to dramatically intensify contrast between the sky and clouds.

Most of us are familiar with the effect that polarized sunglasses have on reducing reflections and cutting glare. Professional *polarizing filters* for cameras can go much further in their effect. And, since most are adjustable, the polarizing effect can be varied. A polarizing filter enables a lens to see much more clearly through the surface reflections of glass and water. These filters also darken blue skies, intensify colors and, in general, heighten visual impact. Once its many applications are understood, a polarizer can become a videographer's most valuable filter.

Special-Effect Filters

star filter: An optical filter that has finely etched crisscrossing lines on the surface that creates fingers of light around bright lights and spectral reflections.

Star filters, which come in a variety of forms, create multicolored lines around bright lights. Depending on the type you choose, you can create four or five fingers of light around bright lights and reflections (spectral highlights). Note the use of a four-point star filter in Figure 1.2 in Chapter 1. The exact effect provided by a star filter is dependent upon lens f-stop. Because of this, if at all possible, the effect should be observed at different f-stop settings. Resulting differences in exposure can generally be controlled through the choice of shutter speeds on CCD cameras.

Sometimes it is desirable to create a dreamy, "soft focus" effect. This can be achieved through the use of a **diffusion filter**. These filters were regularly used in the early cinema to give starlets a soft, dreamy appearance, especially in close-ups. Diffusion filters come in several intensities. A diffusion effect can also be achieved by shooting through a very fine screen wire placed close to the lens or by shooting through a single thickness of a nylon stocking. In this case the f-stop used will greatly affect the final result. A somewhat related effect can be achieved by **fog filters**. They can add a barely perceptible haze to the image or a very pronounced foggy effect.

Before shooting with any type of filter, examine the result on a high-resolution monitor. Once a scene is taped, it is impossible to undo the effect. It should also be noted that whenever a filter is used with a video camera, the black level of the video (as seen on a waveform monitor) is slightly raised. Because of this, it is advisable to automatically or manually readjust camera setup or black level whenever a filter is used.

FIGURE 3.26
Professional video cameras have at least one filter wheel behind the lens, which can be rotated into position as needed. Typically, a filter wheel contains two neutral density filters, one or more color correction filters, one or more special-effect filters and an opaque "cap," which will protect the camera's target when the camera is not in use. Some cameras have two independent filter wheels, which makes it possible to use more than one filter at the same time.

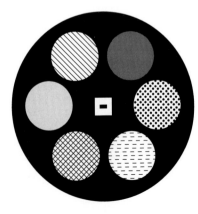

Camera Filter Wheels

Professional video cameras have a filter wheel located behind the lens that can hold several filters (Figure 3.26). Individual filters can be rotated into the lens path as needed. Typically, a filter wheel will contain two neutral density filters (ND-1 and ND-2), two or more color correction filters (including one that can reduce the blue-green effect of some fluorescent lights), one or more special effect filters (including the previously discussed star filter) and an opaque "cap,"

FIGURE 3.27
A matte box is a small bellows device mounted on the front of the camera. It can serve two purposes: a lens shade and a holder for filters and special-effect patterns. Instead of circular glass filters placed over the lens, comparatively inexpensive colored gels 4 inches square (gelatin filters) can be inserted into the back of the matte box.

which will protect the camera's target when the camera is not in use. Some cameras allow for two overlapping filter wheels, which means that more than one filter can be used at the same time. It should be noted, however, that some filters, such as polarizing filters, must be mounted in front of the camera lens to be most effective.

MATTE BOXES

Since glass color correction filters are rather expensive—especially being as large as they need to be to fit over the end of a zoom lens—professional film and video camera operators often make use of a **matte box**. As shown in Figure 3.27, a matte box is a small bellows device mounted on the front of the camera.

Instead of circular glass filters, comparatively inexpensive colored gels 4 inches square (gelatin filters) can be inserted into the back of the matte box.

Matte boxes can also hold small cutout patterns or masks. For example, a keyhole-shaped pattern could be cut out of a piece of cardboard and used to give the illusion of shooting through a keyhole. The f-stop and focal length used and distance of the mask from the lens affect the sharpness of the keyhole outline. Many of these effects are now more easily and predictably achieved with a special-effects generator. Matte boxes act as an adjustable lens hood to prevent strong light from hitting the surface of the lens at an oblique angle.

SUMMARY

The lens and its associated accessories represent the critical first step in achieving video quality and in exercising creative control over the video image. There are two types of lenses: prime, with a fixed focal length, and zoom, with a variable focal length. The angle of view of a lens is directly related to focal length: the shorter the focal length, the wider the angle of view, and the longer the focal length, the narrower the angle of view.

Although focal length appears to affect depth of field (the area in focus along the lens axis), this appearance is based on differences in camera-to-subject distance and target image size. It also seems that focal length alters spacial relationships between objects in a scene. This too is based on an unequal comparison of image areas. The target image size associated with a wide-angle lens hides a lack of sharpness and gives the appearance of a great depth of field. Problems with sharpness and focus are more noticeable in HDTV production. Because of the close lens-to-subject distances normally associated with the use of a wide-angle lens, this lens also appears to increase spacial relationships between objects. The reverse will be true for longer focal lengths: spacial relationships will appear to shrink.

Image stabilizers can greatly reduce the effects of an unsteady camera, including the image instability associated with videotaping while in a car or airplane. There are two types of camera mounts for lenses: C-mounts and bayonet mounts. The lens opening or iris of a lens controls the amount of light reaching the target and, thus, the image exposure. Iris settings are calibrated in f-stops. The larger the f-stop number, the smaller the iris opening, and the greater the apparent depth of field will be. The reverse is also true. The "speed" of a lens is equal to its widest f-stop opening.

Lenses are coated to reduce surface reflections. Because this coating is easily scratched, lenses must be properly cleaned and always covered with a lens cap when not in use. Although auto-focus lenses can reduce focusing errors in some situations, they are not normally used in professional production because of a number of associated problems.

The macro setting on a lens allows for extreme close-ups. If the back focus on a zoom lens is out of adjustment, the lens will shift focus as it is zoomed. There are a wide variety of filters and lens attachments that can creatively alter images, including colored filters, neutral density filters, low-contrast filters, polarizing filters, star filters, diffusion filters and fog filters. A matte box can hold filters and cutout forms and also serve as an adjustable lens hood.

KEY TERMS

angle of view	lens extender
aperture	lens flare
aperture setting	lens speed
auto-focus lens	lens shade (hood)
auto-iris	low-contrast filter
back focus	macro
bayonet mount	matte box
C-mount	neutral density (ND) filter
camcorder	polarizing filter
colored filter	prime lens
contrast filter	range extender
depth of field	servo-controlled zoom
diffusion filter	snap zoom
f-stop	soft-contrast filter
focal length	star filter
fog filter	supplementary lens
follow focus	t-stop
full-focus lens	ultraviolet filter
geometric distortion	VL bayonet mount
internal focus	zoom lens
iris	zoom ratio

Video Cameras | 4

From the lens we turn to the actual camera and its associated equipment. In this chapter we'll examine camera CCDs and tubes, video levels and resolution, camera viewfinders, prompting devices and camera mounting equipment. We'll also look at the basic types of cameras: studio, portable, convertible, electronic cinematography and high-definition.

THE CAMERA IMAGING DEVICE

The heart of a video camera is the target, the light-sensitive imaging device that translates the light from the lens into an electronic signal. Video cameras use two types of imaging devices: CCDs and tubes. In this chapter we will explain how each produces the luminance part of the video signal; in the next chapter we'll discuss how they create color. As we'll see, the principle of **photoemission,** or the conversion of light into electrical energy, is central to the operation of camera CCDs and tubes.

CCD Cameras

Although tube-type cameras were used in television for more than 40 years, most cameras being manufactured today use CCDs, or charge-coupled devices. On the outside a CCD looks like the miniaturized integrated circuit, or "chip," that is relied upon for almost all of today's electronic equipment. (CCDs are also called chip cameras.) One thing makes it different. On top there is a small window (Figure 4.1), which is the target. Excluding high-definition cameras, most of today's broadcast-quality CCD cameras have an image size of ½ or ⅔ inch (measured diagonally from one corner of the target to the other). Put

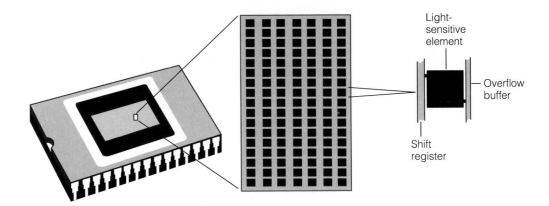

Light-
sensitive
element

Overflow
buffer

Shift
register

FIGURE 4.1

Most TV cameras rely on CCDs (charge-coupled devices) to convert the light from the camera lens into an electronic signal. On the top of the chip there is a small window called the target, which is ½-inch or ⅔-inch across (measured diagonally). Within this area there are from a few hundred thousand to several million light-sensitive points (pixels). If too much light hits a pixel, the voltage overflows the shift register and is drained off into the overflow buffer.

another way, the target area of a CCD is about the size of the nail on your little finger. Within this area there are from a few hundred thousand to several million light-sensitive points. Each of these points, or **pixels,** acts as a photoconductor, a light sensor whose electrical conductivity is changed by the absorption of light energy. The electrical energy released by any one pixel is in direct proportion to the amount of light focused on that point by the camera lens.

CCDs have many advantages over camera tubes:

- The sharpness of a CCD does not diminish around the edges of the picture as it does with camera tubes.

- There is no geometric distortion of the image with CCDs.

- CCDs can handle much higher brightness and contrast ranges.

- The life of a CCD is equal to the life of a typical integrated circuit, which is almost indefinite.

- Much less power is required by CCDs, a major advantage for battery-powered, portable equipment.

- CCDs can operate under very low light levels.

- CCDs are much more rugged than camera tubes.

- Bright lights do not "burn into" CCDs, resulting in a negative afterimage.

- CCDs are unaffected by magnetic fields or *microphonics* (disturbances in the picture resulting from vibration or loud noise).

- CCDs typically have a higher **signal-to-noise ratio** (the ratio between the desired video information and interfering video noise).

- CCDs do not require special setup and registration (color alignment).

- The electrical currents that result from light hitting a CCD can be "read out" (sampled) at different speeds, creating what is, in effect, an electronic shutter.

CCD Shutter Speeds   Unlike the shutters used in still cameras, the shutter used in CCD cameras is not mechanical. It is simply the duration of time that the light-induced charge is allowed to build before being transferred out of the **shift register,** an electronic memory bank (see Figure 4.1). With speeds as high as 1/10,000 second in CCD cameras, most any movement can be frozen without blur or smear (Figure 4.2).

By setting a CCD camera at its "normal" shutter speed of 1/60 second, the sampling is done at the maximum time allowed by the field rate of the TV system. This represents the maximum exposure possible with normal scanning. But, under very low-light conditions—especially where little or no action is

FIGURE 4.2
To reduce blur, CCD cameras rely on electronic shutters that limit exposure from 1/60 to 1/10,000 second. As shown by this picture of a wave crashing onto rocks along a Newfoundland coastline, even at a shutter speed of 1/1,000 second, movement can be frozen. (See also Figures 4.3A to 4.3D.)

involved—some video cameras have a provision to let the light-induced charge build for double and quadruple the normal time. Although this results in much brighter video, if there is any action, a pronounced stroboscopic effect will be obvious. This will be discussed in more detail later.

As the light level increases and there is a need to freeze action or reduce exposure, faster shutter speeds can be selected. Most professional CCD cameras have speeds of 1/60, 1/100, 1/250, 1/500, 1/1,000, and 1/2,000 second. Some go beyond this to 1/4,000, 1/8,000, and 1/10,000 second. (The exact sequence of numbers may vary, depending upon the make and model of the camera.) The higher speeds (1/1,000 second and above) make possible clear slow-motion playbacks and freeze-frame still images. Figures 4.3A to 4.3D show the effect of shutter speed on action.

Shutter Speeds and F-stops Just as in traditional still photography, with CCD cameras there is a direct relationship between shutter speed and f-stop. Table 4.1 illustrates this.

You will note that each time the shutter speed is doubled, the lens must be opened up one f-stop to provide the same net exposure. This means that each of the combinations shown (1/250 second at f/8, 1/2,000 second at f/2.8 etc.) represents the same exposure or video level. The relationship between shutter speed and CCD exposure is illustrated in Figure 4.4.

TABLE 4.1
Typical Relationship Between CCD Shutter Speed and Exposure

CCD shutter speed:	"normal"	1/100	1/250	1/500	1/1,000	1/2,000	1/4,000	1/8,000	1/10,000
Corresponding f-stop:	16	11	8	5.6	4.0	2.8	2.0	1.4	1.2

(a)   (b)   (c)   (d)

FIGURE 4.3

This roller coaster shows the effect of shutter speed on stopping action. Figure 4.3A was shot with a shutter speed of 1/60 second (the normal shutter speed for a CCD camera); Figure 4.3B was shot at 1/250 second; Figure 4.3C was shot at 1/1,000 second; and Figure 4.3D was shot at 1/2,000 second. Since the roller coaster was going at exactly the same speed in each photo, it is the increasing shutter speed that reduces the blur caused by movement. Note also that the closer the subject is to the lens, the more likely the motion will blur the camera image.

Stroboscopic Effects with Shutter Speeds A stroboscopic effect can occur in CCD cameras when very high (above 1/250 second) and very low (below 1/60 second) shutter speeds are used.

At shutter speeds below 1/60 second the camera must repeat the information on fields and frames more than once (to allow exposure to build) before moving on to new information, so there are fewer frames produced. If no movement is involved, this will go unnoticed. However, with movement, the loss of frames results in a discontinuity in action and a jerky, stroboscopic effect. In spite of the somewhat questionable "special effect" this provides, there are occasions—primarily very low-light news and documentary situations—where imperfect video will be better than no video at all (Figure 4.5).

When shutter speeds faster than 1/250 second are used, action tends to be cleanly frozen into crisp, sharp still images. Without the slight blur that helps smooth out the transition between successive frames, we may notice a subtle stroboscopic effect when we view rapid action. Even so, the overall effect of the faster shutter speeds is to make images clearer—especially in slow-motion playbacks.

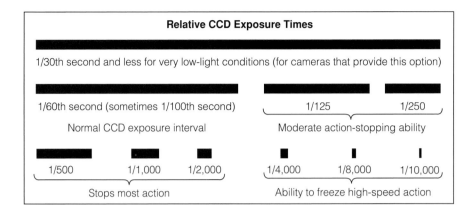

Relative CCD Exposure Times

1/30th second and less for very low-light conditions (for cameras that provide this option)

1/60th second (sometimes 1/100th second)

Normal CCD exposure interval

1/125   1/250

Moderate action-stopping ability

1/500   1/1,000   1/2,000

Stops most action

1/4,000   1/8,000   1/10,000

Ability to freeze high-speed action

FIGURE 4.4
Just as the speed of the mechanical shutter in a 35mm still camera affects film exposure, the electronic shutter in CCD video cameras influences CCD exposure. Each time the shutter speed is doubled (from 1/500 to 1/1,000 second, for example) the amount of light (exposure) is cut in half. Conversely, dropping the shutter speed from 1/250 to 1/125 second will double CCD exposure. Speeds above 1/2,000 second are rarely necessary to stop action. Their main value is in reducing exposure under bright sunlight to achieve selective focus effects. Some cameras can reduce frame rates to 1/30 second, making possible photography under extremely low light levels.

CCD Problems   Although most of their original problems have been solved, professional quality CCD cameras still have a few disadvantages, compared to tube cameras.

- Standard CCDs don't lend themselves to conversion to the new wide-screen, high-definition aspect ratios as readily as tube cameras do.

- Because CCDs are permanently cemented into place when they are installed in the factory, it is not possible to make back focus adjustments in multiple-CCD cameras to compensate for the problems exhibited by some lenses.[1]

- When operated in very high or very low temperatures CCDs can exhibit problems.[2]

- Although fewer CCDs than tubes go bad, pixels occasionally develop problems responding to light, resulting in extremely small spots in the video image.[3]

- Some of the less expensive CCD cameras exhibit vertical **smear** (a trailing image) when bright lights or objects appear in the scene.

Camera Tubes

Camera tubes date back to the early 1920s and the invention of the iconoscope tube by Vladimir Zworykin and the image dissector by Philo T. Farnsworth. These developments made television possible. Improvements in this basic imaging-tube technology resulted in the widely used orthicon and vidicon tubes associated with the era of black-and-white television. When color was developed and three and four camera tubes were needed, the smaller Plumbicon and Saticon tubes were introduced. Today, tube cameras are limited to special applica-

FIGURE 4.5
Most CCD cameras will produce acceptable pictures under as little as 1 footcandle (11 lux) of light. Even so, for optimum quality most require a basic light level of 90 to 160 footcandles.

1. **Chromatic aberration** is the major problem here. This is the characteristic of some lenses to bring certain colors (generally reds) into focus at a slightly different back focus point. With tube cameras, the red channel can be adjusted to compensate, but there is no such adjustment with most CCD cameras. Therefore, CCD cameras require high-quality, color-corrected lenses.

2. This is normally evidenced by a loss of pixel response, as shown by colored specks in the video. Except in extreme circumstances this problem will disappear when the camera is brought back to its normal temperature range.

3. Because of imperfections in the manufacturing process, it is almost impossible to manufacture a CCD without some "dead" pixels. Modern CCD camera circuitry takes this into account and electronically (and imperceptibly) fills in these dead spots with video information from adjacent pixels.

tions. Some HDTV cameras use HARPICON tubes.[4] Although many of the original problems associated with tubes have been reduced or eliminated, there are some problem areas. The most consequential is **burn in**. If bright lights or even bright spectral highlights from shiny objects are focused on the target of a tube, it can retain a negative afterimage. The longer the exposure and the brighter the object, the greater the potential problem. In extreme circumstances, such as when a camera is pointed at a bright light or the sun, the tube will suffer permanent damage and have to be replaced. Since tubes are quite expensive, this can be very costly.

VIDEO RESOLUTION

Now that we've covered the primary imaging devices for cameras, we can examine some important attributes of camera video. One of these is resolution. *Resolution* refers to the ability of a video camera to reproduce the fine detail transmitted by the lens. The higher the resolution, the sharper the picture.

resolution: The ability or degree to which a camera system can distinguish and reproduce fine detail.

Determining Resolution

Charts that contain squares or wedges of fine black lines are used to measure resolution. Within specific areas of these *resolution charts* or *test patterns* there are numbers such as 200, 300 etc. that refer to the number of *lines of resolution* within a specific area. (See Figure 4.6.) By filling the camera viewfinder with the resolution chart and observing the point where the lines appear to lose definition and blur together (as shown on a high-resolution monitor) the limits of sharpness for CCD and tube cameras can be determined. For example, if you can distinguish the individual lines at 500 but not at 600, you would say that the resolution limit of a particular camera system is 500 lines.[5] The best NTSC-type cameras can resolve 800 horizontal lines; HDTV cameras typically exceed more than 1,200 horizontal lines. As shown in Figure 4.6, vertical resolution is considered separately from horizontal resolution.

resolution chart: A test pattern that shows camera sharpness and the condition of the camera system.

test pattern: Any one of a number of standardized electronic patterns or camera charts intended to evaluate specific video qualities such as linearity and resolution.

Vertical and Horizontal Resolution

Before we can get more precise about resolution, we need to distinguish vertical resolution from horizontal resolution. **Vertical resolution,** or the limit of sharpness that can be reproduced along a vertical axis, is restricted by the number of scanning lines the TV system uses. Simply put, if you had a test pattern with 700 vertical lines you couldn't expect the 525-line NTSC television system to be able to reproduce it.[6]

There is also a limit on **horizontal resolution**, or the number of horizontal elements that can be reproduced. Although some TV cameras can reproduce

---

4. *HARPICON* stands for high-gain avalanche rushing amorphous photoconductor. A HARPICON tube uses a light-multiplying target material to make the tube more than 10 times as light-sensitive as a standard Saticon tube. Because it can resolve more than 1,200 TV lines, this tube is a good choice for some high-definition applications.

5. Although the quick procedure outlined is adequate for evaluating the general performance of cameras, the only technically precise method involves going a step further and determining the *depth of video modulation*. This involves using an oscilloscope to determine how well the camera system responds to the individual lines.

6. Because of technical limitations relating to the actual number of active scanning lines and the interlaced approach to scanning fields and frames, vertical resolution will always fall significantly below the total number of scanning lines in the TV system. With CCD cameras, the number of pixels in the target also imposes an upper limit on resolution.

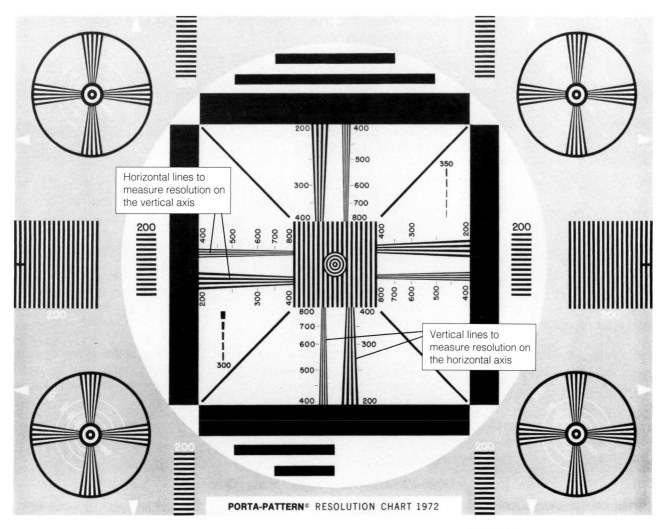

Horizontal lines to measure resolution on the vertical axis

Vertical lines to measure resolution on the horizontal axis

PORTA-PATTERN© RESOLUTION CHART 1972

FIGURE 4.6

Resolution charts are used to measure the amount of detail a camera can reproduce. By filling the camera viewfinder with a resolution chart and observing the point where the lines appear to lose definition and blur together, the limits of sharpness for a camera can be determined. Note that vertical and horizontal resolution are measured separately.

800 horizontal lines, these are only visible on video monitors *within* the station. Once an NTSC signal is broadcast and it reaches homes, resolution is reduced to fewer than 340 lines. The limiting factor is primarily the bandwidth of the TV channel, which, as noted in Chapter 2, is 4 MHz for NTSC. PAL and SECAM systems can do better with 100 additional scanning lines and 5 MHz bandwidths. Closed-circuit (wired) NTSC television distribution systems can go to about 8 MHz, or a resolution of about 640 lines. Satellite-to-home reception falls somewhere in between standard over-the-air broadcasting and closed-circuit television.

Since home receivers can only reproduce up to 340 lines of resolution in standard NTSC broadcasting, the question arises, why use cameras with resolutions of up to 800 lines? Since there are resolution losses throughout the TV process, the sharper the picture is to start out with, the sharper it will end up at the home receiver.

Depending upon the system, HDTV productions can start out with a 30 MHz bandwidth. This means that, initially, these systems have a horizontal resolution many times greater than standard NTSC video. However, the 30 MHz bandwidth is typically *compressed* for the transmission and distribution process. **Data compression,** which is commonly used in digital electronics, reduces the bandwidth of audio and video signals so that the signal will take less space and, therefore, be easier to record and transmit. The trick is to compress the signal without losing too much picture detail or introducing **artifacts** (picture aberrations) that will significantly degrade quality.

MINIMUM LIGHT LEVELS FOR CAMERAS

footcandle: The measure of light intensity used in non-metric countries. The number of lumens per square foot.

lux: Unit of light intensity used in metric countries. One footcandle is equal to 10.74 lux.

Television cameras require a certain level of light (target exposure) to produce good-quality video. This light level is measured in footcandles or lux. A *footcandle,* which is a measure of light intensity from a candle at a distance of 1 foot (under very specific conditions), is used in non-metric countries for measuring light intensity.[7] Countries on the metric system use *lux*. A footcandle is equal to about 10.74 lux.

Although they will produce acceptable pictures under much lower light levels, most professional video cameras require a basic light level of 90 to 160 footcandles to produce an optimum quality picture. At this level of illumination the camera lens aperture can be between f/4 and f/11—a desirable range, technically. As the light level increases, the iris of the lens is stopped down to maintain the proper target exposure—just as the iris of a still camera must be stopped down so that film of a certain speed won't be overexposed.

Under low light levels the iris of the lens can be automatically or manually opened up—all the way to its maximum aperture. Beyond this point, the video will quickly start to look dark with a major loss of detail in the shadow areas. To help compensate for low light levels, professional cameras have built-in gain control (video amplifying) circuits that can be switched in. Through the use of these multiposition gain control switches on the camera or the CCU, these circuits can amplify the video signal in steps from 3 to about 28 units (dB). Using these circuits, some CCD cameras can produce acceptable video under light levels that are much too dim to read this page. But the greater the video "boost" (amplification), the greater the sacrifice in picture quality. Specifically, video noise will increase, and color clarity will diminish. However, less than optimum video quality is often better than no video at all. This is especially true when you are doing important television news (ENG) stories.

LIGHT MULTIPLIERS

For situations that require video under even less light, so-called light multipliers or "night viewing devices" are available. The most refined of these can "see" under conditions that seem pitch black to the human eye. These devices use fiber optics and solid-state circuitry to amplify light. Many create a monochrome (greenish) image that is slightly blurry. In recent years news camerapersons have found these devices useful on ENG cameras for covering nighttime stories—especially when artificial lighting would call attention to the camera and adversely affect the story being covered.

CAMERA SETUP

Two adjustments are basic to setting up CCD cameras: setting the video level and white (color) balancing. With tube-based cameras, registration is also required. White balancing and registration will be covered in the next chapter.

---

7. As the United States inches its way to the metric system, *lux* has slowly been replacing *footcandles*.

Camera setup is controlled at the camera CCU, often with the help of base stations and memory cards.

Base Stations

Although each studio camera has its own CCU circuitry, most studios now use digitally controlled cameras that tie into a single base station. The base station is used to handle the complex camera setup procedures for all studio cameras from one control point. As adjustments need to be made, they can either be made for all cameras simultaneously, or each camera can be switched to the base station for individual adjustment. A memory unit within each camera is able to maintain the established settings, even when the camera is not switched into the base station. Since the microprocessor memory unit in the camera is battery-powered, it can also retain settings after the camera is shut off.

The move to digitally controlled cameras has not only made possible base station control, but has eliminated the large, heavy camera cables (typically containing more than 100 wires) that were associated with studio cameras. These have now been replaced with small, lightweight **triax** (three-conductor coaxial) cables.

Memory Cards

Many cameras now also make use of credit card–sized programmable "memory cards." After one camera is set up and the settings programmed into the card, the card can be inserted into each camera and the setup information instantly transferred. This ensures that each camera is set up in the same way. Memory cards are especially helpful in multiple-camera field production where cameras are not tied into a central base station.

VIDEO LEVEL CONSIDERATIONS

As we've noted, target exposure is determined by the iris setting of the camera lens. Ideally, video levels should be somewhat evenly distributed between 7.5 (the blackest-black) and 100 (the whitest-white) in the picture. (See Figures 4.7A and 4.7B.) But, as we'll see, often things don't start out being ideal.

FIGURE 4.7
Normal video levels are somewhat evenly distributed between 7.5 (the blackest-black) and 100 (the whitest-white) in the picture. Figure 4.7B shows how the video in photo 4.7A would appear on a waveform monitor. The remaining photos and corresponding waveform distributions (Figures 4.8A through 4.13B) show problem video situations.

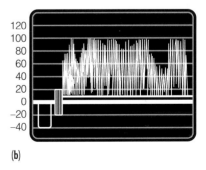

(b)

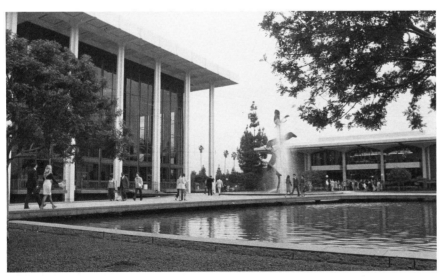

(a)

Contrast Range

The human eye can handle differences in contrast (or brightness) of 1,000 to 1; color slides, about 400 to 1. But in broadcast video the acceptable contrast range drops to about 30 to 1.[8] This means that **TV white,** or the lightest part of the picture, should not be more than 30 times brighter than **TV black,** or the blackest part of the picture.

In terms of reflected light, this 30-to-1 range means that subject matter can reflect from 3 percent to 90 percent of the light hitting it (3 $\times$ 30 = 90).[9] Subject matter that reflects 3 percent of the light (TV reference black) includes dull black paint, black velvet, and new blue jeans.

In addition to white skies, windows in the background etc., there is much subject matter that can cause a video camera to exceed an acceptable contrast range. White paint, white plaster and a terra-cotta white surface can all reflect more than 90 percent of the light hitting them. New fallen snow in direct sunlight also exceeds the 90 percent maximum. One of the most common mistakes that students make in video field production work is to include overly bright subject matter in scenes (bright skies, white buildings etc.), which causes a severe darkening of skin tones.

Overexposure

If the target of the camera is significantly **overexposed** from having too much light on the target, the waveform monitor will show a white level that is above 100. Left uncorrected, one of two things can happen. The system will **clip** or cut off the top of the video range at 100, or it will compress (push down) the video range so it stays between 7.5 and 100.

Clipped Whites Although clipping off the top end of the video may at first seem to be a good solution, in many cases important detail in the lighter areas of the picture can be lost in the process. The clipped areas, especially if they are large, will lack detail and have a chalky, burned-out appearance (see Figures 4.8A and 4.8B). The effect will be evident on the waveform monitor because the top of the pattern will look flat and cleanly lopped off instead of being irregular or jagged as it should be.

Tonal Compression The second way of handling an excessive contrast range—compressing the gray scale—also creates undesirable effects. This **tonal compression** means that most of the objects in the picture (including skin tones) will be reproduced much darker than they should be. In fact, if the bright area influencing the video is large and quite bright, skin tones can go completely black, and an individual in the scene will become a silhouette, which generally is not the desired result. As Figures 4.9A and 4.9B show, this problem can often be eliminated by reducing the contrast ratio with fill light. As we've noted—and this bears repeating more than once—such things as bright skies, interior shots with windows in the background or even white walls used as a background can all cause tonal compression.

8. CCD cameras can easily handle 40-to-1 contrast ranges. But we must keep in mind that contrast ranges are reduced by the weakest links in the chain: the transmission and reception process, and the home receiver. When a picture is viewed on a home TV set, the maximum brightness range, depending upon the viewing conditions, can drop to 20 to 1. We'll compromise by citing a 30-to-1 contrast range.

9. This assumes that the subject matter is evenly lit. When lighting varies from one part of the scene to another, different brightness values will result.

(a)

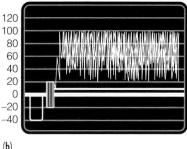

(b)

FIGURE 4.8

When whites are clipped (generally because of camera overexposure), the lighter areas of the picture will lack detail and have a chalky, burned-out appearance (Figure 4.8A). The effect will be evident on the waveform monitor (Figure 4.8B) because the top of the pattern will look flat and cleanly lopped off instead of being irregular or jagged. Compare Figure 4.8B with Figure 4.7B.

Controlling Excessive Contrast Ranges

White clipping and tonal compression are obviously unsatisfactory solutions to coping with an excessive contrast range. Assuming that you need to preserve important detail outside of the normal 30-to-1 range, there may be two solutions. First, you may be able to alter the lighting by putting more light on the dark areas and reducing the light on offending bright areas. Lighting will be covered in Chapter 6. The second option is a technical adjustment called gamma correction.

Gamma correction refers to electronically changing or re-shaping the black-to-white response curve of a camera so that the resulting video will fall within an acceptable range. This is done on the camera's CCU and is best left to a video technician. Although gamma correction results in subtle changes in other areas of the camera's white-to-black (gray scale) range, it can eliminate the clipping or tonal compression that would otherwise take place.

FIGURE 4.9

One of the most common problems encountered by videographers is the tonal compression that results when a subject is photographed against an overly bright background (Figure 4.9A). This problem can be controlled either by eliminating the overly bright background, or (as was done here) by using fill light to reduce the contrast ratio (Figure 4.9B).

(a)

(b)

CCD cameras have a major advantage over tube cameras in handling excessive contrast ratios because excess video levels are drained off into a buffer (Figure 4.1) before they can affect video quality. Taking an extreme example, a momentary shot taken of the sun with a CCD camera results in the same (maximum) video level as photographing a white piece of paper. Not only would a shot of the sun ruin most camera tubes, but the resulting white level would be so great that all other tones in the picture would instantly turn black.

AGC (automatic gain control): Circuit that automatically maintains proper audio or video level.

Video cameras have special problems with an excessive brightness or contrast ranges if automatic gain control (*AGC*) and **auto-iris** (also called **automatic exposure control**) circuitry are used to maintain video levels. Since most simple consumer-type camcorders rely on these automatic features, it is difficult to compensate for exposure problems with this type of equipment. Some of these cameras do allow you to manually adjust the iris or use a backlight switch. A *backlight switch* opens the iris about two f-stops to compensate for scenes with strong back light. This option should be used whenever you encounter backlit scenes or scenes with bright backgrounds. (This, of course, assumes you can't avoid them in the first place.)

backlight switch: Camera control that overrides auto-iris system and opens the iris two or three f-stops. Commonly used in backlit situations where auto-iris would result in dark skin tones and underexposure.

Professional cameras allow you to switch off AGC circuitry and set video levels manually with the aid of a waveform monitor or zebra stripes. **Zebra stripes,** which are a striped pattern that indicate areas of maximum video level, can be switched into the viewfinder picture during the setup phase of a camcorder. They are used as a guide to adjust camera levels so that reflections or small undesired bright areas don't provide unintended reference points for TV white. In doing ENG work many videographers simply use the camera viewfinder as a reference while manually adjusting the camera's iris. This assumes a good-quality viewfinder image and adequate personal experience.

Handling Spectral Highlights

spectral highlights: Bright reflections from shiny subject matter that often cause spikes on a waveform monitor and video brightness range problems.

Spectral highlights, or reflections from bright, shiny objects, create special contrast range problems, especially if they involve large areas of a scene. As we've noted, AGC circuits in cameras often routinely bring down white levels so that the resulting bright "spikes" of video will be within the normal 7.5 to 100 IRE unit range. As a consequence, other video areas will become much too dark (Figure 4.10A). Since there is no important detail in spectral highlights, the most desirable solution is to manually raise the video level (gain) of the camera by opening the iris until the important white areas reach 100. This restores the normal tonal range. At this point, of course, the spikes from the spectral highlights will be considerably above 100 (Figure 4.10B). But these can be eliminated by using the camera's white clip feature (Figure 4.10C). Some of the newer CCD cameras can (within limits) sense the presence of spectral highlights and automatically clip them.

Camera Underexposure

Underexposure (insufficient light on the target) results in low video levels. On a waveform monitor this is immediately obvious since the peak video level may only come up to 50 or so IREs (Figures 4.11A and 4.11B).

If video is initially left at a low level and then raised or boosted later in the video recording or transmission process, the resulting picture will generally look grainy and of low technical quality. This undesirable graininess is called **video noise.** (Audio has a similar problem when a low-level signal is boosted so that hiss and general system noise become evident.)

(a)

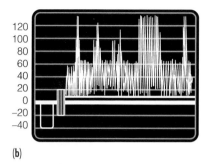

(b)

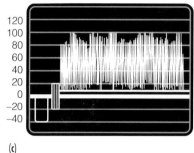

(c)

FIGURE 4.10

If left uncorrected, reflections from bright subject matter (such as the reflections from the fountain, the windows and the water in this scene) can create special contrast range problems. Note in Figure 4.10B that when the entire video scale (including the spikes of white from the reflections) is brought within a normal video range on a waveform monitor, some of the more important elements in the picture become much too dark (Figure 4.10A). Since there is no important detail in these reflections, the most desirable solution is to manually raise the video level (gain) of the camera by opening the iris until the more important white areas of the picture reach 100 on the waveform monitor. At this point, the spikes of video that go beyond 100 can then simply be eliminated by using the camera's white clip feature (Figure 4.10C).

(a)

FIGURE 4.11

Camera underexposure (insufficient light on the target) results in low video levels (Figure 4.11A). On a waveform monitor this is immediately obvious, since the peak video level may only come up to 50 or so (Figure 4.11B). If video is initially left at a low level and then raised or boosted later in the video recording or transmission process, the resulting picture will typically look grainy and be of low technical quality.

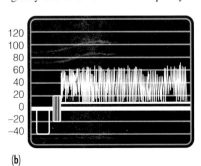

(b)

Camera Black-Level Considerations

Two controls on the CCU affect the black level: the pedestal or setup control and, to a lesser degree, the iris setting.

Setting the Pedestal Control   After either physically capping the lens so that no light can enter or using a button on the CCU that automatically accomplishes the same thing, the *pedestal* or **setup** (black-level) control can easily be observed on a waveform monitor. The pedestal is then adjusted up or down to bring the black level to exactly 7.5 on the scale. The use of a waveform monitor in setting levels is especially important in multicamera productions when each camera must be perfectly matched to avoid annoying level (and possibly color) shifts when different cameras are switched on-line. When the CCUs of several cameras are routed through a single waveform monitor and base station, the common pedestal or setup control is referred to as a *master black control*.

The black level on cameras being used in single-camera productions (most ENG work, for example) can be set without a waveform monitor by simply pushing the automatic black-level setup button. When this is done the camera is, in effect, capped so no light strikes the target, and the black level is then automatically set to 7.5.

Figures 4.12A and 4.12B show what happens when the black level is too high. Note that blacks have been pushed up into the brighter areas of the picture. As a result, they have been replaced by gray. Without true blacks, much of the important detail in the picture is lost.

If the darker parts of a video camera's picture are "crushed," "bunched up" or compressed down to the bottom of the waveform pattern (see Figure 4.13B), the picture will be highly contrasty and contain large pools of black as shown in Figure 4.13A. Much important detail is also lost when the black level is too low. (Very old films often show this tendency because of shortcomings in early motion picture film.)

You might logically think that setting levels with a waveform monitor should just be a matter of setting the brightest object in the picture to 100 and the darkest object to 7.5. Although that sounds totally reasonable, normal on-camera subject matter often does not lend itself as a reference in setting camera levels—for two reasons. On a waveform monitor display it is often difficult to determine which specific objects in a scene represent TV white and which should be considered TV black. Second, even if such objects are found, they may be too small to easily locate in the waveform monitor's complex display pattern. Fortunately, there is a better way.

Using Chip Charts

Chip charts (Figure 4.14) are routinely used in studios for setting video levels. The chart should be placed at the point in the scene where the talent will appear. All the lights required for the scene should be turned on. With the camera focused full-frame on the chip chart, camera levels should be adjusted so that the brightest step on the chip chart registers 100 on the waveform monitor. The blackest-black on the chip chart has 3 percent reflectance and should appear at the 7.5 point.

Although adjusting the camera iris primarily affects the white level, you will also notice the black level changes to a slight degree. Therefore, whenever one adjustment is made, the other may have to be changed slightly.

When the iris and black levels are properly set, you should be able to clearly see on a (well-adjusted) monitor each gray scale step of the chip chart (Figure

pedestal: In video, the black level as displayed on a waveform monitor.

master black control: An adjustment on one or more video cameras which controls the blanking, pedestal or black level of the video.

chip chart: A test chart consisting of shades of gray from TV white to TV black used for setting up cameras.

(a)

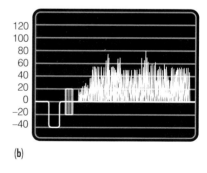

(b)

FIGURE 4.12

When the camera black level is set too high, there are no true blacks. Consequently, much of the important detail in the picture is lost. Note in Figure 4.12A that blacks have been replaced by gray. This is also apparent on a waveform monitor (Figure 4.12B).

4.14).[10] When the chip chart is removed from the scene, you should be assured of optimum tonal rendition on normal subject matter.

Subjective Elements of Video Levels

Sometimes technical standards differ from aesthetic ideals. We've noted that ideal video levels start at 7.5 and (in a somewhat evenly distributed manner) extend to 100 on the waveform monitor. This assumes a "normal" scene, one

10. Because of printing limitations, a clear distinction between each of the gray scale steps is difficult to achieve in this textbook illustration.

FIGURE 4.13

If the blacks are "crushed," or compressed down to the bottom of the waveform pattern (Figure 4.13B), the picture will contain large areas of black (Figure 4.13A). Much important detail in the darker area of the picture is lost when the video black level is too low.

(b)

(a)

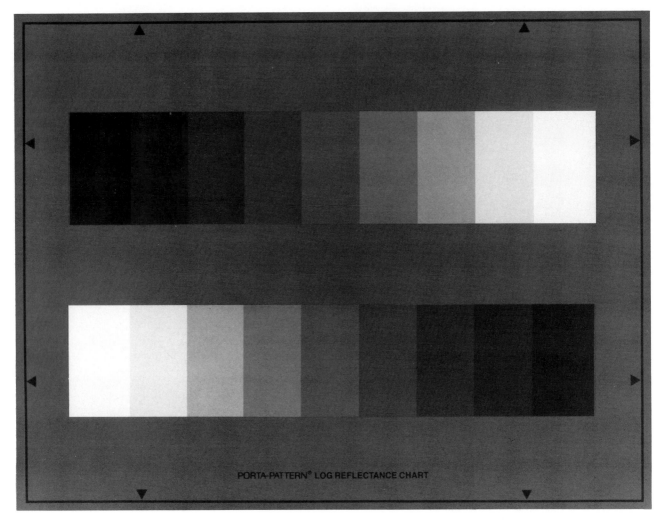

PORTA-PATTERN® LOG REFLECTANCE CHART

FIGURE 4.14

Chip charts or gray scales are routinely
used in studios for setting video levels.
With the camera focused full-frame on
the chip chart, camera levels should be
adjusted so that the brightest step on
the chip chart registers 100 on the waveform monitor. The blackest-black on
the chip chart should appear at the 7.5
point.

that contains elements in the TV white and TV black range. Occasionally, there
are situations where this will not be true. A wide-angle scene showing dense
Los Angeles smog or the fog of a New England coastline may not contain any
true blacks. In fact, if the black level were brought down to 7.5, it would destroy
the true tonal (gray scale) values in the scenes. In this case, after the black level
has been set on TV black, you can let the black level for the actual scene float
significantly above 7.5. Only in this way would the resulting video realistically
depict the original subject matter.

In unusual circumstances the white level might also be an issue, as, for
example, in a dramatic segment where the lights momentarily go off in a room.
Without special instructions, problems will result when a videotape operator
(with an eye on technical standards rather than artistic concerns) reacts by
automatically cranking the video level up to a full 100 percent. In such cases the
intended effect of a carefully crafted dramatic scene can be destroyed.

In searching for a solution that will meet both technical and artistic needs,
some producers and engineers suggest that at least one element in every scene
have approximately a 3 percent reflectance (TV black) and another a 90 percent
reflectance (TV white). If the objects are large enough to be evident on a
waveform monitor, but not so large that they detract from the effect the producer-director wants, technical standards will be met, and the intended result

can be ensured. In the fog scene, a small, black foreground object could serve as TV black. In the dramatic scene where the lights temporarily go out in a room, a streetlight visible through a window could act as a white reference to help ensure that the remaining video is held down to its intended (low) level.

THE CAMERA VIEWFINDER

We now turn to a major component of all video cameras, the viewfinder. The viewfinder is actually a small TV screen connected to the output of the camera's CCU. Studio cameras generally have 7-inch viewfinders designed to be viewed with both eyes at a distance of 1 or 2 feet. Portable cameras commonly rely on 1.5-inch images that are viewed with one eye with the help of a magnifying lens. Although the viewfinders of some cameras display color images,[11] a black-and-white image is sometimes preferred. There are at least three reasons:

- The resolution or clarity of a monochrome image is generally superior, which makes focusing easier and more accurate.
- The black-and-white viewfinder requires less power than a color viewfinder, which is an important consideration in a portable camera.
- The electronics of a black-and-white viewfinder take up less space.

A black-and-white viewfinder also allows production personnel to evaluate *color compatibility,* or how successfully the colors translate into black and white. (Certain elements in a scene may be clearly distinguishable in color, but these distinctions may merge together into the same tones when the picture is translated into black and white.)

color compatibility: The ability of different color subject matter to translate into a black-and-white picture and maintain adequate tonal contrast and separation.

Although field cameras now use viewfinders that warm up in one or two seconds, studio cameras typically require ten seconds or so to form a stable picture. Until tube-type viewfinders are replaced by flat, solid-state devices, they will remain the one element in a camera that requires a warm-up period.

Viewfinder Status Indicators

In an effort to communicate information about the camera's status to the operator, camera manufacturers have added an array of **status indicators** to viewfinders. Portable cameras generally have a greater number of these, because there is no external CCU and the total control of the camera rests with the operator. There are often one or more miniature colored lights around the edges of the video image. A small red light at the top of the viewfinder generally indicates that the tape is rolling and the camera's signal is being recorded.

status indicators: The collection of various lights, patterns and alphanumeric characters visible in and around a video camera viewfinder that shows the operating condition of the camera, recorder and battery.

There are also indicators that are superimposed over the basic video image, such as patterns, written material and various electronic masks. Masks include white lines indicating the safe areas and, in the case of an HDTV camera, lines showing the smaller 4 × 3 aspect ratio. Other indicators may signal that the camcorder battery is about dead, that there is insufficient light for acceptable video, or that the camera needs color balancing. You will want to consult the camera's instruction manual to learn what the specific boxes, bars and lines appearing over the video are designed to indicate.

Some messages may be in plain English. The superimposed message *tape remaining: 2 min.* in a camcorder viewfinder is hard to misinterpret. Also difficult to misinterpret is a voice from a small speaker in the side of a portable

---

11. Viewfinders with color images are preferred by camera operators doing sports because the colored jerseys of the two teams are easier to distinguish during a fast-moving game.

camera saying "there is one minute left on the videotape." Optional voice status reports (in the language of your choice) are now being used on ENG/EFP cameras made by at least one manufacturer.

Adjusting the Viewfinder Image

To be useful, viewfinders must accurately reflect the nature and quality of the video coming from the camera. Because the viewfinder is actually a miniature TV screen, the image is subject to brightness, contrast and focus problems, as well as the occasional lack of proper image centering. Adjusting the viewfinder image in no way affects the video coming from a video camera, but adjustments to the camera video will affect the viewfinder image.

To make sure that the contrast and brightness are set correctly, the camera's built-in, electronically generated color bars can be switched on and examined in the viewfinder. With many cameras the colors will not be visible in the viewfinder, but the brightness and contrast controls can be adjusted until a full, continuous range of tones is visible, from solid black to white.

Although brightness and contrast problems in a viewfinder image can easily be recognized and fixed, **linearity** problems (the absence of geometric distortion) may not be as apparent. Therefore, viewfinders should be periodically checked with a test chart and a well-adjusted TV monitor.

Checking Viewfinder Accuracy

To check the accuracy of a viewfinder image, a video monitor has to be found that has, itself, been perfectly aligned with the help of a test pattern. The output of the camera is then hooked up to the monitor, and the camera is focused on a test pattern so that the outermost edges of the pattern just fill the viewfinder image. Any discrepancy between the viewfinder image and the monitor image should then be obvious. Image centering and linearity problems will have to be corrected with the help of an engineer. Although the flat, solid-state viewfinders now being used on some cameras eliminate linearity and focus problems, the clarity of their pictures doesn't (yet) equal that of a tube-based viewfinder image.

Viewfinder Sharpness

On some viewfinders the brightness and contrast settings (which are interrelated in their effect) also influence image sharpness. Generally if either of these is excessively high, there will be a loss in picture sharpness. If a tube-type viewfinder image becomes somewhat fuzzy and hard to focus, it may be an electronic rather than an optical problem. The sharpness of the viewfinder image is primarily dependent upon the viewfinder's electrical focus setting. Since this is an internal setting, it will have to be adjusted by an engineer.

Although wearing eyeglasses is not a problem with studio cameras, it is with portable cameras. Since the camera eyepieces are designed to fit against the face, if eyeglasses are used, the operator may not be able to clearly see all four corners of the viewfinder image. To solve this problem, portable cameras have adjustable magnification eyepieces that can accommodate a wide variety of magnification needs. Cameras that don't have built-in adjustments will normally accommodate correcting lenses that screw over the eyepiece. With proper eyepiece correction, operators should not need their glasses to see a clear viewfinder image.

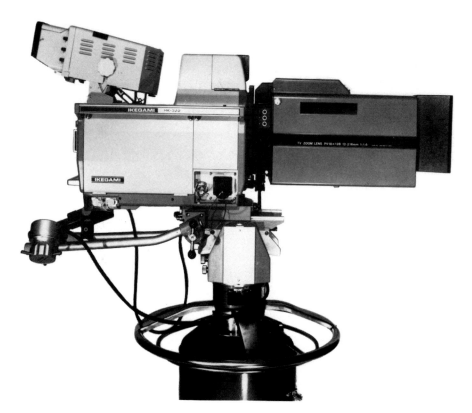

FIGURE 4.15
Studio cameras are the largest and least portable of the various types of cameras. They are characterized by large viewfinders, zoom lens housings that are often as large as the camera itself and conspicuous tally lights. Studio cameras are normally mounted on pedestals that enable them to be smoothly trucked and dollied around a studio floor.

BASIC CAMERA TYPES

Studio Cameras

The largest and least portable of the various types of cameras is the studio camera. Studio cameras (Figure 4.15) are characterized by large viewfinders, zoom lens housings that are often as large as the camera itself and conspicuous tally lights. Studio cameras are mounted on heavy pedestal devices that enable them to be smoothly trucked and dollied around a studio floor. Generally, these mounts (to be discussed later) also make possible adjustments in camera height.

Studio cameras also allow for headsets for personal communication with other production personnel (Figure 4.16). These are referred to as PLs (for private lines or production lines), or in some cases *intercommunication lines*. Many camera systems have two communication channels. Generally, one is used for production crew communications (Figure 4.17), and the second one is used to handle engineering concerns.

Most studio camera viewfinders can be switched to a special-effects feed from the control room switcher. This makes it possible for camera operators to take a direct role in setting up a video effect involving their cameras.

Portable Field Cameras

In addition to being much smaller, cameras designed for field production (Figure 4.18) differ from studio cameras in several ways. First, the lenses associated with field production are generally much smaller and less technically sophisticated. The zoom lenses on many studio cameras have shot boxes that can

FIGURE 4.16

Headsets are used on studio cameras so that camera operators can talk to and hear other production personnel. Although camera operators normally plug their headsets into their cameras, other production personnel, such as floor directors, sometimes use wireless headsets. The two-way radio receivers and transmitters give the users much more freedom to move around the studio and control room.

FIGURE 4.17

Many PLs (production lines or inter-communication systems) have two lines: one for production crew communications and a second one to handle engineering concerns. Here a floor director talks to the director during a commercial break.

electronically memorize several preselected zoom position and focus settings. A push of a button by an operator or a signal from a computerized robotic camera control system (to be discussed below) will cause the lens and camera to move to a preprogrammed shot. This level of sophistication is seldom needed in the field. Because field cameras must be compact and highly portable, their viewfinders are typically only 1.5 inches compared to the larger viewfinders associated with studio cameras.

FIGURE 4.18

In addition to being much smaller, cameras designed for field production differ from studio cameras in four ways: the lenses are smaller, they get their power from an attached battery, their viewfinders are typically only 1.5 inches compared to the 7-inch viewfinders associated with studio cameras, and they have built-in camera control units (CCUs).

Instead of having the CCU (camera control unit) located at a remote point so functions can be controlled by a technician, portable cameras have their CCUs located within the camera itself. This means that with field cameras all camera functions, such as color balance, video levels etc., are adjusted at the camera. Except when doing multiple-camera field work, field cameras seldom have a need for normal PL (production line) communication. Consequently, some field cameras do not contain plugs and amplifier circuits for headsets.

The final area of difference between studio and field cameras relates to the camera's power supply. Whereas the studio camera's multiconnector cable carries the power for the camera (along with the video signals, PL communications etc.), many field cameras get all of their power from an attached battery.

Convertible Cameras

Although many cameras are designed either for studio work or field production, some manufacturers have seen the value in making *convertible cameras* — cameras that can be altered to serve the needs of both kinds of work (Figure 4.19). Three areas of modification are associated with converting cameras from one configuration to the other:

- The size and type of viewfinder are switched.
- The power supply and its associated cabling are changed so that in its studio configuration the convertible camera can be routed through a CCU and possibly a base station.
- The zoom lens and associated cabling and electronics are changed.

Electronic Cinematography Cameras

One type of video camera has been designed especially for single-camera video production. The **electronic cinematography** or **EC camera** is a high-quality video camera designed to replace the traditional motion picture camera in single-camera video productions. Many of these are HDTV cameras.

The EC camera resembles a 35mm motion picture camera in size, weight, basic operation and, in particular, in its ability to use standard fixed-focal-length (prime) lenses.

HDTV Cameras

In outward appearance, an HDTV camera (Figure 4.20) may resemble either a studio camera or an EC camera. Although all of the major features and components of an HDTV camera are the same as the cameras we've discussed, there are three basic areas of difference. First, to handle the extra resolution required for HDTV, the zoom lens must be of better quality. (Among other requirements, HDTV lenses must be able to resolve at least three times the detail that normal NTSC camera lenses can.) Second, since there are several HDTV standards, some HDTV cameras are capable of creating video in more than one standard. A third difference is that the HDTV camera viewfinder shows a 16 × 9 instead of a 4 × 3 picture ratio.

Camcorders

The final type of camera, the camcorder, is either an all-in-one camera and recorder unit, or a small portable camera designed to be directly attached to

FIGURE 4.19
A convertible camera can be altered to serve the needs of both field and studio work. As noted in the text, at least three types of modifications are involved in switching from a field to studio configuration: the size and type of viewfinder are switched, the power supply and its associated cabling are changed, and the zoom lens and its cabling and electronics are changed.

convertible camera: A video camera especially designed to be quickly switched between studio and field use.

FIGURE 4.20

In outward appearance an HDTV camera resembles a studio camera. However, there are three basic differences: the zoom lens must be of better quality in an HDTV camera, the viewfinder shows a 16 × 9 instead of a 4 × 3 picture ratio, and some HDTV cameras are capable of creating video in more than one television standard.

(docked with) a videotape recorder. For news and documentary work camcorders (Figure 4.21) have now replaced the separate camera and recorders that previously had to be awkwardly strung together by cables.

CAMERA MOUNTS

Originally, mounts were required for television cameras because they weighed up to 240 pounds. Now, even though some high-quality video cameras weigh less than 2 pounds, mounts are still important, primarily because they enable an operator to smoothly control camera movement.

FIGURE 4.21

A camcorder is either a combination *camera* plus re*corder* or a small camera designed to be directly attached to (docked with) a small videotape recorder. For news and documentary work camcorders have now replaced the separate camera and recorders that previously had to be (rather awkwardly) strung together with cables.

FIGURE 4.22
With a shoulder mount, the weight of a portable video camera or camcorder can be equally distributed over the front and back of the mount, making it unnecessary to support the weight of the unit with the hands. This leaves the hands free to lightly steady the unit on the shoulder while operating the controls. Although shoulder mounts should never be considered a regular substitute for a tripod, they often must be used in news and documentary work where setting up a tripod is not practical.

shoulder mount: A frame that supports a camcorder unit so that it can be balanced and supported on the shoulder. Shoulder mounts are commonly used with ENG cameras.

body brace: A type of camera mount that attains some measure of stability by resting on the shoulder and chest or belt area.

Body Mounts

There are two basic types of camera body mounts: the kind that rests on the body (generally the shoulder) and the type that uses a body harness to support the camera through a system of counterbalanced springs and levers.

With a ***shoulder mount*** the weight of a portable video camera or camcorder can be equally distributed over the front and back of the mount making it unnecessary to support the weight of the unit with the hands (Figure 4.22). The hands can lightly steady the unit on the shoulder making it relatively easy to operate the controls. In doing EFP work, shoulder mounts should never be considered a suitable substitute for a tripod. However, they often must be used in news and documentary work where setting up a tripod is not practical.

A ***body brace*** goes one step further than a shoulder mount by adding a belt support. Although this type of support is more stable than the shoulder mount alone, in fast-moving news situations camera operators find that the body brace can interfere with personal movement.

One of the most sophisticated types of body mounts consists of an elaborate harness with a camera arm attached. The arm is connected to a number of counterbalancing and stabilizing springs (Figure 4.23). Going under brand names such as **Steadicam** and **Panaglide,** the spring-balanced arm of these camera stabilizers can, within limits, absorb and cancel the motion of a camera operator who is walking, going up a flight of stairs, or even running. An attached high-intensity viewfinder can be seen at a distance of 2 to 3 feet (to allow for maximum camera movement).

The major disadvantage of this type of stabilizer — apart from its relatively high cost — is that it is quite heavy. Sustained shooting can tire out the most hardy camera operator. Even so, they make possible impressive camera moves and follow shots — shots that were previously impossible.

With the advent of lightweight video cameras an even simpler mount is being used (Figures 4.24A to 4.24C). Instead of a body harness and heavy counterbalancing springs, this type of stabilizer relies on a simple weighted arm to counterbalance the weight of the camera. Like its larger and more sophisticated brother, it also features a high-intensity viewfinder suitable for viewing at a distance.

FIGURE 4.23
One of the most sophisticated types of body mounts consists of an elaborate harness with a camera arm attached. Going under brand names such as Steadicam and Panaglide, the spring-balanced arm of these camera stabilizers can, within limits, absorb and cancel the motion of a camera operator who is walking, going up a flight of stairs or even running. To allow for maximum camera movement the attached high-intensity viewfinder can be seen at a distance of 2 to 3 feet.

FIGURE 4.24
With the advent of lightweight camcorders, a small, light, counterbalanced mount has gained favor. Instead of a body harness and heavy counterbalancing springs (Figure 4.23), this type of stabilizer relies on a simple weighted arm to counterbalance the weight of the camera. This unit features a high-intensity, flat CCD viewfinder.

FIGURE 4.25
With the help of an image stabilizer, cars, boats and helicopters can effectively be used as "moving platforms" for camera shots. CCD shutter speeds above 1/250 second reduce the effects of blur associated with motion.

Vehicle Mounts

Often with the help of an optical image stabilizer, cars, boats and helicopters can effectively be used as "moving platforms" for camera shots (Figures 4.25 and 4.26). A variety of camera mounts (sometimes called camera clamps) that can be attached to supporting structures in vehicles are available.

Tripods

Whenever possible, video cameras should be mounted on a tripod or studio pedestal. Not only do they make possible steady, professional-looking video, they also contain a pan head (to be discussed below) that allows for controlled pans and tilts.

Tripods, the three-legged supports that are as old as photography itself, are the simplest to use. Because each leg can be separately adjusted for height, it is possible to level a tripod on a hillside, stairs or uneven ground (Figure 4.27). Many tripods have a bubble-type level, which can be used to level the camera. Some tripods have "elevator" columns, which can be cranked up to raise the height of the camera. Unfortunately, when the column is extended, the camera often starts to become shaky. Standard tripods are indispensable for video field work when the camera doesn't have to be dollied or trucked.

Tripod Dolly The larger and more sturdy tripods can be locked into three-wheeled bases and rolled from one shooting position to another. Although the simple tripod dolly does not allow for smooth, on-the-air trucks and dollies the way a studio camera pedestal does, a rolling tripod (a tripod with an attached wheel base) can be used for moving the camera from place to place. Within limits (when there is the luxury of a smooth floor), a rolling tripod can be used for doing limited dollying and trucking while on location.

Most lightweight field cameras have a hole in the center of the bottom base plate that accepts a threaded screw from the tripod. With a few turns of this

FIGURE 4.26
A variety of camera mounts are available that can be attached to supporting structures in vehicles. Although pickup trucks and convertibles make ideal moving platforms, camera clamps are also available for mounting cameras on the sides of cars. A fill light is often required to lighten deep shadows.

FIGURE 4.27
Tripods, which are as old as photography itself, are essential for steady, professional-looking, on-location video. Because each leg can be separately adjusted for height, it is possible to level a tripod on a hillside, stairs or uneven ground. Many tripods have a bubble-type level, which can be used to level the camera.

screw you can lock down the camera on a mount. Instead of a tripod screw, larger cameras make use of a mounting plate. Some of these can be quickly attached to a camera support with a single lever. One type of mounting plate, the **wedge mount,** is associated with large studio cameras and pedestals.

Camera Pedestals

The standard camera mount for studio work is the pedestal (Figure 4.28). Pedestals are designed to move smoothly across a studio floor, even while the camera is "hot" (being recorded or is on the air, "live"). The base is triangular-shaped with steerable sets of wheels at each corner. A large steering ring in the middle of the pedestal controls the direction of the wheels. The operator normally has two steering options. First, all three sets of wheels can be locked so that they always stay parallel. In this mode all of the wheels turn together through the action of the steering ring. By the use of a foot control on the base of the pedestal, the steering mode can be changed so that only one set of wheels can be steered. This mode, which resembles the steering action of a tricycle, enables the pedestal to be rotated.

Adjustable cable guard "skirts" at the bottom of the pedestal cover the wheels and come within a fraction of an inch of the floor. Consequently, when the pedestals are rolled across the studio floor they will push cables out of the way instead of rolling over them.

A center column in the pedestal allows for the vertical adjustment of the camera. This enables the camera operator to adjust camera height by **pedding up** or **pedding down.** Although some pedestals use a hand crank to move the center column up or down, most professional pedestals make use of a column of compressed air (nitrogen) or lead weights within the pedestal to counterbalance the weight of the camera on the center column. This makes raising or lowering

FIGURE 4.28

Pedestals are designed to move cameras smoothly across a studio floor, even while the camera is on-line, or on the air. The base is triangular-shaped with steerable wheels at each corner. A large steering ring in the middle of the pedestal controls the direction of the wheels. Counterbalanced weights or compressed gas allow the camera height to be smoothly adjusted. The column locking ring locks the vertical movement of the center column at any desired point. The snap lock on the column is primarily a safety device that anchors the column in the down position. The three wheels in the base of the pedestal can be controlled in two ways by the steering mode controls. In one mode the direction and movement of all three wheels are locked to the rotation of the steering ring. The steering mode controls can also be switched so that only one wheel is locked to the steering control and the other two wheels are free to turn as needed.

FIGURE 4.29

The crab dolly consists of an electrically controlled arm mounted on a wheeled base. This type of camera dolly permits a smooth transition in camera heights — generally from about 1 foot to more than 5 feet. The camera operator sits on a small seat and rides up and down with the arm. A second operator can push and steer the dolly across a smooth surface or over specially laid tracks (see Figure 4.30).

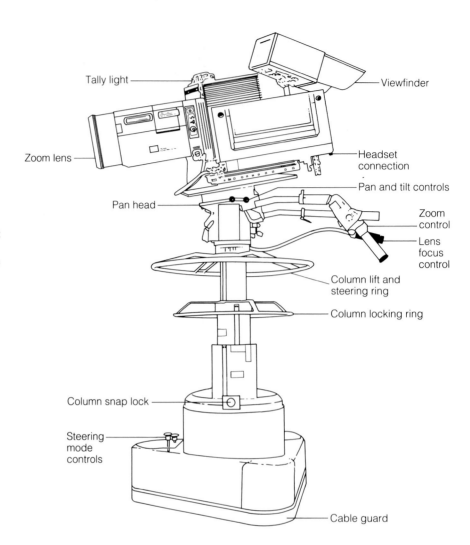

the camera smooth and effortless. The normal vertical range of a pedestal is from 2 to about 5 feet. A ring similar to the steering ring but smaller in diameter is often used to enable the operator to lock the vertical position of the camera.

Crabs and Cranes

The **crab dolly,** the mainstay of the 35mm motion picture camera mounts, consists of an electrically controlled arm mounted on a wide-wheeled base (Figure 4.29). Crab dollies permit a smooth transition in camera heights — generally from about 1 foot to more than 5 feet. The camera operator sits on a small seat and rides up and down with the arm. A second operator can push and steer the dolly across a smooth surface or over specially laid tracks. The four wheels of the dolly steer together in a parallel fashion. Since this looks a bit like the way sand crabs move, the device has been given the name *crab dolly.*

Some crab dollies have special wheels designed to be used with tracks or

FIGURE 4.30
Some crab dollies have special wheels designed to be used with tracks, or rails. Although laying down rails for a tracking shot is time-consuming, it can produce a smooth, professional-looking shot.

rails (Figure 4.30). Although laying down camera tracks or rails for the camera to roll over is a time-consuming task, rails can provide smooth, professional-looking follow shots.

Cranes (Figures 4.31A and 4.31B) allow for an even greater vertical range than a crab dolly. Many cranes can bring the camera down to floor level and then, depending upon the model, raise the camera to 25 feet. Cranes normally consist of a large, hydraulically controlled or counterweighted arm mounted on a heavy base with four sets of wheels.

crane; camera crane: A camera mount on a long arm capable of raising a camera and camera operator to a high vantage point.

(a)

(b)

FIGURE 4.31
Cranes allow for an even greater vertical range than a crab dolly. In Figure 4.31A a mini-crane is being used to shoot above people standing along the sidelines of nationally televised football game. Figure 4.31B shows another type of mini-crane. Some large cranes can bring the camera down to floor level and raise it to more than 25 feet. In many applications camera jibs (Figure 4.32) have advantages over camera cranes.

FIGURE 4.32
With the advent of lightweight cameras in television, cranes have given way to camera jibs, which are much smaller, lighter and easier and faster to maneuver. All adjustments, including the panning, zooming and focusing of the camera, are remotely controlled by a single operator seated in front of a video monitor. Because of the speed at which camera jibs can glide along the floor or swoop into the air, they have added new levels of artistic energy and ebullience to television production.

camera jib: Remotely operated, crane-like camera mount that can typically move a camera from floor or ground level to a height of 10 or more feet.

fluid head: The pan head of choice for EFP cameras because its internal parts move through a heavy viscous fluid, making very smooth pans and tilts possible.

FIGURE 4.33
Because of their light weight and ability to smooth out pans and tilts, fluid heads are preferred for most field production. As the name suggests, the internal parts of the head are made to move through a heavy, viscous liquid—an action that smooths out camera movement.

Camera Jibs

With the advent of lightweight cameras in television, cranes have given way to *camera jibs,* which are much smaller, lighter and easier and faster to maneuver (Figure 4.32). All operations, including panning, zooming and focusing, are remotely controlled by a single operator seated in front of a video monitor. Because of the speed at which camera jibs can glide along the floor or swoop into the air, they have added new levels of energy and ebullience to television production.

PAN HEADS

We now move to the essential camera-to-camera mount interface: the pan head. This is what will give us smooth control over panning and tilting and will enable us to lock down the camera. There are four types of pan heads: fluid, cam, friction and geared.

Fluid Heads

Because of their light weight and ability to smooth out pans and tilts, *fluid heads* (Figure 4.33) are preferred for most field production. The internal parts of the head are spring balanced and move through a heavy, viscous liquid—an action that moderates and restrains camera movement. Since fluid heads will resist rapid changes in direction, they can occasionally be a problem in covering a fast-moving athletic event like hockey. However, on most fluid heads the "drag" or freedom of movement can be adjusted over a wide range.

Cam Heads

Cam heads are normally used with studio-type cameras mounted on pedestals. These pan heads make use of several "cams" or cylinders to control and smooth

FIGURE 4.34
Gear heads, or geared heads, which have long been the choice for 35mm motion picture work, now are used in single-camera HDTV production. The two large wheels at the back of the pan head can be turned (or spun) to bring about extremely smooth and carefully controlled pans and tilts. Since the camera is supported entirely by the two gear chains, a pan handle isn't needed.

out the pan and tilt movements. Tilt and pan drag controls can vary the resistance to these movements. Ideally, the controls should be adjusted so there is enough resistance to keep the camera shot from appearing to "float" up and down and from side to side when the operator is trying to keep a steady shot. At the same time, there should not be so much resistance that panning and tilting cannot be smoothly done. Tilt lock and pan lock controls on the cam head are used to lock down the camera so the cameraperson can safely walk away from the camera after a production.

Friction Heads

Friction heads, which are associated with simple tripods, are the least expensive type of pan head. By turning the pan handle of the tripod clockwise until it is tightened down, both the vertical and horizontal movement of the pan head can be locked. (Some friction heads have separate controls for the locking and panning movement.) Friction heads are ideal for simple "locked down" work with lightweight cameras. Even though the larger models incorporate a counterbalancing spring to control movement, smooth pans and tilts are difficult with friction heads.

Gear Heads

Although **gear heads** (sometimes called *geared heads*) are not often used in NTSC video production, they have long been the choice in 35mm motion picture work (Figure 4.34). They are now widely used in single-camera HDTV productions. With gear heads, two large wheels at the back of the pan head can be turned (or spun) to bring about extremely smooth and carefully controlled pans and tilts. Since the camera is supported entirely by the two gear chains, a pan handle isn't needed. Although extremely smooth and well-controlled pans and tilts are possible with gear heads, they take experience to operate and do not lend themselves to covering fast-moving or unpredictable subject matter.

(a)

(b)

FIGURE 4.35
Robotic cameras are widely used in TV stations and network facilities. Instead of requiring an operator behind each camera, one operator working at a central, computer-controlled panel in the TV control room can preprogram and remotely control the movement of all studio cameras (Figure 4.35B). Although robotic cameras are useful for shows that have established and predictable shot patterns, they are not suitable for spontaneous, unpredictable shows.

CAMERA BALANCE

When using any type of head, camera balance is important—both for the comfort of the operator and the safety of the equipment. If a camera is correctly balanced, it will not have to be held in place by the operator, nor will it tend to fall forward or backward (a rather dangerous condition) when the tilt drag is minimized. Most cameras have an adjustment in their base that can shift the center of gravity of the camera forward or backward to accommodate different weights of lenses and associated equipment.

LOCKING DOWN CAMERAS

Whenever a camera is left unattended, the pan and tilt controls should be locked down. Even if a camera is perfectly balanced, it can be bumped or someone can trip over a cable causing the camera to spin and hit a nearby object. Even worse, it could become temporarily overbalanced and crash to the floor. Not only should the pan and tilt controls be locked down after a production, but the lens cap should be placed over the lens. After use, cameras should be moved to the side of the studio and their cables coiled and placed next to them. Depending upon the facility, headsets may also need to be disconnected and stored in a central area.

ROBOTIC CAMERA SYSTEMS

In the late 1980s remotely controlled robotic cameras started showing up in production facilities (Figure 4.35A). Instead of requiring an operator behind each camera, one operator working at a central, computer-controlled panel in the TV control room can preprogram and remotely control the movement of all studio cameras (Figure 4.35B).

There are two levels of automation with these systems:

- First is a remotely controlled pan and tilt head (generally tied in with remotely controlled camera functions, like zoom and focus). With this level of automation, cameras are dollied to a specific point in the studio where all of the needed shots will be attainable by just panning, tilting and zooming.

- In the second level of camera automation, these capabilities are added to an automated camera pedestal. This makes it possible for a camera to truck, dolly and even ped up or down by remote control. These pedestals are sometimes referred to as *free-roaming pedestals*. The term *robotic camera* generally refers to a camera unit that incorporates both levels of automation.

Robotic cameras are commonly used on news and interview programs—or any productions that have predictable shot patterns. For each camera, all zoom, focus, pan and tilt settings, as well as exact floor positions for each shot, can be "memorized" by a computer control unit. Once the production is underway, the shots can be precisely recalled, either in a pre-established order or randomly, as needed.

Script-Controlled Robotic Camera Positioning

Some facilities are now specifying camera shots in scripts—primarily in studio-based news production scripts—as they are initially typed into a computer. During the production, as the computer displays the script on the teleprompter, the robotic camera system gets cues from the electronic version of the script to move the cameras to the specified shots. The cameras can even be automatically switched on-line and off-line at the appropriate times. Such a high level of automation assumes that on-camera routines have been clearly established and that few departures from the script are expected.

One question inevitably arises with this level of automation: What happens in a news program if a late bulletin comes along, a videotape doesn't "lock up" (fully stabilize) or someone departs from the script? In such instances the automatic sequence can be temporarily overridden. It is even possible to pull one or more stories from the news lineup (complete with associated camera shots) to make up for lost time. The automated system will then automatically compensate for the change(s) and give you a revised list of scheduled times for the remaining elements in the show. (If only it were as easy to get the talent and crew to instantly adjust to such last-minute changes.)

Although zoom, focus, pan and tilt settings are easy for robotic pedestals to accurately and consistently replicate, floor positions (which may require the camera to dolly or truck to various studio positions) are a bit more difficult. Various systems for automatically establishing camera locations are used.

With one system, sensors in the camera pedestal are guided by one or more tape strips that have been put on the studio floor. An *X* may represent a "home" or reset position. If a camera loses its bearings, it will return to the *X* to "zero out" any error before resuming its shot sequence. Some robotic systems depend upon grid wires embedded in the studio floor. Early systems, such as that used by NBC news, relied upon tracks in the floor. An example of the effective use of robotic cameras is in Great Britain's House of Commons. Although the cameras do not need to truck or dolly, their pan, tilt, zoom and focus controls have been preprogrammed so that at a touch of a button a camera can instantly zoom in on any of a hundred seats. CNN, the Cable News Network (Figure 4.36), is able to remotely control cameras in various affiliated studios around the country from its Atlanta headquarters.

All robotic camera systems contain collision avoidance sensing. This means that the camera can sense obstructions in its path, and when it gets within 20 or so inches of another object, refuse to move closer.

Since CCD cameras (without their viewfinders turned on) require little power, some robotic studio pedestals are wireless. Rechargeable batteries in the pedestal power all operations including a radio transmitter that relays the cam-

FIGURE 4.36
Robotic cameras are used on news and
interview programs — or on any productions that have predictable shot patterns. For each camera all zoom, focus,
pan and tilt settings, as well as exact
floor positions for each shot, can be
memorized by a computer control unit.
Once the production is underway, the
shots can be precisely recalled, either
in a preestablished order or randomly.

cue cards: Large white cards used by on-
camera talent to help them remember dialogue. Black markers are normally used to
write material in large letters.

soft copy prompter: A camera prompting
system where the image displayed originates
in computer memory rather than from a
camera image of hard copy (paper).

era's signals to the control room. Wireless cameras solve the problem of robotic
cameras getting tangled in cables.

Although robotic cameras are now being relied upon for shows with predictable shot patterns, they can't replace operators in productions that develop
spontaneously and unpredictably.

PROMPTING DEVICES

People who work in front of the camera use various prompting methods to aid
on-camera delivery. News reporters working in the field typically rely on hand-
held note cards or a small notebook containing names, figures and basic facts.
They generally memorize their opening and closing on-camera comments and
then speak from the notes (or even read a fully written script) while continuing
with off-camera narration.

Some on-camera people prefer large poster-board *cue cards* with the script
written out with a bold black marker. But cue cards have three disadvantages:

- They are rather difficult and time-consuming to prepare.
- They require the aid of an extra person (a card puller).
- Talent must constantly look slightly off to the side of the camera to see the
  cards.

Some on-camera people have mastered the technique of fully writing out
the script, recording it on an audio cassette machine, and then playing it back in
an earphone while simultaneously repeating their own words to the camera. A
foot- or hand-controlled switch starts and stops the playback as needed. Although this technique demands great concentration (not to mention reliable audio
playback procedures), once mastered, it can result in highly effective on-camera
delivery.

A camera prompter or teleprompter is the most relied upon form of prompting, especially for long on-camera segments (Figure 4.37). There are two types
of camera prompters: **hard copy,** where the original script has been typed on
paper or written on a plastic roll, and the more widely used *soft copy prompter,*
where the text is displayed from computer memory.

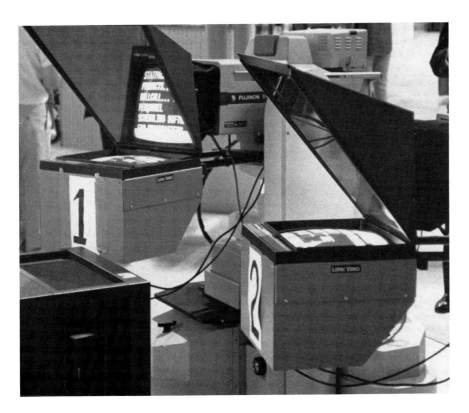

FIGURE 4.37
Camera prompters, which display a script at the point of the camera lens, are the most relied upon form of prompting for on-camera talent. Hard copy prompters that use rolls of paper (Figure 4.38) are now being replaced by computer-based prompting systems.

Hard Copy Prompters

Most hard copy prompters use long rolls of paper on which the script has been typed in large letters in short (two- to four-word) lines. A camera placed above the copy (Figure 4.38) picks up the image of the slowly moving script. The speed of the prompter is controlled by a hand-held speed regulator — operated by either a prompter operator or the talent themselves. A high-contrast video image from the prompter camera is reflected into a half-silvered mirror mounted at a 45-degree angle in front of the camera lens (Figure 4.39). The image of the text as seen by the prompter camera must be electronically reversed left to right so that the resulting mirror image will appear correct. Since the mirror is only half-silvered, it ends up being a two-way mirror. First, it reflects the image of the moving text from the video screen. Second, being semitransparent, the mirror allows much of the light from the subject matter being photographed to pass through its surface to the camera lens. When the talent looks at the prompter mirror to read the text, it appears as if they are looking right at the camera lens — and, therefore, the audience. In order to avoid the appearance of constantly staring into the camera lens, most on-camera people who use prompters periodically glance at their scripts — especially in order to emphasize facts and figures.

A few field prompters rely on clear rolls of plastic mounted above or to the side of the camera. The script is written on the plastic in large black letters. Since a light source is used behind the clear plastic, the resulting image can be very bright — an important consideration when shooting under sunlit conditions.

Soft Copy Prompters

In recent years soft copy prompters have largely replaced hard copy prompters. Soft copy prompters bypass the paper or plastic (hard) copy and directly display

FIGURE 4.38
With the hard copy prompter, the script is written out on long rolls of paper and then moved past the camera (top of picture) at a controlled rate. The square in the center of the picture indicates the words that are visible to the talent at any one time.

FIGURE 4.39
Studio prompters make use of a high-contrast image from a video monitor (bottom of picture). The image of the text is reflected in a half-silvered mirror placed directly in front of the camera lens. Since the mirror is only half-silvered, the camera lens can still get an image of the talent through the mirror. If a color video monitor is used, text can be color-keyed to set off different speakers, special instructions to the talent etc.

output on a video screen. The extra step of printing out a prompter script for a camera is not required. This has several advantages. First, because the text is a direct, electronically generated image, it is sharp and easy to read. Revisions are easy to make without the legibility problems resulting from crossed-out and inserted words on paper copy.

With soft copy systems, once the script is entered into the computer (Figure 4.40), it can be displayed in the variety of formats required for different phases of the production — including the standard prompter format (narrow lines with large bold letters). Soft copy prompters are available for both studio and field work. If a color prompter monitor is used, text can be color-keyed to set off different speakers, special instructions to the talent etc.

Considerations in Using Prompters

When using any type of on-camera prompting device there is always the important issue of camera-to-subject distance. If the camera is placed close to the talent (making it easy for them to read the prompter), the constant left-to-right movement of their eyes as they read can be distracting to an audience. Moving the camera back and zooming in reduces this problem by narrowing the left-to-right motion of the eyes, but at the same time, the extra distance makes the prompter harder to read.

There is also another area of compromise. We've mentioned the term *half-silvered mirrors,* which implies that exactly 50 percent of the light from the scene will pass through the mirror to the lens and 50 percent of the light from the text will be reflected toward the talent. In actual fact, mirrors can be obtained with different reflectance ratios. In brightly lit settings talent prefer that more than 50 percent of the light from the prompter text is reflected toward them, since it makes the copy easier to read. However, changing the reflectance ratio to favor the prompter image (possibly to a 60-to-40 ratio) means that less than 50 percent of the light from the scene will enter the camera lens. This increases the already existing light-loss problem associated with the use of an on-camera prompter. Once again, the only solution is one of a mutually acceptable compromise.

FIGURE 4.40
Portable computers, such as this one, make it possible to take a computer-based prompting system into the field. Once the script is entered into the computer it can be electronically reformatted in the various formats required for the different phases of production.

SUMMARY

Video cameras use two types of imaging devices, CCDs and tubes. For most work, CCD or "chip cameras" are preferred because of their many advantages. Camera tubes and CCDs are based on the principle of photoemission, the conversion of light into electrical energy. One of the most important attributes of a camera imaging device is resolution—the ability to reproduce fine detail. Although the broadcast process limits video resolution, the sharper the original camera image, the sharper the image will be on the home receiver. Even though video cameras can reproduce scenes under very dim light, normally, sacrifices in image quality result unless the light level is about 75 or more footcandles.

A 30-to-1 contrast ratio is considered maximum for scenes. Cameras that encounter subject matter that exceeds this range either clip the whites in the scene or compress the tonal range of the gray scale. Chip charts are used to set up cameras, with the blackest part of the scale (3 percent reflectance) representing TV black and the whitest part of the scale (90 percent reflectance) representing TV white. The black level is controlled on the CCU by the pedestal or setup control, and the white level is set by the camera's iris control. On the waveform monitor TV black should be set at 7.5 and TV white at 100.

Camera viewfinders contain status indicators that provide information about a camera's (and often a VCR's) operational status. There are five basic types of cameras: studio, portable, convertible, EC and HDTV. A single base station can be used to control the operating status of several cameras at the same time.

There are various types of camera supports including shoulder mounts, tripods, pedestals, crab dollies, cranes and jibs. Pan heads allow operators to smoothly control pan and tilt functions, as well as to lock down the camera when it is not in use. Robotic pedestals and cameras are used in productions that have predictable shot patterns.

Soft copy prompters are replacing hard copy prompters for general production. The image of the copy for most types of prompting devices is reflected in a half-silvered mirror over the camera lens. This allows the talent to look directly into the camera lens while reading a script.

KEY TERMS

AGC (automatic gain control)
artifacts
automatic exposure control
auto-iris
backlight switch
body brace
burn in
cam head
camera jibs
chip chart
chromatic aberration
clip
color compatibility
convertible camera
crab dolly
crane
cue cards
data compression
EC camera

electronic cinematography (EC)
fluid head
footcandle
friction head
gamma correction
gear head
hard copy prompter
horizontal resolution
linearity
lux
master black control
overexposure
Panaglide
ped down
ped up
pedestal (black level)
photoemission
pixel
rails

resolution
resolution chart
setup
shift register
shoulder mount
signal-to-noise ratio
smear
soft copy prompter
spectral highlights
status indicators
Steadicam

test pattern
tonal compression
triax
tripod
TV black
TV white
underexposure
vertical resolution
video noise
wedge mount
zebra stripes

Color | 5

A knowledge of the color television process will not only add to the effectiveness of your productions, but it can eliminate many production problems. In this chapter we will examine such things as color temperature, additive and subtractive color, how color cameras and receivers work, how color is used to communicate meaning and how the vectorscope can be used to ensure accurate and consistent color quality.

LIGHT

Television is primarily a medium of light. As shown in Figure 5.1, white light is actually composed of a spectrum of colors from red to violet. Later in the chapter we will explore the interaction of specific colors and see how this interaction forms the basis for color television. Before we can do that we need look at an

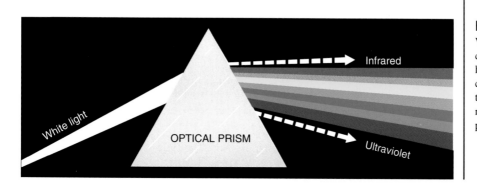

FIGURE 5.1
White light is actually a mix of all colors from red to violet. As shown here, a prism can separate the various colors from white light. In somewhat the same way, a color TV camera separates component colors out of a color picture.

FIGURE 5.2

The color temperature of light ranges from a candle flame at about 1,000 degrees Kelvin to more than 10,000 degrees Kelvin for the light of a clear blue sky. Although the human eye will more or less automatically correct for different color temperatures, unless color correction takes place within video cameras, the resulting picture may be either too red or too blue.

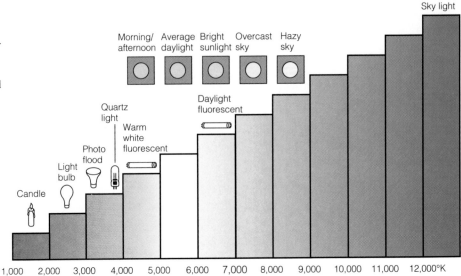

important dimension of light—one that is often so subtle as to be invisible to the eye.

Color Temperature

hue: Refers to specific color without the dimensions of brightness or saturation.

color temperature: The dominant color of a light source measured in degrees Kelvin.

The dominant color or *hue* of light can be measured by its *color temperature,* specified in Kelvin (K) degrees. The bluer the light source, the higher its color temperature; the redder the light source, the lower its color temperature. This may seem confusing until you remember that when a piece of metal is heated it first becomes red hot and then, as it gets even hotter, it becomes white hot. Because the temperatures involved are so high, the **Kelvin scale** is used.[1]

Table 5.1 lists the typical color temperature for a variety of light sources. As you can see, the color temperature of light can vary by many thousands of degrees Kelvin. Figures 5.2 and 5.3 show how these relationships look in color.

Color Standards Two color temperatures are recognized as standards: $5,500°K$[2] for normal daylight and $3,200°K$ for incandescent studio lights. Because incandescent light is actually an orange-yellow color compared to sunlight, there has always been the problem of "inside" and "outside" color balance. Since the two standards are 2,300 degrees apart, errors become obvious (Figure 5.4). If a video camera is color balanced for inside lighting and outside scenes are taped without color balancing, subject matter will end up being rather blue-looking. Conversely, if a video camera is color balanced for daylight

1. Although the concept of Kelvin temperatures goes beyond this discussion, it is based on heating a "perfect black-body radiator" (an enclosed carbon block that does not reflect light, for example) and noting the spectral distribution of light emitted at progressive temperatures. Therefore, the actual temperature of a specific light source being used is not the same as its Kelvin temperature.

2. The color temperature of average daylight is influenced by three factors: time of day, longitude and latitude and atmospheric conditions. Consequently, average daylight may be listed as being anywhere from 5,400 to 5,600 degrees Kelvin. Unlike color temperatures in the 3,200-degree range (where even a 100-degree change can be noticeable) changes of several hundred degrees Kelvin at 5,000 plus degrees are difficult for the eye to detect.

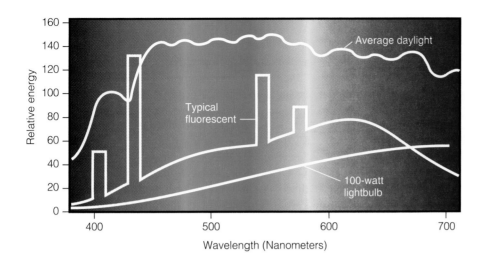

FIGURE 5.3

Three light sources are compared: daylight, incandescent light and a fluorescent lamp. Note that incandescent light (at the bottom of the illustration) contains a much higher percentage of reddish-yellow light than daylight (the wavy line at the top of the drawing). Although fluorescent lamps vary in color temperature, unless they are specially designed for TV work, they typically have "spikes" in the blue and green areas. Although the eye does not normally notice this, the resulting pictures from film and some video cameras will have a pronounced blue-green cast.

(which can actually vary from 5,000°K to as high as 25,000°K) and then scenes under incandescent light are taped, the inside scenes will have a pronounced orange cast.

Since most camera viewfinders do not reproduce color, errors will not be realized until the videotape is later played back on a color monitor. Attempts at correcting this type of color error in postproduction are generally not completely successful.

Professional video cameras are normally balanced for 3,200°K. When these cameras are used outside in daylight, a yellow-red (straw-colored) filter located behind the lens is rotated into the light path of the lens. This shifts the sunlight to 3,200°K. The basic 3,200- to 5,500-degree correction is one of two types of color adjustment used in video cameras. Once the inside-outside correction is made by rotating a filter into the lens path, more subtle adjustments are made electronically through the white balance control. This will be discussed in more detail later.

FIGURE 5.4

There is a color temperature difference of 2,300 degrees between daylight (on the right side of this photo) and the incandescent light (illuminating the left side of the model's face). When both color temperatures are present in the same scene, accurate color balance is not possible.

TABLE 5.1

Typical Color Temperatures in Degrees Kelvin

Candle flame	1,900
100-watt light bulb	2,850
Quartz studio light	3,200
Warm-white fluorescent lamp	4,500*
Average daylight	5,400–5,600
Daylight fluorescent lamp	6,500*
High-intensity arc light	6,600
Hazy or overcast sky	7,500
Clear blue northerly skylight	25,000

*Many fluorescent tubes have strong bands of color in the blue and green spectral areas, which may result in pronounced green or blue tones with some video cameras. (See Figure 5.3.)

APPROXIMATE COLOR CONSISTENCY

approximate color consistency: The human ability to automatically make corrections for changes in color temperature. For example, a white piece of paper will appear white under both daylight and incandescent light, even though the actual color will vary more than 2,000°K.

Through a process called *approximate color consistency,* the eye automatically adjusts to color temperature changes. As an example, if you look at a white piece of paper in sunlight, you have no trouble verifying that it is white. When you take the same piece of paper inside under normal incandescent light, it still *looks* white. But, the paper is now reflecting yellow light. (By all objective measures, a yellow [3,200°K] light falling on a white object will result in a slightly yellow object.) But because you know the paper is white, your mind says, "I *know* the paper is white"; and so, through approximate color consistency, you (unconsciously) adjust your internal color balance and see the paper as white. In so doing you shift all of the other colors slightly, so you can perceive them in their proper relationship.

This helpful adjustment mechanism means that our color perception can easily be fooled. A simple experiment demonstrates this. First, an audience is put in a dark room. Without telling them what's going on, they are shown a color slide of a familiar scene. But the slide has a slightly bluish cast. In a few minutes (with the help of approximate color consistency) the audience makes the necessary mental adjustment, and the slide looks acceptable. At this point a new slide is substituted — one of the same scene, but this time with a perfectly accurate color balance. The audience will now see the perfect slide as having a pronounced yellow cast (the complement of blue).

Unlike the subjects in the slide experiment, a television viewer who has a light on in the room or who can see sunlight coming through the window makes color comparisons based on these visible standards. In fact, in order to judge the accuracy of color we require some type of *color standard* within our field of vision. But moviegoers sitting in a completely dark theater are like the subjects in the slide experiment; without a visible standard of comparison, they regularly make psychological corrections for slight color shifts. This makes color balance in TV production more of an issue than it is in theatrical films.

SIMULTANEOUS CONTRAST

simultaneous contrast: The effect of a surrounding tone or color on a specific color or tonal value. Certain color combinations or brightness values, when placed next to each other, interact and affect each other.

In addition to approximate color consistency, there are other perceptual color interactions. When we look at a bright, saturated color, the color of the surrounding area will tend to shift toward that color's complement — the color directly opposite on the color wheel (Figure 5.5). This also means that complementary colors placed next to each other will tend to exaggerate each other. This phenomenon is called *simultaneous contrast.* For example, if red is placed next to cyan, both the red and the cyan will seem more pronounced. If a woman with red hair wants to emphasize her hair, she will wear a cyan or green dress, and not a red or yellow dress.

Simultaneous contrast can also cause colorless areas to take on color. A bright cyan object can make a colorless background take on a rose-colored hue. This can be a problem when it is important to preserve the appearance of delicate colors. Placing tuna fish in a bright red dish in a commercial can make the tuna fish appear green — an effect that would not please an advertiser.

Simultaneous contrast has implications for wardrobes and backgrounds. Since the appearance of skin tones is generally the most crucial element in a scene, production personnel must watch for interactions between brightly colored backgrounds and skin tones. Colors such as yellow or red can rob skin tones of "a healthy color," while others, such as green or blue, can enhance skin

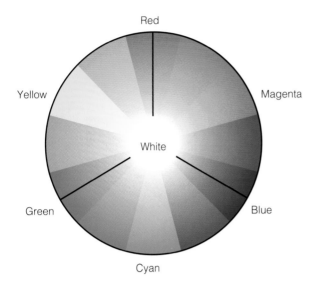

FIGURE 5.5
Becoming familiar with this additive color wheel is the key to understanding many color-related issues in TV production. The primary additive colors—red, green and blue—are indicated by the dark lines. The remaining colors—magenta, cyan and yellow—are secondary colors. Colors directly opposite each other (blue and yellow, for example) are called complementary colors.

tones. By studying the color wheel, color combinations can be found that will either enhance or detract from a desired effect.

Simultaneous contrast also affects the perception of black and white tonal values. If a medium gray object is viewed against a black background it will appear lighter than when the same object is viewed against a white background.

One final color consideration should be mentioned: the effect of reflected color. A woman standing next to a brightly lit green wall may find the side of her face partially illuminated by the green light reflected from the wall. This effect, which can take place when any object is near a highly saturated color, will disappear when the subject moves out of range of the offending color.

SUBTRACTIVE AND ADDITIVE COLOR

Color television is primarily based on the physics of additive color. Problems in understanding additive color often center on confusion with the better known subtractive color process that governs the mixing of paints and pigments. The two are, in a way, exactly opposite.

Subtractive Color

The color of an object is determined by the colors of light it absorbs and reflects. When white light falls on a piece of red paper, the paper appears red because it subtracts (absorbs) all colors of light except red. If you paint an object blue, you add a kind of filter to the surface of the object that absorbs all colors except blue (Figure 5.6).

When all of the primary **subtractive colors** of magenta, cyan and yellow[3] pigments are mixed together, the result is black—or a dark shade resembling mud. All color is essentially absorbed (Figure 5.7). The light that is absorbed (subtracted) is transformed into heat. This explains why a black object gets much warmer in sunlight than a light-colored object that tends to reflect all colors.

3. Red, yellow and blue are often given as the subtractive primaries. However, in most printing applications, including the making of photographic prints, magenta, yellow and cyan are most commonly used.

FIGURE 5.6

The principles of subtractive color govern the mixture of paints and pigments. An object appears blue, for example, because the pigment in the blue paint subtracts all colors in white light except blue.

complementary: Colors that are approximately opposite each other on the color wheel. Blue and yellow are complementary colors.

When a colored filter is used on a camera (either behind the lens in a filter wheel or in front of the lens) the same type of color subtraction results. For example, a pure red filter placed over a camera lens will absorb all colors except red (Figure 5.8). Filters tend to subtract colors that are *complementary* (those colors directly across from them on the color wheel) and pass colors that are similar (colors near them on the color wheel). (Refer to Figure 5.5.) A cyan filter will block red and reduce the amount of yellow and magenta light that passes through. The same filter will pass cyan and most green and blue. The same general relationship applies to the other colors and their complements.

FIGURE 5.7

The primary subtractive colors used in color photography and color printing are yellow, cyan and magenta. Note than when the three primary colors are mixed, there is a subtractive effect and the result is black. In contrast, note in Figure 5.9 when the three primary colors are mixed in additive color, the result is white light.

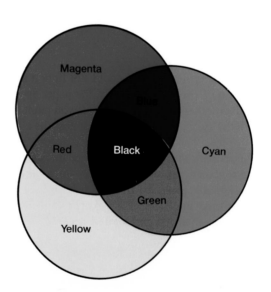

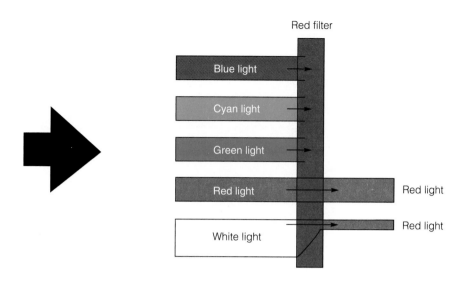

Red filter

Blue light

Cyan light

Green light

Red light → Red light

White light → Red light

FIGURE 5.8

Contrary to what is widely believed, a colored filter does not change the color of light, but subtracts dissimilar (complementary) colors. In this illustration, note that a red filter subtracts all but red light. A cyan filter placed to the right of the red filter in this illustration would absorb the remaining red light.

Additive Color

Thus far we have been talking about the effect of mixing paints or pigments. When colored lights are mixed together, the result becomes additive rather than subtractive. Thus, when the ***additive primaries*** (red, blue and green light) are mixed together, the result is white light. This can easily be demonstrated with three slide projectors. If a pure-color filter is placed over each of the three projector lenses—one red, one green and one blue—the result will be the same as illustrated in Figure 5.9. When all three primary colors overlap (are added together) white light is created. You will see from Figure 5.9 that magenta is a combination of red and blue, yellow is a combination of green and red, and cyan is a combination of blue and green.

By extending this additive concept slightly, it should be obvious that by combining the proper mixture of red, blue and green light, virtually any color can be produced. Therefore, in color television a maximum of only three colors (red, blue and green) is needed to produce the full range of colors in a color picture. The standard additive color wheel (Figure 5.9) is the key to understanding many issues in color television. Note that the overlap of two primary colors creates secondary colors: magenta, cyan and yellow. From Figure 5.9 you can also see that if a primary and a secondary color are mixed (two colors exactly opposite each other on the color wheel), the result is also white. Again, note that instead of canceling each other, as they did with subtractive colors, these complementary colors combine for an additive effect. (One definition of *complementary* is "to make whole.")

THE COLOR TV CAMERA

As we've suggested, all colors can be broken down into percentages of red, blue and green. It then follows that a color TV camera only has to be able to recognize a maximum of three colors in order to reproduce a color picture. The first thing a color camera has to be able to do, therefore, is to divide color scenes into red, blue and green.

additive primaries: Red, blue and green. Colors that, when added together in different combinations, create white and all other colors.

FIGURE 5.9

If lights with red, blue and green filters were projected onto a white screen, the principles of additive color would govern the result. Note that when two primary colors overlap, the result is a secondary color (magenta, cyan or yellow).

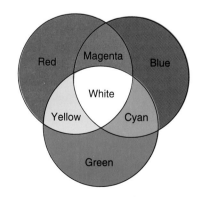

Red — Magenta — Blue

Yellow — White — Cyan

Green

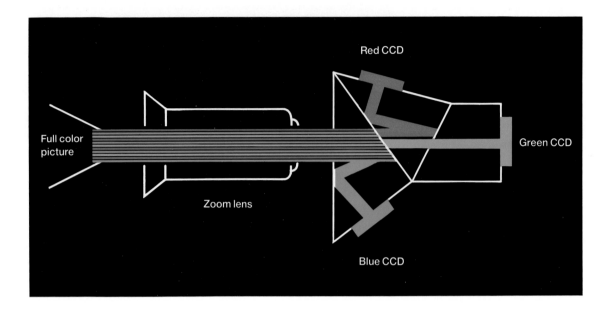

FIGURE 5.10

Dichroic filters within a video camera's prism block divide the light from the lens into three primary colors. A color picture can thereby be defined in terms of percentages of these three colors.

dichroic filter: An optical device that passes or reflects only certain wavelengths of light. Normally used in three-CCD color cameras to separate red, blue and green.

How the Camera Sees Color

The full-color image seen by the color TV camera lens first goes into a **prism block** containing *dichroic filters* (Figure 5.10). This unit divides the full-color picture into the red, blue and green primaries and directs each color to one of three CCDs. Strictly speaking, the CCDs (or tubes) in color cameras are color blind. A red CCD does not actually respond to the red color; only to the presence or absence of light. A yellow object is seen by the video camera as being a percentage of red and green light — or, simply as a combination of signals from the red and green CCDs. A blue-green, or cyan, object translates into a percentage of green and blue. Therefore, every color in a scene can be defined as a percentage of signals from the camera's three **chroma channels** (color channels).

That takes care of color, but how does a color camera detect pure black or white? Since white is the presence of all colors, the camera's three chroma channels respond to pure white as the simultaneous presence of all three colors. And, of course, black is simply the absence of all three colors.

You might assume from the above that white is the result an *equal mix* of the three primary colors. Unfortunately, it's not that simple. For one thing, the human eye does not see all colors with equal brightness. The eye is much more sensitive to yellowish-green light than to either blue or red light; in fact, several times more sensitive. Due to the greater sensitivity of the eye to the green-to-orange portion of the spectrum, a mix of equal percentages of red, green and blue colored light will not appear white. Because of this, and because of the nature of the color phosphors used in TV picture tubes, the actual color mix used in color television ends up being about 30 percent red, 11 percent blue and 59 percent green.[4]

4. Because of attempts to make picture tubes brighter, there have been changes in TV picture tube phosphors in recent years. Consequently, the original NTSC red, blue and green color standards have been unofficially modified by TV set manufacturers. Even so, the basics of this discussion remain valid.

One- and Two-Chip Cameras

Some color cameras have only two CCDs, and most consumer camcorders have only one CCD. In these cases, filters with microscopic color stripes are placed over the CCD(s). These filters (together with some sophisticated electronics) are able to break down the full-color picture into selected primary colors. Through the use of these filters, one-chip color cameras can be made so small (Figure 5.11) that they can be hidden almost anywhere. Although the one- and two-CCD (or tube) cameras can deliver excellent color quality, they can not equal the quality of good three-CCD or three-tube cameras.

A Little Algebra

Thanks to a little algebra, color cameras and color TV systems don't have to always work with three colors. For example, in the equation $A + B + C = 100$, if the values of A and B are known, it is easy to figure out C. In the same way, in the television process it is not necessary to know the values of all three primary colors — only two. If a TV camera were focused on a white card and the red channel registered 30 on the waveform scale and the green channel registered 59, you would know that the missing factor (blue) would have to be 11, since $30 + 59 + 11 = 100$. Because of this, the NTSC TV transmission process can work with only two color signals.

White Balancing a Video Camera

Since we know that red, blue and green must be present in certain proportions to create white, white balancing (color balancing) a camera becomes a matter of simple math — which is done by electronic circuitry. First, the appropriate filter must be rotated into place behind the camera lens to set the basic white balance to either *incandescent light* or *daylight*. Then, with the camera zoomed in and focused full frame on a white card, the operator pushes a *white balance* button, and the camera's chroma channels are automatically adjusted to produce pure white. This process is referred to as **white balancing** the camera.[5]

5. Simple consumer-type camcorders often have automatic color balance. A sensor on the camera electronically white balances the camera for (what seem to be) prevailing conditions. Since this type of color balance can easily be fooled, users can end up with scenes that are very blue or very yellow — especially when mixed light sources or strong dominant colors are present. With some of these cameras you can override this automatic feature and set the camera for specific light sources.

white balancing: Electronically adjusting a camera's chroma channels for a light source so that white will be reproduced as true white. Most cameras can automatically white balance when the operator fills the screen with a white card and pushes a white balance button.

FIGURE 5.11
One-chip color cameras are being made so small that they can be placed almost anywhere. All that is needed for this peanut-sized CCD camera and lens system is a small CCU.

Going from sunlight to shadow will necessitate rebalancing the camera. In fact, any time the dominant light source in a scene changes in some way, the camera must be white balanced. Not to do so risks having colors change from scene to scene — a problem that can become particularly vexing during editing. Even the passage of one or two hours will change the Kelvin temperature of sunlight.

It is possible to "lie to the camera" to create interesting effects. A "warm" (golden) color bias in a scene can be created by white balancing the camera on a light blue card; a rose-colored scene results from white balancing on a light cyan card.

Most video cameras and postproduction equipment allow for the manual adjustment of color. Referring to the color wheel (Figure 5.5), it should be evident that a picture that has too much yellow can be corrected by adding blue. (Since yellow is not a primary, you can't electronically subtract yellow.) If the picture has too much green, there are two choices: add red and blue or subtract green. If the snow in a scene looks slightly pink, or grass is blue, you should now be able to see what adjustment needs to be made.

Although white balance can be electronically altered to some degree in postproduction, it is always best to start out with proper white balance at the camera. Since white balance involves the interrelationship of three colors, it is not always possible to adjust just one color later in the production process without affecting the others.

Luminance and Chrominance Signals

As we've noted, a color TV camera first decodes the full-color picture into three signals: red, blue and green. From these the basic black-and-white, or luminance, signal can be determined (red + blue + green = white). This luminance signal is then used as a base for the broadcast video signal (and, of course, for the basic signal used by black-and-white receivers).

chrominance: Color. Also, a TV camera color channel.

But what about the color or ***chrominance*** part of the broadcast signal? To simplify the transmission process, only two colors need to be broadcast along with the luminance signal (since the third signal can be figured out by the home color TV receiver). Therefore, the final NTSC signal consists of a luminance signal within which is embedded (interleaved) information on two colors.[6]

But how does the luminance and chrominance information get turned into a color picture in a home receiver? In a sense, the process used by a TV set to reproduce a color picture is the reverse of what originally took place in the camera.

TV PICTURE TUBES

The inside of the picture tube has three types of small dots or stripes: those that will glow red, blue or green when hit by a stream of electrons (Figures 5.12 and 5.13). Electron beams scan the picture in a left-to-right, top-to-bottom fashion. (This basic scanning process was discussed and illustrated in Chapter 2.)

Because of the precise alignment of the **shadow mask** and the dots or stripes on the inside surface of the picture tube (Figure 5.12) each of the three

---

6. Although a full explanation would go far beyond the level of this text, electronic data on two "intersecting vectors" on the color wheel are used: cyan-to-orange and magenta-to-green. Assigning a value to a specific color is similar to plotting a value on the *X* and *Y* axes of a graph; any color of the rainbow can be designated by values along the cyan-to-orange and magenta-to-green axes.

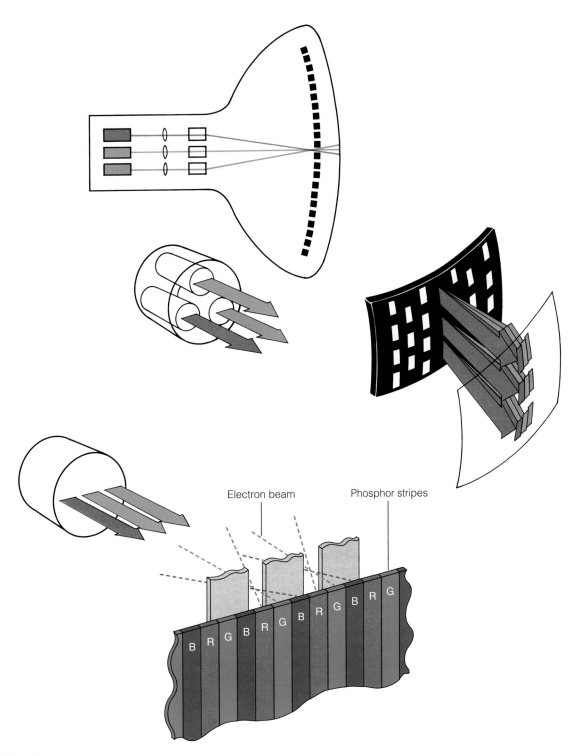

Electron beam

Phosphor stripes

FIGURE 5.12

The most common type of TV screen is based on a vacuum tube. Although the workings vary somewhat between manufacturers, all are based on the principle of one or more electron beams (guns) hitting red, blue and green phosphor dots. As the beam scans back and forth across the inside surface of television tube, it causes the microscopic red, blue and green areas to glow in proportion to respective areas in the original scene. By studying the illustrations, you can see how the angle of the electron beam causes it to hit specific color areas. An aperture grill, commonly called a shadow mask, keeps the electron beam(s) from hitting the wrong color phosphor areas.

FIGURE 5.13

In a vacuum tube display the color picture results from a blending by the eye of the millions of microscopic red, blue or green illuminated phosphor points. Depending upon the type of color tube, these can either be dots or stripes. All commonly encountered colors can be created by some combination red, blue and green. When all of the points are illuminated, the eye perceives the effect as white.

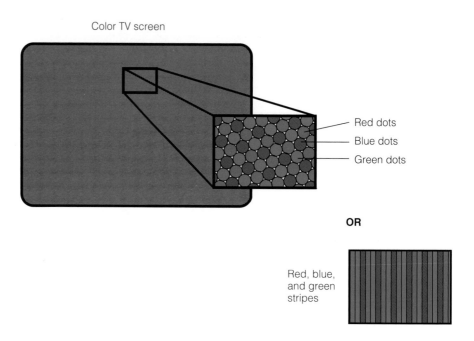

electron beams can only hit and illuminate one color of phosphor. The "red" electron gun can only hit red phosphor dots or stripes; the "blue" gun can only illuminate blue dots or stripes etc.

You will remember in discussing the color video camera that the camera sees every color as some combination of red, green and blue. In reverse fashion, a color TV set creates specific colors in terms of a combination of red, green and blue. The intensity or brightness of each of the electron guns is varied according to voltages associated with the red, blue and green colors originally seen by the color camera. (For the sake of simplicity at this point, we've jumped over the step of changing the three colors to two colors before broadcast, and then converting the two colors back into all three primaries in the receiver.) The red, blue and green dots or stripes on the surface of the TV tube (Figure 5.13) are so small that they blend together at normal viewing distances. More on that in a moment.

LCD COLOR DISPLAYS

More and more TV sets, camera viewfinders and computer screens are using flat, solid-state LCDs (liquid quartz displays). In one type, the **passive matrix display,** pixel points respond to a color TV signal by either passing or blocking light from a background source of illumination. Color is created by the interaction of red, blue and green polarizing filters (Figure 5.14). A more recent approach, called the **active matrix display,** has found greater favor because it can create a brighter, sharper picture. With this type of CCD display, light is perceived directly from glowing red, blue and green pixel points. There are two major advantages to LCD displays: they operate on much less power than a picture tube, and since they are flat, LCDs take up much less room.

RECOMPOSING THE COLOR IMAGE

Regardless of whether a TV picture tube or a LCD display is used, it is the eye that finally combines the microscopic red, blue and green dots or stripes into a

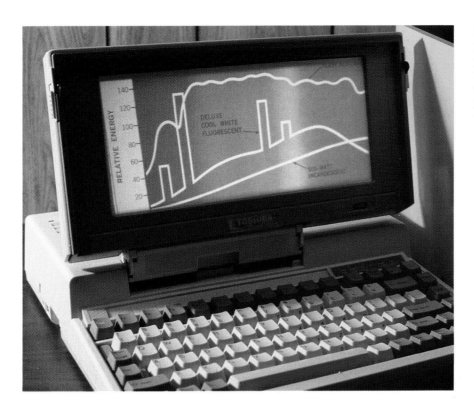

FIGURE 5.14
Flat color displays are used in computers, camera viewfinders and in some TV sets. Although these displays tend to be expensive, they consume less power and are smaller and lighter in weight than picture tubes.

full-color picture. At normal viewing distances the eye cannot distinguish the individual dots or stripes of color—only the resulting mix.

The color printing used in a book or magazine relies on the same basic process. If you look at a color reproduction in this book (or the surface of a color TV screen) with a 20-power, or greater, magnifying glass, the individual colored dots become apparent. However, when viewed normally, you can readily see that the eye "mixes" the dots into a full-color image.

Through the color television process outlined in this chapter, *most* colors can be reproduced.

ACCURATE COLOR REPRODUCTION

We say most colors. The triangle inside the horseshoe-shaped diagram in Figure 5.15 represents a color range that can be accurately reproduced by the phosphors used in standard consumer TV sets. Although the colors outside the shaded area can be distinguished by the human eye, these highly saturated (deep, rich) colors can't be accurately reproduced by today's TV systems. This is the cause of some disappointments in TV production.

Analysis of Color in the TV Process

For many years no one had systematically analyzed the strengths and weaknesses of the color TV process—or could adequately explain the "surprises" that resulted with certain color combinations. To try to uncover weaknesses in the TV system, an extensive study was conducted some years back in which more than 500 colors were systematically tracked through the TV process. Two major areas of weakness were discovered: the inability of the TV camera to correctly respond to certain colors and the inability of TV picture tube phosphors to reproduce certain colors.

FIGURE 5.15
This diagram illustrates the range of colors visible to the eye and the somewhat more restricted range (inside the triangle) that can be reproduced by today's color TV systems. The area marked *a* represents the color of standard incandescent lights (3,200 degrees Kelvin). The area marked *b* is 5,500 degrees Kelvin, or the approximate color temperature of standard daylight. Colors outside the triangle tend to be highly saturated colors that are beyond the ability of standard TV systems to produce. These colors are almost never encountered in paints or pigments.

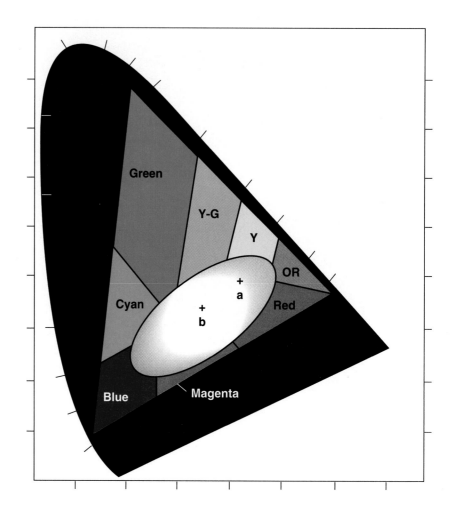

In particular, highly saturated colors—especially those in the blue-green area—were transformed into dark gray or black. Desaturated colors (very light colors containing much white light) were also lost. Typically these delicate shades simply paled out into light gray or white.

Beyond these problem areas, the study found that colors between red-orange and magenta and between violet and blue "wandered" from their true values. For example, if an artist highlighted a red apple with different shades of red and red-orange (for the sake of shading and dimension), these subtle differences ended up as identical hues on a color television set. Although it was found that metallic colors (gold, silver, brass) retained their shimmering qualities, the nature of these colors was often distorted. For example, gold often tended to appear greenish.

Exact results vary with equipment, of course (and new equipment is introduced almost on a monthly basis). Even so, since the findings point to some unexpected variations in color reproduction, directors need to make use of a high-quality color monitor to observe how critical colors in a scene are being reproduced.

Plotting Accurate Color

Although a waveform monitor cannot be used to evaluate color quality, it will indicate if a color signal is present. A **color burst** signal will be present if video equipment is generating a basic color signal. (Refer to Figure 2.12 in Chapter

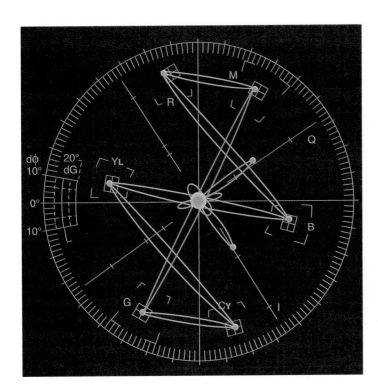

FIGURE 5.16
The vectorscope plots color in terms of hue and amplitude. Note the six small boxes inside the circle. These show the ideal positions of the three additive primary and the three additive secondary colors from a color test chart (Figure 5.17). The distance the plotted colors appear from the center of the display represents the purity of the colors.

2.) Without this signal, a color receiver will switch to a monochrome or black-and-white mode.

As we've noted, color can be rather subjective. Therefore, we need a way of accurately measuring or plotting the primary and secondary colors so that they (and the colors they create) can be accurately and consistently reproduced. This is the role of the *vectorscope*. In a sense a vectorscope is a color wheel with the information electronically filled in. Note in Figure 5.16 that the face of a vectorscope has six small boxes inside the circle. These represent the areas where the electronic signal from the three additive primary and the three additive secondary colors should appear.

If a color camera is focused on a test chart that contains these six primary and secondary colors, or if a tape machine is playing back a videotape of an electronic color test pattern (Figure 5.17), each of the six colors should appear within its appropriate box. Colors that fall outside of their designated areas will not be accurately reproduced.

All six colors can easily be *simultaneously* shifted in one direction or the other by shifting the phase of the color signal. However, if some of the colors fall inside their designated areas and some don't, the task becomes more difficult. Then, each of the primary and secondary colors has to be individually adjusted until it is brought into its designated area.

In addition to hue (color), the vectorscope also shows the amplitude, or *saturation* (purity), of each color. Color saturation, which is measured in percentages, is indicated by how far out from the center of the circle the color is displayed.

Part of the process of setting up a camera involves making sure that the colors from an internally generated *electronic test pattern (ETP)* appear in their proper places on the vectorscope. Before a production is recorded, a minute or so of ETP precedes the program material on the tape. This is used to align playback equipment for proper color before the videotape is played.

vectorscope: A CRT instrument that displays the phase and saturation of the primary and secondary video colors. Used to align cameras and equipment.

saturation: The purity of a color; its freedom from black or white.

electronic test pattern (ETP): An electronically generated pattern used for setting up video systems. Includes, among other things, the primary and secondary colors.

FIGURE 5.17
The standard SMPTE (Society of Motion Picture and Television Engineers) color test chart is used in conjunction with a vectorscope (Figure 5.16) to accurately set up and balance cameras, videotape machines and other pieces of video equipment.

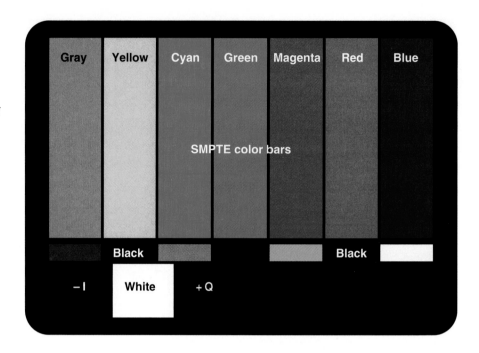

"Good" Color vs. "Real" Color

It might be assumed that television viewers want to see colors reproduced as faithfully and realistically as possible. Surprisingly, this is not really true. Studies have shown that color preferences, especially in the United States, lean toward exaggeration. Viewers prefer to see skin tones "healthier" than they actually are—as well as grass a bit greener and the sky a bit bluer than normal. In terms of the vectorscope, this preference does not mean that hues are inaccurate, only that they are stronger and more saturated.

TUBE REGISTRATION

Unlike CCD cameras, tube cameras require registration. If the images from the three tubes do not precisely overlap, double- or even triple-colored fringes will appear around objects. This is similar to the registration problems newspapers can have in printing when certain colors in a photo or comic strip "wander" outside of their boundaries. In color printing or in color television this results in a blurry picture with strange color fringing around the edges of objects.

Since the tubes in multitube cameras can both physically and electronically shift in alignment—often as a result of being transported from one place to another—multitube cameras regularly require a process called registration. **Registration** is the alignment of the color tubes so that each of their images ends up being perfectly superimposed over the others. Special black-and-white test patterns will quickly show color fringing if one or more tubes is out of alignment.

COLOR RESOLUTION

Resolution, as discussed in Chapter 4, relates to monochrome, or black-and-white, images. Color resolution (or the sharpness of the individual color channels) is seldom mentioned in camera or monitor specifications for two reasons.

(a)

(b)

FIGURE 5.18
A single person working with one of today's desktop video systems can do animation sequences that a few years ago required scores of artists and hundreds of thousands of dollars worth of equipment. Desktop video systems can also replicate almost any video effect done by dedicated special-effects equipment.

First, it was discovered early in experiments with color TV that the human eye perceives detail primarily in terms of differences in brightness (luminance) rather than differences in color. Therefore, it is unnecessary to add high-resolution red, blue and green signals to the existing black-and-white signal in order to maintain picture detail. In NTSC television it was found that two rather low-resolution color signals could be interleaved (placed within) the existing broadcast luminance signal and achieve adequate color quality. This also meant that a completely new broadcast system did not have to be introduced.

COLOR COMPATIBILITY

Although almost all U.S. homes have color TV sets, some second and third sets are black-and-white. Advertisers in particular want to make sure that brand names translate well from color into black and white, that is, that they are color compatible.

To illustrate this issue, a number of years ago a national advertiser discovered to its dismay that although the bright red letters of their brand name stood out boldly against the blue background when seen in color, the letters were almost indistinguishable from the background when seen on black-and-white sets. Of course, close-ups of a product are of little value to advertisers if the brand name can't be read.

To keep elements from blending together in black and white, good directors must make sure there is sufficient tonal contrast (as well as sufficient color contrast) between important elements. Monochrome camera viewfinders, as well as the monochrome monitors in the control room, are a good guide to color compatibility.

COLOR EFFECTS

The understanding of color opens the door to a wide variety of video applications. Today, with desktop video animation systems (Figure 5.18A) elaborate computer-generated programming can be created (Figure 5.18B). In addition, a

FIGURE 5.19

With today's special-effects equipment, a single video source can be bent in a variety of configurations — including being folded back like a piece of paper. Starting with images from four video sources a wide variety of cube effects are possible. A three-dimensional box can be created, rotated, "exploded" or even disassembled.

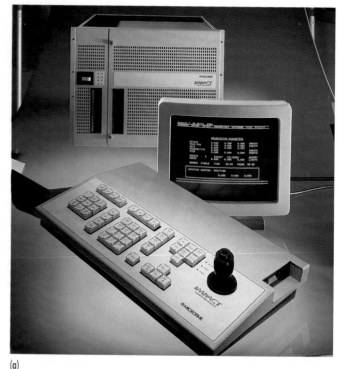

(a)

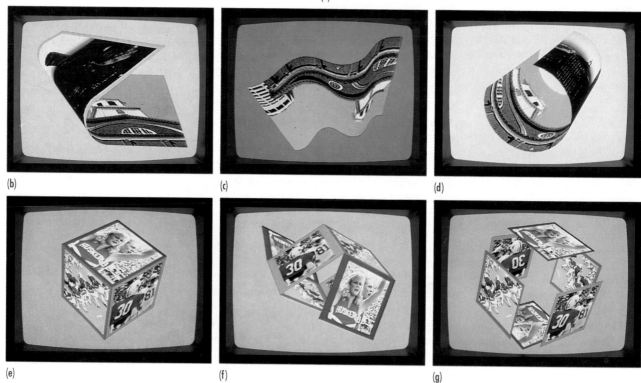

(b)   (c)   (d)

(e)   (f)   (g)

wide variety of effects are possible with dedicated visual effect equipment (Figures 5.19A to 5.19G). Computer-generated scenes are also becoming more life-like. Figures 5.20A to 5.20F show key steps in creating a scene with a computer system. Once created, the scene can also be animated. We'll discuss some of these possibilities in more detail in later chapters.

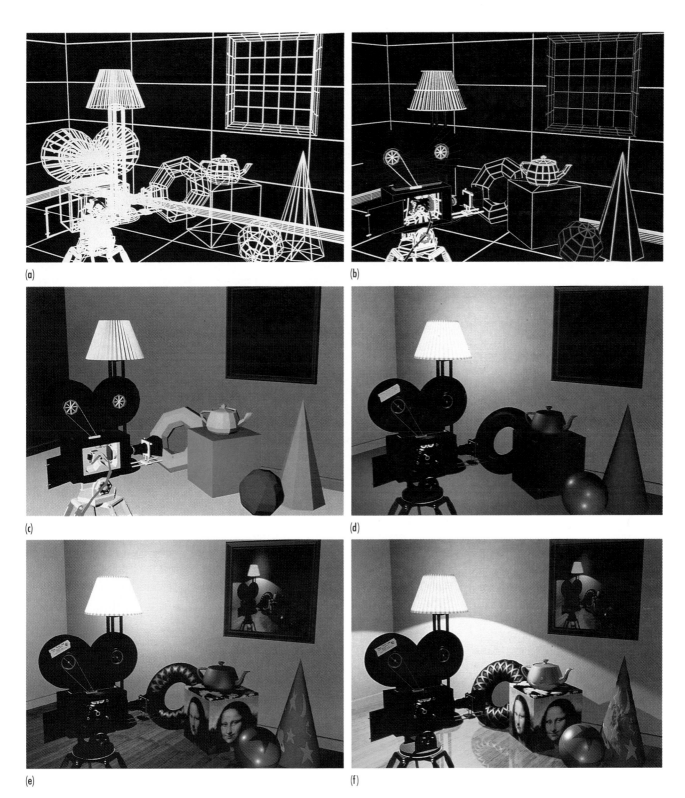

(a)   (b)

(c)   (d)

(e)   (f)

FIGURE 5.20

Today's computer equipment can be used to design scenes with lifelike quality. As shown in Figures 5.20A through 5.20F, this is done in steps. In Figure 5.20A the basic outline of the room and subject matter is created on the computer screen. Color is added to the lines in Figure 5.20B. In Figure 5.20C shading and highlights are added. In step four (Figure 5.20D), the scene begins to take on a realistic quality. Texture mapping is added in Figure 5.20E. And, finally, the addition of shadows and reflections complete the scene (Figure 5.20F). *(All photos copyright © 1990 Pixar, rendered by Thomas Williams and H.B. Siegal using Pixar's PhotoRealistic RenderMan™ software.)*

SUMMARY

Television is primarily a medium of light. An important dimension of light is color temperature, measured in degrees Kelvin. Two Kelvin standards are important: 5,500 degrees for the color temperature of average daylight and 3,200 degrees for studio lighting. Although color shifts as low as 100 degrees can be noticed at 3,200°K, at higher color temperatures a much greater color temperature shift is necessary before it will be noticed (and possibly seen as objectionable to the eye).

Without a visible standard of reference, the eye will readily adjust (within limits) to color temperature shifts through approximate color consistency. Another human attribute that affects color perception, simultaneous contrast, results in complementary colors intensifying each other. Undesirable interactions can also take place between adjacent colors—especially if they are highly saturated complementary colors.

The principles of subtractive and additive color control the color television process. Color television cameras rely on dichroic filters to separate full-color scenes into red, blue and green components. These three primary colors are converted to electronic information on two complementary colors, and this is interleaved within the basic luminance signal before transmission. In a TV receiver the luminance signal and the encoded color information is converted to red, blue and green color signals. These are used to illuminate microscopic red, blue or green dots or stripes on the surface of the picture tube or color LCD. The eye blends the three colors together into a color mix almost identical to the original color image seen by the color camera. Although the color television process can reproduce most colors accurately, some colors end up being distorted or lost. Color compatibility, or the ability of colors to translate well into black-and-white values, still should remain a consideration for production personnel.

TV cameras must be white balanced to compensate for different lighting conditions. First, the camera is set for either incandescent (indoor) light or daylight. Then a white card and white balance circuit are used to electronically white balance the camera. Unlike CCD cameras, tube-type cameras must be registered with a test chart to eliminate tube misalignment that results in color fringing.

KEY TERMS

active matrix display
additive primaries
approximate color consistency
chroma channels
chrominance
color burst
color temperature
complementary
dichroic filter
electronic test pattern (ETP)
hue

Kelvin scale
passive matrix display
prism block
registration
saturation
shadow mask
simultaneous contrast
subtractive colors
vectorscope
white balancing

Lighting | **6**

Lighting can be one of the director's most powerful tools in establishing a mood or communicating a feeling (Figure 6.1). Lighting can emphasize important details, or completely hide them; it can impart a menacing and malevolent look to a scene, or add a comfortable and congenial atmosphere. Just as sound must be controlled in audio, light must be skillfully managed in television production to produce the desired results. Some lighting directors refer to lighting as "the art of casting shadows" since, as we'll see, it is actually shadows and not light that establish the important visual attributes of subject matter.

In this chapter we'll be looking at six areas of lighting:

- Light intensity, coherence and color temperature.
- The effect of lighting angles on the appearance of subject matter
- Light sources and their characteristics
- Lighting instruments
- Studio lighting setups
- On-location lighting issues

THE EVOLUTION OF TV LIGHTING

One of the major differences between the "video look" and the (often preferred) "film look" centers on lighting. Historically, there has been a greater understanding of lighting among lighting directors and directors of photography in film than among their counterparts in video. For one thing, video started out using simple, flat lighting—the kind that was necessary to cover multiple camera angles at the same time. Early TV stations, in fact, went so far as to use large

FIGURE 6.1

As video has begun to emulate the more artistic dimensions of film, there has been a greater emphasis on using creative lighting to interpret scenes and create dramatic moods. Compared to standard broadcast systems, high-definition television is much better at retaining the shadow detail and subtle shades of color—both of which are important to a dramatic scene such as this.

banks of fluorescent lights on floor stands in their studios. From an engineering standpoint this may have looked good on a waveform monitor, but on the TV screen it looked flat, lifeless, and artistically poor.

Except for working within a more limited brightness range, there is no reason video directors can't make use of the same effective, well-developed principles of lighting as their counterparts in film. As video, especially HDTV, has begun to emulate the more artistic dimensions of film, there has been a greater emphasis on creative video lighting (Figure 6.1).

Before light can be successfully controlled, its three basic characteristics must be understood: coherence (quality), intensity (quantity) and color temperature.

LIGHT COHERENCE

coherence: A descriptive dimension of light that characterizes its hardness or softness. The harder a light source is, the more coherence it is said to have. Professional photographers refer to coherence as light *quality.*

Coherence (also called **quality**) is the attribute of light that defines its "hardness" or "softness." In Figures 6.2A and 6.2B all the objects are the same. The intensity and the color temperature of the lights are also exactly the same. The only difference between the photos is the coherence of the light used. (We'll return to these photos in a moment.) Coherence is probably the least understood and the most neglected of the three variables.

Hard Light

Light that is transmitted directly from a small point source results in relatively coherent (parallel and congruous) rays. This gives the light a hard, crisp, sharply defined appearance. The light from a clear, unfrosted light bulb, a focused

(a)

(b)

FIGURES 6.2A and 6.2B

In both of these photos the objects are identical — and so are the intensity and the color temperature of the lights illuminating them. The only difference between the two photos is the coherence of the light used. Figure 6.2A was shot with standard studio lighting; Figure 6.2B with a lighting tent (see Figure 6.11).

spotlight, or the noonday sun in a clear sky all represent hard light sources. Hard light casts a sharp, clearly defined shadow — the kind that, unfortunately, results in undesirable shadows of boom microphones on backgrounds. Several types of lighting instruments are used in TV to create hard light, including the beam-spot projector and the more commonly used ellipsoidal spotlight (Figure 6.3).

When hard light is used to illuminate a face, imperfections in the skin stand out. The result is less than flattering. But in other applications, such as bringing out the texture in leather, or the engraving on an expensive piece of jewelry, this can be an advantage. In a dramatic scene a hard light source is sometimes used to simulate bright sunlight coming through a window.

Lighting Angles and Quality   The angle at which light strikes a subject is extremely important in defining its appearance. This angle establishes the depth, form and texture of subject matter. A hard light source used at an oblique angle (65 to 95 degrees on either side of the camera) will bring out maximum surface detail (see Figures 6.4A and 6.4B). This is because when surface shadows are created, texture (surface detail) is emphasized (Figures 6.5A and 6.5B). Later in the chapter we'll cover the recommended angles for the various lights on a subject.

FIGURE 6.3

Several types of lighting instruments produce "hard" light, including this ellipsoidal spotlight. In a dramatic scene a hard light source can simulate bright sunlight coming through a window. When hard light is used to illuminate a face, imperfections in the skin stand out and the result is less than flattering. But, in other applications, such as bringing out the texture in leather, or the engraving on an expensive piece of jewelry, this effect can be an advantage. (Compare Figures 6.4A and 6.4B.)

(a)

FIGURES 6.4A and 6.4B
When a hard light source is used at an oblique angle, the surface detail of this ivory jewelry box is maximized. Figure 6.4A was taken with soft lighting and Figure 6.4B with a hard light source 80 degrees from the camera position.

diffuser: An attachment that fits over the front of a lighting instrument and softens the quality of the light.

soft light: Wide aperture lighting instrument that produces a very diffused source of illumination.

umbrella reflector: A white or silver umbrella with a bright light placed near the center and used for creating soft light.

flat lighting: Soft, even lighting that produces minimal shadows and minimizes the depth and dimension in subject matter.

Soft Light

Soft (diffused) light has the opposite effect of hard light—especially when lighting angles are also controlled. As shown in Figures 6.6A and 6.6B, soft light hides surface irregularities and detail. Spun glass or stainless steel *diffusers* are used over the front of lights to soften and diffuse their beams (Figure 6.7). At the same time, diffusers also reduce the intensity of light. Large *soft lights* (Figure 6.8) are used in production studios to create a broad, even area of light.

Because of their size, soft lights are difficult to work with in the field, so EFP videographers often rely on *umbrella reflectors* to create a soft lighting effect. As you can see in Figure 6.9, this lightweight, portable source of soft light is simply a light bounced off of a silver or white umbrella-like reflector. Since soft light tends to hide lines, wrinkles and blemishes, it is desirable in doing "glamour" work (Figure 6.10).

A soft light source placed close to the camera minimizes surface detail and creates a *flat lighting.* Although it has certain applications, especially in extreme close-up work where shadows would obscure important details, flat lighting leaves subject matter somewhat "dimensionless." When used over a large area, it can impart an arid and sterile-looking appearance.

FIGURES 6.5A and 6.5B
Note how a hard light source at an angle of about 70 degrees from the camera (Figure 6.5A) creates the shadow areas (Figure 6.5B) necessary to emphasize surface detail. The effect of this setup is illustrated in Figures 6.6A and 6.6B.

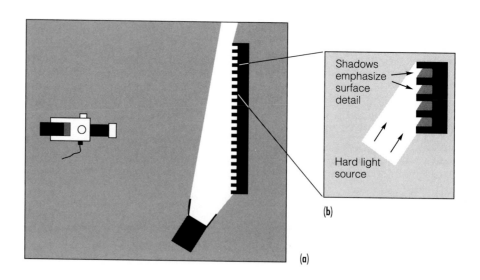

Shadows emphasize surface detail

Hard light source

(b)

(a)

(a)   (b)

FIGURES 6.6A and 6.6B

The photograph in Figure 6.6A was taken with soft lighting. As a result, the surface of the object shows minimal surface detail with soft, muted colors (not visible in this black-and-white picture). When a hard light source is used (Figure 6.6B), surface detail is maximized and colors are much brighter. (Note shadow of flower on the surface of the tombstone.) It is important to note that the intensity of the light in each of these photos is exactly the same.

FIGURE 6.7

Spun glass or stainless steel diffusers are used over the front of lights to soften and diffuse their beams. Soft (diffused) light has the opposite effect of hard light—especially when lighting angles are also controlled.

FIGURE 6.8

Soft lights are used in production studios to create broad, even areas of light. Because soft light tends to hide skin imperfections, it can create flattering effects.

FIGURE 6.9

Umbrella reflectors provide light similar in quality to a soft light, but they are much more portable. Although seldom used in multicamera production, they are often seen in single-camera, on location productions.

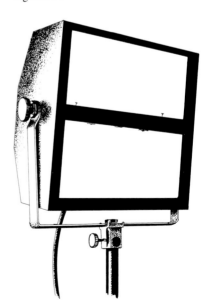

The ultimate in soft, shadowless light is produced by the **lighting tent.** (See Figures 6.11 and 6.2A and 6.2B.) Although extreme, upon occasion this approach is the only way to solve major spectral highlight (reflection) problems from small, highly reflective objects. A lighting tent is easy to devise; a white sheet is simply suspended in tent-fashion over the subject matter. The tent must completely surround the subject(s) while leaving the smallest possible opening for the camera lens. By focusing several lights around the exterior of the tent, a soft, omnidirectional light is created that provides an ultra-soft, shadowless illumination. A lighting tent also solves the problem of studio crew members and equipment being visible in mirrored surfaces, such as silver pitchers or chrome tea kettles.

Most subject matter will look best when illuminated with a light source somewhere between hard light sources used at oblique angles (designed to bring out maximum surface detail) and ultra-soft light (designed to hide surface detail and minimize reflections).

FIGURE 6.10

Soft lighting can soften facial features, hide minor skin blemishes, and enhance the beauty of the human face — but with the loss of some texture, form and dimension.

COLOR TEMPERATURE

The second attribute of light, color temperature, was introduced in Chapter 5. Referring to Figure 5.4, you can see the difference between the two basic color standards: 3,200°K for the incandescent lamps used in studios and 5,500°K for average daylight. Beyond this basic information, we need to elaborate a bit on several color temperature issues.

Sunlight's Varying Color Temperature

Although we've said that sunlight is about 5,500°K, the color of sunlight can actually vary rather greatly — depending on the time of day, the amount of haze or smog in the air and geographic longitude and latitude. Because of its angle to the earth in the early morning and late afternoon, sunlight must travel through more of the earth's atmosphere. The result is that more blue light is absorbed

FIGURE 6.11

A lighting tent produces the ultimate in soft, shadowless light. Upon occasion this approach is the only way to solve major reflection problems. Figures 6.2A and 6.2B show the difference a lighting tent can make.

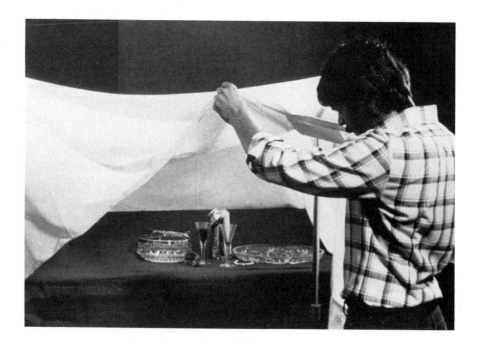

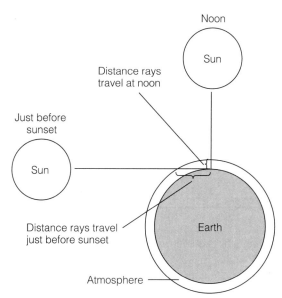

Noon

Sun

Distance rays
travel at noon

Just before
sunset

Sun

Distance rays travel
just before sunset

Earth

Atmosphere

FIGURE 6.12
Because of its angle to the earth in the early morning and late afternoon, sunlight must travel through more of the earth's atmosphere. The result is that more blue light is absorbed than red (shorter wavelengths of light are more readily absorbed) and the color temperature of the sun is shifted toward red. During midday the temperature of direct sunlight rises to about 5,500°K.

than red (shorter wavelengths of light are more readily absorbed) and the color temperature of the sun is shifted toward red. (See Figure 6.12.) During midday the temperature of direct sunlight rises to about 5,500°K. However, if the day is hazy or overcast, the Kelvin temperature may go up to 8,500°K. Pure skylight (coming through a window, for example) can reach even higher color temperatures. Left uncorrected, skylight will impart a cold, blue look to skin tones—generally not a desirable effect.

Related Technical Continuity Problems

Because of the significant variations in color temperature that can be encountered in doing on-location work, it is important to remember to white balance video cameras whenever lighting conditions change. For about two hours after sunrise and two hours before sunset, color temperature changes rapidly. And, if the sun moves in or out of cloud cover, color temperatures (and light quality) will dramatically change. Although these changes may not be too obvious to the eye, they can present major problems when you attempt to match successive scenes during editing. These color temperature and light quality examples represent two types of **technical continuity problems** (scene-to-scene technical inconsistencies) that you can encounter in video production.

technical continuity problem: Any one of several types of unintentional changes in video or audio quality. Examples are unintended changes in color balance or changes in audio levels during the course of consecutive shots.

LIGHT INTENSITY

The last characteristic of light that is essential to control is intensity. As we noted in an earlier chapter, light **intensity** is measured in foot candles or lux.

Typical Foot Candle Intensities

To provide some points of reference, sunlight on an average day ranges from 3,000 to 10,000 foot candles; TV studios are lit at about 200 foot candles; a bright office has about 40 foot candles of illumination; moonlight represents about 0.01 foot candle; and starlight measures a mere 0.000005 foot candle. Although most TV cameras need at least 75 foot candles for good quality, most can produce acceptable pictures under only a few a foot candles of light.

LIGHT METERS

Light meters are used to measure light intensity. As we will see, being able to establish rather exact foot candle or lux intensities for the various lights is important in production. There are two types of meters: reflected and incident.

Reflected Light Meters

A **reflected light meter** measures the amount of light being reflected from (off of) the main subject matter in a scene. This is the type of built-in light measurement system used in most still cameras. In determining exposure times, this type of meter assumes that all subject matter reflects 18 percent of the light falling on it—a so-called average scene. A reflected light meter can be easily fooled by non-standard subject matter. For example, readings taken from snow scenes, white sand or scenes with bright backgrounds will result in underexposure of skin tones when the camera erroneously "assumes" that the overall reflectance is only 18 percent. (People often have difficulty understanding how pictures taken of people standing in the middle of a bright, sunlight beach can come out *under*exposed.)

Conversely, if you were photographing a scene of a spotlighted subject in the center of a large black backdrop, the assumption of an overall 18 percent reflectance would also be wrong. In this case, because of the large black background, the reading would be much too low, resulting in overexposure of the central subject matter. Under these conditions the subject would end up looking like a chalky-white ghost.

The accuracy of reflected light readings can be improved by using a spot meter. **Spot meters** are a type of reflected light meter that can measure light within a 3- to 5-degree angle of acceptance. Whereas general reflected light meters are best used within a few feet or even a few inches from a subject, spot meters make possible light readings from a distance. Because they can zero in on specific objects in a scene, they can provide more accurate readings. This capability makes it possible to determine (and control) the contrast ratio of a scene. Using a spot meter, a lighting director can simply stand in the position of a camera and compare the contrast values of subject matter in a scene. If there are five or more f-stops difference between important subject matter, the contrast ratio has been exceeded. This ratio can then be reduced either by throwing more light on the dark areas or by reducing light intensity on bright areas.

Incident Light Meters

Whereas a reflected light meter is valuable in determining contrast ratios in a scene, an **incident light meter** can tell you how bright the various lights on a set are. As we've noted, instead of measuring the amount of light reflected from subject matter, incident meters measure the amount of light falling on the subject. Therefore, to get an accurate reading with this type of meter you must point it at the light you are measuring (while standing at the exact spot the talent will assume). Some incident-type meters read directly in foot candles or lux; others require a conversion scale to arrive at these values.

Significant unevenness in lighting around a scene causes variations in video and can result in dark or even washed out skin tones. It is possible to walk around a studio set with an incident light meter and quickly find dark or "hot" areas where lighting needs to be adjusted.

There is another reason for being able to accurately measure light on a set. By subtly manipulating the brightness in the primary and secondary areas of a scene, you can achieve a sophisticated means of visual control. Since our eyes are drawn to light areas, you can use light to shape and control pictorial composition and emphasize the scene's center of interest. The implications of this will be discussed in more detail in the chapter on composition.

CONTROLLING LIGHT INTENSITY

Of course, it does little good to know how to measure the brightness of lights if we can't control their brightness. There are several ways of doing this.

First is light-to-subject distance. As the distance between a light source and the subject increases, the light is spread out over a larger area and the intensity decreases. Put more precisely, the intensity of light from an unfocused light source decreases according to the inverse-square law. We'll leave precise foot candle calculations to the mathematicians[1] and illustrate this concept with a simple illustration. If you have 1,600 foot candles of light at a distance of 10 feet, and double the light-to-subject distance to 20 feet, you will end up with only about 1/4 the original light, or 400 foot candles. If you triple the distance to 30 feet you will end up with about 178 foot candles. And finally, if you increase the distance to 40 feet (four times the original distance) you end up with only about 100 foot candles of light. See Table 6.1.

By keeping this general concept in mind, you will be able to quickly vary the intensities of lights to conform to needed lighting ratios.[2]

Another way to control the intensity of light is with **scrims** (Figure 6.13). By using single or double thickness scrim over a light, its intensity can be cut 30 to 60 percent.

Many lighting instruments can be *focused,* and this also influences intensity. By using a lever or a crank, the beam of these lights can be *pinned down* and concentrated over a narrow area, or *flooded out* to cover a larger area.

TABLE 6.1
Light Distance/Brightness Relationship

1/2 the original distance = 4 × the light
2 × the original distance = 1/4 the light
3 × the original distance = 1/9 the light
4 × original distance = 1/16 the light

1. Although you seldom need to calculate things down to the foot candle, in case you are interested, here's how you do it. To find the change in illumination caused by a change in distance, take the factor by which the distance is increased, square it and invert the result. Example: by moving a light from 12 to 24 feet there is a distance change of 2 ×. If you square that you have 4; and 4 inverted is 1/4. If you started out with 200 foot candles of light you would end up with 50 foot candles of light, which means you end up with one-fourth the original illumination.

2. As the efficiency of lighting instruments is increased by the use of a focusing reflector and one or more lenses, this example will cease to be completely accurate. However, unless various types of lighting instruments are mixed, this approach is adequate to determine the placement of lights for needed brightness ratios. When lighting instruments are mixed (e.g., when Fresnels and scoops are used on the same scene), exact intensities can be determined with an incident light meter.

FIGURE 6.13

One way of controlling the intensity of light is with scrims. By using a single or double thickness scrim over a light, intensity can be cut 30 to 60 percent. Note the two round scrims fastened to the top of the case in this portable lighting kit.

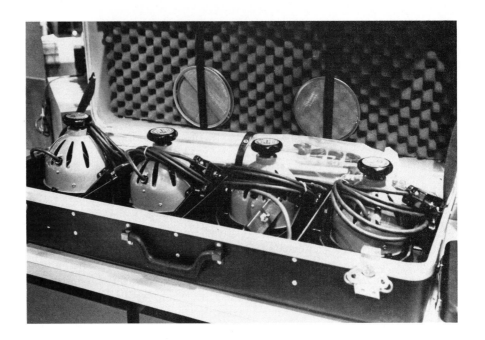

Finally, brightness can be reduced in incandescent lights by reducing the voltage to the lamps with dimmers. Unfortunately, this also affects color temperature. A rough rule of thumb is that for every 1-volt drop in the voltage to an incandescent light, the color temperature is reduced by 10°K (Figure 6.14). Since the human eye can detect a 200°K color shift in the 2,000°K to 4,000°K range, this means that a studio light can only be dimmed by about 20 percent (in relation to the other lights) without having a noticeable effect on color balance.

Having discussed the three basic attributes of light — quality, quantity and color temperature — we turn to various artificial light sources and their characteristics.

INCANDESCENT LIGHTS: PROBLEMS AND SOLUTIONS

Thomas Edison found that by passing an electric current through thin filaments of carbonized threads in a glass-enclosed vacuum, a stable, bright glow could be created. He also discovered two other things: the amount of light rises with voltage, and beyond an optimum voltage, the life of the lamp quickly diminishes — and burns out.

FIGURE 6.14

For every 1-volt drop in the voltage to an incandescent light, the color temperature is reduced by about 10°K. Since the human eye can detect a 200°K color shift in the 2,000°K to 4,000°K range, this means that a light can only be dimmed by about 20 percent (in relation to the other lights) without having a noticeable effect on color balance.

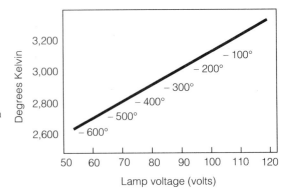

The Problem of Incandescence

During the operation of a normal incandescent lamp (like the 75- or 100-watt lamp you may be using to read this book) atoms of the tungsten filament are slowly "boiled off." This results in three undesirable effects. First, these atoms are deposited on the inside of the glass envelope of the bulb. As the lamp gets older this darkens the bulb and reduces the light output up to 60 percent. Second, these tungsten deposits can drop color temperature 100 to 200 degrees over the life of the lamp. And finally, as the tungsten atoms are boiled off, the filament gets thinner, eventually burning in two.

The Solution

These problems are solved with the tungsten-halogen lamp. **Tungsten-halogen** lamps (also called *quartz lights*—for quartz-iodine) are the primary type of lamp used in studio production. Like standard incandescent lamps, they use a tungsten filament. However, the major shortcomings of incandescent lamps are virtually eliminated with quartz lights. During the time the tungsten-halogen lamp is operating, bromine, which has been added to the gas inside the lamp, combines with the "boiled off" tungsten atoms to create tungsten-halide. The tungsten half of this combination then combines again with the tungsten filament. This means that the leftover halide is then free to combine with more boiled off tungsten atoms. If you have followed this chemical progression, you can see that this cycle not only serves to maintain the tungsten filament, but solves the problem of tungsten being deposited on the inside of the lamp.

quartz light: Tungsten-halogen light. A high-intensity light consisting of a tungsten-halogen filament and a quartz or silica globe.

In order to sustain the tungsten-halogen cycle, the transparent wall of the lamp must be several hundred degrees Celsius. This means that if the lamp is operated at a reduced voltage (which drops the temperature below 250°C), blackening of the bulb will occur and the life of the lamp will be shortened. This is a significant issue because dimmers, which are commonly used to reduce the intensity of lamps, operate on the principle of reducing voltage.

Normal glass can't be used at the high temperatures associated with tungsten-halogen lamps, so the lamp envelopes are made out of quartz. (See Figures 6.15 and 6.16.) At the same time, the operating temperature of several hundred degrees centigrade comes close to the melting point of some materials. Once the temperature goes up above 400°C, the lamp and its mount can melt. It is therefore important for lamp housings to have good ventilation and cooling.

There is one more important consideration in using quartz lamps. While the lamp is on, any foreign material clinging to the exterior surface of the enclosure, including fingerprints, will cause a localized heat buildup. This quickly results in lamp failure. To avoid getting fingerprints on a lamp when it is changed, you should use a handkerchief or glove.

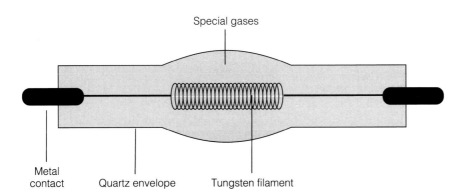

FIGURE 6.15

Tungsten-halogen (quartz) lamps differ from normal incandescent lamps. Special compounds are injected into the lamp to preserve color temperature and lamp life. Since normal glass can't be used at the high temperatures associated with tungsten-halogen lamps, the lamp envelopes are made out of quartz.

FIGURE 6.16
Lights used on location are almost all built around the tungsten-halogen (quartz) lamp. This particular light has two-way barn doors (black metal flaps), which can be used to mask off the sides of the light's beam. There are also four-way barn doors, which can mask off the top and bottom edges of the light beam as well.

HMI LIGHTS

HMI lights were originally developed in Germany in the 1960s to aid television crews who needed a small, efficient and intense on-location light source. The inventor of the HMI knew that battery-powered incandescent lights were a major problem in video field production. Because of their inefficiency, 80 percent of the energy for incandescent lights is converted into heat. (The figures are better for tungsten-halogen or quartz lights: 65 percent of the energy goes into heat, and 35 percent is transformed into light.)

HMI, which stands for Hydrargyrum Medium Arc-length Iodide, emits an intense light that is the same color temperature as sunlight. But the problems surrounding the uneven spectral response associated with discharge-type lights was solved by the addition of specific chemicals in the HMI tube. Like tungsten-halogen lamps, the glass enclosure of HMI lights contains bromides. A tungsten-bromide cycle is initiated that keeps the inside of the bulb from darkening.

HMI lights generate less heat than incandescent lights. This is often an important consideration when shooting inside in a confined space. The less heat generated, the more comfortable it will be for talent and crew. Makeup also holds up better.

Unlike incandescent or tungsten-halogen lamps, voltage drops in HMI lights produce an increase rather than a decrease in color temperature. But HMI lights have a voltage-correction feature built into their power supply. Minor changes in voltage — common at different times of the day in many cities — do not result in fluctuations in light output or color temperature. Since HMI power requirements are significantly less than for incandescent lights, the electrical problems are reduced.

A special circuit in the base of the power supply furnishes a one-second, time-controlled ignition voltage necessary to start the HMI light. A warm-up time of about one minute brings the light up to 90 percent of its maximum output. After three minutes there is full stabilization of both intensity and color. Although intensity cannot be controlled by dimming, scrims and mechanical shutters (similar to venetian blinds) can be used to reduce light levels.

The main disadvantage of the HMI light is the large, heavy high-voltage power supply that is needed. (See Figure 6.17.) Even so, because of their color temperature, efficiency and high light output, HMI lights are an excellent choice for on-location production — especially for filling shadows caused by sunlight.

FIGURE 6.17
Although smaller in size, the HMI Fresnel light on the left is actually brighter than the large arc Fresnel on the right. The HMI light also stays cooler and uses less power. Its main disadvantage is the need for the heavy ballast (transformer) shown at the bottom left of the picture.

PROBLEM LIGHT SOURCES

Standard Fluorescent Lamps

Fluorescent lamps belong to the group of lighting devices known collectively as **discharge lamps**—glass tubes filled with metal vapor, with electrodes at each end. Electric current passed between the electrodes ionizes the vapor, which begins to glow, producing light. Unlike tungsten-type lights, standard fluorescent lamps have a broken spectrum. Instead of a relatively smooth mix of colors from infrared to ultraviolet, fluorescent light has sharp bands or spikes of color—primarily in the blue-green areas. Even though the eye will not notice these spikes, they can result in color shifts in video.

The Daylight Fluorescent   A popular fluorescent tube, the daylight fluorescent has a color temperature of 6,300°K. This high color temperature, together with the bands of color, means that blue tones will be exaggerated and reds will be rendered slightly gray and dull. Although the latest generation of CCD cameras are much better at handling the problems inherent in standard fluorescent lamps, they still can't completely or consistently solve these problems. For one thing, there are about 30 different types of tubes in use, each with slightly different color characteristics.

Warm-White Fluorescent   The standard consumer-type fluorescent lamp that causes the least color temperature problems is the warm-white fluorescent with a color temperature of 3,000°K. Although this light is slightly yellow compared to the 3,200°K incandescent standard, the tube will produce satisfactory results—assuming the camera is white balanced on a white card and assuming perfect color fidelity isn't a major goal. If regular productions in a specific daylight fluorescent-lit location must be done (and unwanted color shifts are resulting from existing tubes), it may be better to replace all the lamps with warm-white fluorescent (or comparable) tubes. Some manufacturers also make plastic "sleeves" that can be slipped over tubes to change their color characteristics.

Color-Balanced Fluorescent

Thus far in this discussion we have used the term *standard fluorescent lights*. In recent years some fluorescent-tube manufacturers have started producing high-intensity fluorescent bulbs which smooth out the normal spikes in the standard fluorescent spectrum. It should be noted, however, that these are special lamps and not the kind you normally encounter in offices, meeting rooms, schools and homes. Since standard fluorescent lamps are apt to produce undesirable (and generally unpredictable) results, some videographers make it a habit to switch off the fluorescent lights in a room and set up their own incandescent light sources.

Other Discharge Lights

Other types of discharge lamps can cause much more severe color problems than standard fluorescent lamps. One type, high-pressure sodium vapor lamps, used primarily for street lighting, produces a brilliant yellowish-orange light that will drastically skew color balance. Operating at even higher pressures are the mercury vapor lamps, sometimes used for large interior areas such as gymnasiums. These produce a greenish-blue light.

Suffice to say, to avoid unpleasant surprises with any standard discharge-type light it is wise to do a test using a good color monitor.

MIXED LIGHT SOURCES

In on-location production situations **mixed-sources** will often be encountered. An example is a room that is partly illuminated by incandescent light and partly lit by sunlight coming through a window (Figure 5.4). If the camera is color balanced with the incandescent light, the areas lit by sunlight will appear blue and cold. Conversely, if the color balance is done in an area lit by sunlight, the remaining areas will appear yellow. Videographers, who don't have time to completely control the problem by blocking out one of the light sources, should color balance on the dominant light source and hope the secondary (weaker) source will not be too distracting. (Of course, what you can "get by with" will be much different in a news piece than it will in a cosmetic commercial.)

There are, of course, better solutions for handling mixed-sources. The simplest is to close the curtains or venetian blinds in the room and set up incandescent lights designed for on-location production. Another approach is used for more demanding single-camera film and HDTV dramatic productions: putting large sheets of straw-colored gel over the windows. (*Gels* are colored pieces of heat resistant transparent plastic, available in more than one hundred colors.) The proper gel will bring the color of the exterior daylight to 3,200°K—the same color temperature as the incandescent lights. This daylight-to-incandescent gel (designated as N85) also serves one other important function: it reduces the intensity of the exterior light so that is comes closer to matching the level of the interior light.

Occasionally it is desirable to change the color of incandescent or quartz lights to 5,500°K (daylight). In Figure 6.18 the incandescent lights are being changed to match the sunlight coming through the window. This is done by covering the lights with a daylight-blue gel. Unfortunately, this also reduces the output of the lights by about 40 percent—a rather significant loss when you need to balance the intensity of the lights with sunlight.

gel; gelatin: A piece of optically pure colored, translucent material used to filter the light from a lighting instrument.

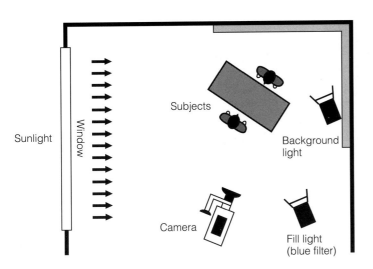

FIGURE 6.18
Occasionally it is desirable to shift the color temperature of quartz lights to 5,500°K — the color temperature of daylight. In this setup all of the lights are being filtered to 5,500°K to match the daylight coming through the window at the left. ENG cameras often use dichroic filters over camera-mounted lights to change their color temperature from 3,200°K to 5,500°K. When shooting outside in sunlight, the lights can then be used to fill harsh shadows.

USING COLOR AS A PROP

Since the color of light suggests specific meanings and associations, sometimes having mixed light sources in a scene is desirable. For example, moonlight is typically simulated by slightly blue light. (Since it is reflected sunlight, its being blue compared to incandescent light would be logical.) This color association could be used in lighting a dramatic night scene of a burglar looking through a window. But since even a full moon has an intensity of only about 0.01 foot candle, it would be impossible with standard production equipment to produce a well-exposed video image by moonlight. But dramatic television, like "Hollywood," frequently has to make things seem real through fabrication. In this case an incandescent light with a blue gel placed behind and above the burglar would simulate moonlight. A second incandescent light inside the house (possibly with a light yellow or straw-colored gel to enhance the effect) would suggest normal nighttime interior house light. To look realistic, the interior light would also need to be somewhat stronger than the moonlight.

Color is also used to suggest other things: a flickering straw-colored light for fire, intense flashes of blue light for lightning, and a blue light that occasionally changes in intensity to simulate the light of a TV set. Colored lights can also be used to make backgrounds more interesting. For example, spotlights with colored gels can be focused on a gray cyc to create (with a flip of a switch) an interesting background for a studio setting. Production settings will be discussed in Chapter 11.

LIGHTING INSTRUMENTS

We've discussed various sources of artificial light used in television production. Now we need to look at the various lighting instruments that direct, shape and house these light sources.

The Fresnel Light

The light that for several decades has been the primary source of illumination in most film and TV studio productions is the Fresnel (pronounced fra-nell) light. The Fresnel lens in the front of the light (named for the person who

FIGURE 6.19
The primary source of illumination in most film and TV studio productions is the Fresnel light. The Fresnel lens in the front of the light consists of concentric circles that both concentrate and slightly diffuse the light. Fresnels provide an ideal mix between hard and soft light. (Note that both lights in Figure 6.17 are Fresnels.)

devised it) consists of concentric circles that both concentrate and slightly diffuse the light (Figure 6.19). Fresnels provide an ideal mix between hard and soft light.

Fresnels are specified by the wattage of their lamps and by the diameter of their lenses. Wattage ranges from 500 to 10,000. The most common lens sizes are 6, 8 and 10 inches. Although less common, Fresnels are also available with $4\frac{1}{2}$-inch, 12-inch and 16-inch lenses.

The distance between the lamp and the Fresnel lens can be adjusted to either spread out (flood), or concentrate (*spot* or *pin*) the light's beam. The beam width of some Fresnels is adjustable over a 10-to-1 ratio, which means the beam can be varied from about 12 to 35 degrees. This adjustment provides a convenient control over the intensity of the light.

Barn Doors **Barn doors** are adjustable black metal flaps attached to the sides of the Fresnel light. There are **two-way barn doors** that provide masking from two sides (Figure 6.16) and **four-way barn doors** (two sets of flaps) that can simultaneously shape the top and bottom and the sides of the light. Barn doors provide an important way of masking off unwanted light, especially when the Fresnel's beam is flooded out (generally as a way of reducing central-area light intensity). Because barn doors are mounted close to the light source, they provide a soft and unnoticeable cutoff to the edges of the light. Occasionally, however, it is necessary to sharply define the edges of the light. For this, the flag can be used.

flag: Metal or cloth-covered rectangle placed in front of a light to mask off the beam or produce a precise shadow.

Flags *Flags,* which are also primarily used with Fresnel lights, consist of any type of opaque material that can block and sharply define the edges of the light source. Typically, flags are devised from either 8-by-10-inch or larger metal or cardboard sheets, or from pieces of aluminum foil. Double or triple thicknesses of aluminum foil are often preferred for small flags because they are easy to shape and can stand the heat associated with lights. Flags are generally either clipped to stands or attached to the outer edges of barn doors.

The farther away they are used from the light source, the more sharply defined the light cutoff will be.

Filter Frames   Other attachments to Fresnel lights include **filter frames** that can hold the following:

- One or more scrims that reduce light intensity of the light
- One or more diffusers that soften the light
- A colored gel that alters the color of the light

All of these have been introduced earlier. Most filter frames are a part of a one-piece barn door attachment that slides over the front of a Fresnel light.

Safety Considerations   Even when not using a scrim, diffuser or gel, safety-minded lighting directors keep a rabbit wire insert in the frame holder of Fresnels at all times.[3] Fresnel lenses, which are rather thick and heavy, have been known to shatter from heat; and falling pieces of glass from a light positioned 15 or so feet overhead can obviously pose a severe threat to those working below.

Scoops

A somewhat softer light than the Fresnel spot is provided by a *scoop* (Figure 6.20). Scoops are available in 12- to 18-inch diameter sizes. They are equipped with tungsten-halogen lamps that are frosted or (for a slightly harder light) unfrosted. Their wattage ranges from 500 to 2,000. Unlike the Fresnel light, which is enclosed by the lens, scoops are open-faced with large, matte-surface metal reflectors. Some have a focusing control that provides a limited adjustment on the spread of the light beam.

Broads

Broads (for broad-beam lights) give a slightly harder and more defined light than the Fresnel. They normally have a rectangular-shaped front with a bright, pebbled reflector. Lamps for broads are available from 500 to 1,000 watts, frosted or unfrosted.

Ellipsoidal Spots

Rounding out the list of lighting instruments commonly found in production studios are ellipsoidal spotlights. The *ellipsoidal spotlights* (Figures 6.21 and 6.3) produce a hard, focused beam of light. Used with gels, they can project colored pools of light on a background. Some ellipsoidals have slots at their optical midpoint that accept a **cookie (cucalorus)** — a small metal pattern that can be used to project a pattern on a background. As you can see from Figure 6.22, many designs are available. When projected behind subjects, they can be used to suggest a location, such as an office, church or jail cell.

Pattern projectors, which are designed to project more elaborate backgrounds, take the ellipsoidal-cookie combination a step further. Some of the patterns are made in a large loop that can be electrically moved through the beam of light. These patterns (especially when thrown slightly out of focus

FIGURE 6.20
A somewhat softer light than the Fresnel spot is provided by a scoop. Scoops are available in 12-inch to 18-inch-diameter sizes, and they range from 500 to 2,000 watts. Unlike the Fresnel light, which is enclosed by the lens, scoops are open-faced with large, matte-surface metal reflectors. Some have a focusing control that provides a limited adjustment on the spread of the light beam.

scoop: A floodlight, often used as a fill light, that has an elliptical matte-finish reflector.

ellipsoidal spotlight: Spotlight that uses a lens to produce a sharply defined beam of light.

3. Rabbit wire, which consists of 1/4-inch crisscross mesh, is placed in filter frames. Chicken wire, which has a larger mesh and is not quite as sturdy, is also used. If a Fresnel lens breaks, large pieces of glass should be held in place by the wire.

FIGURE 6.21

The ellipsoidal spot (see also Figure 6.3) produces a hard, focused beam of light. Used with gels, they can project colored pools of light on a background. Some ellipsoidals have slots at their central focus point that accept a "cookie" (cucalorus)—a small metal pattern that can be used to project a pattern on a background. As you can see from Figure 6.22, many designs are available.

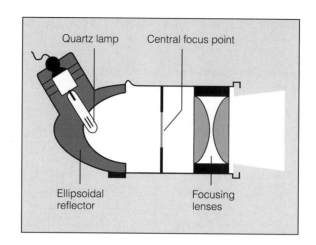

Quartz lamp   Central focus point

Ellipsoidal reflector   Focusing lenses

behind subjects) can suggest such things as slowly moving clouds in a blue sky or trees going by outside a train window.

Thus far we have discussed the major types of lamps and lighting instruments. But lighting isn't a matter of just hanging lights wherever it's convenient until some overall level of intensity is reached. The lighting instruments we've introduced are intended to fulfill specific roles within an overall lighting design. In a typical lighting setup, lighting instruments may serve as follows:

- Keys
- Fills
- Backs (back lights)
- Background lights

FIGURE 6.22

Ellipsoidal patterns (often called cookies) can be placed in the light to project patterns on backgrounds. In addition to just providing interesting backgrounds, they can suggest a location, such as an office, church or jail cell. These are just some of the patterns that are available.

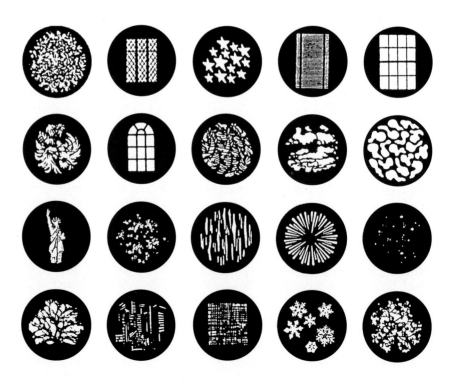

In describing the function of each of these we'll assume a standard, three-point (three-light) setup—the kind that can be used for all standard subject matter. We'll concentrate on the so-called formula approach to lighting, an approach that can be relied upon to produce excellent results for most of your studio and on-location productions. We'll also look at special-purpose lighting.

THE KEY LIGHT

As the name implies, the *key light* (Figures 6.23A and 6.23B) is the main light and the light that most affects the appearance of subject matter. In terms of coherence or quality, it should be in the middle of the hard-to-soft range.

In three-point (formula) lighting the key light is placed at an angle of between 30 and 45 degrees from either the left or the right of the camera. Forty-five degrees is best, because it brings out more texture and form in the subject, plus it gives more room for trucking the camera left or right during a production. For the sake of consistency, the 45-degree angle will be used throughout this discussion. If multiple cameras are being used, the key light angle should be set in reference to the camera that will take most of the close-ups.

The Rule of Simplicity

The key light also creates the **catchlight** in eyes—the (single) spectral reflection in each eye that gives the eyes their "sparkle." Often personnel unexperienced in proper lighting techniques try to put lights everywhere, feeling somehow that "more is better." Not only does this result in a multitude of catchlights in eyes, but it generally results in flat, lifeless lighting. Using multiple key lights on talent areas not only violates the basic tenet of three-point lighting, but it creates a confusing horde of shadows. As lighting director Steven Taibbi says, the only things that are probably less appealing than multiple, "butterfly" nose shadows are "raccoon eyes" and three-chin shadows! All this brings us to one of the maxims in lighting: *the simpler the design, the better the effect.*

key light: The brightest frontal light on a scene. A light that establishes the form, dimension and overall appearance of a subject.

FIGURES 6.23A and 6.23B
As its name implies, the key light is the main light and the light that most affects the appearance of subject matter. When used to illuminate people, the key should be in the middle of the hard-to-soft range. Note in Figure 6.23B, however, that by itself, the key light casts dark shadows on the side of the model's face. The addition of a fill light, to be discussed later, will solve this problem.

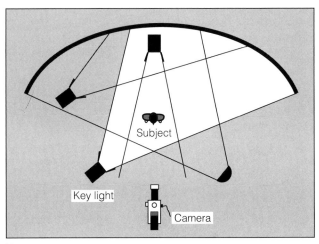

(a)

(b)

To the Right or to the Left?

We mentioned that the key light can be placed either to the left or right of the camera. Four considerations influence where the key should be placed:

- The subject's best side (Flaws on one side of the face can be minimized by placing the key on the opposite side.)
- The visible or assumed location of a source of light on the set (in a dramatic scene, the location of a window or table light, for example)
- Consistency (It is generally illogical for people sitting together to be keyed from different directions.)
- Convenience (Space limitations may make it easier to put the key on one side or the other of the camera.)

The Key's Vertical Angle

We have established the horizontal angle for the key light as being approximately 45 degrees to the left or right of the subject in relation to the camera. One other key light angle should be considered: elevation. This angle is also commonly 45 degrees (Figure 6.24).

Some lighting directors prefer to place the key right next to the camera or at a vertical angle of less than 30 degrees. Sometimes in limited, on-location conditions this may be necessary. However, three problems can result: the full illusion of depth and form will be sacrificed, there is a risk of having shadows from the key light appear on the background, and talent are forced to look almost directly into a bright key light when they try to look at their camera. (The last can make reading a teleprompter very difficult.) Ideally, when the talent face their close-up camera they should see their key light 45 degrees off to one side of the camera, at an elevation of about 45 degrees.

Keys and Boom Mics

Since the key light is the brightest light on subjects, it's the one that will create the darkest shadows. One of the main problems encountered is shadows on the background. Shadows from boom mics can be minimized by positioning the boom parallel to (directly under) key lights. (Later, we'll see that by controlling subject-to-background distances and background lighting, boom shadows can be further reduced or eliminated.)

FIGURE 6.24
The ideal vertical angles for each of the main lights in three-point lighting are illustrated. The only light not shown, the background light, can be placed in any position or angle that provides an even light over background areas.

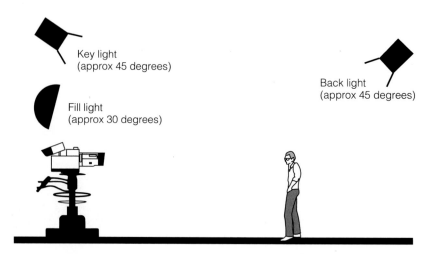

FIGURE 6.25
When shooting on location during the day the sun will normally be your key light. However, direct sunlight from a clear sky results in harsh shadows and an excessive brightness range. Aside from using a fill light, one solution is to use a Griffolyn screen (a fine, white, open weave material) to change direct, harsh sunlight into a soft light source.

The Sun as a Key

When shooting on location during the day, the sun will normally be your key light. Direct sunlight from a clear sky results in an excessive brightness range between highlights and shadow areas. Without fill light, harsh shadows will result. Aside from using a fill light (to be discussed in the next section), one solution is to filter the sunlight through a large white screen. Note in Figure 6.25 that a Griffolyn screen is being used to change direct sunlight into a soft light source. Thin white bedsheets stapled to large frames are also sometimes used.

On an overcast day the diffused sunlight will provide a much better (softer) source of light. If the diffused sunlight is coming from behind the subject, it can provide good back lighting, while the ambient light from the overcast sky furnishes soft front lighting. With the proper cloud cover this can result in flattering lighting. In camcorders with automatic exposure control, underexposure will result unless the backlight switch (discussed in Chapter 4) is used. On other types of cameras you can manually adjust the iris for the best tonal rendition.

There are other issues in using the sun for on-location lighting. Since the "high-noon" effect (with sunlight directly overhead) produces dark eye shadows, it may be best to shoot sun-lit, on-location productions in mid-morning or mid-afternoon when the sun is at an elevation of 30 to 45 degrees. (Of course, where the sun is at a particular time depends upon the season and the longitude and latitude of your location.) If subjects can also be oriented so that the sun (the key light) ends up being 30 to 45 degrees off to one side of the camera, lighting will be best — especially if a fill light is used to slightly fill the shadows caused by the sun.

THE FILL LIGHT

Whether in the field or in the studio, the key light establishes the dimension, form and surface detail of the subject. However, without fill light this one light source produces heavy, distracting shadows (Figure 6.23B). The purpose of the *fill light* is to partially (but not entirely) fill in the shadows created by the

fill light: A soft light used to partially fill in the shadows caused by the key light. Typically, one-half the intensity of the key light.

FIGURE 6.26

The purpose of the fill light is to partially (but not entirely) fill in the shadows created by the key light. Without fill, the key light produces heavy, distracting shadows (Figure 6.23B).

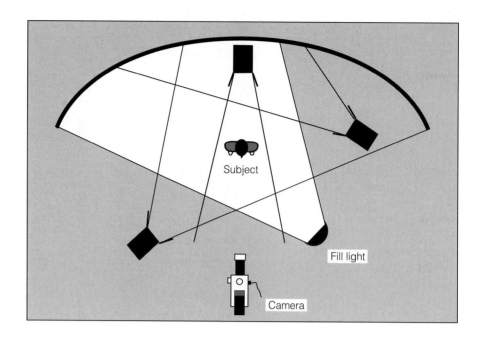

reflector board: A silver or bright white surface used to reflect light onto a subject. Often used outside to soften and fill in the light from the sun.

FIGURE 6.27

Large reflector boards such as this are often used outside in single-camera productions to fill in shadows caused by the sun. Because of their highly reflective surface, they will reflect light over a greater distance than the simple white panel reflectors commonly used for close-ups in ENG work. (See Figures 6.28, 6.29A and 6.29B.)

horizontal and vertical angles of the key light. In the studio the fill light is placed on the opposite side of the camera as the key. It can be positioned at any point from right beside the camera to 45 degrees away. However, it is safest to place the fill 45 degrees from the camera. With the key and fill each 45 degrees from the camera position, an angle of 90 degrees is created between the two lights (Figure 6.26). By lighting a full 90-degree area, an important margin of safety is created in case subjects unexpectedly move and camera angles have to be changed during the production. (Having to stop a production to change the position of lights can represent a time-consuming and costly delay.)

Although the vertical angle for the key should be about 45 degrees, the vertical position of the fill is less critical (Figure 6.24). Generally the fill is placed just above camera height, which means it ends up being slightly lower than the key. A vertical position of 30 degrees is commonly suggested for the fill light. In this position it can easily do what it's intended to do: *partially* fill in the shadows created by the key light.

We've suggested that the fill light should be "softer" than the key. A soft light source is able to subtly fill in some of the key's shadows without creating a second catchlight in the eyes. Although a good choice for a studio fill light is a scoop, for interior, on-location settings you will find a scoop is a bit large and unwieldy. In this case a portable quartz stand light—the same type you used for a key light—can be used with a diffuser (Figure 6.7). The diffuser not only softens the light, but it can appropriately reduce its intensity. For exterior scenes in sunlight either an appropriately filtered quartz light or an HMI light can be used as a fill.

Another approach to fill light is using a white or silver *reflector board* (Figure 6.27). Outside, when the sun is being used as a key, the reflector board can be positioned to reflect sunlight into the shadow areas. White board reflectors are commonly used in ENG work to do the same thing (Figure 6.28). Figures 6.29A and 6.29B show the effect of using a white board in sunlight to fill shadows and decrease the contrast ratio. If the sun is hitting the subject's

FIGURE 6.28
White reflector boards are often used in ENG work to fill in shadows caused by harsh sunlight. Since they reflect a softer, less intense light than shiny reflector boards (Figure 6.27), they must be used closer to the talent. Figures 6.29A and 6.29B show the effect of using a white reflector board.

right side, the reflector board will need to be positioned on the left side of the subject, just out of camera range. Reflector boards can be clipped to a stand or held by an assistant.

Inside, especially in single-camera production setups, a key light can be bounced off of the board (Figures 6.30A and 6.30B) to provide a soft light, or, if the key light puts out a wide beam of light, part of the key light illumination can be reflected on to the subject (Figure 6.31).

(a)　　　(b)

FIGURES 6.29A and 6.29B
Figure 6.29A shows the harsh effect of direct sunlight. In Figure 6.29B, a white reflector board was used and the contrast ratio was brought within an acceptable range.

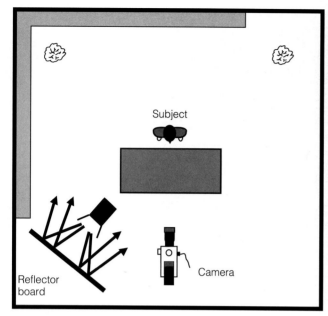

(a)

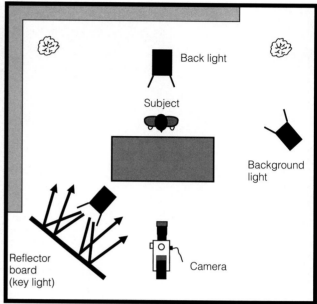

(b)

FIGURES 6.30A and 6.30B
A light bounced off a white or silver reflector (Figure 6.30A) will provide a soft source of illumination for an interview. As we will see, the addition of a back light and background light (shown in Figure 6.30B) will add depth and dimension to the picture.

FIGURE 6.31
If the beam from the key light covers a wide enough area, part of the light can be redirected for fill. A silver or white reflector at close range will provide the needed 2-to-1 lighting ratio (with the key twice as bright as the fill).

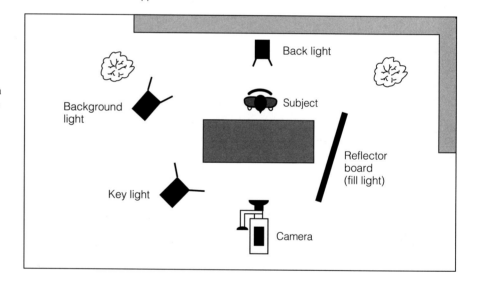

THE BACK LIGHT

back light: Light directed from behind and above the subject and used to add separation and dimension to a scene. Slightly stronger than front light.

With the key and fill lights, two points of three-point lighting have been covered. The third point is represented by the back light. The function of the **back light** is to separate the subject from the background by creating a subtle rim of light around the subject. (See Figures 6.32A and 6.32B.) You will note from Figure 6.32A that the back light (sometimes called a *hair light*) should be placed directly behind the subject in relation to the close-up camera.

Fresnels are commonly used for backlights. Compared to the key, a smaller, lower wattage instrument can be used for two reasons. First, back lights are often placed closer to the subject than the key light, and second, with subjects confined to a limited area (like a chair) the light can easily be "pinned down" to concentrate the beam.

In determining the position of the back light, remember that from an over-

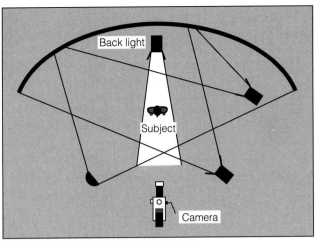

(a)

(b)

FIGURES 6.32A and 6.32B
The function of the back light is to outline and separate the subject from the background. You will note from Figure 6.32A that the back light should be placed directly behind the subject in relation to the camera.

head perspective you should be able to draw a straight line from the lens of the close-up camera, through the subject, directly to the back light. (See Figure 6.32A.) If a back light is placed too far off to one side, it will spill around one side of the subject and leave the other side dark.

Although the elevation of the back light is often dictated by conditions, a 45-degree angle is most desirable. (Refer back to Figure 6.24.) If the back light is too low, it will be picked up by the camera; if it's too high it will spill over the top of the subject's head, lighting up the tip of the nose. (This has been called the "Rudolph effect" after a well-known reindeer.)

By using only back lights with no front lighting, a silhouette effect can be created (Figure 6.33). This can be used for dramatic effect or to hide someone's identity. In trying to successfully eliminate all front lighting, watch out for reflected light from walls or the floor. Occasionally, predominant back light alone can add drama to video—especially if clear details are less important than dramatic effect (Figure 6.34).

In addition to the main subject, there is also one other aspect of a scene that needs to be lit: the background.

FIGURE 6.33
By using only back lights and background lights (no keys or fills) a silhouette effect can be created. This can be used for dramatic effect or to hide someone's identity.

FIGURE 6.34
Although it may exceed the TV brightness ratio, predominant back light (in this case, hazy sunlight with no fill) can add a dramatic effect to a scene. Note that shadow detail is sacrificed here for dramatic effect.

BACKGROUND LIGHTS

background light: Light intended to illuminate a background. Generally about two-thirds the intensity of the key light.

Background lights (Figure 6.35) are used to illuminate the background area and add needed depth and separation between scene elements. Once the background light is added, the lighting setup is complete.

Figure 6.36B shows the effect of the key, fill, back and background lights. Note in Figure 6.36A that the three lights (key, fill and back light) form the points of a triangle; hence, this kind of lighting is also referred to as triangular lighting.

Many different types of lights can be used to illuminate backgrounds, including Fresnels, scoops and broads. In fact, it makes very little difference as long as you are able to throw an even light across the background (and not hit unintended subject matter in the process). The evenness of the light on the background is especially important when chroma key is being used. (Chroma key will be covered in Chapter 9.)

There are special lights designed to be used as background lights. Some lights are intended to be hung from the ceiling and some are designed to be placed on the floor (whenever they can be hidden from view). The lamps in background lights are mounted in an offset position in relation to the reflector,

FIGURE 6.35
The background light(s) can be placed anywhere that will provide an even light across all background areas while not being seen in camera shots. Scoops and Fresnels can be used, as well as special background lights.

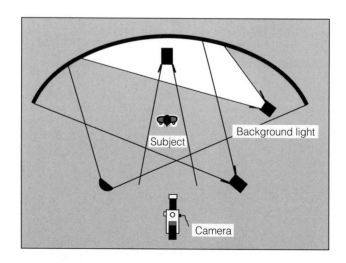

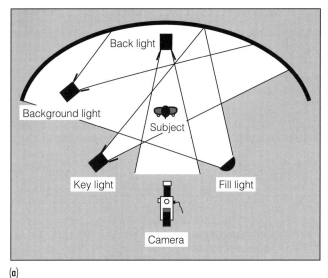

(a)

(b)

FIGURES 6.36A and 6.36B
In Figure 6.36A all lights are in place: key, fill, back and background lights. The result is shown in Figure 6.36B. To achieve this effect each light must be at the proper intensity.

which means they will throw a beam of light at an angle. This enables them to be used as close as 3 to 5 feet from a background.

The four lights we've thus far discussed, keys, fills, backs and background lights, are basic to all good lighting design.

LIGHTING RATIOS

One more important aspect of three-point lighting remains to be covered: lighting ratios. Since the key light is the dominant light on the subject, it is stronger than the fill light. In color production the fill should normally be one-half the intensity of the key. This key-to-fill difference is expressed in terms of a *lighting ratio*.[4] If the key light is twice as bright as the fill, the ratio will be 2 to 1. Using the 2-to-1 ratio, if the key light is 200 foot candles, the fill will be 100 foot candles. Although many lights may be used in a scene, the lighting ratio always refers to the ratio between the key and fill lights.

The purpose of controlling the key-to-fill ratio is to control the form, dimension and surface texture in subject matter. For general production work (in color[5]) the 2-to-1 ratio gives the best overall rendition (refer to Figure 6.36B). To achieve dramatic effects, and occasionally to meet the needs of special subject matter, other ratios can be used. More on that later.

Lighting ratio is not the same as contrast ratio. The latter is the difference in brightness (reflectance value) between the brightest and darkest subject matter

lighting ratio: The intensity relationship between the key and fill lights with the key light representing the larger number. Typically 2 to 1 for color and 3 to 1 for black-and-white television.

---

4. In still photography lighting ratios are sometimes measured in a different way: by comparing reflected light readings from the highlight and shadow areas of a scene. When properly done with a spot meter, this is a more accurate approach. However, for most applications it is simplier and faster to determine lighting ratios by measuring the difference between the intensity of the key and fill lights.

5. In black-and-white television and photography, the key-to-fill ratio is normally 3 to 1. This slightly higher ratio provides the needed visual separation that color would otherwise provide.

in a scene. Of course, since the amount of light an object reflects is dependent upon the amount of light falling on it, the contrast ratio is directly influenced by the lighting ratio.

If a foot-candle meter isn't available to establish the proper lighting ratios, a standard photographic light meter can be used. The f-stop differences between the intensity of lights can be translated into lighting ratios. (See Table 6.2.) As an example, to achieve a standard 2-to-1 ratio, a light meter could be used to make the key light one f-stop more than the fill. The key light in this example could (when measured by itself) call for an exposure of f/16 and the fill light (by itself) an exposure of f/11.

Occasionally, it is desirable to minimize or smooth out the surface detail of subject matter. If highly diffused key and fill lights are used close to the camera, there will be a flattening of the appearance of subject matter and a minimizing of surface detail and texture. Reducing the key-to-fill lighting ratio to 1 to 1 (with the key intensity equal to the fill intensity) adds to this effect. (Compare Figures 6.4A and 6.4B.) Although form and dimension will be sacrificed, flat lighting can minimize wrinkles and skin problems and create a soft, flattering effect for the human face. (Refer back to Figure 6.10.) This might be important in a cosmetic commercial, for example.

In contrast, by increasing the key-to-fill ratio to 5:1 and beyond, surface detail and texture will be emphasized—especially if hard key light is used at an angle from 65 to 85 degrees (Figure 6.4B). By manipulating these three areas of lighting—coherence, key-fill angles and lighting ratios—a striking level of control can be exercised over the appearance of subject matter.

BACK-LIGHT INTENSITY

To provide the subtle rim of light around subjects, the back light has to be slightly brighter than the key light. In the case of an on-camera person, back-light intensity will depend on the hair color of the subject and what he or she is wearing. Subjects who have brown hair and clothes in the low to mid-gray range will require a back light one and one-half times the intensity of the key. Assuming a key light intensity of 150 foot candles, the back light will be 225 foot candles. The f-stop approach (Table 6.2) to figuring the ratio can be used by making the back light two-thirds of an f-stop brighter than the key light. An Afro hair style and a dull black coat will take considerably more back light than a blond wearing light clothing. Be careful to observe the effect on a monitor or in the camera viewfinder.

With subjects who have hair and clothing of similar reflectance, the intensity of the back light is not too difficult to determine. The problem comes in with

TABLE 6.2

Lighting Ratio	F-stop Difference
1 to 1	no difference (flat lighting)
2 to 1	1 f-stop (general color work)
3 to 1	$1\frac{2}{3}$ f-stops (general black-and-white)
4 to 1	2 f-stops (low-key dramatic effect)
8 to 1	3 f-stops (low-key dramatic effect)

dark hair and a light coat, or blond hair and dark clothing. In such cases the beam of the back light(s) can be partially masked off with barn doors so that the brightest part of the beam will hit the dark areas.

The color temperature of the back light is not nearly as critical as that of the key and fill lights. Within limits, dimmers can be used. In fact, a slight yellow color shift in the back light (which can also be created by a light, straw-colored gel) will improve the performance of a chroma keyer (see Chapter 9), which is set to key out a blue background. Dark hair sometimes picks up a blue cast and produces a ragged, tearing effect with a chroma keyer. Going a step further, the use of two back lights is helpful to a chroma keyer that has trouble deciding what to key out of the scene and what to leave in. The use of two back lights will be discussed later.

BACKGROUND LIGHT INTENSITY

Because the background is of secondary importance to the center of interest, it should receive a lower level of illumination. Generally, the intensity of background lights should be about two-thirds the intensity of key lights. This will ensure that the central subject matter stands out slightly from the background. In case you have forgotten Math 101, you can get two-thirds of any number by multiplying it by 2 and dividing the result by 3. Therefore, if the key is 200 foot candles, the light falling on the background should measure about 130 foot candles. If you are using a photographic meter to set light intensities, the background light(s) should read one-half to two-thirds of a stop less on the exposure meter than the key light.

Since backgrounds are typically two-dimensional (flat) and of secondary importance to the main subject matter, the placement of the lights and their angles is not critical. But, the light across the background should be even—especially for chroma key. By walking along the background with a light meter, any dark or bright areas can be quickly found.

Subject-to-Background Distance

Shadows on backgrounds from mic booms, moving talent etc. can be distracting and annoying. Background lights will lighten but normally not eliminate shadows. However, by moving subjects 9 or more feet away from a background, you will find (if the key is at an elevation 45 degrees) that shadows will end up on the floor instead of on a wall. (Recall that under the discussion of the key light, we also stressed the need to position boom mics parallel to keys in order to minimize boom shadows on backgrounds.)

Sometimes it is necessary for talent (and therefore a boom mic, if one is being used) to move in close to a background. The use of a large softlight (Figure 6.9) will render shadows invisible—if you don't mind the soft, diffused look it will create in the video.[6]

There is another reason that adequate subject-to-background distance should be maintained: by altering the intensity and position of background lights, you can make separate lighting adjustments on the background without affecting the main subject matter. This will provide the opportunity to control the tonal range and even the color brightness of the background. Unduly dark backgrounds can

6. Because of resolution losses in the broadcast transmission process, soft lighting will look sharper on a control room monitor than it will on a home TV receiver. This difference should be kept in mind in evaluating all lighting.

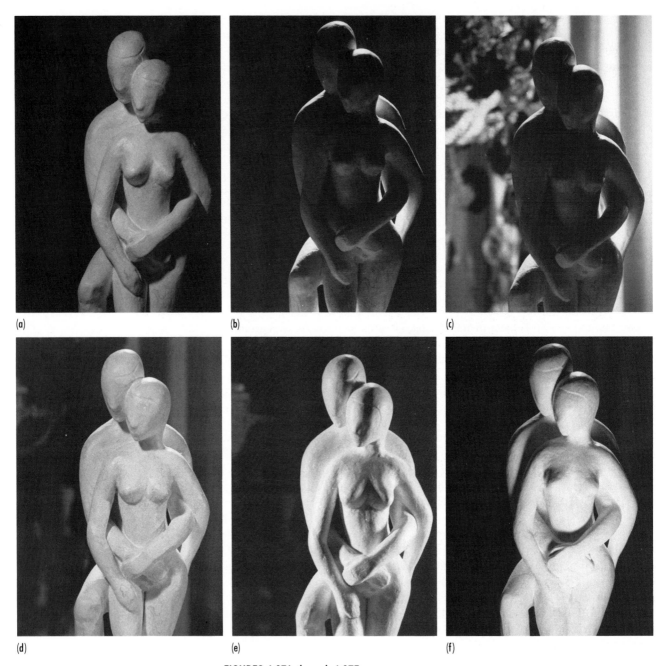

FIGURES 6.37A through 6.37F

This series of photos is designed to help you see the effects of various lighting setups. Figure 6.37A shows the stark effect of a single key light. Although this might be desirable for a specific dramatic scene, it has little use in day-to-day television production. A single back light (Figure 6.37B) highlights the subjects and separates them from the background. The addition of a background light (Figure 6.37C) brings the subjects into proper perspective in their surroundings. This effect can be used whenever you want to hide the identity of someone on camera. When a key, fill, back light and background light are combined, the subjects become fully visible, with normal form and dimension. Combining a key, fill, back light and low-level background light produces the standard three-point lighting effect (Figure 6.37D). Exaggerated depth and dimension are created when cross-keys are used, one at 95 degrees to the left and one at 95 degrees to the right of the camera (Figure 6.37E). Unfortunately, this also creates a shadow area directly in front of the camera. Finally, in Figure 6.37F the key light is put at the feet of the figures, creating an eerie effect.

be "brightened up" by using a higher level of illumination, and bright, intrusive backgrounds can be "brought down" by lowering background illumination.

Once lighting is understood in terms of quality, intensity, angles, lighting ratios and the effect of keys, fills, back lights and background lights, a variety of effects can be created. Figures 6.37A through 6.37F show just a few lighting effects with a simple subject. The caption explains the light(s) used for each figure.

THE LIGHTING GRID

In most television studios, lights have to be regularly moved to accommodate a variety of productions. Therefore, a system had to be developed that would allow a limited number of lights to be quickly moved and plugged in at any place within the studio. The *lighting grid,* which consists of a network of crisscrossed pipes mounted a few feet from the ceiling, serves this purpose. Since lighting grids are normally at heights of 15 or more feet, large, rolling ladders or wheel-based light platforms are used to hang the lights.

A *C-clamp* mounted on the yokes of studio lights makes it possible to attach lights at any point on the grid. A half-inch, open-ended (or crescent-type) wrench is normally used to tighten down a large setscrew in the C-clamp. Because lights are heavy and would pose a severe threat to safety if they fell, a **safety chain** is also routinely used. (C-clamps have been known to come loose or even break when a light was accidentally hit by a mic boom.) Once a light is mounted, the safety chain is looped over the pipe and snapped to the frame of the light.

Normal AC plugs are not used on grid-mounted lights. Instead, three-conductor twist lock connectors are the norm (Figure 6.38). Typically, grid pipes carry the AC power and provide connectors for plugging in lights. Grid connectors are normally numbered to make quick identification possible in lighting control.

lighting grid: A crisscross arrangement of pipes suspended below the studio ceiling used to hold lights.

C-clamp: A screw-down clamp used to mount lights to studio grid pipes and lighting stands.

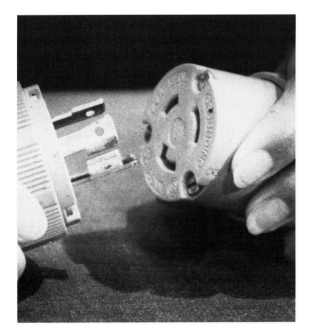

FIGURE 6.38
Most studio lights use a twist lock connector. Not only are these more rugged than standard AC connectors, but their locking feature helps ensure that the connectors will not unexpectedly pull apart.

FIGURES 6.39A and 6.39B
Figures 6.39A and 6.39B show lighting setups for multiple subjects. Note that the basic three-point lighting approach has simply been duplicated for each talent position. With each subject separately lit (as opposed to lighting several people with one set of lights) you can tailor the lighting to meet the needs of each individual.

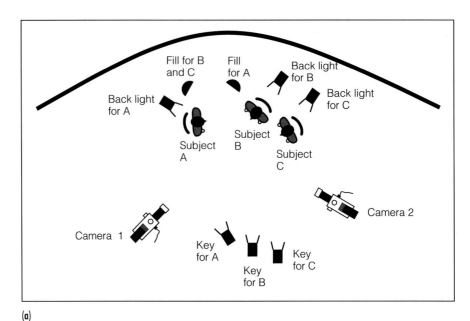

(a)

(b)

APPROACHES TO LIGHTING MULTIPLE SUBJECTS

Thus far, our discussion and illustrations have covered the lighting of one subject only. Unfortunately, things aren't always this simple. Figures 6.39A and 6.39B show lighting setups for multiple subjects. If you examine the figures carefully, you will note that the basic, three-point lighting approach has simply been duplicated for each talent position. This is the safe way of lighting several subjects in one setting—especially if you know which camera will be shooting the close-up of each subject. (Remember, you should establish your key and fill angles from the perspective of the close-up camera.) With each subject separately lit (as opposed to lighting several people with one set of lights) you can tailor the lighting to each individual subject. This can be important in accommodating blond hair, bald heads and wide variations in clothing, skin tones etc.

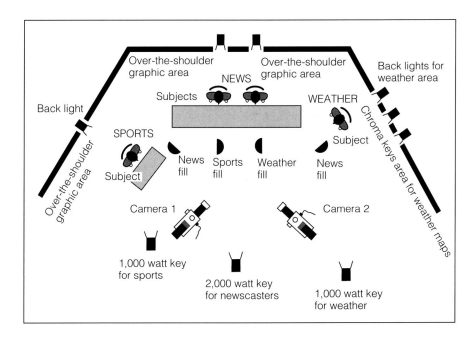

FIGURE 6.40
In lighting news, sports and weather sets we often must light the talent for two camera positions. The anchor position is lit so that close-ups can be taken from two angles. One angle provides a simple close-up of the person. The second angle allows a background space for over-the-shoulder visuals. Note that from both angles the appropriate key-fill effect is retained. In determining the placement of keys and fills we must also be sure that no one's face will be dark, even when they turn away from the camera and talk to the person next to them.

Barn doors are commonly used to keep lights intended for one person from spilling over onto another person or area.

News, Weather and Sports

Once the basic technique of three-point lighting is understood, you can move on to lighting more complex productions.

In doing news, sports and weather we often must light the talent for two (and sometimes more) camera positions. Figure 6.40 shows a typical studio news setup. Note that the anchor position is lit so that close-ups can be taken from two angles. One angle provides a simple close-up of the person. The second angle allows a background space for over-the-shoulder visuals. Note that from both angles we retain the appropriate key-fill effect. In determining the placement of keys and fills we must also be sure that at no time—even when on-camera people turn away from the camera and talk to each other—will the side of anyone's face be dark. Of course, every studio situation will be different. But the object is to arrive at good lighting through well–thought-out planning while avoiding the temptation of just putting lights everywhere so that you will automatically cover every conceivable angle. (The flat, lifeless effect will quickly reveal a lack of knowledge or planning.)

Multiple-Purpose Lights

Sometimes, because of limitations in lighting instruments, the proximity of subjects, or the number of subjects on camera, multiple subjects can be treated as a single subject while still adhering to the three-point lighting setup. For example, in an interview setup with four people behind a desk, a single key and single fill light can be aimed at all four subjects. Two back lights (or possibly even one) can be used for all four people. Although you can, upon occasion, use one back light for multiple subjects, remember that it is only by using a separate back light for each subject you will be able to control for variations in hair, clothing etc.

FIGURE 6.41

Sometimes lights can be used for multiple purposes. Here, the basic three-point lighting setup is achieved with only three lights. Note that the key light for A also serves as a back light for B; and the key for B serves as a back light for A. A single fill light serves both subjects.

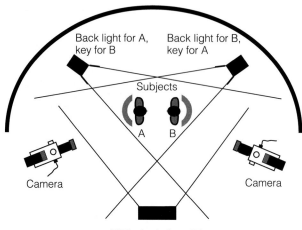

In Figure 6.41 note that the key light for each subject is also serving as the back light for the other. If distances are carefully controlled, the lights can be 50 percent brighter as back lights than in their role as keys. This can work well under carefully controlled situations where you know in advance the color of each person's hair (or, in some cases the lack of hair), and the color of clothes that will be worn by each person. The position of the chairs in this case will be especially critical to lighting intensity. Once lighting is set up in this situation, neither chair can be moved without altering the lighting ratios.

Approaches to Area Lighting

So far we've covered subjects conveniently confined to one place. But what if one or more subjects must be free to roam around while on camera? There are four ways this can be handled.

First, the entire area can be flooded with a ***base light,*** which is an overall, even fill light. Important close-up camera talent positions can then be keyed with lights at twice the intensity of the base light. A small piece of tape placed on the floor will provide marks for the talent to hit as they move from one major camera position to another. With this approach you will probably not want to restrict the beams of the lights with barn doors any more than necessary, since illuminated areas should be kept large enough to give talent a margin of error in missing their marks.

Using a Stand-In Lighting at the various positions can be checked on camera by having a ***stand-in*** (a person of similar height and skin color and wearing similar clothing as the talent involved) slowly walk through the positions. During the show's dress rehearsal (with the actual talent) any remaining problems can be noted. These can be fixed during the break between the dress rehearsal and the actual production.

The second approach to lighting talent who must be free to roam involves keying, filling and backlighting the entire area. Here, the whole working range — assuming it's not too large — is treated as a single subject. This will require a powerful (high-wattage) key light positioned at a great enough distance to cover the entire set. If the key is placed in the center of the set, 90 degrees to the back wall, the angle will be appropriate for cameras positioned at each side of the set. One or more scrimmed Fresnels can serve as fills. (Scoops would probably not throw light far enough to cover a large area.) If more than one key has to be used to cover the area, they should be positioned as close together as

base light: Even lighting used over a set or production area. Sometimes, a set is initially lit with a base light, and then the key back lights are added.

stand-in: An individual who resembles the main talent and can substitute for them during specific phases of production. Often used during lighting setups.

possible to reduce the problem of multiple shadows and multiple catchlights in eyes. Multiple back lights will have to be used. They should be aimed so that they produce slightly overlapping pools of light over the whole talent area. The talent should be able to walk from one area to another without obvious variations in back light.

The third approach to lighting a large area is to divide the set into individual areas and key, fill and backlight each area. Often, large interior settings are divided into four parts for keying, filling and back lighting. Typically, the lights at the edge of each of these areas will just begin to merge. With this approach it is important to make sure that close-ups will not be in the transition points between lighted areas. Keep in mind the sources of light that may be suggested by the setting — visible table lamps, windows etc. Place the key lights so they will be consistent with these suggested sources of illumination.

The last solution to lighting a large area could be used to simulate an interior at night. This technique would use a lighting ratio of about 4 to 1 or 6 to 1, and the talent would move in and out of specifically defined set areas. Only important, close-up areas would be lit, leaving the rest of scene relatively dark. With this approach it is especially important to place keys so that they are consistent with the visible or suggested sources of light within the setting. If a person were sitting next to a reading lamp, the key would have to be angled so that the light would appear to be coming from the table light. This approach to keying, which is called *following source,* is widely used in dramatic productions. In some cases you may want to use a low-level base light over the entire set to cover "in-between areas," to keep them from going completely dark.

HIGH-KEY AND LOW-KEY LIGHTING

The nighttime interior setting described above is an example of low-key lighting. Contrary to what is sometimes written, *low key* and *high key* do not refer to the overall intensity of the key and fill lights, but to their ratios and angles. **Low-key lighting,** which produces a predominance of shadow areas, is created with a high key-to-fill ratio (6 to 1 and beyond) and oblique key angles. This would be used for dark looking, dramatic night scenes etc. (Refer back to Figure 6.1 for an example of low-key lighting.)

In contrast, **high-key lighting** is bright and upscale. It uses a low key-to-fill ratio with barely perceptible shadow areas. Daytime beach scenes, the interiors of offices under fluorescent lighting etc. would be high key.

SINGLE-CAMERA VS. MULTIPLE-CAMERA LIGHTING

At the beginning of the chapter we noted that compared to film, video often looks flat and dimensionless and that the reason largely centers on lighting. At this point we can delve into the reasons for this difference.

Since film is almost always shot with a single camera (representing a single subject-to-camera angle), lighting can be optimized for every scene and take. While a studio news show can be shot (and lit for) only two cameras, a typical television sit-com involves three or four cameras spanning almost 160 degrees. Since the director needs to be able to cut to any camera at any time, the lighting must be able to "hold up" throughout this entire range. To avoid the possibility of having any shadow areas, the "safe" way of lighting this type of production is to light relatively flat, using multiple key lights to cover every possible camera angle. This means that dimension and form — the things that can make film scenes so much more effective — are lost.

following source: The use of lights in a lighting design that are consistent with the apparent sources of light within the room or setting. If a table lamp in a scene is visible and supposedly turned on, subjects near the lamp should be keyed so that the lamp appears to be supplying their illumination.

low-key lighting: Lighting characterized by a high key-to-fill ratio that results in predominant shadow areas. Typically used for night scenes in dramatic productions.

high-key lighting: Lighting characterized by minimal shadows and a low key-to-fill ratio.

FIGURE 6.42
Unlike single-camera productions, most situation comedies have to be lit to accommodate three or four camera angles at the same time. This means that lighting ends up being somewhat flat. While the high-key effect (minimal shadow areas) makes the production look brighter, there is a loss of depth and dimension.

Although this high-key effect may be somewhat appropriate for TV situation comedies (Figure 6.42), in dramatic productions it leaves much to be desired. Fortunately, as we will see in Chapter 16, single-camera video production is now able to take advantage of the same lighting strategies afforded to filmmakers. One of the major strategies is called following source.

FOLLOWING SOURCE

In the late 1980s, television production moved to CCD cameras, which are similar to film cameras in their ability to handle contrast ranges. Instead of a basically flat lighting approach, lighting directors such as George Dibie brought the lighting techniques to television that had long been associated with film.[7] Dibie said that because of today's CCD cameras he could now ". . . light for my video cameras exactly the way I light for film cameras." Whether you are simulating day or night, the most important thing is to follow source, according to Dibie. "Windows, doors, lamps . . . these are the sources of light in a scene. [For] . . . one camera or multiple cameras, you deal with the feel of the source." The technique of following source has now become a standard approach in many dramatic productions.

7. George Spiro Dibie, a lighting director who received three Emmys for his innovative film and television work, was for many years president of Hollywood's American Society of Lighting Directors.

In following source, a lighting director must first determine where the obvious sources of illumination *are* (if they are visible) or *might be* (if they are not). If none is obvious, it becomes a matter of where a logical source of illumination might be. In a scene in a seedy flophouse this might be a bare light bulb hanging in the center of the room. It then becomes a matter a keying important camera close-up positions so that they are consistent with this suggested source of illumination. In the case of the flophouse, a dramatic effect could be achieved by crisscrossing hard light sources above the set so that actors seem as if they are illuminated by a bare light bulb. This effect can then be filled to achieve the desired lighting ratio: a 4-to-1 ratio for a basic effect, a 6-to-1 to 10-to-1 ratio for a harsher, more dramatic effect.

In Figure 6.43 the young girl is being primarily lit from behind. The source here is a window. In the studio the same effect is commonly achieved by using a *kicker light,* a light coming from behind and to one side of the subject. Kicker lights can simulate windows, table lamps and fireplaces.

LIGHTING CONTROL EQUIPMENT

Whereas lighting directors used to use AC patch cords and large patch panels to route specific lights to specific dimmers and switches, today, studio lighting is switched electronically at a *lighting board* (a centralized lighting control device). Figures 6.44A and 6.44B illustrate two types of lighting boards. Whatever system is used, it must provide a way of turning on and off (and possibly dimming) the various lights in the studio from one central point.

FIGURE 6.43
This young girl is being lit from a window behind her. In the studio the same effect is achieved by using a kicker light, a light coming from behind and to one side of the subject. Kicker lights can simulate windows, table lamps and fireplaces.

(a)

FIGURES 6.44A and 6.44B
Figures 6.44A and 6.44B illustrate two types of lighting boards. Normally, each AC outlet in the studio lighting grid has a number, and these are assigned to specific dimmer circuits (and groups of dimmers) by entering their numbers on a keypad. A video display terminal (VDT) shows the studio lighting grid and light-dimmer assignments.

(b)

kicker, kicker light: A light typically placed between the back light and the fill lights. Sometimes used to simulate the light from a window behind a subject.

lighting board: A centralized control system for studio lights. Most lighting boards allow for the dimming of lights and include provisions for controlling each AC outlet in a studio *lighting grid*.

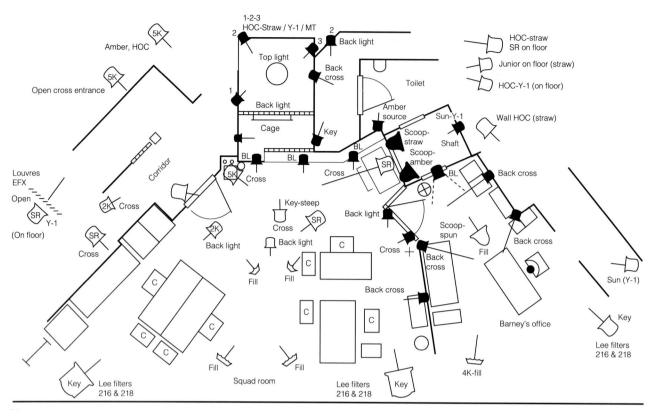

(a)

(b)

FIGURES 6.45A and 6.45B

In many complex sets, such as this setting for the *"Barney Miller"* series, lighting is designed to illuminate areas instead of specific people. Although a detailed analysis of this plot is beyond the scope of this book, the drawing (Figure 6.45A) provides an idea of the complexity of such lighting plots. This particular set took two people more than 10 hours to light. George Dibie provided this "simplified" lighting plot. Figure 6.45B shows the effect of this lighting design.

In some lighting control devices a key pad is used to enter the numbers of the grid connector positions being used. Once this is done lights can be individually controlled or grouped and regulated together as a subgroup. The more sophisticated lighting boards can be programmed with settings on hundreds of lights. A complete production containing numerous scenes, each involving scores of lights (even at different dimmer settings), can be programmed so that during the production the lighting pattern of each scene can be instantly recalled. A video display terminal (VDT) is commonly used to display how the lights are configured.

CREATING A LIGHTING PLOT

In a large production a lighting director (after reading a script and consulting with the director and others) will draw a *lighting plot,* a drawing to scale with all lights indicated. (Figure 6.45A is an example of a lighting plot. Figure 6.45B shows the effect of this lighting design. We'll discuss the process of doing scale drawings in Chapter 11.) The lighting director will pay particular attention to the close-up positions, as decided by the director. Assistants will then use the plot when they hang the lights. With the help of one or more stand-ins and lighting assistants, the lighting director can then check the final effect on a monitor.

lighting plot: A detailed drawing, generally to scale, showing the placement of each light in relation to talent positions and scenic elements.

ON-LOCATION LIGHTING

Lighting Packages

Today's producer of short, on-location segments needs lights that are lightweight, portable and easy to set up. To meet this need there are *lighting kits* consisting of several 420-watt to 2,000-watt, open-faced tungsten-halogen lights with stands. (See Figure 6.46.) Many of these portable lights can be focused; that is, their beams can be pinned down or flooded. Most portable lights accommodate barn doors for masking off the sides of the beam and square frames for attaching gels, scrims and filters.

Setting Up On-Location Lighting

The three-point lighting setup already discussed will provide excellent results in the field. Figures 6.47A and 6.47B show an on-location lighting setup in a small office for the A (interviewee) and B (interviewer) camera positions. (Reverse-angle, single-camera setups for interviews will be discussed in Chapters 15 and 16.)

Because of time or space limitations, it is often not possible to set up a key, fill, back and background lights—especially when doing fast-paced ENG work. It then becomes a matter of knowing what compromises can (safely) be made.

First, a reflector can be used as a fill light (refer back to Figure 6.31). This will save a bit of time by eliminating the need to set up a separate light.

Next, a single soft front light can replace both the key and fill. Either an umbrella reflector key light (Figure 6.9) or a light bounced off a white card (Figures 6.30A and 6.30B) will work. The light source should be placed 20 to 30 degrees off to either side of the camera. In a small office or room, much of this soft light will carry over to the background. If the background is close behind a subject, this may eliminate the need for a background light. (Since you are using a diffused light source, shadows will be less noticeable.) An extra light

FIGURE 6.46
Today's producer of short, on-location segments needs lights that are lightweight, portable and easy to set up. To meet this need there are lighting kits consisting of several 420- to 2,000-watt, open-faced tungsten-halogen lights with stands.

FIGURES 6.47A and 6.47B
Single-camera, on-location interviews are normally taped in two segments. Two videotapes, an A-roll and a B-roll, are made. First, the person being interviewed is lit (Figure 6.47A). With the camera focused on this person, the interviewer (off camera) asks the questions needed, and the answers are recorded. At this point the camera and lighting are reversed (Figure 6.47B). A B-roll tape is then made of the interviewer asking all the questions (over again) on camera. Various interviewer reaction shots are also shot at this time. This process will be covered in more detail in Chapters 15 and 16. Note that because of the small size of the office, the fill and key lights provide the background light. In larger rooms a separate background light would add depth and separation to the video.

can be used as a back light. Depending upon the background, you may want to forgo the back light and use the second light as a background light. Either will provide some degree of subject-background separation.

The simplest and quickest lighting setup for doing a short interview is to use a single light bounced off the ceiling. (See Figures 6.48A and 6.48B.) The bounced-light approach works best with low, white or light-gray ceilings. The white acoustic tile commonly found in offices works well. Bounced light creates a soft even light throughout the room, an effect that is similar to what we are used to seeing with overhead fluorescent lights.

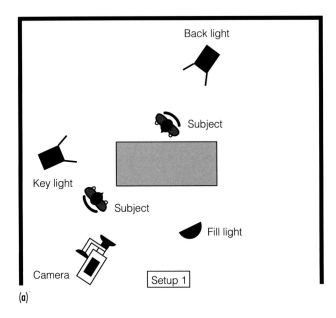

(a)

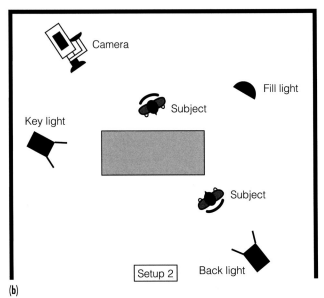

(b)

(a)

(b)

FIGURES 6.48A and 6.48B
For doing short, on-location interview segments, the quickest and simplest lighting setup is bounced light. This technique works best in rooms with low, white or light-gray ceilings. Bounced light creates a soft, even light throughout the room, an effect that is similar to overhead fluorescent lighting. In large rooms with light ceilings, the lighting setup shown in Figure 6.48A can be used. For smaller rooms with light walls and ceiling this can be modified as shown in Figure 6.48B.

Occasionally, a light mounted on top of a camcorder can be aimed at the ceiling for a bounced-light effect. In this case the camera (and attached light) should be placed far enough back from the subject so that the light will come down at an acceptable angle. If the light is too close to the subject, dark eye shadows will result. If the walls of the room are a light, neutral color, they will reflect part of the bounced light and more fully fill in shadow areas.

To help compensate for the color that the ceiling and walls add to the light, remember to color balance the camera under the bounced (rather than the direct) light. Bounced light will not work, of course, if the ceiling is too high or too dark. While bounced light solves the problem of uneven lighting, its disadvantage is that the effect is often too soft; i.e., it hides the texture, form and dimension of subject matter.

CAMERA LIGHTS

ENG and EFP Work

In spot news work, where quality is secondary to getting a story, single, tungsten-halogen lights (called **sunguns**) are sometimes used as a sole source of illumination. These lights can be mounted on the top of the camera (Figure 6.49) or held by an assistant. Although these lights can be plugged into a wall socket, for the sake of portability they are generally powered by batteries — sometimes by the same batteries that power the camera.

The quality from a camera-mounted light leaves much to be desired. As a result of the straight-on angle involved, picture detail and depth are sacrificed. Because of the relationship between distance and light intensity, the detail and color of foreground objects often become washed out, and objects in the distance typically go completely dark. For this reason a camera light works best if important subject matter is at about the same distance from the camera. This type of light provides the same questionable quality as the familiar single-flash-on-the-camera does in still photography.

There are other disadvantages in using a camera-mounted light; it can be intrusive and even disruptive. This rather bright light mounted right above the camera lens tends to make subjects quite conscious of the presence of the camera. Consequently, it often becomes rather intimidating to subjects. Exposure can also be a problem. As subjects move toward or away from the camera, or, as in a fast-breaking news story, people momentarily cross the camera's path,

FIGURE 6.49
In spot news work where quality is secondary to getting a story, single tungsten-halogen lights (called sunguns) are sometimes used as a sole source of illumination. These lights can be mounted on the top of the camera or held by an assistant. They are generally powered by batteries—sometimes by the same batteries that power the camera.

the camera's auto-iris may constantly readjust—at the expense of good exposure on the center of interest. But since the object of news work is often just to "get the story," poor video is better than no video.

Camera Lights on Studio Cameras

In multiple-camera studio productions, small Fresnel spotlights are sometimes mounted on the top of studio cameras to serve as an **eye light.** These eye lights are used to supplement studio lighting—especially when the basic lighting is not adequate. They are generally switched on to lighten eye shadows and add sparkle (a catchlight) to the eyes. Although they may make up for lighting deficiencies in difficult situations, they can also introduce problems. In addition to the flattening and distance effects already discussed, when a camera with a camera light is moved during a multiple-camera production, the change in lighting may be noticed in other camera shots.

USING EXISTING LIGHT IN ENG WORK

Considering the shortcomings of the single camera-light approach in ENG/EFP work and the difficulty involved in setting up multiple lights, it is often best to use **existing light**—the natural light present at a location. With today's sensitive CCD cameras, this is generally not a problem (Figure 6.50). Existing light is actually more realistic (and honest) since it represents actual conditions. Even so, existing light can present three problems:

1. The light may be of mixed color temperatures: a mixture of incandescent, fluorescent or even daylight from a window.

FIGURE 6.50
In doing ENG and EFP work, it is often best to use existing light—the natural light present at a location. With today's sensitive CCD cameras, this is generally not a problem—even when using 1/250 or 1/500 second shutter speeds to stop action.

2. The overall light level might be too low. Although office areas are typically lit at 40 foot candles (which is well within the capability of CCD cameras), some stories must be taped in convention halls, meeting rooms etc., where the light level can be much lower. This means that cameras will have to use wide f-stops, often aided by the camera's built-in sensitivity boost.

3. Finally, the contrast ratio between lights may be too high. This is the most common problem. For example, the source of light may be coming from the wrong direction, creating dark shadows in critical areas, or the light can consist of hard, overhead light that creates eye shadows. In this case moving a table lamp, closing the blinds or curtains or switching on or off selected lights in the room will often solve the problem.

LIGHT PLACEMENT PROBLEMS

Setting Up Lights

Unlike the studio situation where lights are hung from the lighting grid, on-locations lights are mounted on light stands. Key and fill lights are generally easy to position; stands are just placed at 45 degrees on either side of the camera. Back lights are another issue. They can't be hung from a lighting grid as they can in a studio, and a light stand behind the subject would be seen on camera. There are two possible solutions.

First, a back light may be clipped to the top of a book case or an exposed rafter—or any convenient, out-of-view anchoring point. If this option isn't available, you might consider assembling a *lighting goal post* out of plastic pipe and clipping the light to the center. One or more back lights can be hung from the middle, and the wires can be taped to the pipe. The top and sides of the goal

FIGURE 6.51
Two back lights provide a "wrap-around" rim of light around subject matter. They can be used when you want to add luster and brilliance to hair, or when two close-up cameras from slightly different angles must be used on a subject.

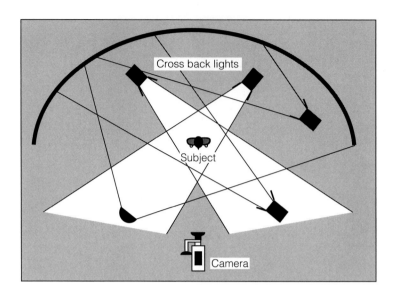

post should, of course, be outside the range of the widest shot. Many videographers carry a number of links of inexpensive, PVC plastic pipe (available in any hardware store) that can be quickly assembled in a variety of configurations.

The second solution is to use **cross back lights** (Figure 6.51). The two back lights are put on floor stands behind and on either side of the subject, just out of camera range. Many lighting directors prefer this effect because the lights spill around the sides of the subject giving a better subject-background separation.

POWER PROBLEMS

In setting up on-location lighting it is often necessary to figure out how many lamps a fuse or circuit breaker can handle. Although the standard (house current) voltage in the United States is between 110 and 120, in doing calculations it is common to assume a voltage of 100. This not only makes it is easier to do calculations, but it automatically provides a safety factor. By assuming a voltage of 100, the following formula can be used:

$$\text{amps} = \frac{\text{watts}}{100}$$

Therefore, a 500-watt lamp would draw 5 amps. A 20-amp fuse or breaker could handle up to 2,000 watts; a 30-amp fuse up to 3,000 watts, etc.

When setting up multiple lights, the wattage must be added. If a 1,000-watt key light, a 500-watt fill, a 500-watt back light and a 750-watt background light were all on the same 20-amp circuit, the combined amperage would blow a fuse or breaker. (Actually, it might take a few minutes to heat up the breaker enough to trip it — just long enough to get a good start on taping a segment!)

To keep from overloading a single fuse or breaker, it will often be necessary to run extension cords from separately fused circuits, possibly from an adjoining room. But, if they are not made of heavy gauge wire, long extension cords can lower voltage to lamps, resulting in drops in color temperature.

Since limited power on some locations — especially in older homes — is often a problem, upon occasion you may have no choice but to bring in an electrician to run a temporary, high-amperage line from the main fuse box. In remote areas a generator truck especially designed for film and television work may have to be rented. Although they use a gasoline- or diesel-powered engine, because of extensive sound-proofing they are virtually silent (an important consideration when you are doing sound recording on location).

THE ART OF LIGHTING

In describing the basic techniques for lighting in this chapter we've covered approaches that will provide highly acceptable results for most production work. At the same time, no attempt has been made to cover complex lighting needs. (Entire books have been written on that subject.) The lighting required for sophisticated, multiple-camera dramatic productions requires the skills and artistic ability of an experienced lighting director. The skills of such a person go far beyond the basic principles of lighting to an ability to creatively compose a lighting scheme that represents an artistic interpretation of both the scene and its role within the entire script. At this level of sophistication lighting moves into a true art form.

SUMMARY

The basic characteristics of light are coherence, quantity and color temperature. Each represents an important creative variable for television lighting.

A hard light source at an oblique angle brings out surface detail; soft light sources close to the camera hide surface detail and minimize depth and form. In on-location production, color temperature, which varies with time of day and cloud cover, must be carefully controlled from scene to scene to avoid postproduction technical continuity problems.

In setting up lighting, the intensity of various lighting instruments can best be measured by an incident light meter. Light intensity is commonly controlled by pinning down and flooding out the beams of lights, altering light-to-subject distance and (in the case of HMI lights) with the use of shutters. Dimmers, which alter color temperature, must be used with care. Standard fluorescent lights belong to a group of discharge-type lights that have an uneven and broken color spectrum that can result in undesirable color shifts.

Four types of lighting instruments commonly used in studios are Fresnels, scoops, broads and ellipsoidal spots. Barn doors and flags are used to mask off the edges of light. The three-point lighting technique typically uses a Fresnel as a key and a soft light source such as a scoop for a fill. A brightness ratio between the key and the fill of 2 to 1 is commonly used in color television. For normal subject matter a Fresnel at about one and one-half times the intensity of the key can be used as a back light. Background lights are normally two-thirds the intensity of the key.

In exterior, on-location productions the unobstructed sun (at the proper angle) can be used as a key, but for close-up work a fill in the form of a reflector or incandescent light at 5,500°K must be used to eliminate harsh shadows. In recent years lighting for television has come much closer to that of film. This move has included the principle of following source.

Lighting boards are used in the studio to control the lighting outlets in the overhead grid. Modern lighting boards can memorize hundreds of light settings, which can then be recalled as needed during a production.

In ENG work, where time and space are often limited, various compromises can be made in three-point lighting including using a reflector as a fill, using an umbrella reflector in the place of a key and a fill and using bounced light. Under the right conditions, existing light can be used on locations. For news and documentary work this is actually the most realistic and honest type of lighting. Although they are often necessary in ENG work, where just "getting the story" is the object, camera lights (sunguns) are the least desirable type of lighting.

In doing on-location production, care has to be taken not to exceed maximum wattage of fused circuits. Beyond the lighting setups described in this chapter, lighting moves into an area of creativity and experience reserved for those who make a thorough study of lighting effects and how they can be used to interpret scenes and convey moods.

KEY TERMS

back light	key light
background lights	kicker light
barn door	light meter
base light	lighting board
broads	lighting grid
C-clamp	lighting plot
catchlight	lighting ratio
coherence	lighting tent
cookie	low-key lighting
cross back lights	mixed-sources
cucalorus	pattern projector
diffusers	quality (coherence)
discharge lamp	quartz light
ellipsoidal spotlights	reflected light meter
existing light	reflector board
eye light	safety chain
fill light	scoop
filter frame	scrim
flags	soft light
flat lighting	spot meter
following source	stand-in
four-way barn doors	sunguns
gels	technical continuity problem
high-key lighting	tungsten-halogen light
incident light meter	two-way barn doors
intensity	umbrella reflector

Audio | 7

In this chapter we'll look at the following topics:

- The nature of sound and its role in television production
- Microphones and their use
- Monophonic, stereophonic and surround-sound recording and playback techniques
- The use of audio patching, control and mixing devices
- Sound synthesizers and MIDI
- Hard disk editing and editing workstations

AUDIO QUALITY

During the first few decades of television much more attention was paid to video than audio. But, in the late 1980s this started to change. Several things made the difference.

Originally, network programming had to go through hundreds of amplifiers as it made its way across the country. The constant reamplification of the analog signals introduced noise and distortion. Ironically, at that time good-quality sound in a TV set was a bit of a liability; it simply made the audio problems in the system more obvious. Today, TV network programming is distributed directly to stations by satellites, without the need of constant reamplification.

The next thing that spurred a greater interest in audio quality was the shift to TV stereo, using a system referred to as *MTS,* for multichannel TV sound. Listeners, used to the high quality of their stereo music systems, expected similar quality from television stereo. The basic stereo effect was enhanced in

MTS (multichannel TV sound): General designation for a stereo TV system.

159

1990, when productions started using various surround-sound and "dimensional sound" techniques that further widened and enhanced the perceived stereo effect.

Before discussing the basic audio production concepts used in television, sound itself must be understood.

AMPLITUDE AND FREQUENCY

Sound has two basic characteristics that must be controlled in production: amplitude and frequency.

Amplitude

amplitude: The strength of a video or audio signal.

decibel (dB): Unit of sound amplitude or loudness. See **dB/SPL** and **dBm**.

In sound, *amplitude* refers to loudness or volume level. It is measured in units of sound called *decibels,* or **dB.** There are two types of decibels. The first, **dB/SPL** (for sound pressure loudness), is a measure of acoustic power. This unit is used to measure the loudness of the sounds we hear throughout the day. Table 7.1 shows the loudness of various day-to-day sounds.

One hundred thirty dB/SPL is considered the threshold of pain and the point at which permanent ear damage can start.[1]

The second use of the term *decibel,* is **dBm** (for milliwatt reference level). This is the measure of audio-based electrical power—the kind displayed on the meters found in audio studios. In production we are primarily interested in dBm, commonly referred to as just dB.

One of the meters that displays this amplitude is a VU meter (volume units meter). As we will see, because of some limitations in the basic VU meter, newer versions, such as peak program and loudness meters, are preferred in many applications.

1. Exposure to sound levels of 130 dB/SPL and higher for a period of 20 minutes can cause permanent, irreversible hearing impairment. The U.S. Government's Occupational Safety and Health Act limits exposure to sounds at 115 dB/SPL to 15 minutes. As noted in Table 7.1, the sound level at some contemporary music concerts has been measured at 140 dB/SPL.

TABLE 7.1
Typical Sound Levels in Decibels

Sound	Average Decibels (dB/SPL)
Some contemporary music concerts	140
Jet aircraft taking off	125
Subway express train (close)	105
Niagara Falls, noisiest spot	95
Heavy traffic	85
Interior of car at 40 mph	75
Dept. store/noisy office	65
Normal conversation	60
Soft background music	30
Quiet whisper, 5 feet	20
Sound studio	15
Outdoor "silence"	10

Two versions of the basic VU meter are illustrated in Figures 7.1A and 7.1B. One scale (−20 to +3) represents volume units in dB (dBm) and another scale (zero to 100) is the modulation percentage (percentage of a maximum signal). Contrary to what logic might dictate, the zero dB point on a VU meter does not represent zero sound but, in a sense, the opposite—the maximum desirable sound level. This may seem confusing until you realize that the zero dB point on the meter is not comparable to zero dB/SPL; it's just an electrical reference point. Therefore, we commonly have sound levels on the VU meter that register in negative decibels—just as we have minus degrees (below zero) temperatures on the Fahrenheit scale.

The amplitude of the signal going through audio equipment must be carefully controlled throughout the production process. If the sound is allowed to pass through analog equipment at too low a level, noise will be introduced that will later become obvious when the sound level is increased to a normal amplitude. If the audio level is too high (appreciably above zero dB on the VU meter), objectionable distortion will result.[2]

We noted in Chapter 4 that the eye can handle a much greater contrast range than video cameras. Our ears have a similar advantage. We can comfortably hear a much greater *dynamic range* (loudness range) than our audio equipment can handle. For this reason the loudness range of many naturally occurring sounds (Table 7.1) must be reduced in audio production by raising the level of the softest sounds and lowering the level of the loudest sounds.[3]

Frequency

The second aspect of sound, **frequency,** relates to the basic **pitch** of the sound (how high or low it is). Frequency is measured in **hertz (Hz)** or cycles per second (CPS). A person with exceptionally good hearing will be able to hear sounds from 20 to 20,000 Hz.[4]

A frequency of 20 Hz would sound like an extremely low-pitched note on a pipe organ, almost a rumble. At the other end of the scale, 20,000 Hz (20 KHz) would be the highest pitched sound that can be imagined—even higher than the highest note on a violin or piccolo.

Since both ends of the 20 to 20,000 Hz range represent rather extreme limits, FM radio and TV concentrate on the range from 50 to 15,000 Hz. Although this doesn't quite cover the full range that can be perceived by people with good hearing, it does cover almost every naturally occurring sound. Taking some musical instruments as an example, the lowest note on a string bass is 36 Hz, and the highest note that can be played on a piccolo is about 3,520 Hz.

Timbre   Most sounds do not consist of just one pure tone or frequency. In fact, pure tones do not exist naturally and can only be generated with a tuning fork or special audio equipment. While naturally occurring sounds may have a dominant frequency or pitch, they are also accompanied by a rich and complex combination of other sounds and frequencies. If this were not the case we would only need one instrument in an orchestra, because middle C (or any

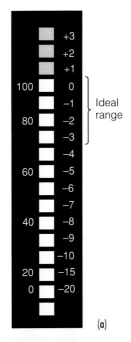

(a)

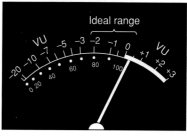

(b)

FIGURES 7.1A and 7.1B
Two versions of the basic VU meter are illustrated in these figures. On most meters one scale represents volume units in dB (−20 to +3) and the other scale is the modulation percentage (percentage of a maximum signal: 0 to 100).

dynamic range: The range between the weakest and loudest sounds that a particular piece of equipment can effectively reproduce.

---

2. Although in the discussion of dB/SPL and dBm it is necessary to distinguish between the two, in the remainder of this discussion the commonly used (and abbreviated) designation *dB* will be used instead of *dBm*.

3. The greater dynamic range of FM radio over AM radio is one of the reasons that classical music (with its inherently great dynamic range) sounds so much better on FM radio. Even more important, an FM signal is capable of reproducing a much greater frequency response than AM.

4. Men normally cannot hear sounds that are quite as high in pitch as women can. For men with good hearing, the range 16 to 16,000 Hz is sometimes given.

other note) played on a piano and middle C played on a bassoon, trombone, violin or guitar would sound exactly the same — a tone of about 240 Hz.

Timbre is the characteristic of sound that allows us to differentiate middle C as played on a piano from middle C as played on a French horn — or middle C as sung by any of several vocalists. The American Standards Association tackled the rather difficult task of defining **timbre** by describing it as "that attribute of auditory sensation in terms of which a listener can judge that two sounds similarly presented and having the same loudness and pitch are dissimilar." (You may hope that no one will ask for that definition on your next test!) Although this is a rather confounding definition, given the attributes of timbre, it is difficult to do much better. Timbre includes **harmonics** or **overtones** — sounds that are multiples ($2 \times$, $3 \times$, $4 \times$ etc.) of the basic pitch. In the case of a violin hitting a high C (at about 2,093 Hz), there would be harmonics (to varying degrees) at 4,186 Hz ($2 \times 2,093$), 8,372 Hz ($4 \times 2,093$) and 12,558 Hz ($6 \times 2,093$ Hz). The latter frequency, 12,558 Hz, explains why we need audio systems capable of detecting and reproducing sounds above 10,000 Hz. Harmonics of snare drums, symbols and even a string bass can also go beyond 10,000 Hz.

Harmonics are also related to the amplitude of musical notes. A very soft note played on a flute is almost a pure tone. But as the tone becomes louder, more harmonics are added. On a violin, harmonics are controlled in part by the movement of the fingers on the strings. So, while it is the fundamental frequency that establishes the basic pitch of a musical sound, harmonics add the richness and texture to the tone — and differentiate one instrument (or one voice) from another.

In addition to harmonics, timbre also consists of the complex interactions between sounds. A note played on a piano or guitar will be affected by the physical design of the instrument, and sound textures characteristic of the instrument will be created. This is one of the reasons middle C played on a Stradivarius violin sounds different from middle C played on an inexpensive, mass-produced violin.

It is only by being able to accurately reproduce the full richness, texture and dimension of instruments, voices and musical passages we can do justice to musical performances. The job of a musician or vocalist is to produce harmonious and mellifluous tones — a task many spend a lifetime trying to perfect. Our job in production is to reproduce these sounds as faithfully and realistically as possible.

The Amplitude-Frequency Relationship

Even though sounds of different frequencies may technically be equal in loudness as shown on a VU meter, human hearing may not perceive them as being equal. Just as the eye does not perceive all colors (frequencies of light) as being of equal intensity, the ear does not perceive all frequencies of sound as being equal in loudness. Figure 7.2 shows the frequency response of the human ear to pure tones of 85 dB/SPL and to music — a rich combination of tones — also at 85 dB/SPL. Note that, regardless of whether the sound consists of pure tones or music, the ear responds to them in a different way than a good-quality microphone does (Figure 7.3). Because of the reduced sensitivity of the ear to high and low frequencies, they must be louder to be perceived as being equal to other frequencies. For example, a 25 Hz tone would have to be many times louder than a tone in the 1,000 to 10,000 Hz range to be perceived as being equal in loudness.

If this is the case, the question arises, why not make mics with frequency/sensitivity response patterns similar to the ear? This might be a good idea if all

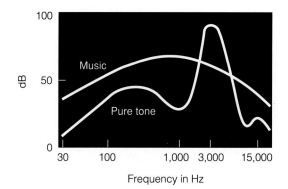

FIGURE 7.2

The ear perceives sounds of the same loudness differently, depending upon their complexity. This figure shows the frequency response of the human ear to pure tones of 85 dB/SPL and to music (a rich combination of tones) also at 85 dB/SPL. Although the two curves are quite different, they show one pattern: the ear has a reduced sensitivity to high and low frequencies.

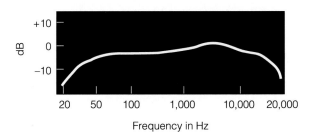

FIGURE 7.3

The frequency response of a good microphone should be fairly smooth and flat from about 30 to about 15,000 Hz. The slight peak at about 8,000 Hz on this mic response pattern is intentional; it emphasizes a frequency area associated with speech intelligibility.

listening conditions were the same, but the room, the speakers and the listener all affect the way sound will be perceived. In particular, the size of a room, together with how walls and objects within the room reflect sound, greatly influence sound perception. Some frequencies might be unnaturally emphasized by resonance within a room; others might be canceled or absorbed. Even the age of the listener will influence how frequencies will be perceived.

The only practical solution to this wide range of variables is to carefully maintain the frequency/loudness relationship during the recording and transmission process and then let the listener adjust these characteristics to suit specific playback conditions and personal preferences.

SHAPING PLAYBACK RESPONSE

The adjustment of frequency/loudness characteristics is primarily the purpose of the **bass** (low frequency) and **treble** (high frequency) controls on amplifiers. More sophisticated playback equipment will include a ***graphic equalizer*** (Figure 7.4), which goes a step further and allows specific frequency bands to be individually adjusted for loudness. These controls make it possible to tailor playback to the size and acoustics of a listening area. Unfortunately, with home TV receivers this level of control over the frequency/loudness relationship is typically reserved for **component** TV systems (systems that have separate tuners, video monitors and audio amplifiers).

Some audio equipment has additional controls. A **presence** control can add clarity to audio by increasing the level of sounds in the upper mid-range (6,000 to 10,000 Hz) area and attenuating (rolling off) sounds below 100 Hz. Using the presence control is often desirable for clearer reproduction of the human voice.

The **loudness** control is intended to compensate for a loss of bass when sound is reproduced at low levels. (At low levels most speakers do not respond

graphic equalizer: A series of adjustable frequency filters designed to vary the amplitude of successive parts of the audio spectrum.

FIGURE 7.4
A graphic equalizer allows control over specific frequency bands of the audio spectrum. Not only does this make it possible to enhance audio playbacks by emphasizing and attenuating certain frequency ranges, but audio playbacks can be tailored to the needs of specific listening conditions.

as well to bass; therefore, a bass boost is necessary to restore a realistic frequency response.)

Once equipment is set up to conform to specific playback conditions in a production facility, controls should not be varied.[5] This is the only way that you will be able to consistently evaluate and compare sound from a variety of programming sources.

LOUDNESS-PERCEPTION ISSUES

The fact that the human ear does not hear all frequencies equally leads to some audio problems. Broadcasters have been accused of transmitting commercials at a louder level than the program material. There are two explanations for this perception. Both have implications for television production.

First, commercials are typically recorded on modern equipment, capable of full-range frequency response. Old movies, to use a contrasting example, have sound tracks that are limited in their frequency response[6]—especially in the higher frequencies where the ear is more sensitive. Viewers will turn up the sound on old movies, only to discover a few minutes later that a commercial (with its greater proportion of higher frequencies) seems very loud. But on a VU meter there may be no difference between the old movie and the commercial.

5. Sound engineers are always looking for full-range sound sources for use in the evaluation of audio equipment and listening conditions. Some use one or more of the following CDs (compact discs): *Jazz,* by Ry Cooder (Warner Bros.); *Face Value,* Phil Collins (Atlantic); *Mussorgsky: Pictures at an Exhibition,* Jean Guilou, organ (Dorian); and any high-quality recording of Pachelbel's *Canon.*

6. Because of limitations in early optical sound track recording technology and inherent limitations in the optical recording process, optical tracks—especially in older films—did not respond to sounds above about 5,000 Hz. The ear is more sensitive to sounds that are slightly higher, in the 6,000 to 10,000 Hz range.

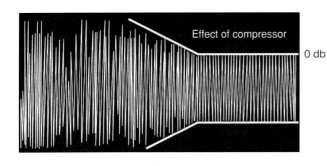

FIGURE 7.5

Audio compressors bring up low amplitude sounds and pull down the amplitude of loud sounds. As a result, the average loudness is held much closer to zero dB. Audio that has been compressed seems louder than non-compressed audio.

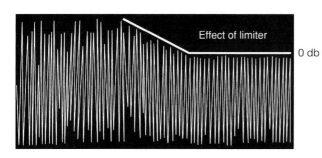

FIGURE 7.6

Audio limiters are a kind of safety device that keeps audio levels from exceeding zero dB. They are not as sophisticated as compressors or AGC circuits.

AMPLITUDE CONTROL DEVICES

Audio Compressors

Commercials may seem louder for another reason. Commercial producers commonly use a piece of audio equipment that raises average loudness. An *audio compressor* brings up low amplitude sounds and pulls down the amplitude of loud sounds (Figure 7.5). As a result, the average loudness is held much closer to zero dB. Program audio that has been compressed seems louder than non-compressed audio.

audio compressor: Audio-processing circuit that reduces dynamic range by simultaneously raising low audio levels and lowering high levels so that a higher average audio level is achieved.

Audio Limiters

An *audio limiter,* which is not as sophisticated as a compressor, is widely used in video production equipment. Unlike compressors, which are designed to affect both ends of the dynamic (loudness) range at the same time, a limiter is simply a kind of safety device that keeps audio levels from exceeding zero dB (Figure 7.6).

audio limiter: An electronic device intended to restrict the maximum amplitude of a signal.

AGC Circuits

The automatic gain control, or AGC, circuits, widely used in portable videotape recorders, go a step beyond limiters. If the average level of the audio is low, these circuits will raise it; if it is high, they will bring it down (Figure 7.7). AGC circuits are rarely used in the studio, where audio goes through an audio board (Figure 7.8). Here, an audio person's job largely centers on maintaining proper audio levels.

Although AGC circuits can free a video production person from having to worry about manually controlling audio levels (which has undoubtedly saved many productions from silent disaster), they cannot intelligently respond to

FIGURE 7.7
Automatic gain control (AGC) circuits are widely used in portable videotape recorders. If the average level of the audio is low, these circuits will raise it; if it is high, they will bring it down. AGC circuits can create problems in specific recording situations.

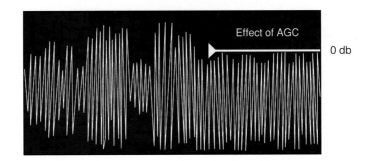

varying audio situations. Since AGC circuits are designed to maintain peak levels regardless of the nature of the audio, they end up making annoying background sounds louder whenever no other sound is present. This means that during pauses in dialogue the loudness of background noise will increase as the circuit (which can't differentiate between the sounds you want and the ones you don't) tries to bring background noise up to a maximum level. If subsequent audio processing circuits used during editing also have AGC circuits—each bringing up background noise to a higher level—this problem will be quickly compounded.

In addition to bringing up objectionable background sound during quiet moments, AGC circuits can also introduce a reverse problem. Since they respond to loud noises by pulling down audio levels for several seconds, words can be lost during a conversation when an AGC circuit reacts to a loud sound (such as someone bumping the microphone). AGC circuits also have a slight delay in their response. As a result, the first word spoken (especially after a period of silence) can be loud and distorted. Assuming an AGC circuit can't be shut off, production personnel sometimes try to get around this problem with an intentional *false start*. They will have the talent say a few words ("Hello, are we ready?") one second before the "real" dialogue. This allows the AGC circuit to adjust itself to the level of the speaker. During audio editing, the false start can easily be cut out.

FIGURE 7.8
An audio board (audio console) is the central controlling device for all audio within a production facility. Although a board such as this looks complex and even intimidating, it primarily consists of the same pattern of controls repeated over and over again for each available source.

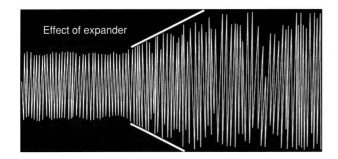

FIGURE 7.9
Audio transmitted over telephone lines or by satellites often ends up being overly processed and suffering from a restricted dynamic (loudness) range. As shown here, an audio expander, can restore audio to its normal dynamic range. In the process it can reduce background noise.

The last problem area for AGC circuits is in recording music. An important part of music, of course, are the distinctions — sometimes very subtle distinctions — between the loud and soft passages. Once these are lost, as they can be when an AGC circuit (or an overly active audio compressor) is used, many of the important nuances of music are sacrificed. Although AGC circuits don't have the magnitude of control over dynamic range that sophisticated compressors do, still, in recording long musical passages, the natural dynamic range of the music will be preserved by switching off AGC circuits and manually **riding gain** (making regular manual adjustments to audio levels as needed).

riding gain: Continually monitoring and controlling the level of a video or audio signal.

Some ENG field cameras have sound level indicators visible in the viewfinder. This means that the operator can ride audio gain as video is being taped. However, many times the camera operator is too busy with video concerns to worry about audio levels. Although the quickest solution is just to switch in an AGC circuit, a better approach is to use a separate audio person; someone with a good set of earphones and a clear view of a VU meter.

As we've noted, AGC circuits have their problems. Even so, when the limitations we've discussed are kept in mind, AGC circuits can free you from having to constantly ride gain, especially during EFP and ENG work. Like most of the automatic devices in video production, it's simply a matter of understanding what they can do — and being able make them work for you instead of against you.

Audio Expanders

To complete the discussion of amplitude control devices, we should mention the audio expander. Often, audio transmitted over telephone lines or satellites ends up being overly processed and suffering from a restricted loudness range. An *audio expander* can restore audio to its normal dynamic range and, in the process, reduce noticeable background (ambient) noise, hiss and hum (Figure 7.9).

audio expander: An electrical circuit that increases the dynamic range of an audio signal.

PEAK PROGRAM AND LOUDNESS METERS

When it comes to keeping up with the effects of compressors, expanders and the needs of digital signal processing, the basic VU meter (invented more then 50 years ago) has some shortcomings. It primarily represents average volume levels and doesn't give an accurate indication of loud, transient (very brief) sounds. A gunshot, clap of the hands or a single beat of a drum will cause a VU meter (Figure 7.1B) to jump; but, being somewhat sluggish, the needle will not reflect the true magnitude of the sound before it reverses its movement. Therefore, loud sounds of short duration can easily exceed maximum allowable levels without being noticed.

FIGURE 7.10

Loud sounds of short duration can easily exceed detection with normal VU meters. Peak program meters (PPM) are not only able to keep up with quick bursts of sound, but they hold the reading for a fraction of a second so it can be observed.

FIGURE 7.11

Although the PPM meter (Figure 7.10) solves the problem of loud, transient sounds, it does not reflect the loudness of sounds as perceived by the ear. Loudness meters (also called loudness monitors) not only can keep up with short sound bursts, but show loudness as humanly perceived.

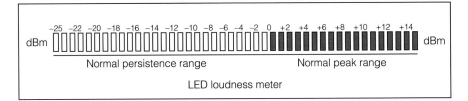

To solve this problem the **peak program meter (PPM)** was introduced (Figure 7.10). Not only is the PPM able to keep up with the maximum level of quick bursts of sound but, in addition, most PPM meters are designed to hold the reading for a fraction of a second so it can be observed.

Although the PPM meter solves the problem of loud, transient sounds, it does not reflect the loudness of sounds as perceived by the ear (Figure 7.2). **Loudness meters** (also called **loudness monitors**) are preferred by many audio engineers because they address both of these issues (Figure 7.11).

Needles vs. LEDs

Both needles (Figure 7.10) and light-emitting diodes, or **LEDs** (Figure 7.11), are used as indicators on sound meters. Since LEDs have no moving parts, there is no physical inertia to overcome; thus, they respond faster to transient sounds. The graph-like audio display associated with LEDs can also be superimposed over video, combining both an indication of video and audio in a single display (Figure 7.12).

Although any one of the level indicators we've discussed can be used to monitor and control audio levels, to simplify our discussion we'll henceforth just refer to them all in a kind of generic way with the term *VU meter*.

FIGURE 7.12

The graph-like audio display associated with the loudness meter can also be superimposed over video. This type of display in an ENG camera viewfinder is valuable to camera operators who must handle both audio and video from the camera.

FREQUENCY RESPONSE AND AUDIO QUALITY

Note in Figure 7.3 that the frequency response of a good-quality microphone does not vary to any significant degree from 50 to 15,000 Hz. This means that this microphone will rather accurately reproduce sounds throughout this range. The slight peak in the curve (at about 8,000 Hz) is not accidental. You will recall that this is the area associated with presence, the frequency range associated with voice and music clarity.

Generally speaking, the flatter the frequency response of a microphone, the better (and, unfortunately, the more expensive) it is. If you look at the specs (the printed technical specifications) of an inexpensive microphone you will often find that its frequency response contains significant—sometimes even rather abrupt—variations within the audible range.[7] This indicates that the microphone will unnaturally emphasize or de-emphasize certain frequencies. Although to some degree it is possible to clean up the frequency response of a poor microphone in postproduction, even the most sophisticated audio postproduction (sweetening) techniques cannot work miracles.

Even though a flat frequency response is best for microphones (and all audio equipment), it should be noted that it is often desirable to attenuate (reduce) the level of sounds below about 27 Hz—the lowest note on a piano. Below this point the low frequency sound from moving air in a studio, low-frequency vibrations etc. can load the audio signal with undesirable noise. Although this type of low-frequency energy may not be audible, it is often visible on a VU meter as existing in a "silent" studio.

MICROPHONES AS TRANSDUCERS

Any piece of audio equipment—microphone, amplifier, tape machine or audio speaker—can adversely affect the fidelity of sound. However, it is the **microphone** (the initial device that transduces sound waves into electrical energy) and the **audio speaker** (the device that changes electrical energy back into sound waves) that typically represent the weakest links in audio quality. Only sounds that are electronically generated, such as those produced by an audio synthesizer, do not need to go through a microphone to be reproduced. Everything else—the human voice, musical instruments etc.—must have its sound converted into electrical energy before being recorded or broadcast. We will divide microphones into two basic categories for discussion: transducer types and application designs.

When we talk about microphone transducer type we are talking about the type of generating element that transforms sound waves into electrical energy. But before we can discuss these, we need to cover directional characteristics.

DIRECTIONAL CHARACTERISTICS OF MICROPHONES

A microphone is selected for specific purposes on the basis of its attributes. One of the most important of these is its *directional characteristics*. There are three basic directional categories: omnidirectional, bidirectional and unidirectional.

---

7. It is sometimes difficult to rely on published specs to accurately judge microphones and loudspeakers. Frequency response curves are sometimes "smoothed" or averaged; consequently, some dips and peaks may not be evident.

FIGURE 7.13

Mics with non-directional, or omnidirectional, patterns, are equally sensitive to sounds coming from all directions. Although this would have advantages in radio (where several people could be seated around a single microphone), in television it is almost always more desirable to use directional mics. Directional mics can reduce unwanted sounds (behind-the-camera noise, ambient on-location noise etc.) while maximizing sound coming from talent.

omnidirectional mic: Non-directional mic. A microphone pickup pattern where sounds are received more or less equally from all directions.

bidirectional: A microphone pickup pattern with two primary areas of sensitivity, typically in a figure-**8** pattern.

cardioid: A slightly directional, heart-shaped pattern of microphone sensitivity.

Omnidirectional Mics

Also called **non-directional** mics, *omnidirectional mics* are equally sensitive to sounds coming from all directions (Figure 7.13 shows the sensitivity pattern for an omnidirectional mic). Although this characteristic would have advantages in radio (where several people could stand or be seated around a single microphone), in television it is almost always more desirable to use directional mics. A directional mic reduces unwanted sounds (behind-the-camera noise, ambient on-location noise etc.) while maximizing sound coming from talent.

Bidirectional Mics

You will note from Figure 7.14 that a *bidirectional* sensitivity pattern (**polar pattern**) means that the mic is primarily sensitive to sounds from two directions. Until the advent of stereo, bidirectional (also called **figure 8**) sensitivity patterns had limited use in television (although they are commonly used in radio interviews). Later we will see that this pattern has important applications in stereo.

Unidirectional Mics

There are actually four subdivisions in the **unidirectional mic** category: cardioid, supercardioid, hypercardioid and parabolic. Although these titles sound a bit formidable, they simply refer to how narrow the mic's pickup pattern is. Figure 7.15 represents a simplified comparison of the three most commonly used sensitivity patterns.

Cardioid   The *cardioid* (pronounced car-DEE-oid) pickup pattern is so named because it vaguely resembles a heart shape (Figure 7.16). Mics

FIGURE 7.14

Bidirectional mics are primarily sensitive to sounds from two directions. Until the advent of stereo, bidirectional (also called figure-8) mics had limited use in television.

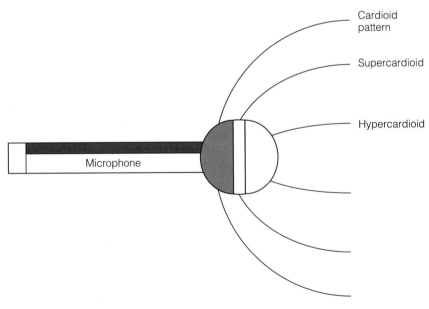

FIGURE 7.15

Professional microphones are selected for specific applications on the basis of a number of attributes—the most important of which are the mic's directional characteristics. In this (highly simplified) drawing three directional patterns are illustrated: cardioid, supercardioid and hypercardioid.

using a cardioid pattern are sensitive to sounds over a wide range in front of the mic, but relatively insensitive to sounds coming from behind the mic. Although this pattern might be useful for picking up a choir, the width of a cardioid pattern is too great for most TV applications. When placed 8 or more feet from a speaker, it tends to pick up unwanted, surrounding sounds—including reverberations from walls.

Supercardioid As the name suggests, the *supercardioid* is even more directional than the cardioid sensitivity pattern (Figure 7.17). When this type of mic is pointed toward a sound source, interfering (off-axis) sounds tend to be rejected. This polar pattern is similar to that of our ears as we turn our head toward a sound we want to hear and try to ignore interfering sounds.

Shotgun and line mics (Figure 7.18) are types of supercardioid mics widely used in on-location television production. They provide good pickup when used off camera at a distance of 8 to 15 feet from the talent.

Hypercardioid and Ultradirectional Even more directional are the *hypercardioid* and **ultradirectional** response patterns. Although their narrow angle of acceptance means that off-axis sounds will be largely rejected, this also means that they have to be accurately pointed toward sound sources. Regular adjustments have to be made if the talent moves. Some highly directional shotgun mics are included in the hypercardioid category.

Parabolic *Parabolic mics* (Figure 7.19) represent the most highly directional type of mic. Figure 7.20 illustrates how these mics work. The parabolic reflector can be from 18 inches to 3 feet in diameter. Because of the parabolic shape of the reflector, all the sounds along a very narrow angle of acceptance will be directed into the microphone from the surrounding reflector. Parabolic microphones can pick up sound at distances of 300 or more feet. These mics are not a practical choice for studio or general field production work, but they are often used in sports.

Although all directional mics favor sounds coming from one direction, they still have some limited sensitivity to off-axis sounds. This means that ambient noise—if it's loud enough—can still be a problem. For on-location work, a good set of padded earphones is indispensable for an audio operator. Constant audio monitoring is especially important when using hypercardioid and ultradirectional mics.

PROXIMITY EFFECTS

The use of highly directional microphones in general and parabolic microphones in particular results in a partial loss of some frequencies. This loss is not because of a weakness in the microphone. Sound traveling over a distance loses low frequencies (bass) and, to a lesser extent, the higher frequencies (treble). Con-

FIGURE 7.16

Mics using a cardioid pattern are sensitive to sounds over a wide range in front of the mic, but relatively insensitive to sounds coming from behind. Although this pattern might be useful for picking up a choir, the width of a cardioid pattern is too great for many TV applications.

supercardioid: A moderately directional microphone response pattern.

shotgun mic: A highly directional microphone capable of picking up sound over a great distance.

hypercardioid: A highly directional mic pickup pattern.

parabolic mic: A highly directional microphone application design that uses a reflector in the shape of a parabola to focus sound into a mic.

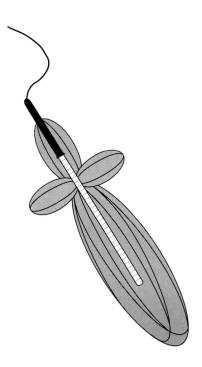

FIGURE 7.17

As the name suggests, the supercardioid is even more directional than the cardioid sensitivity pattern. When this type of mic is pointed toward a sound source, interfering (off-axis) sounds tend to be rejected. This polar pattern is similar to that of our ears as we turn our head toward a sound we want to hear and try to ignore interfering sounds.

FIGURE 7.18
Shotgun and line mics are widely used in on-location television production. They provide a highly directional pickup and are normally used at a distance of 8 to 15 feet from the talent.

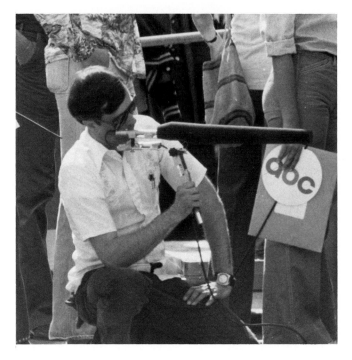

FIGURE 7.19
Parabolic mics are the most highly directional type of mic. They can pick up sound at distances of 300 or more feet. Parabolic microphones are not a practical choice for studio or general field production work, but they are often used in sports.

proximity effect: The exaggeration of low frequency response associated with most microphones when they are used at very close distances. Some microphones have built-in adjustments that can compensate for proximity effect.

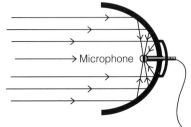

FIGURE 7.20
Parabolic mics work on the basis of a parabolic reflector, which directs all sounds along a very narrow angle of acceptance into the microphone at the center.

versely, microphones used at a close distance normally create what is called a *proximity effect*—exaggerated low frequency response.

This knowledge is important for postproduction editing. When directional microphones are used at different distances, the sound perspective or audio presence (balance of audio frequencies and other acoustical characteristics) can change slightly with each change in microphone distance. If the resulting problem is not corrected in postproduction, the sound presence or perspective will annoyingly shift with each edit. With a graphic equalizer (Figure 7.4) the frequency response of a directional microphone (or any audio source) can be reshaped to help bring about a consistent presence to the audio. This step takes place during a postproduction phase called audio sweetening.

MICROPHONE TRANSDUCER TYPES

Although there are several transducer designs used with microphones, three — the ribbon, the dynamic and the condenser — are most used in professional production.

Ribbon Microphones

The *ribbon mic,* which is also called a **velocity mic,** uses a thin corrugated aluminum ribbon suspended by springs between the poles of a magnet (Figure 7.21). Sound waves hitting the ribbon cause it to vibrate within the magnetic field. This in turn generates a minute electrical current, which is amplified many thousands of times.

Although ribbon mics are used in radio, they have limited use in television production. They are primarily found in announce booths (Figure 7.22) where they can enhance an announcer's voice by bringing out some of its more mellow characteristics. Since the ribbon is quite sensitive to moving air, two things must be kept in mind. First, the proper working distance between announcer and microphone must be maintained to avoid objectionable "pops" or plosive sounds created by pronouncing words with initial *b*'s and *p*'s. Twelve inches is a good working distance for a ribbon mic — and, in fact, for most types of microphones. Second, moving air (especially outdoors) can easily "rattle the ribbon," resulting in an unpleasant noise, or even damage to the mic.

Ribbon mics are larger than other types of mics. When you add to this the fact that their ribbon is quite sensitive to shock and moving air, they are a poor choice for ENG and EFP work.

Dynamic Microphones

The *dynamic mic* (also called a **moving-coil** microphone) is considered to be the most rugged type of professional microphone (Figure 7.23). In a dynamic microphone, sound waves hit a diaphragm attached to a fine coil of wire (Figure

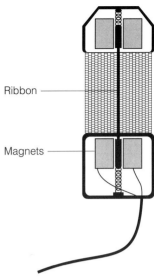

FIGURE 7.21

The ribbon mic uses a thin aluminum ribbon suspended by springs between the poles of a magnet. Sound waves hitting the ribbon cause it to vibrate within the magnetic field. This in turn generates a minute electrical current, which must be amplified many thousands of times.

ribbon mic: A type of microphone that makes use of a metal ribbon suspended in a magnetic field. When sound waves strike the ribbon, the resulting vibratory movement of the ribbon creates a minute voltage.

dynamic mic: A rugged type of microphone with a diaphragm attached to a moving coil suspended in a magnetic field.

FIGURE 7.22

Ribbon mics are primarily found in announce booths where they can enhance an announcer's voice by bringing out some of its more mellow characteristics. Since the ribbon is quite sensitive to moving air, ribbon mics have limited use in general television production.

FIGURE 7.23

The dynamic mic is considered to be the most rugged type of microphone. The hand-held mics used by ENG reporters and stage performers are generally dynamic mics.

7.24). Since the coil is suspended in the magnetic field of a permanent magnet, any movement of the coil as a result of sound waves hitting the diaphragm generates a small electrical current.

Many dynamic microphones are non-directional when it comes to the lower frequencies, but somewhat directional in their response to higher frequencies. Knowing this, problems created by a shrill or sibilant speaker can be reduced by putting the speaker slightly off to one side of the mic.

Although the technical quality of a typical dynamic microphone may not always equal the best condenser microphone, the ability of a dynamic mic to withstand shock, major temperature fluctuations and high humidity has made it the first choice for television field production. The hand-held mics used by ENG reporters and stage performers are generally dynamic mics. Even so, when optimum sensitivity and quality are prime considerations, condenser mics are often preferred.

FIGURE 7.24

In a dynamic microphone, sound waves hit a diaphragm attached to a fine coil of wire. Since the coil is suspended in the magnetic field of a permanent magnet, any movement of the coil as a result of sound waves hitting the diaphragm generates a small electrical current.

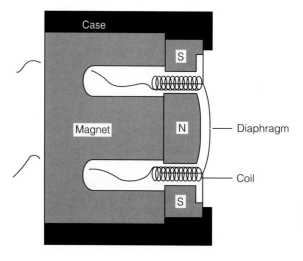

Side view

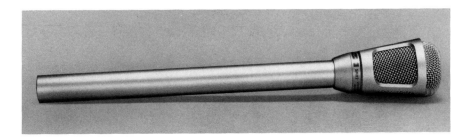

FIGURE 7.25
Although condenser mics (also called capacitor or electret condenser mics) can equal or exceed the quality of other types of microphones, they are not as rugged as a dynamic mic and problems can result from using some models in adverse weather conditions.

Condenser Microphones

Condenser microphones (also called **capacitor** or **electret** mics) are capable of delivering extremely high audio quality (Figure 7.25). They are basically omni-directional, but the polar pattern on some models can be altered to make them unidirectional. Although condenser mics equal or exceed the quality of other types of microphones, they are not as rugged as a dynamic mic, and problems can result from using some models in adverse weather conditions.

These mics work on the principle of an electric condenser or capacitor. An ultrathin metal diaphragm is stretched tightly above a piece of flat metal or ceramic (Figure 7.26). In most condenser mics a power source maintains an electrical charge between the elements. In one type, the electret mic, the capac-itor is permanently charged at the factory.

With condenser or electret mics, sound waves hitting the diaphragm cause fluctuations in an electrical charge. Since this voltage fluctuation is extremely small, it must be greatly amplified by a preamplifier (pre-amp). The pre-amp can either be located within the microphone housing, or (in the case of a small, clip-on microphone) in a outboard electronic pack that can be put in a pocket or attached to a belt (Figure 7.27).

Because they require a pre-amp, condenser mics, unlike ribbon and dynamic mics, require a source of power. This can either be from an AC power supply or from batteries. An AC power supply has the advantage of being more reliable than batteries, but it can also be somewhat limiting. Using batteries solves the external power problem, but introduces a problem of its own. At the end of their life cycle — which, depending upon use, may be a year or more — the batteries go out without warning. For this reason two miniature condenser mics are often used together for important live or taped productions. If one mic goes out, the other can immediately be switched on. This double microphone technique is called *dual-redundancy*.

Front plate (diaphragm)
Air space
Back plate

Battery-powered amplifier

FIGURE 7.26
Condenser mics have an ultrathin metal diaphragm that is stretched tightly above a piece of flat metal or ceramic. In most condenser mics a power source maintains an electrical charge between the elements. In the electret type, the capacitor is permanently charged at the factory.

condenser microphone: A microphone that detects sound by amplifying changes in electrical capacitance between two closely spaced plates.

dual-redundancy: The use of two identi-cal condenser microphones on a subject, one intended as a backup in case the pri-mary mic goes out.

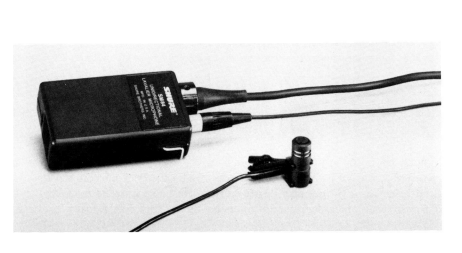

FIGURE 7.27
Condenser mics require a preamplifier. It can be located within the microphone housing, or (in the case of this small, clip-on microphone) in an outboard electronic pack that can be put in a pocket or attached to a belt.

FIGURE 7.28
The most commonly used audio connectors include XLR (Canon) connectors on the left. Both the female and the male versions are shown. Next are standard miniature (3.5 mm) connectors and (on the right) an RCA phono connector. Note that the miniature connectors differ slightly. One (the second from the right) has a floating center contact separated by black insulating bands. This additional contact shows that it is a stereo connector.

Although condenser mics require a power supply, the use of a preamplifier means they deliver a higher level signal — which generally translates into greater microphone sensitivity. Condenser mics also tend to be very responsive to high and low frequencies, giving them a full, clean, crisp sound. Because the transducer elements can be made very small, condenser mics can be easily hidden.

Before considering application designs, we should discuss a few other issues related to the basic elements of a mic. We'll begin with impedance.

MICROPHONE IMPEDANCE

Impedance mismatches between microphones and associated amplifiers, recorders and mixers, will adversely affect audio quality. Although this might seem like a fairly technical topic, **impedance** is simply a unit of electrical resistance expressed in ohms (a term that is abbreviated with the symbol Ω). The abbreviation for impedance, as found on microphones, amplifiers etc. is the letter Z. Microphones fall into two categories: high impedance (high Z) and low impedance (low Z). Microphones from 50 to 600 ohms are considered low impedance; those rated over 10,000 ohms are considered high impedance. If you encounter major audio distortion, check to see that microphone impedance matches equipment needs. If it doesn't, all is not lost; you can change impedance (high to low, or low to high) with a matching transformer.

BALANCED AND UNBALANCED LINES

Related to the issue of impedance is another seemingly technical issue (which is actually not all that technical) that affects audio quality: balanced and unbalanced lines. Most of the mics that are used with audio cassette machines and consumer-type camcorders use **unbalanced lines**. This isn't a major problem with short mic cables. But with long extension cables, and especially if mic lines are not in perfect condition, you will quickly encounter noise, pops, hum and other undesirable audio problems. Professional mics and camcorders rely on **balanced lines**. The basic difference is one wire; unbalanced lines use two wires, balanced lines use three. (With stereo there is an additional wire in each case.) The little monophonic miniconnectors used on cassette and camcorder mics (Figure 7.28) have only two conductors. Professional mic connectors are normally *XLR connectors,* which have three wires. Again, adapters are available that will convert lines from unbalanced to balanced, and balanced to unbalanced.

ELECTRICAL INTERFERENCE PROBLEMS

Care must be taken in using any kind of a microphone around electrical equipment. Fluorescent lights can induce an annoying buzz in audio. Computers and certain types of medical equipment, especially if they are near audio cables or equipment, can also create noise. Running mic cables parallel to power cords often creates problems. The solution to hum or buzz in audio is often as simple as moving a mic cable a few feet.

Sometimes noise problems are the result of a break in a ground wire or the outer shield of a mic cable. To work properly mic cables require near perfect conductivity through both their internal wires and the outer shield (ground) of the cable.

APPLICATION DESIGN

Earlier we talked about the basic microphone transducer types: ribbon, dynamic and condenser. The application design of the mic shapes the transducer to specific applications. We will discuss 11 applications: personal (including lavaliere and clip-ons), hand-held, wireless (RF), PZ, headset, contact, suspended, hidden, line, stereophonic and quadraphonic.

Personal Microphones

Personal mics can be either a condenser or dynamic mic. They are either hung from a cord around the neck (a *lavaliere* or *lav mic*) or clipped to clothing (a **clip-on mic**). Condenser-type personal mics can be made quite small and unobtrusive (Figure 7.29)—an important consideration whenever there is a need to conceal a microphone.

    Placement of Personal Mics   When attaching a personal mic, it should not be placed near jewelry or decorative pins. When the talent moves, the mic will often brush against the jewelry and create major, distracting noise. Beads, which have tendency to move around quite a bit, have ruined many audio pickups.

    If a personal clip-on mic is attached to a coat lapel or to one side of a dress, you will need to anticipate which direction the talent's head will turn. Personal mics are designed to pick up sounds from only about 14 inches away. If an individual turns away from the mic, not only will the distance from mouth to mic be increased to about 2 feet, but the person will then be turned away from the microphone as well.

FIGURE 7.29
Condenser-type personal mics can be made quite small and unobtrusive—an important consideration whenever there is a need to conceal a microphone. This mic is only 0.2 inch by 0.3 inch.

XLR connector: A standard, three-prong professional audio connector. Also called Canon connector.

lavaliere, lav mic: A small, personal microphone clipped to clothing or suspended from a cord around the neck.

FIGURE 7.30

Hand-held mics are often dynamic because they are better at handling the sound overloads associated with some performers. It is best if the mic is tilted at about a 30-degree angle, rather than being perpendicular to the mouth.

sibilance: A splattering, hissing vocal sound commonly caused by the combination of *s* sounds and poor audio equipment.

pop filter: A screen placed over a microphone that reduces the effect of speech plosives and wind.

windscreen: A small fabric or foam rubber cover for the top of a microphone that reduces or eliminates the sound of moving air or wind.

FIGURE 7.31

In addition to reducing the effect of plosives, windscreens can eliminate a major on-location sound problem: the effect of wind moving across the grille of the microphone. Otherwise, even a soft breeze can create a turbulence that can drown out a voice.

Hand-Held Microphones

Hand-held mics (Figure 7.30) are often dynamic mics because they are better at handling the sound overloads associated with some performers. Because these mics are often used at close distances, some special considerations should be mentioned. First, it is best if the mic is tilted at about a 30-degree angle and not held perpendicular to the mouth. Speaking or singing directly into mic often creates unwanted *sibilance* (an exaggeration and distortion of high-frequency *s* sounds), pops from plosive sounds (words with initial *p*'s and *b*'s) and an undesirable proximity effect (an exaggeration of low frequencies). Because of proximity-effect problems with hand-held mics, some manufacturers include an adjustment on the mic case that reduces bass response below 150 Hz. This also serves to reduce handling noise. One manufacturer has three adjustments: *V1* (some bass attenuation) for normal hand-held work, *V2* (significant bass attenuation) when the mic needs to be held close to the mouth to reduce background noise and *M* (a flat frequency response) when using the mic on a stand placed several feet away from musical instruments. Other manufacturers use other designations to indicate various degrees of **low frequency roll-off** (attenuation).

Although most hand-held mics are designed to be used at a distance of about 8 to 16 inches, this distance may have to be reduced in high-noise situations. *Pop filters,* which are designed to reduce the pops from plosive sounds, are built into many mics.

Microphone Windscreens   *Windscreens* (Figure 7.31) can reduce or eliminate a major on-location sound problem: the effect of wind moving across the grille of the microphone. Even a soft breeze can create a turbulence that can drown out a voice. During field productions, a properly fitted windscreen should be used on all mics, including exposed personal mics. In an emergency, a small square cube of soft, porous foam rubber cut to fit over the end of the microphone can be used.

Positioning Hand-Held Mics When a hand-held mic is shared between two people, audio level problems can be avoided by holding the mic closer to the person with the weaker voice. Inexperienced interviewers have a tendency to hold the mic closer to themselves. The resulting problem is compounded when the interviewer has a strong, confident voice, and the person being interviewed is somewhat timidly replying to questions.

PZ Mics

PZ (sometimes abbreviated *PZM*) stands for *sound pressure microphone*. This mic relies entirely on reflected sound. In specific situations (such as when placed on a table top) a PZ mic will provide a pickup that is superior to that of other types of mics.

Headset Mics

The headset mic was developed to serve the needs of sports commentators (Figure 7.32). Normally, a unidirectional dynamic mic with a built-in pop filter is used. The padded double earphones carry two separate signals: the program audio and the director's cues. Having the mic built into the headset assures a constant mic-to-mouth distance—even when the announcer moves from place to place.

Contact Mics

As the name suggests, contact mics pick up sound as a result of being in direct physical contact with the sound source. These mics are generally mounted on musical instruments, such as the surface of an acoustic bass or near the bridge of a violin. Contact mics have the advantage of being able to eliminate interfering external sounds and not being influenced by sound reflections from nearby objects. Their flat sides distinguish them in appearance from small personal mics.

FIGURE 7.32
The headset mic was developed to serve the needs of sports commentators. Normally, a unidirectional dynamic mic with a built-in pop filter is used. The padded double earphones normally carry two separate signals: the program audio and the director's cues.

FIGURE 7.33

Wireless (RF) mics can be an ideal solution whenever microphone cables are a problem. In a wireless mic, a basic dynamic or condenser microphone is connected to a miniature FM (frequency modulation) radio transmitter. A receiver located within the production area picks up the signal.

RF mic: Wireless mic; radio frequency mic. A combination microphone and miniature broadcast transmitter that eliminates the need for mic cables.

WIRELESS MICROPHONES

Wireless mics can be an ideal solution whenever microphone cables are a problem (Figure 7.33). In a wireless mic, a basic dynamic or condenser microphone is connected to a miniature FM (frequency modulation) radio transmitter. Because the mic's audio signal is converted into an FM radio frequency signal, these mics are commonly referred to as *RF mics*.

Types of Wireless Mics

There are two types of wireless mics: the self-contained (all-in-one) unit and the two-piece unit. Figure 7.33 shows a self-contained, hand-held unit where the mic, transmitter, battery and antenna are all within the microphone housing. When small, unobtrusive clip-on mics are desirable, a two-piece unit is the best choice (Figure 7.34). Here the mic is connected to a separate transmitting unit that can be clipped to the belt, put in a pocket or hidden underneath clothing.

Wireless Mic Applications

Since they solve many of the problems associated with using off-camera mics, wireless mics are now widely used in both studio and on-location productions. Today, some camcorders even have built-in receivers for wireless mics, thus eliminating the vexatious mic cable connecting the reporter or interviewer to the camera.

Transmitting-Range Considerations

As we've noted, the audio detected by a wireless mic is converted to a low-power RF signal. This signal is transmitted either by an internal antenna (within the mic's case) or by an external antenna, generally in the form of a short wire attached to the bottom of a separate transmitting unit. In the latter case the antenna should be kept straight and not folded over or coiled up—which can happen if the unit is shoved into a pocket. Some wireless personal mics make use of a loop of wire inconspicuously worn around the neck like a necklace. Under optimum conditions wireless mics can reliably transmit over more than a 500-foot radius. This distance is reduced to 50 feet if obstructions are present.

FIGURE 7.34

When small, unobtrusive clip-on mics are desirable in a wireless mic, a two-piece unit is the best choice. Here the mic is connected to a separate transmitting unit that can be clipped to the belt, put in a pocket or hidden underneath clothing.

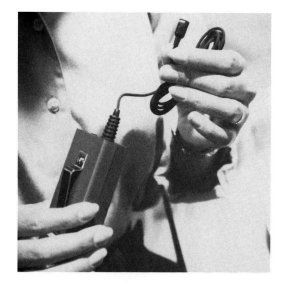

Interference Problems

RF mics can have problems with dead spots and distortion and fading caused by interference from nearby objects—especially if those objects are metal. The latter results in multipath reception (Chapter 2) with the reflected signal interfering with the primary signal. This can be particularly bothersome if the talent is moving and the audio begins to rapidly fade in and out. As we will see, this problem can often be easily fixed.

In addition to multipath reception, RF mics can experience interference from other sources of RF energy. Because of FCC limitations, the FM mic signal must be of relatively low power. As a result, other radio transmitters can interfere with the signal (*RF interference*). Even though they are on different frequencies, nearby radio services emit harmonic signals that, if strong enough, can be picked up on the wireless mic frequency. In order for a wireless FM mic signal to be reliable, its RF signal must be at least twice as strong as an interfering RF signal.

RF interference can also take other forms. Most good-quality RF mics transmit on frequencies above the standard FM radio band in either the highband VHF range or in part of the UHF band. In some regions of the country some of these frequencies are used by navigation buoys, hydroelectric equipment, broadcast control signals and TV stations using the higher UHF TV channels. Therefore, before use, the frequencies of RF mics must be checked against existing transmitters in a specific area.[8]

RF interference: An unwanted radio frequency signal that interferes with an audio or video signal.

Wireless Mic Receiving Antennas

There are two types of wireless mic receivers. **Non-diversity** receivers use a single antenna mounted on the back of the receiver. This type of antenna is most prone to multipath reception problems—especially if the talent moves from place to place. Two antennas are used in *diversity antennas.* Since the two antennas can be placed some distance apart, it is assumed that any time one antenna is not picking up a clear signal the other one will. To keep the signals from interfering with each other, electronic circuitry within the receiver is used to automatically select the stronger and clearer of the two signals at any one moment.

With either diversity and non-diversity receivers, multiple wireless mics can be used at the same time by putting each on a different frequency. Assuming enough clear frequencies are available, it is possible to use up to 16 wireless mics together.

diversity antenna: A radio-frequency (RF) mic system using two or more receiving antennas in an attempt to eliminate or reduce multipath interference.

USING OFF-CAMERA MICS

With the exception of contact mics, we have thus far been talking about microphones that are attached to, or held by, the talent. There are many instances in television production when it is desirable to place a microphone off camera. Some examples follow:

8. As noted, RF mics operate in either the VHF or UHF range of frequencies. There can be problems with TV interference in either range. In Chicago, for example, there are no TV stations on Channel 8, so wireless mics can use that area of the RF spectrum. In Tampa, Florida, Channel 8 is in use, so the same frequency range is unusable. The TV interference issue can sometimes be avoided by using so-called traveling frequencies (160 to 171 MHz). But in certain areas of the country even this range is used by navigation buoys. Wireless mic dealers, such as Shure Brothers in Evanston, Illinois, can provide information on frequencies in use in various regions of the United States.

FIGURE 7.35
For on-location production a supercardioid or narrower pickup pattern should be used as an off-camera mic. Wider patterns tend to pick up surrounding noises, which could easily interfere with dialogue.

- Because a visible mic wouldn't be appropriate, as in the case of a dramatic production
- When a mic cord would restrict the movement of talent
- When too many people are in the scene to use multiple personal, hand-held or RF mics.

Because of their non-directional nature, omnidirectional or simple cardioid-patterned microphones used at a distance of 10 or more feet will quickly start picking up extraneous sounds and, depending on the acoustics of the situation, cause the audio to sound hollow and off-mic. Consequently, only a supercardioid or narrower pattern should be used as an off-camera mic (Figure 7.35). But even these mics will not solve the problem of excess reverberation or echo within a room.

Room Acoustics

Whenever a room has smooth, unbroken walls or uncarpeted floors, reverberation can be a problem. Even moderate reverberation is enough to reduce the intelligibility of speech and make audio sound hollow. Since the ear hears rather selectively, this problem may initially go unnoticed unless audio is monitored with high-quality earphones. Moving mics closer to the subjects is the simplest solution, but this is not always possible. Other solutions include adding sound absorbing materials to walls,[9] or placing objects within a scene that will break up sound reflections. The problem of sound reflections from parallel walls is commonly solved in TV production by designing three-sided sets so that walls are not parallel (Figures 7.36A and 7.36B).

9. If too much sound absorbing material is used, audio can end up sounding unnaturally "dead" — like a recording done in an open field. An ideal setting provides a slight bit of "life" (reverberation) to the sound without in any way interfering with speech intelligibility.

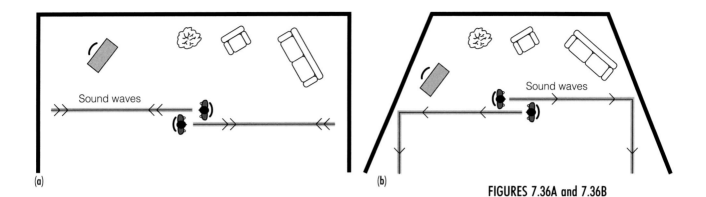

Hanging and Slung Microphones

Hanging and slung microphones are useful for covering sound from a large area, such as a choir or orchestra. They can be of any type: condenser, dynamic or even ribbon.

Microphones can be slung or suspended over a performance area by tying them to a grid or fixture just above the top of the widest camera shot. Suspended microphones should be checked with the studio lights turned on to see that they do not create shadows on backgrounds or sets. Once hung, the slung or hanging mic cannot be moved during a scene. Since it is sometimes desirable to be able to follow the movements of talent, a fishpole or a boom mic is often a better choice.

Fishpoles

As the name suggests, fishpoles consist of a long pole with a mic attached to one end (Figure 7.37). Some have a counterbalancing weight on the opposite end. An operator equipped with an audio headset can move the microphone to correspond with changes in camera shots and talent positions. Supercardioid and hypercardioid mics mounted in a rubber cradle suspension device called a ***shock mount*** are commonly used with a fishpole.

FIGURES 7.36A and 7.36B
The problem of sound reflections from parallel walls is common to most rooms (Figure 7.36A). In TV production this can be solved by designing three-sided sets where walls are not parallel. Not only will this reduce reverberation within the room, but it facilitates lighting.

shock mount: A rubber or spring-based mic holder that reduces or eliminates the transfer of sound or vibration to the mic.

FIGURE 7.37
As the name suggests, fishpoles consist of a long pole with a mic attached to one end. An operator equipped with an audio headset can move the microphone to correspond with changes in camera shots and talent positions. Depending upon the camera shot, the fishpole can be either suspended above or below the speaker's head.

(a)   (b)

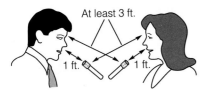

FIGURE 7.38
Unless precautions are taken, cancellation can be a problem in multiple-mic audio pickups. One solution, illustrated here, is to follow the "three-to-one" rule. This rule states that mics must be at least three times farther from each other than they are from a speaker.

Microphone Booms

Microphone booms range from a small giraffe (basically a fishpole mounted on a tripod) to a large perambulator boom that takes two people to operate.

The giraffe, or small studio boom, has an adjustable central column and a telescoping arm with a reach of 10 to 15 feet. The tripod legs are mounted on wheels. The microphone at the end of the boom can be swiveled to the left or right by the operator.

The largest booms are reserved for studio use. (Refer back to Figure 6.42 in Chapter 6.). They have a hydraulically controlled central platform where operators sit while controlling four things: the left or right movement of the boom arm, the reach of the arm, the left-to-right panning of the attached microphone and vertical tilt of the microphone. Generally operators are also provided with a video monitor and a script holder so that they can move the boom according to changing shots. The counterbalanced boom arm can extend from 10 to 30 or more feet and can follow action over a wide stage area. A second operator, if needed, can roll the entire boom from one place to another.

Hidden Microphones

It is often possible to hide microphones close to where the on-camera talent will be seated or standing and eliminate both the need for personal or hand-held mics and the problems that mic cords present. Microphones are often taped to the back of a prop or hidden in a table decoration.

When several mics are used on a set, each mic not being used should be turned down or switched off until needed. This not only reduces total ambient sound, but eliminates phase cancellation. **Phase cancellation,** which results in low-level and hollow sounding audio, occurs when two or more mics pick up sound waves that are out of phase. (See Figure 7.38.) When multiple mics are used on a set, there are four safeguards against phase cancellation:

1. Place mics as close as possible to sound sources.
2. Use directional mics aimed at sound sources.
3. Turn down mics any time they are not needed.
4. Carefully check and vary distances between the sound sources and multiple mics to reduce or eliminate any cancellation effect.

As shown in Figure 7.38, a speaker's primary mic should be placed at one-third the distance (or less) of any other mic. If a good solution to phase cancellation is not impossible, in an emergency an engineer can electrically reverse the phase of one mic.[10]

Line Mics

The most commonly used off-camera mic in electronic field production is the **line mic.** Line microphones are a type of highly directional shotgun mic surrounded by a dark-gray foam rubber or a fur-like windscreen (Figure 7.39). With their directional housing, the mics are about 2 feet long, although some even more directional versions are as long as 8 feet.

Line mics are normally of the condenser type. They are widely used in video field production because of their high quality and because they can be

---

10. This procedure involves switching (reversing the connections on) the two central wires to the cable connector. This should be done only as a last resort. A few audio boards have a provision to do this with a switch.

FIGURE 7.39
The most commonly used off-camera mic in electronic field production is the line mic. Line microphones are a type of highly directional shotgun mic surrounded by a dark-gray foam rubber or a fur-like windscreen. Because line mics are quite directional, they require someone just outside the camera's view to keep them carefully aimed at the sound source.

successfully used at distances of 20 or more feet. Because line mics are quite directional, they require someone just outside the camera's view to keep them carefully aimed at the sound source.

STEREO

Our ability to locate a particular sound is possible in part because we have learned to understand the minute and complex time-difference relationship between sounds in our left and right ears. If a sound comes from our left side, the sound waves from that sound will reach our left ear a fraction of a second before they reach our right ear. This time difference is called a *phase difference*. Depending upon the location of a sound, we might also note a slight difference in loudness between sounds that occur on our left vs. sounds coming from our right. This also helps us to locate sounds.

The Stereo Effect

There are several approaches to creating the stereo effect in TV production. First, there is *synthesized stereo,* where the stereo effect is simulated electronically. A slight bit of **reverb** (reverberation or echo) adds to the effect. Although this is not true stereo, when reproduced through stereo speakers the sound will be perceived as having more dimension than monaural sound. The synthesized approach is often supplemented (and much improved) with the addition of a true stereo soundtrack of associated music or environmental sound.

synthesized stereo: An approach to creating a simulated stereo effect from one or more monophonic audio signals.

Multitrack Stereo Recording

Next, a true stereo effect can be created during postproduction. By recording the various sources of sound on separate audio tracks, they can later be "placed" in any left-to-right sound perspective. Separate audio tracks can be devoted to narration, music and various prerecorded effects. (See Figure 7.40.) Recorders are available that will record from eight to more than 40 separate audio tracks on a single piece of 1-inch or 2-inch audio tape. Even more audio tracks are available by synchronizing two or more, multitrack recorders together with SMPTE time code. (Time code will be discussed in Chapter 15.) During the editing phase, the audio from the numerous tracks is mixed together—often

FIGURE 7.40
Computer-based audio editing systems allow complex overlays of stereo sounds. Note in this illustration that 14 audio sources are present in the time interval represented in the left half of this frame. Computer control allows each sound to be modified as needed and then moved forward or backward in time (generally to synchronize it with points in accompanying video).

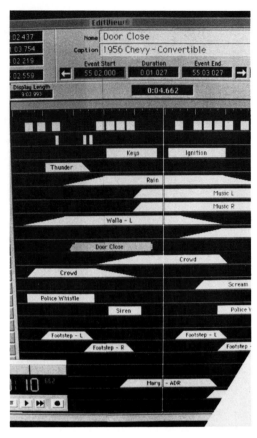

under computer control—to provide the desired mix between the various audio sources. By keeping the original multitrack tapes—a procedure that should always be followed in sophisticated audio production work—changes can later be made by simply loading the original multitrack tape, rerecording the tracks that need to be changed and then redoing the mix. We'll discuss this in more detail later in the chapter.

In recording a sophisticated contemporary music session, the various instruments do not even need to be in the recording studio at the same time. Vocal parts and instruments can simply be recorded on separate audio tracks. Performers recording their specific parts rely on earphones to hear playbacks of previously recorded material. Later, the various tracks are creatively mixed together to achieve the best artistic effect.

Keeping the various tracks separate not only provides maximum flexibility in doing a final stereo mix, but an instrument or vocalist can be rerecorded, if needed, without having to redo the entire session.

By manipulating the sound-phase relationships between the individually recorded sources and placing sounds on the left-to-right stereo perspective, an engineer can completely construct a physical orientation of a music group. Any instrument or vocalist can be placed at any point along the left-to-right perspective. This placement may bear little resemblance to their original location in the recording studio. This process of individually recording the separate sound elements not only makes it possible to control the placement and balance between each sound source, but each track can be separately enhanced with reverberation, filtering etc.

The multiple-track recording method is preferred in contemporary music because it affords maximum postrecording flexibility. In contrast, recordings of classical music and orchestras are often done with only one (strategically placed) stereo mic. In this case, the sound mix and balance are the responsibility of the conductor. The job of the recordist is simply to capture this carefully crafted result by placing a high-quality stereo mic in a central, acoustically desirable place in the auditorium.

Recording Live Music in Stereo

In recording live music in stereo we generally expect the dominant (instrumental or vocal) melody to be placed in the center of the stereo perspective. Beyond this, there is considerable latitude in the placement of audio sources in the left-to-right stereo perspective. First, you will want to pay attention to the balance of instruments and sounds. Although you may want to keep strings and brass instruments in separate areas of the left-to-right perspective, putting all of the "heavier-sounding" instruments in one channel results in an unbalanced effect. Through the use of pan pots (to be discussed later) and individually miced (miked) instruments you can create a pleasing balance between the channels.

In recording background music, the placement of sounds on a left-to-right stereo spectrum can be left to the creative instincts of an audio engineer. But when the sources of sound appear on screen, it's a different matter. When there is an obvious visual reference, the directional aspects of stereo need to conform to what the viewer sees on the screen. In this case an audio engineer must mix multitrack recordings together to maintain a believable on-screen audio perspective. While the multitrack recording technique outlined is good, it is time-consuming. Luckily, there is an easier way.

STEREO MICS

The simplest solution to stereo recording is to use an all-in-one **stereo mic,** which is basically two mics mounted in a single housing. The mic can be hand-held, mounted on a camera or suspended from a boom or studio grid.

To give maximum control over directional characteristics, most stereo mics use two condenser elements placed about one and one-half inches apart. The upper element can be rotated over 180 degrees to provide a variety of offset angles. Numerous directional patterns can generally be selected.

Stereo mics can give an adequate stereo effect—especially in applications where audio can be successfully miced from one location. Even so, this approach is limited in its ability to provide optimum **stereo separation** (a clear and distinct separation between the left and right stereo channels). Part of the problem rests with the proximity of the mic elements within a mic housing. With our ears (which are 8 inches or so apart) there is a phase (time) difference in sound as it reaches our left and right ears. As we've noted, this phase difference plays a major role in human stereo perception. Although this difference can, to some degree, be added to the signals of all-in-one stereo mics, many technicians prefer (when conditions allow) to use two separate mics. Two approaches are used: the X-Y and the M-S techniques.

The X-Y Micing Technique

In **X-Y micing** two slightly directional (cardioid) mics are suspended next to each other. One is directed to the left at a 45-degree angle, the other to the right at 45 degrees (Figure 7.41). Sound from a central source reaches each mic at

FIGURE 7.41

In X-Y stereo micing two slightly directional (cardioid) mics are suspended next to each other. One is directed to the left at a 45-degree angle, the other to the right at 45 degrees. The two channels can then be mixed as needed to create the needed stereo perspective. For most television applications, the M-S micing technique (Figure 7.42) is preferred.

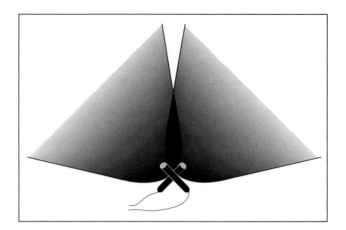

the same time and at the same loudness. Sounds to the left or right of the mics will be detected in the left-channel or right-channel mics in direct proportion to their position and loudness. When the sounds are reproduced through the left- and right-channel speakers of a stereo system, they assume the phase and loudness characteristics appropriate to their original position in the scene.

Although the sound quality of the X-Y method is excellent when reproduced by a stereo system, it can end up sounding a bit "muddy" when reproduced in monaural — especially in the critical center-stage (middle-of-the-scene) position. Since many TV sets are still monaural, the X-Y approach has not found favor in TV production.

The M-S Micing Technique

mid-side (M-S) micing: A stereo micing technique commonly used in broadcast television that provides maximum flexibility in postproduction. Important centered sounds are sharper and more stable than those produced by the X-Y method.

The second major approach to stereo recording is the **mid-side,** or M-S, technique. There are three advantages to the M-S method:

1. It sounds better than the X-Y method when reproduced by a standard mono TV sound systems.

2. The stereo effect can be readily changed as needed during production and postproduction.

3. Middle and high frequencies do not lose sharpness and definition in the critical center-stage position.

FIGURE 7.42

In the M-S stereo micing technique bidirectional and unidirectional (supercardioid) mics are used together. The bidirectional mic's polar pattern is aligned so that its areas of maximum sensitivity are parallel to the scene. Areas of minimum sensitivity are toward the camera (which tends to reduce off-camera noise) and toward the center of the scene (the area covered by the directional mic). The M-S micing technique allows for maximum control over the stereo effect.

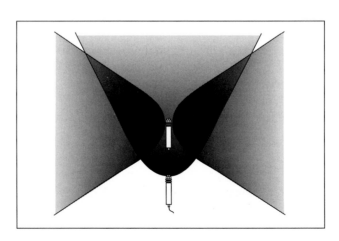

In the M-S technique, bidirectional and unidirectional (supercardioid) mics are used together. The bidirectional mic's polar pattern, which is shaped like a figure 8, is aligned so that its areas of maximum sensitivity are parallel to the scene (Figure 7.42). This means that the areas of minimum sensitivity are oriented toward the center of the scene and toward the camera. The dead spot that is directed toward the camera ends up being an advantage, because off-camera noise is reduced. The second dead spot, the one oriented toward the center of the scene, is covered by the directional mic.

The outputs of both mics are fed through a complex audio matrix circuit that uses phasing differences to produce the left and right channels. Adjustments to this circuit allow considerable latitude in varying the overall stereo effect.

MAINTAINING A STEREO PERSPECTIVE

Stereo TV has a major ongoing sound perspective problem because camera angles and distances shift with each new camera shot. It is almost impossible — and, in fact, it would be rather disconcerting in most instances — for the stereo perspective to shift with each change in camera angle. For example, if the sound of the ocean, nearby machinery or a playground flipped to the right and back again with each reverse-angle shot, it would be rather disorienting to a listener/viewer.

Concessions in Stereo Perspectives

To solve this problem, "inventive concessions" in stereo sound perspectives are regularly made. In the case of an ocean sound effect, a sound mixer might place the ocean in a left-to-right perspective that matches a wide-angle establishing shot and then — especially if the subsequent dialogue close-ups are short and numerous — simply maintain that original stereo perspective in subsequent shots. Although, strictly speaking, the stereo perspective would not accurately conform to close-ups, this concession would be better than flipping the ocean back and forth with each cut.

Using Pan Pots

Another solution — especially if the close-up dialogue shots are long — is to use a pan pot to subtly shift the ocean slightly with each shot so that a true left-to-right stereo perspective is simulated. A *pan pot* consists of two faders (volume controls) hooked together so that they move simultaneously, which can be used to slowly move a source of sound from one stereo channel to the other. (The role of faders will be discussed more later in the chapter.)

pan pot: An attenuator-based device that can "place" a sound to varying degrees in a left or right stereo channel.

Holding Dialogue to "Center Stage"

To ensure maximum intelligibility — especially for monophonic audio systems — the dialogue for the typical one- and two-shots associated with dramatic productions should be kept in the center of the stereo perspective. There are two reasons for this. First, in most cases this will conform to the visual perspective shown on the screen. Second, since the dialogue can be recorded on one audio track instead of two, it will greatly simplify both audio production and postproduction. As we've previously suggested, a stereo effect can then be added with background sounds, off-camera dialogue etc.

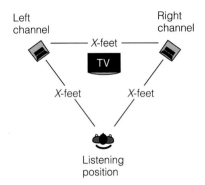

FIGURE 7.43

Stereo audio should be reproduced through two good-quality speakers, placed at equal distances from the TV set. The distance between the speakers depends on the distance of the listener; the farther back the listener is, the greater the distance should be between the speakers.

surround-sound: A system of sound recording and reproduction that goes beyond stereo in its dimensional perspective and approximates quadraphonic sound.

Stereo in Sports Coverage

Generally, in sporting events a general background stereo pickup of the crowd is mixed in with a monophonic feed from the play-by-play narration. If there are two announcers, pan pots can be used to place them slightly to the left and right of center. Having individual mics directed fully into either a left or right channel, as is sometimes done, makes the announcers sound unrealistically isolated from each other.

Sometimes a stereo mic mounted on a sideline camera will be mixed into existing program audio when that camera is switched up. This would be appropriate to pick up the sound of cheerleaders or sideline activity.

Guidelines for Stereo Placement

Stereo placement is a creative decision, and no set of rules can be established that will cover every situation. But there are two guidelines: First, try to simulate an authentic stereo reality whenever possible. The second guideline—actually more of a caveat—is even more important. It is almost never desirable to use a production technique that diverts viewer attention away from production content. It is better to hold back on authenticity rather than introduce effects that will call attention to themselves.

Stereo Playback

The final stereo signal should be reproduced through two good-quality speakers, placed at equal distances on each side of a TV set. The speakers are normally positioned from 9 to 12 feet apart and aimed at about a 45-degree angle toward the viewer. The distance between the speakers depends on the distance of the listener; the farther back the listener is, the greater the distance should be between the speakers. The best listening area for stereo is shown in Figure 7.43.

SURROUND-SOUND TECHNIQUES

Whereas stereo covers about a 120-degree frontal perspective, *surround-sound* and **quadraphonic**[11] sound systems attempt to reproduce sounds in both the front and back of the listener—a full 360-degree sound perspective. Today, many productions are done in surround-sound, although the number of homes equipped with surround-sound decoders is still limited.[12] In playing back true surround-sound or quadraphonic sound, at least four speakers are needed (Figure 7.44).

Admittedly, a 360-degree sound perspective is a little difficult for television production. Not only does this perspective not match the limited visual area, but placing four or five speakers an equal distance from all listeners/viewers strains the decorative schemes of most TV living rooms. There is another way.

By analyzing the way we hear sounds, psychoacoustic researchers have

11. Although there are historical differences between the two, the goal of both is to create a 360-degree sound ambiance, while maintaining a strong "center-stage" component.

12. In 1992, two U.S. systems, the Dolby Surround system and the Sure HTS Stereo Surround system, provided equipment for most productions using surround-sound. Both systems required the surround-sound signal to be encoded in the broadcast audio signal before transmission and then decoded for multiple speakers when received in the home.

come up with a surround-sound system that uses only two speakers. One version, introduced during Super Bowl XXIV, expands the stereo sound perspective significantly — even adding the illusion of a vertical dimension. To achieve the expanded effect, multichannel audio recordings are digitized and fed into a computer during postproduction. A special six-axis joystick (that also telescopes vertically to represent height) is used to place audio sources in specific sound perspectives. Although the system has the advantage of needing only two speakers, the four- or five-speaker approach is capable of much greater realism.

Quadraphonic Mics

For surround-sound TV applications, **quad mics** that have four mic elements within a single housing can be used. Typically, an upper capsule containing two mic elements picks up sound from the left-front and right-rear. Another capsule, mounted below this one, picks up sound from the right-front and left-rear. In postproduction the four audio tracks can be mixed with tracks of music and effects (M&E) to develop a full surround-sound effect.

SINGLE AND DOUBLE SYSTEM SOUND

Single System Recording

Sound recorded directly on the videotape as a production is shot is referred to as **single system** recording. This approach is used in news and documentary work. Today's VTRs and VCRs (videotape recorders and videocassette recorders) can record from two to eight channels of audio along with the video. Four channels are adequate for most professional needs. However, complex stereo techniques require more audio channels than are available on videotape machines. To meet these needs there is double system recording.

Double System Recording

In *double system* recording a multitrack audio recorder is synchronized with a VCR and used to record up to 40 separate audio tracks. Recording each source of audio on a separate track provides maximum flexibility in the postproduction phase. Double system sound recording has been the standard for motion picture production since the earliest days of sound.

MIC CONNECTORS AND CORDS

To ensure reliability, audio connectors (refer back to Figure 7.28) must always be kept clean, dry and well-aligned (without bent pins or loose pin connectors). Although the audio connectors themselves must be kept dry, in field production mic cables can be strung across wet grass, or even through water, without ill effects (assuming the rubber covering has not been damaged). If you must work in rain or snow in the field, moisture can be sealed out of audio connectors by tightly wrapping them with plastic electrical tape. It should be emphasized that this applies to mic cables only. If AC power is used in the field for the camera, lights or recorder, these extension cables and connectors must *always* be kept dry.

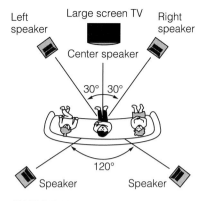

FIGURE 7.44

Whereas stereo covers about a 120-degree frontal perspective, surround-sound and quadraphonic techniques attempt to reproduce sounds in both the front and back of the listener — a full 360-degree sound perspective. Most systems require that listeners sit approximately in the middle of four or five speakers.

double system recording: A production approach, normally used to meet complex audio recording needs, that records pictures and sound with two separate recording devices. Normally, video is recorded on a VCR and audio on a multitrack audio recorder.

FIGURE 7.45
Although turntables (foreground) used to be the central source of all music in radio stations and production facilities, they are now primarily used for library music originally released on $33\frac{1}{3}$ rpm and 45 rpm records.

SOURCES OF PRERECORDED AUDIO

Thus far, we've discussed audio production in terms of "live" pickups with mics. But, of course, much audio comes from prerecorded sources: turntables, tape machines, DCCs, CDs, DATs and disk drives.

Turntables

Although records used to be the primary source of prerecorded material, they have now been largely replaced by tapes and CDs. The first records to be widely used rotated at 78 rpm. The high rotation speed and the hard surface of 78s combined with normal wear and tear to quickly result in noisy playbacks. Next, $33\frac{1}{3}$ rpm monophonic records were introduced—the so-called long play (LP) records. This was a big improvement, both in terms of quality and recording time. The final record format to be widely used was the 45 rpm format with its large center hole. Both the $33\frac{1}{3}$ rpm and the 45 rpm records were introduced in the single-channel monophonic format; later, stereo was added to both. For several decades records dominated audio production (Figure 7.45).

Regardless of their speed, records share a common problem: the surface noises (pops and scratches) that build up with use. Although noise reduction devices can be used, some loss of audio quality (frequency response) results. To get around some of these problems, in the 1970s radio stations started making copies of their records on audio tape cart machines.

Cart Machines

cart; cartridge: A plastic container with audio or videotape that threads automatically when inserted into a record or playback machine. In contrast to a cassette, the tape is commonly connected in a continuous loop.

Cart machines (**cartridge machines**) contain a continuous loop of 1/4-inch audio tape within a plastic cartridge (Figure 7.46). Although tape lengths vary from 15 seconds to one hour, most carts are 30 seconds and 60 seconds (used for commercials and public service announcements) and three minutes (for musical selections). One of the advantages of cart machines is that they automatically cue themselves (move to the beginning of each segment) and start almost instantly—a feature that makes "tight" audio edits possible. The first cart machines were analog, but in the late 1980s, digital cart machines were introduced.

The functions of the basic controls on cart machines—*start, stop, play* and *record*—are self-evident, except possibly for one thing. In order to record on some cart machines the *record* button has to be held down as the *play* button is pressed.

Carts rely on inaudible tones recorded on the tape to cue up segments. To speed cuing, some machines accelerate tape transport between the point when one segments ends and the start of the next segment. If there is only one "cut" (segment) on the cart, the "next segment" will be the beginning of the tape loop.

Carts are used in postproduction for recording and playing back background sound and narration. Short audio segments can be recorded on a cart ("carted") and then "rolled in" as needed, either manually or under the automatic control of a video editor.

Reel-to-Reel Tape Machines

Except for multiple-track recording and meeting special audio editing needs, reel-to-reel tape machines (Figure 7.47) have limited use in TV production. The highest quality reel-to-reel tape machines run at 15 ips (inches per second). In most of today's audio production the $7\frac{1}{2}$ and $3\frac{3}{4}$ ips speeds are most common.

Editing Reel-to-Reel Tapes   Occasionally, there is a need to precisely edit a variety of audio segments that has been recorded on a reel-to-reel machine. Although the all-electronic approach is faster and easier, some "purists" still prefer the older, more direct, method. If you have the time and patience to edit reel-to-reel tapes, it is possible to fine-tune a narrative segment to the point of eliminating "ah's" from sentences, and even taking *s*'s off of words.

FIGURE 7.46
Cart machines (cartridge machines) contain a continuous loop of 1/4-inch audio tape within a plastic cartridge. Although tape lengths vary from 15 seconds to one hour, most carts are 30 seconds and 60 seconds (used for commercials and public service announcements) and three minutes (for musical selections). The first cart machines were analog, but in the late 1980s, digital cart machines were introduced.

FIGURE 7.47
Except for multiple-track recording and meeting special audio editing needs, reel-to-reel tape machines have limited use in day-to-day TV production. In the late 1980s, DAT (digital audio tape) machines were introduced, which not only improved audio quality but allowed for the computer control of audio segments.

FIGURE 7.48
Many "purists" still prefer to edit audio with a reel-to-reel tape machine by physically cutting and splicing the tape. With single-track recordings, smoother edit transitions will result if tape is cut and spliced on a diagonal, as shown.

Five things are needed: a grease pencil, a single-edge razor, a pair of scissors, a roll of audio splicing tape and an editing block. A 1/4-inch audio tape **editing block** holds the audio tape at the desired points for cutting and splicing (Figure 7.48). Some splicers are simply aluminum blocks with a channel to hold the tape and vertical groves for cutting the tape with a razor. Others have built-in blades for cutting the tape and a holder and guide for affixing the audio splicing tape.

A reel-to-reel tape machine is required that provides the operator with clear access to the playback head. Most reel-to-reel recorders have three sets of heads arranged in the following left-to-right order: the **erase head** that erases existing material as new segments are recorded, the **record head** that records new audio when the machine is in the record mode and the **playback head** that plays back recorded material.

The first point to be located on the tape is the beginning point for the material you want to eliminate. While playing the tape at the normal speed you can quickly stop it when this approximate point is found. Then, while carefully listening to the audio, the machine's reels can be manually rocked back and forth until the precise point is located. (The higher the tape speed used in recording the original material the easier it is to edit at precise points.) The grease pencil is used to put a mark on the back of the tape in the middle of the playback head at the precise beginning point in the audio you want to eliminate. The ending point for the audio you want to eliminate (the starting point for the next segment) can then be found and marked in the same way. The area between the two marks represents the tape to be removed. Removing this segment is simply a matter of cutting out the section of tape between the two marks, butting the ends together and then carefully splicing them with the special adhesive splicing tape.

In making splices in this way several things must be kept in mind. First, tape edits should not be obvious. Depending upon the pace of the production, you may need to see that there is a natural pause between the segments. (Once a piece of audio tape is removed, it is difficult to put part of it back in.) Second, in single-track monophonic recordings it is best to cut the audio tape at an angle. Most editing blocks allow for this. Angled cuts provide a "softer" audio transition between segments, reducing the possibility that edits will be noticed. With stereo tracks, however, a vertical cut will be necessary to ensure that the left and right channel transitions are simultaneous.

In physically cutting and splicing a tape, it is assumed that no reverse-direction tracks are needed on the tape (some reel-to-reel tapes can be flipped over like audio cassettes and recorded in the reverse direction). You will also need to consider the effect a splice will have on a multitrack tape. Whatever cutting and splicing you do will obviously affect all of the tracks on the tape at the same time.[13]

Compact Discs (CDs)

Because of their superior audio quality, ease of control and small size, CDs (compact discs) have become a preferred medium for prerecorded music and sound effects (Figure 7.49).

Like all digitized audio, the original analog signal (generally from a microphone) is first converted to a digital signal by an analog-to-digital converter. An image of the digital data is "stamped" into the surface of the CD in a process

13. Reel-to-reel tapes have several basic formats: full track (one monophonic audio track extending across the full width of the tape); two-track reversible (one monophonic track on each side of the tape, which allows for recording in each direction); two-track stereo (left and right channels only); and four-track stereo (two tracks of stereo for both the forward and reverse direction tape directions). Some tape formats also reserve tracks for time code.

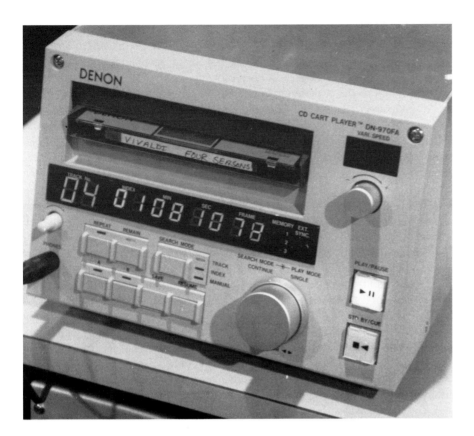

FIGURE 7.49
Because of their superior audio quality, ease of control and small size, CDs (compact discs) have become a preferred medium for prerecorded music and sound effects. CDs are easier to label and store if they are put in cartridges.

that is similar to the way LP records (with their analog signals) are produced. When a CD is played, a laser beam is used to illuminate the digital pattern encoded on the surface. The reflected light (modified by the digital pattern) is read by a photoelectric cell.

The overall diameter of a typical audio CD is a little less then 5 inches (120 mm). The program area is a band of groves only 33 mm wide, located between the 50 mm and 116 mm points. A typical CD contains a 1.6 μm wide spiral track, which, if unwound, would come out to be 3.5 miles (5.7 km) long. The width of the track is one-sixtieth the size of the groove in an LP record, or one-fiftieth the size of a human hair! Because of the minuscule size of the track, imperfections in the mechanics or optics of a CD player, or in the CD itself, will cause immediate problems.

CD Defects   Occasionally, surface stress occurs in the CD manufacturing process, resulting in disc warp. If the surface of the CD is sufficiently warped, the automatic focusing device in the CD player will not be able to adjust to the variation. The result is mistracking and loss of audio information.

CDs can also have other manufacturing problems, including pinholes, air bubbles and black spots. Some of these are an inevitable part of the CD manufacturing process. It is only when the areas involved become relatively large (100 μm for bubbles, 200 μm for pin holes and 300 μm for black spots) that they cause audio problems. These defects can often be spotted when the CD is held so that light is reflected from its surface.

By far the most common types of CD problems stem from things that happen to the CD *after* it is manufactured. Although CDs don't build up surface noise the way records do, scratches, fingerprints, dust and dirt on the CD surface will cause loss of digital data.

Automatic Error Correction   CD players attempt to compensate for manufacturing or handling problems in three ways: error correction, error concealment (interpolation) and muting. For small problems, error-correcting circuitry within the CD player can detect lost data (dropouts) and, based on the existing digital sound at the moment, accurately supply the missing data.

If the loss of data is more substantial and the CD player can't automatically "figure out" what has been lost, error-concealing circuits can automatically build an "audio bridge" across the missing information by substituting data that conforms to (blends in with) existing audio. In most cases the substituted (interpolated) data will be so similar to the lost data, that the effect will not be detected. However, if error-concealing circuitry has to be invoked repeatedly within a short time span, the result will become noticeable. In loud passages you may hear a series of clicks or a ripping sound. Error concealment will generally not be noticed during quiet passages.

When a large, contiguous block of data is missing or corrupted, the CD player will simply mute (make silent) the audio until good data again appears. A large scratch on the surface of a CD can cause audio to disappear for some time, giving the impression, when audio returns, that the player has skipped tracks.

Programming CD Playback   In addition to their high quality and compact size, one of the major advantages of CDs is their ability to be programmed for instant starts at precise points. This makes it possible for an audio operator or a video edit controller to trigger preset musical transitions and audio effects at preprogrammed points—and to instantly re-cue them as needed. The only audio playback systems that are more versatile are computer disk drives. These will be discussed later in the chapter.

Mini Disk (MD)   In 1992, Sony introduced the **mini disk (MD)**, a scaled-down version of the CD, with both record and playback capabilities. The $2\frac{1}{2}$-inch MD, which is based on a magneto-optical disk enclosed in a protective cartridge, is about half the size of a standard CD. The disks can record up to 74 minutes of digital audio using a data compression technique that eliminates unnecessary portions of the audio range. Although the sound quality is better than an analog audio cassette, it isn't as good as a standard CD. One of the major advantages of MDs over audio cassettes is their almost instant ability to randomly access desired segments. New shockproof and vibration-proof technology makes it possible for the MD to successfully record and play back audio under adverse conditions.

In order to foil attempts at illegally making digital copies of commercial (copyrighted) recordings, MDs use the Serial Copy Management System. This system relies upon a signal in the recordings that can be detected by an electronic component (chip) in the mini disk player. When the signal is present, it is not possible to make a digital copy of the copyrighted material. (In some instances analog copies are possible, however.) This copy management system is also used in digital audio tapes.

Digital Audio Tapes (DAT, RDAT)

digital audio tape (DAT): A digital audio recording format utilizing a tape cartridge containing 3.81 mm wide metal particle tape.

Digital audio tapes (DATs) can record and play back with an audio quality that exceeds what is possible with CDs. The 2-inch by $2\frac{7}{8}$-inch DAT cassette contains audio tape 3.81 mm wide and is about two-thirds the size of a standard analog audio cassette (Figure 7.50). The two-hour capacity of a DAT cassette is 66 percent greater than a standard 80-minute CD.

DAT exists in two forms: one for general consumer (home) use and one, referred to as RDAT (recordable digital audio tape), for professional applica-

FIGURE 7.50
DAT (digital audio tape) machines can record and play back with an audio quality that exceeds what is possible with CDs. Encoded into the audio signal of professional DAT recordings is an IEC SubCode time code reference that can be used by production equipment to start, stop and cue tapes.

tions. Because of the potential for **pirating** (making illegal copies of commercial recordings), the Serial Copy Management System, discussed under mini disks, is also used in consumer DATs. This makes it impossible to make digital copies of commercial tapes, although analog copies can sometimes be made. RDAT players, which are designed for professional applications, do not have the same copy limitations.

DAT systems (Figure 7.51) use a headwheel that spins at 2,000 rpm — similar to a videocassette recorder. Encoded into the audio signal of a DAT recording is a *control subcode* that can be used for several types of data, including (in professional models) a time code reference.

DAT Time Code   In early 1992, a time code system was introduced by several manufacturers that makes it possible to automatically cue and control DATs (specifically, RDATs) with split-second accuracy. The system, referred to as the **IEC SubCode Format,** also ensures that tapes recorded on one DAT machine can be played back without problems on any other machine using the

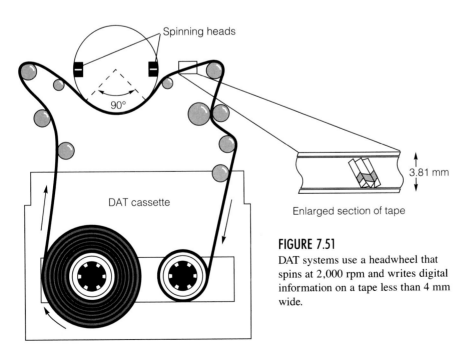

FIGURE 7.51
DAT systems use a headwheel that spins at 2,000 rpm and writes digital information on a tape less than 4 mm wide.

FIGURE 7.52
With sophisticated audio consoles you can manipulate specific characteristics of audio including adding reverberation, changing the left-to-right placement of stereo sources and shaping frequency characteristics of individual audio sources.

time code format. The DAT version of SMPTE time code involves a sophisticated technique of translating hours, seconds and video frames (one-thirtieth of a second intervals) into a signal that can be recorded with the digital audio. Since the time code format has been designed to be universal, it can be used with any of the world's video standards.

DAT time code is especially valuable in postproduction where time codes can be used to accurately synchronize a wide range of audio sources with video. In audio and video workstations, DAT machines can be programmed to automatically cue themselves, and start and stop as needed. The major problem with DATs is the **access time.** Compared to CDs or MDs, DATs take much more time to cue up a needed segment.

Digital Compact Cassette (DCC)

During the mid to late 1980s the medium of choice for prerecorded music at the consumer level was the analog cassette. Although these cassettes are sometimes pressed into service in professional audio production, their quality falls significantly short of rivaling the standards of CDs and DATs. In 1992, much of this quality difference was eliminated with the introduction of *digital compact cassettes (DCCs)*. Instead of using a rotating head the way DAT machines do, the DCC system relies on a stationary head very similar to those used by the analog cassette system.

digital compact cassette (DCC): An audio recording system that records a digitized audio signal on an audio cassette using non-rotating heads.

In order to capture the great amount of digital data necessary, the DCC system greatly compresses information by splitting up the audio spectrum into 32 separate frequency bands and processing them to conform to the characteristics of human hearing. After compression, the DCC system is able to use a data rate of only 770,000 bits per second. Although this is considerably less than the 2.5 million bits per second used by DAT technology, it is still adequate to capture most of the dynamics of audio.

In addition to basic audio information and time codes, DCC recordings also include other digitally encoded information: song titles, artist names, record labels and basic indexing information.

THE AUDIO CONSOLE

The sources of audio we've been discussing must be carefully blended and controlled in the production and postproduction processes. As we noted in Chapter 1, this is the role of the audio console, or audio board (Figure 7.52). Audio consoles are designed to serve six functions:

1. To amplify the level of incoming signals

2. To provide level (volume) adjustments for audio sources through the use of visual references (VU, peak program or loudness meters)

3. To allow for the mixing (blending together) of multiple audio signals

4. To manipulate specific characteristics of audio (alter the left-to-right "placement" of stereo sources, shape frequency characteristics, change the phase of microphones, add reverberation to audio, etc.)

5. To allow for the aural monitoring of individual sources, as well as the total effect (mix) of audio

6. To route the combined effect to a transmission or recording device

Audio Inputs

Even though audio boards can control scores of audio sources, these sources break down into two categories: mic-level and line-level inputs. As the name suggests, **mic-level** inputs handle the extremely low voltages associated with microphones. **Line-level** inputs are associated with the outputs of amplified sources of audio, such as CD and tape players. Normally these are **hard wired** (permanently wired) into the audio console.

Audio Console Controls

The audio console (or audio board) uses two types of controls: faders and switches. *Faders* (volume controls) can be either linear (Figure 7.53) or rotary (Figure 7.54) in design. Faders are also referred to as **attenuators** or *gain controls*. **Rotary faders** are commonly called *pots* (for potentiometers). **Linear faders** are also referred to as **vertical faders** and **slide faders**.

Normal audio sources should reach zero dB on the VU or loudness meter when the pot or vertical fader is one-third to two-thirds of the way up (open). Having to turn a fader up fully in order to bring the sound up to zero dB indicates that the original source of audio is coming into the console at too low a level. In this case, the probability that there will be background noise in the audio source increases. Conversely, if the source of audio is too high coming into the board, "opening" the fader very slightly will cause the audio to immediately hit zero dB. The amount of fader control over the source will then be limited, making smooth fades difficult. This brings up an important attribute associated with some faders.

Some fader controls are *step attenuators* that range from zero resistance to the incoming audio signal to maximum resistance (a total blocking of the audio signal). Rather than smoothly moving through their range, step attenuators progress in discrete steps from one resistance value to another, with no "in-between" points.[14] Moving across individual steps becomes noticeable when incoming sound is at too high a level, and the step attenuator can only be used

FIGURE 7.53
Linear faders are also referred to as vertical faders and slide faders. Since the scale on the fader represents levels of attenuation (resistance), the smaller the number, the louder the audio.

fader: A volume control or potentiometer used to control the amplitude of an audio signal.

gain control: A volume-controlling device manipulated by either a sliding fader or a rotating knob.

pot: A potentiometer. A control that uses variable resistance to alter the intensity of audio and video signals.

---

14. Step attenuators, which are primarily associated with rotary faders, are designed to withstand constant use. Compared to faders that rely on a continuously varying resistance (which can exhibit a static noise with age) they are easier to clean and service.

FIGURE 7.54
Until recently, almost all attenuators (volume controls) were the rotary type pictured.

input selector switch: A switch found on many audio control boards that can route specific sources of audio to a single audio console input.

at its lowest positions. At these points it becomes impossible to smoothly fade out or precisely control the level of an audio signal.

Since faders use a system of varying resistance, zero resistance means that the fader is turned up to its maximum point—that no resistance is being placed in the path of the audio signal. Maximum resistance means that the fader is totally blocking the audio—that the volume control is down all the way. To reflect the various states of attenuation (resistance) the numbers on some faders are the reverse of what you might think: the numbers get higher (reflecting more resistance) as the fader is turned down. Maximum resistance is designated with an infinity (∞) symbol. When the fader is turned up all the way, the number on the pot or linear fader may indicate 0—for zero resistance.

Input Selector Switches

Since it is assumed that audio sources will not be used at the same time, the number of inputs that can be fed into an audio board generally exceeds the number of faders. *Input selector switches* are used to direct specific sources of audio through specific faders. Figure 7.55, a simplified block diagram of an audio console, illustrates three sources (inputs) of audio to each fader or **audio channel**.

But audio needs can be unpredictable. On a specific occasion you might need both mic-1 and CD-2 at the same time. Since the input switch will not allow you to control both sources with the single fader, you have a problem. One solution is to redirect one of the audio sources to another fader by using a **patch panel** or **patch bay**. In a patch panel **patch cords** or solid-state switching circuits are used to redirect sources of audio. A more recent approach is to use a touch-screen or mouse-controlled computer control system (Figure 7.56). Simply by touching (or clicking on) the appropriate boxes, various audio sources can be connected.

Whatever method of patching is used, any one source of audio can be selected and directed into a specific fader. Going back to our previous example, TT-1 (turntable 1), which is connected to the third fader, could be disconnected (assuming the turntable wasn't going to be used), and CD-2 could be patched into that fader channel. We then could control the volume of music on CD-2 with fader 3 while simultaneously controlling the level of an announcer using mic-1 with fader 1. By repatching the inputs to specific faders, you can tailor sources of audio to available faders to meet specific needs.

FIGURE 7.55
This simplified block diagram of an audio board shows how a selector switch can be used to assign one of three audio sources to each fader. Note that the output of each fader can be directed to a cue speaker, an audition speaker or to program out. The master gain fader simultaneously controls the output of all faders.

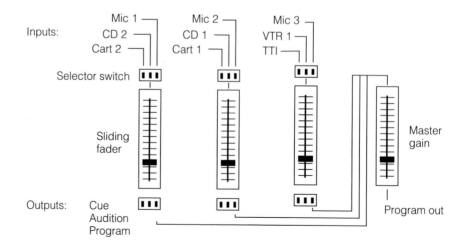

Level Control and Mixing

In addition to switching in the proper audio source at precisely the right time (a formidable task in itself during fast-paced productions) one of the audio operator's primary tasks is to maintain proper audio levels (Chapter 1). But the skillful mixing of audio goes far beyond watching a VU meter. Audio operators must monitor and control the total subjective effect as heard through the **audio monitor** (the audio speakers that reproduce the final output of the audio board).

Control Room Monitors

Professional audio control rooms must have high-quality stereo monitoring systems that can accurately reproduce the full range of sound—from at least 50 to 15,000 Hz—without appreciable distortion. Normally, there is a fader on the audio board that controls the speakers in the control room (the control room monitor). This fader does not affect the level of **program audio,** the final audio mix that will eventually emerge from the audio console.

Although it is desirable to have a high-quality stereo audio monitoring system, this may not provide an accurate representation of the audio as received on relatively inexpensive monophonic TV sets—the kind that many viewers have. To hear how the final stereo mix will be reproduced on these TV sets many audio control rooms have the capability of monitoring program audio through a single, 4- to 6-inch speaker. By occasionally switching the audio to this monophonic speaker, an operator can get an idea of how the audio will sound on many TV sets, and make minor adjustments as necessary. Two things should be checked: the effect these speakers (with their limited bass and treble response) will have on the audio mix, and what is more important, the clarity of monophonic audio, especially in the crucial "center-stage" position where dialogue is normally placed.

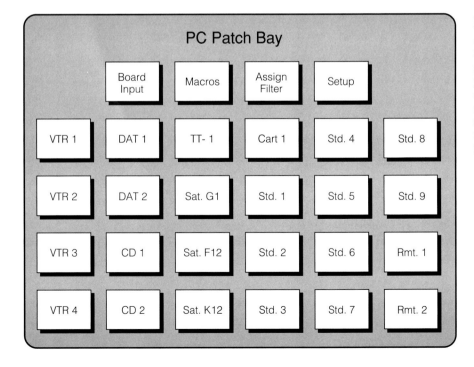

FIGURE 7.56

As desktop computers gain more and more ground in production, traditional patch panels and solid-state audio patching is being replaced in some cases by audio control programs. By simply touching the computer monitor screen or clicking on the appropriate box with a mouse, audio sources can be routed to appropriate destinations.

Audition and Cue Channels

You will note in Figure 7.55 that each of the audio channels can be sent in one of three directions: (1) cue, (2) audition or (3) program. Selecting *program* will direct the audio through the master gain control to the final output of the board. As the name suggests, the **audition channel** allows audio to be "previewed," audio levels set and quality evaluated without going out through the board for recording or transmission.

audition channel: An audio monitor system enabling a technician to listen to, preview and cue audio sources before sending them through the audio console.

The **cue channel,** which is similar to audition, is primarily associated with manually cuing records and reel-to-reel tapes. Depending upon how quickly the tape machine will start when *play* is pressed, a half second or so of lead time might be needed for the machine to come up to full speed. Records are typically cued up by a process called slip-cuing. In *slip-cuing* a record, the stylus of the tone arm is placed on the leading groves of a desired band (cut) of music and the record is manually rotated back and forth until the starting point is found. The record is held with the fingers as the turntable is started. Depending upon how fast the record starts when released, it might need to be backed up about one-quarter of a rotation from the desired starting point. Once the record is cued, the channel is switched to *program.* **Wowing** the record (when the record is heard coming up to speed) is the result of too tight a cue.

slip-cuing: Method of cuing records that involves moving the record forward and backward until the precise starting point of a selection is found. Allows for the instantaneous start of a selection as needed.

In order to differentiate between the audio from cue speakers and the outgoing program material (and to make sure that a record is not accidentally being cued up on the air) many audio operators prefer that cue speakers be of low quality—even a very "squawky" quality. This makes the source of the audio clearly discernable. (This is one of the few cases where an inexpensive piece of equipment can be an asset.)

Master and Sub-Master Gain Controls

Master Gain Control   In Figure 7.55 note that the signals from the three faders (audio channels) on the left all go into a master gain control. This fader simultaneously controls the level of all audio channels on the board and establishes the final output of the console—the program audio. Figure 7.55 represents a rather simple audio board. Although the basic principles illustrated will remain the same, most audio consoles will be more complex, having more inputs and faders—and even several sub-master controls.

sub-master: A volume control that enables an operator to group a number of different audio or lighting sources together and control them with one fader.

Sub-Masters   A *sub-master* is a fader that controls a group of audio channels. For example, all studio mics can be assigned to a sub-master and faded up or down together.

Background Music Levels

Now we come to the all-important subjective elements of audio mixing. Taking a common example of an announcer talking over CD music, if we try to run both the music and announcer's voice at zero dB, the music will drown out the announcer's words. Letting the music peak at about minus 10 dB, and letting the voice peak at zero dB, will probably provide the needed effect: dominant narration with supporting but non-interfering background music. The level of the music will typically be increased somewhat during long pauses in narration, and then brought back down *just before* narration resumes. The exact music level will depend upon the nature of the music itself: whether it is inherently bright and intrusive or soft and mellow. Instrumental music is preferred as a background to narration. However, if the music has lyrics sung by a vocalist (definitely not recommended as background to narration) they will have to be much lower so as not to compete with the narrator's words. Chapter 19 will discuss other considerations in the use of music.

As long as the final mix from the audio board is maintained at about zero dB for maximum levels (you will not want to bring up intentionally soft musical passages to zero dB, of course) the proper mix and blending of audio sources should be left up to the ear.

AUDIO FOLDBACK

It is sometimes necessary to allow studio performers to hear selected audio from the audio board. In the case of a dramatic production this could be a sound effect of a doorbell or a phone ringing. To eliminate audio *feedback* (howl or squeal caused by a mic picking up its own audio from a speaker) studio speakers are normally "muted" (cut off) whenever a studio mic is "open" (switched on). Therefore, when it's necessary for specific audio to be heard in the studio, a special audio speaker called a *foldback speaker* is used. Generally, an audio source (such as a DAT player with a prerecorded sound effect) can be routed through a foldback channel on the audio board and then to the studio foldback speaker. It is important that the volume of this speaker be kept low. Otherwise an echo of the original sound will be picked up by a studio mic. In contemporary music productions, foldback speakers are routinely used so that performers can hear backup singers, musical accompaniment etc. In this case the speakers are often put in front of them—either hung from the grid or placed on the floor.

feedback: Sound regeneration caused by a microphone picking up the output from its own speakers, which results in a ringing sound or a high-pitched squeal.

foldback speaker: PA-type speaker intended to be heard only by talent. Often used in music concerts so performers can hear accompaniment from surrounding instruments.

Lip Sync Presentations

In musical productions vocals are often prerecorded and played back through studio speakers while the performer sings along with (mimes) their own prerecorded singing. This is done for three reasons:

1. The vocalist will be moving and possibly even facing in different directions during the performance, thereby making it difficult to keep him or her on mic at all times.

2. The vocalist will be dancing during the production and would be too out of breath to sing at the same time.

3. The vocal involves complex interactions with other singers or musicians.

The prerecorded musical selection is then played from a tape machine when the number is introduced. The studio mics are not used, but the singer neverthe-less tries to sing along with his or her own words and maintain *lip sync* with the prerecorded words. (If there are no mics on in the studio, the normal studio speakers can be used without a problem.) The number of close-ups on the singer will be governed by how good he or she is at staying in synchronization (lip sync) with the music.

lip sync: Having an on-camera performer mouth words to a prerecorded soundtrack to make it appear as if he or she is actually singing during a production.

MULTIPLE-MICROPHONE SETUPS IN THE FIELD

Audio can be controlled relatively easily in the studio where a wide variety of audio sources can be routed through an audio console, but in the field it can be a different matter.

If only one mic is needed in the field, it can simply be plugged into one of the audio inputs of the camera. But when several microphones are needed (and their levels must be individually controlled and mixed), a small portable audio

FIGURE 7.57

Portable AC- or battery-powered stereo audio mixers are available that will accept several mic or line-level inputs. Most mixers have from three to six stereo input channels. Since each pot can be switched between at least two inputs, the total number of channels that can be addressed ends up being more than the number of faders.

mixer is the best solution (Figure 7.57). The use of an audio mixer requires a separate audio person to watch the VU meter and maintain the proper level on each input.

Portable AC- or battery-powered audio mixers are available that will accept several mic (or even line-level) inputs. The output of the portable mixer is plugged into a high-level VTR audio input (as opposed to a low-level mic input).

Most portable mixers have from three to six input channels. Since each pot can be switched between at least two inputs, the total number of channels that can be addressed ends up being more than the number of faders. However, just as in the case of an audio console, the number of sources that can be on at the same time is limited to the number of pots on the mixer. In addition to the faders that control the inputs, there is a master gain control that controls the levels of all inputs simultaneously and a pot for headset volume.

Using Audio From PA Systems

In covering musical concerts or stage productions, it is possible to use an appropriate line-level output of a public address (PA) amplifier and feed it directly into a high-level input of a mixer. (The regular speaker outputs from the PA amplifier *cannot* be used.[15]) A direct line from a professionally mixed PA system will result in better audio than using a mic to pick up sound from a PA speaker.

MUSIC SYNTHESIZERS AND MIDI INTERFACES

Synthesized Music

synthesized music: Music created entirely by electronic means without the use of traditional musical instruments.

Whereas mainstream TV dramatic productions used to require a full orchestra to create background music, the majority of the music we hear in today's network productions is synthesized. *Synthesized music* is electronically created — sometimes by only one musician. Working with electronic keyboards and an array of electronic equipment, these electronic musicians can realistically simulate anything from a harmonica to a full symphony orchestra.

15. Speaker outputs can't be used for two reasons. First, the impedance is normally 8 ohms, and this will result in a serious impedance mismatch for line-level inputs. More important, the power level for speakers is normally so great that it would seriously damage the input amplifier of a mixer.

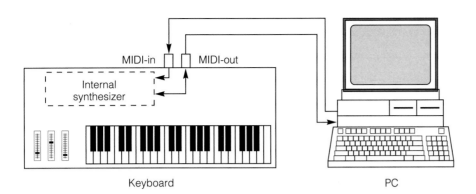

FIGURE 7.58

The MIDI system is credited with starting a technological revolution in modern music. Using MIDI, musicians can interconnect a full range of keyboards, computers and music synthesizing devices to a desktop computer to produce an unrestricted range of musical sounds and effects.

MIDI

In the early 1980s a complete set of system hardware and software standards was adopted for electronic music. This standard is referred to as **MIDI** for Musical Instrument Digital Interface. The MIDI system is credited with starting a technological revolution in modern music. Using MIDI, musicians can interconnect a full range of keyboards, computers and music synthesizing devices to produce an unrestricted range of musical sounds and effects. Normally, a computer is used as a central controlling device (Figures 7.58 and 7.59).

A central feature of composing with MIDI is the building of layers of musical sounds from sampled segments. **Sampling** in this context involves digitally recording sounds or musical segments from live or prerecorded sources. Once a sound is sampled, it can be endlessly modified. Musical segments can

MIDI: Musical Instrument Digital Interface. A standardized interface system allowing various pieces of digital audio equipment, including computers, to work together.

sampling: Digitally recording sounds or short musical segments from live or prerecorded sources. Once a sound is sampled, it can be endlessly modified. Sampling is used in MIDI-based sound creation systems.

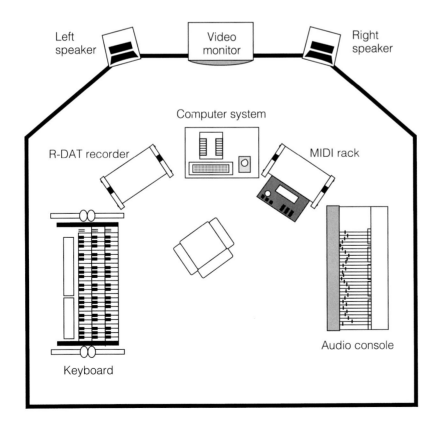

FIGURE 7.59

A central feature of composing with MIDI is the building of layers of musical sounds from sampled segments. Musical segments can be cut and pasted in somewhat the same way a writer uses a word processor. Most of the music heard in today's network productions is produced in MIDI composing/sweetening studios similar to the one shown. Figure 7.60 shows how a computer screen might look during a MIDI session.

FIGURE 7.60

Although MIDI and sound editing software vary greatly, all represent sounds as a linear progression of various sources (layers) of sound. By selecting a layer with the cursor, any characteristic of that audio sequence can be changed, including the point at which it synchronizes with video.

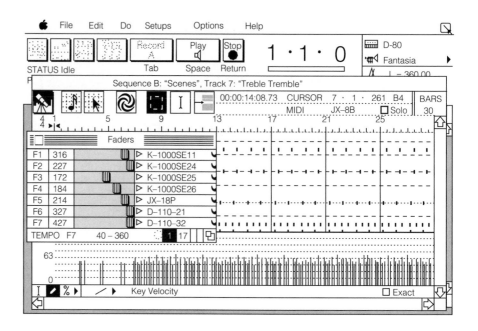

be cut and pasted in somewhat the same way a writer uses a word processor. (See Figure 7.60.) Starting with a simple beat, an electronic composer can add electronic instruments, one by one, until a complete musical group is realistically created. It is possible to alter the tempo of music without changing its pitch. You can also do **tempo mapping** by assigning time code numbers to specific points in video and automatically shrink or expand the music to fit the designated video intervals. In television production, MIDI devices can be synchronized with SMPTE time code, and music and sound effects can be precisely keyed to specific scenes and transitions.

Since MIDI composing and editing is non-destructive to the original sampled sounds, you are free to try a variety of effects. Whenever you don't like something you have done (which might be most of the time when you are experimenting), you can readily "undo" your last edit decision—or even your last few decisions—and instantly be back where you started so you can try something else.

TAPELESS EDITING SYTEMS

Tapeless recording (also called **hard disk recording**) makes use of computer storage devices such as disk drives that allow an operator to digitally record sounds and then play them back almost instantly, in any order. This lays the foundation for tapeless editing. At its most basic level, tapeless editing makes use of a desktop computer using software that is configured to visually represent audio segments on the screen. Once audio is recorded on the computer disk, it becomes an easy task to call up segments, make modifications and mix multiple audio tracks together into a stereo or mono track. Just as with the MIDI equipment discussed, audio can be time-compressed, expanded, filtered, echoed, raised and lowered in pitch and even played backward as needed (Figure 7.60). With enough hard disk storage, an entire digitized sound-effects library can also be put on the disk for instant recall during the editing process.

As editing demands expand beyond a basic desktop computer, we move to dedicated audio editing equipment, referred to as editing workstations.

FIGURE 7.61
For sophisticated audio editing — and
especially for conforming audio to
video — there are editing workstations.
Since both audio and video sequences
are visually represented on the computer screen, music, narration and
sound effects can be slowly "shuttled"
back and forth to synchronize them
with specific points in an edited video
production.

Editing Workstations

For sophisticated audio editing — and especially for conforming audio to video —
there are **editing workstations** or *tapeless workstations* (Figure 7.61). Although
the term can mean many things, an *editing workstation* generally refers to a
sophisticated time-code-based, computer-controlled audio editing system that
allows audio to be synchronized with video. Workstations are often used in the
audio sweetening phase of video production. Since both audio and video sequences are visually represented on a computer screen, music, narration and
sound effects can be "shuttled" (moved) back and forth to synchronize them
with specific points in an edited video production. (Refer back to Figure 7.40.)
When an audio segment is completed, it can be outputted in final form to an
audio tape or videotape recorder.

tapeless workstation: An audio or video
editing console, or workstation, that typically uses computer disks as a recording
medium.

AUDIO QUALITY CONSIDERATIONS

Audio quality can be no better than the weakest link in the audio chain —
microphone, amplifiers, recorder, recording tape, playback mechanics and electronics and audio speakers. When properly used, today's high-quality audio
amplifiers almost never represent a limitation on quality. One critical point,
however, is the audio heads on the recorder. Dirty, misadjusted or magnetized
audio recording and playback heads will quickly affect high frequency response
and playback level.

Audio Head Problems

If the level or quality of the audio as played on one tape machine is noticeably
different from another, there may be three possible explanations: head clog, a
magnetized head or loss of head alignment.

Head Clog   Although some of today's audio and video recorders are
equipped with self-cleaning heads, problems can still occur if the microscopic

head clog: A loss of an audio or video signal resulting from dirt in the microscopic gap of a record-playback head.

gap in audio (or video) heads is clogged with dirt or the oxide coating of the recording tape.[16] This is referred to as **head clog**. Moderate head clog only results in a loss of high frequencies. When it's more severe, there may be either a partial or complete loss of the audio signal.

Head clog requires cleaning the audio heads, either with a Q-tip dipped in an appropriate cleaning agent or with a special cleaning tape. There are both "dry" and "wet" types of head-cleaning tapes. A dry cleaning tape is simply put in the recorder/player and played for a specified length of time. Since most cleaning tapes are somewhat abrasive, care should be taken not to exceed the recommended time. A so-called wet head-cleaning tape (actually, it's only slightly damp) uses a solvent-cleaner, which must be applied to the tape before it's used. Although less convenient, wet cleaning tapes more readily dissolve residue clogging the microscopic gap in tape heads.

With machines using spinning heads (DATs, VCRs), the machine may have to be opened up to take care of a severe case of head clog. But the heads in these machines are easily damaged. If you are not totally confident in your ability to take the top off your DAT or VCR to clean the heads, leave this servicing to a technician. (These heads are expensive to replace.) The heads of analog audio recorders and DCC machines are sturdier, more accessible and much easier to clean.

Magnetized and Misaligned Audio Heads   Audio playback heads depend upon their ability to respond to the minute magnetic patterns recorded on an audio tape. If the heads themselves become slightly magnetized, audio quality will be degraded. Demagnetizing tools are available that can demagnetize record/playback heads.

Through continued use the audio heads in analog recorders and players can become misaligned. Correcting this involves monitoring a special audio test tape while physically repositioning the heads with set screws. Aligning audio heads, which shouldn't have to be done very often, is best left to a technician.

Other aspects of audio, such as production communications (PLs or production lines) and audio and video editing concerns will be discussed in future chapters.

SUMMARY

Audio has two basic characteristics that must be understood and controlled: frequency, measured in Hz, and amplitude, measured in dB/SPL and dBm. AGC circuits and limiters are commonly used to control audio level. Audio compressors, limiters and expanders go a step further and modify dynamic range. The level of audio sources can be visually monitored by VU meters, peak program meters and loudness meters. Audio equipment used in broadcast production should be able to accurately reproduce a frequency range of at least 50 to 15,000 Hz.

Three types of transducer elements are used in broadcast microphones: moving coil, condenser and ribbon. Three general directional classifications are recognized for mics: omnidirectional, bidirectional and unidirectional. When the free movement of talent is a prime concern, wireless (RF) mics are often used. Highly directional condenser-type line or shotgun mics are commonly used on location to pick up sound from off-camera positions. On-camera mics include

16. Even though this chapter deals with audio, we'll refer to both audio and video recorders for two reasons. First, the audio on many VCRs is recorded with the video heads (Chapter 10). Second, DAT recorders are similar to VCRs in both their design and operation.

personal (lav and clip-on mics) and hand-held mics. Boom mics are commonly used in studios when it is undesirable or impractical to use personal mics. Often in TV production each audio source is individually miced and recorded on a separate audio track. During postproduction these tracks are mixed down into a single stereo track. Pan pots are used in stereo to shift the perceived spacial position of audio sources.

Sources of prerecorded audio include turntables, CDs, MDs, cart and reel-to-reel tape machines, DCCs and DAT players. The audio console or board, which represents the central mixing/controlling device for audio, amplifies the incoming signals, provides a visual reference for audio levels, allows for the selection of numerous audio sources, permits the mixing together of multiple audio sources, provides a way of checking audio sources and effects before use and allows for the critical monitoring of the final result.

KEY TERMS

access time
amplitude
attenuator
audio channel
audio compressor
audio expander
audio limiter
audio monitor
audio speaker
audition channel
balanced line
bass
bidirectional
capacitor
cardioid
cart (cartridge) machine
clip-on mic
component
condenser microphone
cue channel
dB
dBm
dB/SPL
decibel (dB)
digital audio tape (DAT)
digital compact cassette (DCC)
diversity antenna
double system
dual-redundancy
dynamic mic
dynamic range
editing block
editing workstation
electret condenser mic
erase head
fader
feedback
figure-8 response
foldback speaker

frequency
gain control
graphic equalizer
hard disk recording
hard wired
harmonics
head clog
hertz (Hz)
hypercardioid
impedance
IEC SubCode Format
input selector switch
lav (lavaliere) mic
LED
linear fader
line-level
line mic
lip sync
loudness
loudness meter
loudness monitor
low frequency roll-off
mic-level
microphone (mic)
MIDI
mid-side (M-S) micing
mini disk (MD)
moving-coil mic
MTS (multichannel TV sound)
non-directional
non-diversity antenna
omnidirectional mic
overtone
pan pot
parabolic mic
patch bay
patch cord
patch panel
peak program meter (PPM)

phase cancellation
pirating
pitch
playback head
polar pattern
pop filter
pot
presence
program audio
proximity effect
quad mic
quadraphonic sound
record head
reverb
ribbon mic
riding gain
RF interference
RF mic
rotary fader
sampling
shock mount
shotgun mic
sibilance
single system

slide fader
slip-cuing
stereo mic
stereo separation
sub-master
supercardioid
surround-sound
synthesized music
synthesized stereo
tapeless recording
tapeless workstation
tempo mapping
timbre
treble
ultradirectional
unbalanced line
unidirectional mic
velocity mic
vertical fader
windscreen
wireless mic
wowing
XLR connector
X-Y micing

Composition | 8

THE ELEMENTS OF COMPOSITION

Why do certain paintings endure over the centuries and become priceless, while others quickly move into oblivion? Although art critics have been trying to explain that for centuries, most agree that the difference hinges on an elusive element called artistic talent. Although we don't know all of the factors of talent, we do know that, in the case of art, it goes far beyond a familiarity with basic elements, such as paint, brushes and canvas, to an ability to creatively control these elements to create an emotional experience in the viewer (Figure 8.1).

In painting, an understanding of paint, brushes and canvas is considered rudimentary. This could be compared to the understanding of lenses, VCRs and editors for videographers. In art, as in videography, those who never get beyond a basic understanding of the tools of the trade — as essential as that might be — never distinguish themselves. At best, they will be considered good technicians. It is only after we master our tools and are able to employ them in creative ways to effectively communicate important ideas that our work will be considered praiseworthy and even exemplary.

Form vs. Content

If a scene in a production is striking, dramatic or humorous, we will tend to overlook minor technical weaknesses. On the other hand, a scene can be well-exposed, be in sharp focus, have perfect color balance and be well-lit (i.e., have good *form*) and still be empty of emotional meaning and impact (be void of meaningful *content*). This leads us to the following adage: *Content takes precedence over form*. In other words, the intended message in a production is more

FIGURE 8.1
Successful art, as well as notable videography, goes far beyond an understanding of the tools of the medium to an ability to creatively control these tools to create an emotional experience in the viewer. Here a production unit works on a scene in an art gallery for an institutional video.

important than technical excellence or flashy embellishments. Nevertheless, significant technical problems—poor sound, a jittery camera or a moving boom shadow in the background—will quickly divert attention away from "the message"—content.

The Best Work Is Invisible

All of the elements of production—lighting, music, sound and editing—are best when they can solidly support and enhance content and, at the same time, go by unnoticed by the average viewer. When production elements call attention to themselves, either because they are poorly done or because they are ostentatious, attention is shifted away from the content. In short, production work is generally best when it is, to the average person, invisible. (Of course, if it went by unnoticed or unappreciated by those who know production, we wouldn't have so many awards for film and television given out each year.)

A Director Directs Attention

Although we generally assume that the term *director* refers to the person's role in directing (steering) the work of production personnel, the term actually has a more important meaning: one who directs the attention of viewers. Generally, the "message" has already been set down by the writer. The director's role then becomes one of directing the viewer's attention to a sequence of elements that will impart the intended meaning to the viewer.

In a sense the director is a tour guide for viewers. But instead of saying, "If you will look out the window on the left of the bus, you will see . . . ," a good director cuts to a close-up of whatever is important for the audience to see at that moment. As we will see when we talk about editing in Chapter 15, this would be considered an ***insert shot,*** a close-up of something important within the overall scene. The use of an insert shot is simply a way of directing attention. It forces the audience to look at an aspect of the overall scene and, at the same time, brings out details that may not be apparent.

Good tour guides also help their audience understand things by adding significant information along the way. Good directors do the same. This could be considered a *cutaway*—cutting away from the central scene to bring in related material. In an interview with animal rights activists, the director might cut away to footage of women arriving at a gala event in full-length fur coats.

One of the major roles of production tools is also to enhance the basic message. Music is a production tool when it enhances the atmosphere, tips us off to danger or sets the mood for romance. Lighting can instantly suggest a cheerful atmosphere or a dark, dim and seedy environment. As we will see in Chapter 11, sets and props can readily do the same; in a dramatic production, they can also tell us a great deal about a character. A good example of this is an ***atmosphere introduction,*** where a director tips us off to important things about characters by introducing us first to their surroundings. Starting a dramatic production with a slow pan across a bright, immaculate, airy penthouse apartment garnished with ultramodern furniture and paintings can tell us a lot about the person who lives there. Very much in contrast to this example is Figure 8.2. Would this setting tell you something about a person who chooses to live there?

In a general sense, all of the techniques we've been discussing can be included in the general term *composition*. (Many of them will be elaborated upon in later chapters.) For the remainder of this chapter, we'll concentrate on a narrower and more traditional definition of the term.

insert shot: A close-up shot of something within the basic scene that is used to show features or details.

cutaway: The use of a shot that is not part of the basic scene but that is relevant to it and occurring at the same time. In an interview a cutaway is commonly used to show the interviewer's reaction to what is being said.

atmosphere introduction: Beginning a video segment with a scene or series of scenes intended to establish the conditions, habitat or environment of the central subject matter.

FIGURE 8.2

By showing an audience an establishing shot of this cabin in the woods, much can be communicated about the people who live there—even before we see them. In terms of composition, note how the trees form a frame for scene, both on the left and the right.

PICTORIAL COMPOSITION

composition: The controlled ordering of elements in a scene designed to provide the strongest artistic arrangement and the most effective communication of a central idea.

dynamic composition: Elements of composition related to the moving image and to the interrelationship between scenes.

Composition is the controlled ordering of elements in a scene or series of scenes, designed to bring about the clear communication of an intended message. The principles of both static composition and dynamic composition apply to television production. **Static composition** not only covers the inherent content of fixed images like paintings or still photos but also covers the basic elements that make up video scenes. *Dynamic composition* goes a step further and considers the effect of time: moment-to-moment change. This change can be within a single shot (primarily camera or talent moves), or it can apply to the overall effect of scene selection and editing.

By carefully studying the most enduring and aesthetically pleasing paintings over the centuries, as well as the most effective film and video scenes during the past 50 years, certain artistic principles emerge. These principles govern things we'll be discussing: the use of leading lines, framing, the placement of the center of interest and the balance of mass and tone.

Rules vs. Guidelines

Even though these principles seem rather clear, they should always be considered guidelines and not rules. Composition is an art and not a science. If composition were totally a science, it could be dictated by a fixed set of rules and would end up being rigid and predictable, without room for creativity — and we could probably turn the whole process over to computers.

Since composition is part art, the guidelines can occasionally be broken. But when they are, it is generally by someone who understands the principles and recognizes when they can be successfully transcended for greater impact. Most people break the guidelines without being aware of them. The results speak loud and clear: weak, confusing and amateurish-looking work.

The following sections introduce 15 guidelines for composition. A number of related subtopics are loosely organized around them.

CLEARLY DELINEATE YOUR OBJECTIVES

First, **clearly delineate your objectives and adhere to them throughout the production.** The objectives or central intent of a production can be anything from an exercise in plain escapism to a treatise on spiritual enlightenment.

This guideline applies to the total production and to each shot within the production. Few people would start writing a sentence without any idea of what they wanted to say. Visual statements are no different. If you don't know the specific purpose of the shot in the total production, you cannot expect your audience to somehow come away with a clear message. In fact, whatever meaning the shot might intrinsically contain will probably be confused or even buried by irrelevant and distracting elements.

Good writers, producers, directors and editors know the purpose of each scene. In a documentary they might say, "In this sequence we need to show the alienation these young people feel toward their parents." Once that point is made, the documentary will move on to other points. In a dramatic production a director could tell an editor, "In these scenes we need to hint at the love that Alice is beginning to feel for Jerry." Knowing the idea that needs to be conveyed influences everything from the elements to be included in every shot to the timing of every edit. So, before you roll tape on any shot, have two things clearly established in your mind: the specific reason for the shot, and the purpose of the shot within the overall production. "I couldn't resist it; it was such a pretty shot," is not a legitimate reason for including an extraneous scene in a production — no matter how pretty or interesting it is.

Bit Rate and Boredom

In electronics the term *bit rate* refers to the amount of data (or bits of information) transmitted per unit of time. By twisting this term slightly we can apply it to television production. The "data" in the case of production content, however, is quite diverse; it consists of such things as ideas per second, concepts per second, thrills per second, laughs per second and surprises per second.

The speed at which this information (data) is presented is directly related to the ability of a production to hold viewer interest. This speed has rapidly risen in recent years. If information is presented either too slowly or at a level that is beneath an audience, the production is perceived as being boring. If it is presented too quickly or in too abstract a fashion, an audience can become lost and frustrated. In either case the audience will quickly consider other media options.

We can clearly see this "bit rate acceleration" in long-running TV series. Compare specific soap operas of five years ago to the same productions as they are being done today. In order to stay competitive (i.e., hold an audience), the writing and production have had to change greatly. These programs now feature exotic locations, faster cutting, greater and more frequent emotional swings, faster-moving and richer story lines and, of course, regular dips into those two ingredients relied upon to increase the flow of viewer adrenalin: violence (and the threat of violence) and sex (and the possibility of sex).

In novels, authors used to spend many pages elaborately setting scenes. Now readers are apt to say, "Enough! Get to the point!" TV writers used to be content to follow a single dramatic idea (plot) for an entire show. Today, to hold an audience dramatic television typically consists of numerous plots and subplots intricately woven together. In terms of assimilated ideas per unit of time, viewers have simply become much more demanding.

"But," the question is often asked, "isn't good production always good production, no matter how much time passes?" Unfortunately, from a commercial perspective, the answer is no. For example, to the uninitiated most of yesterday's classic films are rather boring; most simply move too slowly to hold the attention of today's audiences. *"Citizen Kane,"* considered by many film historians to be this country's greatest film, is now difficult to get a group of average people to sit through. The film is also in black and white. Color represents an extra informational dimension. Electronically as well as psychologically, color represents more "bits per second" of information. The more information an audience perceives per unit of time (up to a point, of course), the more engrossing the production seems to be.

Nice, but Not Essential

Including non-essential material in a production slows down the communication of information; and *slow* is almost the same as *boring* in today's fast-paced film and television fare. This brings us to an important maxim: *If in doubt, leave it out.* Once you know the purpose of a production or a sequence within a production, include only what's relevant to support that idea. Each and every scene in a good film or television production should add information to the idea, message or emotion being developed.

Depicting Emotional States

It is in depicting emotions that we often find the greatest difficulty. Seemingly unrelated scenes of people running through stalled city traffic, lines of people pushing through turnstiles and jamming escalators, wouldn't be irrelevant to establishing a frenzied state of mind in a character trying to cope with life in the city. But a shot of "a darling little girl with a red ribbon in her hair" standing alone would not only leave the audience wondering what her role was, but would probably mislead them into believing that there is a relationship between her and the central character.

Finally, a good director and editor know when a point has been made and when to move on. As we will see in the chapters on editing, there are important implications here for how long scenes should be. For now we can summarize this aspect of composition as follows: A scene, or series of scenes, should never be continued for one second longer than it takes to convey the essential information to the intended audience. It is better to leave your audience wanting more than less. When they want less, your production is in trouble.

In the case of our frenzied character, a rush-hour montage of a few scenes will quickly establish the pressures surrounding the central character. Having then made that point, we will want to move on, possibly to show our character's lack of success in coping with it all.

MAKE SURE SCENES HAVE UNITY

The second guideline for composition states that **scenes should have unity**. If a good film or prize winning photo is studied, it is generally evident that the elements in the shot have been selected or arranged so that they "pull together" to support the basic idea. That idea may just be an abstract feeling. When the elements of a shot combine to support a basic visual statement, the shot is said to have *unity*.

This second guideline also applies to such things as lighting, color, costumes, sets and settings. You might, for example, decide to use muted colors throughout a production. Or you may want to create a certain atmosphere with low key lighting or by using wardrobes and settings with earthy colors and a lot of texture. By deciding on certain appropriate themes you can create an overall feeling or "look" that will give your production unity.

DESIGN THE SCENE AROUND A SINGLE CENTER OF INTEREST

The third guideline applies to individual scenes: **Design the scene around a single center of interest**. Before rolling tape on a scene, ask yourself what major element in the shot communicates your basic idea. Starting with the most obvious, it may be the person speaking, or it may be something quite subtle and symbolic. Whatever it is, the secondary elements should support the scene and not draw attention away from it. Multiple centers of interest may work in three-ring circuses where viewers are able to fully shift their interest from one event to another. But competing centers of interest within a single visual frame weaken, divide and confuse meaning.

Again, think of each shot as a statement. An effectively written statement is cast around a central idea and swept clean of anything that does not support, explain or in some way add to that idea. Consider this "sentence": "Woman speaking, strange painting on the wall, coat rack behind her head, interesting brass figurines on desk, sound of airplane flying by, man moving in background. . . ." Although we would laugh at such a sentence, some videographers are prone to create visual statements that include such unrelated and confusing elements.

Developing an Objective Eye

To be able to understand this aspect of composition, you must be able to detach yourself from a scene and objectively view it as simply a collection of visual elements. Once you are able to stand back and see a scene as a collection of "things," you can start to organize, arrange and include or exclude those "things" that do not support your message. In a particular shot, this might be a coat rack, an empty chair in the background or an object on a desk that momentarily ends up being more interesting than the intended center of interest.

We are not suggesting that you eliminate everything except the center of interest—just whatever does not in some way support (or, at the least, does not detract from) the central idea being presented. A scene may, in fact, be cluttered with objects and people, as, for example, an establishing shot of a person working in a busy television newsroom. But each of the objects in the scene should fit in and belong, and nothing should upstage the intended center of interest. A master (wide) shot of an authentic interior of an 18th-century farmhouse may include dozens of objects. Each of the objects, however, should add to the overall statement: "18th-century farmhouse." An interview with a scientist may take place in an office full of scientific apparatus. But the apparatus belongs there and represents the "natural habitat" of the scientist. Assuming that you are focusing on the scientist, just make sure that these supporting elements are in a visually secondary position.

Remember that the viewer has a limited time—generally only a few seconds—to understand the content and meaning of a shot. If some basic meaning doesn't come through before the shot is changed, the viewer misses the point and can become frustrated.

Using Selective Focus

The eye sees selectively and in three dimensions; it thereby tends to exclude what is not relevant at the moment. It is easy for the eye to focus on a particular object and not be conscious of others. If you are talking to someone you will probably not be distracted by a coat rack directly behind the person's head. A TV camera does not see in the same way—just as the microphone is not able to hear selectively and screen out the sound of a passing airplane or a nearby conversation.

However, a camera "sees" in two dimensions, and not selectively. For if you were to videotape an interview with a woman in an office similar to the one described before, the coat rack might appear to be growing out of her head. Assuming for some reason that the coat rack can't be moved or the camera angle can't be shifted to exclude it, you might be able to throw it out of focus by using **selective focus**. Remember from Chapter 3 that shooting from a distance and using a wide f-stop and a zoom lens at an extended focal length (zoomed in) decrease depth of field and increase the selective focus effect. In order not to be distracting, competing objects need to be thrown far enough out of focus so that our eye will not be drawn to them (Figure 8.3).

A Basic Component of "the Film Look"   Part of the "film look" is based on selective focus. Early films were not highly sensitive to light, and lenses had to be used at relatively wide apertures (f-stops) to attain sufficient

FIGURE 8.3
By using selective focus, objects that would otherwise detract from the center of interest can be thrown far out of focus. Here, viewer attention is forced to the center figurine.

exposure. This was fortunate, in a way. By focusing on the key element in each shot (and throwing those in front of and behind that area out of focus) audiences were immediately led to the scene's center of interest—and were not distracted by anything else. Even with today's high-speed film emulsions, directors of photography in film strive to retain the selective focus effect by lowering light levels. This is one of the elements in the so-called film look, which many people admire.

The same principles that have worked so well in film can also be used in video. By throwing foreground and background objects out of focus, the videographer can reduce visual confusion—while directing attention to the center of interest.

This level of image control takes extra planning when you use today's highly sensitive CCD cameras. The auto-iris circuit often adjusts the f-stop to an aperture that brings both the foreground and background into focus. To make use of the creative control inherent in selective focus, high shutter speeds, neutral density filters or reduced lighting levels must be used. The control of lighting is also important in another way

Using Lighting to Focus Attention

Recall from Chapter 6 that the eye is drawn to the brighter areas of a scene. This means that the judicious use of lighting can be a composition tool—in this case to emphasize important scenic elements and to de-emphasize others. Barn doors and flags are commonly used with lights to downgrade the importance of elements in a scene by making them slightly darker.

Shifting the Center of Interest

In static composition, scenes should maintain a single center of interest; in dynamic composition, centers of interest can change over time.

Although our eye may be dwelling on the scene's center of interest, it will readily be drawn to movement in a secondary area of the picture. Movement can therefore be used to shift attention. Someone entering the scene would be a good example.

We can also force the audience to shift their attention through the technique of *rack focus,* changing the focus of the lens from one object to another. Figures 8.4A through 8.4C show how focus is shifted as the sleeping woman becomes aware of the ringing telephone, picks it up and starts talking. Initially, we want the audience to be aware of the sleeping woman, not the phone; then, when it starts ringing, we want to call attention to the phone; finally, in Figure 8.4C, we want to bring the two together.

rack focus: Shifting camera focus from one part of a scene to another, thereby forcing a shift in audience attention.

Shifting Attention With Sound

In stereo and surround-sound we can shift attention from the center of interest to another area through sound placement. This is typically accompanied by movement, as, for example, when something that originally held a secondary role at one side of the frame suddenly comes to life and becomes the center of interest. There are many examples of this in horror films.

OBSERVE PROPER SUBJECT PLACEMENT

The fourth general guideline for composition is **observe proper subject placement**. In "gun-sight fashion," most weekend snapshooters, armed with their automatic, point-and-shoot cameras, feel they have to place the center of inter-

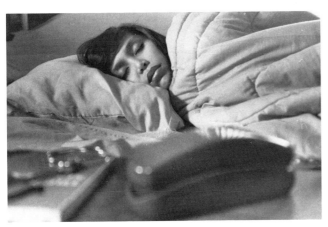

(a)

(b)

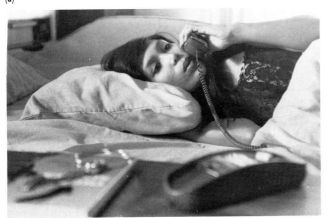

(c)

FIGURES 8.4A through 8.4C

We can force the audience to shift their attention during the course of a scene by using rack focus. Figures 8.4A through 8.4C show how attention can be shifted. Initially, we want the audience to be aware of the sleeping woman, not the phone (Figure 8.4A); then we want to call attention to the phone when it starts to ring (Figure 8.4B); finally, in Figure 8.4C, we want to bring the two together.

FIGURE 8.5
In the rule of thirds the total image area is divided vertically and horizontally into three equal sections. It is often best to place the center of interest somewhere along the two horizontal or two vertical lines. Composition can often be made even stronger if the center of interest falls near one of the four cross-points. (See Figures 8.16 and 8.17.)

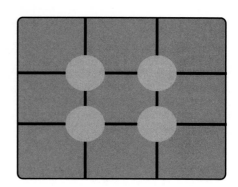

est — be it Uncle Henry, Spot the dog, or the Eiffel tower — squarely in the center of the frame. Strangely enough, the center of the frame is seldom the best place for the center of interest — for a snapshot or a video scene.

Rule of Thirds

Except possibly for close-ups of people, it is often best to place the center of interest near one of the points indicated by the rule of thirds (Figure 8.5). In the **rule of thirds** the total image area is divided vertically and horizontally into three equal sections. Although it is often best to place the center of interest somewhere along the two horizontal and two vertical lines, generally, composition is even stronger if the center of interest falls near one of the four cross-points. (See Figures 8.6 and 8.7.) But remember, we are speaking of a *rule* of thirds, not *law* of thirds.

rule of thirds: A composition guideline that suggests putting the center of interest near one of four points. These four areas are at the cross-points of two vertical and two horizontal lines that divide the frame into equal segments.

Handling Horizontal and Vertical Lines

Weekend snapshooters also typically try to make sure that horizon lines are perfectly centered in the middle of the frame. This severely weakens composition by splitting the frame into two equal halves. According to the rule of thirds, horizon lines should be either in the upper third or the lower third of the frame. In the same way, vertical lines shouldn't divide the frame into two equal parts. From the rule of thirds we can see that it's generally best to place a dominant vertical line either one-third or two-thirds of the way across the frame.

Even if we place dominant horizontal or vertical lines at points suggested by the rule of thirds, there is one more thing to keep in mind. It is generally best to break up or intersect dominant, unbroken lines with some scenic element. Otherwise, they may serve to divide the composition. A horizon can be broken by an object in the foreground (Figure 8.8). Often this can be done by simply moving the camera slightly. A vertical line can be interrupted by something as simple as a tree branch. (Videographers have been known to have someone hold a tree branch so that it projects into the side of a shot in order to break up a line or make composition more interesting.)

CREATE A PATTERN OF MEANING

The fifth guideline for effective composition is **use scenic elements to create a pattern of meaning**. Most people are familiar with the ink blot tests used by psychiatrists. Presented with a meaningless collection of shapes and forms, individuals draw from their own background and thoughts and project their own

FIGURE 8.6
The palm trees at the left and top of picture frame the scene. Note the balance in this scene and how the mountain appears at one of the cross-points in the rule of thirds (Figure 8.5).

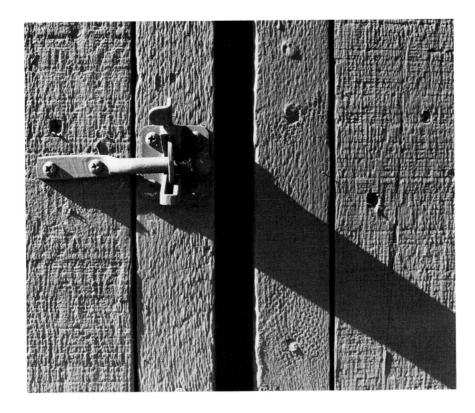

FIGURE 8.7
By following the rule of thirds and using light to bring out detail, something as mundane as an old door latch can be made into an interesting photographic study. Note that the composition would be destroyed if the photographer had chosen to put the door latch in the center of the photo.

FIGURE 8.8

It is generally best to intersect dominant, unbroken horizontal or vertical lines with scenic elements. Otherwise, the lines will divide (and weaken) the composition. If the figures on horseback in this photo were both below the horizon line (instead of intersecting it) the strong horizon line would divide the photo.

meaning onto the abstract images. ("That looks like a mother scolding her son"; or "That looks like a school being crushed by a bulldozer.")

In the same way, if a variety of objects appear in a still photo or video scene, we, possibly even unconsciously, try to make sense out of why they are there and what they represent. We assume that things don't just come together by accident (Figure 8.9).

Good directors take advantage of this tendency and pay careful attention to the specific elements included in a scene. The most obvious example of this is in the atmosphere introduction (mentioned earlier in the chapter), where a director will open on a scene full of clues about the central characters — long before we see them. Early morning shots of a room littered with beer cans, overflowing ash trays, overturned chairs and shoes would not only suggest what happened the night before, but would tell us a lot about the kind of people who were there.

Elements in a shot may be bold and obvious, or they may be subtly designed to suggest almost subconscious meaning. Film critics have spent many hours discussing the symbolism and subconscious levels of meaning in films by directors such as Frederico Fellini. Quite in contrast to the highly abstract meaning of many Fellini films is the concrete meaning required for news and documentary work.

While the director of a dramatic piece should, ideally, be a master at creating illusions and emotional effect, the job in ENG and documentary work is to clearly show things the way they are and let events and facts speak for themselves. This does not rule out striving for new and creative ways of presenting subject matter. Often, it is only by presenting the familiar in a new way that an audience is awakened (or possibly reawakened) to the reality of it.

The Concrete and the Abstract

Whereas in news the object is to present images as completely and clearly as possible, a shot in a dramatic production should *lead* viewers toward intended meaning without being totally concrete. Most intelligent viewers want a bit of room to think and interpret on their own. The term, *on the nose,* is used in

FIGURE 8.9
The fifth guideline for effective composition suggests that we use scenic elements to suggest meaning. We assume that things don't just come together by accident. If a variety of objects appear in a still photo or video scene, we try to make sense out of why they are there and what type of "story" or message they represent.

feature film writing to denote script dialogue or shots that have gone too far in "saying it all." In deciding just how far to go along the abstract-to-concrete continuum, videographers must know their target audience. Intelligence and education are related to an ability to understand abstract ideas. This is why simplistic presentations are resented by adults and also why the classics in music, art, literature, TV and film are not widely appreciated.

Considering the economic realities of the marketplace today, videographers (who wish to be successful) do not have the luxury of blithely going along "doing their own thing" and not concerning themselves about whether their audience will understand it. Good composition is primarily effective visual communication, and the most effective communication takes place when a videographer understands an audience and is able to steer the middle path between being totally concrete and "on the nose," and being so abstract that the audience misses the intended message.

Including Multiple Levels of Meaning

Is it possible to have it both ways? Yes, sometimes. Films and television programs can be designed to have multiple levels of meaning. One of the more obvious examples is a James Bond (007) film. Children can watch these films and enjoy the action and spectacle; adults can readily recognize another level of meaning: specifically, the many sexual double entendres. On a somewhat more sophisticated level there are films like *"The Graduate,"* where new levels of symbolism and meaning can be discovered with each viewing.

Movies and television seek a broad-based appeal. If a writer (and director and editor) can "layer" a production with multiple levels of meaning and successfully provide something for everyone (which is, admittedly, not an easy task), the production will have a much greater chance of success. Although many examples could be given, let's just look at a scene from one film. The closing scene in *"The Graduate"* can be, depending upon the viewer, interpreted in at least two ways. Some will say (and will want to believe) that the film has a happy ending; others, equipped with clues that are integrated within scenes

(a)

(b)

FIGURES 8.10A and 8.10B

Leading lines are used to move viewer attention to a scene's center of interest. These lines can be obvious (as the lines in the walkway in Figure 8.10A), or implied, as in Figure 8.10B. In Figure 8.10B our eyes tend to follow the eyeline of the volleyball players. In so doing, we are led to the ball at the top right of the picture.

throughout the film, will say just the opposite. Possibly what the real meaning of the ending is, doesn't matter, as long as it provides an efficacious experience for different people.

USE LEADING LINES

The sixth guideline for visual composition within a scene is **use leading lines to direct attention**. The boundaries of objects in a shot normally consist of lines: straight, curved, vertical, horizontal and diagonal. Our eyes travel along these lines as they move from one part of the frame to another. Knowing this, it becomes the job of videographers to use these lines to lead the attention of viewers to the parts of the frame they wish to emphasize—especially toward the

FIGURES 8.11A and 8.11B

In addition to moving our eyes around the frame, lines can suggest meaning in themselves. A predominance of curved lines in a scene (Figure 8.11A) suggests grace, movement and beauty. Sharp, jagged lines (Figure 8.11B) connote disharmony and even violence.

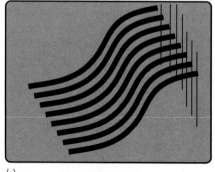

(a)

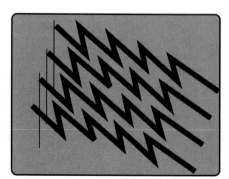

(b)

(a)   (b)

FIGURES 8.12A and 8.12B
By putting objects at one or more edges of a scene, a shot can be framed. Note how the tree and branches frame this photo (Figure 8.12B) of the Hollywood sign. Framing keeps viewer attention from wandering away from subject matter you want to emphasize.

leading lines: The use of either visible or implied lines within a scene to direct the eye to a specific location; generally, to the scene's center of interest.

center of interest. When used in this way these lines are referred to as *leading lines* because they are selected or arranged to lead the viewer's eyes toward the center of interest (Figures 8.10A and 8.10B).

In addition to moving our eyes around the frame, lines can suggest meaning in themselves. Straight, vertical lines suggest dignity, strength, power, formality, height and restriction. Horizontal lines suggest stability, openness and rest. Diagonal lines can impart a dynamic and exciting look. Curved lines suggest grace, beauty, elegance, movement and sensuality. Sharp, jagged lines connote violence or destruction, and broken lines suggest discontinuity. (See Figures 8.11A and 8.11B.)

FRAME CENTRAL SUBJECT MATTER

The seventh guideline for effective composition is **frame central subject matter**. By putting objects at one or more edges of the picture, a shot can be framed. Framing a scene holds attention within the shot and keeps viewers' attention from wandering away from important subject matter. To cite a common example, a leaning tree branch at the top of a scenic shot breaks up a bright sky and acts as a visual barrier or "stop point" for the top of the frame. (See Figures 8.12A and 8.12B.) Framing a shot also adds depth and dimension.

USE PERSPECTIVE CONTROL

The eighth guideline is **use perspective control**. Although many people assume that "the camera never lies," the interpretation of scenes can be significantly altered through lighting, camera angles and lens focal length. As noted in Chapter 3, camera positions and lens focal length alter the apparent perspective in a shot, as well as the apparent distance between objects. A minimal camera-to-subject distance coupled with a short focal length lens (or a zoom lens in its widest position) exaggerates perspective. Parallel lines will be wide apart in the foreground of the picture and rapidly and dramatically converge after a short distance. By using perspective control, quite different impressions about a subject can be conveyed (Refer back to Figures 3.11A and 3.11B in Chapter 3.) The ability to control these production elements represents another important tool for presenting subject matter.

FIGURES 8.13A and 8.13B
The tone (brightness and darkness) of objects in a scene suggests weight. Against medium to light backgrounds dark objects seem heavier than light objects (Figure 8.13A). This is brought back into balance in Figure 8.13B by making the light object larger than the dark one. Large objects seem heavier than small ones.

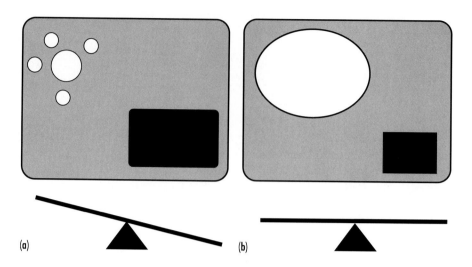

(a)   (b)

MAINTAIN TONAL BALANCE

The ninth guideline for effective composition is **maintain tonal balance.** The tone (brightness and darkness) of objects in a scene suggests weight. Against medium to light backgrounds dark objects seem heavier than light objects (Figure 8.13A). Once you realize that brightness influences mass, you can begin to "feel" the visual "weight" of objects within a scene — and strive for balance.

BALANCE MASS

Somewhat related to maintaining tonal balance is the 10th guideline: **balance mass.** Just as a room would seem out of balance if all of the furniture were piled up just on one side, a scene must be balanced to be aesthetically pleasing. Regardless of their actual physical weight, large objects in a scene seem heavier than small ones (Figure 8.13B). By objectively viewing the elements in a scene, you will learn to see their psychological weight in composition. To do this it helps to imagine a fulcrum or balance point at the bottom center of each of your shots (Figures 8.13A and 8.13B).

Several things can be done to try to balance a shot: the camera can be panned to the left or right, a new camera angle can be selected, or the lens can be zoomed in or out to include and exclude objects. Seldom will things actually have to be moved around.

USE THE PSYCHOLOGICAL EFFECTS OF COLOR AND TONE

The choice and arrangement of colors and tones in a scene can convey a particular message. Thus, the 11th guideline is **make use of the psychological effects of color and tone.**

We know that a dark scene that contains large shadow areas (a dark bedroom or a back alley at midnight) produces a far different feeling than a scene that is brightly lit (the stage of a variety show or a beach at noon). A predominance of bright or dark areas in a scene conveys meaning itself, regardless of what else is going on.

Just as the selection of lighting and monochrome values suggests mood and meaning, so does the choice of color. Producers, directors, set designers and wardrobe persons need to be aware of the messages colors can convey. In general, bright colors can add energy to a scene, whereas a serene, harmonious and stable look will result from the use of lighter (desaturated) hues.

Color preferences among different groups are also important in programming decisions—especially in commercials designed to appeal to a specific demographic group. Women tend to prefer magenta to red hues and delicate tints, while men tend to prefer more conservative blues and more saturated colors. Children are first attracted to the color red, a finding that has not escaped the attention of toy manufacturers.

People also prefer to see colors "in their place." Magenta-to-red colors are popular—until they are brought into a kitchen setting. Bright green can be attractive—until it becomes associated with the walls of a bedroom or hospital.

Surrounding colors also affect color preference. When a color is used near its complement, its preference rating usually rises—as long as the complementary color is subdued and not brighter or more intense than the original color.

Just as people prefer a balance between mass and tone in composition they also prefer a color balance as seen on the color wheel. In particular, they prefer a balance between calming and stimulating colors. In balancing the colors in a scene you should be aware that it will take a greater area of "cool" colors to balance "hot" colors.

Even though people prefer a balance in the colors of a scene, there are many times when a television producer or director will want to intentionally skew this balance to achieve an intended effect. For example, scenes that contain predominately cool pastel colors, such as light greens, will result in an entirely different effect than scenes consisting of fully saturated, hot colors, such as deep orange and burgundy. The first might help convey an atmosphere of undefiled beauty and tranquility; the second, an atmosphere of decadence and perversion.

Finally, our eye initially tends to be drawn to the "warmer" areas of a picture. So, all things being equal, things that are yellow, red and orange will be noticed before those that are blue, green or purple.

AVOID MERGERS

The 12th guideline for composition is **avoid mergers**. There are tonal mergers, dimensional mergers and border mergers.

Tonal Mergers

Tonal mergers result when important objects in a scene appear to blend together and lose their identity. This may be because they are out of focus, because the objects are of similar tonal or color values or because of lighting problems.

Objects that are clearly of different brightness or color when viewed with the naked eye may end up being indistinguishable on the TV screen because of differences in illumination. Objects placed at different distances from a light will vary greatly in tonal value, depending on the level of illumination they receive. We've all seen flash pictures where someone in the foreground of the picture ends up being a washed out "white ghost" and someone in the background is completely black and without any trace of skin color.

tonal merger: An undesirable visual blending of different objects in such a way that they cannot be clearly distinguished.

FIGURE 8.14
Dimensional mergers can cause scene elements to run together. At worst, they look ludicrous, such as when a fountain, tree or lamppost is seen jutting out of an unsuspecting person's head. The student who snapped this photo of the author didn't realize that the lamppost would add an absurd look to the composition. (Then again, maybe he did!)

Dimensional Mergers

dimensional merger: A composition problem often caused by lighting or tonal contrast problems where objects at different distances in a scene merge together and cannot be adequately distinguished.

Next are ***dimensional mergers***. We've noted that the eye sees selectively and in three dimensions. By closing one eye, a videographer can often get a better idea of how a scene will appear when the third dimension is removed. At best, dimensional mergers can cause important scene elements to run together and lose meaning; at worst, they look ludicrous, such as when a fountain or tree is jutting out of an unsuspecting person's head (Figure 8.14). Although selective focus and the use of a back light can alleviate this problem, the best solution, when possible, is to recompose the shot by either shifting the camera angle or rearranging the elements.

Border Mergers

border merger: A composition problem in which subject matter is awkwardly and inappropriately cut off at the edge of the video frame.

The last type of merger, the ***border merger,*** occurs when subject matter is cut off by the edge of the frame — at an inappropriate point. A side view of a car showing all but the back wheels will probably give you an uncomfortable feeling that the back end of the car is just hanging in air without visible back support. A shot of an individual cropped at the knees looks awkward. Cropping off feet or hands in a shot gives a similar result. A shot of a woman in a strapless dress cropped just above the top of the dress gives the illusion she is "topless." Tightening or loosening the shot would solve the problem in each case.

CONTROL THE NUMBER OF PRIME OBJECTS

The 13th guideline for effective composition is **control the number of prime objects in the scene**. An odd number of primary objects provides stronger composition than an even number. In Figure 8.15A the two-object composition seems divided. The addition of a third object in Figure 8.15B seems to add

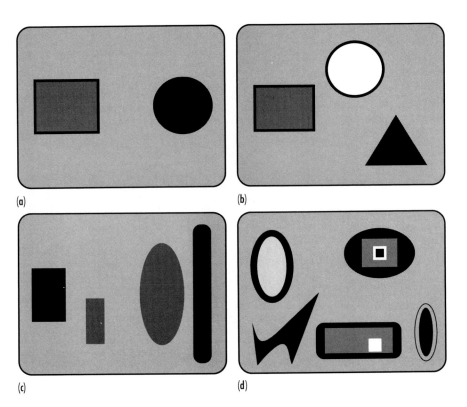

(a)   (b)   (c)   (d)

FIGURES 8.15A through 8.15D
An odd number of prime objects in a scene augments balance. With only two objects (Figure 8.15A), the composition seems divided. The addition of a third object (Figure 8.15B) seems to add unity. Again in Figure 8.15C, an even number of objects makes the composition seem divided. Adding a fifth element improves the composition (Figure 8.15D). Beyond five primary objects, the complexity of the shot becomes such that the number of objects is less important.

unity. Again in Figure 8.15C, with an even number of objects, the composition seems divided. Rearranging the objects and adding a fifth element improves the composition (Figure 8.15D). Beyond five primary objects the complexity of the shot becomes such that the number of objects is less important.

BALANCE COMPLEXITY AND ORDER

The 14th guideline is **balance complexity and order.** This aspect of static composition can be stated with the following rule: Complexity without order produces confusion; order without complexity produces boredom. A medium shot of a banana against a medium-gray background will probably end up being a rather dull visual experience. Add a few apples, some grapes and an interesting fruit bowl and you'll have a more engaging picture (with the banana still standing out from the darker colors). But throw in 500 randomly arranged bananas on top of this and you'll end up with a visual muddle. The most interesting composition is a balance between order and complexity.

USE THE DIRECTION OF MOVEMENT

The final guideline is **use the direction of movement.** Where action moves *from* and *to* is significant. Movement from dark areas to light areas can symbolize liberation or emotional uplift. Upward motion—even something as simple as an individual getting out of a chair—catches attention because it suggests progress or advancement. Downward motion often connotes the opposite (a man collapsing into an overstuffed chair).

Action that progresses toward the camera is more powerful than action that

FIGURE 8.16
A canted shot (a tilted camera angle, also called a dutch angle) is often used to connote might, energy or domination.

canted shot: A shot in which the subject matter appears tilted (running up or down hill) on the screen.

moves away from the camera. The object itself may be moving, or the camera shot may change through a dolly or zoom. Often, televised speeches are worked out with camera operators so that the camera is zoomed in to add emphasis to a certain part of the speech. With this in mind, it is generally better (psychologically) during a speech to dolly in for emphasis and then cut (rather than zoom) back, as necessary, to a medium or wide shot.

Left-to-right movement is more engaging than right-to-left movement. The most engaging type of movement is diagonal, especially when it's from the lower left of the frame to the upper right. A ***canted shot*** (a tilted camera angle, also called a **dutch angle**) is often used to connote energy or power (Figure 8.16).

SUMMARY

It is only when we are able to go beyond a mastery of the basics of production to an ability to use production tools to effectively communicate important ideas that our work will be considered exemplary. Although content always takes precedence over form, problems with form (such as technical problems) can easily obscure content. The best production work should be transparent; it should go unnoticed by the average viewer.

In addition to directing the work of production personnel, one of the major roles of the director is to direct attention. Insert shots and cutaways are commonly used to direct viewer attention to important information.

In its most basic sense, composition is the controlled ordering of elements in a scene or series of scenes, designed to bring about the clear communication of an intended message. Static composition covers the content of fixed images, and dynamic composition goes a step further and considers the effect of time. The guidelines of composition can be broken by those who know how to transcend them in specific instances in order to achieve a greater visual impact.

Fifteen guidelines for composition were discussed: (1) Clearly delineate your goals and adhere to them throughout the production. (2) Strive for unity. (3) Design scenes around a single center of interest. (4) Observe proper subject placement. (5) Use scenic elements to create a pattern of meaning. (6) Make use of leading lines to direct attention. (7) Frame central subject matter. (8) Use perspective control. (9) Maintain tonal balance. (10) Balance mass. (11) Make use of the psychological effects of color and tone. (12) Avoid mergers. (13) Control the number of prime objects in the scene. (14) Balance complexity and order. (15) Create meaning by making use of the movement direction.

The speed at which information is presented is related to the ability of a production to hold viewer interest. This speed has rapidly risen in recent years due to the sophistication of media audiences. If information is presented either too slowly or at a level that is beneath an audience, the production is perceived as being boring. If information is presented too quickly or in too abstract a fashion, an audience can become lost and frustrated. One of the largest factors in this regard is being able to understand and meet the needs and expectations of the target audience. Considering the effect that irrelevant and extraneous material has in slowing down and confusing the central focus of productions, one of the major axioms today is: *If in doubt, leave it out.*

The techniques of selective focus, rack focus and lighting control and the use of color, movement and sound are important in directing audience attention. Composition is often strongest if the rule of thirds is followed for subject placement. News and documentary pieces need to be rather concrete. It is desirable to aim the content of a dramatic piece at a point in the concrete-to-abstract continuum that allows room for personal interpretation. By creating multiple layers of meaning, the base of appeal for a production will be strengthened and broadened.

KEY TERMS

atmosphere introduction
border merger
canted shot
composition
cutaway
dimensional merger
dutch angle
dynamic composition

frame
insert shot
leading lines
rack focus
rule of thirds
selective focus
static composition
tonal merger

9

Video Control and Effects

A *production switcher* (Figure 9.1) is to video what an audio console is to audio: a master controlling and mixing device. Production switchers serve two production phases. First, they are used to switch (edit) a production in real time when decisions on shots and effects are done by the director as a show is recorded or broadcast. Second, they are used in postproduction when the a video switcher and all its effects capabilities are tied in with the videotape editing process.

Today's production switchers go far beyond the simple switching and mixing of video sources. They commonly include a SEG (special effects[1] generator) or DVE (digital video effects) unit[2] which can shrink, expand, flip, spin, wipe and combine images in a multitude of ways. In fact, it seems impossible to envision a visual effect that can't be done with one of today's most sophisticated SEGs. Unlike film, where visual effects, or **opticals,** take days or weeks to complete, in video, effects can be set up and examined immediately. With digital video a sequence of highly complex visual effects can be slowly "built" element by element, electronically memorized and then played back at a touch of a button. Because of video's advantages in doing visual effects, many of today's film effects are created in high-resolution video and then transferred to film.

1. Since special effects are not all that special any more, many feel that the term *visual effects* is more appropriate.

2. It is difficult today to make a clear distinction between *production switcher, postproduction switcher, special effects generator, digital video effects unit,* and *digital video manipulator.* All of these terms are used to describe switching/visual effects units. Facilities that require elaborate visual effect capabilities commonly have one or more separate video effects units designed to supplement the basic production switcher.

FIGURE 9.1
A production switcher is to video what an audio console is to audio: a master controlling and mixing device. Switchers serve two production phases: first, to switch (edit) a production in real time, and second, for postproduction where the switcher's effects capabilities can be tied in with the editing process.

COMPUTER-BASED SWITCHING AND EFFECTS

In recent years dedicated switchers—especially for postproduction work—have been replaced to some degree by computer-based systems that can do a wide variety of postproduction tasks, including titles, graphics and video effects. The introduction of the Video Toaster system for the Amiga computer in 1990 represented a major step in this direction (Figure 9.2). It was at this point that affordable, broadcast-quality video effects became available to a wide range of

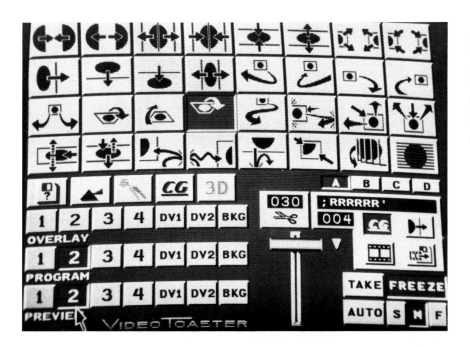

FIGURE 9.2
With the introduction of the Video Toaster system, affordable, broadcast-quality video effects became available to a wide range of video users. Many of the on-screen symbols used in this desktop computer system are designed to look like elements of a standard video switcher.

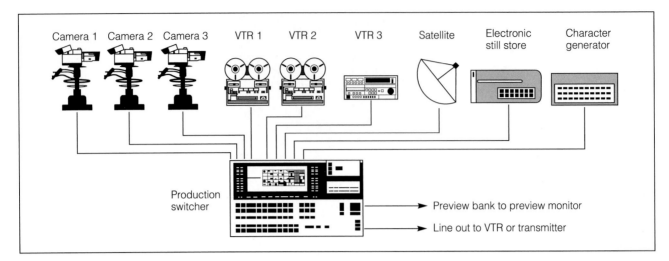

FIGURE 9.3
A variety of video sources can be handled by a production switcher. In this illustration three cameras, three videotape machines, a film chain, a satellite receiver, an electronic still store device and a character generator can be accommodated. Video from each of the sources is assigned to a specific button on the switcher.

video users. Many of the on-screen symbols used in these computer-based systems are designed to look like elements of a standard video switcher. Therefore, a familiarity with the operation of a video switcher will help in understanding and operating computer-based systems.

In this chapter we'll cover the basics of switching and visual effects. In the next two chapters we'll go more into detail on how the effects are used—especially in postproduction.

ELEMENTS OF VIDEO SWITCHING

Note in Figure 9.3 how a variety of video sources can be handled by a production switcher; in this case three cameras, three videotape machines, a film chain, a satellite receiver, an electronic still store device (containing hundreds of still photos in electronic form) and a character generator (for electronically creating titles, credits, graphics and animated visuals). Also note in Figure 9.3 that the video from each of the sources is assigned to a specific button on the switcher.

In contrast to the switcher illustrated in Figure 9.4, more sophisticated production switchers (Figure 9.5) have many rows of buttons—not to mention an ample assortment of switches, knobs and levers. Initially, all this looks quite intimidating. But, as you can begin to see by comparing Figure 9.5 to Figure 9.4, many of these buttons actually control the same video sources.

Regardless of how simple or complex the switcher, the most important row of buttons is the program bus.

FIGURE 9.4
Some basic switching functions are illustrated in this simplified switcher drawing. Sophisticated production switchers have many rows of buttons—not to mention an ample assortment of switches, knobs and levers (Figure 9.5).

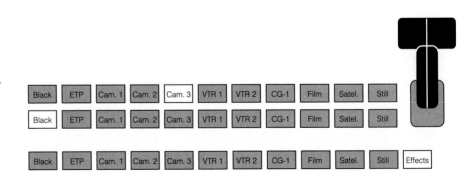

FIGURE 9.5
Initially, all the buttons and levers on a switcher look intimidating. However, as you will discover, many of the buttons on a large production switcher simply duplicate several times over the buttons shown in Figure 9.4.

The Program Bus

It is the row of buttons called the ***program bus,*** or *direct-take bus,* that determines what video will be directed to *line out* or *program.* This is probably the most used row of buttons (bus) on any switcher. Pushing a button on the program bus results in an instant switch (cut) from one video source to another. In Figure 9.6 you can see that the button marked *Cam. 1* is illuminated. As a result, the video from camera 1 is appearing on the line out monitor. If the button marked *Cam. 2* were pushed, the video from camera 2 would instantly[3] appear on the line out monitor (and the light under the *Cam. 1* button would go out as the light under the *Cam. 2* button lit up). In short, you have cut from camera 1 to camera 2. And, of course, pushing any other button on the program bus results in an instant switch to that video source.

program bus: The master bus on a video switcher that determines the final output of the switcher.

3. Technically, it is not always "instantly." The switching electronics have to wait until the interval between video frames before the switch can be made; otherwise the picture would roll on the screen until the new picture got into "sync." Since pictures are completely scanned every thirtieth of a second in NTSC television, the maximum delay in switching from one video source to another will always be less than one-thirtieth of a second—not exactly the kind of delay anyone needs to sit and worry over!

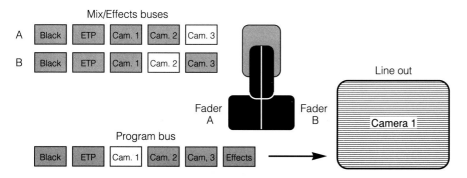

FIGURE 9.6
Pushing a button on the program bus results in an instant switch (cut) from one video source to another. Here, the button marked *Cam. 1* is illuminated. As a result, camera 1 is appearing on the line out monitor. If the button marked *Cam. 2* were pushed, the video from camera 2 would appear on the line out monitor.

FIGURE 9.7

The *Effects* button on the right side of the program bus represents the combined output of the mix/effects (M/E) bank. Two levers called fader bars determine how much video from bus A and bus B will be directed to the *Effects* button. The left fader bar controls the output of bus A and the right fader bar controls the output of bus B. Since the fader bars are in the down position, camera 2 is being directed through the *Effects* button to line out.

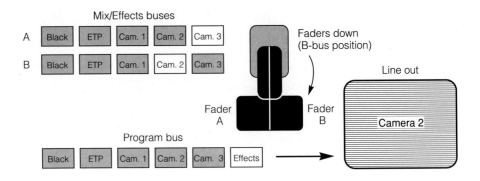

TD (technical director): The individual who operates the control room switcher and is in charge of various technical aspects of a production.

M/E: Mix/effects bank. A double row of buttons on a switcher that can be used for video effects.

fader bars: A pair of levers on the switcher that allows for gradual changes in video levels. They can be used to produce superimpositions, dissolves, fades, keys or wipes at different speeds.

During the course of a normal production the *TD (technical director)* or *switcher* (the person running the production switcher) will rely primarily on the program bus to cut from video source to another. It is only when a visual effect is desired—primarily a dissolve, fade, wipe or key—that it is necessary to use another part of the switcher.

Mix/Effects Buses

Note in Figure 9.7 that the last button on the right of the program bus is labeled *Effects*. This stands for **mix/effects bank** (or *M/E*). This button represents the combined output of the two rows of buttons above the program bus: one marked *A* and one marked *B*. Two levers called *fader bars* (generally locked together so they move at the same time) determine how much video from bus A and bus B will be directed to the *Effects* button on the program bus. The left fader bar controls the output of bus A and the right fader bar controls the output of bus B. They are configured to work in reverse of each other, so when both bars are in the up position the video output of the A-bus is maximum and the output of the B-bus is zero. Conversely, as you move the levers to the down position the video output of the A-bus goes from 100 percent to zero, as the video from the B-bus goes from zero to 100 percent.

Note in Figure 9.7 that the fader bars are in the down position. This means that whatever video source is selected ("punched up") on the B-bus will be directed to *Effects* on the program bus. But it is not until the *Effects* button on the program bus is actually pushed that the video source will go to the line out monitor.

Let's look at an example. In Figure 9.7 you will note that the button marked *Cam. 2* on M/E bus B is illuminated, and the fader bars are in the down (B-bus) position. Since the *Effects* button is pushed on the program bus, camera 2 is

FIGURE 9.8

If you start with the setup shown in Figure 9.7 and move the fader bars to the top position, the video from camera 3 can be directed through the *Effects* button to the line out monitor. In so doing, you have dissolved from camera 2 to camera 3.

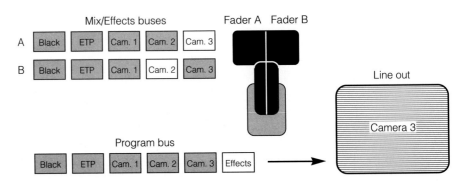

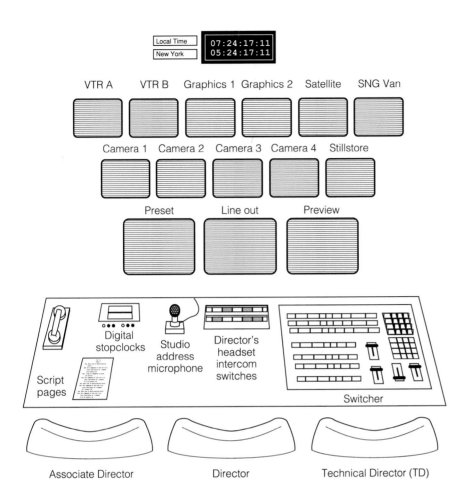

FIGURE 9.9
This shows a typical setup for a TV control room. The line out monitor shows the video being sent to a videotape machine for recording, or, if the production is live, the picture that is being sent to the transmitter. In some control rooms one monitor may serve both previewing and presetting functions; in others there may be two such monitors.

visible on the line out monitor. Note also in Figure 9.7 that *Cam. 3* is punched up on M/E bus A. Therefore, by simply moving the fader bars to the top position, as shown in Figure 9.8, the video from camera 3 can be directed to the line out monitor.

PREVIEW/PRESET MONITORS

Of course, when the *Effects* button is pressed on the program bus, anything set up on the mix/effects bank will go immediately to line out. As we will soon see, it is important to check (and adjust) visual effects before they are "officially seen." This is the role of monitors called ***preview monitors*, preset monitors** or **mix/effects monitors**. (See Figure 9.9.) In some control rooms one monitor may serve all previewing and presetting functions. In others there may be two such monitors: one for previewing upcoming video sources and the other for setting up (presetting) visual effects.

In Figure 9.10 you will note that an additional row of buttons called the ***preview bus*** has been added under the program bus. (The preview bus may also be placed near the top of a switcher.) Any video source, including the output of mix/effects, can be punched up on this bus and viewed on a preview monitor—without in any way affecting the video on the program bus. As we've noted, one of the primary purposes of preview monitors is to set up and adjust visual effects; even simple ones like the super.

preview monitor: A video monitor that can be used to check any camera or video effect before use.

preview bus: A switcher bus, generally connected to a preview monitor, used for setting up and checking video sources before use.

FIGURE 9.10

Here, an additional row of buttons called a preview bus has been added under the program bus. Any video source, including the output of mix/effects, can be punched up on this bus and checked before use. If you stop the fader bars midway between the A-bus and B-bus positions, you will get both video sources at the same time — one over the other. (See Figure 9.12A).

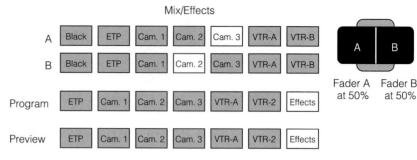

Program = Super

VISUAL EFFECTS

Supers, Faders and Dissolves

From what has been said, you might assume that if you stop the fader bars midway between the A-bus and the B-bus you will get both video sources at the same time — one over the other (Figure 9.10). That's true. When one image is superimposed over another in this way it is called a ***super***. Before the development of electronic keying, all titles, program credits, subtitles etc. were supered over background video sources. Unfortunately, this results in lowered video levels (50 percent video) in both pictures — and a slightly muddy result.[4,5]

But, supers do have their place — if only in passing. ***Dissolves*** are the result of moving the fader bars from one bus position to another so that, in the process, the images overlap for a brief period of time. If it takes three seconds to move the fader bars from one bus to another the result is a *three-second dissolve*. In some switchers and software-based switching systems, dissolves are done without fader bars; you simply enter the sources involved and program the switcher for a one-second dissolve, a three-second dissolve or whatever.

Another use of the fader bar is to do a ***fade***. Let's look at an example of how you could fade out of camera 3 (to black) and then fade up (from black) to camera 2. Referring back to Figure 9.8, you would first punch up *Black* (in place of *Cam. 2*) on the B-bus. When the time came to fade to black, you would move the fader bars to the B-bus (down) position. This would be your fade to black. You would then punch up *Cam. 2* on the A-bus. When you moved the fader bars to the up (A-bus) position, camera 2 would slowly appear. Figure 9.11 compares three visual effects described so far: cuts, dissolves and fades to black.

Occasionally — maybe if you are planning to do a production involving a ghost — it might be desirable to hold a super for a period of time. Unlike a key, which is electronically inset *into* a background source of video, in supers both video sources are slightly transparent (Figure 9.12). As noted before, this can have a slightly muddy result. But it would be useful for supering ghosts (which,

super: Superimposition. A double-exposure effect that predates the key in which two video sources can be seen on the screen at the same time.

dissolve: Simultaneously fading out of one picture while fading in another. There is a momentary superimposition of the two images midway through the effect.

fade: Making video appear from black (fade in), or the reverse, making a video signal slowly disappear to black (fade out; fade to black).

4. To reduce the muddy effect and provide the brightest possible titles, the blanking level on the camera with the title cards is normally brought down to zero (as seen on a waveform monitor) and the white level brought up to 100. By altering the blanking and video gain in this way, you can often take out unwanted details. These same adjustments are made for cameras being used as key sources for titles (to be discussed later).

5. When colors are supered over each other an additive effect is produced. For example, when green is supered over red, the result is yellow. (Refer to Chapter 5 for an explanation of additive color.)

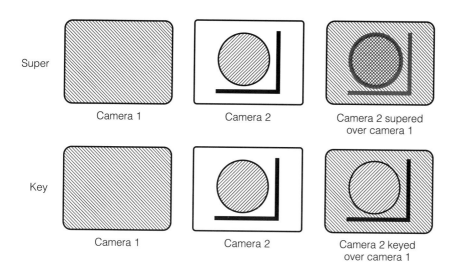

Super — Camera 1   Camera 2   Camera 2 supered over camera 1

Key — Camera 1   Camera 2   Camera 2 keyed over camera 1

FIGURE 9.11

You can use either a *super* or a *key* to get two sources of video on the screen at the same time. However, the results are different. A super is like a double exposure: two video sources appear in the same place simultaneously. For titles, a key gives in a much clearer effect.

according to occasionally reliable sources, are supposed to be partially transparent) over a background scene. The figure of the ghost, in this case, could be shot against a black background with one camera and that camera image superimposed over another video source (let's say the interior of an 18th-century house). Objects, especially bright objects, in the background video source (the eerie room) would then be visible *through* the ghost, thus preserving their reputation for being semitransparent.

What if you want to fade to black from a super? First, there are two things you *won't* want to do. Punching up *Black* on either the A-bus or the B-bus (Figure 9.10) will result in a partial loss of the super (and, in our example, either an instant loss of the ghost or the room). Punching up *Black* on the program bus would result in an instantaneous (and abrupt) cut to black. Neither would look good.

There are two acceptable solutions. On many switchers the fader bars on a mix/effects bank can be unlocked and moved independently. When each is moved to its zero-video position (Figure 9.13) the result would be a graceful fade to black. Moving them in the opposite directions (each to its maximum position) should definitely be avoided. This could result in 200 percent video: 100 percent from the A-bus and 100 percent from the B-bus.[6]

6. If a waveform monitor is visible (which it is in most large production facilities), the bars can sometimes be split in this direction to bring the video up to a full 100 percent. But exceeding 100 percent video can cause serious quality and image stability problems.

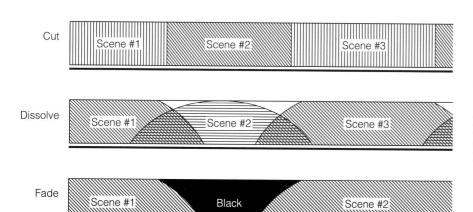

Cut — Scene #1   Scene #2   Scene #3

Dissolve — Scene #1   Scene #2   Scene #3

Fade — Scene #1   Black   Scene #2

FIGURE 9.12

Instantaneous switches from one scene to another are called *cuts*. When scenes momentarily overlap during a transition it is called a *dissolve*. Finally, in the bottom example the scenes are divided by a momentary *fade* to black. Momentary fades to black are often used to signify changes in time or location.

FIGURE 9.13

In many switchers the fader bars on a mix/effects bank can be unlocked and moved independently. When each is moved to its zero-video position, the result is black. Moving them in the opposite directions should definitely be avoided. This results in 200 percent video: 100 percent from the A-bus and 100 percent from the B-bus.

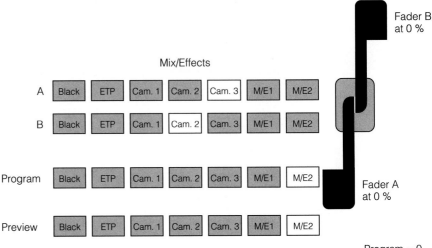

Multiple Mix/Effects Sources

On a switcher with two or more mix/effects sources, fading to black from a super could be done in at least two other ways. In Figure 9.14, M/E-1 could be routed through M/E-2. In this case M/E-2 will simply treat the output of M/E-1 as it would any other video source. The super you've set up on M/E-1 could then be faded to black with the fader bars on the second M/E bank. (To send the final result to *program* or *line out,* M/E-2 must, of course, be punched up on the program bus.)

With switchers that have two M/E banks it is possible to put an effect over an effect (if, for some reason, you have a need to do that). This is done by feeding the output of one M/E bank through another M/E bank. In the process you add whatever effect you have set up on M/E-1 to M/E-2. This is referred to as **double re-entry.** Some switchers even have three M/E sources and are capable of **triple re-entry.**

With this we move from the simple mix aspect of M/Es (supers, fades and dissolves) to the effects component (keys and wipes). On most switchers there are buttons to the right of the M/E banks to select a mix, key or wipe (Figure 9.15).

double re-entry: A switcher that permits the output of one mix/effects bus to be re-entered into another mix/effects bus for further video manipulation.

triple re-entry: A video switcher system in which the results of one mix/effects bank can be directed through another, and then the results of that can, in turn, be directed through a third mix/effects bank, thus combining three layers of video effects.

FIGURE 9.14

In addition to being able to fade to black as shown in Figure 9.13, there is a better way on switchers with two mix/effects banks. *M/E-1* and *black* are selected on M/E-2. You can then fade out of any M/E-1 effect by fading to black on M/E-2. Note that *M/E-2* has been selected on the program bus.

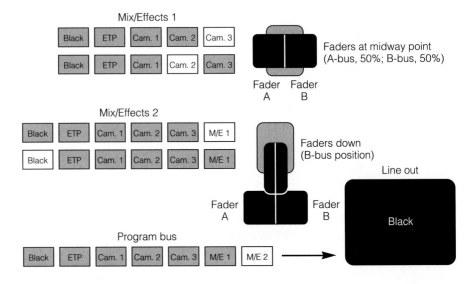

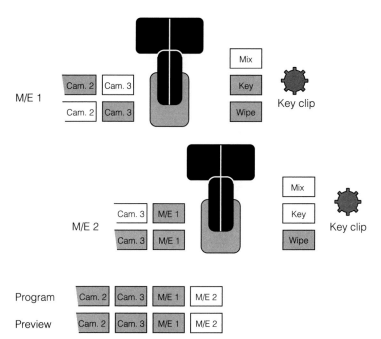

FIGURE 9.15
Although there are limited uses for simple mix functions on switchers, when we move to the key and wipe modes a whole range of keys, wipes and special effects becomes possible. (Note the *mix, key* and *wipe* buttons on the right of the fader bars.)

Luminance Keys

You will note from Figure 9.12 that (except for the production requirements of ghosts) the effect of a key is much better than a super. Unlike a super, with a standard **luminance key** the two video sources are not placed on top of each other. Instead, an area of the background video is electronically "cut out," and the second video source (the *key source*) is inserted into the empty space. In a basic key the specific area cut out is determined by the shape of the bright areas (luminance) of the second key source (the video being keyed into the background). With a key, the two images can't interfere with each other as they do with a super since only one source of video will be visible at any one point. This also means that both video sources can be used at 100 percent of their levels, and not just 50 percent as in the case of the standard super.

key source: A video source keyed into background video.

Internal and External Key Sources

A distinction between an external key and internal key is made on some switchers. An **internal key,** the one we've been talking about, involves two sources: a background and a key source. The roles of the key source (the video to be inserted into the background video) are (1) to define the shape of the area that is to be cut out and (2) to supply the video that will fill the cutout area. With internal keys, the background video is selected on one M/E bank and the key source on the other. Once you push a button marked *key* next to a M/E bank (Figure 9.15) and the fader bars are moved toward the bus with the key source, this video is then inserted (keyed into) the background video.[7]

7. In an effort to reduce the number of banks on switchers, **delegation controls** are commonly used to assign different roles to banks. On some switchers the preview bank can be delegated as a key source selector. As we've noted, production switchers vary considerably in their features and operation, so no attempt can be made in this chapter to provide a guide to the operation of all switchers.

Camera 1
Background video

Camera 2
Key pattern

Camera 3
Key fill pattern

Final result

FIGURE 9.16
When a third video source is involved in a key it is referred to as an external key. In this case the first video source (Camera 1) is the background camera and the second source (Camera 2) defines the area to be cut (keyed) out of the background. Camera 3 shows the content for the key pattern. The last frame shows the final result.

There is also another type of key, which involves a third video source. This is referred to as an **external key**. Just as in the case of the internal key, the first video source is the background camera and the second source defines the area to be cut (keyed) out of the background. But, in the case of an external key (sometimes called *third camera key*) a third video source represents the content that will be put into the area defined by the second video source (Figure 9.16). When *external key* (not shown in the illustrations) is selected on a switcher, the video from a designated bus becomes the "third camera."

Downstream Keyers

downstream keyer: A device that allows titles to be keyed over a line out signal.

With a *downstream keyer* (Figure 9.17) the key is added to the video after it leaves the switcher ("downstream" from the program bus). Putting the keyer downstream means that a M/E bank on the SEG can be freed up for other purposes. The effect of a downstream key can be previewed (and adjusted) before use by punching it up on an effects monitor. Most downstream keyers have two sets of fader bars: one to fade the key in and out and the second to

FIGURE 9.17
When a downstream keyer is added to a switcher, a mix/effects bank can be freed up for other purposes. Most downstream keyers have two sets of fader bars: one to fade the key in and out and the second to fade the entire downstream video signal to black. CG-1 and CG-2 represent two character generators used to key titles and credits over the final video. The effect of downstream keys can be previewed (and adjusted) on an effects monitor.

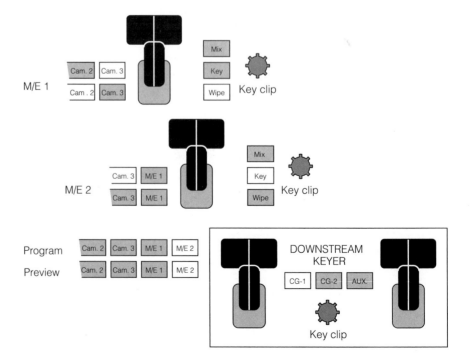

fade the entire downstream video signal to black. This would be used if you wanted to fade a downstream key to black at the end of a production.

Adjusting the Key Source

The final result of a luminance key is dependent upon the luminance (video level) of the key source. A control called a *key clip* (sometimes called a **clipper gain knob**) is provided on the switcher to adjust this level (Figure 9.17). Before keys are used, they must be checked (and generally adjusted) with this control. Too much level from the key source and the key will smear across the background picture; too little and the edges of the key image will look thin, tear and, in extreme cases, not be visible at all. Key clip adjustments should be made while carefully observing the result on an effects monitor. By adjusting this control you can drop out middle tones in video and create interesting high-contrast effects (Figure 9.18).

Unless the background video is significantly different in tonal and color values from the keyed-in information, there can be a legibility problem with keyed-in text. Several additional key adjustments are provided that can help this problem.

Altering Key Colors

It is possible with most of today's switchers and character generators (CGs) to change the color (and associated color attributes) of the keyed-in material with hue, saturation and brightness controls (Figure 9.19). In some switchers these controls are referred to as *colorizing controls*. When the switcher provides the video to be keyed into the area cut out by the key source, it is referred to as a **matte key**. In this case the key source simply defines the shape of the matte and the switcher fills in a color that has been selected on the colorizer. Mattes also

FIGURE 9.18
The key function on a switcher opens the door to many special effects. Here, all middle tones are dropped out with the key clip control, and the effect is a stark black-and-white image.

key clip: A control on a video effects unit used to set the threshold level for color or luminance keying.

colorizing control: A knob that can move through the entire range of colors and be used to select any color for electronic effects.

FIGURE 9.19
It is possible with most of today's switchers and CGs to change the color of keyed-in material with the hue, saturation and brightness controls. Note the color wheel represented on the hue control. A variety of wipe patterns are shown at the top of the drawing. The edges of these wipes can be modulated (made to fluctuate) with the pattern modulation control. The frequency and amplitude controls affect the nature of the modulation.

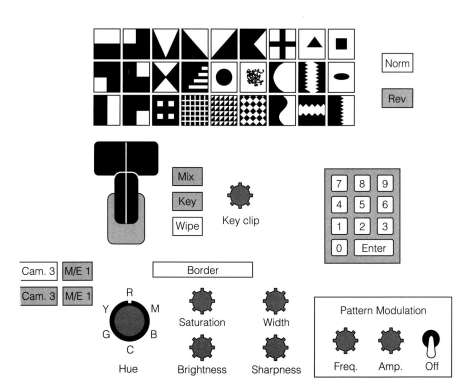

FIGURE 9.20

Unless special precautions are made, text can become illegible when keyed over a complex background. One solution is to add an edge or border to the keyed-in material. You could use light letters with black edging (center). If the letters still look flat, a drop shadow can be added to increase legibility and suggest depth (bottom).

drop shadow: Shadows, generally electronically produced, that are added around letters.

chroma key: An electronic matting effect that keys out, or removes, a portion of video of a specific color. Another video source is then substituted for the removed area. Generally, a deep, saturated blue is used as a keying color.

chroma key blue: A deep shade of blue commonly used in backgrounds intended to be keyed out and replaced with other video. See *chroma key.*

apply to external or third-camera keys, but in this case instead of the switcher filling in the matte, the third camera supplies the video.

Title Keys and Legibility

If you were trying to key letters over a complex background, using a matte key to add color to the letters (Figure 9.20) would be the first step toward improving legibility. But two questions remain: How will the colored letters show up on monochrome TV sets? and Will the letters still be legible if you key the letters over a mixed or changing background—one with a variety of colors and tones?

The solution in both cases is to add an edge or border to the keyed-in material. In the case of written material you could use either white letters with black edging (black borders) or black letters with a white border (Figure 9.20). And, if the letters on an edged key still look a little flat, a shadow effect (*drop shadow*) can be added to suggest depth. Additionally, on many CGs you can change the color of the border and the drop shadow.

Chroma Key

So far we have been talking about luminance keying. There is another type of internal key called *chroma key* that is based upon color in the background video rather than on the luminance of the key source.

Chroma key is a matting process, similar in concept to what is used for many film visual effects. With chroma key, an area represented by a selected color is removed from the background video while the rest of the picture remains. At the same time, video from a second source is inserted into the void. (See Figures 9.21A through 9.21C.)

Although any color can be keyed out of the background video, it is obviously best to select a color that will cause the fewest problems. It is also simpler, technically, to use a primary color. If red were keyed out of a scene, there would be a risk of keying out flesh tones (and, therefore, people) since skin tones contain red. Interestingly, skin tones also contain quite a bit of green, so this color can also be a problem. This leaves the third TV primary, blue. Not only do skin tones contain virtually no blue hues, but, as you may remember, TV white contains only 11 percent blue (whereas it contains 59 percent green and 30 percent red). Selecting a shade of blue reduces the danger of accidentally keying out important video from the background scene.

Chroma Key Blue   But there are many shades of blue, so a shade has to be selected that will present the fewest problems with the largest variety of on-camera subject matter. A highly saturated (pure) royal blue, now dubbed *chroma key blue* is commonly used for chroma key. This shade—officially recognized by some paint suppliers—can be found in the background of many TV studios. But there are still two possible problems.

First, whatever color is selected for the chroma key will restrict the range of colors that can be used in sets and wardrobes. When keying out a certain shade of blue, anything in the background picture containing that color will be keyed out. It simply disappears. A person wearing a blue coat on camera might suddenly find that the coat has been electronically removed and video from another camera substituted in its place. The second problem involves shadows. Deep shadows in a scene are often seen by TV cameras as being bluish. These shadow areas can sometimes exhibit a tearing effect around their edges, especially if the keyer is improperly adjusted. For this reason, lighting with chroma key must be kept quite even across the set and high lighting ratios must be avoided.

(a)

(b)

(c)

FIGURES 9.21A–9.21C

Chroma key is a matting process, similar to what is used for many film visual effects. With chroma key, a selected color is removed from the background video while the video from a second source is inserted in its place. Here, the blue background is removed behind the two seated figures (Figure 9.21A) and another background, in this case a scale model of a city (Figure 9.21B), is picked up on another camera and combined for a final effect (Figure 9.21C).

Chroma Key Applications

At most TV stations chroma key is now used primarily to key in maps, satellite images etc. behind the weatherperson. Since TV weathercasters can't see the keyed-in visuals, but only a blank, blue wall behind them, they must rely on video monitors to show them the composite picture. A video monitor is typically placed at each end of the weather set just out of view of the camera. When weathercasters appear to be pointing to various spots on the map, they are actually using one of the monitors as a guide in directing their hand to invisible (to them) spots on the blue background behind them. (This obviously takes a bit of practice.)

In many special-event field productions the setting for the event—be it a football stadium, civic auditorium, concert hall or the scene of a disaster—can be keyed in behind a commentator. This gives the impression, which might be considered unacceptably misleading in some situations, that the commentator is actually at the event. Only one camera would be needed at the event for background video; the other could be focused on the commentator, who could be comfortably seated in an air-conditioned, chroma key–equipped studio hundreds of miles away!

Beyond the basic weather and special event–type applications of chroma key, there are much more sophisticated uses. Chroma key can put actors into animated backgrounds and into scale models of anything from 18th-century farmhouses to the interior of a spaceship. Of course, building scale model backgrounds can be done at a fraction of the cost of building full-size sets. In the PBS production, *"Alice Through the Looking Glass,"* chroma key was used throughout the production to supply an ever-changing assortment of fantasy settings for the actors.

Actors can even be made to appear to sit on a chair or lie down on a bed that exists only in the scale model background. To do this, a solid, full-size object, having the scaled-up dimensions of the miniature chair or bed in the background must be constructed and painted chroma key blue. In the case of an actor sitting down on a chair, a 20-inch high, chroma-key blue plywood cube could be placed at the exact location of a scaled-down chair in the model background. When an actor sits on the blue cube, it would appear as if he were sitting on a chair in the background.

Actors can even be made to appear to go through doors of a miniature background setting. In this case, a door-sized opening could be cut to the chroma key background. When an actor moved through this "door," it would seem as if he were going through the door of the scale model house.

Chroma Key Problems   Using chroma key in this way has its own special set of problems (some would say "challenges"). First, actors must learn to act against a large chroma key backdrop, void of any scenery or props. In order to show the actor's feet, the acting backdrop must be constructed so that the floor and background of the acting area smoothly and unobtrusively blend together in one, continuous chroma key tone.

The next problem area for chroma key relates to creating a good, clean keying edge around the actors. Dark or black hair may reproduce slightly blue. This can result in a ragged edge around heads or even cause a tearing effect as the chroma keyer tries to decide where subjects end and the chroma key background begins. As we've noted (in Chapter 6), for chroma key, some lighting directors use light straw-colored (yellow-amber) gels in all back lights. A slightly amber rim around subjects cancels the blue in the hair and aids in clean keying.

The final problem area involves keeping the chroma key background unblemished. Dirt, smudges, creases and, in fact, any significant variation in the background can cause problems. Even footprints on a chroma key floor resulting from dirt on the shoes of actors can cause problems.

Taking the Shadow With the Actor   When chroma key was first developed it only keyed the actors into a background and did not take along their shadows. (Since shadows on a blue background also end up being a shade of blue, they simply disappeared along with the background.) We expect a person working close to a background to cast a shadow. To solve the problem of shadowless people, chroma keyers were developed that could detect an actor's or announcer's shadow on a chroma key background (even those disturbing multiple shadows that accompany bad lighting setups!). With their shadows intact, the images of actors or announcers could then be combined with background video for a convincing effect.

Panning, Tilting and Zooming With Chroma Key   Another initial problem with chroma key was the inability to pan, tilt or zoom the cameras involved. If you panned with an actor as he crossed a chroma key background, you got the strange impression (from the perspective of the keyed-in background) that he was walking while standing still. If you zoomed in, things got even more interesting: you would find that your actor was inexplicably growing larger from the perspective of the background.[8]

---

8. Of course, if you need to see someone shrink or get larger as part of a special effect, this may be just the technique you are looking for.

The answer to these problems is to use motorized (robotic) pan heads, pedestals and zooms controlled by a computer. The computer can lock all the movements of two cameras together. When the camera with the actors pans, tilts or zooms to follow movement, the camera on the miniature background will simultaneously move—but in precise, scaled-down degrees. As an example, let's say that the background was built to a scale of 1 centimeter equals 1 meter. If the talent camera is panned 1 meter to the right to follow a talent move, then the camera focused on the background will automatically move right 1 centimeter. When viewed on a monitor, it appears as if the actor is simply walking across the background setting as the camera pans to keep pace. The same is true, of course, for zooms; when the talent camera zooms in or out, the "slave" camera focused on the miniature background simultaneously zooms in and out in scaled-down increments.

At this point, you should recognize the origin of many of the attention-getting visual effects you see on television. In recent years the quality of chroma key effects has been greatly enhanced by the use of high-definition video. To achieve maximum quality, effects are often done with in high-definition digital equipment and then transferred to NTSC video for broadcast.

Wipes—5,000 Ways to Change a Picture

Cuts, dissolves and fades are three ways of making a video transition. One of the leading manufacturers of video switchers has asserted that there are 5,000 types of transitions possible with today's sophisticated production switchers. As yet, no one has stepped forward to challenge the statement. With only three transitions covered, does this mean that we have 4,997 left to discuss? Fortunately, the rest all come under one category: the wipe.

A general definition for a *wipe* is "an electronically generated pattern that forms a moving border between two video sources." This border can take a multitude of forms; it can have a hard, sharp edge or a soft, blurred edge; it can consist of a band of any color, and it can be modulated (made to fluctuate) in many ways. By pushing a pattern selector button on the SEG, selecting *wipe* on the switcher, and then moving the fader bars from one selected video source to another, the pattern selected will form the moving transition between the two video sources.

In addition to the patterns that may be shown on the buttons on a switcher (Figure 9.19), on many SEGs hundreds of other basic patterns can be stored in electronic memory. A printed menu is used to select the pattern needed. The corresponding number is entered into the SEG with a keypad (Figure 9.19).

In a *modulated wipe,* the boundary line is made to ripple by the modulating action of an electronic signal (sine wave). Both the frequency and amplitude of the modulating signal can be varied to suit the mood of the transition.

Many switchers have *Normal* and *Reverse* buttons on wipes, which allow greater flexibility in the direction that wipes move, depending upon which way the fader bars are moved (Figure 9.19). If a wipe moves from left to right in the *Normal* mode when the fader bars are moved from the A-bus position to the B-bus position, it will also move from left to right when the bars are moved from the B-bus position to the A-bus position. However, what if you want to wipe left to right and then quickly back again (right to left) to another picture? When the *Reverse* button is pushed, moving the fader bars from the B-bus to the A-bus will reverse the movement of the wipe: it will then move from right to left. (Even with the *Reverse* button pushed, the wipe moves in the normal left-to-right direction when the fader bars are moved from the A-bus to the B-bus.)

Keying in Background Graphics   One of the most common applications of the wipe is to put background visuals in a newscast (Figure 9.22).

wipe: Visual effect where one video signal gradually replaces another through the action of a moving line or pattern of demarcation.

FIGURE 9.22
One of the most common applications of the wipe is to put background visuals in a newscast. This technique is referred to as a corner insert. Although a corner insert might not seem like a wipe, it is typically just a rectangular wipe pattern stopped partway through a transition.

corner insert: A square or rectangular key insert into a segment of a background picture. Generally used in news to show graphics behind a newscaster.

freeze-frame: A still image captured from action on a videotape or film.

This technique is referred to as a ***corner insert***. Although a corner insert might not seem like a wipe, it is typically just a rectangular wipe pattern stopped partway though a transition. Using a M/E box pattern for a corner insert rather than relying on a rectangular-shaped chroma key area in the studio background is preferred for two reasons: it provides more flexibility in positioning and sizing the visual, and it gives a more consistently reliable result.

On many switchers splitting the fader bars and moving them independently provide control over both the size of the rectangle and its vertical and horizontal dimensions. These adjustments can be important in masking off the top, bottom or sides of a visual.

Any source of video that can be punched up on a mix/effects bank can be used as a background visual. On most switchers this limits video to sources that are "in sync" with other sources of video coming into the switcher. Non-synchronous sources of video must first go through a **framestore synchronizer** to bring them into sync with the background video before they can be used in a M/E bank.

Framestore synchronizers also allow *freeze-frames* (still pictures from any still or moving video source) to be used as visuals. Still frames from the beginning scene of a videotape are sometimes used over a newscaster's shoulder as the tape is introduced. Then the tape is rolled and taken full screen. Selected freeze-frames from a show are sometimes used to roll closing credits over at the end of the production.

On many switchers full-frame visuals can be digitally enlarged or reduced to appropriately fit into a corner insert or chroma key area. When it is not critical to keep the horizontal and vertical proportions of the picture in the same ratio, it is possible to vertically and horizontally shrink or stretch a visual. Generally, small adjustments in the vertical or horizontal size of a visual can be made without being noticed.

Digitally expanding or compressing the size of a video source also has other uses. Let's say a boom mic accidentally ends up being visible at the top of a scene. During postproduction the picture can be slightly enlarged to eliminate the mic. With allowances for diminished picture quality, even bigger enlargements can be made if, for example, you wanted to call attention to a specific element in a scene in of an ENG tape.

Auto-Key Tracking

An **auto-key tracking** (or *chroma key tracking*) feature on many switchers keeps the size and area of the keyed-in information constant when the background camera is zoomed or repositioned. If you were to zoom out on a newscaster (and thereby reduce the size of the chroma key area behind him or her) the auto-key tracking feature would automatically resize the keyed information to correspond with the reduced size of the chroma key area. This feature also makes it possible to remove a corner insert by shrinking it down to a dot, or to do the reverse: expand it from a point until it takes over the full frame of the video.

Another control, a **joystick**, or *positioner* (Figure 9.23), can be switched in and used to move a corner insert to any part of the background video. The joystick is also used to position a bright circle to provide a **spotlight effect.** This effect slightly darkens background video and overlays a highlighting circle around an area that you want to call attention to.

positioner: A video effects control that can move an inserted key source to any position in background video.

Programming Visual Effects

Even in this introductory discussion you can begin to see that the steps involved in setting up and executing visual effects can become rather complex. Often it is difficult to go through all the necessary setups in a short time — especially when a production, such as a commercial, calls for a rapid sequence of many visual effects. When you add to this the necessity of cuing up and starting and stopping a variety of video and audio segments (and presetting their levels) before they are needed, things start bordering on the impossible — at least for a mere human being.

For some time manufacturers have provided many SEGs with the ability to memorize a sequence of steps and play them back at a touch of a button. This

FIGURE 9.23

A joystick, or positioner, can be switched in to move a corner insert to any part of background video. The joystick is also used to position a bright circle to provide a spotlight effect on background video.

means that a series of events can be broken down into steps and then "chained" into one, continuous sequence. At a touch of a button the sequence can be automatically executed. This makes it possible to slowly go through the steps (checking the results and making adjustments as necessary) while the SEG unit records in memory everything you do. At any point the sequence can be run in real time to check the effect. When everyone is satisfied with the effect, the sequence of steps involved can be saved on a floppy disk for future use. Using this approach, it would be possible to load into memory the standard visual effect sequence regularly needed for a newscast and then start the sequence at the push of a button each time it was needed.

COMPUTER-BASED SYSTEMS

Desktop Video

dedicated equipment: Electronic equipment designed for a specific purpose, as opposed to computer-based or software-based equipment.

desktop video (DTV): Video effects and editing controlled with a desktop computer.

Thus far we have primarily concentrated on separate pieces of hardware designed to do specific jobs. This approach is referred to as a hardware-based approach using *dedicated equipment* because each piece of equipment (hardware) is intended for (dedicated to) a specific task. In the early 1990s this concept started to change when it became practical to consolidate the functions of many separate pieces of production hardware in a computer. This became known as a software-based system. Since a desktop computer is used, it is also referred to as *desktop video.* By adding a few circuit boards to a computer and installing specially designed software programs, you can accomplish the following:

- Do production, postproduction and master control switching
- Create a full range of broadcast-quality visual effects
- Design elaborate graphics for productions
- Key in written material (titles, credits etc.) with a plethora of fonts and typefaces to choose from
- Do two- and so-called three-dimensional animated sequences

Suddenly, production sequences that had previously required an assemblage of specially designed pieces of hardware could all be done in front of a single computer terminal. And you could do these things without having to sacrifice any of the computer's other capabilities. (Computer graphics and animation will be discussed in Chapter 11.)

Desktop video came along at about the same time Hi8 and S-VHS camcorders were introduced. Both developments represented major steps forward in low-cost quality production. This meant that for the first time sophisticated production techniques became available to a wide base of video users.

Amiga, Apple and IBM Desktop Video Standards

Three basic industry computer standards are used in these computer-based systems: Amiga, Apple and IBM. Unlike the basic Apple and IBM approach to video display and processing, from the start Amiga engineers patterned their electronics after the NTSC broadcast standard. This made it simpler and less expensive to modify the Amiga for NTSC video production. Taking advantage of this fact, the Newtek Corp. invested five years in designing hardware and software for the Amiga that could replicate the functions of a video switcher, video effects generator, character generator and graphics creation system. They dubbed their system the Video Toaster. Although the initial configuration was

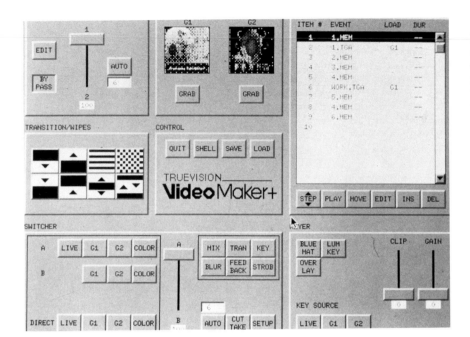

FIGURE 9.24
In addition to a basic video switching
capability, desktop video systems typically include the following effects: luminance keyers, standard and animated
wipes (page turning, mosaic transitions, spray paint effects etc.) and
freeze-frame and framestore
capabilities.

limited to only four external video inputs (plus additional internal sources of
video), this was found to be adequate for meeting many basic production and
postproduction needs.

Referring back to Figure 9.2, you can see that the menu of options on the
screen represents many basic video switcher functions. You can also switch to
several other screens (or, in some cases, add "window" displays on top of the
basic display) that give you control of the systems's other video capabilities.
(See also Figure 9.24.)

There are similar systems for the Apple and IBM computer standards. In
addition to a basic switching capability, these systems typically include the
following video effects: luminance keyers, standard and animated wipes (page
turning, mosaic transitions, spray paint effects etc.) and freeze-frame and framestore capabilities. The last item allows you to "grab" (capture) selected still
frames from a video source. These frames can then be used as background for
titles or modified in a variety of ways with a *paint program* (Figure 9.25) to
create elaborate visuals. Typically, a **chroma processor** is also included. This
allows you to modify video colors—all the way from subtle shifts in chroma (to
restore the proper color balance in scenes) to transforming a basic video source
into an unrecognizable piece of abstract art.

The functions of computer-based editing and video effects are controlled in
four ways: with a standard computer keyboard, by touching appropriate areas of
the screen with a finger (a so-called **touch-screen system**), by using an electronic pencil (Figure 9.25) or by "clicking" on screen icons (symbols) with a
hand-controlled mouse (Figure 9.26). These approaches to computer control
will be discussed in more detail in Chapter 11.

Like the Amiga, the IBM **computer platform** (a readily modified basic
computer system) has an *open architecture*. This means it is possible for a wide
range of companies to manufacture video-related plug-in boards, without having
to go through IBM. In many cases adding or upgrading video hardware is as
simple as opening the computer, plugging a new board into an empty slot, and
installing new software. Although upgrading Apple-type computers is often
not as easy, the basic design of the more advanced Apple computers favors

paint program: A computer program designed to create and modify graphics.

open architecture: A computer platform
that allows for the easy addition of circuit boards produced by a variety of
manufacturers.

FIGURE 9.25
Sophisticated electronic graphics systems (paint programs) use an electronic pencil to select options from an on-screen menu and to draw, trace and color on-screen art. Some examples of what these systems can do are shown at the end of Chapter 5.

high-speed video display techniques. For this reason there have been scores of production-related software programs designed for the Apple computer.

Multitasking

As we've suggested, one of the most valuable characteristics of the computer is its ability to do a wide variety of production-related (and even non-production-related) jobs. The latest generation of computers can do several jobs simultaneously. This is called *multitasking*. Although computers are fast — and getting faster each year — occasionally you will find yourself waiting for the computer to finish a specific task before you can go on to the next one. With multitasking you can start the computer on one task, and while it's busy doing that you can pop up another task-related window of functions on the screen (Figure 9.27) and start the computer working on something else. Meanwhile, in the background the computer will continue to work on the first assignment.[9] Assuming you can keep track of it all — and we very quickly learn about our human limitations here — you could conceivably have the computer working on four or five production-related tasks simultaneously.

But even if you are not up to making full use of the computer's ability to simultaneously work on several tasks at the same time — and few of us are — multitasking will make it possible for you to switch back and forth between tasks without having to drop (dump) one computer program and replace it with another. For example, you could readily switch back and forth between following a script in your word processing program and editing a related production. During the process of editing you may find a need to call up other computer programs. You might see that some scenes need color correction, that you need to add titles, subtitles or credits over some scenes or that some animated video transitions and video effects should be added. After all of these software programs are loaded, something really important, like lunch, might come along. By popping up yet another task window over all of this, you could find the

multitasking: A computer-based system that can do more than one task at the same time.

FIGURE 9.26
Most basic desktop video systems use a keyboard and a mouse to control the various functions. Because of their comparatively low cost and many features, desktop video systems have made a major impact on video production.

9. Tasks such as calculating the vectors for an elaborate graphics display involve millions of computer operations. Since it may take the computer some time to perform them, multitasking allows you to go on to some other task while the computer simultaneously works on these calculations in the background.

FIGURE 9.27
With multitasking you can start the computer on one task and, while it's busy doing that, pop up another task-related window and start the computer working on something else.

phone number of your favorite pizza palace and have the computer dial the number for you.

Each of these tasks requires a different computer program. With multitasking you can load all of the programs required and then switch between them as needed. The number of programs you can use at one time depends primarily on three things: the amount of random-access memory (**RAM**) available in the computer, the type and speed of the computer's central processing unit (**CPU**) and the computer's data storage capacity.[10] But the computer's usefulness doesn't stop here.

RAM: Random-access memory. A computer's basic working memory that holds information only as long as the computer is turned on.

CPU: Central processing unit. The heart of a computer that processes information according to the instructions received from software.

Transmitting and Receiving Production Data by Modem

Today, various types of production information are routinely exchanged between computers in different locations. The computers might be in different parts of a building, a city or even in different parts of the world. You might want to send or receive script revisions, an edit decision list, a graphic, a video effect programming sequence or some other production-related information. For this you need to know about computer modems. A **modem,** which stands for *mo*dulator-*dem*odulator, is a device that changes digital computer data into analog audio tones that can be transmitted over telephone lines. Modems also allow users to tap into vast electronic "libraries" of graphics and information. By joining a **computer network** that specializes in the needs of people working in video production, professionals can share resources and exchange data and information on specific projects. In addition to national networks such as CompuServe that have specialized divisions, there are numerous electronic bulletin board services (**BBS**), especially in New York and Southern California, that cater specifically to the needs of people working in production.

modem: (modulator-demodulator) A device that converts digital information from a computer to analog sound signals that can be transmitted over telephone lines. At the receiving end the modem can convert the sound back into digital information.

BBS: Electronic bulletin board system. An electronic source of text, images and computer programs available over telephone lines by computer modem hookups.

10. Even though various data compression techniques are routinely used to reduce the amount of storage space needed for desktop video, computer storage space generally has to be upgraded to 100 MB (megabytes) or more.

Keeping Video Effects in Perspective

The production technology we've been discussing in this chapter is capable of effects that are only limited by our imaginations. Faced with an ever increasing array of video effect opportunities, it is easy to get lost in creative possibilities. In so doing, it is easy to forget the real goals of the production.

A person who puts on airs is said to be *affected,* meaning that he or she is artificial, contrived, phony, pompous and pretentious—not exactly flattering adjectives. When television productions are overly *effect*ed (with a profusion of dazzling but meaningless effects), the same adjectives apply. As noted earlier, anything that distracts from the central message weakens a production. Therefore, the bottom line in the use of effects is this: they can be justified only when they in some way supplement or enhance the intended message of a production.

ROUTING AND MASTER CONTROL SWITCHERS

Although the production switcher or SEG is often just referred to as "the switcher," there are actually three other types of switchers: postproduction switchers, routing switchers and master control switchers.

Postproduction switchers are similar to the dedicated switchers we've covered thus far in this chapter. The primary difference is that postproduction switchers are designed to be interfaced with editing equipment to automatically carry out programmed editing sequences. Instead of being controlled by an operator, a postproduction switcher is typically controlled by the computer software associated with the editing system.

As we will see in the chapters on editing, desktop video systems and editing workstations are also used for postproduction switching. (Editing workstations, which are more specialized than desktop video systems, are all-in-one editing stations designed specifically to handle a full range of professional audio and video editing needs. See Chapter 7.)

The next type of dedicated video switcher is a routing switcher. **Routing switchers** serve the same basic function for video that patch panels do in audio. They make it possible to reassign video inputs to the various pieces of video equipment as well as to select among various video sources for a limited number of switcher inputs. As in audio, there are three types: one relying on patch cables (Figure 9.28A), one that is keypad-based and one that relies on a CRT display (Figure 9.28B). In the last case a computer-type mouse or a touch screen is used to select and interconnect the various video sources.

The *master control switcher* resembles a small production switcher. Its function is to handle changes in programs; specifically, to select the needed video and audio sources from control rooms, tape machines and satellite services. (Refer back to Figure 1.13 in Chapter 1 for a photo.) Other than not having the same visual effect capabilities of a production switcher, there are two major differences. First, it has the capability of simultaneously switching audio and video (*audio-follow-video*) to the transmitter or distribution system. Second, since the switching sequence involved in station breaks can be very complex, many of these switchers can be programmed to automatically handle a sequence of steps with split-second accuracy. Although the cost of such automated equipment is high, this is offset by the fact that a single commercial can represent thousands of dollars in revenue. A switching error that causes even the beginning or end of a commercial to be lost can result in having to provide free air time to rerun the commercial (a **make-good**).

postproduction switcher: A video switcher designed to meet the specific needs of editing and that is capable of interfacing with two or more videotape machines.

master control switcher: Video switcher with limited video effect capabilities designed to serve the specific needs of a master control area. Most such switchers control video and audio simultaneously.

audio-follow-video: A switcher that automatically switches audio with its corresponding video.

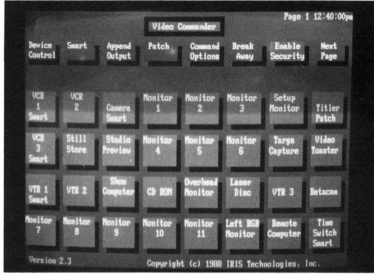

(b)

(a)

FIGURES 9.28A and 9.28B

A video routing switcher serves the same basic function for video that a patch panel does in audio—to assign a limited number of video inputs to the various pieces of video equipment. As in audio, there are three types: one relying on patch cables (Figure 9.28A), one that is keypad-based (not shown) and one that uses on a CRT display (Figure 9.28B). In the last case a computer-type mouse or a touch screen is used to select and interconnect the various video sources.

SUMMARY

There are four types of dedicated video switchers: production switchers, post-production switchers, routing switchers and master control switchers. Many of today's production switchers incorporate the functions of an SEG (special effects generator), a DVE (digital video effects) unit and a DVM (digital video manipulation) unit.

The production switcher represents the central switching and image manipulation device in the production facility. The program bus is used to select the output of the switcher. This output can be any video or any mix/effects (M/E) source. Fader bars are used in M/E banks to make transitions from one bus to another. A wide variety of wipe patterns can be selected to make patterned transitions from one video source to another. Joysticks are used to position boxes, circles and other geometric patterns within a background picture. In keys and matte keys, video is electronically removed from a background picture and video from another source is inset into the area. Keys are generally used for inserting titles, credits and background visuals into a production. In one widely used type of matte key (chroma key), video of a particular color (generally royal blue) is removed from a background video source, and video from another source replaces it.

A routing switcher serves to initially route video to specific sources, such as VTRs and switcher inputs. A master control switcher is the final switching device that directs the audio and video output of various tape machines and studio control rooms to the transmitter or program distribution service. Today, desktop video systems bring the functions of switchers, character generators, chroma manipulation, framestore devices and graphic creation systems to desktop computers.

KEY TERMS

audio-follow-video	key source
auto-key tracking	luminance key
BBS	make-good
chroma key	master control switcher
chroma key blue	matte key
chroma processor	mix/effects monitor
clipper gain knob	mix/effects (M/E) bank
colorizing control	modem
computer network	multitasking
computer platform	open architecture
corner insert	opticals
CPU	paint program
dedicated equipment	positioner
delegation control	postproduction switcher
desktop video	preset monitor
dissolve	preview bus
double re-entry	preview monitor
downstream keyer	production switcher
drop shadow	program bus
external key	RAM
fade	routing switcher
fader bars	spotlight effect
framestore synchronizer	super
freeze-frame	TD (technical director)
internal key	touch-screen system
joystick	triple re-entry
key clip	wipe

Video
Recording

10

In this chapter we'll look at the various approaches to recording video, including the strengths and weaknesses of each.

A few decades ago programming produced by local stations either had to be done on film or live. Film, which had been around for almost 100 years, was an excellent medium for recording images and sounds. But for broadcasting there were a couple of major problems. First, because of its need for processing, film represented a delay of at least several hours before it could be broadcast. Second, film was costly, especially for doing full-length programs. Video, on the other hand, was immediate and comparatively inexpensive. But video also had a major problem. There was no way of preserving the live image, except by kinescope recording (focusing a motion picture camera on a video monitor and making a film of a program). Because kinescopes were of low quality, were expensive and necessitated time-consuming processing, they were seldom used for locally produced programming.

This all changed in the mid-1950s when the first practical video recorder was developed by the Ampex Corp. in California. The first machines required 2-inch-wide tape that cost $500 per reel and could only record 30 minutes of programming (Figure 10.1). Even so, it opened up whole new vistas of possibilities in video production, including the tape delay of programming originating on the East Coast (so it could be played back at the appropriate time for the different time zones across the United States).

With the exception of prime-time dramatic productions, much of television programming today is produced on videotape and relayed by satellites to stations across the country. In contrast to the blurry old kinescope recordings of yesteryear, today's videotape recorders routinely reproduce television programming that is technically indistinguishable from a live show. Even when productions originate on film, they are almost always transferred to videotape before broad-

FIGURE 10.1
The first practical video recorder required 2-inch-wide reels of tape that cost $500 each. They could only record 30 minutes of black-and-white video. Even so, these machines opened up whole new possibilities for television, including the tape delay of programming originating on the East Coast (so it could be played back at appropriate times for different time zones).

cast or distribution. In the area of non-commercial, institutional television, almost all programming is produced on videotape.

Videotaping a production has many advantages:

- Mistakes can be corrected during postproduction.
- Program content can be improved in a multitude of ways through editing.
- Program segments can be reorganized and rearranged for optimum effect.
- The length of a program or segment can be shortened or lengthened to fit programming needs.
- Production costs can be saved by scheduling TV studio facilities for optimum efficiency.
- Programming can be time-shifted to conform with time zones and personal preferences.

A QUICK LOOK BACK AT THE TECHNOLOGY

The electronic recording of broadcast programming can be traced back to the German AEG Magnetophon audio recorder in the mid-1940s. Once the basic technology for recording audio arrived in the United States, experiments began to extend the concept to video. But, the 4-million Hz NTSC bandwidth was far more difficult to record than the 5 to 10,000 Hz bandwidth associated with early audio recorders.

In order to capture this wider bandwidth, the first experimental efforts to record video attempted to move the tape 200 to 300 times faster than the tape in an audio recorder. In theory it seemed like a good idea. To accomplish this some of the early experimental VTRs (videotape recorders) used tape reels that were almost 6 feet in diameter, and even then could manage to record only a few minutes of black-and-white video. The tape also had to travel at a speed of 4,000 ips (inches per second), which is equal to more than 225 miles per hour. Not

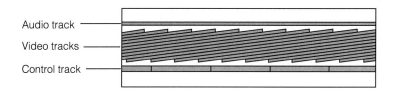

Audio track
Video tracks
Control track

FIGURE 10.2
Videotape machines today are of the helical type. Since the tracks are slanted and long, analog-type helical machines are able to record a complete video field in a single pass of a head. The control track consists of electronic pulses that help keep the video frames in synchronization.

surprisingly, early experiments often resulted in wall-to-wall tape when something malfunctioned during the high-speed recording process. In the early 1950s Crosby Electronics, RCA and the BBC (British Broadcasting Corp.) all came up with various types of videotape machines. Unfortunately, none were really practical.

The Two-Inch Quad VTR Debuts

It was a small, six-man team at Ampex in 1956 that first demonstrated a practical videotape machine. The approach they patented ended up being a world standard for three decades. Instead of trying to move the tape at a high enough speed to record millions of cycles of information each second (no one was having much success with that idea), the Ampex team reached the needed speed by simultaneously moving the videotape and the recording heads. The effect—a little like walking up a moving escalator—combined both speeds. This allowed the tape to go at the slower and more manageable speed of 15 ips. These tape machines used 2-inch-wide tape and four video heads placed 90 degrees apart on a spinning headwheel. The headwheel rotated perpendicular to the horizontal movement of tape. As the tape moved past the spinning headwheel, each of the video heads recorded 16 horizontal lines. This meant that the headwheel had to turn eight times in order to piece together a complete 525-line picture. These machines weren't exactly portable; each weighed 1,350 pounds—not counting the three, floor-to-ceiling racks of associated electronics.

Because there were four heads on the machine and the video fields were transversely scanned in segments, the system was variously referred to as "segmented," "quadruplex" and "transverse" recording. Eventually, these tape machines were just referred to as **quad machines**.

Helical Tape Machines Take Over

The concept for the helical-type recorder, which eventually succeeded the quad machine, was actually experimented with in early VTR work. But it took some time to solve all of the technical problems. Today, almost all videotape machines are of the helical type. The name, *helical,* comes from the head-scanning pattern that resembles a spiral. (See Figure 10.2.) Instead of the recording heads spinning almost perpendicular to the moving tape as they did with quad machines, the heads of helical machines record long tracks that are almost parallel to the moving tape. (See Figure 10.3.) Since the tracks are much longer, helical machines are able to record a complete video field in a single pass of a head. This eliminates one of the major problems with quad machines: getting the four segments to match when played back.

The first helical machines used 2-inch videotape, just as the quad machines did. By 1963, improved technology made it possible to reduce tape width to 1 inch. In the 1970s, 1/2-inch recording tape appeared; and in the 1980s, some helical VCRs started using tape that was 8 mm wide.

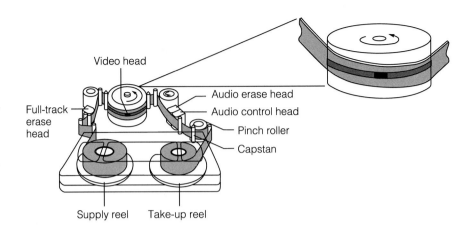

FIGURE 10.3
Videocassette recorders (VCRs) all work in basically the same way. The tape from a cassette is automatically threaded into the VCR so that it is wrapped around the video heads and pulled past the audio heads by the capstan roller. Since the video heads are spinning at the same time the tape is moving, the combined speed makes it possible to record the high frequencies associated with video.

THE VIDEO RECORDING PROCESS

In all types of video recorders the **video head** transfers the signal from the video source to the recording tape. Videotape consists of a strip of plastic backing coated with a permanent layer of microscopic metal particles embedded in a resin base. These particles are made of materials such as iron or cobalt, which are capable of holding a magnetic charge from the video heads. The video heads are made from a highly permeable material that can be quickly magnetized by an electric current, in this case a current responding to changes in a video signal. A microscopically small opening between the heads focuses the varying magnetic fluctuations within the gap. As the heads rapidly move across the tape, the varying magnetic fields affect the alignment of magnetic particles in the tape's magnetic coating. Thus, a magnetic "imprint" is created in the videotape corresponding to the original video signal.

When a videotape is played back, the process is reversed; the magnetic imprint on the tape induces magnetic changes in the video heads, which are in turn converted into minute voltages. After being amplified millions of times, these voltages can be brought back to the level of a normal video signal.

THE TIME-BASE CORRECTOR ARRIVES

TBC: (time-base corrector) Electronic device that corrects time inconsistencies in a camera or videotape recorder's signal.

Shortly after the invention of 2-inch quad recording, a number of smaller, non-broadcast tape formats were developed. They all had one major drawback: because of mechanical and electronic instabilities, they could not meet the technical requirements of the Federal Communications Commission (FCC) for broadcasting. It was the invention of the time-base corrector in 1973 that changed this. The **time-base corrector,** or *TBC,* can take the signals from small cameras and non-broadcast-quality VCRs and correct the variations in the high-speed scanning and timing pulses so they meet FCC broadcast standards.[1] If not corrected, the likelihood of the pictures rolling, fluttering and evidencing variations in the scanning lines (Figure 10.4) is much greater.

Once the TBC became available, a whole new realm of video equipment

1. Today's TBCs go far beyond simple time-base correction. Many can hold a complete video frame in memory, making it possible to bring any non-synchronized video source into synchronization with another piece of video equipment (such as a video switcher). This full-frame window of correction (referred to as *infinite correction*) is also important in accepting signals from a variety of unsynchronized sources, including satellite and microwave feeds and consumer VCRs.

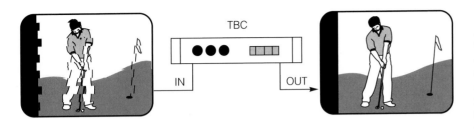

FIGURE 10.4
A time-base corrector, or TBC, can take the signals from small cameras and non-broadcast–quality VCRs and correct variations in the high-speed scanning and timing pulses. If not corrected, the likelihood of the pictures rolling, fluttering and evidencing variations in the scanning lines is much greater.

was suddenly available for broadcast use. In a short time the TBC revolutionized television news. Videotape machines, which previously could only be transported in a medium-sized truck, suddenly could be carried from place to place by one person. Small video cameras and recorders could then be used for on-location, broadcast-quality production, just the way film cameras had for decades.

VTR/VCR CLASSIFICATIONS

Eventually, three general classifications of VTRs and VCRs[2] emerged: consumer, professional and *prosumer* (a combination term reflecting high-quality consumer equipment often good enough to be used professionally). In addition, an **industrial video equipment** classification is recognized that typically falls somewhere between the prosumer and professional categories.

prosumer video equipment: A combination term denoting equipment that lies between professional and consumer-quality video equipment.

VTR INPUTS AND OUTPUTS

VTR Inputs

Today's VCRs record video, audio and often an indexing signal called time code. (Time code will be discussed in Chapter 15.) In addition to the connections for these signals, VCRs generally provide a number of other input options. Most allow for an external sync cable. With *external sync* the VCR can be "locked" (brought into video synchronization) with an external device, such as a sync generator or video switcher. Some tape machines also provide a connection that will interconnect them with an editor or edit controller.

external sync: As opposed to internal sync, video synchronizing pulses from an external source, such as a sync generator. Used to synchronize multiple pieces of equipment.

VCR Outputs

Although the stereo and monophonic audio outputs of VCRs are standard, high-level outputs, with video there are more choices. Specifically, there are composite, Y/C and component outputs.

Composite Video

A **composite video signal** contains luminance, chrominance and sync information all multiplexed together into a single signal. This general approach to combining the various parts of the video into one composite signal for VCR

2. The term *VTRs,* or *videotape recorders,* refers to reel-to-reel machines with separate supply and take-up reels. The 1-inch, type-C VTR is an example. The term *videocassette recorders,* or *VCRs,* refers to systems that use a plastic enclosure that houses both the supply and take-up reels. S-VHS, Hi8, Betacam and MII are examples of VCR formats. Since VCRs are most common, this term is generally used throughout this text.

generations: The number of copies away from an original tape. The first generation is a copy of the original recording; the second generation is a tape dubbed from the first generation, etc.

Y/C: Refers to the separate processing of the luminance (Y) and chrominance (C) video signals. Separate Y/C signals offer a number of advantages over a single composite signal.

recording is referred to as **color under**. (Color information is, in a sense, put under luminance information in a restricted-bandwidth signal.) Although it's convenient to have an all-in-one signal, sacrifices have to be made. This results in the following problems:

- Quality is reduced when the full bandwidth of the color signal is reduced and multiplexed into one signal.
- Interactions take place between the various signals—further reducing quality.[3]
- Once combined, the various components of the signals can't be fully reconstituted into their initial forms, complicating later signal-processing techniques.

With composite video, quality quickly deteriorates when tapes are copied. After the third or fourth generation, video may be unusable.[4] The exception here is the 1-inch, type-C format, which, although composite, uses much wider luminance and chrominance bandwidths. Six *generations* of copies are possible with type-C.

Y/C Video Signals

In the *Y/C* approach to recording, the color (C) signal is kept separate from the luminance (Y) signal. At the same time, the color information is given a wider bandwidth, which means that, compared to composite recording, more color information can be retained. To retain this quality advantage throughout the production process, much of today's postproduction equipment has separate Y and C inputs.

It was the development of the new metal videotape formulations that made it possible to record wider chrominance and luminance bandwidths in Y/C recordings. As you might assume, Y/C machines have both inputs and outputs for the luminance and chrominance signals.

Component Video Signals

In **component signals** (sometimes called Y, C, C) there are three signals: a luminance signal and two color signals. By combining the red, blue and green colors into two signals instead of one, most signal interactions are eliminated. (As we noted in Chapter 5, if you know the values of two color signals, the third color can be electronically deduced.) In component recording (primarily the D-1 format, to be discussed later), color information is recorded on separate tracks from the luminance.

Even with the seeming advantages of component recording, Y/C recording has gained favor, primarily because the new metal videotape formulations have meant higher Y/C quality while, at the same time, allowing producers to take advantage of simpler and less expensive equipment. When tape copies are limited to five generations or less, it is difficult to distinguish between component recordings and high-quality Y/C recordings.

---

3. Interference between the luminance and chrominance channels causes a variety of problems: chroma noise, edge sparkle, ringing (edge shadows), color displacement, loss of color resolution and a greater likelihood of moire patterns (a wavy, sometimes moving pattern associated with closely spaced lines).

4. The original is considered the first generation; a copy of that tape is the second generation, etc.

ACQUISITION FORMATS

We previously noted that with composite, color-under machines there is a significant loss in quality when the tapes have to be copied, a necessary step in doing editing and special effects. There is a reasonably satisfactory way around this problem, however. It is possible to use a format such as S-VHS (Figure 10.5) or Hi8 and immediately ***bump it up*** (copy it, or *dub it*) to a higher quality Y/C or component format before postproduction work starts. When this is done, the S-VHS or Hi8 is considered an ***acquisition format***, a format that is only used to acquire the initial footage. Although the results may not be as good as starting out with a higher quality formats, the procedure offers the advantage of being able to use compact, lightweight S-VHS and Hi8 equipment in some professional applications.

In presenting this background to videotape recording we have mentioned several videotape formats. Now it's time to discuss them in more detail.

bump up: To copy segments from one videotape format to a larger or higher quality format.

acquisition format: Typically, footage shot on S-VHS or Hi8 intended to be transferred to a higher quality format in order to retain better quality during subsequent editing and copying.

ONE-INCH PROFESSIONAL STANDARDS

For many years after quad machines faded from the scene, professional video recording around the world relied on the 1-inch tape format. Not only was the 1-inch tape smaller, cheaper and easier to ship and store, but there were fewer equipment problems. Three versions were used: type-A, type-B and type-C. Type-A was altered extensively, and in 1978 emerged in the form of type-C. Type-B was widely used in Europe.

One-Inch Type-C

Type-C was the first videotape system to offer good still-frame and slow- and accelerated-motion playback capabilities (Figure 10.6). By the mid-1980s, type-C had replaced the original 2-inch quad standard for making studio masters of

FIGURE 10.6
Type-C was the first videotape
system to offer good still-frame
and slow and accelerated motion
playback capabilities. In the late
1980s the dominance of the 1-
inch, type-C format for general
recording started to fade.

productions and for doing final, high-quality editing. Only in the late 1980s did
the dominance of 1-inch type-C start to fade. When high-definition VCRs were
introduced in the late 1980s, modified type-C machines were used to record the
HDTV signal.[5]

THREE-QUARTER-INCH VIDEOTAPE

With the invention of the TBC, a videotape format that had been introduced by
Sony Corp. in the 1970s was quickly adopted for broadcast field production. The
3/4-inch U-matic format, which introduced the concept of a cassette to video,
was originally intended for home use. Unlike the 1-inch and 2-inch open-reel
VTRs that have to be threaded by hand, the 3/4-inch machines automatically
threaded their own tape when the VCR was started. But because of the high cost
of 3/4-inch machines, the format did not catch on in the home market; instead,
it found a home in institutional television settings.

It should be noted that throughout the history of videotape, there has been
a proliferation of incompatible formats — more than 40 in all. Some of these
formats appeared (often with great fanfare), only to disappear within a year or
two. This left those who invested in the equipment not only stranded with
outmoded equipment, but with tapes that couldn't be played on any other machine. For this reason, getting manufacturers to agree on a standard has always

5. The 1,125-line, 60-field HDTV signal carries four times the video information of a standard
NTSC color signal. For this reason the writing speed of high-definition recorders is considerably
higher than NTSC recorders.

been a critical issue. Since all major Japanese VCR manufacturers agreed on the 3/4-inch format (and by this time Japanese manufacturers dominated the VCR marketplace), the almost universal acceptance of the 3/4-inch cassette was assured.

This wide acceptance, together with the advent of the TBC, resulted in the format being adopted as standard for most non-studio broadcast work. But since the 3/4-inch format could not equal the quality of quad machines or 1-inch helical VCRs, it was primarily used when portability of equipment was an issue, as it generally is in news and documentary work.

The major problem with the 3/4-inch format is that its quality becomes marginal to unacceptable when recorded material has to go through three or more generations. Most of the quality limitations in the 3/4-inch format result from its color-under recording approach. But on the plus side, not only did the 3/4-inch cassette concept make the handling and loading of tape much more convenient but the plastic cassette kept harmful dirt, dust and finger marks off of the tape surface. In addition, a record lockout feature was included. A small red plastic button, which could be removed from the bottom of the cassette, made it impossible to accidentally record over material.

The great investment the video industry had in 3/4-inch equipment kept it alive for some time after the introduction of smaller, better quality formats. Before we get to these, however, we need to hold to a bit of a historical sequence by discussing the Betamax and VHS consumer formats.

BETAMAX

The **Betamax** format, which was introduced by Sony Corp. in 1976, was the first *consumer equipment* format to become widely accepted. Hundreds of thousands of Beta-type machines have been sold throughout the world. The original Beta format went through several revisions, mostly to extend playing time. Nevertheless, Betamax lost favor, and by the early 1990s it had virtually disappeared from the scene.

consumer equipment: Relatively inexpensive audio and video equipment intended for general, non-professional use.

VHS

Although the **VHS** (Video Home System) format was introduced a full year after Betamax, it attracted immediate attention because of its two-hour playing time — a feature that the early Betamax machines didn't share. This feature not only made it possible to record televised feature films and football games but later ushered in what was to become a major attraction for VCR sales: movie rentals.

Seeing the advantage of VHS (and possibly finally coming to grips with the American passion for football and films), the Betamax manufacturers (primarily the Sony Corp.) quickly moved to increase Beta's playing time. They did this by slowing down the tape speed and reducing the width of the recording tracks. Not to be outdone, VHS manufacturers then did the same. In response, Beta's playing time was again increased. Seeing that they had dropped into second place again in the maximum time competition, VHS manufacturers again increased their playing time. Before it was over, VHS, with its slightly larger cassette, could (with special tape) record eight hours of programming on a single cassette — more than enough for most any need.

When attention swung away from maximizing recording time to audio and video quality, Sony moved on to Super Beta. The VHS manufacturers then introduced their own high-quality HQ machines. But by this time, the VHS momentum had turned the tide, and the Beta-VHS war was all but over. By 1990, VHS not only had taken over the home VCR market, but all VCR manufacturers (including Sony) were making VHS machines.

In addition to using the Beta and VHS machines to record and play back programming, the move to home VCRs took the "home movie" market away from Super-8 film. Those who had files of Super-8 films found it was easier to transfer them to the inexpensive ½-inch cassettes and show the films on their TV sets. Once transferred, there was no worry about threading projectors, setting up screens or having the Super-8 films accumulate more dirt and scratches with each showing. Those who took home "movie making" seriously, invested in ½-inch videotape editors and started doing creative postproduction work.

In 1983, one of the major Japanese companies, JVC, introduced a small version of the VHS cassette referred to as **VHS-C**. Since the new cassette was about half the size of the standard VHS cassette, this made it possible to significantly reduce the size of camcorders. Although original VHS-C cassettes could record only about 20 minutes of material, the latest versions can record for more than 30 minutes. VHS-C cassettes can be played in VHS machines with the use of an adapter.

Eight Millimeter Video

There is one more important consumer format we need to mention: **8mm video**. With the introduction of 8mm video camcorders by Eastman Kodak in 1984, the size and weight of the basic camcorder dropped more than 50 percent.[6] The tape cartridges, which are 3.7 inches by 2.5 inches by 0.6 inch, are about the size of a standard analog audio cassette. Production facilities that switched from 3/4-inch to 8mm video reported major savings in shipping and storage costs.

In order to obtain a high-quality video signal with the small format, tapes were developed that had **pure metal** and **metal evaporated** coatings. Since this new tape technology made it possible to record and play back at much higher signal levels, these tapes were quickly adopted for other video and audio recording formats.

The first battery-powered camera and recorder VCR units introduced in 1966 were bulky, two-piece units awkwardly strung together by cables. (The cameras weighed seven pounds and the recorders 23 pounds.) By 1980, the separate units had merged into a single, lightweight **camcorder** (camera-recorder).[7] Even though VHS and 8mm camcorders gained wide acceptance in the consumer (home user) arena, quality limitations discouraged their use at the professional level.

Compact-8

In 1992, a compact version of the Hi8 cassette called **compact-8** was introduced. The smallest of these units can fit into a pack of king-sized cigarettes and is capable of 30 minutes of recording time. Compact-8 can be played on a standard 8mm video player with the help of an *adapter shell* similar to the adapter used to play VHS-C cassettes on standard VHS machines. With cameras this small and inconspicuous, "totally hidden video" takes on a whole new meaning.

adapter shell: A holder for the VHC-C and Compact-8 formats that allows their cassettes to fit into a standard VHS and 8mm players.

6. In 1984, Eastman was the first company to start selling 8mm camcorders; but a short time later, the company decided to get out of the VCR business.

7. Sony introduced the first camcorder in 1980 as a replacement for Super-8 film, which had been around since 1932. Today, camcorders fall into two categories: the all-in-one units and the dockable units. Although slightly larger, the dockable units allow the camera to be disconnected from the recorder. This means the units can be easily switched — a definite advantage when a unit malfunctions or when it's time to upgrade the camera or the recorder.

PROSUMER FORMATS

S-VHS

Although VHS won the consumer VCR battle against Beta, VHS manufacturers did not rest on their laurels. Research and development continued, and in 1987 a high-band version of VHS called *S-VHS* (super VHS) was introduced. The wider bandwidth of S-VHS meant that more than 400 lines of horizontal resolution were possible on a first-generation recording. Consumers sitting in front of their TV sets found that this level of picture clarity exceeded what they were used to seeing with the best over-the-air programming.

But they weren't the only ones to notice the resolution advantage of S-VHS. Professionals who had been using 3/4-inch equipment noted that the first-generation picture quality of the 1/2-inch S-VHS format was superior to what was possible with standard 3/4-inch equipment. Unfortunately, after about the third generation this superiority disappeared. But some news and documentary producers, who were anxious to take advantage of the small, lightweight and comparatively inexpensive S-VHS equipment, found that they could bump up an original S-VHS recording to a professional format for editing and copying — without suffering a major loss in quality. Consequently, by 1990 some broadcast stations had started using S-VHS in news and documentary work. S-VHS is *backward compatible;* that is, standard VHS tapes can be played on S-VHS machines, but the new S-VHS tapes can't be played on standard VHS machines.

S-VHS: An improved version of the VHS system offering both higher video resolution and better audio quality.

Hi8

At the same time that S-VHS was being developed, Sony was busy working on its own high-band consumer video format: *Hi8*. The first generation of Hi8 camcorders was introduced in 1989. Although the Hi8 videocassette is much smaller than the VHS or VHS-C cassettes (Figure 10.7), it offers the same high, first-generation quality. It also has a time-code address track that facilitates editing.

Hi8: A 8mm videotape format developed by Sony that is of higher quality than the standard 8mm format. Often used as an *acquisition format.*

FIGURE 10.7
Although the Hi8 videocassette is much smaller than the VHS or VHS-C cassettes, it offers the same high, first-generation quality. It also has a time-code address track to facilitate editing.

Like S-VHS, Hi8 attracted the attention of news and documentary producers looking for a small, lightweight and inexpensive alternative to traditional broadcast-quality equipment. This can be important. In covering high-risk foreign news assignments, S-VHS and Hi8 equipment is considered "expendable." If it is confiscated, badly damaged or has to be left behind, there is no great financial loss.

With the professional acceptance of S-VHS and Hi8, the lines between professional, industrial and consumer equipment have become blurred. For the first time, expensive technology does not stand in the way of serious videographers wanting to produce news and documentary pieces for broadcast.[8]

HALF-INCH, BROADCAST-QUALITY ANALOG FORMATS

In the mid-1980s the Sony Corp., RCA and Panasonic introduced two new, broadcast-quality recording formats that used ½-inch videocassettes: Betacam and the M-format. Because they were much smaller than the ¾-inch cassettes, for the first time (in the professional arena) it was possible to combine a broadcast-quality camera and recorder into one unit. By increasing the tape speed and recording the luminance and chrominance information separately, a dramatic increase in quality was realized.

Betacam

Sony, which pioneered development of the ½-inch Betamax videocassette for home use, introduced their professional ***Betacam*** format in 1981. In 1986, they improved this with Betacam SP (for superior performance). Because the improved version rivaled or exceeded the quality of 1-inch, type-C recording, some

Betacam: A broadcast-quality format developed by Sony and used in several types of camcorders.

8. To prove the point an employee of KCET, the Los Angeles PBS affiliate, bought a Hi8 camera at a local camera store, traveled alone to Russia, and produced a documentary that subsequently aired on the PBS network.

FIGURE 10.8
Sony, which pioneered development of the ½-inch Betamax videocassette for home use, introduced Betacam, a professional format, in 1981. After some improvements, it was found that Betacam rivaled or exceeded the quality of 1-inch, type-C recording. Some facilities started relying on Betacam for both studio and non-studio production.

FIGURE 10.9

This is a typical playback unit for the MII format. Betacam and MII are two of the most widely used formats in on-location productions. MII makes use of a metal particle tape, which can record for more than 90 minutes on a cassette. The format has four audio tracks, including two recorded with the video heads.

facilities started relying on Betacam for both studio and non-studio production (Figure 10.8).

Unlike the rival MII format, which must use special tape, Betacam SP can use either metal particle tape or the standard, readily available, oxide-coated Beta tapes. And, unlike the M format, the improved SP version of Betacam is compatible with the original Betacam format.

The M Formats

The ½-inch, broadcast-quality format introduced by Matsushita (Panasonic) and RCA in 1986 was called the M format because the tape is wrapped around the video head assembly in an M-pattern. Like Betacam, it was a Y/C format.[9]

In 1985, the M-format was significantly improved with the release of the MII format (Figure 10.9). MII uses metal evaporated tape (Figure 10.10), which can record for more than 90 minutes on a cassette. The original two M-format audio tracks were increased to four with MII. These two new tracks are recorded

9. For those who demand technical accuracy, we should mention that there is a basic technical difference between the Betacam and M-format systems. Betacam records two video tracks side by side on a videotape: a luminance track and a chrominance track consisting of two, color-difference, time-compressed signals. The M format also records two signals, a luminance and a chrominance, but the chrominance signal consists of two color-difference signals multiplexed together by frequency.

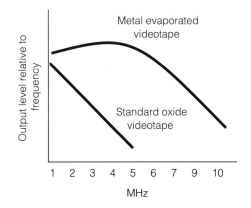

FIGURE 10.10

Do high-quality metal types really make a difference? This graph illustrates that the playback level and frequency response of metal evaporated tape are significantly higher than that of standard oxide tapes.

with the high-speed video heads using an FM signal. The audio signal is switched into a part of the video track as the video is being recorded. Unlike the limited-quality audio tracks that are recorded longitudinally along the top and bottom of the videotape, the quality of these additional audio tracks extends throughout the full 20 to 20,000 Hz audio spectrum.

Five generations are possible with MII. Like Betacam SP, recording quality equals or exceeds the 1-inch, type-C, reel-to-reel VTRs. By the late 1980s the NBC television network and many of its affiliated stations had standardized on the MII format for video field production work.

DIGITAL VIDEO RECORDING

The digital recording of video, as represented by videodiscs and digital video-tape machines, holds significant quality and editing advantages over the analog-type systems we've discussed thus far. Since the digital signal is recorded in terms of clearly defined "off" and "on" (or 0 and 1) pulses, there is no generational loss in making digital copies. A fifth-generation recording from the best analog VCR shows signs of deterioration. A fifth — or even a 50th — generation of digital video is not significantly different from the original. This advantage is important in postproduction, when video sometimes has to go through several generations of special effects.

Equally important, the signal-to-noise ratio of digitized video remains consistent through repeated stages of amplification and signal processing. (The signal-to-noise ratio is the degree to which video or audio information stands out from background interference. The higher the signal-to-noise ratio, the clearer and stronger the signal will be. See Figure 10.11.) Because sophisticated error-correction equipment is normally used with digital equipment, digital play-backs are highly immune to normal video problems.[10]

Finally, digital video can be directly processed by computer equipment without going through analog-to-digital conversions. This has opened the door to a wide variety of editing and special-effect possibilities, most of which can be done with today's generation of desktop computers.

Videodisc

The first system to use digital video was videodisc players. In their operation videodisc players are almost identical to CD players discussed in Chapter 7. Unlike videotape machines, the first generation of consumer-type videodisc systems could not record programs — only play back prerecorded materials. However, by the early 1990s a practical recordable disc system was in use (Figure 10.12). This brought many of the advantages of the videodisc (such as high-speed random access to recorded information) to video production.

FIGURE 10.11

The signal-to-noise ratio is the degree to which video or audio information stands out from background interference (noise). The higher the signal-to-noise ratio that production equipment is capable of delivering, the clearer and stronger the audio and video signals will be.

10. These include dropouts, velocity errors, impact errors, moire patterns and general color errors.

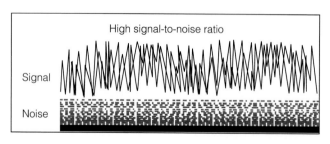

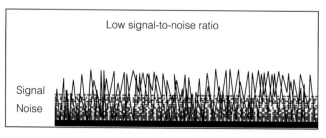

FIGURE 10.12
Although the first consumer-type videodisc systems could not record programs, by the early 1990s recordable disc systems such as this one had been developed. One of the major advantages of a videodisc system is that the access time needed to find segments is typically only a fraction of what is required by videotape machines.

There are several videodisc systems, including optical, magnetic, magneto-optical and phase change. One of the more popular designs works in the same way as an audio CD (discussed in Chapter 7). As the videodisc spins at a rate of 1,800 revolutions per minute, a narrow laser beam hits the surface of the disc. The image of the information digitally encoded in the track is reflected into a light-sensitive cell and converted into a digital signal (Figure 10.13).

The phase change optical drive uses disc cartridges that can hold up to 1 GB (one billion bytes) of digital information. Discs are referred to as *rewritable,* since they can be used to both record and play back data. With a billion bits of data on a disc it would seem like a hopeless task to be able to locate a specific bit of information. Not at all; the machine can find any precise point on the disk in less than one second. Because of their small size, their high video and audio quality capabilities and their ability to quickly access information in a random order, videodiscs have found acceptance in random-access video editing, a topic that will be covered in Chapter 14.

Digital Videotape Advantages

Digital audio recorders have been in use for some time, but the greater bandwidth of video signals delayed the introduction of digital video recorders until the mid-1980s. Digital recording has a number of advantages over the analog formats we've discussed.

- As we noted, a digital videotape can be copied more than 50 times without significantly affecting quality, an important consideration in postproduction sessions that require numerous layers of video effects.

- Because of the error-correction circuitry, the effects of problems such as dropouts and disturbances caused by abrupt or severe VCR movements are not apparent.[11]

- Digital videotapes have a much better shelf life than analog tapes, which means they are better suited for storage and archival use.

- The audio and video quality of digital recordings exceeds the best analog recordings.

By the early 1990s three digital formats were in general use.

11. In a demonstration, a D-2 portable VCR was repeatedly dropped with a force of 30 g with no noticeable effect on the audio or video being recorded on played back.

FIGURE 10.13

As the videodisc spins at a rate of 1,800 revolutions per minute, a narrow laser beam hits the surface of the disc. The image of the digitally encoded information is reflected into a light-sensitive cell and converted into a digital signal. In the write-once disc the "pits" are etched permanently into the recording medium with a laser beam. On a rewritable disc the digital "image" of the signals is not permanent. They are held in a magnetic field in a special medium and can be changed (rewritten) with a laser beam.

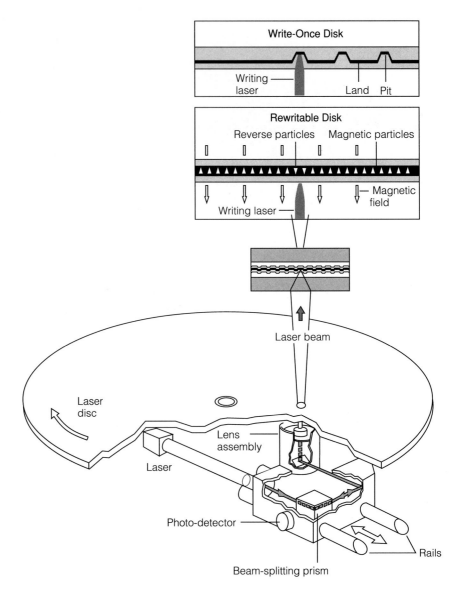

D-1, D-2 and D-3 formats: Videotape systems that record signals in terms of digital information and afford a number of advantages over analog videotape systems.

The D-1 Format

The *D-1 format* is a digital component format that retains two digitized chrominance signals and a luminance signal throughout most of the production and postproduction process. By keeping these signals separate, D-1 makes possible elaborate and multiple layers of chroma keying and **compositing** (bringing together numerous generations of video). However, because three discrete signals are involved, D-1 requires more elaborate video processing equipment. In addition to creating elaborate video effects, D-1 offers an important advantage in doing video animation and in building complex graphics.

The D-2 Format

Although the **D-2 format** relies on a composite signal, for most production and postproduction work the quality of D-2 is indistinguishable from D-1. Only in doing highly demanding and complex postproduction effects does the difference become significant. At the same time, D-2 is more practical because it does not

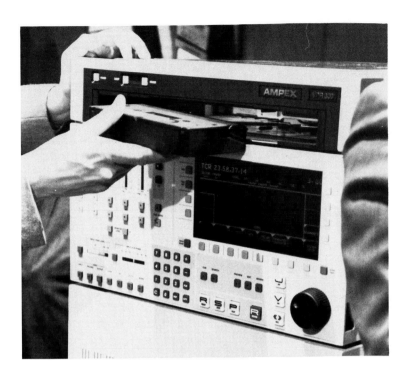

FIGURE 10.14
In appearance, D-2 machines resemble a ¾-inch analog VCR. However, these digital machines use special cassettes and have four digital audio channels.

require complex signal processing equipment. In appearance, D-2 machines (both tabletop and portable) resemble the 3/4-inch analog machines discussed earlier (Figure 10.14). However, they use their own type of cassettes that provide for four digital audio channels.

The D-3 Format

During the 1992 Olympics in Barcelona, Spain, a 1/2-inch digital format referred to as the **D-3 format** first received widespread attention (Figure 10.15), although prototypes had been introduced at the National Association of Broadcasters

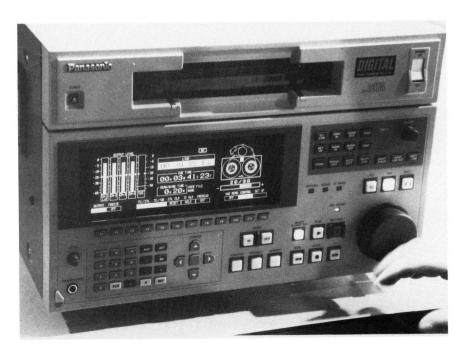

FIGURE 10.15
During the 1992 Olympics in Barcelona, Spain, ½-inch, D-3 digital recorders such as this first received widespread attention. This was the first time that a major event was primarily covered with digital equipment.

FIGURE 10.16

The D-3 recording system is typical of the complexity of today's professional VCRs. Note that a total of four digital (also called PCM for pulse-code modulation) audio tracks are recorded, two at the top and two at the bottom of the video tracks. Ten helical heads spinning at 5,400 rpm are necessary to record and play back audio and video. It takes six helical tracks to record a single video field. The speed of the video heads combines with the speed of the moving tape to create a total head-writing speed of 24.4 meters per second.

confidence heads: VCR audio and video playback heads that immediately play back signals after they are recorded. In this way signals can be monitored for quality as recordings are being made.

convention in Atlanta, Georgia, in 1989.[12] By using more than 200 cameras and recorders and taking advantage of a digitized signal through most of the recording and the production and postproduction processes, significant gains in video and audio quality were realized.

Since 1/2-inch cassettes are used, the recorders can be made smaller than either D-1 or D-2 recorders, which makes them practical for a camcorder. Although small, the cassettes can record up to 125 minutes on metal evaporated tape.

The D-3 recording system is typical of the complexity of today's professional VCRs. Figure 10.16 shows the various tracks. Note that a total of four high-quality digital (also called PCM for "pulse-code modulation") audio tracks are recorded at the top and bottom of the video tracks. Ten helical heads spinning at 5,400 rpm are necessary to record and play back audio and video. Four of the heads record video, four are *confidence heads* (that can immediately play back the audio and video signals as they are being recorded), and two heads are erase heads. Three stationary heads record a cue track, a control track and a time code track along the edges of the tape. It takes six helical tracks to record a single video field. Since the speed of the video heads combines with the speed of the moving tape, the combined movement creates a head-writing speed of 24.4 meters per second (almost 9,000 Km/hr!).

Computer Disk Video

With the advent of high-capacity computer disks, it was found that digitized video could be recorded on computer hard disks and a wide variety of editing and postproduction special effects were possible. As we will see in Chapter 15, desktop computers are now being used for recording and editing video segments. Audio and video are simply loaded onto hard disk memory from videotape. Thereafter, the segments can be almost instantly called up in any order and combined and manipulated as needed with special-effects equipment. When finished, the product can then be output to a videotape. We'll discuss these procedures more in Chapter 15.

12. New models of equipment are typically unveiled at either the NAB (National Association of Broadcasters) or the SMPTE (Society of Motion Picture and Television Engineers) conventions. The NAB convention has for many years been the world's largest annual broadcasting convention.

FIGURE 10.17
Instead of using videotape or a computer disk to record programming, solid-state video recorders save video information in computer chips. Because no tape or moving parts are involved, maintenance is all but eliminated.

SOLID-STATE RECORDING

Instead of using videotape or a computer disk to record programming, solid-state[13] video recorders save video information in computer chips. Standard computer RAM (random-access memory) microchips (Figure 10.17) and **flash EPROMs** are used.[14] Because no tape or moving parts are involved with solid-state storage devices, mechanical maintenance problems are eliminated.

Since the information is stored in digital form, it lends itself to a full range of video effect and image processing possibilities. Even more important than all of these advantages, video images can be recalled from solid-state memory in any order and at any playback speed. This is a great advantage in doing editing and special effects. There are two basic types of solid-state memory chips: volatile and non-volatile.

Volatile Memory

Since standard computer RAM memory relies on a regular refreshing voltage to hold the stored information, this type of memory is referred to as *volatile memory.* Captured audio and video information must be transferred to videotape or computer disks before the power is shut off—otherwise, it is instantly lost. Volatile RAM chips are quite fast in both the recording and readout phases.

volatile memory: Digitized information stored in a computer or microprocessor that remains only as long as there is electrical power.

13. The *solid-state* designation may seem strange until you recall that at one time all electronic amplification and signal processing relied upon vacuum tubes. Rather than a vacuum, solid-state devices are composed of comparatively solid materials. Included in this general solid-state category are transistors that amplify electronic signals and ICs (integrated circuits consisting of hundreds or thousands of transistors, resistors, diodes and capacitors).

14. *EPROM* stands for erasable programmable read-only memory, which, admittedly, is rather contradictory jargon. The term is associated more with a type of chip than with the chip's capabilities.

Delays in getting information in and out of RAM chips are measured in **nanosecond** (billionths of a second) intervals, which gives you some idea of the level of performance of solid-state devices. This almost instantaneous record and playback capability makes RAM memory useful in editing, where segments must be randomly accessed and instantly recalled in real time during the post-production process.

Non-Volatile Memory

Recently, flash EPROM chips have been introduced that retain information even in the absence of a power source. This type of memory is called **non-volatile.** Although not as fast as RAM chips in the recording phase, they are much smaller and take much less power than hard disks — the standard, high-capacity recording medium for computers. To date, flash EPROMs are only capable of recording short audio and video segments. However, it is assumed that by the mid to late 1990s non-volatile solid-state devices will be able to accommodate full-length television programs. When technology reaches this point, we'll probably be recording our HDTV programs on miniature plug-in modules,[15] and videotape will join kinescope recorders and 78 rpm phonograph records in New York's Museum of Broadcasting.

FILM VS. ELECTRONIC RECORDING

Until 1973, 16mm film dominated news and documentary production. However, as we've noted, with the invention of TBCs, this changed. Suddenly, the small cameras and VCRs that had previously been limited to non-broadcast production found acceptance for EFP and ENG work. Many benefits were immediately realized.

First, with the help of microwave equipment and satellite uplinks, video field production could be done live — a development that dramatically changed TV news. Even when content is recorded, videotape makes possible the instant confirmation of content and technical quality; something that has to wait several hours with film. Unlike film editing, the editing or postproduction phase of video production can be computer controlled. This not only saves time but provides a wide array of postproduction video effects.

Relative Costs

Unlike film, tape is reusable. When film stock and processing are added together, the cost of videotape, especially when it is reused, comes out to be a small fraction of the cost of film. But this is also a mixed blessing; the tendency to reuse videotape has meant that the record of many events is lost when the tape is reused. This sometimes presents problems when attempts are made to do historical documentaries.

During the time when the cost per minute of doing productions on videotape was rapidly dropping, the cost of using film was increasing. Today, the minute-for-minute cost of 16mm film and processing is more than a thousand times greater than that of broadcast-quality video recording. The cost of 35mm film, the format used for professional film production, exceeds even this figure.

15. Ironically, they will probably look similar to the plug-in information modules first shown in *"Star Trek"* 25 years ago.

The Advantages of Film

Even though more and more production is being done on videotape, major dramatic works continue to be done with 35mm film. There are several reasons for this.

First are the historical reasons. After more than 100 years of 35mm film production, a rich and highly sophisticated tradition has grown up around film. Unlike video production, where newcomers may quickly find themselves functioning as camerapersons and even in some cases as directors, the feature film tradition typically involves a long, highly competitive apprenticeship. Less motivated people tend to drop out in favor of those who are more talented, persistent and dedicated.

Because of this rich heritage, film's production and postproduction processes have not suffered from a lack of talent or a lack of supporting industries. In Southern California alone, there are thousands of companies that specialize in various aspects of film production. Comparing the closing credits of a major feature film with those of a typical video production provides some measure of the differences in personnel and specializations that still exist between the two media.

For decades film has enjoyed consistent worldwide standards. A 16mm film can be broadcast on any of world's broadcast systems (regardless of the broadcast standard) and a 35mm film can be shown in almost any theater in the world. Video, on the other hand, has not only progressed through numerous tape formats, but there are now a half dozen incompatible broadcast standards being used in various parts of the world.

Technical Quality Compared

It is commonly believed that, as viewed on television, the quality of 35mm motion picture film is better than video. Much of this belief is based on less than equal comparisons. If we are talking about the artistic differences, then film has a definite advantage—for basically historical reasons. But as more and more film-style video production is being done, especially in single-camera HDTV production, this gap is rapidly disappearing.

Although artistic differences between film and videotape are difficult to measure, purely technical differences are not. This brings us to the following statement: If production conditions are controlled and if comparisons are made on the basis of technical quality, the best 35mm film will be slightly inferior to the best video — *when the final result is broadcast*. The reason becomes obvious when the production process for each medium is traced.

First, it is important to realize that if a signal from a video camera is recorded on the highest quality videotape process, no discernible difference will be noted between the picture coming from the camera and the picture that is later reproduced by videotape.

With film intended for broadcast the process is far more complex. First the image is recorded on negative film. The original negative film is used to make a master positive, or intermediate print. From the master positive a "dupe" (duplicate) negative is created; and from that a positive release print is a made. This adds up to a minimum of three generations. At each step things happen: subtle color and quality variations are introduced by film emulsions and processing, there is a general optical degradation of the image, and the inevitable accumulation of dirt and scratches on the film surface starts. After all of these steps, the film release print is projected into a video camera to convert it to an electronic signal — which is where the video signal started in the first place.

image enhancer: An electronic circuit that intensifies contrast in lines of separation between objects, thereby giving the appearance of greater sharpness and detail.

To understand the film-video difference, we must also bear several other factors in mind. Film is capable of resolving several times more detail than standard video. But since it loses much of its sharpness in its route from film camera to television camera, image enhancement is used when the film is converted to video. (An *image enhancer* electronically sharpens the border transitions or edges around subjects, increasing the appearance of sharpness.) Although image enhancement sharpens the overall film image, once lost, subtle details cannot be "enhanced back" into existence.

But sharpness isn't everything. Many people think the slightly soft look associated with film on television is actually one of its advantages. The soft ambience surrounding the film image is subconsciously, if not consciously, associated with Hollywood film making. At the same time, the slightly sharper image of video is associated with news and the live coverage of events—subject matter that by its nature is generally very much in contrast to the normal fare of feature films.

Coping With Brightness Ranges

The next area of technical difference between film and video is the way in which the two media handle brightness ranges. Until recently, video cameras simply could not handle the brightness range of film. If film exposure is carefully controlled, a bright window in the background of a scene, for example, will not adversely affect the reproduction of surrounding tones. With the limited brightness range associated with video cameras the same bright window would significantly darken surrounding tones. As a result, many producers preferred film. However, when the latest generation of CCD cameras are manually set up (as opposed to relying on automatic settings), brightness range capabilities end up being similar to film. A video engineer with a knowledge of gamma (contrast) control can set up a CCD camera so that critical tonal areas are virtually identical to film. In fact, if the "film look" is important, there are adjustments and electronic devices that can make video indistinguishable from film.[16]

Single-Camera, Multiple-Camera Differences

Purely technical considerations aside, the primary underlying difference between film and video lies in the way it is shot. Film is shot in a single-camera style, and video is normally shot using a multiple-camera production approach. In film, each scene can be carefully set up, staged, lit, rehearsed and shot. Generally, a number of takes are made of each scene and the best one is edited into the final production. (As they strive for perfection in today's high-budget feature film productions, some directors shoot scenes twenty or more times.) Quite in contrast, video is generally shot with multiple cameras covering several angles simultaneously. With the exception of single-camera production (Chapter 16), multiple takes with video are the exception rather than the rule.

Film vs. Videotape Equipment Costs

We've noted that videotape is far less costly than using film. However, offsetting this savings is the initial cost of video equipment. Depending on levels of sophistication, the initial investment in video production and postproduction equipment can easily be ten times the cost of film equipment. The cost of

---

16. To distinguish film from video many people study the image for dirt—an unavoidable aspect of the film medium. However, to fool the experts, in one film-video comparison video engineers developed a device that superimposed random specks of electronically generated "dirt" on the video image!

maintaining professional video equipment is also greater. On the other hand, there is a substantial cost savings in using video for postproduction. For these and other reasons film productions intended for television are routinely transferred to videotape. This transfer can take place as soon as the film comes out of the film processor. Reversal of the negative film to a positive image—complete with needed color correction—can be done electronically as the film is being transferred to videotape. From this point on, all editing and special effects are done by the video process.

Even for film productions intended for theatrical release, major time and cost savings can be realized by transferring the film to videotape for editing. Once edited, the videotape is then used as a reference for editing the film.

In recent years some producers have found they can save money by shooting productions film-style with high-definition video and then transferring the final edited production to film for general release.

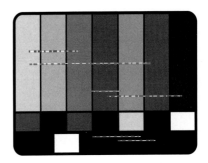

FIGURE 10.18
Dropouts are momentary losses of a video signal. Videotape imperfections, dirt on the tape or in the video heads or a momentary loss of tape-head contact all result in dropouts.

VCR OPERATIONS

From this general background, we turn to some specific information on videotape recording. Regardless of the format, VTRs and VCRs have a number of common features.

The five basic functions on any videotape machine are: play, record, stop, rewind, fast-forward and pause. Although VCR functions are basically self-explanatory, two things should be mentioned. In order to put some machines into the record mode, the *Record* button has to be held down, and then the *Play* button pressed. A small red light indicates when the machine is recording. Since the recording process erases previously recorded material, the tape should be checked to make sure there is nothing on it that should be saved. If in doubt, the tape can generally be fast-forwarded past the material to an unused or less questionable tape segment.

Unlike *Stop*, which disengages the tape from the head, the *Pause* button on most machines keeps the tape in contact with the spinning video heads—ready for an instant start in either the record or playback modes. If left too long in the pause mode, however, the heads will wear away the recording surface of the tape. This will not only damage the tape and result in dropouts (Figure 10.18) but it can cause head clog. Once the microscopic gaps in the video heads are clogged with any kind of matter, recording and playback are impossible. At best, a slightly snowy picture will result from head clog; at worst the picture will roll, break up and rival a full-blown snowstorm.

Some tape machines have confidence heads that are able to play back the recorded signal a fraction of a second after it has been recorded. Without confidence heads, the operator only monitors the video from the camera and has no indication of recording problems.

Spot-Checking a Tape

Unfortunately, many machines do not have confidence heads, and the effects of dropouts or head clog are not realized until the tape is played back in the camera viewfinder or on a TV monitor. It is for this reason that tapes should be *spot-checked* (checked at various spots) after recording. Many VCR operators only look at the last few seconds of the tape assuming that if anything went wrong, the problem carried through until the end of the tape. Although this is a safe assumption in most cases, for important productions an ever safer approach is to do end, middle and beginning checks. (Occasionally problems develop early in recording process and later clear up.)

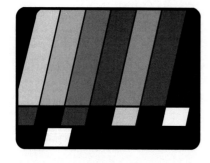

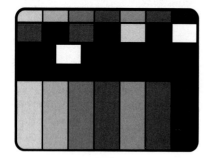

FIGURES 10.19A and 10.19B
Video problems include a loss of horizontal sync where a picture pulls to the side (Figure 10.19A) or completely collapses into horizontal stripes. Loss of vertical hold results in the picture rolling (Figure 10.19B). If the problem is with the monitor or TV set itself, an adjustment of the vertical or horizontal controls generally locks the picture in.

dropout compensator: An electronic device that can, on a limited basis, restore momentary losses of video information due to videotape *dropouts*.

FIGURE 10.20
Video noise is normally the result of low video levels or dirty video heads. In the latter case, "playing" a head-cleaning tape for a few seconds will often solve the problem. Some machines have self-cleaning heads.

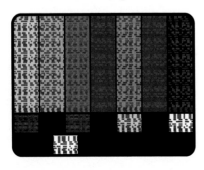

Full spot checks are done by stopping the tape at the end of the recording, rewinding it a few feet and checking the last five or ten seconds of the tape; then rewinding the tape to about the midpoint and checking again; and, finally, rewinding the tape to the beginning and checking the first five or ten seconds of the recording. During spot checks, operators should do the following:

- Check for absolute image stability (no horizontal jitter or vertical flutter or roll). See Figures 10.19A and 10.19B.

- Check for the presence of dropouts or video noise. Dropouts are generally the result of bad spots in the videotape. Assuming the material can't be easily rerecorded and the dropouts aren't too bad, there are electronic **dropout compensators** that can unobtrusively fill in missing data as the tape is edited or copied.[17] Video noise (Figure 10.20) is normally the result of low video levels (reflecting low light levels) or dirty video heads. In the latter case, "playing" a head-cleaning tape for about five seconds will often solve the problem.

- Check for general sharpness and picture quality. If the video is being played back in the field through the camera viewfinder, remember the small image represents a limited indication of how the final picture will look. Even so, it can reveal problems. When you are miles from a repair facility, as you often are in video field production, remember that even though a segment may have a technical problem, it is often wise not to record over it. When a major technical problem is emerging, the second attempt sometimes produces even worse results. Today's sophisticated signal-processing equipment will sometimes solve instability problems and salvage the original recording.

- Check for good audio quality, including an acceptable balance between audio sources. The presence of most kinds of noise can't be completely eliminated in postproduction. Moderate variations in audio levels, however, are easy to fix.

- Finally, check on difficult or questionable camera moves, including pans, zooms, dollies and trucks. When possible, shoot two or more takes of scenes—especially scenes involving complex camera moves.

BASIC VCR ADJUSTMENTS

The VCR Skew Control

The **skew control** found on some VCRs controls videotape tension, which in turn affects the length of the video tracks recorded or "read" from the videotape. This tension is adjusted by tape guides, which hold the moving videotape around the video heads. Improper skew adjustment is typically indicated by **flagging**, or a bending and wavering of vertical lines at the top of the frame (Figure 10.21A).

Although the skew adjustment is disabled when a VCR is in the record mode, this adjustment may need to be made when tapes are played back—especially on a machine other than the one they were recorded on. Most skew controls have a center "indent" position that indicates a normal setting. As VCRs get older, the needed tension may go beyond the range that can be adjusted by the skew control. When this happens an engineer or person familiar with the operation of the VCR can adjust the internal tape guides so that the skew adjustment once again falls within the normal range of control.

17. Dropout-compensation circuitry is often part of time-base correctors and framestore synchronizers. Digital VCRs have this circuitry built in.

Tapes that have been played many times, stretched or subjected to high temperatures often require a skew adjustment before they can be played. Because not all TV set and video monitor electronics react the same to video problems, you will probably find that skew problems show up differently depending on the equipment used.

Occasionally, it is necessary to try to play back a taped segment that has skew problems so severe that the picture can't be stabilized. In this case a sophisticated time-base corrector may help, especially one that goes beyond time-base correction and totally reprocesses the video and sync portions of the signal. (See footnote 1.)

The VCR Tracking Control

Tracking refers to the ability of a VCR to precisely (and generally automatically) align itself with the narrow video tracks recorded on the tape. As with skew, the tracking control is only used to correct problems during tape playback. On most videotape formats, tracking errors show up in the form of either a horizontal band of video noise (Figure 10.21B) or, in severe cases, in a total breakup of the picture. When tracking errors show up it is generally because the playback machine and record machine do not agree on the precise location of the video tracks. Some VCRs have tracking level meters. This is simply a readout of the overall amplitude of the recorded video signal. If automatic tracking fails to work and tracking falls below the optimum level indicated on the meter, the tracking control should be adjusted for maximum signal.

Occasionally, poorly recorded tapes have tracking levels too low for a stable playback. Sometimes trying the tape on a different machine will help.

COMMON VCR METERS AND STATUS INDICATORS

In addition to the meter for tracking, most VCRs will have a number of other status indicators. There should be one or more meters for monitoring audio levels. Professional machines, especially those used for editing, often incorporate video level indicators as well. These may be in the form of meters, LEDs (light-emitting diodes) or direct digital readouts. Video meters only indicate the maximum video level and tell nothing about the quality of the video signal. (The video could conceivably consist of nothing but a blank screen.)

The SMPTE time code reading is also displayed on many professional VCRs. (Time code will be discussed in detail in Chapter 15.) Machines that do not display time code generally have a tape index or tape counter readout. This is often a readout similar to the mileage indicator in an automobile. Since many of these are based on an internal geared connection rather than an electronic signal from the tape, they cannot be relied upon for highly accurate cuing. In addition, there is no way to reliably convert these numbers into minutes or seconds. On the other hand, SMPTE time code, which represents hours, minutes, seconds and video frames, is accurate to within one-thirtieth (and in some cases one-sixtieth) of a second.

MAINTAINING VIDEOTAPE

In the early days of videotape recording, both videotape and record-playback heads had a rather short life. Although both have been greatly improved, there are still some problems that should be understood.

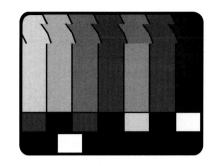

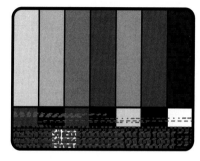

FIGURES 10.21A and 10.21B
Skew and tracking problems result from improperly adjusted VCRs. With some videotape formats, improper skew adjustment is indicated by flagging, a bending and wavering of vertical lines at the top of the frame (Figure 10.21A). On some formats tracking problems evidence themselves with snow or a general breakup in the bottom or top of the video frame (Figure 10.21B).

FIGURE 10.22
A momentary head-to-tape separation of only 4 microns (one-twentieth the size of a human hair) will cause a tape dropout. Videotape also sheds microscopic particles during use. These particles can gradually fill in the gap in record-playback heads, resulting in both dropouts and increased head and tape wear.

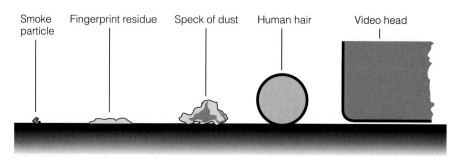

Videotape will "shed" microscopic particles during use. These particles can gradually fill in the gap in record-playback heads, resulting in both increased head and tape wear and a microscopic separation between the tape and the tape heads. This separation will lower the video signal and cause dropouts. A momentary head-to-tape separation of only 4 microns (which is one-twentieth the size of a human hair) will cause a tape dropout (Figure 10.22).

Videotape should not be stored in temperatures that exceed 80 degrees Fahrenheit. Some types of tape stored at 90°F will only last about a year. It has been shown that videotapes can be destroyed in less than one hour when stored at 150 degrees. A cassette sitting in the sun in a closed car will quickly reach that temperature. In the summertime, automobile glove compartments and trunks can also exceed 150 degrees. Temperature problems will especially affect material that has already been recorded on the tape.

A process called **packing the tape** is recommended when a new tape is used for the first time. This process, which involves fast-forwarding the tape to the end and then rewinding the tape again to the beginning, accomplishes two things. First, the inevitable variations in tape-wind tension will be minimized—variations can cause recording problems. Second, any loose oxide on the tape that has been shed will have a chance to drop away from the tape before getting lodged in the record-playback heads.

While discussing videotape, a word of advice should be passed along about bargain tapes. The high consumption of videotape—especially tapes intended for the home market—has spawned the manufacture, packaging and marketing of videotape of questionable quality. This tape not only provides poor (and sometimes even nonexistent) results, but it can get jammed in machines, and it's abrasive surface will severely cut short the life of video heads. For consistent results stick to brand names you have heard of. Although you might be able to buy videotape packaged by the Fly-by-Night Tape Company for a dollar or two cheaper than a respectable brand, it's little consolation when a tape jams or you are left staring at a snowy screen. When good-quality videotape is stored properly and kept in a reasonably dry and dust-free environment, it should last for several hundred "passes" (record and/or playback sessions). Assuming good-quality videotape is used, video heads should last for about 1,000 hours of use.

SUMMARY

The first practical videotape machine was a quadruplex machine developed by Ampex Corp. in 1956. After several decades, helical-type machines took over. In order to record the high video frequencies involved in television, videotape machines use the combined writing speed resulting from simultaneously moving the recording heads and video tape.

Videotape consists of a strip of plastic backing coated with a permanent layer of microscopic metal particles, such as iron or cobalt, embedded in a resin base. The metal particles are capable of holding a magnetic charge from the moving video heads. The resulting magnetic "imprint" within the tape's coating can be read back by the playback heads of a videotape machine. Although both analog and digital video recorders are in general use, digital machines offer an number of important advantages.

The time-base corrector (TBC) made it possible to use small cameras and VCRs in news and documentary broadcast applications. Video recording methods that do not rely on tape include videodiscs, computer disks and solid-state recording.

Electronic video recording techniques offer many advantages over film in the areas of cost, speed, postproduction versatility and technical (but not necessarily artistic) quality. Although film stock and processing costs are many times higher than video, film has the advantage of a relatively permanent image, worldwide standards and somewhat lower equipment and equipment maintenance costs.

KEY TERMS

acquisition format
adapter shell
Betacam
Betamax
bump up
color under
compact-8
component signal
composite video signal
compositing
confidence head
consumer equipment
D-1, D-2 and D-3 formats
dropout compensator
8mm video
external sync
flagging
flash EPROM
generation
Hi8

image enhancer
industrial video equipment
metal evaporated tape
nanosecond
non-volatile memory
packing the tape
prosumer video equipment
pure metal tape
quad machines
skew control
S-VHS
TBC (time-base corrector)
time-base corrector
tracking
type-C videotape machine
VHS
VHS-C
video head
volatile memory
Y/C

11 Sets and Graphics

First impressions are critical in television production. It is during the opening 10 seconds or so of a production that a viewer's hand often hovers over the TV's remote control ready to jump to a more interesting option. Although the establishing shot of a show should tip off an audience as to the nature and atmosphere of a production, it also does something else: it reveals much about the level of sophistication and general quality of the production. A major part of this impression rests with several things we will be focusing on in this chapter: sets, props, staging and graphics. We'll start with some definitions.

SETS, PROPS AND STAGING

sets: Scenery and properties supporting the suggested locale, idea and mood of a production.

props: An abbreviation for the term *property*; things that are used, generally by a talent, on a production set.

staging: A temporary structure used for a production setting.

By *sets* we are referring to the basic supportive scenery, furniture and general background of scenes. *Props,* which are used within sets, can be divided into set props and hand props. **Set props** are items used to embellish the set: lamps, pictures on a wall, books in a bookcase, curtains on a window etc. As the name suggests, **hand props** are things that are to be used by the talent: a telephone, newspaper, wine glass, book, screwdriver, typewriter etc. And finally, *staging* refers to the process of bringing all these elements together to create the atmosphere and mood for a production, as well as a suitable working environment for the talent.

Large production facilities will have a set designer, **art director** or **scenic designer** (Figure 11.1) whose job it is to work with a producer-director throughout the design, construction and staging process. In smaller facilities, sets and props may be the responsibility of the show's lighting director or producer-director.

FIGURE 11.1
Large elaborate production facilities will have a set designer and art director whose job it is to work with a producer-director throughout the design, construction and staging process. This model was made for an Academy Awards presentation. In smaller facilities sets and props may be the responsibility of the show's lighting director or producer-director.

FIVE TYPES OF STUDIO SETS

To organize the discussion we'll divide sets into five categories: neutral, representational-supportive, symbolic, realistic and fantasy. The first two, neutral and representative-supportive, are the most widely used.

Neutral/Indeterminate Sets

As the name suggests, a ***neutral (indeterminate)*** set plays a neutral role in the production; that is, it is not intended to directly influence the production's central theme. In its most basic form *neutral* could be considered to mean "nothing," since this type of set often starts out as either a cyc (Figure 11.2) or a blank wall. However, neutral sets are often embellished in various ways to provide interesting (but non-intrusive) patterns and designs. Terms that describe specific fundamental types of neutral sets are *limbo* and *cameo*. A ***cameo background*** is completely black, as opposed to a ***limbo background,*** which can be any solid tone or color.

Since there is nothing in a neutral or indeterminate set to distract viewers from the center of interest, attention is not divided. At the same time, unless it is creatively used, a neutral background can end up being as exciting as last week's baseball scores. But as we will see, with a dash of creativity a neutral set can be embellished in many engaging ways.

The Studio Cyc   The basic cornerstone for a neutral set is the cyc. As you can see from Figures 11.2 and 11.3, a cyc (cyclorama) is a large, seamless backdrop. It can be made of canvas, muslin, plaster or any material that can be finished so that corners and seams will not be visible. Most studio cycs are made of a tightly stretched ceiling-to-floor canvas or muslin and cover two or three studio walls in an L or U shape. Since the cyc can gently curve undetected around a 90-degree turn in the corner of a studio, there are no visible corners.

neutral (indeterminate) set: A production set that does not suggest a specific setting or locale.

cameo background: A totally black background.

limbo background: A background of any color or brightness that has no discernible detail.

FIGURE 11.2

The basic cornerstone for a neutral set is the cyc (cyclorama). A cyc is a large, seamless backdrop made of canvas, muslin, plaster or any material that can be finished so that corners and seams will not be visible. The ground row is designed to let the bottom of the cyc merge seamlessly into the floor. (See also Figure 11.3.)

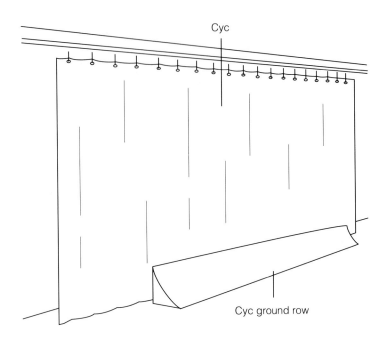

Cyc

Cyc ground row

ground row: Row of lights at the bottom of a cyc (generally hidden from cameras) that provide even illumination across the front surface of the cyc.

Through the use of a cyc ***ground row*** (Figure 11.3) it is possible to make the bottom of the cyc blend into an appropriately painted floor so that even the wall-to-floor transition becomes invisible. When this is done, a full *infinity effect* (a background without boundaries) can be created.

By carefully controlling background lights on a cyc, it can be made into anything from a stark white background suitable for silhouettes to a cameo (black) background. In the latter case the central subject matter must be far enough away from the cyc to keep keys, fills and general ambient light from hitting it. By using separate background lights on a cyc, shadows from foreground objects can be erased.

FIGURE 11.3

Most studio cycs are made of a tightly stretched ceiling-to-floor canvas or muslin and cover two or three studio walls in an L or U shape. Since the cyc can gently curve undetected around a 90-degree turn in the corner of a studio, there are no visible corners.

FIGURE 11.4
This 1960s background represents the theme "Lifestyles of the '60s." Although the full set will be visible in a wide shot, when close-ups are shot of the participants, this busy background will intentionally be thrown out of focus.

Curtains   At one time no respectable television studio was without at least two colors of curtains. Since they were hung by roller clips on tracks around the walls of the studio, the curtains could be quickly pulled into place to provide an instant background for just about anything. (Having "instant backgrounds" was an important consideration before videotape when everything produced in the studio had to be done live.) Nowadays no respectable TV production routinely uses plain curtains for backgrounds—unless they can be disguised or embellished in some unusually impressive way.

But curtains do have their uses, especially if you really can't see them. Since black velour drapes reflect almost no light, they are great for creating cameo backgrounds. To keep the background black, background lights should not be used. Barn doors can be used on keys and fills to keep as much light off the background as possible. (However, a moderate amount of light spilling on the black velour drapes probably won't spoil the cameo effect.) A limbo effect can be created by using a wrinkle-free curtain in a medium tone or color stretched tightly behind subjects. Moving subjects away from the curtain and throwing it out of focus help ensure that the background retains its limbo quality.

Representational-Supportive Sets

In *representational-supportive* sets, the most commonly used type of studio set, the background elements characterize the subject matter and may even be a vital element in the show. News, sports and weather sets with their news props and chroma key backgrounds fit this category. Note in Figure 11.4 that the 1960s background represents and supports the theme of "Lifestyles of the '60s." In Figure 11.5 the background graphics and visuals are an essential part of an instructional program on geometry. Game shows, where the talent must flip cubes or point to questions or clues, are another example. Shadows are often a problem with this type of set because the talent must sometimes work only a few feet from the background. As noted in Chapter 7, the use of softlights will alleviate the problem.

representational-supportive set: A production setting, such as a news or weather set, designed solely to support the function of the production.

FIGURE 11.5
These background graphics and visuals are an essential part of an instructional program on geometry. Shadows are often a problem with this type of set because the talent must sometimes work only a few feet from the background. As noted in Chapter 6, the use of effective background lighting and overall soft illumination will alleviate the shadow problem.

symbolic set: A non-realistic setting intended to suggest an environment or setting—often somewhat abstractly.

Symbolic Sets

Symbolic sets suggest a real and complete setting, without requiring you to include all the details. With this type of set a cyc is sometimes used as a "background screen" on which realistic shadows and patterns can be projected. Examples would be venetian blinds, suggesting an office; bars, representing a jail cell; or colored patterns, suggesting the stained glass windows of a church. To add believability, foreground objects are generally used in conjunction with symbolic backgrounds.

For example, you can suggest an office setting (especially if you can get by with only a close-up or medium shot of an individual) by projecting the shadow of venetian blinds in the background and then adding a real desk and possibly a coat rack. Adding "busy office" sound effects can complete the effect. A prison cell can be suggested with the shadow of prison bars on a wall. Add one shady character in prison garb sitting on a cot, and the effect is complete.

A **gobo,**[1] a scenic piece through which a camera shoots, is also a useful device in these cases (Figure 11.6). When objects are used as gobos, the camera can zoom through them or dolly around them to add authenticity. In many cases, a symbolic set, coupled with realistic sound effects befitting the particular environment, will be all that's needed for complete believability.

Obviously, much time, effort and money can be saved with a symbolic reality set compared to going all the way to a realistic set. Sometimes, however, it's necessary to shoot a scene from a variety of angles. In this case, the realistic or replica set may be the only choice.

Realistic or Replica Sets

realistic set: A production setting that appears (from the camera's viewpoint) to be authentic.

replica set: A production setting that is a copy of, and is designed to look exactly like, a well-known site.

Realistic or *replica sets* appear (at least from the perspective of what the camera sees) to be authentic settings. The sets for dramas (Figure 11.7A) and situation comedies (Figure 11.7B) are generally of this type. Although replica sets should

1. In film the term *gobo* has a different meaning; it is an opaque piece of material used to mask off a beam of light.

FIGURE 11.6
When objects are used as a gobo, the camera can zoom through them or dolly around them to add authenticity to the setting. In many cases an appropriate gobo, coupled with a few realistic background elements, will be all that's needed for complete believability.

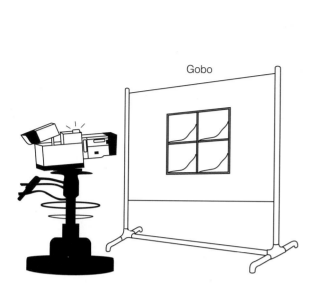

(a)

FIGURES 11.7A and 11.7B
Realistic or replica sets appear (at least from the perspective of the camera) to be authentic settings. The sets for dramas (Figure 11.7A) and situation comedies (Figure 11.7B) are generally of this type. Although replica sets should appear in all respects to be authentic, a number of adjustments are normally made to accommodate production needs.

(b)

FIGURE 11.8
Because there is generally no need for accurate and intricate detail, fantasy sets sometimes don't even exist in the literal sense; they are just computer creations electronically keyed in behind actors. This process was discussed in Chapter 9. Here, a computer operator creates a background for a fantasy production.

appear in all respects to be authentic, a number of adjustments are normally made to accommodate production needs.

First, since the effect of a wide-angle lens on master shots slightly exaggerates distances and perspectives, replica sets are often slightly scaled-down versions of "real-life" settings. Second, to accommodate camera angles, and sound and lighting needs, room interiors are normally constructed with only two or three walls.

Fantasy Sets

fantasy set: A television setting that is abstract or bears only limited resemblance to a realistic setting.

As the name suggests, **fantasy sets** bear little resemblance to anything real. They are often abstract and stylistic, and end up being bizarre and deliberate distortions of reality. Because there is generally no need for accurate and intricate detail, fantasy sets sometimes don't even exist in the literal sense; they are just computer creations (Figure 11.8), which are electronically keyed in behind actors. This was discussed in some detail in Chapter 9.

TONAL VALUE CONSIDERATIONS

A 10-step gray scale is typically used as a reference in assigning brightness values to sets, props and wardrobe. With limbo backgrounds it is best to create background tonal values that are either two to four gray scale steps darker or two or three steps lighter than talent skin tones. Even when there is an obvious color difference between the background and the central subject matter, there also needs to be adequate monochrome tonal separation in order to retain color compatibility.

Backgrounds that are too light (reflecting more than about 70 percent of the light falling on them) will often cause skin tones to darken as the typical TV system compresses the brightness differences down to a range that it can handle. The brightest step on the gray scale is actually light gray (TV white) that reflects

FIGURE 11.9
Special heat-resistant gel materials are available in hundreds of colors from lighting supply companies. If ellipsoidal spotlights are used on backgrounds, clearly defined circles of colored light can be created through the use of these gels. A colored gel over the front of a Fresnel light (which has been focused down to a narrow beam of light) will provide a softly defined pool of colored light.

70 percent of light. If the background contains very bright areas, or the light on the background is several times greater than the light on the central subject matter, you can inadvertently end up with a silhouette effect.

When using a neutral set such as a cyc, the easiest way to control and adjust background brightness is to route the background lights through dimmers and observe the effect of various settings on a video monitor. At low dimmer settings there will be a considerable color temperature shift in the lights, of course; but, since skin tones are not involved, this will probably not be a problem.

The normal gray limbo effect of a cyc can be modified by the use of colored gels over background lights. Special heat-resistant gel materials are available in hundreds of colors from lighting supply companies (Figure 11.9). If ellipsoidal spotlights are used on backgrounds, clearly defined circles of light can be created. Because the beams of Fresnels are slightly diffused, they end up providing softly defined pools of colored light on backgrounds.

Overlapping pools of colored lights from spotlights will also create interesting additive color effects. By referring back to the principles of additive and subtractive color in Chapter 5, you can see how a multitude of secondary colors can be created by overlapping colored lights. Keep in mind that when gels are placed over lights they act as filters, and there is a subtractive color effect. For example, when both a yellow gel and a cyan gel are placed over a light, the result is green. But when the colored lights from spotlights combine on the cyc, there is an additive effect. Where red and green lights overlap, the result will be yellow.

Other background effects can also be created with lights. By using large, high-wattage ellipsoidal spots with cookies or pattern projectors, interesting shadows can be projected across the surface of a cyc. Figure 6.22 in Chapter 6 illustrates some of the patterns available. A similar effect can be devised by using a gobo-type pattern illuminated with a large ellipsoidal spot (Figure 11.6). Rather surprising additive shadow interactions can result by using multiple spotlights with colored gels directed at a single gobo pattern. Results can be unpredictable, so experimentation is the key.

FIGURE 11.10
Softwall flats consist of frames made of 1-by-3-inch wood covered with canvas or bleached muslin. A number of flats are normally joined together with lash-lines to create a full background.

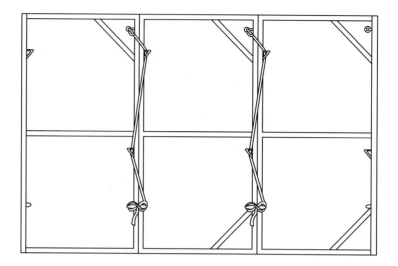

flat: A single unit of scenery. See also *softwall flat* and *hardwall flat*.

softwall flat: A set piece consisting of wooden frames covered with canvas or burlap.

hardwall flat: A set piece used for the background of a set, generally composed of a wooden frame covered with a rigid material such as plywood. See also *softwall flat*.

BASIC SET BUILDING BLOCKS

TV studios must be able to accommodate a variety of sets to meet ever-changing programming needs. Since studio space is generally limited, it is also necessary to construct sets so that they can be quickly and easily taken down (struck) and then removed for storage whenever they are not being used. To meet these needs sets are typically made up of lightweight sections called *flats*. Flats are from 8 to 12 feet high and are typically 4 feet wide. There are two basic types: softwall and hardwall.

Softwall Flats

Softwall flats consist of frames made of 1-by-3-inch wood covered with canvas or bleached muslin (Figure 11.10). A number of flats are normally joined together to make a background. Softwall flats are light, easy to strike and store (Figure 11.11) and easy to repaint. Their major disadvantages are that the muslin or canvas can be easily torn, and they will show wear with continuous use. Softwall flats are an excellent choice, however, for dramas and specials. They can be painted to depict almost any interior or exterior background.

By studying Figure 11.10 you can see how softwall flats are constructed. The canvas or muslin is stretched over the wooden frames and attached to the edges with staples and glue. The surface is then coated with a flame-proof sealer before painting. Matte (dull) surface paints are used to avoid glare from key and fill lights.

Hardwall Flats

Because of their greater durability, hardwall flats are the basic set pieces used by most production facilities. *Hardwall flats* are made from one-by-three or two-by-four frames covered with composition board or paneling. (The 1/4-inch wood paneling used in many homes and offices is an example this covering.) A visit to a building supply house will reveal a tremendous range of designs and surfaces available.

Creating Your Own Surface Designs   If, by chance, you can't find a ready-made design to meet your needs, you can cover the frames with a

material such as composition board and then paint on your own finish. Since
composition board is normally dark brown, it may need one or two coats of
light-colored paint before you can add a design (Figure 11.12). *Stippled patterns*
are designs created by applying paint with a coarse brush, sponge, wrinkled
paper or even a cloth. To retain the pattern, the paint should be applied in a
stamping motion rather than being stroked onto the surface. This technique can
be helpful in suggesting stone, cement or earth. In addition to making the
background more interesting, texture is desirable on flats to hide the inevitable
smudges, fingerprints, gouges etc. that will accumulate with use.

FIGURE 11.12
Since composition board is normally
dark brown, it may need one or two
coats of light-colored paint before a design can be added.

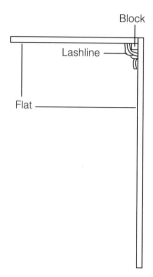

FIGURE 11.13

With the help of a block of wood to support the corner, the lashline technique can be used to form a 90-degree to 120-degree angle between two flats.

Wallpaper and Contact Paper   Wallpaper and contact paper can also be used to cover the composition board. A visit to a large wallpaper store will reveal a myriad of patterns, textures and colors. Contact paper and some types of wallpaper have a self-sticking backing—an improvement over the earlier approach of having to mix white paste in a bucket and apply it to the back of the paper with a large brush.

Ready-Made Panoramic Scenes   Even complete panoramic scenes that can be pieced together are available. These scenes often cover a series of flats that are placed on the other side of windows in a realistic or replica set. When viewed through the windows they give the appearance of a realistic outside scene. The level and color of light on the scene can suggest midday, morning or evening. Imitation trees or shrubbery between the window and the scene can add authenticity.

Surface Problems   Regardless of the choice of covering for hard-wall flats, a shiny surface can cause major problems by creating reflective hot spots. Metallic and reflective surfaces can be very pretty in a room, but for television it is best to be on the safe side and select a surface with a non-reflective, matte finish. It is also good to check a pattern on camera. Many wallpaper stores will allow you to take a sample to the studio to check out on camera. (Or you could take an ENG camera to the store and check out a variety of patterns all at once.) Be sure to study effect at the proper *working distance*. Some patterns can look good when photographed close up, but will blend into confusion when seen in the background of a setting.

Joining Flats

Settings based on either softwall or hardwall flats generally require that several flats be joined together. This can be done in several ways. Figure 11.10 shows the fastest method for joining flats: *lashlines*. You will note in Figure 11.10 that flats can be constructed so that a rope can be tightly strung back and forth between cleats on the flats and then secured at the bottom. With the help of a block of wood in the corner, the same lashline technique can be used to form a 90-degree to 120-degree angle between two flats (Figure 11.13).[2] Added stability

2. In designing sets, 90-degree angles are seldom desirable. Sound, lighting and camera-angle problems are alleviated by using larger angles.

FIGURE 11.14

Stability can be added to the lashline technique of joining flats (Figure 11.13) by nailing a one-by-three across the corner. To simplify the removal of the nails, "two-headed nails" are used. They have one head about one-quarter of an inch below the other to ensure the nails aren't driven in all the way in.

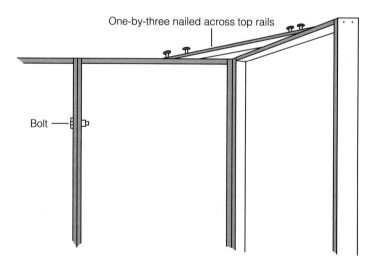

is achieved by nailing a one-by-three across the corner (Figure 11.14). To simplify the removal of the nails when the set is struck, nails should not be driven all the way in (Figure 11.14). "Two-headed nails" are an even better solution; they have one head about a quarter of an inch below the other to ensure that a nail can never be driven in all the way.

Note in Figure 11.14 that instead of a lashline, a bolt or even a C-clamp can be used to join flats. Although these approaches take a bit longer, they add stability. Figure 11.15 shows two other techniques: L-plate fasteners and pin hinges. These fasteners require the perfect alignment of the mounting hardware on flats; otherwise, there will be problems. There will either be a visible gap between the flats (as the hardware loosens), or you will not be able to join the flats together (if the hardware is too closely spaced or becomes twisted or out of position).

If the flats are well constructed and joined tightly together (by whatever means), the breaks between the flats should be invisible to the television camera.

Self-Supporting Set Pieces

Figure 11.16 shows *twofold* and *threefold* set pieces in semiclosed positions. These are simply hardwall flats that have been joined with hidden hinges. If you use this approach, you will probably want to make the flat frames out of one-by-fours or two-by-fours. Twofolds and threefolds are self-supporting, as long as they aren't opened up completely. They can be made large enough to represent a corner or even three walls of a small room, office, kitchen or whatever. Although twofolds and threefolds are fast and convenient to use, they have the disadvantage of being hard to move and store.

To add dimension to a setting, it is often desirable to bring set pieces forward, away from walls. This generally means that these set pieces must be able to stand on their own; in other words, they must be freestanding. A pole cat (Figure 11.17) or an L-brace (Figure 11.18) can make this possible. *Pole cats* are hollow pipes with spring-loaded extension pieces at the top. They are designed to fit between the floor and a grid pipe. Note in Figure 11.18 that with the help of a sandbag an L-brace tied to the bottom rail of a flat can make the flat self-supporting. (Heavy canvas bags filled with 20 to 30 pounds of sand can

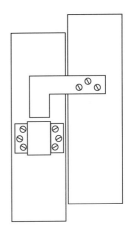
L-plate fastener

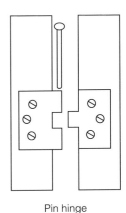
Pin hinge

FIGURE 11.15
L-plate fasteners and pin hinges require almost perfect alignment of the mounting hardware. Otherwise, you will either not be able to join the flats together, or there will be visible gaps between them.

twofold set: A freestanding, two-section set, hinged at the midpoint.

threefold set: A freestanding, three-section set, hinged in two places.

pole cat: A pole with spring-loaded, telescoping sections placed between the floor and grid pipes and used to attach scenery and set pieces.

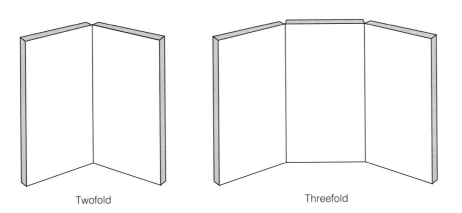
Twofold   Threefold

FIGURE 11.16
Twofold and threefold set pieces are simply hardwall flats that have been joined with hidden hinges. They can be made large enough to represent three walls of a small room, office or kitchen. Although they are fast and convenient to use, they have the disadvantage of being hard to move and store.

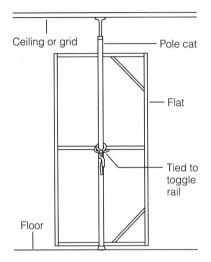

FIGURE 11.17

To add dimension to a setting, it is often desirable to bring set pieces forward, away from walls. This generally means that they must be freestanding. A pole cat (shown) or an L-brace (Figure 11.18) makes this possible.

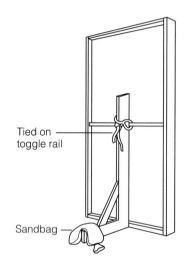

FIGURE 11.18

With the help of a sandbag, an L-brace tied to the bottom rail of a flat can make the flat self-supporting. There are no rules on how many L-braces and sandbags are necessary to hold up a section of flats. Just make sure that if you err, it's on the side of too many, rather than too few.

canvas drop: A canvas background that can be lowered into place from the studio grid.

serve a variety of purposes in anchoring sets.) There are no rules on how many L-braces and sandbags are necessary to hold up a section of flats. But just make sure that if you err, it's on the side of too many, rather than too few. The sight of a set coming down upon an announcer's head during a show can tarnish a station's image!

Painted Canvas Drops

Taking a page from the history of vaudeville, some set designers use a series of painted canvas drops to provide "instant backgrounds" for a variety of segments. *Canvas drops* are large canvas backdrops containing a variety of scenes. They can be quickly lowered into place with fly lines. It is possible to have a series of canvas drops, one behind the other. As you can see from Figure 11.19, pulling on fly lines causes the canvas drop to roll up from the bottom and disappear into the studio grid. A variety of backgrounds are possible, from abstract designs to highly realistic scenes. The drops can easily be repainted with new scenes. Added perspective and realism is possible through the use of foreground objects (Figure 11.20).

Seamless Paper

The quickest background to "construct" is made with seamless paper. It is available from most display houses in 9-by-36-foot rolls in a variety of matte surface colors. Seamless paper can be rolled along a studio wall and quickly stapled to a flat surface. (With a little experience, a power stapler and an agile

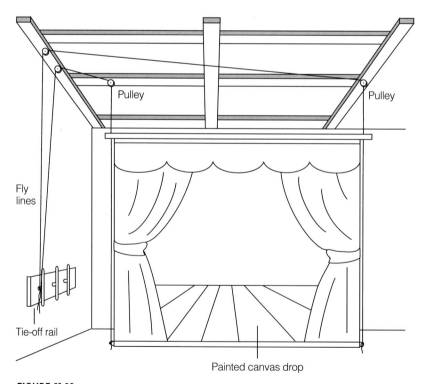

FIGURE 11.19

Pulling on fly lines causes the canvas drop to roll up from the bottom and disappear into the studio grid. A variety of backgrounds are possible, from abstract designs to highly realistic scenes (Figure 11.20). The drops can easily be repainted with new scenes.

FIGURE 11.20
By using foreground objects, added perspective and realism are possible with a background drop. Here, the real objects blend almost imperceptibly into the background painting.

assistant you can cover a 25-foot background with seamless paper in less than 60 seconds!) Although large areas can be quickly covered, a small section of seamless paper is often used to provide a quick colored background for a small space, such as behind an announcer. Even though the paper is a heavy gauge — somewhere between paper and cardboard — it still has the disadvantage of being easily torn and wrinkled.

Polystyrene Set Pieces

Polystyrene blocks represent one of the most interesting materials to work with in designing sets and set pieces. These featherweight hardened foam blocks are available at many lumber supply houses. They come in 4-by-8-foot blocks from 1 to 12 inches thick. Polystyrene blocks can be painted and suspended from grid pipes or affixed to background sets.

Interesting shapes and designs can be sculptured and embossed into polystyrene blocks with carefully applied applications of paint thinner. The paint thinner causes a chemical reaction with the polystyrene that instantly eats away designs or patterns. The paint thinner can be used in several ways: it can be poured down a sheet to result in a "stalactite" effect; it can be carefully painted on the polystyrene to form designs and crude letters; or it can be sprayed on to provide more interesting patterns and effects.

Petroleum-based paints will cause the same chemical reaction as the paint thinner. So, to keep paint from reacting with polystyrene, it should be painted only with a latex-based paint. (But, then again, you may want to experiment with some effects by intentionally using petroleum-based paints.)

Columns

Occasionally it is desirable to construct columns for a setting. Figure 11.21 shows the basic types: pillars, pylons, periaktas and sweeps. In Figure 11.22 you can see how the periakta can rotate to create a variety of background pictures or designs. Simple, self-supporting columns — especially if curves are involved —

FIGURE 11.21

There are four basic types of columns: pillars, pylons, periaktas and sweeps. Simple, self-supporting columns — especially if curves are involved — can be devised from a wooden understructure covered with cardboard and then painted.

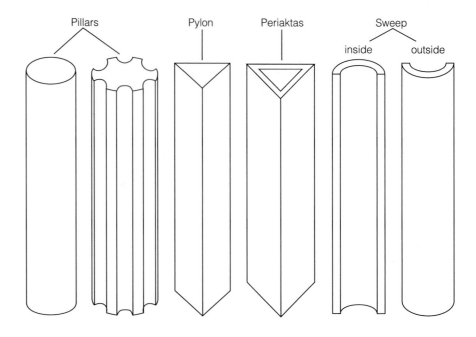

can be devised from a wooden understructure covered with cardboard and then painted. Since they have flat surfaces, pylons and periaktas (Figure 11.21) can be covered with the same materials that are used for hardwall flats.

The Floor as Part of the Set

With today's camera jibs that can sweep from floor level to a height of 20 feet or more, it is easy to get high camera angles on sets. As a result, the floor has become a much more important consideration in set design. Figure 11.23 shows a model set done for a retrospective on U.S. actions in Cambodia during the Vietnam War. Other possibilities for floors include painted geometric patterns,

FIGURE 11.22

Periaktas can rotate to create a variety of background pictures or designs. During a commercial break in a show, they can even be changed to coincide with a new topic.

FIGURE 11.23
With today's camera jibs that can sweep from floor level to a height of 20 feet or more, it is easy to get high camera angles on sets. As a result, the floor has become a much more important consideration in set design. This is a scale model set done for a production documenting U.S. actions in Cambodia during the Vietnam War. Other possibilities for floors include painted geometric patterns, bricks, cobblestones and pathways with imitation grass on either side.

bricks, cobblestones and pathways with (imitation) grass on either side. Since it can be scrubbed off, poster paint is sometimes used on floors to meet temporary needs.

Risers

Although some studios place their news, sports and interview sets directly on the studio floor, there are important advantages to elevating sets 4 to 12 inches with *risers*. Since most on-camera talent is seated, risers can elevate them to the point of being approximately level with camera lenses.

riser: A small platform.

Risers provide three advantages:

- They result in better talent-to-camera eye contact.
- It is easier on camera operators (providing straight-on camera angles).
- They generally provide a better visual perspective (cameras are not looking down on subject matter).

Depending on height and load-bearing needs, the frames can be constructed of anything from two-by-fours to two-by-twelves. The framework can then be covered with ½-inch or ¾-inch plywood. As long as risers are solidly built, you generally don't need to worry about a perfectly finished job, since they will probably be covered with carpeting. Besides providing an attractive covering, carpeting cuts down on noise when talent has to move from place to place. Attractive designs can be made by fitting together different sizes, shapes and colors of carpeting.

It is also possible to make risers out of thick polystyrene blocks. But, since the polystyrene is relatively soft, it must be covered with a material that will evenly distribute weight over its surface. One-eighth-inch plywood covering can be used for this. The plywood must be held in place with nails long enough to anchor it into the polystyrene material. The plywood can then be painted or covered with a rug. Compared to the all-wood risers, the polystyrene risers are cheaper, lighter and quieter. But, of course, they are much less durable.

FIGURE 11.24

To draw a floor plan you start with a diagram of the studio that shows the overall outline of the empty studio. To aid in the placement of lights and pole cats, the positions of ceiling grid pipes are indicated. The floor plan is important not only to indicate the positions of sets, props and scenery, but in determining camera positions.

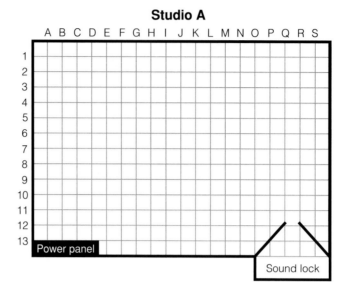

Risers are generally constructed in 4-by-4 or 4-by-8-foot sections. Not only does this make them easier to store, but the sections can be assembled in various configurations. For a choir or band, for example, you may want to stack some on top of each other to provide several elevations.

Modular Scenery

Ready-made "building block" modules are commercially available for sets that can be arranged in a variety of patterns. This commercial approach to sets is ideal for production facilities that do not have their own set designer or workshop. A wide variety of configurations are available.

DRAWING FLOOR PLANS FOR SETS

Although it may not be necessary with neutral or fantasy sets, with replica and representational sets, it is generally wise to draw a floor plan of the set before construction gets underway. A floor plan is an overhead, non-perspective drawing, done to scale.

To draw a floor plan, you start with a **studio floor plan** that shows the overall outline of the empty studio (Figure 11.24). To aid in the placement of lights and pole cats, the positions of ceiling grid pipes may also be indicated in the studio floor plan.

studio floor plan: A scale drawing of a studio area showing where scenery and props (and sometimes lights and cameras) are to be placed.

The floor plan is important not only to indicate the positions of sets, props and scenery, but in determining camera positions. When you have limited studio space, close-up shots will not be a problem, but the important master or cover shots might be. A master shot may not be possible if your cameras can never get wide enough to show more than bits and pieces of a set at one time. If, for example, you determine that the maximum angle of acceptance of your lenses is 45 degrees, that the set you plan to build is 40 feet wide and you will only be able to move your camera 15 feet away from the background—you have a problem! In this situation you will, at best, only be able to see a part of your set at any one time. (Without the perspective of a cover shot, your audience will never be able to understand the geographical relationships between things in your scene.) Set materials and labor are expensive, and construction time is generally limited, so you don't want to discover problems such as this after a set is built.

By referring back to the lens angle-of-acceptance guidelines in Chapter 3, you should be able to estimate both the maximum and minimum camera distances required for needed shots. A protractor or a clear piece of plastic with camera lens angles marked on the surface will provide a quick guide to possible camera positions.

A floor plan drawn to scale can also answer other questions. For example, it can tell you if you will you be able to fit all of the desired furniture or set pieces into a set. And even if you can, will there be enough room left over for an actor to easily get up from a sofa and stroll over to a table? And, how about that 8-foot bookcase in the prop room? Will it fit into the area between the front door and the breakfast bar? Such questions can be answered by trying out options, either on paper or on a computer screen. On paper, a scale of 1/4 inch to 1 foot, or 2 centimeters to 1 meter, can be used. Drafting paper with 1/4-inch or 2-centimeter light blue squares can be used for making scale drawings. Once you get used to it, you will probably find that the metric ratio of 1:50 (2 cm = 1 m) is easier to work with than 1/4 inch to 1 foot.

Computer programs are also available that allow the ready manipulation of set pieces and props. The basic studio floor plan and drawings of available set pieces are generally stored in computer memory to be retrieved as needed. Additional props and scenic elements can be designed on the computer screen and integrated into drawings. Once you have the basic elements in place, the props can be easily moved around on the computer screen to try out various options. Camera positions and lens focal lengths can also be determined. When the drawing is completed, an inventory of needed props can be printed out along with the final version of the drawing. For elaborate productions a producer may want a full sketch of the set.

FIGURE 11.25
To head off problems with a new set it is often desirable to build a scale model and check it out on camera. Because of the ability of the camera to show a model full screen, you can get a realistic idea of the final effect.

TOOTHPICKS AND TWO-BY-FOURS

To head off problems with a new set it is sometimes desirable to build a scale model and check it out on camera before starting to build the full-size set (Figure 11.25). When it comes to building materials, toothpicks (or maybe more accurately, balsa wood sticks) are much cheaper and easier to modify than sets made from two-by-fours. Because of the ability of the camera to show a model full screen, a realistic idea of the final effect is possible. A scale model set is particularly valuable in seeing how a camera will render specific shades of paint. And, of course, it is much easier to repaint a 4-square-inch section of a model set than a 9-square-yard section of a full-size set. In general, color schemes can be experimented with, spatial relationships checked, camera angles figured out and even lighting and micing problems foreseen, by working with a scale model. Figure 11.26 shows a scale model of the set for an Academy Awards production.

A scale model can be put together in a few hours with cardboard, balsa wood and glue. A visit to the local toy store for doll furniture can also save a lot of time. To get an idea of how actors will look in the set, you could even go the extra step of keying actors into the set, as described in Chapter 9.

We now turn to the second major topic of the chapter, television graphics.

FIGURE 11.26

This scale model of an Academy Awards set was designed months before the actual telecast. It was only after many changes were tried that construction of the actual set got under way.

TELEVISION GRAPHICS

The 4 × 3 Aspect Ratio

Visuals designed for the NTSC, PAL or SECAM broadcast systems must conform to the 4 × 3 aspect ratio. When visuals are designed on the screen of a electronic graphics generator (to be discussed below) this is fairly easy—you just keep things within the boundaries indicated. But often in developing graphics for television you need to rely on existing drawings or photos.

A graphic that is 8 inches wide, needs to be 6 inches high (2 times the 4 × 3 ratio) to stay within a 4 × 3 aspect ratio; and a graphic that is 9 inches high will have to be 16 inches wide to correspond to a 16 × 9 aspect ratio. But, without checking a visual on a camera—a time-consuming process—how can you determine whether a picture that is $5\frac{3}{4}$ inches wide and $3\frac{1}{2}$ inches high will work?

For this you need a proportional scale, such as the one illustrated in Figure 11.27. Using this scale you can find new dimensions for artwork that needs to be reduced or enlarged. You will see, for example, that the following are all in the 4 × 3 ratio: 5-by-$3\frac{3}{4}$, $6\frac{2}{3}$-by-5 and 10-by-$7\frac{1}{2}$.

As you search for graphics, you will quickly find that all of the materials you need will not conveniently present themselves in the appropriate aspect ratio. (It's an imperfect world out there!) Sometimes non-essential material can simply be cropped (cut) off on the top, bottom or sides of the visual. Occasionally, it is possible to electronically change the proportions of a visual—shrink it horizontally or vertically—to bring it into the 4 × 3 ratio. Often, however, visuals will become unacceptably distorted when shrunk or stretched in this way. In such cases related information, generally in the form of text, can be added at the side of the visual.

Safe Areas   The safe title and safe actions areas were introduced in Chapter 2. These safe areas are particularly important to graphics. (Refer back to Figure 2.17.) Remember that although the basic subject matter should be

FIGURE 11.27

With a proportional scale you can find the new dimensions for artwork that needs to be reduced or enlarged.

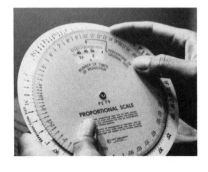

FIGURE 11.28
This figure indicates the safe area that must be kept in mind in designing graphics in the 16 × 9 aspect ratio. Unlike standard broadcast systems, there is greater control of overscanning with high-definition systems. Therefore, only one safe area (for both action and written materials) is used. Figure 2.17 in Chapter 2 shows the safe areas for NTSC television.

confined to the safe action area, it is best to keep written material within the safe title area.

The 16 × 9 Aspect Ratio

The proportional scale shown in Figure 11.27 can also be used for the 16 × 9 aspect ratio. For example, 4-by-7-inch, 14-by-8-inch, 18-by-10-inch and 25-by-14-inch graphics would all conform nicely to the 16 × 9 aspect ratio. Figure 11.28 indicates the safe area that must be kept in mind in designing graphics to the 16 × 9 aspect ratio. Unlike standard broadcast systems, there is greater control of overscanning with high-definition systems. Therefore, only one safe area (for both action and written materials) is used.

It is wise to design 16-by-9-inch visuals so that they can be used with standard (4 × 3 ratio) broadcast systems. Not to do so seriously limits the marketability of the material. Unless a special wide-screen-to-NTSC conversion process is planned (Chapter 2), this means that essential information should not be placed at the sides of the 16-by-9 frame.

Coping With Vertical Graphics

We know that 35mm slides intended for projection on a screen can be shot either horizontally or vertically, depending upon the nature of the original subject matter. The same holds for photos and graphics intended for the print media. Unfortunately, this is an advantage that television does not share. There are four ways of dealing with vertical visuals.

- First, the visual can simply be cropped into a horizontal format through camera framing. Unfortunately, cropping the visual in this way sometimes results in the loss of important subject matter.

- The second solution is to tilt the camera up or down as the graphic is shown (Figure 11.29). This is sometimes done to slowly "reveal" some significant aspect of the picture at the right time. While this has the advantage of adding movement to a static visual, it is difficult to do smoothly and takes more time than just presenting the visual all at once. More importantly, it is often desirable to see the entire visual at the same time.

- The next—and slightly inelegant—solution to this problem is to pull the camera back and tolerate empty areas to the left and right of the visual. With most switchers a rectangular wipe can be selected to "box in" and add a

FIGURE 11.29
One solution to accommodating vertical graphics is to tilt the camera up or down as the graphic is shown. This is sometimes done to slowly "reveal" some significant aspect of the picture at the right time.

(a)

(b)

FIGURES 11.30A and 11.30B

Another way of changing the ratio of a graphic is to use digital effects to change its horizontal and vertical proportions. Here the 4 × 3 (Figure 11.30A) and 16 × 9 (Figure 11.30B) versions of this drawing show little perceptible distortion. This technique can only be used with a limited number of visuals because of the objectionable distortion that can result.

boarder to the visual. At the same time the visual can be cropped as needed. After this is done, the outside (empty) areas around the visual can then be filled with a solid color. In some situations the visual can be moved completely to one side of the frame and text, or other material can be added to the screen.

- The last way of dealing with a vertical graphic is to use digital effects to change its horizontal and vertical proportions. As we've noted, because of the resulting distortion, this can only be done with a limited number of visuals. In Figures 11.30A (4 × 3 ratio) and 11.30B (16 × 9 ratio) this technique is used with little perceptible distortion.

Legibility of Written Material

Legibility refers to the readability of written material after it goes through the television process. As we've noted, legibility suffers much more in the standard broadcast process than it does when the video is distributed by satellite, cable or closed-circuit television. It is probably wise to hold to a "worst case scenario" and design graphics so that details will survive a low resolution broadcast process (specifically, about 200 lines of resolution, which is equivalent to slightly impaired reception on a typical NTSC home receiver).[3] This means a type size should be selected that is at least one-twentieth the vertical size of the video frame. The legibility of font (type) sizes that are less than one-thirtieth the size of the frame will be lost on some receivers.[4] These ratios assume full-screen visuals, as opposed to graphics that will appear in only part of the TV frame (such as behind a newscaster).

To maximize legibility letters should

- be bold, rather than consisting of thin lines,
- not be narrow or condensed, and
- not have striped or hatched designs.

As we noted, these readability guidelines are for full-frame visuals. If a

3. As we noted in Chapter 2, there is a difference between the resolving power of the 525-line NTSC system of broadcasting and the 625-line PAL and SECAM systems. And, of course, high-definition television is able to resolve several times the detail of either the 525-line or 625-line systems. But, since it is often necessary to convert one system to another, we are covering guidelines that will produce acceptable results with any of these systems.

4. This may not always be an accident. It would seem that some television advertisers who are required to make certain "delicate disclosures" select type sizes that fall significantly below these guidelines. We are probably safe in assuming that this does not happen by accident.

visual is designed as a corner insert behind a newscaster or narrator, all important elements (including text) will have to be much larger. With background visuals no specific guidelines can be given, since legibility requirements will depend upon final size.

With this as a background, we can now turn to the various ways of creating visuals for television. We'll discuss three basic types of television graphics: camera cards, 35mm slides and electronically generated graphics.

Camera Cards

In the past, 11-by-14-inch **camera cards** used to be used for almost all TV graphics. Included were super or key cards consisting of white letters on a black background. These were used for opening titles, closing credits and, in between these, the names and titles of on-camera guests. *Full value* camera cards, or pictures and drawings containing a full range of tonal and color values, were also common. These primarily consisted of photos, many of which were AP or UPI newsphotos transmitted to the station by a fax-type machine. The camera cards were commonly stacked on a card holder or music stand. At the appropriate time in a newscast a studio camera would quickly swing around to get a close-up of a card. By placing tabs on the sides of the cards, they could be quickly pulled by an assistant.

full value visual: Television visual that contains a full range of tones from black to white.

Although camera cards have largely been replaced by other graphic systems, they still have some advantages:

- They remain the fastest approach to putting a graphic into a production (an important factor in fast-breaking news stories), and they allow for last-minute modifications.
- They readily allow for pans and tilts (and in some cases, zooms) to slowly reveal subject matter, or to add movement to what is an essentially static visual form.
- They can be held by on-camera talent and have important areas pointed out.
- They are the most direct and least less expensive way to incorporate a visual into a production.

But camera cards also have disadvantages:

- They can tie up a camera that could be used for other things.
- They normally require a card holder (music stands are often used) with special lighting.
- Since they often require extreme close-ups, their use calls for careful camera positioning, framing and focusing.
- Some zoom lenses have problems focusing at the distances required.
- Compared to slides and electronic still store, they are larger and more difficult to store and retrieve.
- They sometimes require the help of a studio assistant — especially when cards have to be changed (pulled) during a production.
- With age, camera cards can quickly show signs of wear.

Thirty-Five-Millimeter Slides

Slides taken with 35mm cameras used to be heavily relied on to illustrate commercials, station breaks and news stories. Although they are not used nearly as much as they used to be, slides have several advantages over camera cards:

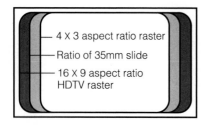

FIGURE 11.31

The 3 × 2 aspect ratio of 35mm slides falls conveniently in between television's 4 × 3 and 16 × 9 video aspect ratios.

- They are smaller and easier to index and store.
- Once loaded into a projector, 35mm slides can be rapidly accessed without the reframing and refocusing problems associated with camera cards.
- Organizations such as the Associated Press find they are a convenient, easy to manage and relatively inexpensive format for supplying news visuals to stations. (Even so, fax-type newsphoto machines are still used for important, late-breaking news.)
- Since 35mm film is used by professional and amateur photographers around the world, television has ready access to a wealth of visual material.
- Since the image from slides results from light passing through the slide rather than light being reflected from the surface of a visual, more subtle color and tonal values and greater brightness ranges are possible with slides.
- The 3 × 2 aspect ratio of slides falls conveniently in between the 4 × 3 and 16 × 9 video aspect ratios (Figure 11.31).
- While small production facilities typically have provisions for converting slides to video,[5] they are not necessarily quipped with electronic still-store equipment (images stored on computer disks).
- Slides are a convenient medium for capturing images for use in electronic still-store devices.
- The high resolution, superior color and tonal rendition of slides make them an ideal medium for high-definition television.

The disadvantages of slides include the following:

- They require time-consuming processing.[6]
- Unless slides are mounted and sealed in glass frames, dirt and dust quickly collect and become visible.
- It is difficult to do just a few visuals at one time, since 35mm transparency film comes in 12-, 24-, and 36-exposure rolls.
- Unlike visuals that are electronically stored, slides require physical handling; a process that risks damage, loss and improper loading into a projector (sometimes resulting in slides being reversed left to right or upside down).

Electronic Still Cameras

Electronic still cameras operate in the same basic way as a standard 35mm camera (Figure 11.32). However, instead of using film they record images electronically — often on 2-inch computer-type disks. Although originally introduced for the home (consumer) market, electronic still cameras seem to have found a home in professional television and print journalism applications instead. In production they offer a number of advantages over film cameras:

- No film processing is involved.
- Images can be immediately verified on a color monitor.
- The digital image can be color corrected, cropped, manipulated and easily combined with other images.

5. Reasonably good results can be obtained by simply projecting a 35mm slide onto a good-quality screen and picking up the image with a TV camera. Assuming the projected image is large enough, it is also possible to enhance the effect by panning, tilting and zooming the video camera.

6. Although Kodachrome, especially in its slower speeds, is one of the highest quality slide (transparency) films available, only a few labs around the country are equipped to process it. In contrast, labs in all major cities can use readily available E6 technology to develop films such as Ektachrome, Fujichrome and Agfachrome.

FIGURE 11.32
Electronic still cameras operate in the same basic way as a standard 35mm camera. However, instead of using film, they record images electronically — generally on 2-inch computer-type disks.

- In news work, images can be transmitted via telephone lines from any point in the world.[7]
- Although the quality does not equal the best slide film, the two-million-pixel CCDs used in some electronic still cameras provide quality that exceeds the capability of NTSC television and approaches the limits of high-definition television.
- Costs are lower in the long run because the camera disks can be used over and over.
- With the appropriate equipment, the electronic images can be directly converted into a color print (Figure 11.33).

7. Since the image is digital, a complete color image can be transmitted by a computer modem in a matter of minutes. This is an important consideration in covering news stories, especially in foreign locations. Totalitarian governments have been known to ban satellite video transmissions on important (but politically delicate) events; but, they have found it far more difficult to censor computer data transmitted by telephone. Shortwave radio has also been used to send video still frames.

FIGURE 11.33
The images from electronic still cameras can be printed out electronically with equipment such as this. Images from these cameras can be immediately verified (without processing) on a color monitor and color corrected, cropped and manipulated. The electronic images can also be transmitted via telephone lines from any place in the world. The small computer-type disk on the table can hold 50 video frames.

FIGURE 11.34
Standard video cameras are commonly used to capture still pictures. A desktop computer equipped with a frame-capture card, plus a video camera mounted on a copy stand are the basic requirements. Once the image is displayed on the computer monitor, a full range of image manipulation techniques becomes possible.

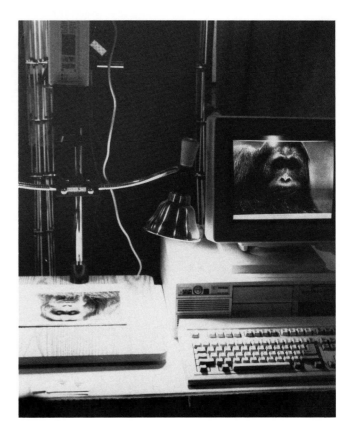

Standard video cameras are commonly used to capture still images. A desktop computer equipped with a frame-capture card, plus a video camera mounted on a copy stand are the basic requirements (Figure 11.34). Once the image is displayed on the computer monitor, a full range of image manipulation techniques become possible. After the desired effect is achieved, the electronic image can be stored on a computer disk for future use. These images become the basis for much of the artwork for news visuals, public service announcements (PSAs) and commercials we see every day on television. (See Figure 11.35.)

Electronic Still Store

Whatever the original medium—camera cards, slides, electronic still cameras or standard video cameras—there are many important advantages to filing visuals in an electronic still-store device.

- They can be retrieved almost instantly and in any order during a production.
- Unlike film, they are stored in an electronic form, which means there is no deterioration of quality over time.
- Their digital form allows for direct special-effect manipulation.
- Images can be received or transmitted over telephone lines.
- Large inventories of visuals are available for downloading (electronic transfer from one computer to another) from many "image banks" across the country.

Most still-store devices rely on computer-type disk drives to store images. Since digitized pictures require a great amount of storage space, high-capacity

FIGURE 11.35
The images captured with video cameras and manipulated by computers become the basis for much of the artwork for news visuals, public service announcements (PSAs) and commercials we see every day on television.

disk drives are required. Both dedicated (hardware-based) still-store units and desktop computer (software-based) units are used.

ELECTRONIC GRAPHIC SYSTEMS

It is impossible to clearly distinguish between character generators, titlers, paint programs, frame-creation systems, 2-D (two-dimensional) animation, 3-D (three-dimensional) modeling and image processing systems. So to simplify things, we'll just put all of these into a single category: *electronic graphic* systems.

electronic graphics: Titles, credits, drawings etc., produced electronically.

Some electronic graphic systems are dedicated, which means they are hardware-based and designed to just do specific things (see Figure 11.36). Others are

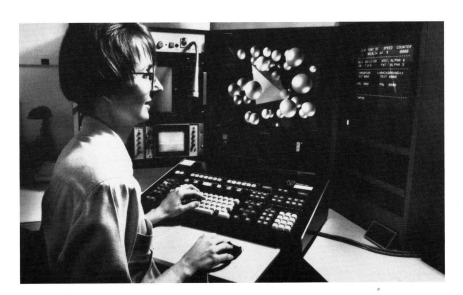

FIGURE 11.36
Some electronic graphic systems, such as this one, are dedicated, which means they are hardware-based and designed to just do specific things. In contrast, graphic systems that use a standard desktop computer platform are software-based.

FIGURE 11.37

Somewhere in between the simple titles and the lifelike pictures are the weather graphics we see each night on the news. Units such as this can start with the daily satellite pictures from the national weather service and then generate localized maps and overlays appropriate to a geographical area. Simple animated sequences showing the movement of weather systems are a common part of these graphic systems.

based on a standard desktop computer platform and are software-based. In their most sophisticated form, electronic graphic systems can create animated 3-D modeling rivaling real-life subject matter. The color pictures at the end of Chapter 5 illustrate some of the possibilities.

Somewhere in between the simple titles and the lifelike pictures are the weather graphics we see each night on the news. Dedicated units such as the one shown in Figure 11.37 can start with the daily satellite pictures from the national weather service and then generate localized maps and overlays appropriate to a geographical area. Simple animated sequences showing the movement of weather systems are a common part of these graphic systems.

Some common functions of today's basic electronic graphic units include the following:

- A wide range of font (typeface) styles (see Figure 11.38)
- Variable font sizes (in some cases all the way from letters that are too small to read to a single letter that will fill the TV screen)
- Choice of colors for letters, figures and backgrounds
- Choice of edging and drop shadows (see Figure 9.20 in Chapter 9)
- Ability to blink words on and off to attract attention
- Choice of graphic building blocks (vertical and horizontal lines, boxes, patterns etc.)
- Ability to scroll words vertically (**roll**) or horizontally (**crawl**) through the frame
- Ability to assign numbers to graphic pages once they are created and almost instantly recall specific pages on demand
- Ability to call up stored electronic pages either manually, by entering an identifying number, or automatically, in a programmed sequence
- Ability to incorporate pictures from sources, such as a VTR or studio camera
- Ability to move or change vertical and horizontal proportions of selected elements

Condensed typefaces can be hard to read.

Script isn't too clear.

Serif can blur and be hard to read.

A simple, modern typeface such as this,

or possibly even this, is much better.

FIGURE 11.38
A wide range of font (typeface) styles
are available with most of today's
graphic systems. These include font
sizes that range from letters that are too
small to read to a single letter that will
fill the TV screen. As illustrated here,
not all fonts are suitable for TV.

- *Anti-aliasing* capabilities; the ability to smooth out the "sawtooth" effect around curves and angled lines (Figure 11.39)

In addition, some more elaborate systems offer the ability to do two more tasks:

- Complex layering for 2-D animated sequences
- Programmed, vector-based (pseudo) 3-D animation sequences that allow images to be rotated to show full dimensionality

These latter two areas will take some explanation.

anti-aliasing: Smoothing a sawtooth,
jagged effect around curved and diagonal
lines in electronic graphics through the use
of electronic filters.

Electronic Animation

Traditional animation requires the drawing and painting of 24 or 30 frames (pictures) every second to correspond to film or TV frame rates. This means that an animated film requires in the neighborhood of 130,000 separate pictures (90 minutes × 60 seconds × 24 frames per second).[8] However, when a high-end computer is used, all of the drawings necessary to get a subject or object from point A to point B can be "filled in" (figured out) by the computer. By only having to supply key drawings, the animation process is greatly simplified. This also means that the computer can immediately show the results of an animated sequence in real time; something that can't be done with traditional animation.

FIGURE 11.39
Professional graphic systems are
equipped with anti-aliasing capabilities — the ability to smooth out the
"sawtooth" effect around curves and
angled lines.

8. These drawings are normally done by creating several layers of transparent, acetate *cels,* which can be independently moved during the frame-by-frame process of photography. This makes it unnecessary to totally redraw every element of each frame. In many types of action, frames can also be repeated.

Electronic Image Layering

Traditional film animation also depends upon layers of acetate cels, each containing an element of the overall picture that must move separately from the rest. When the camera shoots a picture of the combined layers, they merge into one image. Electronic 2-D animation uses the same principle; however, instead of existing on acetate, the various layers exist in computer memory. With some animation systems it is possible to create more than 10 layers, each of which can be modified and controlled without affecting the rest.

To show movement in typical Saturday morning cartoon style, the different layers can be moved at different speeds. Thus, from the viewpoint of the viewer or camera, a kind of motion-related dimensional perspective is created for objects that are supposedly at different distances from the camera. Since the computer is not responsible for calculating and showing the dimensionality of the various objects, this type of animation is referred to as 2-D animation.

THREE-DIMENSIONAL TELEVISION

There are various techniques for creating actual 3-D (stereoscopic) images on a screen. All depend upon delivering slightly different images to the left and right eyes. These two images correspond to the separation that exists between our two eyes. Although this change in perspective or viewpoint is only separated by a few inches, it's enough to create the illusion of depth and dimension. True 3-D systems, therefore, must be able to simultaneously photograph two images from separate perspectives and display them separately to the left and right eyes.

Given the proper equipment and conditions, 3-D techniques can be quite impressive with still photos and slides. Results have been much less spectacular with moving images, however. In order to keep the left and right images separate, various types of glasses have been devised, which separate a display into two images. With bright, high-resolution computer images, glasses with red and blue filters have been used that primarily pass red light to one eye and blue light to the other. When one of the 3-D images is reproduced on the screen in red and other in blue, a 3-D effect can be achieved.[9] But, because the system depends upon color filtering, full color rendition is lost.

Over the years a number of TV stations around the country have broadcast 3-D films and TV programs.[10] However, because of the glasses required and the less-than-spectacular results, to date 3-D video has not met with wide acceptance. With this background in "real" 3-D reproduction, we can move onto what is called pseudo 3-D—the appearance of three dimensions created on a standard two-dimensional TV screen.

Vector-Based 3-D Modeling

pseudo 3-D system: A computer-based vector graphic system capable of being used to do drawings that, rather than appearing flat, seem to have three dimensions.

vector-based graphic system: A computer-based drawing system in which the appearance of three dimensions is created by being able to rotate or move the subject matter. The moving perspectives (vectors) are automatically calculated and created on the screen by the software involved.

In vector-based *pseudo 3-D systems* the appearance of three dimensions is created over time. Pseudo 3-D graphic images give the illusion of 3-D by extrapolating what a 3-D drawing of an object would look like when rotated. In *vector-based graphic systems* a set of descriptive coordinates (vectors) for an

9. Various TV games, including some of the Nintendo games, rely on the same technique. Film has been somewhat more successful using polarized lenses on both projectors and viewing glasses. The images are kept separate by polarizing one image vertically and one horizontally. This technique has not been widely accepted for three reasons: the glasses become uncomfortable after a period of time, the images are often a bit dim, and differences in eyesight affect the 3-D effect.

10. TV station KTLA in Los Angeles, which has experimented with many new production innovations over the years, has had sporadic programming in 3-D for almost a decade.

object is used as a basis for computing new positions, angles and perspectives. Objects can be made to automatically move from point A to point B while turning and revealing apparent depth and dimension.

So-called high-end dedicated graphic systems (optimum quality at correspondingly high prices) compute pixel-by-pixel addresses for every point on an object for every increment of movement. Once the initial information is entered into the computer (image shape, size, movements, changes in perspective etc.) the computer may require from a few minutes to many hours to figure out the frame-by-frame changes for every pixel point on the screen as objects move from point A to point B. Because of the computing demands inherent in doing really elaborate vector-based animation, it is reserved for computers that can do a hundred million or more calculations per second—a feat that probably should not be tried on your pocket calculator!

FIGURE 11.40
With desktop computer graphic systems either a mouse or a trackball (shown here) can be used to control the movement of the cursor (the on-screen visual reference point).

CONTROL OF ELECTRONIC GRAPHIC SYSTEMS

Regardless of their level of sophistication, electronic graphic systems are basically controlled with a computer-style keyboard.[11] In addition, either a mouse or a trackball (Figure 11.40) can be used to control the movement of a cursor (visible reference point on the screen) as it is moved from place to place.

Keyboard, Mouse and Trackball Controls

With some graphic systems—especially those that are based on a desktop computer—keyboard functions are introduced by hitting the escape (Esc) key followed by any other key, or by holding down either the control (Ctl) key or the alternate (Alt) key while pressing another key. A mouse or trackball commonly supplement the keyboard, especially for pull-down menus.

Pull-Down Menus

Most graphic systems rely, at least to some degree, on pull-down menus to select options (Figure 11.41). Selections are made with a mouse, a trackball or, in some cases, by an electronic pencil. With many programs a special key, such as the alternate (Alt) or escape (Esc) key, moves you to the pull-down menus, and then the arrow keys on the keyboard are used move the cursor to various points within the menus. Hitting a return or enter key initiates the function. If you are using a mouse or trackball, you normally have to hold down a button while moving through the menu of options. When you release the button you activate the highlighted function.

Although pull-down menus provide a simple and systematic approach to accessing functions, they can be time-consuming to use—especially for functions that must be accessed repeatedly. There are faster ways. Although they take a bit longer to learn, most graphic systems provide direct access to functions in one of three ways:

- Through dedicated keys on a drawing palette
- By *function keys* (normally arranged at the top of an IBM-style keyboard and labeled *F1* through *F12*)
- By assigning functions to special key combinations (macros)

---

11. All of the approaches in this section apply as well to computer editing systems (Chapters 14 and 15) and other computer-based production equipment.

FIGURE 11.41

Most graphic systems rely, at least to some degree, on pull-down menus to select options. Selections are made with a mouse, a trackball or by keys on the computer keyboard.

Since macros represent a major time-saving device in working with almost any computer-based program, they merit some explanation.

Macro Control Sequences

With many computer-based graphic programs it is possible to customize the program by having it memorize a sequence of commands in a user-created mini-program called a **macro**. (Some computer systems refer to this as *scripting*.) The entire sequence can then be "played back" any time with only one or two keystrokes. This is similar in concept to the telephones that can be programmed with frequently used telephone numbers that be recalled by just pushing one or two keys. Computer macros, however, are a bit more complex, because they are capable of memorizing complex sequences.

Macros may be temporary held in computer memory, to be used for just one session, or saved for use during subsequent sessions. Temporary macros, which are held in volatile memory, disappear from memory at the end of the session. Permanent macros are saved in non-volatile memory (generally on a computer disk) and need not be reprogrammed to be used in subsequent sessions. (But, of course, whenever desired, they can be erased and new sequences assigned to the same initiating keys.) Whatever the computer-based application—graphics, animation or editing—macros can save considerable time.[12]

Electronic Palettes

Dedicated electronic graphic units (as opposed to software-based systems) typically supplement the keyboard and pull-down menus with a separate **electronic palette** that uses an **electronic pencil**. The electronic pencil, which takes the place of a mouse, is more natural for many people to use—especially when doing on-screen drawings. Dedicated keys around the drawing palette give direct

---

12. If the graphic system does not have a built-in macro capability, or it is limited, a separate macro program can be loaded before the graphic program. In some cases these will allow you to create more than 100 macros.

access to the indicated functions without having to keep in mind keyboard commands or move through a series of pull-down menus. (See Figure 5.18A in Chapter 5.)

Touch-Screen Control

Some graphic systems have touch-screen controls where the operator chooses functions by touching the screen with an electronic pen. Although this represents the simplest and most direct means of controlling graphic programs, it generally requires the operator to repeatedly pick up and put down the electronic pencil in order to move between touch-screen control and the keyboard entry of data. Although this seems like a pretty simple task, when it has to be repeated hundreds of times during a day it can become rather bothersome.

Voice Control

Whenever a computer-based system involves constantly moving from one command to another, voice control is an attractive option. With this system a *voice recognition module* within the system is programmed to recognize commands from specific operators. To reduce the possibility of surrounding noise interfering with voice commands, headsets are commonly used. Some systems are programmed to recognize a basic menu of the voice commands from any operator. However, a much higher level of reliability is possible when individual operators program the system to recognize their own voice and sets of commands. Thereafter, whenever the command word or phrase is repeated, the system should be able to recognize it and instantly invoke the programmed sequence. Voice control can greatly speed up the actions in computer-based systems.

voice recognition module: A computer system that can recognize certain voice commands and respond appropriately.

SUMMARY

Sets refer to basic supportive scenery in a production. Props, which are used within sets, include set props and hand props. *Staging* refers to the process of bringing these elements together to create a working environment for on-camera talent. The set designer, art director or scenic designer's job is to work with a producer-director throughout the design, construction and staging processes.

There are five categories of sets: neutral, representational-supportive, symbolic, realistic and fantasy. One of the most versatile and widely used neutral sets is the cyc. A 10-step gray scale is commonly used in assigning brightness values to sets, props and wardrobe. Cameo backgrounds are totally black; limbo backgrounds can be any solid, unbroken color or tone. Background lights can be used to control the tonal and color values of backgrounds. Gels are used over spotlights to create background colors, while ellipsoidal spotlights with cookies are used to create abstract or realistic shadows on backgrounds.

Both softwall and hardwall flats are used in television. Both are fastened together by lashlines, bolts and hinges to create various types of backgrounds. Hardwall flats finished with wood paneling or wallpaper are commonly used to simulate interior settings. To facilitate lighting, subjects should be kept from 9 to 12 feet away from backgrounds. A background that is inexpensive and quick to put up can be made by stapling 9-foot-high seamless paper to walls.

Today, with cameras mounted on remotely controlled jibs that can easily get high angles on sets, the floor has become an important part of many settings. Risers are used to both elevate (seated) talent to convenient camera heights and to supplement scenic design. Commercially made modular set pieces are available that can be used like building blocks to create a wide variety of set designs.

A floor plan, which is an overhead scale drawing of the basic set pieces and props in a production, is also commonly used to indicate the position of lights and cameras. Close-up shots of scale model renderings of sets can be used to get a realistic idea of how sets will look on camera before actually being built.

Although camera cards used to be used for almost all television graphics, they have now almost entirely replaced with slides and electronic graphics. Television graphics either have to be in a 4 × 3 or 16 × 9 aspect ratio. Since up to 80 percent of the outside parameter of a broadcast picture can be cut off by the time the picture appears on home receivers, all important subject matter (including all written material) should be confined to an inner "safe area."

For most graphic applications hardware- and software-based graphic systems are replacing camera cards and slides. After a computer animation system is programmed with basic drawings, it can create 2-D and (pseudo) 3-D animation. This eliminates the tens of thousands of individually prepared drawings that were typical in traditional, frame-by-frame animation.

Hardware- and software-based graphic systems are controlled in a number of ways including a standard computer-type keyboard, a mouse, a trackball, an electronic pencil, user-defined macros and voice recognition.

KEY TERMS

anti-aliasing	pole cat
art director	props
cameo background	pseudo 3-D system
camera card	realistic set
canvas drop	replica set
crawl	representational-supportive set
electronic graphics	risers
electronic palette	roll
electronic pencil	scenic designer
fantasy set	set props
flats	sets
full value visual	softwall flat
gobo	staging
ground row	studio floor plan
hand props	symbolic set
hardwall flat	threefold set
limbo background	twofold set
macros	vector-based graphic system
neutral (indeterminate) set	voice recognition module

Scripts and the Creative Sequence | 12

There are some parallels between writing a script for a production and drawing a blueprint for a building. A successful architect needs to understand the possibilities of modern building materials, as well as the basic steps involved in constructing a building. The same way, a good scriptwriter should understand the capabilities of today's latest production tools, as well as the television production process. In this chapter we are not only going to examine scriptwriting, but the whole creative sequence, including the following:

- Principles of script form and content
- Defining the needs and interests of the target audience
- The role of treatments, program proposals and storyboards
- Budget considerations
- The preproduction and production phases
- Script conventions and formats

FORM AND CONTENT

A script has two dimensions: form and content.[1] In an earlier chapter we touched on these when we likened form to the medium and content to the message. But since form and content are — when you get right down to it — the quintessential aspects of production, we now need to look at them more carefully.

1. Many of the concepts in this section are based on the ideas of Richard Colla, an accomplished television and film director.

FIGURE 12.1

Depending upon its size, a production may involve only a few simple steps, or dozens of production phases. A step-by-step sequence for a rather sophisticated dramatic production is outlined here.

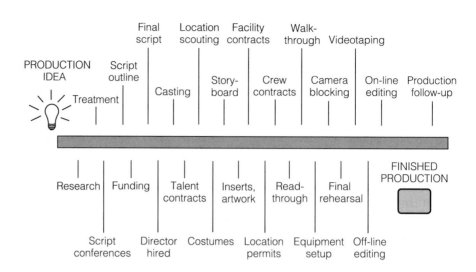

THE 15-STEP PRODUCTION SEQUENCE

Identify the Goals of the Production

Step 1. First, and foremost, *there must be a clear formulation of the goals and purposes of the production.* The best way to this is to ask some questions. Beyond the essential requirement of capturing and holding attention, we need to ask what the production is primarily intended to do: instruct, inform, entertain or possibly to generate feelings of pride, or social, religious or political need? Possibly its purpose is to create a desire in the audience to take some action. Or maybe, quite candidly, the primary purpose is simply to hold the attention of the audience through a series of commercial messages.

If there is no clear agreement on the purpose of a production, it will be impossible to evaluate success. (How do you know if you've arrived at your destination, if you don't know what your destination is?) Most productions, of course, have more than one goal. We'll elaborate on some of these a little later.

Analyze Your Target Audience

Step 2. Clearly define and investigate your target (intended) audience. The programming preferences of television audiences differ, based on such things as age, sex, socioeconomic status and educational level. Program preferences are also different in different areas of the United States (North, South, urban, rural etc.). Regional variations can in part be seen in differences in the local programming broadcast in different parts of the country—and occasionally by noting the films and network programming that some stations refuse to air.

Compared to standard broadcast television, institutional television, which includes corporate and educational video, has different needs and expectations. Here, too, there are demographic characteristics, such as age, sex and education. But in institutional television the producer and scriptwriter have to be keenly aware of the audience's experience, education, needs and expectations. To underestimate the education or experience and inadvertently talk down to an audience insults them. To overestimate education or experience and talk over everyone's head is probably even worse—you lose them, and they can become totally frustrated with the presentation.

But whatever type of television script you are writing — commercial or institutional — *the better your know the needs, interests and expectations of your audience, the greater the probability of your success.*

Review Similar Productions

Step 3. *Investigate similar productions done in the past to determine the probability of success of your idea (vision and goal).* If you can consistently predict this one, you have an exceptional career awaiting you on television; what's more, you can probably name your own salary. Since totally reliable predictors have not been found for determining a production's success, the best we can do is conduct some research and ask some hard questions. These include:

- Has the idea been done before? If so, with what results?

- How will the proposed production differ from the successful and unsuccessful efforts of the past? (If you are going to make some mistakes, at least make some new ones!)

- What will the life span of the production be? (Will it become quickly dated, or is it the type of production that can be replayed over time?)

- Does the production contain elements that will engage an audience? Pathos, action, sex, violence and beauty have been relied upon for centuries. But there may be other reasons for watching: a need to improve oneself, a need to know or understand issues or concepts, a need to be a more successful and productive worker (and reap the advantages of promotion, higher pay, greater respect and a higher social status).

- Finally, with all of these things in mind, there is the all-important consideration: how attractive will the production be to an advertiser or underwriter?

Determine Value and Marketability

Step 4. *Determine the overall value of the production to a sponsor or underwriter.* Obviously, underwriters or advertisers want some sort of return on their investment. Although we will cover ***costing-out*** (determining the production costs of) a production in Chapter 13, here we want to make sure we can justify production expense in terms of some sort of gain or return. To do this, we must ask several questions. First, what is the probable size of the audience? To determine this, you must know whether it will be a one-shot presentation or whether production expenses can be recouped over time by presenting it to other audiences.

> *costing-out:* The process of figuring out the costs of a production.

Generally, the larger the audience, the more marketable a production will be to an underwriter or advertiser. At the same time, simple numbers don't tell the whole story. Let's say an advertiser has a product intended for young people (athletic shoes or jeans, for example). In this case, a production that draws a large percentage of this age group will be more valuable than a production that has a larger overall audience, but a lower percentage of young people.

Once the potential value of a production to an advertiser or underwriter is determined, this must be balanced with the projected cost of producing and presenting the production. This is the return on the investment; the nefarious *bottom line,* or *payback.* In commercial television this payback is generally in the form of increased sales and profits. But, the return on the investment may take other forms, such as the expected moral, political, spiritual or public relations benefit derived from the program.

Develop a Treatment or Production Outline

Step 5. Next, *commit the idea to paper*. There are several steps to this. They span the interval from the initial proposal to the final shooting script.

After the initial decisions are made in Step 1, the producer generally commissions a treatment. A ***treatment*** (often called a ***program proposal*** in non-dramatic production) is a written summary of the production idea. It may be just a couple of pages, or in the case of a dramatic production, it may be 30 or more pages. A treatment is written as an aid in presenting and getting agreement on the focus and direction of the production. It may also be used to interest key people, especially financial backers, in supporting the production. A treatment should cover the focus of the production or in the case of a dramatic production, the basic story-line. Also included are the locations and talent required, and sometimes even a key scene. In non-dramatic productions the approximate times of the segments and basic production needs are also included. Anyone reading the treatment should be able to get a clear idea of the whole production. If there is disagreement on the program concept, it will be much easier to change elements at the treatment stage rather than after the complete script is written.

After the treatment is approved, a full script is requested. At this point the remaining research is commissioned. If the script called for someone watching TV in a 1960s ***period piece*** (a production that takes place during a specific historical era), we'd need to check on what television shows were being broadcast at that time.

Generally, the first version of the script is considered a draft, the first of several revisions. Throughout this process, a number of *story conferences* or *script conferences* typically take place as the script is revised and developed. Here, such things as audience appeal, pace, problems with special interest groups etc. are thrashed out, and alternative ideas are considered. If the director is "on board" (Step 7) at this time, he or she may be a part of these conferences.

Finally, a version emerges that is more or less acceptable to everyone.[2] However, even the version of the script used to start a production may not be *final*. In some instances revisions on a scene continue right up to the moment it's shot. Writers have been known to sit on the set of a major motion picture and crank out revised pages on almost a minute-by-minute basis. Each revision is issued on a different-colored paper, so that the cast and crew will not confuse it with an earlier version.

As the name suggests, a ***production outline*** is a list of the basic elements in the production, generally noted in the order they are to take place. It is used primarily in planning and organizing the production phases of the project.

Depending upon the production, a storyboard may be requested. A ***storyboard*** consists of (generally rather rough) drawings of key scenes with corresponding notes on dialogue, sound effects and music. Figure 12.2 shows the storyboard for a music video. Storyboards are common in short productions,

---

treatment: A summary of a film or video script that includes a description of the characters and the story plot. Often samples of action or dialogue are included.

program proposal: A treatment. An outline of the basic elements of a proposed production. Often used to interest investors or talent in the production.

period piece: A dramatic production that takes place during a specific historical time period.

production outline: A preproduction outline of the basic elements or steps involved in doing a specific production.

storyboard: A series of rough drawings of the basic shots or scenes in a planned production. They normally include a brief written description of the associated action and audio.

---

2. Hollywood production studios are notorious for radically altering script ideas. Following weeks and months of story conferences (and after numerous people have insisted on including their particular ideas in the project) the script may only vaguely resemble the original idea. Joseph Dominick (*"The Dynamics of Mass Communication,"* third edition) talks about a program proposal centering on a Peace Corps worker in a foreign country. After going through the committee process, it ended up being about a country agent working in the Southwest United States. When it got to this point, the writer quit the project.

3. There are many notable exceptions to this. For example, Alfred Hitchcock felt that the time he spent thinking through scenes and drawing out sketches represented the real creative focus of his work. Actually shooting the scenes was, in his mind, a bit anticlimactic. In the present era George Lucas is known to commission intricate storyboards for his key scenes.

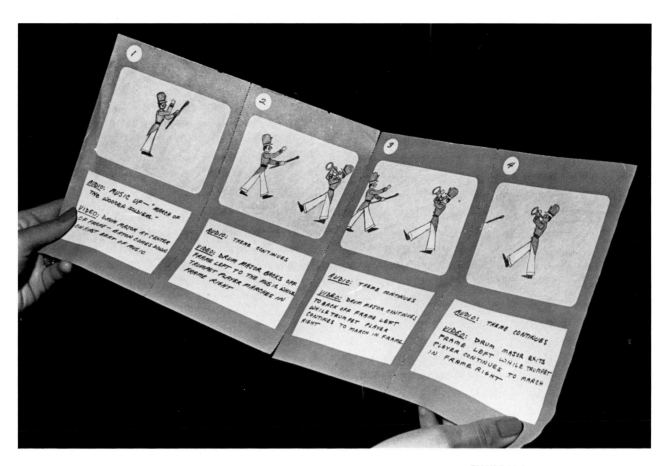

FIGURE 12.2

A storyboard consists of (generally rather rough) drawings of key scenes in a production with corresponding notes on dialogue, sound effects and music. In addition to hand-sketched storyboards (shown) storyboards are often done by computer.

such as commercials and public service announcements; they are somewhat less common in dramatic productions.[3] The ideas of set designers and costumers, as well as the angles and shots envisioned by the director, all go into the these drawings. Storyboards are especially useful in conveying basic production concepts to advertisers and underwriters.

Develop a Production Schedule

Step 6. Next, *a tentative production schedule should be developed.* Often, broadcast or distribution deadlines will dictate the **production schedule** (the written timetable listing the time allotted for each production step). If a corporate video production must be completed in time for an international conference, for example, you will need to outline a realistic production schedule that can ensure the completion of the production by that time. Missing the deadline could make the production worthless to the corporation (which, in turn, wouldn't contribute much to your job security).[4]

production schedule: A daily agenda showing time periods for specific phases of a production.

4. Ironically, as I was writing this I received an invitation in the mail to visit a leading television equipment manufacturer for an open house in their new location. Although I was impressed with the eye-catching invitation, when I checked the date I found that the open house was last week. The postmark indicated that there was not an undue delay in the mail, so it would appear that someone didn't meet the deadline for preparing or mailing the invitations. Since the company is a large one, I assume that in addition to unsold television equipment, they are stuck with a lot of coffee and doughnuts.

Commission Key Personnel

above-the-line: Budgetary division focusing on non-technical, creative expenses. Included are the producer, director, writer and the on-camera talent.

Step 7. From here on, the various production steps will overlap and in many cases take place simultaneously. But it is at about this point that *key, above-the-line production personnel should be brought on board*. **Above-the-line** personnel include the writer, producer, production manager and director. (The Glossary contains more information on the above-the-line and below-the-line production divisions.) A promotion director may be assigned to document and publicize the various phases of production.

Select Locations

Step 8. Next, *locations are selected*. In a major production a **location manager** will be hired to find locations that are as similar as possible to the ones outlined in the script. More and more, as audiences expect authenticity in productions, footage is being shot at the actual locations depicted. Cities that encourage TV and film production have film commissions that supply photos and videotapes of interesting shooting locations in their area. These commissions provide information on usage fees, if any, and people who need to be contacted. They generally also assist in getting the necessary permits, licenses and bonds (see Step 11 below).

Often—especially in high-budget productions—it will be necessary to arrange for modifications of on-location settings. This might include rooms that have to be repainted or redecorated, signs that have to be changed etc.

Decide on Talent, Costuming and Sets

Step 9. Decisions are made on talent, costuming and sets. Depending upon the type of production, talent interviews, auditions and casting may take place at this point. Contracts are then negotiated and signed. (If you are lucky enough to be able to afford well-known actors, they will have probably been chosen early in the preproduction process and their contracts will be negotiated at this point.) Once final decisions are made on actors, costuming can start.

During this phase, set design and construction will also get underway. After a set designer is engaged, he or she will review the script, possibly do some research, and then discuss initial ideas with the director. If these are accepted, sketches of the set or sets can be made and plans drawn up. Once these are approved, construction can begin.

Rehearsals, from initial walk-throughs to the final dress rehearsal, can then be scheduled. Even though sets are not done, the talent can start reading through the script with the director to establish pace, emphasis and rudimentary blocking. Once the sets are finished, final blocking and dress rehearsals can take place (Figure 12.3).

Engage Remaining Production Personnel

Step 10. Decisions are made on remaining staff and production facility needs. Arrangements are made for key technical personnel, equipment and facilities, including the rental of equipment and rehearsal and production facilities. Transportation, catering (from food and refreshment trucks) and on-location accommodations (for overnight stays) must also be arranged.

If unions are involved, their contracts will include job descriptions and specific responsibilities. Working hours, including graduated pay increases for overtime hours, will also be spelled out. In addition, unions often set minimum standards for transportation and the quality of meals and accommodations.

FIGURE 12.3
Once the sets are finished, final blocking and dress rehearsals can take place. Here, a visual effect for a institutional video is being rehearsed.

Obtain Permits, Insurance and Clearances

Step 11. Necessary access permits, licenses, security bonds and insurance policies are arranged. In major cities and in many foreign countries, it is not possible to just go to the location of your choice, set up your tripod, and start taping. Except for spot news and short documentary segments, permits are often required. Many semipublic interior locations, such as shopping malls, also require "filming"[5] permits. Depending on the nature of the production, liability insurance and security bonds may be necessary in case an accident is directly or indirectly attributed to the production. In some locations the controlling agency will limit exterior production to certain areas and to specific hours. If there is a street scene and traffic will be affected, it will be necessary to arrange for special police.

Included in this category are a wide variety of clearances. They range from permission to use prerecorded music to reserving satellite time. If clearance cannot be obtained, alternatives must be quickly explored.

Determine Supporting Production Elements

Step 12. As this work progresses, *program inserts can be selected and second unit work started.* Arrangements can now be made for shooting and acquiring VTR or film inserts, still photos and graphics. If possible, existing *stock footage* is secured (for a fee) from film or tape libraries located around the country. If suitable footage is not available or it does not meet the needs of the production, a second unit may have to be hired to produce needed segments. **Second unit** work is production done away from the main location by a separate production crew. It may not involve the principal actors or on-camera talent. If the script

stock footage: Scenes from a film or tape library that show common (generally exterior) scenes, which can be used in a production for a fee. This eliminates the time and expense involved in shooting or re-creating the footage.

5. Although many videographers understandably resist applying the term *filming* to video, some government agencies do not make these professional distinctions.

for a dramatic production calls for a specific building in Chicago, for example, a second unit can shoot the necessary exterior shots of the building in Chicago, while the interior shots (which are supposedly taking place within the building) are actually shot in New York (where the actors are living).

Initial decisions on music are made at this point. Copyright clearances and royalties must be worked out for music and visual inserts (these will be covered in more detail in Chapter 19).

Start the Production Sequence

Step 13. *The production goes into rehearsal and shooting.* Depending on the type of production, rehearsal may take place either minutes or days before the actual shooting. Productions shot live-on-tape (without stopping except for major problems) must be completely rehearsed before taping starts. This includes early walk-through rehearsals, camera rehearsals and one or more dress rehearsals (discussed in Chapter 1). Productions shot single-camera, film-style, are taped one scene at a time. Rehearsals generally take place right before each scene is taped.

Begin the Editing Sequence

Step 14. After shooting is completed, *tapes are reviewed by the producer, director and videotape editor, and editing decisions are made.* For major productions, the editing process is done in two phases.

off-line editing: Editing or making editing decisions from a time-coded copy (work print) of the original videotapes. Once off-line editing decisions are made, they are used in on-line editing to create the final edited master from the original videotape footage.

on-line editing: Using the original videotapes to make the final edited master.

edited master: The final tape created during the editing process.

First is *off-line editing*, where decisions are made using copies of the original tapes. Off-line editing decisions are made by editing an analog copy of the original footage, usually on one of the smaller videotape formats. Using this edited tape and an EDL (edit decision list) as a guide, the production then moves to the *on-line editing* phase, where much more sophisticated (and expensive) equipment is used. At this point a high-quality video format is used in making the *edited master,* the final edited version of the tape. During this final editing phase, all necessary sound sweetening, color balancing and special effects are added. (These topics will be covered in more detail in Chapter 15.)

Do Postproduction Follow-up

Step 15. Finally, *follow-up reports, production evaluation, promotion and distribution are completed.* Although most of the production crew will be finished at this point, there is still much in the way of follow-up work to be done. Final bills have to be paid, financial statements totaled, and the success or failure of the production determined. Broadcast television has ratings; in institutional television there may be tests, evaluations or simply informal viewer feedback to consider.

PLANNING THE SCRIPT

With this basic overview of the production process outlined, let's back up and examine the key element in the whole production process: the script.

There are semiscripted shows and fully scripted shows. In the first category are interviews, discussions, ad-lib shows and many demonstration and variety shows. The script for a **semiscripted show** resembles a basic outline, with only the show segments and their times indicated. This type of show puts considerable pressure on the director and talent to keep things on track as the show progresses (Figure 12.4).

FIGURE 12.4
The semiscripted show puts considerable pressure on the director, technical director and talent to keep things on track as the show progresses.

As the name suggests, the script for a **fully scripted show** lists the complete audio and video for each second of the production. In the fully scripted show, overall content, balance, pace and timing can be carefully worked out before the production starts. Unpleasant surprises are thereby minimized.

The Concrete-to-Abstract Continuum

Documentary and hard news pieces should be reasonably concrete; that is, they should (ideally) present information so clearly that the possibility of misunderstanding is eliminated. This type of script will be quite different in approach and structure from a script for a feature, a soft news piece, a music video or a dramatic production. In the latter instances it is often even desirable to not be too concrete — to allow room for personal interpretation.[6]

Let's look at two examples. An instructional video on the operation of a new computer program would need to be as concrete as possible. Given the nature of computers and computer programs, information would have to be presented in a highly structured, step-by-step fashion. Although the material should be presented in a creative, interesting and possibly even humorous way, the success of the production would rest on each member of the audience getting the same clear idea of a specific sequence of operational procedures. If the people in the audience walk away from the production confident that they can operate the

6. In film the range from *realism* to *formalism* (or expressionist) could be likened to the concrete-to-abstract continuum presented here.

computer program covered, the production would be a success. And the success of the production would be easy to evaluate when these people were subsequently confronted with the new program.

In contrast to this very concrete production would be a feature piece on jazzercise or new fashions. Given the fact that the audience has undoubtedly seen scores of television segments on fashion, the first challenge would be how to approach the segment in a fresh, creative, attention-getting way. Considering this challenge, actually doing the piece would probably be the easy part. Unlike stereo components or computers, fashions are not sold on the basis of technical specifications. Fashions appeal largely to ego and emotions. In doing the fashion piece, therefore, we are not as interested in communicating facts as in generating some excitement about new fashions — generating an emotional response. (Does this sound familiar?)

Likewise, a soft news piece on jazzercise would not emphasize facts as much as action. Its purpose would be to communicate something of the feelings surrounding exercise (and the feelings that go along with having a slim, trim, fit body). We should also admit that part of the attraction to the piece would probably be a certain amount of "sex appeal."

Structuring the Script

Once the intent and focus of the production are established and the characteristics of the audience are known, the various program elements can be selected and arranged.

In scripting content, a *logical sequence* is, of course, the most natural, especially when information must be presented in a concrete, step-by-step fashion. An example would be the instructional computer piece already mentioned. Often, however, it is desirable to abandon a structured, linear presentation, which can sometimes be pretty boring and predictable. In dramatic productions the technique of using flashbacks, or presenting **parallel stories** (two or more stories running concurrently) is often used to stimulate interest. The primary consideration is to create a sequence that will provide aural and visual variety and offer the most interesting variations in pacing. A production outline can be helpful in organizing these elements.

Working Around Weaknesses in Interviews

For better or worse, interviews are the mainstay of many, if not most, nondramatic productions. Because of this, and because of the difficulty involved in making most interviews interesting, they merit special attention.

Within limits, the credibility and authenticity involved in getting information directly from a credible source is better than having a narrator present the same information. Even if sources for interviews are not highly effective speakers, at least you are getting information "right from the horse's mouth," so to speak. This alone tends to offset presentation weaknesses. Even so, badly needed video and audio variety can be introduced into interview-centered programming by regularly switching to new speakers in new locations. Unless the person being interviewed on camera is an unusually gifted speaker or is recounting a highly dramatic, engaging event, interviews should be broken up into short segments and intercut with related material. You will also want to select only the most cogent elements from the interview. Keep in mind that once we see what someone looks like on camera, very little can be gained by holding the same shot while the person continues to talk. Interest and pace can be increased by staying with the audio track while cutting in related B-roll footage.[7] (This technique will be covered in more detail in Chapters 16 and 17.)

Organizing and Writing an Interview-Based Production   Turning dozens of reels of interview and B-roll material into a coherent (and even illuminating) production is a formidable task. An experienced writer with a good memory may only need to review the interview and B-roll footage while making periodic notes on topics and time codes. Writers who prefer a more systematic approach start out by getting a transcript of the interviews typed up on a computer (ideally, with regular time code references). This is especially valuable if there are numerous, lengthy interviews. Once the material is on computer disk, word or phrase searches can be done to quickly locate key words or topics in the various interviews. The related segments can then be condensed, rearranged and assembled right on the computer screen to provide the most logical flow. Most word processing programs allow the interview transcript to be reviewed in one window while the script is written in another. There is no need to retype the interview segments you decide to use; it is simply a matter of cutting and pasting text from one computer screen window to another.

Narration is written to explain or amplify points or to establish bridges between segments. (This will generally be read by an announcer over B-roll footage.) Once the narrative backbone of the production is in place, the writer can go back and (whenever possible) add relevant B-roll footage. The B-roll video is used with the narration or substituted for static, on-camera interview shots. Once the script is finished, a videotape editor can use the time code references and the written text to locate the beginning and ending points of the needed segments.

MATCHING PRODUCTION TECHNIQUES TO CONTENT

In writing the script, you must be alert at each moment to use the most effective way of getting ideas across. Sometimes you can best do this by asking yourself some questions. What will best illustrate a necessary point: a narrator, a short clip from an interview, an electronically animated sequence, a graph or a still photo? As you pull the elements together, think of yourself as watching the show, and try to visualize exactly what's going on at each moment. It is said that the great musical composers can hear each instrument in their heads as they write. In the same way, effective scriptwriters should be able to visualize scenes as they write their scripts.

PACING THE PRODUCTION

In establishing the pace of the production, there should not be long, slow periods or even long periods of fast pacing. Either will tire an audience. Except for short, fast-paced montages, scene segments should be at least three seconds in length. Conversely, only a scene with plenty of action or intensity will be able to hold an audience for more than a minute. As we've suggested, the most important parts of your production are the beginning and ending. To capture and hold attention, productions must engage the audience quickly. And to leave an audience with a positive impression, your production must have an effective ending. In between you have to keep interest from drifting by varying pace, emotional content and presentation style.

---

7. *B-roll* traditionally refers to any video footage that depicts, supports or visually interprets what is being said. Today, however, so-called B-roll is often used as part of the production structure to establish major points.

BASIC SCRIPTWRITING GUIDELINES

Although a complete guide to writing the various types of scripts used in television is beyond the scope of this chapter, some basic principles can be outlined. First, it should be emphasized that writing for the visual media is different from writing for print. Those writing for publication enjoy advantages that their counterparts in television don't have. For one thing, a reader can go back and reread a sentence. If a sentence is not understood in a television production, it is lost; or worse, the listener is distracted for some time trying to figure out what was said. With the written word, the reader is guided by such things as chapter divisions, paragraphs, subheadings, italics and boldface type. And in print the spelling of sound-alike words can indicate their meaning. (You might have a bit of difficulty preparing pastry with a calendar. But it wouldn't be too difficult with a calender.)

Since narration should be read in a conversational style, the standard rules of punctuation sometimes aren't followed. Commas and ellipses (three dots) are commonly used to designate pauses. Often, complete sentences aren't used . . . just as they aren't used in normal conversation. Although such usage is inconsistent with proper written form, the overriding consideration in writing narration is clarity.

The way we perceive information also complicates things for the scriptwriter. When we read, we see words in groups or thought patterns. This helps with meaning. When we listen, information unfolds for us *one word at a time*. This means that to make sense out of the sentence, we must retain the first words in memory and add them to all subsequent words until the sentence or thought is complete. If the sentence is too complex or takes too long to make its point, meaning is missed. Even worse, the listener's normal reaction in such cases is to dwell on the troublesome sentence to try to figure it out—thereby missing subsequent points.

Video scripts are written in what has become known as the broadcast style. With allowance for sentence variety, this means that video scripts use short, concise, direct sentences. All unnecessary words are weeded out: do not say, "at this point in time" when you mean "now." In writing for the ear it is especially important to eliminate "verbal fog." For example, which of these news story leads do you think would be most apt to capture your attention:

1. A man and a woman are listed as being in critical condition in St. Joseph's hospital today after being shot by a female assailant. The shooting took place at the house of the assailant's former boyfriend.

2. In an apparent fit of jealous rage a 29 year-old woman smashed through the front door of a former boyfriend's house this afternoon and fired three shotgun blasts at him and a female companion. The victims are listed in critical condition at St. Joseph's hospital.

Consider these lead sentences:

1. On Friday night the Sea Lions captured the state basketball title. After some disappointing opening games, Coach Jim Smithers decided that additional practice sessions were necessary for a successful season. These apparently paid off Friday night as the Sea Lions squeaked past the Winnetka Warriors 81 to 78.

2. After three disastrous opening games, no one believed the Sea Lions had an ice cube's chance at the state title. According to Coach Jim Smithers, "After the first few games it was pretty obvious that we had an awful lot of catching up to do. I figured the only way we'd get a shot at the title was to

practice longer and harder than anyone else." On Friday night the extra work paid off. The Sea Lions wrestled the State Basketball title away from the Winnetka Warriors 81 to 78.

Consider these as well:

1. Following an extended illness, President Teddy Roosevelt passed away a few minutes ago at Washington Memorial Hospital, where he had been a patient since October 17th.

2. The president is dead. The news was delivered to a stunned and weary crowd outside of Washington Memorial Hospital just a few moments ago.

And, finally, these:

1. The board's action helped the program to once again function.
2. The program is being rejuvenated by the board.

In writing a script, remember to prefer the active voice over the inactive voice; to prefer nouns and verbs over adjectives; and to prefer specific words over general words. Avoid dependent clauses at the beginnings of sentences. Also remember that attribution should come at the beginning of a sentence ("According to the Surgeon General . . .") rather than at the end of the sentence, which is common in newspaper writing.

Since viewers are used to having the video relate to the audio, the basic guideline *correlate audio and video* should be kept in mind. If viewers are seeing one thing and hearing about another, they can become confused. Watch out, however. This can lead to the "see Dick run" approach. If you can clearly see what is happening on the screen, it can be annoying to also be told exactly what you are seeing.

GUARDING AGAINST INFORMATION OVERLOAD

Although the purpose of many TV scripts is to impart information, if the script is packed with too many facts, the viewer will become confused, lost and frustrated. The average individual can only absorb a limited amount of information at a time. It is better to effectively cover a little bit of important material than to try to say it all and inundate viewers with a torrent of information they can't possibly retain.

Not only is the amount of information important, but so is the pacing of that information within the presentation. You need to give the viewer a chance to process each idea before moving on to the next point. The best approach in dealing with crucial information is to first signal the viewer that something important is coming up. Next, present the information as simply and clearly as possible. Finally, reinforce the point through repetition or with an illustration or two.

In summary, here are six important rules to remember in writing for television:

- Assume a conversational tone through the use of short sentences, informal words and contractions.
- Avoid complex sentence structure, including beginning sentences with dependent clauses.
- Provide adequate logical structure; let viewers know where you are going, which points are key concepts and when you are going to change the subject.
- After making an important point, expound on it; illustrate it.

- Pace the presentation of important ideas; give your audience a chance to digest one concept before moving on to another.
- Don't try to pack too many facts into one program.

VIDEO PROTOCOL

Some people argue that, unlike writing, video and film don't have any standardized grammar (i.e., conventions or structure). This is debatable. Although paragraphs, subheadings and chapter divisions aren't as apparent in television as they are on the printed page, nevertheless the TV audience has become somewhat adept at picking up the meaning of various audio and video transition devices.

The slow *lap dissolve* in video and the *cross-fade* in audio (where two sources momentarily overlap) often signal a transition. They are commonly used to signal a change in time or place. The "meanwhile, back at the ranch" phrase used in early westerns was often punctuated by a lap dissolve from a scene in town to a scene at the ranch. Just in case the transition was somehow missed, there might also be a cross-fade in the music at the same time. We quickly got the idea.

Fade-ins and **fade-outs**, which also apply to both audio and video, can be likened to the beginning and ending of book chapters. They consist of a two- or three-second transition from a full signal to black and silence. These transitions normally signal a major division in a production. Generally, this also consists of a passing of time. Traditionally, **teleplays** (television plays) and **screenplays** (film scripts) start with *fade-in* and close with *fade-out*.

In the process of scriptwriting, a number of other phrases and abbreviations are commonly used. First, there are those that describe camera shots. **Cuts** or *takes* are instant transitions from one video source to another. Put in grammatical terms, shots can be likened to sentences: each shot is a visual statement. In describing shots in a scriptwriting, remember that cutting from a static scene to a scene with motion accelerates tension and viewer interest.[8] Conversely, cutting from a scene with fast-paced movement to a static scene can bring about a sudden collapse of tension.

Cover shot, master shot or *establishing shot* are all designations for a wide shot (**WS**) or long shot (**LS**) that gives the audience a basic orientation to the geography of a scene. In the relatively low resolution medium of NTSC television, they are visually weak, simply because important details aren't easy to see. Cover shots should be used only long enough to orient viewers to the relationship between scene elements. Thereafter, they can be momentarily used as reminders or updates on scene changes. In the video column of video scripts the shorthand designation *LS* is normally used. Occasionally, you will see the abbreviations **XLS**, for extreme long shot, or **VLS**, for very long shot.

Except for dramatic shock value, a long shot should not be immediately followed by a close-up. The transition is too abrupt. A medium shot or medium long shot should come in between. Other shot designations you will find in scripts include the following:

- **MLS:** medium long shot or **FS** (full shot). With people, this is a shot from the top of their heads to their feet.

lap dissolve: Fading one video source out while simultaneously fading up on (going to) another source. Midway through a lap dissolve, both signals will be present in equal proportions.

cross-fade: The process of bringing down one audio source while simultaneously bringing up another.

take: A single shot. In single-camera production a specific shot often requires several takes before it meets the approval of the director.

cover shot: An establishing wide-angle or long shot of a set used both to establish the relationships between subject matter in a scene and to momentarily cover problems with mismatched action.

master shot: A wide, all-inclusive shot of a scene that establishes major elements. Often in single camera, film-style production action and dialogue are taped from the master shot perspective before the closer insert shots are done.

establishing shot: A wide shot meant to orient the audience to an overall locale and the relationship between scene elements. Generally used at the opening of a scene.

---

8. We are talking here about subject movement, not camera movement. Abruptly cutting from a static camera shot to a shot where the camera is rapidly panning, tilting or zooming is one of the editing "no-nos" that we'll discuss in Chapter 15.

- **MS:** medium shot. When applied to talent, an MS is normally a shot from the waist up.

- **MCU:** medium close-up. On a person, a shot cropped between the shoulders and the belt line.

- **CU:** close-up; a head and shoulders shot. A relatively straight-on CU is the most desirable for interviews. Changing facial expressions, which are important to understanding a conversation, can easily be seen. CUs are commonly used for insert shots of objects when important details need to be shown.

- **XCU:** extreme close-up. On people this is generally reserved for dramatic impact. The XCU shot may show just the eyes or mouth of an individual. With objects an XCU is often necessary to reveal important detail.

A **two-shot** or **three-shot** (also 2-S and 3-S) designates a shot of two or three people in one scene.

Although it doesn't indicate the closeness of a shot, the term *subjective shot* in a script indicates that the audience (camera) will see what the character sees. Often, it indicates a hand-held camera shot that moves in a walking or running motion while following a character. Subjective camera shots can add drama and frenzy to chase scenes.

subjective shot: A camera shot that appears to take the viewpoint of a person (generally one of the actors).

Camera angles are also sometimes indicated on scripts. Included are *bird's-eye view, high angle, eye level,* and *low angle.* A *canted shot,* or *dutch angle* shot, is tilted 25 to 45 degrees to one side, causing horizontal lines to run up or down hill. Although a writer occasionally feels it necessary to indicate camera shots and angles on a script, this is an area that is better left to the judgment of the director. Even so, you may find the terms *camera finds,* to indicate the camera moves in on a particular portion of a scene; *camera goes with* to indicate the camera moves with a person or object; *reverse-angle shot* to indicate a near 180-degree shift in camera position; and the term *widening* to signal a zoom or dolly back. The terms *various angles* and *series of cuts* indicate a variety of shots — generally on some specific subject matter. Writers use the term *quick cut to* in order to emphasize a fast cut.

reverse-angle shot: Used in dialogue scenes where a shot of someone speaking is followed by a shot of a person who is listening. Normally taken from over the shoulder at an angle of about 140 degrees.

In addition to these basic script terms, there are a number of other abbreviations used in scriptwriting. (See the sample scripts later in this chapter.)

- **EXT** and **INT:** exterior (outside) and interior shot.

- **SOT:** sound-on-tape. This indicates that the voice, music or background sound will be from a videotape audio track.

- **SOF:** sound-on-film.

- **VTR:** videotape recording.

- *VO: voice over.* This refers to narration heard over a video source. It can also refer to narration heard at a higher level than a source of music or background sound.

VO (voice over): Any time an announcer's voice is heard over video but the announcer is not shown.

- **OSV:** off-screen voice. The voice indicated on the script is from a person who is not visible.

- **MIC** or **MIKE:** microphone.

- **POV:** point of view. Dramatic scripts will often note that a shot will be seen from the point of view of a particular actor.

- **OS shot:** over-the-shoulder shot. The picture shows the back of one person's head and possibly one shoulder. (These are also designated as O/S and X/S shots.)

- **ANNCR:** announcer.

- **KEY:** the electronic overlay of titles and credits over background video.

F/X: Special audio or video effects.

- **SFX** or *F/X:* special effects. These may be audio special effects (audio FX) or video special effects—although, admittedly, neither is all that "special" any more.

SCRIPT FORMATS

To conclude this chapter we'll examine the two script formats used in video production: the basic video script and the dramatic (film-style) script.

News, Documentary and Commercial Scripts

Unlike dramatic scripts, to be discussed later, video scripts show no real consistency in their format. Most divide the page into two columns, allotting about one-third of the page to the video and about two-thirds to the audio (Figure 12.5). In some cases the page is equally divided (Figure 12.6). To facilitate reading by the talent, the audio text should be double spaced. Instructions in the audio or video column should be single spaced.

Unlike film scripts, capitalization in video scripts is not standardized. The announcer's words are often written in upper- and lowercase and the instructions in all capitals. However, announcers who have become used to reading news wire copy in all caps often prefer that the parts of the script intended for reading be printed in capital letters.

Shot-by-Shot and Master-Scene Formats

Although the dramatic script format originated with film, it is widely used in television, especially in dramas, sitcoms and single-camera productions.

Even though creativity is a much-sought-after component in script *content,* it is not admired when it comes to dramatic script *formats.* Script ideas must be communicated as quickly and accurately as possible. There is no time to try to figure out what the writer intends. Major variations in accepted script formatting are immediately chalked up to ignorance and inexperience—not the work of a serious or professional writer. Dramatic scripts are either written in the shot-by-shot or master-scene style.

shot-by-shot style: As opposed to the *master-scene style,* which outlines only general scenes, the *shot-by-shot style* lists each individual shot.

Note that in the **shot-by-shot style** (Figure 12.7), scenes are numbered, and basic camera directions are given. Because some directors feel that deciding on the shots is their job and not the job of the scriptwriter, many writers feel it's safer (not to mention easier) to use the master-scene approach. Exceptions occur when it's necessary to explain complex shot sequences or when the writer intends to direct the final production.

Note in Figure 12.7 that many words and phrases are capitalized. At first glance the use of caps in a film script seems a bit arbitrary, but capitalization actually follows set rules. The first time characters appear in a scene, their names are capitalized. Unlike video scripts, where abbreviations are used for CU, ECU, LS, MS, these designations are spelled out and put in all caps: CLOSE-UP, EXTREME CLOSE-UP, LONG SHOT, MEDIUM SHOT.

Capitalized words and phrases are also meant to stand out and indicate specific actions, effects or sounds. For example, specific visual effects are capitalized: REVERSE ANGLE, SLOW MOTION, FREEZE FRAME, MONTAGE, SERIES OF SHOTS, TWO-SHOT etc. Also capitalized are camera directions: CAMERA TILTS UP, CAMERA ZOOMS IN, CAMERA PULLS BACK TO REVEAL. Sometimes the word *camera* is not used: "we WIDEN TO REVEAL . . . , or "we PAN ACROSS room to SHOW. . . ." Actions and

Cactus Cable Company

VIDEO	AUDIO PAGE 1
VTR open, tape #328, cut 1 "Video Showcase"	((audio theme: "Happy Holiday"; establish for 10 sec. and fade under for announce.))
Key in title #1: "Video Showcase"	Anncr. GOOD AFTERNOON AND WELCOME TO ANOTHER EDITION
	OF "VIDEO SHOWCASE," A WEEKLY PROGRAM
	FEATURING THE BEST IN VIDEO PRODUCTIONS
	FROM OUR VIEWERS. YOUR STUDIO HOST FOR THE
Key in card #2: "host: Bill Andrews"	SERIES IS BILL ANDREWS.
	((theme up for 4 sec., and face under and out))
Dissolve from VTR to sl. #1 of cameraman underwater.	<u>Bill:</u> DOESN'T THIS LOOK INVITING? THESE ARE
	THE WARM, CLEAR WATERS AROUND AVACO
	ISLAND IN THE BAHAMAS . . . AND YOU
	ARE LOOKING AT DR. JAMES WILLIAMS, A
	LOCAL OPTHALMOLOGIST, AND THE UNDER-
	WATER HOUSING HE MADE FOR HIS SONY 8MM
	VIDEO CAMERA. BUT BEFORE WE TALK TO
	DR. WILLIAMS, LET'S TAKE A LOOK AT
	SOME SPECTACULAR FOOTAGE TAKEN JUST LAST
	MONTH BY TODAY'S GUEST IN THE WATERS
	OF AVACO ISLAND.
Video segment 01:10:36:10 to 01:10:49:21	((music: "Mystic Interlude," cut 4, ET 118; cut runs 2:18; video will run 1;56; no VO, just music.))
	Bill: I THINK YOU WILL HAVE TO AGREE . . . THAT
	WAS SOME OUTSTANDING FOOTAGE. THE VIDEO-
	GRAPHY WAS BY DR. JAMES WILLIAMS, A LOCAL
	OPTHALMOLOGIST, WHO IS TODAY'S GUEST ON VIDEO
	SHOWCASE." DR. WILLIAMS, WELCOME TO THE SHOW.

FIGURE 12.5

Unlike dramatic scripts, there is no real consistency in the format of video scripts. Most divide the page into two columns, allotting about one-third of the page to the video and about two-thirds to the audio. In some cases the page is divided equally (see Figure 12.6). To facilitate reading by the talent, the audio text should be double spaced, and instructions in the audio or video column should be single spaced. Unlike film scripts, capitalization in video scripts is not standardized. Announcers who have become used to reading news wire copy in all caps, often prefer that the parts of the script intended for reading to be printed in capital letters.

FIGURE 12.6

Since no words are spoken in this video, the audio column can be used to elaborate on the video action. This script, which was based on a student video, used numbers and paste-on faces on the sprinkler heads. In writing a script jumping from one column to another, changing spacing etc. can be time-consuming. A number of scripting programs are available for computers, which can make the process much easier.

VIDEO	AUDIO
(ECU) Sprinkler Head #1.	Peter Gunn Theme by Art of Noise.
(ECU) Sprinkler Head #2.	
(ECU) Sprinkler Head #3.	(It smiles.)
(MS) Jeff walking across Plaza toward camera and his car with Sprinkler #3 in foreground.	
As he approaches, we see only his feet.	(Jeff trips on sprinkler.)
(MS) Jeff on ground.	(In pain, he grabs his toe.)
(2-S) Jeff and Sprinkler.	(Jeff tries to pull sprinkler out of the ground. Frustrated, he leaves.)
(ECU) Sprinkler Head.	(It smiles.)
(LS) Jeff walks to his car.	
(MLS) Low angle. Rack focus. Camera focused on Jeff refocuses to reveal Sprinkler #3.	(He admires shiny, new car. He carefully wipes off speck of dust with white handkerchief.)
(MS) Jeff admiring his car.	(Sprinkler comes on, soaking both car and Jeff.)
(ECU) Sprinkler #3.	(Sprinkler stops. It smiles.)
(MS) Jeff taking wrench from car. Camera follows as he sneaks up behind Sprinkler #3.	
(MS bird's eye) Jeff and the sprinkler.	(He repeatedly tries but fails to take sprinkler head apart. Finally he gives up; throws the wrench down.)
(MS) Sprinkler and Jeff.	(Sprinkler sputters water. Jeff gets wet again. Totally exasperated, he gets up and stomps off.)
(ECU) Sprinkler #3.	(It smiles.)
Fade to black.	Fade out music.

related objects are also capitalized: "Mary EXITS THE FRAME," "JERRY PICKS UP the ARTIFACT."

Sounds are also capitalized: "we HEAR a KETTLE WHISTLE," and "She HEARS her father's FOOTSTEPS ON THE STAIRS." If it were only Sherry that heard the footsteps, there would be no capitalization; only sound that ends up being a part of the soundtrack is presented in uppercase. Thus, she *hears*, but we *HEAR*.

In writing actor instructions, note that margins are narrower than for the dialogue. No more than three lines should be typed here; anything beyond that goes in the scene description. Parenthetical directions are used sparingly. The writer should not try to do the actor's job.

```
    SHOT-BY-SHOT STYLE                                          42

       FADE-IN:

 1     INT. KITCHEN OF MASTERSON HOME—MEDIUM SHOT KAREN           1
       MASTERSON—DAY

       KAREN MASTERSON, age 36, quickly moves from the stove to
       the kitchen table.

 2     CLOSE-UP—TOASTER                                           2

       Toast pops up in the toaster.  We SEE KAREN'S HAND quickly
       pull out the toast.

 3     WIDE SHOT—KITCHEN                                          3

       We HEAR a KETTLE WHISTLE.  She quickly moves to the stove
       to turn off the burner.

                           KAREN
                         (calling)
                 Steve, you're going to be late!

       She takes a pan of oatmeal off the stove and pours it in
       four bowls on the kitchen table.  BILLY, age 9, bursts into
       the room.

                           KAREN
                        (continuing)
                 And tell Sherry to get a move on!

 4     MEDIUM SHOT—BILLY                                          4
                           BILLY
                        (sitting down)
                 Mom,Sherry's puttin' lipstick
                 on again; I saw her.

                           KAREN
                         (calling)
                 Sherry!

 5     INT. HALLWAY—MEDIUM SHOT—SHERRY—DAY                        5

       SHERRY MASTERSON, age 12, stops to check her appearance in
       the hallway mirror.  She HEARS her father's FOOTSTEPS ON
       THE STAIRS and quickly turns and walks toward the kitchen.

 6     INT. KITCHEN—WIDE SHOT—DAY                                 6
                           KAREN
                 (carefully looking at
                  Sherry as she enters)
                 Where's your father?
                                            (CONTINUED)
```

FIGURE 12.7
Unlike video scripts, where abbreviations are used for shots (CU, ECU, LS, MS etc.), these designations are spelled out and put in all caps in film-style scripts (CLOSE-UP, EXTREME CLOSE-UP, LONG SHOT, MEDIUM SHOT etc.). In the shot-by-shot approach shown here, scenes are numbered, and basic camera directions are given. Because some directors feel that deciding on the shots is their job and not the job of the scriptwriter, most writers feel it's safer (and easier) to simply write in terms of master scenes (see Figure 12.8).

The (*CONTINUED*) at the bottom of the page doesn't indicate that the script continues; we know it will until the words FADE OUT and THE END appear on the last page. (*CONTINUED*) means that a particular scene is continuing on the next page. At the top of the next page the word *CONTINUED:* is placed at the top-left margin.

A sample of the *master-scene style* is shown in Figure 12.8. Note that almost all of the conventions described in the scene-by-scene style apply, except that camera shots are not routinely listed. However, when a particular shot would

master-scene style: An approach to scriptwriting where only the basic scenes are described. Decisions on the various shots within the scenes are not noted in the script but are left to the discretion of the director.

FIGURE 12.8

In the master-scene style dramatic script, almost all of the conventions described in the scene-by-scene style apply, except that camera shots are not routinely listed. However, when a particular shot would not be anticipated by the reader, it should be noted. In both the shot-by-shot and master-scene approaches, many words and phrases are capitalized. The first time characters appear in a scene, their names are capitalized. Capitalized words and phrases also indicate specific actions, effects or sounds.

MASTER SCENE STYLE

FADE-IN:

INT. KITCHEN OF MASTERSON HOME—DAY

KAREN MASTERSON, age 36, is hurrying around the kitchen fixing breakfast. Two pieces of toast pop up in the toaster and she quickly tosses them on a plate. We HEAR a KETTLE WHISTLE. She quickly moves to turn off the burner.

                    KAREN
               (calling)
          Steve, you're going to be late!

Karen takes a pan of oatmeal off the stove and pours it in four bowls on the kitchen table. BILLY, age 9, bursts into the room.

                    KAREN
               (continuing)
          And tell Sherry to get a move on!

                    BILLY
               (sitting down)
          Mom, Sherry's puttin' lipstick on
          again; I saw her.

                    KAREN
               (calling)
          Sherry!

INT. HALLWAY—DAY

SHERRY MASTERSON, age 12, stops to check her appearance in the hallway mirror. She HEARS her father's FOOTSTEPS ON THE STAIRS and quickly turns and walks toward the kitchen.

INT. KITCHEN—DAY

                    KAREN
               (looking at Sherry
               carefully)
          Where's your father?

STEVE MASTERSON, age 38, enters. He walks up to Karen and kisses her on the cheek.

                    STEVE
          Oatmeal again?

                                        (CONTINUED)

---

not be anticipated by the reader, it needs to be noted. For example, "a close-up of John's hand SHOWS the BLACK INK STAINS." As in the scene-by-scene approach, use as few words as possible to describe things that will be visible to the camera.

Although descriptions should be thorough and even interesting to read, literary excellence should be saved for novels, where it might be more appreciated. According to one experienced script reader, the mark of an amateur is the use of flowery, poetic scene descriptions.

In this chapter we've looked at the basic preproduction and production elements of video productions. Although some basic elements of scripting were introduced, no attempt can be made in one short chapter to cover the real art and technique of scriptwriting. A number of excellent books on scriptwriting are listed in the Bibliography at the end of this book.

In the next chapter on producing, we'll extend many of the things we've discussed here into the production phase.

SUMMARY

Form refers to the basic design, construction and genre of a script; content centers on the script's emotional goals and visions. The quintessential goal of all production is to capture and hold an audience's attention. *Costing-out* a production refers to the process of determining or projecting production costs. The total production process can be broken down into 15 steps. During the scheduling phase of a single-camera production, the segments and scenes of a script are arranged in the most time- and cost-efficient shooting sequence.

There are semiscripted and fully scripted productions. News and documentary productions should be concrete enough not to be misinterpreted. To be most effective, fictional and dramatic productions should leave room for individual interpretation.

With allowance for sentence variety, video scripts must be written for the ear in a conversational tone and in short, concise, direct sentences. Transitional devices include fade-ins and fade-outs, dissolves and cuts and takes. A cover, or master, shot is used to establish the setting and the relationship between actors in a setting. There are two basic script formats: video and film. Film scripts, which are also used in dramatic television, can be written in the master-scene or shot-by-shot style.

KEY TERMS

above-the-line
ANNCR
budgeting
content
costing-out
cover shot
cross-fade
CU
cut
edited master
establishing shot
EXT
fade-in
fade-out
form (script)
fully scripted show
FS
F/X
goal (script)
INT
lap dissolve
location manager
LS

master shot
master-scene style
MCU
MLS
MS
off-line editing
on-line editing
OS shot
OSV
parallel stories
period piece
POV
production outline
production schedule
program proposal
reverse-angle shot
scheduling
screenplay
second unit
semiscripted show
SFX
shot-by-shot style
SOF

SOT

stock footage

storyboard

subjective shot

take

teleplay

three-shot

timing

treatment

two-shot

vision (as part of script content)

VLS

VO (voice over)

VTR

WS

XCU

XLS

Producing and Directing

13

In the last chapter we concentrated on preproduction planning. Here we'll move into the actual production and direction process. Since the jobs of production and direction are often combined in the single hyphenate-role of producer-director, we'll look at many of these merged functions in this chapter. A good place to start is in determining how much the production is going to cost.

COSTING-OUT A PRODUCTION

After the initial phases of preproduction (Steps 1 to 5 in the last chapter) we must confront the major question that underlies all television production in the real world: How much is it going to cost? Even if you have no interest in producing, the better grasp you have on this issue, the better your chances of success. It would be a waste of your time to come up with ideas—impressive as they might be—if they have little chance of being produced.

Of course, to-the-penny production costs won't be known until all of the production steps outlined in the last chapter are completed. Even so, no production company—at least none that expects to stay in business very long—will commit itself to a production without some idea of costs. Various systems have been devised to cost out a production.

First, expenses should be divided into categories. It has been traditional to think of expenses as falling into two broad categories: above-the-line and below-the-line. Although the "line" involved can at times be a bit blurry, above-the-line expenses generally relate to the performing and producing elements: talent, script, music, office services, stock footage etc. *Below-the-line* elements refer to (1) the physical elements involved (sets, props, makeup, costumes, graphics, transportation, production equipment, studio facilities and editing) and (2) the

below-the-line: Production costs associated with technical rather than creative services.

technical personnel required (the stage manager, engineering personnel, VTR operators, audio operators and general labor).

To accurately cost out a production it is necessary to go beyond just above-the-line and below-the-line expenses and divide production into at least 12 categories, as in the following example:

1. Preproduction costs
2. Location and travel expenses
3. Studio, set and construction costs, props and wardrobe
4. Equipment costs
5. Videotape, audio tape
6. Production crew costs
7. Producer, director, writer, creative fees
8. On-camera talent costs
9. Insurance, shooting permits, contingencies etc.
10. On-line, off-line editing
11. Advertising, promotion, publicity
12. Research and follow-up

While these 12 groupings are more useful than just two divisions, they still do not give an indication of the full range of expenses in a production. For this, and to provide an idea of the relative costs of some of the production elements, we'll go a step further and look at the budget categories contained in an actual budget. Figure 13.1 represents a condensation of a budget for a basic, half-hour, studio-centered TV sit-com.[1] Budgets for hour-long TV productions or 90-minute made-for-TV-movies would be even longer and more detailed.

A Typical Institutional or Local Station Production

The budget for a program or series for a local TV station or an institutional production will be a bit different. Since all of the personnel may be already on staff, it will probably just be a matter of shifting priorities to accommodate the new production. Even so, accounting procedures generally require that expenses for using equipment, facilities and staff be determined. Even though they are under the control of the corporation or institution, for accounting purposes they are *not free*. Unless total costs are determined for a production, including figures for depreciation, repair and maintenance, there will be no way of determining such things as costs vs. benefits (to be discussed later). Budget considerations for an institutional production would include the following:

1. Total production-staff time
2. On-camera talent costs
3. Costs of outside personnel and consultants
4. Share of facility and equipment costs
5. Location and travel expenses
6. Set costs, including modifications and new construction
7. Props and wardrobe

1. The best we can do here is provide an overview understanding. Since this actual budget ran 27 pages, a detailed explanation of each of the items would take up most of this book.

FIGURE 13.1
Sample budget.

```
                    Sample Studios, Inc.
                     Production Budget

Date: Sept. 12, 1992

Series (Production) Title      Episode Title        Production No.
  "N.Y. Stories" (30 min.)      "Perilous Business"    74325

Producer                      Director
  R. Sewell, B. Claremont       Alex Williams

                    Shooting Schedule

        Start              Finish           Production

    Date _____     Date _____     Est. Days _____
      Sept. 10, 1992    Sept. 14, 1992           5

                                              SUB-TOTALS
801    Story & Other Rights                      6,300
803    Writing
          Writers Salaries            11,728
          Secretaries, Typists         2,763
          Story Editors—Script Consultant  14,035
          Hyphenate Bonus—TV Only        850
          Character Payment—TV Only      466
          Supplies & Script Printing   1,242
          Abandoned Story Properties    1,720
          Miscellaneous                  115

       Total Writing                            32,919
805    Producer & Staff
          Producer                    37,375
          Associates                   3,317
          Assistants                   1,265
          Secretaries                  2,400
          Supplies                      168
          Miscellaneous Expense         345

       Total Producer & Staff                   44,870
807    Director & Staff                          17,250
809    Talent
          Series Principals
             Mark    —John Watson      31,625
             Matthew—Kevin Ryan         8,625
             Sheila  —Anne Markinson    5,750
             Linda   —Beth Hooper      11,500
             Todd    —David Colston     5,750
             Neil    —Robert Reeves     5,750
             Tom     —Jim Michaels     11,500
             Amy     —Terisa Downs      8,500

          Total Series Principals      89,000
          Freelance                    6,528
          Teachers—Welfare Workers       904

       Total Talent                             96,432
810    Fringe Benefits
          Health & Welfare, Pension Plan  13,738
          Employers Share of Taxes     20,700

       Total Fringe Benefits                    34,438

       TOTAL ABOVE THE LINE                    232,209
811    Production Staff
          First Assistant Director      4,000
          Second Assistant Director & Trainee  2,411
          Script Supervisor              962
          Miscellaneous Expense         1,685

       Total Production Staff                    9,058


                                              (continued)
```

FIGURE 13.1, continued

(continued)

813	Camera		
	First Cameraman	1,460	
	Second Cameraman	4,423	
	Total Camera		5,883
814	Art Department		
	Art Director & Assistants	1,708	
	Draftsmen, Sketch Artists	360	
	Materials, Purchases & Miscellaneous	200	
	Total Art Department		2,268
815	Set Construction & Striking		
816	Special Effects		
	Operating Labor—Provision	286	
	Rentals	58	
	Total Special Effects		344
817	Set Operations		
	Grips—Company	2,825	
	Grips—Other	115	
	Greensman—Water, Refurbish, Reset	174	
	Heating & Ventilation	170	
	Set Watchmen	1,756	
	Dressing Rooms	690	
	Materials & Purchases	195	
	Total Set Operations		5,925
819	Electrical		
	Electricians	1,485	
	Electrical Riggings & Strikings	410	
	Lamp Operators	1,325	
	Electrical Hookups & Rentals	260	
	Powerhouse & Generator Operators	225	
	Globes, Diffusions, Carbons	1,380	
	Total Electrical		5,085
821	Set Dressing		
	Set Decorator	1,215	
	Set Dressing & Warehouse Labor	3,105	
	Set Dressing MFG—L & M	345	
	Set Dressing Cleaning, Dyeing	115	
	Drapery Labor	920	
	Set Dressing & Drapery Purchases	805	
	Carpeting & Fixtures Costs	518	
	Set Dressing Rentals	345	
	Miscellaneous Expense	495	
	Total Set Dressing		7,863
823	Action Props		
	Propmaster & Assistant	2,102	
	Property Dept. & Manufacturing Labor	1,386	
	Food Used in Picture	1,150	
	Action Props Purchases	345	
	Total Action Props		4,983
831	Wardrobe		
	Women's—Wardrobe Woman on Set	2,070	
	Women's MFG—Labor & Materials	575	
	Men's—Wardrobe Man on Set	2,070	
	Men's MFG—Labor & Materials	862	
	Men's & Women's Cleaning & Dyeing	748	
	Purchases & Miscellaneous	282	
	Total Wardrobe		6,607
833	Makeup & Hairdressing		
	Company Makeup Artist	1,492	
	Company Hairstylists	1,250	
	Hairdressing—Wigs, Rentals	172	
	Total Makeup & Hairdressing		2,914
835	Sound (Production)		
	Mixer	1,100	
	Recorder	4,666	

(continued)

FIGURE 13.1, continued

(continued)

	Micman	3,850
	Other Sound Production Labor	149
	Equipment Rentals	403
	Total Sound (Production)		10,168
838	Video Tape (Production)	
	Technical Supervisor & Director	2,129
	Video Operator	1,100
	Video Tape Recordist	1,279
	Utility Cable Man	818
	Maintenance Man	818
	Purchases—Video Master Stock	1,254
	Rentals & Miscellaneous Expense	16,083
	Total Video Tape (Production)		23,481
839	Transportation—Studio & Local Locations	
	Set Operations (Drivers & Vehicles)	988
	Action Props & Set Dressing (D & V)	915
	Wardrobe & Pickup Drivers & Vehicles	1,823
	Driver Captains & Vehicles	1,838
	Equipment Repairs & Maintenance	283
	Total Transportation		5,847
841	Film Production		—
847	Second Unit		—
848	Insert Shooting		—
	TOTAL—SHOOTING PERIOD		90,426
851	Editing & Projection	
852	Video Tape (Post Production)	
	Film to Tape/Tape to Tape	460
	Off Line & On Line Editing	8,447
	Titles	253
	Video Effect	253
	Screening Times	126
	Lay Down/Lay Back	506
	Mix	911
	Audio Effects Sweetening	449
	Audio Stock	190
	Dubs/Dubbing Master/Sub Master	1,647
	Release & Dubbing Sub Master	541
	Stock & Miscellaneous Expense	2,114
	Total Video Tape (Post Production)		15,897
853	Music	
	Arrangers	746
	Copyists	996
	Composer & Supervisor	1,663
	Underscore Musicians	3,881
	Music Editors	1,464
	Rental, Cartage & Miscellaneous	2,133
	Total Music		10,883
855	Sound (Post Production)	
	Underscore Recording	748
	Post Production Mag Sound Transfer	288
	Total Sound (Post Production)		1,036
857	Film & Stock Shots (Post Production)	
	Stock Shots—Purchases	288
	Stock Shots—Library Labor	115
	Post Production Mag Tape & Film	58
	Total Film & Stock Shots Post Production		461
859	Titles, Optical, Inserts		—
	TOTAL COMPLETION PERIOD		28,277
861	Insurance	
	Cast Insurance	1,208
	Negative Insurance	345
	Extra Expense	363
	Total Insurance		1,916

(continued)

FIGURE 13.1, continued

```
(continued)
863     Fringe Benefits                               29,239
866     Unit Publicist & Stillman                        418
867     General Expenses
            Below the Line Group Charges    37,225
            Meals—Studio                     2,392
            Audience Procurement             2,645
                                            ───────
        Total General Expenses                        42,262

        TOTAL—OTHER                                   73,835

        TOTAL BELOW THE LINE                         192,538
        TOTAL ABOVE & BELOW THE LINE                 424,747
        INDIRECT COST                                106,520

        GRAND TOTAL                                  531,267
```

8. Costs for rental equipment, if needed

9. Videotape, audio tape stock

10. Insurance, shooting permits, contingencies etc., if appropriate

11. Facility/equipment costs for on-line, off-line editing

12. Advertising, promotion, publicity

13. Videotape duplication

14. Distribution

15. Research and follow-up

Figure 13.2 shows a blank budget form for a typical institutional production.

RENTING VS. BUYING EQUIPMENT

Note that one of the categories covers rental equipment. It is often more economical to rent equipment rather than buy it. There are several reasons:

1. Production equipment (cameras, lenses, tape machines etc.) tends to become outdated rather quickly. It is not unusual to spend $50,000 on a top-notch CCD camera. If you do, you assume that you will be able to depreciate the cost over a number of years. (See Tables 13.1 and 13.2.) If you were able to pay cash for a $50,000 camera and use it for 10 years, the cost would break down to $5,000 a year, plus repair and maintenance costs. But technology changes quickly in television production. Although the camera might still be reliable after five or more years, compared to the newer models it would probably seem a bit primitive. Parts for repair might even be hard to get.

    If the equipment were rented, several production facilities would probably end up using it. This means that the initial investment could be written off by a rental company more quickly, making it possible to more rapidly replace the equipment with newer models.

2. When equipment is rented, the rental company rather than the production facility is responsible for repair, maintenance and updating. If equipment breaks down during a production, many rental companies will replace it within a few hours without additional cost.

3. Rental can represent an income tax advantage. When equipment is purchased it has to be depreciated (written off) over a number of years. Some-

Author:

Length:

Studio production days:

First shooting date: **Completion date:**

On-location production days:

Location sites:

FIGURE 13.2
Budget form.

SUMMARY OF COSTS	ESTIMATE	ACTUAL
Story, with rights and clearances		
Total script		
Producer and Director with staff		
Talent and benefits		
Wardrobe		
Make-up and hair		
Sets		
Props and vehicles		
Transportation		
Studio/on-location expenses		
Production staff		
Equipment, including rentals		
Lighting, electrical		
Music		

times this time span exceeds the practical usefulness of the equipment. This means that the facility is faced with having to sell the used equipment in order to recoup some of the initial investment. (Colleges often get used equipment in this way, since donated equipment represents a tax write-off.) Rental expenses can be immediately written off of taxes as part of a production expense. Although rules governing income taxes regularly change, deducting the costs of rental equipment has for some people represented a route to a quicker, simpler (and in many cases a greater) tax deduction.

4. When equipment is rented there is greater opportunity to obtain equipment that will meet specific needs. Once equipment is purchased, there is pressure to use it, even though at times other makes and models might be better suited to the specific needs of a production.

APPROACHES TO ATTRIBUTING COSTS

Once the cost for a production is projected or determined, you may need to justify it, either in terms of expected results or cost effectiveness (generally, compared to other productions or production approaches). There are three bases on which to measure cost effectiveness:

TABLE 13.1
Purchase of Video Camera

Purchase Price = $50,000

Period	Now	Year 1	Year 2	Year 3	Year 4	Year 5
Price	$50,000					
Loan Balance	36,750	29,400	22,050	14,700	7,350	
Down Payment	13,250					
Principal Payments		7,350	7,350	7,350	7,350	7,350
Interest Payments		4,778	3,822	2,867	1,911	956
Prop. Taxes		500	500	500	500	500
Insurance		500	500	500	500	500
Maintenance		500	500	500	500	500
Depreciation		7,143	7,143	7,143	7,143	7,143
Total Expense	13,250	13,628	12,672	11,717	10,761	9,806

Cash Over Five Years = $71,834

Tables 13.1 and 13.2 illustrate the cost differences between renting a $50,000 video camera and purchasing it with standard financing. The total cash required over five years for purchasing the camera is calculated by adding the initial investment, the yearly principal and the expenses paid out. This includes a 13 percent interest charge on the balance of the loan at the end of the year. Note that the total cash invested over this period is $71,834. But this figure does not take into consideration depreciation—a major tax deduction. (Depreciation is figured on a straight-line basis and is amortized over seven years.) When this is considered, the total expense to purchase the camera drops to $47,549.

TABLE 13.2
Rental of Video Camera

Rental Fee = $600/day

Period	Now	Year 1	Year 2	Year 3	Year 4	Year 5
20-Day Rental		$12,000	$12,000	$12,000	$12,000	$12,000
Interest		0	0	0	0	0
Prop. Taxes		0	0	0	0	0
Insurance		500	500	500	500	500
Maintenance		0	0	0	0	0
Depreciation		0	0	0	0	0
Total Expense		$12,500	$12,500	$12,500	$12,500	$12,500

In Table 13.2 the cost for renting or leasing the same $50,000 camera is broken down. In this case there is no initial investment, and the yearly costs are merely the sum of the rental ($600 per day) for 20 days, plus insurance. This adds up to $62,500 over five years. Although the expenses to buy are substantially less, there are two additional considerations. First, the sizeable amount of cash required to purchase the camera may mean the difference between being able to go into production and not being able to. Second, depending upon existing tax laws, it should be possible to deduct a sizable portion of the monthly rental fees.

- Cost per minute
- Cost per viewer
- Cost vs. measured benefits

Cost per Minute

The **cost per minute** is relatively easy to determine; you simply divide the final production cost by the duration of the finished product. You will note that the cost per minute for the production in Figure 13.1 comes out to be $24,148.50 (which is not all that expensive, as network productions go). Note that in this case we are basing our figures on a 22-minute total length (29 minutes minus commercial time). For an institutional production, $800 to $1,000 per minute might be typical.

Cost per Viewer

Cost per viewer is also relatively easy to figure out; you simply divide the total production costs by the actual or anticipated audience. In the field of advertising, **CPM,** or cost per thousand, is a common measure. If 100,000 people see a show that costs $5,000 to produce, the CPM would be $50. On a cost-per-viewer basis this comes out to be only 5 cents per person.

Cost per Measured Results

The last category, **cost per measured results**, is the most difficult to determine. For this we must measure production costs against intended results. In commercial television we might sell 300,000 widgets after airing a 60-second widget commercial. If our profit on 300,000 widgets was $100,000 and we spent $100,000 producing and airing the commercial, we would begin to question whether the ad was a good investment.

Of course, once produced, most ads are aired more than once. This means that the cost of future airings simply centers on buying air time. If the cost of TV time was $10,000 and we sold 300,000 widgets each time we aired the commercial, we would then show a profit of $90,000 with each airing—at least until people got very tired of seeing our widget commercial.

Of course, figuring the return on our investment is often not this simple. What if we are also running ads in newspapers and on radio, and we have big, colorful widget displays in stores? Of course, we can lump all advertising costs together in determining the effect of advertising on profits, but then it becomes difficult to determine the cost effectiveness of each medium.

The returns on other types of productions may be even harder to determine. How do you quantify the return on investment on a public service announcement (PSA) designed to get viewers to stop smoking, or to preserve clean air and water or to "buckle up for safety"? Even if before-and-after surveys are done to measure changes in public awareness on these issues, it can be almost impossible to factor out the influence of a particular public service announcement from the host of other voices the public regularly encounters on these issues. Apart from doing in-depth interviews with viewers, we may have to rely largely on the record. If we find that a series of 60-second TV spots increase widget sales by 300,000, we might safely assume that a 60-second PSA might also have at least some influence on smoking, clean air and water and buckling seat belts.

It is the producer, of course, who is primarily concerned with these issues, as well as the general above-the-line considerations such as financing, selecting key actors or talent, coordinating advertising and guiding the overall project.

Beyond this point, the director takes over to handle all the production and postproduction details.

DIRECTING STUDIO PRODUCTIONS

As in the case of the producer, there is no uniform job description for a director. Responsibilities vary considerably, depending upon the situation. In this chapter we'll concentrate on the director's role in studio production. In Chapter 16 we'll cover single-camera, film-style directing, and in Chapter 17 we'll examine the direction of multiple-camera field productions.

Directing Responsibilities

preproduction planning: All planning and preparations for a production that take place before it is videotaped or broadcast.

Although **preproduction planning** may not be the most glamorous aspect of the director's job, it is the most important. A lack of planning regularly translates into compromised quality and weakened production values. Preplanning errors and oversights are costly, not only in terms of their impact on the production, but also in the time spent by talent and crew — the most costly aspect of production. Directors who go into a production saying, "Well I'm not sure how we're going to handle that problem, but I'm sure we'll figure something out once we get under way," are living dangerously (and foolishly). One successful director is fond of repeating the following axiom: *It's only by thinking through every conceivable problem before a production starts that you will be able to handle the totally unforeseen problems that will inevitably arise once the production gets under way.*

The Primary Job of the Director

The director, especially in a complex studio production, can never do it alone. So, first and foremost, the director's job is to get crew and talent to function as a team and, in the process, to bring out the best work in each person. This means the director often ends up working more in the realm of psychology than television technology.

In large-scale productions everyone is normally working under pressure, especially if the productions are done live or live-on-tape. Directors must therefore be able to control their own tension and anxiety (not an easy task when all important production decisions rest on their shoulders) while being sensitive to the concerns, pressures, strengths and weaknesses of the talent and crew. The personalities and temperaments of the talent and crew typically range from the eminently artistic to the pre-eminently logical. A heavy-handed, threatening approach with the wrong person can temporarily destroy the person's effectiveness and turn a bad situation into a disaster.

Any director worth the title can stay on top of things when the crew, talent and equipment perform exactly as they are supposed to. But much of the value and respect that people place on directors rests on their ability to stay in control when, despite all the best-laid plans, things begin to fall apart. A studio camera may go out, a mic may fail, a crew member or on-camera person may suddenly get sick, or a key person may refuse to continue unless some special accommodation is made. When such things happen, the director will suddenly become the sole decision maker and may have to instantly devise a new game plan.

The perspective of unclouded, 20-20 hindsight may show that a decision that had to be made quickly under pressure wasn't the best one. The only consolation is that even an imperfect decision is generally better than no decision

PRODUCTION FACILITY REQUEST FORM

FIGURE 13.3
FAX sheet.

PRODUCTION TITLE: _____ PRODUCTION DATE: _____

SETUP TIME: _____ REHEARSAL TIME: _____

PRODUCTION TIME: _____ DIRECTOR: _____

LOCATION(S): _____

_____VTR _____OFF-LINE COPIES _____

        COMMON TIME CODE START: _____:00:00:00

        MASTER TAPE FORMAT: _____ OFF-LINE FORMAT: _____

_____LIVE STATION LINKS REQUIRED _____

_____VIDEOTAPE INSERTS. LIST FORMATS _____

_____NUMBER CAMERAS REQUIRED; TYPE(S) _____

_____

_____SPECIAL LENS COMPLEMENTS EXPLAIN: _____

_____MICS. SPECIAL AUDIO CONSIDERATIONS: _____

_____

_____LIGHTING EFFECTS. EXPLAIN: _____

_____

_____EXTRA CREW EXPLAIN: _____

_____

at all. Vacillating, giving mixed signals, or not being able to make a decision at a crucial time can result in production paralysis.

Requisitioning Equipment and Facilities

To eliminate conflicts with the needs of other productions and to help ensure that a director can get the talent, crew and equipment that he or she needs, the facilities, crew and equipment needed for a production will normally have to be requested far in advance. Figure 13.3 shows a typical *FAX sheet* (crew/equipment/facilities request form) for a production. In Chapter 17 we'll cover survey forms for on-location productions.

Although production facilities, productions and directing assignments vary considerably, it is still useful to summarize some of the typical responsibilities of a producer-director. During the production phase of a project they will typically:

■ Supervise hiring and assignment of crew members.

■ Oversee facility/location arrangements.

■ Arbitrate necessary contracts, licenses and permits.

■ Hold production meetings with crew to arrange all details of the production.

■ Organize crew and cast meetings, and the rehearsal and taping sessions.

■ See that talent release forms are signed (see Chapter 19).

FAX sheet: Facilities request form. A multicopy form listing all technical facilities needed for a specific production.

- Oversee and make final decisions on equipment, sets and wardrobe.
- Block actors.
- Block camera positions and decide camera shots.
- Rehearse cameras and actors.
- Make final decisions on needed changes.
- "Call the shots" in the control room during rehearsals and tapings.
- Supervise the striking of sets.
- Supervise postproduction.
- Oversee pay disbursements.

Since the director has the final responsibility for all production details, this means that he or she will receive much of the credit if things go right—and most of the blame if they don't! However, to provide maximum opportunity for making creative decisions, directors will typically delegate as many responsibilities as possible. The director will typically assume that camera operators will be responsible for the following:

- Arranging for camera equipment and accessories
- Setting up, checking and possibly aligning cameras
- Working closely with directors during blocking sessions
- Striking camera equipment and accessories after the production

The director will see that the lighting director (LD) does the following:

- Comes up with an overall approach to lighting
- Draws up a lighting plot
- Arranges for necessary lighting equipment and accessories
- Sets up the lighting in the studio
- Checks lighting from all camera positions
- Strikes all lighting equipment/accessories after the production

The director should see that videotape operators perform the following tasks:

- Arrange for the necessary videotape recording and playback equipment.
- Set up all videotape recordings and playbacks.
- Monitor and maintain video quality during recording and playbacks.
- Cue and roll necessary tapes during the production.
- Check the quality of the recordings after the production.

The director should see that audio operators do the following:

- Arrange for audio playback and recording equipment and accessories.
- Select and put all microphones into place.
- Arrange for the playback of prerecorded materials.
- Arrange for and check all audio feeds into the studio, including foldback.
- Properly mix and balance all audio levels.
- Strike all audio recording equipment and accessories after the production.

During a production the director works closely with a continuity person who is responsible for doing the following:

- Records continuity details related to talent, sets and props, especially if the tape must be stopped during a production.

- Releases actors after successful takes.
- Sees that all continuity details are considered before shooting each scene and take (setup).

Directing Strategies

For every visible or audible change that takes place during a production, several behind-the-scenes production steps are typically required. These steps normally involve coordinating the activities of a number of production personnel. Because production involves the activities of various crew members (the number can range from 6 to 60), the director's instructions must be phrased clearly and succinctly. To facilitate this process, some (relatively) standard and (somewhat) abbreviated commands have been devised.

Even the sequence of words in a director's sentence is important. For example, if the director says, "Will you pan to the right and down a little when you lose your [tally light] on camera one?" all camera operators must wait until the end of the sentence before they know who the director is talking to—and then they must remember what the instructions were. However, if the director says, "Camera one, when you lose [your] light, pan right and down a little," the first two words tell *who*, the next four words tell *when*, and the last six words tell *what*. After the first two words crew members know that only camera one's operator is being addressed. This will get the attention of the camera one operator, and the rest of the crew members can concentrate on their tasks. The *when* tells camera one not to immediately pan and tilt, but to prepare for a quick move once the camera tally light is off. Preparation might involve loosening the pan and tilt controls on the camera's pan head and being ready to make the adjustment requested—possibly within the brief interval allowed in cutting to a reaction shot. Delays—even the one- or two-second delay involved in phrasing commands—can make the difference between a tight show and one where the production changes lag conspicuously behind the action.

Although the specific jargon varies somewhat among production facilities, directors tend to use some of the same basic terminology. To illustrate this, the director's PL conversation for the opening of a simple interview show is traced in Table 13.3.

As you can see from Figure 13.4, this simple production uses two cameras, one of which moves from position A to position B. In position A the camera gets the establishing (wide) shot. In position B it gets close-ups and over-the-shoulder shots. Since the guests are different each week and will require different opening and closing announcements, only the show's theme music is prerecorded on the videotape. The opening and closing announcements (and the slate) are read off-camera, live. Excluding the commercial, all of what takes place in Table 13.3 covers about a minute of production time.

Note that at the end of the show the opening wide shot on camera one will again be used. During the 30 seconds or so that the interviewer uses to wrap up the show, camera one will again truck right to the mid-position and zoom back. This shot will be used (possibly with dimmed studio lights) as a background for the closing credits and announce.

Note in the director's dialogue the constant use of the terms *ready* and *stand by*. Although this may seem unnecessarily repetitious, these cues are important. For one thing, crew members are generally attending to several things at once, including listening to two sources of audio: the PL and the program audio. *Stand by* warns them of upcoming actions. They also protect the director. If the director says, "Take one" when the cameraperson is not ready, the audience may see a picture being focused (complete with a quick zoom in and out) or a

TABLE 13.3
Director's Comments for Interview Show

Director's Comments	Explanation
Stand by on the set.	This essentially means "attention" and "quiet." The command is given about 30 seconds before rolling tape.
Stand by to roll tape.	Get ready to start the videotape that will record the show.
Roll tape.	The tape is rolled, and when it stabilizes after about 5 to 10 seconds, a tape operator calls, "Speed." This means the tape is ready for recording.
Ready to take bars and tone.	This is the electronic test pattern (ETP) and audio tone that are recorded at an even zero dB. It will be used when the tape is played back to correctly set up playback equipment for proper video and audio.
Take bars and tone.	This will last from 15 to 60 seconds, depending on technical requirements of the station or production facility.
Stand by camera one on slate; stand by to announce slate.	Camera one's first shot is the countdown slate. This type of slate has visible, flashing numbers and preempts the use of countdown leader.
Take one. Read slate.	The announcer reads the basic program-identifying information; program name and number, date of recording, date of air, director etc.
Ready black. *Go black.*	The technical director cuts to black for about three seconds.
Ready two with your close-up of Smith; ready mic; ready cue.	The show opens "cold" (without an introduction of any kind) with a close-up of Smith. This tease is intended to grab attention and introduce the show's guest and topic.
Take two, mic, cue! *Stand by one on the guest.* *Take one!* *Take two!* *Ready VTR 4* *Ready black.*	Cut to camera two with its close-up of Smith, turn his mic on and cue him to start. Smith introduces subject and makes a quick reference to the guest. When Smith mentions the guest, the director makes a two- to three-second cut to the close-up camera and then back to Smith on camera two.
Roll VTR 4. Go black. *Take it.*	The commercial is rolled. While it is stabilizing, the TD cuts to black. The commercial is taken as soon as it comes up. The audio person brings up the sound on the commercial without being cued. During the commercial, camera one will reposition for the opening wide shot.
Camera one, truck right for a wide shot.	During the commercial, camera one repositions by trucking right to the middle of the set to get the wide shot. The camera zooms back to a wide shot.

Fifteen seconds; stand by in studio. Stand by opening announce and theme; ready one on your wide shot; ready two on a close-up of Smith. Stand by to key in title.	
Take one; hit music; key title.	The wide shot is taken on camera one, the theme music is established, and the title of the show is keyed over the screen.
Fade [music] and read.	The music is faded under and the opening announce for the show is read by an announcer. The opening announce includes the show title, the topic and the show's host.
Ready two with a close-up on Smith. Stand-by mics and cue.	
Take two, mics, cue.	This is a close-up of the show's interviewer, who now fully introduces the day's guest. The host starts the show.
Camera one, arc around for your close-up on the guest.	Camera one moves back to the opening position for the close-up of the guest. Smith covers the interval of the camera move by fully introducing the guest. When the camera is ready, he throws the first question to the guest.
Ready on one.	
Take one.	Guest answers first question.
	(Show continues alternating between close-ups of host and guest. Occasionally cameras will zoom out to get over-the-shoulder shots.)

sudden, ungracious pan or tilt. In this case the director can't blame the cameraperson. No warning was given. However, if a "Stand by" was given in reasonable time, the director has every right to expect the crew member involved to be prepared for the requested action—or to quickly tell the director about a problem.

In doing any production, you want to strive for the strongest possible camera shots at all times. During interviews the eyes and facial expressions can communicate a great deal—often even more than what the person is saying. Profile

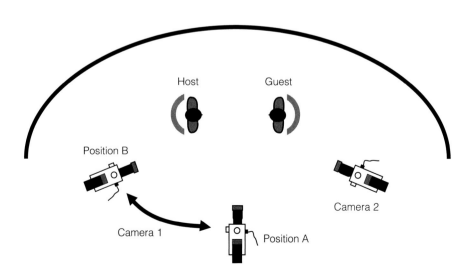

FIGURE 13.4

The production described in the text uses two cameras, one of which moves from position A to position B. In position A the camera gets the establishing (wide) shot. In position B it gets close-ups and over-the-shoulder shots.

shots, even in close-up (Figures 13.5A and 13.5B), are not only weak from a composition standpoint, but much in the way of revealing facial expressions can be missed. This would be equivalent to shooting the close-ups from the center camera position in Figure 13.4. Note how much more engaging the shots are when you shoot almost directly into a person's line of vision (Figures 13.5C and 13.5D). These angles also offer more possibilities for shots. Not only do you have a strong close-up of the person talking, but the over-the-shoulder shot can be used to momentarily cover comments by the person whose back is toward the camera.

The Need to Anticipate

One of the talents essential for a director is the ability to react instantly to changes in action. But *reaction,* no matter how quick, implies delay. This delay might not be too noticeable if a response were possible the instant the director saw the need for a specific action. But the total reaction time is equal to the accumulated time involved in recognizing the need for a specific action, communicating that action to crew members and having them respond.

The solution is for the director to *anticipate* what is going to happen. At first it might seem that this implies precognitive abilities, but it is actually not as difficult as it seems. During an interview an alert director should be able to sense when the interviewer's question is about to end or when the interviewee's answer is winding up. By saying, "Stand by" early and calling for a camera cut a moment before it's needed, a director will be able to cut from one camera to the other almost on the concluding period or question mark of the person's final sentence. By keeping an eye on the off-air monitor in the control room (as opposed to the on-air shot of the person talking), the director will often be able to see when the off-camera person is about to interrupt or visually react to what is being said.

Even the best of directors will miscalculate and occasionally cut to a camera at the wrong time. Possibly the guest suddenly decides to add another thought to a seemingly final sentence, or the interviewer starts to interrupt, but the guest just keeps on talking. In these cases it is sometimes more graceful for the director to stay with the new shot for a few seconds, rather than to quickly cut back to the original camera. The latter rather clearly signals that a mistake was made.

PRODUCING AND DIRECTING A NEWS SHOW

News shows are the most important productions at most TV stations. In addition to representing a TV station's primary means of connecting and interacting with the community it serves, local news generally represents a station's most concentrated source of commercial income. Because newscasts are done live and are generally the most difficult in terms of production sophistication, they are among the most demanding of productions. For these reasons we'll cover news production and direction in some detail. Once these principles are understood, they can be applied to other types of productions. (Chapter 16 will cover the elements of newsgathering and reporting, including the videotaping and editing of stories.)

Approaches to putting together evening newscasts vary widely, and so do the associated personnel and their responsibilities. Compared to their roles in general productions, the roles of the news producer and the news director are different from those of a normal producer and director. In news the news director is in charge of the entire news operation, and the news producer oversees the

FIGURE 13.5

Profile shots (A) and (B), even in close-up, are not only weak from a composition standpoint, but much in the way of revealing facial expressions can be missed. Note how much
more engaging the shots are in this interview if you shoot almost directly into a person's line
of vision, as in (C) and (D). Not only do you have a strong close-up of the person talking
with these angles, but the over-the-shoulder shot can be used to momentarily cover comments by the person whose back is toward the camera.

details of the newscast. But in news there are actually two types of directors:
the news director and the production director (who fulfills the traditional role of
"calling the shots" during the production). Since news is done live, there is
much more pressure on everyone — especially the production director.[2]

2. At the network level, where more than one feed of a newscast is necessary because of different
U.S. time zones, a significant mistake can be eliminated (or a late-breaking news story added) by
editing the delayed version of the newscast.

assignment editor: The individual in a broadcast newsroom who has the responsibility of assigning news and ENG stories to specific reporters.

The *assignment editor* typically decides on the stories to be covered and oversees their assignment to various reporters and videographers. The **associate producer** calculates the times on the segments and puts the script together. In small stations a senior newscaster may function as producer, news editor, assignment editor and associate producer, all in one.

We can now look at the way an evening newscast is handled among the networks and larger TV stations. For lack of a better term, we'll refer to this as *the network approach*.

The Network Approach

Although changes have been taking place in television news as the dominance of network news has diminished and shifted toward the cable news channels, the so-called network model of news is still valuable to examine. In this model a major evening newscast starts to take shape when the news director, producer and key production staff members meet in a rundown meeting at about noon each day. At this session the basic stories that will be pursued are chosen — generally a total of about 25 for a 30-minute newscast. The choice of stories to be developed depends upon four things:

- The importance attributed to them by the news director and producer. "Newsworthiness" is the key element here. (Chapter 16 covers this.) A number of ENG assignments will have previously been made by the assignment editor, and these stories will typically be in development.

- Whether videotape or strong visuals are available to illustrate the story.

- The opinions of bureau chiefs (who are closest to the story) in major cities.

- The importance being assigned to the story by major newspapers (typically, *The New York Times, The Los Angeles Times* and the *Washington Post*) and major wire services, such as the Associated Press.

News Bureaus

package (news package): A completed news segment containing all needed audio and video components, ready for insertion (rolling into) a news production.

Networks and cable news channels typically have news bureaus in major cities — both around the country and around the world. Before the rundown meeting, these bureau chiefs will have submitted a list of stories that have been covered and can be ready in a few hours. As part of putting together their news *packages* (prerecorded, ready-to-broadcast news stories), the bureau chiefs may have already requested and received from the home office background information and file footage to supplement the stories. This information is typically relayed to the bureaus by satellite. The bureaus will typically produce several versions of a story, each a slightly different length. By about 5 p.m. these will have been transmitted back to the home office by satellite. Having two or more versions of a story to choose from gives the news production team greater scheduling flexibility in putting together the evening newscast. These variations are used in two other ways: they provide an additional version of the story for use in a later newscast, and they can be fed by satellite to member stations for use in their own newscasts.

Network News Services

lineup (segment rundown): A listing of the basic elements in a production in the order in which they will appear.

Although network affiliated TV stations generally do not have news bureaus, they do have access to a wide variety of news packages that can be recorded from afternoon and late-night satellite transmissions. Often, based on the *lineup* (a schedule and summary of stories) that has been teletyped to the station a few hours earlier, the news producer or director will have designated specific stories that will (probably) be used in the evening newscast. In addition to these lineups, the networks will also transmit suggested *lead-ins* that can be used by local anchors to introduce the stories.

ABC calls their service the Daily Electronic Feed (DEF); CBS affiliates get Newsfeed, and NBC stations get A-News (Affiliate News). There is also a "late feed" after 11 p.m. EST that primarily highlights the sporting events of the evening. In addition to these sources, some affiliates routinely tape the network evening news and use segments from this.

For **independents** (stations not affiliated with a network), there are a wide variety of news services that provide ready-to-air news packages. Although most of these are delivered by satellite, some videotapes from universities, corporations etc. (often with a public relations motivation) arrive by mail. In addition, many stations also belong to a consortium of affiliated stations, each of which contributes news stories.

With all of these sources of news available, there is never a question of "What can we put on?" It's almost always a problem of "What can we eliminate?" From the 25 or so stories that may have been marked for development during a network rundown meeting, only about 15 to 20 will end up on a 22-minute newscast. Some stories diminish in importance as further details come in; some will have to be cut because of time limitations.

lead-in: The announcer's introduction to an ENG/EFP segment.

Local Station Approaches to News

Since local stations don't have the resources of large news organizations, they have had to develop their own approaches to producing evening newscasts. Instead of a noon rundown meeting, the producer, news director or even the assignment editor will make the decisions on what will and will not be in the newscast. Judgments are generally based on the following considerations:

- The importance assigned to the story by the networks and wire services (if it's a national or international story)
- Whether video footage is available
- If it's a local story, whether the assignment editor has a reporter and crew already working on an ENG package
- The news producer's personal judgment on the story's newsworthiness
- The prominence given to specific stories by the local morning newspaper

NEWS SEGMENTS

The Four-Segment News Format

Local newscasts are generally divided into four or five segments, or blocks. The four-segment approach is most widely used. At the beginning of the newscast (and sometimes even a few minutes before the news show even starts), the top stories of the day will be *teased* (previewed). When possible, appropriate videotape highlights will be included. These constitute what is called a *preshow tease*. Commercials typically follow.

Segment One *(Top Block)* This segment is the longest of the four. Unless there is a rather important local story to report, this segment consists, first of all, of brief coverage of the top national and international stories of the day. (Network affiliates generally leave most of the international news to the networks.) Following this, and for the majority of segment one, the local news will be covered.

Segment Two   This segment contains the remainder of the local news, plus sports or weather. Whereas the first segment contains standard **hard news**, the first part of segment two typically has some **soft news** (features, human interest and possibly even a humorous story). Often a *cover story* (a featured story presented in some depth) will be included in segment two. After this there will be either sports or weather. The decision will be largely based on which is deemed *least* important to the audience. (In order to hold the audience, the most important of the two will be reserved for segment three.)

Segment Three   This segment consists of sports or weather — whatever was not covered in segment two. As time permits, general feature stories illustrated by video footage will be included.

Segment Four   In a four-segment newscast this segment consists primarily of an upbeat closing. The "leave them feeling good" philosophy maintains that after the depressing hard news of the day, you should leave the audience feeling good about the show, the station and the newscasters. (With each rating point worth more than a million dollars in many markets, such things are deemed important!) In segment four you will find such things as the story of the 98-year-old grandmother who cornered a burglar with a sawed-off shotgun, and the latest in doggie designer wardrobes. It is also important to have some "pad material" standing by; stories that can be used, if necessary, to bring the show out on time. Sometimes a *recap* (summary of the leading stories) will also be used for this purpose.

Although segment four may be designed as a "good news" segment, this should never preclude using it to update late-breaking news stories, or even to switch live to a reporter on the scene of an important story. This includes live feeds of important, late-breaking stories that are taken *hot* (directly from the network as they are being sent via satellite).

Between each of the four segments, there are generally one and one-half to two minutes of commercials. Regardless of what the audience thinks of them, prerecorded commercials are welcomed in news production because they provide an opportunity to update times, add or drop stories and relay appropriate messages to crew and on-camera talent.

The Five-Segment News Format

For stations that use a five-segment format, the sports or weather is bumped from segment two down to segment three. The second segment is then fully devoted to general news. This will typically consist of state and regional news, together with some medical news, consumer and business reports and soft news items.

Segment Rundown Sheets

segment rundown (lineup): A listing of the basic elements in a production in the order in which they will appear.

A *segment rundown* (sometimes called a *budget)* is a listing of all of the elements in each of the segments of the newscast. Figure 13.6 shows a typical computerized rundown sheet for a newscast. The news director or associate producer will divide the rundown sheet into four or five segments and decide what will go in each segment. Often, an associate director determines what electronic graphics will be needed and keeps a running total on times as the newscast is planned. Staff writers or the on-camera reporters write the on-camera teases, as well as the lead-ins for each story.

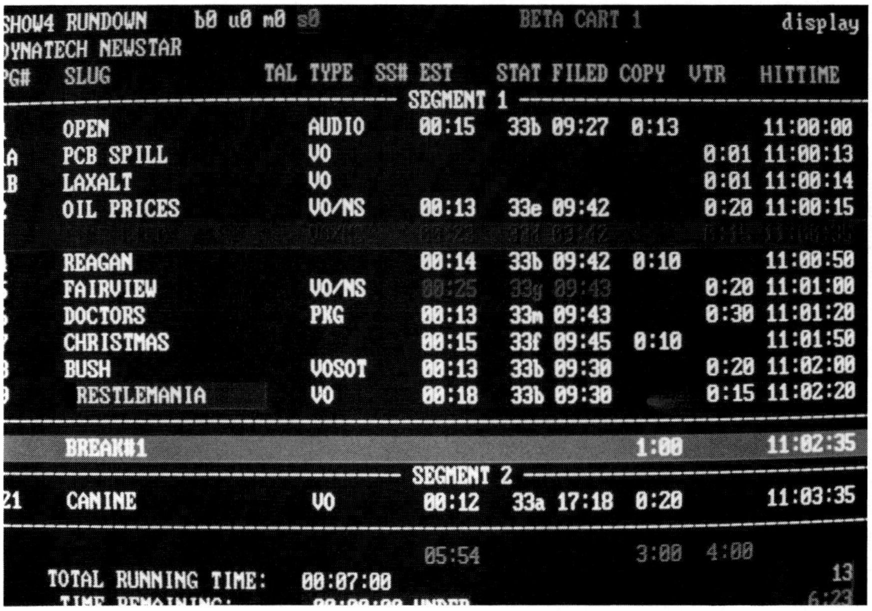

FIGURE 13.6
This is a typical computerized run-down sheet for stories in a newscast. The computer will instantly recalculate total times as segments are added and deleted.

THE NEWSCASTER'S ROLE IN PRODUCTION

As we've noted, in some small TV stations newscasters may function as executive producers, news directors, writers, videotape editors, associate producers and on-air reporters. In some cases they even operate their own teleprompters as they read the news on-air. Quite in contrast, in some large stations newscasters have little say about news content; they simply read a prepared script. At the network level, experienced news anchors typically have executive control over total news content.

NEWSROOM COMPUTER SYSTEMS

Today, producers and directors in news have learned to rely heavily on newsroom computers. Computers are used to do the following:

- Make assignments to reporters and ENG crews
- Efficiently schedule the use of ENG equipment and vehicles
- Selectively capture news from the wire services, using key words indicating topics, cities or local issues of concern to direct stories into computer storage
- Write local news stories and on-camera lead-ins
- Edit, rewrite and update previous stories
- Archive (electronically store) stories and information for later reference
- Format and display all news copy for camera teleprompters
- Organize and (when needed) instantly reorganize the sequence and times of stories
- In some cases, control all studio camera shots during the newscast, including appropriate trucks, dollys, pans, tilts and zooms (Chapter 4)

Although the major stories of the day are often decided early in the day, a lot can happen between that time and the 6 p.m. newscast. Today, computers make it possible to add and delete stories even after the newscast has started.

Since teleprompter copy is also entered into the typical newsroom computer system, stories can be cut and added, and times automatically adjusted. (However, if a director wants a smoothly executed newscast, it is a bit risky to "throw everyone a curve" by suddenly rearranging everything.)

Of course, while changes are taking place in upcoming segments, the newscast must continue. While calling the shots during the on-going newscast, the director must make the necessary adjustments to accommodate upcoming graphics, videotapes and camera shots. If all this sounds like a formidable task, you're right; it's not a job for people who can't make sound decisions under pressure.

QUALITY CONTROL

discrepancy report: A written account of any technical or operational problems or errors that affect broadcast programming.

When major things go wrong in newscasts (as well as in any other type of video production) most production facilities have a **quality control form** or *discrepancy report* that must be filled out (Figure 13.7) to explain what went wrong and why. Problems caused by technical failures (which may need immediate attention) or significant problems resulting from personnel errors are noted. In commercial television, problems affecting the airing of commercials must be explained, so that it can be determined if a make-good (a re-airing of the commercial) needs to take place.

SUMMARY

Whereas production expenses have traditionally been divided into above-the-line and below-the-line expenses, 12 categories provide a more specific breakdown: (1) preproduction costs; (2) location and travel expenses; (3) set construction, props and wardrobe costs; (4) equipment expenses; (5) videotape, audio tape and supplies; (6) production crew costs; (7) producer, director, writer and creative fees; (8) on-camera talent; (9) insurance, shooting permits, contingencies etc.; (10) on-line, off-line editing; (11) distribution, advertising, promotion, publicity; and (12) research and follow-up. It is sometimes more cost-effective to rent equipment rather than purchase it. Production costs can be measured on the basis of cost per minute, cost per viewer, and cost vs. measured benefits. FAX (facility request) sheets are used to request production equipment, facilities and personnel.

One of the most important jobs of a director or producer-director is preproduction planning. The best directors are known for their ability to make intelligent decisions under pressure and bring out the best work in talent and crew. Control room directing competence includes the ability to be decisive, anticipate production needs, give appropriate stand-by cues to crew members and phrase commands in a clear, concise way.

Local news represents the primary means most stations have for connecting and interacting with the community they serve. In many cases it also represents the station's most concentrated source of income. Key news personnel include the news director, the news producer, the assignment editor and the production director. For a 30-minute newscast, about 25 stories are pursued each day. From this, about 15 to 20 will be broadcast. Most will be cut because of time restraints. News bureaus in large cities develop and supply several versions of each story they cover. Not only are satellites used to relay news stories from the field to TV stations, but they are used to relay news stories back and forth between news bureaus and their headquarters, and between various news agencies and their affiliated stations.

Today, newsroom computers control almost every phase of news production and presentation. Most stations use a four-segment approach to structuring their

FIGURE 13.7
Quality control form.

TV-3 QUALITY CONTROL REPORT

Date: _____ Client/Program: _____

Scheduled Time: _____

What Happened: _____
_____
_____
_____
_____
_____
_____
_____
_____
_____
_____
_____
_____
_____

Corrective Action: _____
_____
_____
_____
_____
_____

Recommendations: _____
_____
_____
_____
_____
_____

Submitted by: _____

newscasts. A rundown sheet or budget is used to schedule the various elements in the newscast. Quality control forms—sometimes called *discrepancy reports*—are filled out to note and explain various types of production problems.

KEY TERMS

assignment editor
associate producer
below-the-line
cost per measured results
cost per minute
cost per viewer
CPM
discrepancy report
FAX sheet

hard news
independent (station)
lead-in
lineup
package (news package)
preproduction planning
quality control form
segment rundown
soft news

14

Principles of Editing

Because of the importance of editing to video production, we will devote two chapters to the subject. In this chapter we will look at the principles that govern editing decisions; in the next chapter we'll examine editing procedures and technology.

THE ROOTS OF VIDEO EDITING

When you consider that a modern feature film contains between 500 and 1,000 edits, and a 30-minute TV show 200 or more edits, you begin to appreciate what goes into the editing phase of production. Even so, editing goes far beyond just joining scenes together. This was realized more than 75 years ago when the esteemed Russian director V. I. Pudovkin said, "Editing is the creative force of filmic reality . . . and the foundation of film art." Since then editing has become even more important. In fact, the power and control that a good editor can have over the success or failure of the final production can hardly be overestimated. In the hands of an expert—or, more accurately, an *artist*—editing can establish the structure of the production and control its overall mood, intensity and tempo.

Film dates back to the late 1890s. During the early history of motion pictures, film production consisted of planting the camera in one spot and having the action take place continuously in front of the lens until the reel of film ran out. If problems—major problems—were encountered during the shooting, the whole reel was reshot from beginning to end. The final result was somewhat like watching a stage play from the 20th row of a theater—without the benefit of color or synchronized sound. The film editors of the day were simply technicians given the routine task of cutting out dead footage at the beginning and end of reels and then splicing the reels back together again. It apparently didn't occur to anyone for some time that the camera could be stopped and moved in the middle of the reel, that retakes of short segments could be done, or that scenes on a reel could be routinely cut apart and spliced together in a different order.

Gradually, this approach to editing changed — mostly out of necessity. Someone (probably trying to rush a film to completion) wondered, "Why should I do this whole scene over again from the beginning when I can just re-do the bad part and splice it into the reel?" So, what started out as a way to patch up a mistake ended up (with some refinements) as a way to improve the film.

The film editor's task originally consisted of holding the film up to a light and reviewing the scenes by pulling it through white-gloved fingers. Splices were made by overlapping the two pieces a couple of millimeters at the frame division and using cement (glue) to join the two pieces together. Although refinements were made in handling and viewing the film, the technology of film editing remained basically the same until computer-controlled videotape editing techniques arrived in the late 1970s. Then things started changing rapidly — for both video and film.

Today, film editors routinely use video postproduction techniques to speed up film editing and cut overall production costs. For example, with traditional film editing methods a normal feature film takes about 20 weeks to edit. But this time is cut to only about three weeks if the film is transferred to videotape and electronically edited. Films intended for television are now routinely converted to video almost as soon as they come out of the film processor. In the process the negative color image is reversed, and the first phases of color and brightness correction take place. Once the film is transferred to video, all editing and postproduction work can be done electronically with computer-controlled equipment. If a film copy of the production is later needed, the edited videotape serves as a blueprint. This is not to say that traditional film editing techniques aren't still widely used; they are. But as new generations of film editors arrive on the scene, we will undoubtedly see more and more video-centered editing techniques in film production.

Initial Video Editing Problems

Although crude film editing started almost with the invention of the medium, several decades passed after the invention of television before a system of editing could be devised. Part of the problem was that, unlike film that could be directly viewed, the recorded video "image" consisted of millions of invisible magnetic pulses.

After Ampex Corporation developed the videotape recorder in 1956, it soon became obvious that a primitive form of editing was possible by physically cutting the 2-inch tape and splicing it back together — just as in film editing. But there was a major difference. Tape had to be running at full speed in order for a picture to be visible (see footnote 2). Since the recorded image was invisible, there was no way of looking at the tape to find out where video frame divisions were. When the videotape was spliced back together at the wrong point — an inevitable occurrence when you couldn't see where one picture ended and the other started — the picture rolled and broke up for several seconds.

Finally someone discovered a solution: if you spread a liquid containing a magnetic powder over the edit point, the suspended magnetic powder would cluster around the magnetically affected areas of the tape as the liquid dried.[1] In particular, the electronic control track pulses at the edge of the tape would

---

1. This development is credited to Joe Roizen, one of the most colorful and influential people in the history of early video recording. Joe, who was a friend to many in television, including the author, died in his favorite city of Paris in 1990.

become visible and act as a guide in cutting the tape. Because the edits had to be accurate to within less than 1/64 of an inch, a special editing block with a microscope was used, along with a metallic splicing tape. Even this tedious and time-consuming process resulted in a stable edit only about 60 percent of the time. To make matters worse, tapes that had been cut to make an edit had to be rejected for future use, since the splice point interfered with subsequent recordings. Since 2-inch, 30-minute videotapes originally cost more than $500 each, the whole editing process tended to be frowned upon by cost-conscious executives.

The Dawn of Linear Editing

Then in the early 1960s the Editec company came up with the idea that launched electronic editing. They recorded a precise audio pulse on the second audio track of the 2-inch quad tape at the point where a producer or engineer wanted to make an edit. This reference point was then used by the 2-inch tape for a *pre-roll*, the time needed to stop and rewind itself for about 15 seconds. Once the tape was started at this pre-roll point, it had time to come up to a recording speed of 15 inches per second, stabilize and cut from a playback to a record mode. Instead of splicing various tape segments together, as was done in film, video editing was done by recording the desired segments onto a second tape, one after another, in the desired sequence. Even titles, video effects etc. could be added during the copying (editing) process. Because each segment had to be found, cued and then recorded in sequence (necessitating the stopping of both tapes as each segment was located and cued) this was referred to as *linear editing*.

Although the system worked — which was a breakthrough in itself — this type of editing still had a major weakness: since edit-point decisions were made while the tape was moving, the accuracy of the edit depended upon the reaction time of engineers or directors.[2] With practice and a good night's sleep, they might be able to come within one or two seconds (30 to 60 video frames) of where they wanted the edit. Although one or two seconds seem like a short time, when dialogue or music must be tightly intercut, even a one-second error — either too soon or too late — can make a video production look unacceptably sloppy.

The concept for the helical-type VTR, which was to eventually succeed quad machines, was experimented with during early research into video recording. However, it took until several years after the introduction of quad recording to solve many of the related technical problems. Today, almost all videotape machines are helical. The name helical comes from the head-scanning pattern, which resembles a spiral or helix. Since the helical video tracks are several times longer than quad tracks, complete fields can be recorded with each pass of the video head.

When helical editing machines took over from quad machines, it became possible to slow down the VTR and still see the picture. Not until the CMX company, with some help from CBS and Memorex, developed a computer-controlled editor was electronically controlled, frame-accurate, linear editing possible. From this point on, edits could be consistently controlled to within 1/30 of a second, which is comparable to the accuracy of film editing with its 24-frame-per-second rate.

pre-roll: The time needed between the start of a videotape and the time it stabilizes.

linear editing: As opposed to *random-access editing*, an editing approach that requires edits to be entered and done in the sequence required for the final edited version. Each segment has to be found, cued and then recorded in sequence, which necessitates the stopping of both tapes as each segment is located and cued.

2. With 2-inch quad machines, it took four passes of the heads to record and play back a single video field. Because of this, if the tape was slowed down, the picture broke up and disappeared from the screen. The helical machines (to be discussed later) reproduce a full video field with each revolution of the playback head; therefore, the tape can be inched along or even stopped completely without losing the picture.

Random-Access Editing

CMX was also the first company to try to break away from linear editing and try random-access editing. In *random-access editing,* scenes needed for editing can be called up immediately as needed, in any order. This makes it possible to preview a series of edit decisions in real time, without the need to stop after each edit to locate and cue the next segment. In contrast, a constant need to stop after each edit is not only time-consuming, but makes it difficult to get an idea of the overall pace and timing of the piece. Random-access editing is almost impossible while working with standard videotape because of the time needed to shuffle back and forth to find needed segments on the original tapes. (It can take several minutes to fast-forward or rewind tapes to find segments that are spaced far apart on a large reel; you can't move directly to a needed segment the way you can on a videodisc.)

When originally introduced in the 1960s, the idea of random-access editing was immediately recognized as a good one. Unfortunately, it was far ahead of the existing technology of the day. To originally make the system work, video had to be recorded on huge, cumbersome mechanical discs. A truly practical system of random-access editing had to wait until videodisc technology became practical in the 1980s. By the 1990s two approaches had emerged, one using computers and videodiscs, and the other using computer technology based on solid-state memory.

Videodisc-Based Editing   By transferring original video footage to a computer disk or recordable videodisc, you can take advantage of the ability of these systems to locate segments almost instantly.[3] Once programmed, the edit controller can call up segments in any order, as needed.

RAM-Based Editing   The **access time** is cut down even more when solid-state, or RAM-based memory, is used. When copies of short video segments are needed in the editing process — in doing lap dissolves or special effects, for example — the editing system will automatically copy the needed scenes from videodisc or videotape into RAM. After being used, they are erased and replaced by other segments.

As the cost of solid-state memory chips decreases and their capacity increases, they will not be limited to short segments of video, but will probably replace videodiscs as the sole recording medium for editing systems.

Dedicated and Software-Based Edit Controllers

A software-based edit controller uses a modified desktop computer as a base. Depending upon the software loaded, videotape editing is just one of the tasks it can perform. A dedicated editor, on the other hand, is especially designed to do only one thing: video editing. Dedicated editing equipment was the norm until desktop computer editors started to become available in the late 1980s. However, it was not until the early 1990s that sophisticated video editing hardware and software became widely available for desktop computers (Figure 14.1). As we've previously noted, the Video Toaster system for the Amiga computer was the first, widely used desktop editing system. After this, things changed

random-access editing: The ability of an editing playback system to find and cue successive, non-sequential segments in an editing session before they are needed. This makes it possible for a sequence of edits to be previewed in real time.

---

3. Access time ranges from 20 seconds down to about 9 milliseconds (millionths of a second) for editing systems based on hard disks. The time is longer for optical videodisc systems. For RAM-based editing, the time can be cut down to about 20 nanoseconds (billionths of a second). However, even these "delays" in calling up needed segments can be compensated for by today's editing equipment.

FIGURE 14.1
Dedicated editing equipment was the norm until desktop computer technology became advanced enough to handle sophisticated editing. Here an operator uses a mouse to select a sequence of scenes during an editing session.

rapidly. Many manufacturers started making editing hardware and software, not only for the Amiga, but for the Apple and IBM computer standards.

With this brief historical perspective, we can now turn to some the principles of editing.

CONTINUITY EDITING

Once editing began, it was discovered that the audience didn't have to see *all* of an event in real time in order to understand what was going on. In particular, it was found that routine and uninteresting elements could be left out of a scene, and the audience would just assume they had taken place. It was at this point that *continuity editing* (or *continuity cutting*) to preserve the sequential essence of an event (without showing all of it) was born.

continuity editing (continuity cutting): An editing approach based on either a temporal or logical sequence that centers on maintaining a smooth flow of events.

As editors began to experiment with shortening, rearranging and intercutting scenes, it started to become obvious that the film editor had great power in shaping the meaning of a story. As an example of how rearranging scenes can shape meaning, let's look at what we can do with only two shots: (1) a man glancing up, and (2) another man pulling a gun and firing toward the camera.

In this order it appears that the first man was shot. However, if you reverse the order of these two scenes, an entirely different meaning emerges: the first man is watching a shooting.

Let's look at what we can do with three shots: (1) people jumping from a boat, (2) a burning boat and (3) an explosion.

Edited together in the order given, the shots suggest that people are jumping from a boat seconds before it explodes. A 3-2-1 order suggests that there is an explosion on the boat and then it bursts into flame; as a result, the people flee. In the 2-3-1 sequence, people flee from the boat after a fire causes an explosion. And, of course, there are also the 3-1-2 and 1-3-2 sequences, each suggesting a slightly different scenario.

As you can begin to see, when scores of takes of scenes are available to an editor, which is normally the case in dramatic productions, the editor has considerable power in shaping both the basic continuity and message of the production.

Parallel Cutting

Daytime soap operas typically have several stories taking place simultaneously, as so do most sit-coms and general dramatic productions. This is referred to as **parallel action.** By cutting back and forth between the mini-stories taking place within the overall drama, production pace can be varied and overall interest heightened. Editing segments in parallel action is called *parallel cutting*. The action can be as simple as intercutting between the story of three bank robbers as they try to elude police and the simultaneous work of the police as they try to catch them.

parallel cutting: The alternate intercutting of two stories so that each is regularly updated and both reach a conclusion at about the same time. The stories are generally related in some way.

Early in the history of dramatic television, it was discovered that an audience found watching well-edited, parallel stories more engrossing than simply following one character through a series of events. For the editor, parallel cutting provides many more opportunities to vary the pace and visual variety of a production. (And, if you don't particularly like the story or characters in one of the stories, possibly you will like one of the other stories better.) In some afternoon dramatic productions (soaps), parallel action can be as complex as regularly cutting between five or six concurrent stories.

Continuity Editing in an ENG Story

As an editing example that will serve to illustrate several issues that confront videotape editors, consider the following list of 13 shots for an ENG news story of what appears to be a murder:

1. An extreme close-up of a knife on a street
2. A close-up of a policewoman using a handkerchief to pick up the knife
3. A victim being loaded onto a stretcher
4. A man being handcuffed
5. A close-up of the handcuffed man
6. An ambulance driving off
7. A policeman questioning a bystander
8. A wide shot of the crime scene
9. The handcuffed man being put into a police car
10. A pool of blood on the pavement
11. A wide shot of onlookers
12. A stretcher being loaded into an ambulance
13. A close-up of several bereaved onlookers

There are four main areas for the videotape editor to consider here: logical sequence, creative sequence, ethical suitability and legal suitability.

Often, ENG footage can't be shot in logical sequence. If the ENG cameraperson in the above example arrived just as the man was being handcuffed, this scene would have to be shot first; and it would have to be gotten quickly, or be missed. The next shots on the tape might be of the victim being loaded onto a stretcher, the stretcher being put in an ambulance, and the ambulance driving away. Possibly it would only be after these scenes were shot that the cameraperson would have time to get establishing shots, crowd shots etc.

Here is one way that the videotape editor could arrange the 13 shots:

8. A wide shot of the crime scene

3. The victim being loaded into a stretcher

1. An extreme close-up of a knife on the pavement

4. A man being handcuffed

2. A close-up of a policewoman using a handkerchief to pick up the knife

11. A wide shot of onlookers

5. A close-up of the handcuffed man

13. A close-up of several bereaved onlookers

12. A stretcher being loaded into an ambulance

6. An ambulance driving off

7. A policeman questioning a bystander

9. A handcuffed man being put into a police car

Based on documented experience with TV audiences (if not personal ethics), an editor or news producer would probably deem the close-up shot of the blood on the pavement to be inappropriate for inclusion in the final edit—especially for a dinnertime newscast. If the shots of the man being handcuffed clearly show his identity, a legal issue is raised. What if later facts reveal that the man was only an innocent bystander who in the confusion was mistakenly identified as a murderer? Could he sue the station and its personnel for putting him in a false light?[4] To be on the safe side (and depending on station policy), some camerapersons will include shots of the suspect that do not reveal his identity: scenes from the back, a close-up of handcuffed hands and so on. Other stations would stand on the simple statement, "This man was arrested." These would be some of the legal and ethical considerations in editing this piece. Now, what about the logical and creative aspects?

The rearranged sequence shown above was done in what is probably a logical, time-based (continuity) sequence. Note that there are actually three concurrent stories in this ENG report:

- The sequence of events involving the arrest of a suspect, including picking up the knife

- The events involving picking up and removing the body of the victim

- The ongoing reactions of bystanders to what has taken place and to what is going on

The first job of the editor is to accurately intercut these three concurrent events to (1) preserve the logical sequence of each, and (2) to show their interrelationship. In our example 13 original shots are listed. In an actual news story of this type, there will probably be twice that number of shots taken at the scene. This brings up a related point.

shooting ratio: The amount of tape recorded relative to the amount of tape actually used.

The footage taken vs. the footage used is referred to as the **shooting ratio.** Unlike film, videotape is comparatively cheap, so shooting ratios are not a major concern. The axiom in ENG work is: "Get it all on tape, and we'll figure out later if we can use it." Editors often—even rather routinely—complain about not having enough shots to chose from, but they seldom complain about having too many. Sometimes that extra shot taken almost without reason ends up being an essential editing transition between two shots that otherwise couldn't be used.

---

4. Although this is a thorny legal issue (see Chapter 19), it would depend not only on how the piece was edited, but also, in large measure, on what was said. Saying, "After being identified as the assailant by witnesses at the scene, John Jones, of Canoga Park, was arrested for the murder," is quite different than saying, "A suspect at the scene was taken into custody by police." (The first statement would also complicate getting an impartial jury for a trial.)

With film (which costs hundreds of times more per minute to shoot) the issue is a bit different.

Using Insert Shots and Cutaways

Insert Shots   While holding to the basic continuity of a story, an editor can greatly enhance the look of a production with the prudent use of insert shots and cutaways. An ***insert shot*** is a close-up of something that exists within the establishing (wide) shot. In our example a close-up of the knife on the ground would be an insert shot. (In a wide or medium shot we might see a woman detective either looking at the knife or bending over to pick it up.) We'll have more examples of insert shots later in the chapter.

Cutaways   Ideally, in our crime story there should also be shots that show the responses and actions of people who have in some way been pulled into this event: bereaved friends or relatives of the victim, routine police and paramedic activities and the general crowd. With these shots, we cross the (sometimes rather blurry) line that separates insert shots from cutaways. Unlike insert shots that show significant aspects of the overall scene in close-up, ***cutaways*** *cut away* from the main scene or action for related material. Cutting in a shot of a group of onlookers standing near the crime scene would be an example of a cutaway.

To illustrate another type of cutaway, let's assume that during the late news on the same night, a new development in our story came to light. Another knife was discovered in some trash near the victim. During a live report we might interview the officer in charge from his office at the police station. When he mentions the new finding, we might cut to (*cut away* to) videotape footage taken at the crime scene showing a policewoman examining the second knife. (Of course, with this development we also have the possibility that the man who was arrested was acting in self-defense.[5])

Cutaways, of course, come in many other forms: they could consist of shots of kids watching a parade from a nearby rooftop, or shots of a flaming fantasy dessert being prepared in a kitchen while guests finish their meal in the dining room.

In contrast to news reporting, in dramatic television the producer, director and editor have great latitude in making editing decisions. In fact, it is a major element in the creative process. Editors typically experiment with various editing patterns and sequences before the best one is found. Often during editing a sequence of scenes or shots will be changed from what was indicated in the script. Sometimes this is done to add needed variation in pace; sometimes, after seeing the footage, completely new possibilities emerge.

Altering Expected Continuity

Cutting to continuity (continuity editing) largely involves making edits based on what is expected. Good editors in dramatic television, like good directors, are masters at manipulating audience emotions. To do so, they must sometimes break from the expected.

insert shot: A close-up used to highlight or better illustrate some object or element within a basic scene.

cutaway: A shot that is not part of the primary action but is relevant to it and occurring at the same time. In an interview a cutaway is commonly used to show the interviewer's reaction to what is being said.

---

5. This development illustrates the dangers when either a videographer or an editor makes quick assumptions about what happened at a news scene. In the initial confusion surrounding traumatic events, even eyewitnesses can unknowingly pass on misleading or erroneous information. The history of criminal law has repeatedly shown that "things are often not as they at first appear." Suffice it to say that it is the job of a videographer or editor to *present facts* and not *draw conclusions*.

For example, unfulfilled expectations are often used to create audience tension. Let's take this simple shot sequence as an example: Someone is working at a desk late at night. There is a knock at the door. The person sitting at the desk calls out routinely, "Come in." But a moment later the calm expression on the person's face dramatically changes. Why? We don't know. Where is the shot of who or what just came in? What happens if we don't cut to that expected shot? The audience is then left "hanging" with curiosity and apprehension or, depending on how it's handled, with frustration and resentment.

Here's an example of the latter. A woman has just announced that she has received a priceless heirloom engagement ring from her boyfriend. Another woman looks at the ring closely and exclaims, "That's the largest diamond I've ever seen! And that setting—I've never seen anything like it!" But let's assume that all the while a director holds a two-shot of the two women. As a result, the audience, wanting to see what all the fuss is about, is left with frustration. We obviously need an extreme close-up of the ring. Most editors would also want to use a close-up of the woman speaking and a close-up of the proud possessor of the ring. So, except when you want to intentionally leave your audience hanging for momentary dramatic effect, always keep in mind what you think the audience expects to see at any given moment.

When Effect Precedes Cause   If we see something happen, we then expect to see the response, reaction or consequence of that happening. This is a basic cause-effect or stimulus-response relationship. But *effect* can also precede *cause*. We may see a startled response from someone and then (with our curiosity aroused) be shown what caused it. In fact, many directors in dramatic film and television feel that it is more interesting to regularly show effect before cause. But, regardless of whether cause or effect comes first, we expect to see these relationships tied together, or at least suggested. This is in large measure how we understand story progression and make sense out of a story's message. Occasionally, we can safely assume cause. For example, if we are shown a shot of a man with all the signs of inebriation (effect), we can probably safely assume he had been drinking (cause); if we see a shot of a woman leaving for a skiing trip followed by a shot of her arriving back home on crutches, we will assume she had a skiing accident. In these cases the cause can be safely assumed. But sometimes we need to see (or at least "hear") the cause.

Causality

By slightly expanding the cause-effect or effect-cause relationship, we arrive at *causality*. In a dramatic production it would generally be inappropriate to cut to a shot of someone answering the phone unless we had initially heard the phone ring. (That is, unless you want to suggest they are hallucinating.) A ringing phone brings about a response: the phone is picked up.

A good script reveals causality, both in deed and story line. The job of an editor is to subtly enhance causality—and at times to prolong the cause-effect relationship. For example, we may see a female corpse on the living room floor during the first five minutes of a film but not find out for sure that her husband killed her until 90 minutes later.

But probably just knowing that the husband did it is not enough (maybe for the police, it would be, but not for most viewers). In causality there is also the question of why he did it. This brings up *motivation*. Possibly the murder resulted from revenge, hatred or any of the other age-old motives. But even knowing that the motive was revenge is not enough for a well-thought-out, satisfying production. Since we assume that revenge doesn't occur without a cause, we may want to know the origin of the husband's need for revenge.

Answering this question may necessitate taking the viewer back to an incident in the past. We may be led to discover that the woman had a string of lovers. As a consequence we would also expect to see the suspicion, jealousy, resentment and anger growing in her husband. Finally, we see that these negative emotions can be contained no more. Now we understand. Editors must perceive the dynamics of these cause-and-effect relationships to skillfully handle them.

It might seem that what we've been talking about is relevant only to dramatic productions. But cause-effect relationships are present in all types of productions, even ENG pieces. An ideal ENG piece on a tornado, for example, would show the approaching storm, the effect of this knowledge on the people in its path, including their preparations, the tornado hitting and passing and, finally, the results of the storm. In most news stories, however, we see only the results of causes. Even so, the more logically ENG stories can be assembled, the better an audience will understand the sequence of events. The issue of cause and effect leads into another major topic: relational editing.

RELATIONAL EDITING

In *relational editing,* scenes that by themselves seem not to be related take on an interrelated significance when spliced together. Relational editing techniques cash in on the human tendency to try to draw meaning out of events — even if there isn't any. Many years ago the Russian filmmakers Pudovkin and Kuleshov established this principle in an experiment. They alternated film segments from a long take of a man sitting motionless and expressionless in a chair with several scenes. Included were a close-up of a bowl of soup, a shot of a coffin containing a female corpse and a shot of a little girl playing. To an audience viewing the edited film, the expressionless man suddenly became involved in the emotional scenes — to the point of being a cause or an effect. Although the shot of the actor's face showed no expression, when it was preceded by the shot of the coffin, the audience thought that the actor showed deep sorrow. When the same shot followed the close-up of the food, the audience perceived hunger in his face; and when it was associated with the shot of the little girl, the audience saw the actor as experiencing parental pride. Thus, one of the most important tenets of editing was experimentally established: the human tendency to try to establish relationships among a series of events. In the case of the woman who was shot, what if we preceded the shooting with one of the following shots:

- The woman taking a large sum of money out of a safe
- The woman checking over an airline ticket
- The woman being caught in bed with a lover
- The woman taking a gun out of her purse

If the murder scene described earlier were preceded by any one of these four shots, a different motive for murder would emerge in each case.

ACCELERATION EDITING

We've noted that early films were shot in real time. Today, a film audience would become restless indeed — and in television they would probably quickly turn to another channel — if events in a production were all shown in real time. Let's say you want to tell the story of a girl preparing for an important date. The process of picking out clothes that make the proper "statement," taking a shower, drying her hair, putting on her clothes and make-up, checking the whole effect and

relational editing: In relational editing scenes that by themselves seem not to be related take on an interrelated significance when spliced together.

making necessary adjustments and then driving to some prearranged place, would take at least 90 minutes. That's the total time devoted to most feature films. (And the really interesting part hasn't even started yet.) And if productions were confined to real time, telling someone's life story would also present a bit of a problem.

In film and video production, time is routinely condensed and expanded. The 90 minutes it may take to get ready for the date can be shown in 10 to 15 seconds. In the case of the woman getting ready for a date, this could consist of the following (see Figures 14.2A to 14.2G).

- A shot of woman concluding a conversation on the phone
- A shot of her pulling clothes out of her closet
- A shot of her silhouette through a shower door
- A shot of her blow-drying her hair
- The woman checking the whole effect in the mirror before turning and heading for the door.

This sequence could be followed by a driving shot and a shot of the woman pulling up in front of a prearranged meeting place. Or, if you really want to collapse time (and not make any real points about the woman's preparation for the date), you could just get the tail end of a telephone conversation setting up the date and then cut directly to the woman arriving at the agreed-upon place. Although the latter might seem like a jump cut, audiences have become conditioned to jumping across hours, days and even years in a single cut.

In our getting-ready-for-a-date scenario, let's assume you need to make some dramatic points, either about the importance of the date or the heroine's personality — or both. You could do this by showing something of the woman's preparation for the date. After hanging up the telephone in the kitchen, you could have her exit the frame on the right. From this shot you could cut to a shot of her entering the bedroom at the left of the frame. (This would keep the left-to-right screen direction constant from scene to scene.) If she then tried on six dresses before finding one she liked, that would "say" something — either about the significance of the date or the indecision of the character. (We wouldn't need to *see* her try on the dresses; we would only need quick shots of them coming out of the closet, the woman glancing at the effect in her mirror, and the dresses being rejected and tossed on an ever-growing pile on the bed.) If the importance of the date or the indecision of the character were significant in making a point, we could further emphasize these facts by having her also try several hair styles before she found one she liked.

No matter how we edit this scenario, we will end up collapsing (accelerating) time at many points. The important thing for the editor to keep in mind is not to lose the audience in the trip. If we jumped from a shy, nervous telephone conversation setting up the first date to the two of them settled in on a cruise ship, cruising the Atlantic together, or to the woman three years later with three kids, we might feel a bit confused — or at least feel we had been cheated out of seeing some important phases of the relationship.

Compressing Time

Often it is necessary to make big jumps in time. To do this without losing the audience, obvious clues must be provided.[6] There are ways *not* to do this. Some early movies used the technique of having pages fall off of a calendar. Today

---

6. The stage play and film, "*Same Time Next Year,*" which centers around the changes that time introduces into the lives of two characters, is a good example for study. A more subtle example is the film "*Driving Miss Daisy,*" which traverses several decades.

FIGURE 14.2

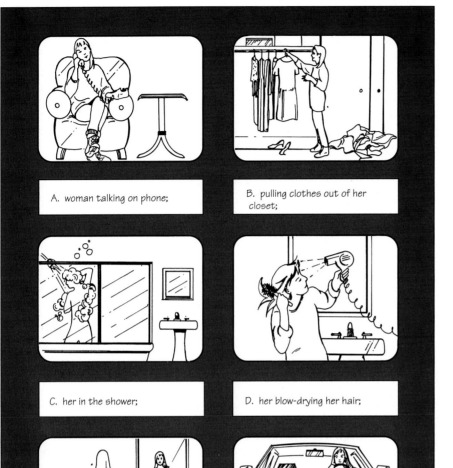

A. woman talking on phone;

B. pulling clothes out of her closet;

C. her in the shower;

D. her blow-drying her hair;

E. the woman checking the whole effect in the mirror;

F. her driving;

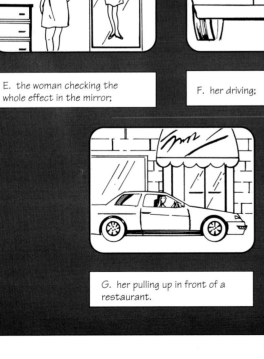

G. her pulling up in front of a restaurant.

this effect would be deemed a bit artificial. Early dramatic films occasionally used an off-screen narrator to announce changes in time and place—also a bit artificial. Dates are sometimes superimposed on the screen—probably a bit more acceptable.

In contrast to using obvious dialogue ("My, how time flies; do you realize it's been six months since we've seen each other!"), good writers, directors and editors can take viewers smoothly backward or forward in time without calling attention to a time-traversing technique. Here are some possibilities:

- References to time slipped into dialogue
- The leaves on trees changing between shots
- A dissolve to black in a summer scene and then a fade up to the same scene showing snow
- Characters obviously aging through the use of make-up
- Children growing up

For smaller shifts in time, they might use these techniques:

- An obvious difference in the color, temperature and position of the sun (for a transition through several hours)
- Changing from high-key daylight to low-key interior lighting (for a transition from day to night)

Expanding Time

In video editing, action is generally compressed; but, occasionally, an editor or director will want to drag out a happening beyond the actual time represented. To illustrate the power of slowing down events, the noted director, Alfred Hitchcock ("*Psycho,*" "*North by Northwest*" etc.) used the example of a scene where a group of people sitting around a dinner table were blown up by a time bomb. In a real-time version of the scene, the people sit down at the table, and the bomb goes off. End of people; end of scene. In the second version the people gather, talk and casually sit down at the dinner table. A shot of the bomb ticking away under the table is shown, revealing to the audience what is about to happen. The guests at the table, unaware of the bomb, continue their banal conversations. Closer shots of the bomb are then intercut with the guests laughing and enjoying dinner. The intercutting continues until the bomb finally blows the dinner party to bits. The latter version understandably succeeds in creating far more of an emotional impact. A similar approach of dragging out events is often used in horror films during a particularly frightening or gruesome scene. And, if for some reason the director and editor don't think this approach will create enough audience reaction, the film or tape can be shown in slow motion—just so we don't miss any of the gore.

THEMATIC EDITING

montage editing: Although the term as used in early film work had a different meaning, today montage editing refers to a rapid, impressionistic sequence of disconnected scenes linked by a variety of transition devices that are designed to communicate feelings or experiences. A montage does not tell a story by developing an idea in a logical sequence.

In *montage editing* (also called **thematic editing**) images are edited together that are related in theme only. Although the term *montage* as used in early film work had a different meaning, today montage and thematic editing refers to a rapid, impressionistic sequence of disconnected scenes designed to communicate feelings or experiences. This type of editing is often used in music videos, commercials and film trailers (promotional clips). In contrast to most types of editing, thematic editing is not designed to tell a story by developing an idea in a logical sequence. The trailer for *"Alien"* (one of the first trailers to use the thematic technique) was produced even before shooting on the actual film was completed. Footage was more or less randomly cut together to conform to the rhythm of the theme music. The intent was simply to communicate action, excitement and danger, not to suggest a story line. Through thematic editing, commercials often highlight good times, romance or adventure. Rather than telling a product's "success story," the commercials are designed to impart a feeling or mood. Thereafter, the sponsor hopes that such phrases as *good times, weekends, oh, what a feeling* or *double your pleasure* will be associated with their product.

Editing Trends

The popularity of music videos (which often use thematic editing) has had an impact on general editing styles. The most significant influence has been in **editing pace** (the number and speed of the edits). Because editing decisions in montage editing are based on a (generally fast) music tempo rather than a story line, generally speaking the pace of general editing and story presentation has dramatically increased in the past decade. It has also meant that viewers have learned to deal with thematic-based editing structures, rather than more structured, time-based presentations.

JUMP CUTS

When we talked about acceleration and thematic editing, we were talking about *intentional* discontinuities in action. Audiences have learned to appreciate the technique of cutting out extraneous footage to keep a story moving. But all discontinuities in action are not good. When one isn't, it's called a ***jump cut:*** a confusing, unsettling or aesthetically rough jump in content. Many weekly television series—those that are shot single-camera, film-style—provide good examples of discontinuity in action.

jump cut: An inappropriate edit between two scenes that, for any number of reasons, keeps the segments from flowing together smoothly and unobtrusively.

- A two-shot of a couple talking on a boat will show their hair blowing gently in the breeze; but in an immediate close-up of one of them, the wind has inexplicably stopped.

- A close-up of an actress may show her laughing, but in an immediate cut to a master shot we see that she is not even smiling.

- A man is walking with his arm around the waist of his girlfriend; but a cut to another angle suddenly shows that his arm is around her shoulder.

- In the master shot we might see an actor start up a flight of stairs; but in the cut to the reverse angle we see him already halfway up the staircase.

Bridging Jumps in Action

Various editing techniques can be used to solve these problems. We'll start with how a jump cut in a major dramatic production might be handled. Using our previous getting-ready-for-a date example, we might see the girl hang up the phone in the kitchen and quickly walk out of the right of the frame. After she exits the kitchen (moving left-to-right), let's assume we then immediately cut to a shot of her entering the bedroom from the right (now moving right-to-left), as shown in Figures 14.3A and 14.3B. The audience is left with a question: Why did she instantly seem to turn a full 180 degrees and start walking in the opposite direction to get to the bedroom?

When successive scenes are shot hours or sometimes even weeks apart (which they commonly are in single-camera video production), it is easy to

FIGURE 14.3

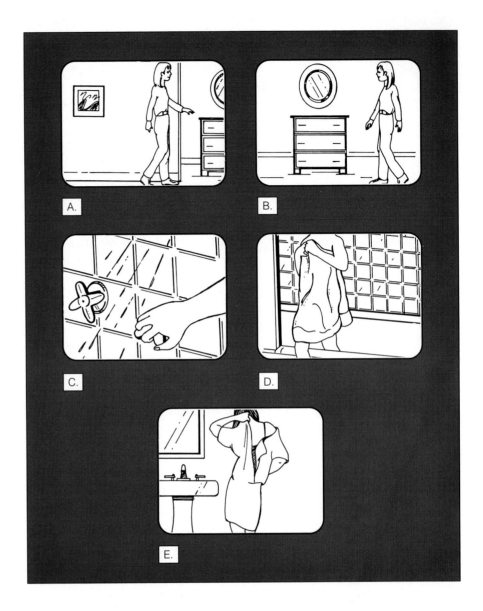

overlook continuity problems such as this. Assuming the director or script assistant didn't catch this problem when the production was shot, the editor and director are faced with a dilemma. Reshooting the sequence after principal photography has been completed would be costly, maybe even virtually impossible, given the time that may have passed and the new commitments of crew and actors. On rare occasions, the scene can be electronically reversed; but this can create major problems with familiar scene elements. (Why does the heroine suddenly have her hair parted on the right?) A better solution would be to insert one or more related scenes. We could suggest a shower by two quick cuts that wouldn't even have to involve the original actor. From the kitchen shot we could cut directly to a quick close-up of a female hand turning on a shower faucet and adjusting the temperature of the water (Figure 14.3C). This could be followed by a quick shot of a towel-draped torso (a stand-in for the actor) emerging from a shower (Figure 14.3D) and quickly exiting the frame on the left.[7]

---

7. In getting needed shots to solve an editing problem, you can often get a *stand-in* to wear the same clothes as the principal actor. By using long shots or shots from the back of a look-alike, you can fool an audience into thinking they are seeing the principal actor. To be on the safe side, you will want to keep these as brief as possible. Although these shots can be done anywhere, you will need to meticulously match the lighting, set etc. of the original scene.

With the introduction of the two brief shower scenes, we have broken the expected left-to-right movement between the kitchen and bedroom shots. But, now we have also introduced another problem, one that a good editor or director should spot. As a student of both human behavior and editing, do you see the problem that remains? We would normally expect to see someone leave a shower in a bathrobe rather than the same clothes they started out with. To solve this problem, we could add one more shot of the female stand-in: a shot of her sliding back into her original dress before leaving the bathroom (Figure 14.3E).

Most jump-cut problems are not as hard to solve as our getting-ready-for-a-date scenario. In most EFP and ENG productions the cameraperson will (or, at least, *should*) take a variety of B-roll shots which can be used as insert shots and cutaways. Although B-roll footage should be designed to add important information to the basic story, it is also used to cover jump cuts in the primary footage. These jump cuts could be the result of mismatches in action, momentary technical problems, or, in the case of interviews, segments that must be removed from long-winded answers to questions.

Bridging Interview Edits

Interviews must be routinely cut down to conform to time limitations. Cutting a section out of dialogue will normally result in an abrupt and noticeable jump in the video of the person speaking. The resulting jump cut can be covered by inserting a three- or four-second B-roll cutaway shot over the jump (while maintaining the edited A-roll audio track). These cutaways are often reaction shots ("noddies") of the interviewer just listening to the person speak (and possibly nodding his head). Since video editors depend greatly on this supplementary B-roll footage to bridge a wide range of editing problems, the director or videographer should always take the time to tape a variety of (B-roll) shots. Otherwise editing problems will be greatly compounded.

The 1-2-3 Formula

Jump cuts not only relate to unacceptable jumps in action; they can also result from major, abrupt changes in subject size. As we've noted, going from the establishing (long) shot directly to a close-up of an individual is quite abrupt. An intermediate medium shot is needed to smooth out the transition (Figures 14.3A, 14.4B and 14.4C). There is a well-established 1-2-3 shot formula that covers this. It starts with (1) a momentary long (master or establishing) shot, then (2) a cut to a medium shot and (3) cuts to various over-the-shoulder and close-up shots.[8] At some point the shot order is reversed. This may be required when it's necessary to back out of a scene, or to accommodate major changes in actor or talent positions. If a scene is long, it may be necessary to occasionally remind viewers where everyone and everything is. When you cut back to a shot in this way, it is referred to as cutting to a ***re-establishing shot.***

re-establishing shot: A wide shot intended to reorient an audience to the basic elements of a scene and their relative positions.

Although this long-shot-to-medium-shot-to-close-up formula is traditional, there will be many times when an editor will opt for another approach. By starting a scene with an extreme close-up—especially of a crucial object—and then backing out, you can immediately focus attention on the scene's center of interest. In a drama the starting close-up could be a snapshot of a child, smashed eyeglasses, a gun, or other key subject matter. From here the camera could dolly or zoom back to reveal the surrounding scene.

8. During the golden age of Hollywood, most studios required this formula approach from all their directors. Among other things, it simplified production by standardizing the directing and editing processes at a time when some studios were turning out several hundred films a year.

FIGURE 14.4
Jump cuts not only relate to unacceptable jumps in action, but also to abrupt changes in subject size. Going from the establishing shot (A) directly to a close-up of an individual (C) is too abrupt. An intermediate medium shot (B) is needed to smooth out the transition.

(a)

(b)

(c)

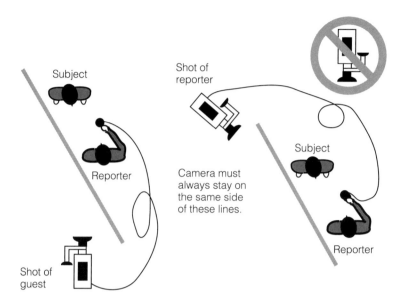

FIGURE 14.5
One example of an undesirable and disorienting angle change is when screen direction is reversed by *crossing the line*. Any time a new camera angle exceeds 180 degrees, you will have crossed the line, and on-screen action will be reversed.

In a dramatic production the impact of a moment might be emphasized by using a **snap zoom** (an extremely rapid zoom) from a medium shot to an extreme close-up, or an abrupt cut from a medium-wide shot to a close-up of a startled person. Note that in these examples the guideline that calls for a smooth transition in shooting distances is violated in favor of a more important concern: dramatic effect. Dramatic effect should always take precedence over normal procedures.

Shooting-Angle Considerations

Another type of jump cut results from cutting to a shot that is almost the same as the one that preceded it. An example would be cutting from one three-shot to another three-shot from a similar angle. Not only is it hard to justify a transition when the new shot is not significantly different, but a cut of this type looks like a mistake. As a result, some videographers adhere to a "30-degree guideline." According to this guideline a new shot of the same subject matter can be justified only if a change of angle of at least 30 degrees is involved. They believe that unless there is a significant change of angle, the audience will not see anything new. Of course, in cutting to a different shot—for example, from a two-shot to a one-shot—this guideline would not apply, since the two shots would be significantly different.

Crossing the Line

Another example of an undesirable angle change is when screen direction is reversed by *crossing the line,* or the *action axis* of a scene. Any time a new camera angle exceeds 180 degrees you will have crossed the line, and action will be reversed (see Figure 14.5). Occasionally, a director will intentionally violate the 180-degree rule for dramatic effect. For example, during a riot scene a director may choose to intentionally cross the line on many shots in order to communicate confusion and disorientation. Assuming that confusion is not the objective, an editor must always remember to maintain the audiences' perspective as edits are made.

Maintaining Consistent Eyelines

When camera shots are being combined in real time, as they are in multiple-camera production, jump cuts are not a problem. However, things are quite different in single-camera production, where one camera must be repeatedly repositioned to get each needed camera shot and angle. Here, the editor must smoothly piece together a variety of shots—generally taped out of sequence over a period of time. (We'll cover single-camera production in Chapter 16.) For example, if an actress is standing and supposedly talking to someone seated in front of her, the director must be certain that when the close-up shot is taped she is looking down at the proper angle for the distance and relative height represented for the other person in the master shot. This is called *maintaining consistent eyelines*. Once the master shot orients us to where everyone is, we expect to see actors conforming to the suggested eyeline angles in their close-ups.

To make it even more difficult to maintain eyeline consistency, speaking parts are sometimes shot without the actors who are being "spoken to" even being present. Rather than stopping the tape during the production when a mistake is made, or keeping the whole cast waiting around after the production or scene is shot, directors often elect to hold just one actor and restage specific shots. A stand-in can replace an actor being addressed, or sometimes an actor will simply deliver his or her lines to "a spot on the wall." This technique is often relied upon to correct lighting, sound or dialogue problems.

TECHNICAL CONTINUITY PROBLEMS

In addition to continuity problems relating to dramatic content, there are also technical continuity problems. A ***technical continuity problem*** is an abrupt and undesirable change in audio or video characteristics.

technical continuity problem: Any one of several types of unintentional changes in video or audio quality. Examples are unintended changes in color balance or changes in audio levels during the course of consecutive shots.

Audio   In audio technical continuity problems include shot-to-shot variations in sound ambience, frequency response or audio level caused by cutting together scenes that were shot under different conditions. Many of these problems can be helped, if not made imperceptible, by technicians skilled in using graphic equalizers, reverberation units and a wide range of sound-shaping equipment. The easiest sound problems to fix—and those that are well within the control of the most basic editing equipment—are those related to minor level variations. Once basic audio levels are established with a VU meter, the editor should primarily rely on "the ear" to make subsequent sound level judgments and adjustments.

More difficult audio problems, such as differences in acoustics or microphone frequency response between successive shots, require the specialized skill and equipment found in a postproduction sound facility. As with the other continuity problems, momentarily cutting in other scenes (with their accompanying audio) will cover minor audio changes in the primary sound track. But even a room full of the latest audio equipment won't solve major audio continuity problems. Quite often—even routinely for major productions—sections of narration have to be rerecorded after shooting has finished. In film this is referred to as **looping,** since the section of the film that needs new audio will be spliced into a loop and run numerous times while an actor watches in a sound-proof booth. The actor then records new audio maintaining the pace, energy and lip-synchronization of the original audio.

Video   In video there can also be continuity problems related to color balance, light levels, camera quality and tape-generation loss. Intercutting scenes from cameras with noticeably different color balance will immediately be apparent to most viewers. Within limits, knowledgeable engineers with the proper equipment can match at least the skin tones from two unmatched video sources. Color shifts in backgrounds, especially in isolated scenes, will often go unnoticed, since the audience has no way of knowing the original color or brightness of the background. (But they do know what skin tones are supposed to look like.) Minor postproduction corrections can also be made for differences in video levels.

MUSIC CONTINUITY CONSIDERATIONS

Another continuity problem relates to background music. When skillfully used, music can smooth the transition between segments and create overall production unity. Except in music-centered productions, music should add to the overall mood and effect without calling attention to itself. Vocals should be avoided, especially when the production contains normal (competing) dialogue. Music should be selected that matches the mood, pace and time period of the production. Ideally, the beginning of the music should coincide with the start of a video segment and end as the segment ends. Of course, this rarely happens, unless the video is specifically edited to match the music.

Conforming Music to Video

If the music runs long (which is generally the case), check to see if a segment can be cut out of the music. This can often be done, especially when a piece contains repetitive sections separated by momentary pauses. The best way of customizing a music section to video is to use a computer-controlled audio editing program. In addition to electronically cutting out musical segments to shorten selections (and repeating sections to lengthen music), segments can be, within limits, digitally compressed or stretched without affecting audio frequency range.

If an audio workstation or computer-based audio editing system is not available, the traditional method of editing reel-to-reel tapes can be used. (Editing 1/4-inch reel-to-reel tape was covered in Chapter 7.) Sections can be cut out, or if you have two reel-to-reel copies of the music, a selection can be lengthened by repeating part of the music. Since the edited music will generally be low in the background, alterations of this sort will probably go unnoticed.

Backtiming Music

If adding or subtracting segments does not work, either because of the nature of the music or because the timing still won't be right, the music can be *backtimed* so that it will conclude with the scene. If the music is longer than the video segment, the music can be started an exact length of time before the beginning of the video segment. At the appropriate point the video can be started, and the music subtly faded in. Here's an example. If a video segment were 1 minute and 43 seconds long, and a music selection 3 minutes and 13 seconds long, the music would be started 1 minute and 30 seconds before the video. Both would then end at exactly the same time. (As you will note in the next chapter, time code greatly facilitates the timing of audio and video segments.) The least desirable solution to music timing is to fade the music out in midstream at the end of a scene. This will be especially noticeable if the music is almost finished or if it has just begun.

backtime: Calculating time for a show backward from the end. This is done to determine when segments should start in order to bring the show out on time.

Tapping Into Music Libraries

Libraries of background music are available that suggest themes (such as "Manhattan Rush Hour," "Serenity" and "Heavy Machinery"). These selections are designed to support video without overpowering it. Since getting the legal right to use music is generally a major concern, these libraries of ready-made, "cleared" music solve this problem as well. (Music clearances and additional guidelines for the use of music are covered in Chapter 19.)

Since music and effects (M&E) generally go together, we should mention that commercial sound libraries also include just about every sound effect you could think of. Most sound effect libraries contain several variations of each category of sound, which eases the problem of making a particular effect blend naturally and realistically into a sound track. When audio workstations or computer-based audio editing is used, sound effect libraries are routinely transferred onto computer disks. They can then be selected from a screen menu, programmed into an editing sequence and recalled instantly as needed.

SEVEN EDITING GUIDELINES

We've noted that production techniques are best when they go unnoticed by the average listener and viewer. Editing, in particular, should be "invisible." Bad editing is intrusive and disruptive; it calls attention to itself. In the interest of making editing as smooth and unobtrusive as possible, seven guidelines should be considered. (Note that, as with the guidelines for good composition, we are avoiding the term *rules*.) In addition to helping make edits as smooth and unobtrusive as possible, the following guidelines also introduce some important editing concepts.

Cutting Between Moving Camera Shots

Guideline 1. Avoid cutting from a moving camera shot to stationary shot, and vice versa. The most obvious example of this is when a camera is rapidly panning across a scene and then there is an abrupt cut to a static camera shot. Although this guideline used to be on the order of a cardinal rule for filmmakers, it is often broken in action-oriented weekly television programs.[9]

A dissolve between two shots that are being panned or tilted at different speeds and in different directions can also be unpleasant and disorienting. However, a cut or dissolve between two panning shots where the pan is at the same speed and in the same direction is acceptable.

Cutting on Subject Movement

Guideline 2. Whenever possible, cut on subject movement. Note that here we are talking about subject movement, not camera movement, as in Guideline 1. When you cut on subject movement, some of the action will be included in both shots. If a woman is getting out of a chair, you can cut at the midpoint. If cuts are motivated by action, the action will divert attention from the cut, making the transition more fluid. In addition, subtle jump cuts are less noticeable, because the viewers tend to be caught up in the action itself.

In cutting to various shots, keep in mind the 30-degree angle guideline

---

9. Everything we see on television should not, of course, be automatically considered good production. Even experienced and knowledgeable directors and editors regularly have to make compromises in the interest of bringing a project in on time and on budget. Given the realities of the business, the objective is often how well a project can be done within these restraints.

already discussed. Not only does it look better, and avoids a possible jump cut, but minor mismatches in action are concealed when the new shot represents a significant change in subject perspective.

Cutting with the action calls for a good eye for detail. To avoid an obvious jump cut, you need to be sure the subject is doing the same thing in exactly the same way in each shot. If you cut from a long shot to a medium shot of someone walking, for example, the cut must be made when the feet are in the same place in both shots. If the director hasn't provided this matched action in each shot, it is up to the editor to add a cutaway to momentarily separate the two (mismatched) shots.

Matching Action   In matching action, not only should the relative position of feet or hands in both shots be the same, but also the rate of movement. In single-camera production where the various camera angles are shot at different times, it is important that actors and directors duplicate the exact action in each take. This duplication also applies to the general energy level exhibited by actors in their voice and gestures. Part of the art of acting is in maintaining consistency in the various takes. To facilitate editing, directors will generally give the editor several takes of each scene.

Often it is necessary to cut to a scene as a person leaves the frame and cut to the next scene as the person enters. An example would be a person walking out of one room and entering another. In this case it is best to cut the first scene as the person's eyes pass the edge of the frame, and then cut to the second scene about five frames (one-sixth of a second) before the person's eyes enter the frame of the next scene. The timing here is significant. It takes about one-sixth of a second for viewers' eyes to switch from one side of the frame to the other. (A person exiting the first scene on the right enters the next scene on the left.) During this time the viewers' eyes are unfocused, and whatever is taking place on the screen becomes a bit scrambled. Because of this "lost interval," some editors prefer to overlap visible action in successive scenes by three to five frames (one-seventh of a second). When this technique is used, not only does the viewer not miss anything, but a kind of "subjective jump cut" is avoided.

Cutting After Subtle Action   Although this guideline stresses cutting on action, when the movement is subtle, editors often prefer to cut just after action ends. An example would be a reaction that only amounts to a shift of the eyes: we hear a door open, a person glances to one side, and we immediately cut to a person entering the room. In this case we use the action to provide motivation for the cut and then make the cut at the precise second the action (the eye movement) ends.

Editor as Magician   When someone in a scene is talking, attention is generally focused on the person's mouth or eyes. Like a good magician, an editor can use this to cover a slight mismatch in action in another area of the frame. In order to know what can and cannot be done, an editor must be aware at every moment of where audience attention is likely to be directed.

Sudden, loud sounds are even used by editors to cover jump cuts. An unexpected loud sound will cause viewers to blink. In the one-fifth of a second it takes to blink, a subtle jump cut will go undetected. Any on-screen diversion can be used in this way.

Motivated Cuts

Guideline 3. Don't make an edit without appropriate motivation. Transitions should be suggested by on-camera action, dialogue or music. In making any transition there is a risk of breaking the concentration of the audience and subtly pulling attention away from the production's central focus. When cuts are motivated by production content, they are most apt to go unnoticed. Let's take the simple scene of a woman who is into a "heavy" discussion with a man. The director wants to show her react to something he said by staring into her glass of wine, taking a sip and then returning her attention to the man (see Figures 14.6A to 14.6F). This scene could be cut (edited together) in several ways, but let's try this:

1. We start with an over-the-shoulder shot of the man as he makes a statement.

2. Once his statement is made, we quickly cut to a reverse-angle shot of the woman as she reacts.

3. As part of her reaction, she quickly glances down into her glass of wine. (Since the scene is becoming emotional, we now need to get in closer on the characters to see expressions and reactions.)

4. Her eye movement together with a need to get closer provide motivation for the cut to a close-up as the woman solemnly takes a sip of wine.

5. She then looks back at the man.

6. This provides motivation to then cut to a close-up of the man (and the scene continues until whatever it is they are discussing is resolved).

Note that not only is each cut motivated, it must be made at a precise time in the action. If editing is done correctly, the cuts should flow so well with the action that they become almost invisible to viewers.

Editing to Accommodate the Medium

Guideline 4. Edit to conform to the strengths and limitations of the medium. Although some might apply the philosophical differences between film and video expounded by theorists such as Marshall McLuhan,[10] Guideline 4 primarily addresses the fact that significant picture detail is lost in the 525- and 625-line systems of broadcast television. The only way to really show needed details is through close-ups. Therefore, it is up to the editor to keep in mind the following precept: *Television is a close-up medium.* Except for establishing shots designed to momentarily orient the audience to subject placement, the director and the editor should emphasize medium shots and close-ups.[11]

In addition to showing detail, close-ups convey intimacy. They are appropriate for interviews, dramas and love stories, but generally not appropriate for light comedy. In comedy the use of medium shots makes it much easier to follow characters around the set. At the same time, medium shots do not seriously and deeply pull the audience into the show's subject matter or the actors' thoughts and emotions. Many comedy directors feel that the use of loose one-shots or even two-shots helps keep the mood light.

In contrast, in interviews and documentary work it is generally desirable to try to "zero in on" a subject's reactions to provide clues to the person's general

10. Marshall McLuhan, who wrote such thought-provoking books as "*Understanding Media*" and "*The Medium Is the Message*," popularized the saying, "We live in a global village." Although he may have been a bit premature in assuming that the reach of television has shrunk the world into a single village, his thoughts nevertheless opened the door to some significant thinking about the media. Based partly on the difference in picture detail in the two media, he also stated that film was a hot medium and television was a cool medium. Students (and professors) have spent decades trying to figure out this distinction. If *cool* and *hot* were ever authentic distinctions between the media, they are probably no longer significant in the era of HDTV.

11. Theatrical film directors must also keep this in mind, since to show a reasonable profit (and often just to break even, financially), most feature films must be picked up by television. Although details in long shots may be discernible in a theater, they often won't be on 525- and 625-line broadcast systems. This must also be kept in mind in designing titles, subtitles and credits.

(a)   (b)   (c)

(d)   (e)   (f)

FIGURE 14.6

The sequence starts with an over-the-shoulder shot of the man as he makes a statement (A). We then quickly cut to a reverse-angle shot to see the woman as she reacts (B). As part of her reaction, she quickly glances down into her glass of wine (C). Since the scene is becoming emotional, we now need to get in closer to see expressions and reactions. Her eye movement together with our need to get close, provide motivation for the cut to a close-up as the woman solemnly takes a sip of wine (D) before looking back at the man (E). This provides motivation to then cut to a close-up of the man (F). The scene then continues until the issue is resolved.

character. Close-ups help do this. At the same time, close-ups of highly undesirable characters can make an audience uncomfortable.

Determining the Length of Shots

Guideline 5. Cut away from a scene the moment the visual statement is complete. Interest quickly wanes in a scene once the essential visual information is conveyed. "Slow-moving" suggests that an audience has grown impatient with the pace of a production. A large part of the responsibility for keeping a production moving rests with editing. Shots with new information stimulate viewer interest — as long as they are presented at the right time.

There are several considerations in determining shot length. The first is the amount of information you wish to convey. In the 13-shot, ENG murder scenario (or was it self-defense?) outlined earlier, the original shot of the knife on the pavement should take only about two seconds, since only two elements need to be communicated at that moment: "knife" resting on "pavement." Because we are probably not interested in what kind of knife it is or the condition of the pavement, two seconds are enough to make this statement—and enough to identify the object later picked up by a policewoman as being the knife we saw.

Accommodating Visual Complexity   Shot length is also dictated by visual complexity. Travelogue shots can often be relatively short, since it may take only a few seconds for the viewer to grasp (or be reminded of) essential information. Examples would be a shot of a beach, a mountain stream or a winding road. If some sort of action is included, the shot will require more time: children playing on the beach, people fishing in the mountain stream or a native family making its way along the winding road with all their belongings. In the case of the native family, you will also want to consider how much information viewers need to know. If the production is *about* the family, you will want to hold the scene long enough for viewers to recognize the individual family members and even start learning things about them. By holding the scene of the family (and even cutting to various angles), you are, in fact, tipping the audience off that this particular family is in some way important to the production. After becoming involved with this family by dwelling on them for a period of time, the audience will naturally develop some expectations. They will assume that the production will either follow this family's story or that the production will at least periodically check on their progress.

In contrast, in montage editing, shots may be only a fraction of a second (8 to 10 video frames) long. Obviously, this is not enough time even to begin to see all of the elements in the scene. But the idea in this case is simply to communicate general impressions, not details.

The next major consideration under this guideline, *subject familiarity,* is illustrated by two brief examples. Since most of us have seen many shots of the Statue of Liberty, a scene showing it would need to be only in the form of a brief, symbolic reminder—probably just three seconds or so. On the other hand, we wouldn't appreciate only three seconds of a strange little green man who just landed his flying saucer on the White House lawn.

Next, cutting rate depends on the inherent or implied tempo of production content. Tranquil pastoral scenes imply longer shots than scenes of downtown New York at rush hour. Although you can enhance and increase production tempo by cutting rapidly during rapid action, this technique can do little to speed up slow action.

Varying Tempo   A well-written script should have periodic swings in tempo. A constant fast pace will tire an audience; a constant slow pace in both production content and editing can quickly put an audience to sleep—or, in television, induce them to look for something slightly more engaging on another channel. If the visual or audio content of the production does not naturally vary, the editor (with possible help from music) will want to try to cut segments in a way that provides changes in pace. This is one of the reasons that editors like parallel stories: pace can be varied by cutting back and forth between stories.

It is often helpful to plot editing pace to see variations over time. This can easily be done by plotting time against the number of edits. If an average 22-minute production (30 minutes minus commercials) has 275 edits, this means that the average scene will be six seconds long. Figure 14.7 shows how the pace

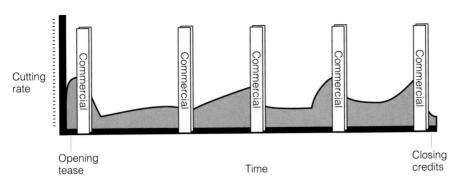

Cutting rate

Opening tease

Time

Closing credits

FIGURE 14.7
This figure shows how the pace of a TV program can vary during a 22-minute period. If an average 22-minute production (30 minutes minus commercials) has 275 edits, this means that the average scene will be six seconds long. Note that the pace may be intentionally increased before commercial breaks to raise and help sustain interest. Cutting rate, however, is not the major criterion for the perceived pace of the production; it is the content. But since cutting rate is often related to the intensity of content, one may reflect the other.

of a TV program can vary during this 22-minute period. The pace may be intentionally increased before commercial breaks to increase excitement and help sustain interest. Cutting rate, however, is not the major criterion for the perceived pace of the production. It is the content. But, since cutting rate should be related to content, one should reflect the other.

Capturing and Holding Audience Interest   In editing segments, guard against peaking interest too soon and letting the remainder of the piece go downhill. Try to lead the segment with something fairly strong (a "hook") that will immediately engage audience interest. Given the many TV channels vying for viewer attention, the first few seconds of a show are crucial to holding an audience. It is during these opening seconds that viewers are most tempted to "channel hop" and see what else is on. Because of this, TV programs often show the most dramatic highlights of the night's program at the beginning, and the nightly newscasts regularly "tease" upcoming stories just before commercial breaks.

In editing news stories it is best to open with a strong audio or video statement and then (once an audience is interested in knowing the details) fill in needed information. But in the process of filling in information, try to gradually build interest until it peaks at the end. This will leave the audience feeling good about the program or video segment.

The Function of B-Roll Footage

Guideline 6. The real story is in the B-roll. Although this editing guideline applies mainly to news and documentary work, it also has implications for dramatic production. Recall that the so-called B-roll contains scenes that supply supplementary information to the main (A-roll) story. In a single-camera ENG interview, the "backbone" information—the interview subject answering the questions—is on one videotape (the A-roll), and supplementary information is contained on a second tape (the B-roll). In a dramatic production the B-roll will consist of insert shots and cutaways.

In an interview the A-roll interview footage typically consists of a rather static looking "talking head." We can almost always make the piece stronger by cutting in supplementary footage. One valuable type of cutaway, especially in dramatic productions, is the ***reaction shot:*** telling reactions from others to what is going on or being said at the moment.

reaction shot: A cut to performer's face that registers a response. Generally a close-up of someone reacting to the central dialogue or action.

Reaction Shots   Reaction shots are desirable because they

- provide important clues to how others are responding to what is being said;

FIGURE 14.8
Cutaway shots move away from the main scene to add related visual information. During all the noise and excitement of a parade, a shot of a child asleep on the sideline would be an example of a cutaway.

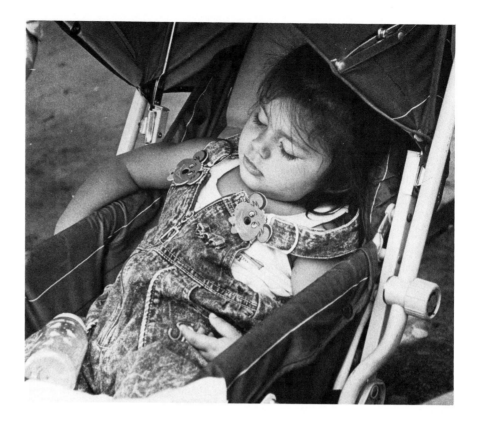

- stimulate the pace of the show;
- introduce visual variety;
- can cover "bad moments" in A-roll footage (such as jerky camera movement, someone walking in front of the camera or the speaker momentarily moving out of the frame);
- make edits possible in the audio track of the speaker.

In a news piece the B-roll consists of scenes that support, accentuate or in some way visually elaborate on what is being said. Using strong supplementary footage increases the amount of information conveyed in a given interval. More information in a shorter time results in an apparent increase in production tempo, and this holds viewer interest.

Insert Shots   Insert shots are also considered B-roll footage. Howard Hawks, an eminent American filmmaker, said, "A great movie is made with cutaways and inserts." As we've noted, insert shots are close-ups and sometimes extreme close-ups of important objects within the basic scene. A news segment that shows a treasury agent holding and talking about counterfeit $100 bills may call for a number of extreme close-ups to show details of engraving problems. A segment on the work of a diamond cutter will need extreme close-up inserts of the diamond as it is marked and cut.

Cutaway Shots   As we also noted earlier in the chapter, cutaway shots move away from the main scene to add related visual information. A cutaway during a parade may show a child asleep in the midst of all the noise and confusion (Figure 14.8). In this case we have cut away from the main event (the parade) to show something which is directly related to it (the sleeping child on the sidelines).

During interviews, cutaways are generally needed to reinforce or illustrate what the speaker is talking about. If an inventor who has just perfected a perpetual-motion machine is being interviewed on his accomplishment, we would fully expect to see his creation. In fact, we would be a bit perturbed if we didn't. If a narcotics agent is being interviewed on finding a major illegal drug lab in your home town, you would expect to see footage of the lab, including where it was located and what was in it.

Once we see the first few seconds of a person speaking, there is generally little advantage in holding this shot. To maintain interest and keep the segment moving, we need to make liberal use of all three types of B-roll footage: insert shots, reaction shots and cutaways.

The Principle of Parsimony

Guideline 7. If in doubt, leave it out. This phrase should be hung in every editing bay. If you don't think that a scene adds significantly to what is being said at the moment, by including it you will probably (at best) slow down story development and (at worst) blur the focus of the production and sidetrack the central message. Let's look at an example of each.

Some novelists used to spend many pages describing settings, right down to the last detail. Today, regardless of how eloquent a writer is, readers quickly grow impatient with such verbosity. In a novel you can skip over such loquaciousness; in television you can't (with the possible exception of fast-forwarding a VCR recording). Television and film viewers, who have become accustomed to rapidly-moving plots and energetic editing, quickly grow restless when a production seems to drag. This is one of the reasons it is so difficult to get an audience to watch classic films. Although they may have many praiseworthy qualities, they just seem to move too slowly for today's audiences.

Although we've talked about the importance of cutaways, there are times where they aren't advisable because they will distract from the central focus of the production. For example, a TV evangelist paid hundreds of thousands of dollars to buy time on national television. His message was engrossing, dramatic and inspiring—or it would have been if the director hadn't chosen to regularly do cutaways to cute kids, couples holding hands, and other interesting things going on in the audience. Although the director undoubtedly thought these cutaways added interest and visual variety, they only succeeded in breaking the mood the preacher had invested considerable time, money and effort to develop. Instead of continuing to follow the message, members of the TV audience were commenting on, or at least thinking about, "that darling little girl with the red ribbons in her hair," or whatever. People watching TV generally have plenty of distractions right in the room where the TV is—we don't need to add any more.

SUMMARY

Electronic videotape editing started in the early 1960s when a pulse was recorded on the videotape to find edit points and pre-roll machines. However, because early quad machines had to be moving at full speed in order for a picture to remain visible, establishing precise editing points was difficult. When helical machines arrived, tape machines could be moved slowly, and edit points could be precisely programmed.

In random-access editing, segments can be programmed into an editor in any sequence, and the editing equipment can locate, cue and display the needed segments without access-time delays. In addition to dedicated editing systems, computer-based editing is now used to meet a wide variety of editing needs.

In continuity editing, segments are arranged in a logical and time-based sequence. Parallel cutting refers to intercutting two or more narratives together in the same production. Insert shots and cutaways are important in supplying needed information and in maintaining visual pace and interest. Causality in editing refers to assembling shots in such a way as to link cause and effect in the minds of viewers. Relational editing techniques rely on the tendency of viewers to try to establish a relationship between successive scenes and events. In acceleration editing, time is compressed by showing only key parts of successive events; thus, an event that may take an hour can be suggested in scenes that may last only a few seconds. Occasionally, for dramatic effect, editing is used to expand time and prolong an event. In thematic editing, segments are assembled around a common theme, without regard to any logical or time-based considerations.

There are many types of jump cuts; but in general, they can be defined as confusing, unsettling or aesthetically rough jumps in continuity. Seven editing guidelines are discussed in this chapter: avoid cutting from a moving camera shot to a stationary shot, and vice versa; whenever possible, cut on subject movement; never make an edit without appropriate motivation; edit to conform to the strengths and limitations of the medium; cut away from a scene the moment the visual statement is complete; the real story is in the B-roll; and if in doubt, leave it out.

KEY TERMS

access time
backtime
continuity editing (continuity cutting)
cutaway
editing pace
insert shot
jump cut
linear editing
looping
montage editing
parallel action

parallel cutting
pre-roll
random-access editing
reaction shot
re-establishing shot
relational editing
shooting ratio
snap zoom
technical continuity problem
thematic editing

Editing Techniques 15

In Chapter 14 we covered some of the principles of editing. In this chapter we move on to editing tools, technology and procedures. The concept behind editing is simple: the tape containing the original footage is transferred (recorded) segment by segment onto a tape in another recorder. In so doing, the original segments can be shortened and rearranged, bad shots can be removed, and audio and video effects can be added. Although the concept is simple, the actual editing process (as it starts to reflect a wide variety of artistic and technical possibilities) can become quite complex.

CONTROL TRACK EDITING

The first automated videotape editing machines kept track of pre-roll and edit points on the tape by electronically counting control track pulses recorded along the edge of the videotape. These pulses are recorded at a rate of 30 per second to correspond to the 30-per-second frame rate of video. This series of pulses, which is referred to as a *control track,* is recorded on an audio-type, linear track as the tape is being recorded. The method of editing that evolved from this process is *control track editing*. In basic control track editing two videotape machines (called a **source machine** and an **edit recorder**) are electronically controlled by an *edit controller* (Figure 15.1). The person doing the editing uses the edit controller to find each segment, mark the beginning and ending edit points and perform the actual edit. We'll go into the specifics later.

Although control track editing is satisfactory for non-demanding applications, it has two major shortcomings. First, it relies on the ability of the equipment to maintain an accurate count of thousands of control track pulses as the tapes go forward and backward at varying speeds. Because of a number of

control track: The portion of a videotape signal consisting of timing pulses associated with video fields and frames. Used in editing and maintaining playback synchronization.

control track editing: Method of editing based on an electronic count of control track pulses for cuing and editing functions rather than SMPTE/EBU time code numbers.

edit controller: The master control panel and associated electronics that control the VTRs etc., associated with a videotape editing system.

393

FIGURE 15.1
In basic control track editing, two videotape machines are electronically controlled by an edit controller. The basic editing process involves locating segments one by one, on the tape in the source machine and sequentially recording them on the tape in the edit recorder.

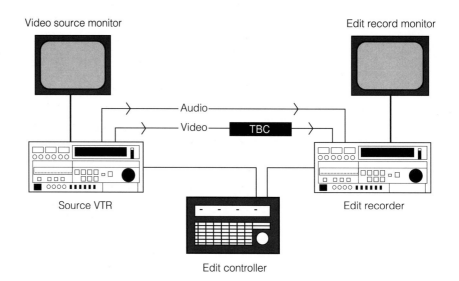

Video source monitor

Edit record monitor

Audio

Video TBC

Source VTR

Edit recorder

Edit controller

technical limitations, absolute accuracy is difficult to maintain. Errors become cumulative. As the tape is moved forward and backward, each successive error compounds the overall error. As a result, edits may eventually end up being off by many frames. Second, since the control track count is valid only during the editing session, once the machine is shut off there is no way to replicate the edit decisions.

SMPTE/EBU TIME CODE

time code: SMPTE/EBU time code. A series of eight numbers identifying the hours, minutes, seconds and frames associated with a specific video frame on a tape.

These problems were eliminated and the videotape editing process was greatly enhanced with the birth of time code. *Time code* is an eight-digit numerical code that can electronically and visually identify each frame in a video production (Figure 15.2). Points on a tape can be specified to an accuracy of 1/30 of a second. (Some equipment allows for "field-rate accuracy," which means that edit points can be indexed to 1/60 of a second.)

The Advantage of Replication

One of the main advantages of time code lies in the ability to record editing decisions and then be able to replicate them (with modifications, if desired) at another time. A designated time code point cannot vary from one editing session to another, from one machine to another or even from one country to another. Editing instructions like "cut the scene when Mary moves away from John" leave much room for interpretation. Even more important, there is the very real possibility that different takes of the same scene will become confused. But even though a tape may be four hours long, the time code 02:13:54:10 refers to one very precise point within that total time.

Time code data on hundreds of edits involving complex video and audio switch points and effects can be electronically stored in a computer-based edit controller (Figure 15.3). Once time code information is entered, the operator can sit back and watch previews of complex edit decisions and make any necessary adjustments before recording the sequence on the edited master.

When initially entered, the time code data goes into the controller's volatile memory. Volatile memory information is retained only as long as the power is

FIGURE 15.2
SMPTE/EBU time code is an eight-digit numerical code that can identify each frame in a video production in terms of hours, minutes, seconds and frames. For precise audio editing some editing systems allow field-rate accuracy (down to 1/60 of a second).

Hours Minutes Seconds Frames

01:03:41:22

FIGURE 15.3
Time code data on hundreds of edits
involving complex video and audio
switch points and effects can be electronically stored in a computer-based
editing system. Once time code information is entered, the operator can sit
back and preview edit decisions and
make necessary adjustments before recording the sequence on the edited
master.

left on. If at all possible, volatile information should be periodically and routinely stored on a more permanent, non-volatile memory form, such as on a $3\frac{1}{2}$-
inch computer disk. In addition, a record of the time code decisions should be
printed out on **hard copy** (computer paper). Since it may take many hours —
sometimes even months — to generate a list of time code decisions for a production, you need to protect data against power failures, brownouts, spilt coffee and
the general range of technical and human problems.

Time Code in Audio

Today, time code has become as important in audio as in video. Because VTRs
are only capable of recording a limited number of audio tracks, productions
involving even moderately complex stereo pickups are routinely recorded with
double-system sound. In this approach a standard VTR is used to record the
video, but the audio is simultaneously recorded on an audio recorder capable of
up to 48 channels (tracks) of sound. Although the audio will eventually be mixed
down to only left and right stereo channels, much greater postproduction control
and flexibility are provided by keeping the audio sources separate until the final
mix-down. This is especially true in modern music, where audio is routinely
reprocessed and remixed during the on-line phase of postproduction. Time code,
which is fed to both the video and audio recorders as the production is done, is
the only practical way to keep audio recorder(s) synchronized with the video
during postproduction.

Interlocking Multiple Machines

The last major advantage of using time code is that multiple audio and video
record and playback machines can be locked together to ensure that they do not
lose sync (synchronization) as a production progresses. Because of tape stretch

and slight differences in machine speeds, this has been a common problem in the past.[1]

Breaking the Code

When time code was initially introduced, several incompatible systems appeared. So in early 1969, the SMPTE (Society of Motion Picture and Television Engineers) acted to establish a uniform system. The resulting standard, which was also adopted by the European Broadcasting Union, was thereafter referred to as *SMPTE/EBU time code*. Since all these initials are hard to say (and audio and video people are notorious for creating quick designations for complex terms) the system is now simply referred to as: *SIM-tee time code*.

Let's look at an example. A time code address of 03, 16, 51, 22 is read as "3 hours, 16 minutes, 51 seconds and 22 frames":

03 :	16 :	51 :	22
Hours:	Minutes:	Seconds:	Frames

Since time code numbers move from right to left when they are entered into an edit controller, you must enter hours, minutes, seconds and frames in that order. By entering only six numbers instead of eight, the machine assumes "00 hours," since the combination of numbers entered would only (as they move from right to left) reach to the minutes designation. The hours designation can go from 00 to 23, the minutes and seconds from 00 to 59 and the frames from 00 to 29. Thirty frames, like five-fifths of a mile, is impossible because 30 frames equal one second. Likewise, 60 minutes in time code is impossible. The next frame after 03 hours, 59 minutes, 59 seconds and 29 frames would change the counter to 04:00:00:00.

Some examples of adding and subtracting time code segments should help in understanding how it works. If one segment were 8 seconds, 20 frames long, and the second segment were 6 seconds, 17 frames long, the total time would be 15:07:

$$08:20 \text{ first segment}$$
$$+06:17 \text{ second segment}$$
$$= 14:37 \text{ or } 15:07 \text{ total time}$$

Note in this example that since 37 frames is more than one second, before we can do our final math we must subtract one second (30 frames) and add it to the total number of seconds. We end up with 7 frames left over (37 minus 30 = 07 frames).

Let's look at another question. If the time code point for entering a video segment is 01:23:38:16 and the out-point is 01:23:45:08, what is the total time of the segment? The answer is just a matter of subtracting the smaller code numbers from the larger numbers:

Out-point:	01:23:45:08	which equals	01:23:44:38
In-point:	− 01:23:38:16		− 01:23:38:16
		Total time	= 00:00:06:22

---

1. Not knowing about these inevitable variations in speed, one TV station filmed a hockey game and recorded the corresponding sound on a reel-to-reel tape machine. Although high-quality equipment was used, within 15 minutes things got considerably out of sync. The television audience was soon baffled when the crowd in attendance maintained absolute silence as their home team made a difficult goal, only to cheer madly a few seconds later when the opposing team leisurely guided the puck up the ice.

FIGURE 15.4
User-bit data can be used to record start and stop cues for triggering various pieces of audio and video equipment during a production or post-production sequence. Here, a sophisticated editing system controls a wide variety of audio and video sources.

Since we can't subtract 16 frames from 08 frames, we have to reverse the procedure followed in the first example; we have to change the 08 to 38 by borrowing a second from the 45. For people who regularly do time code calculations, computer programs and small hand-held calculators are available.

User Bits

Before we turn to other aspects of time code, we need to mention that the digitized SMPTE/EBU signal has room for some additional information beyond the basic hours, minutes, seconds and frames. First, there are error-correcting signals that can detect technical time code errors and be used by the equipment to make necessary corrections. Second, there are **user bits** that can record information about the production—information such as reel number, day and scene number. Because of the limited digital space left over for user bits, they can accommodate a total of only four alphabetic characters or eight numeric digits, or a limited combination of both. Here is an example of a user-bit designation:

R7:S2:T12
for
Reel 7, Scene 2, Take 12.

user bits: Additional digital information that can be recorded along with SMPTE/EBU time code. A limited number of user-bit letters or numbers can be entered to register reel number, date scene, take etc.

Some automated videotape systems utilize the user-bit data area to record start and stop cues for triggering various pieces of audio and video equipment during a production or postproduction sequence (Figure 15.4). As you might assume, user-bit information must be recorded on the videotape along with the original time code.

Drop-Frame Time Code

Before we can go on, we need to understand one more thing about time code: the difference between drop-frame and non-drop-frame. Basic SMPTE/EBU time code assumes a frame rate of 30 per second, but this rate is actually only valid in black-and-white television and some systems of HDTV, not for our standard NTSC broadcast system. For technical reasons, when NTSC color television was introduced, the frame rate was dropped to 29.97 frames per second. Although the difference may seem insignificant, in some applications it can result in problems. If you assume a rate of 30 frames per second instead of 29.97, you end up with a 3.6-second error every 60 minutes. This 3.6-second interval can cut off a sponsor's tag at the end of a program or clip a precisely timed satellite feed in mid-sentence. To correct this error, **drop-frame time code** was introduced. Here is how it works. The error of 3.6 seconds equals an extra 108 frames per hour (3.6 times 30 frames per second). To maintain accuracy, 108 frames must be dropped each hour in such a way as to result in the least amount of confusion. Although the solution devised to solve this problem may be a bit awkward, it works.

First, it was logically decided that the 108-frame correction had to be equally distributed throughout the hour. (It's better to be cheated a few frames here and there than suddenly to have 108 frames disappear in the middle of a scene.) A little math will tell you that if you dropped 1 frame per minute, it would result in a total of only 60 frames per hour. Sixty from 108 leaves 48, so that won't work. If you dropped 2 frames per minute, you would end up with 120 dropped frames per hour instead of 108. That's 12 too many. But, technically, since you can't drop half frames, this is as close as you can get by making a consistent correction every minute. So the problem then becomes one of what to do with the 12 extra frames. The solution is that every 10th minute you *do not* drop 2 frames. In an hour, that totals 12 frames, since there are six 10-minute intervals in an hour.

$$
\begin{aligned}
\text{Error of 3.6 seconds} &= \text{108 frame-per-hour error} \\
\text{Dropping 2 frames/min} &= \text{120 frames (12 too many)} \\
\text{Dropping 1 frame/min} &= \text{60 frames (48 too few)} \\
\text{Solution: drop 2 frames/min, except every 10 minutes} \\
\text{Total} &= \text{108 frames per hour}
\end{aligned}
$$

We can also look at this another way. If you drop two frames each minute, except for every 10th minute (when no frames are dropped) you will have a total of 54 minutes in which frames are dropped. If you multiply the 54 minutes by 2 frames (per minute), you end up with the 108 frames dropped each hour—just the number you need for the 3.6-second correction.

Many edit controllers have a drop-frame/non-drop-frame switch. When you use the drop-frame mode, a signal is added to the SMPTE/EBU time code that automatically lets you and the machine know that drop-frame is being used. Since the frame dropping occurs right at the changeover point from one minute to the next, you will see the time code counter on an editor suddenly jump over the dropped frames every time the correction is made.

Although most production segments run less than an hour, the drop-frame system still keeps timing accurate to within a fraction of a second, no matter what length the segment is. For non-critical applications, such as editing news and industrial television segments, drop-frame isn't needed; in fact, due to its consistent nature (it doesn't skip frames every minute) the non-drop-frame mode makes precise, frame-accurate edits easier. However, if you are involved with producing 15-minute or longer programs for broadcast, or you are producing programming for satellite transmissions (where precise overall timing is generally a must), you should either use an editor with a drop-frame mode or in some way compensate for the error.

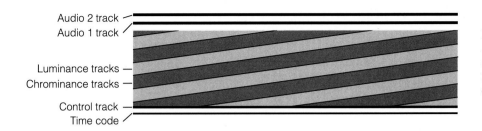

Audio 2 track
Audio 1 track

Luminance tracks —
Chrominance tracks —

Control track —
Time code

FIGURE 15.5
Longitudinal time code is recorded along one edge of the videotape on an audio-type track. This figure shows the longitudinal time code area on a Beta-cam SP tape format.

Adding Time Code

Time code is not an inherent part of videotape in the same way that *edge numbers* are permanently imprinted on motion picture film.[2] With the help of a **time code generator**, the SMPTE/EBU time must be recorded on the videotape as the production is being shot or later, when the tape is being reviewed. Since the time code numbers represent the "address" of needed segments on a videotape, these codes must be logged (written down) so that the segments can later be located. Although logging may seem like a chore, it can save you much time during the editing phase of most productions—and it may save you from using the wrong take of a scene.

Before we move further into this, we need to distinguish between the two basic types of time code: longitudinal and VITC (vertical interval time code), commonly pronounced *VIT-see*.

time code generator: A device that supplies an electronic SMPTE/EBU time code signal to recording equipment.

Longitudinal Time Code

Longitudinal time code is recorded along one edge of the videotape on an audio-type track. Figure 15.5 shows the time code area on a Betacam SP tape format. Other formats use other areas of the tape.

Although the longitudinal system of time code is the easiest to record, it has a number of weaknesses. With the NTSC system of television the complete SMPTE/EBU time code signal consists of 2,400 bits of digital information per second. Although this signal is recorded like an analog audio signal, there is an important difference. When recorded on what is essentially an analog audio track, signal degradation will quickly set in when the tape is copied unless a *jam sync* process is used to regenerate the longitudinal time code as a new copy of the tape is being dubbed. If this isn't done, after several generations a longitudinal signal will be unreliable, especially when the machine is played back at speeds that are slower or faster than normal. (Whenever the time code display freezes on a set of numbers for a moment while the tape is moving, you know that a time code error has occurred.) If a problem is found, the longitudinal time code can be rerecorded. As we will see, with vertical interval time code and some of the newer time code recording techniques, problems with longitudinal time code recording have been all but eliminated—even when a machine is operated in a search mode. In a **search mode** a tape is played back either faster or slower than normal to facilitate the process of finding and marking precise edit points. Typical editing machines can be **jogged** at just a few frames per second or run at between 10 and 50 times normal speed while retaining a recognizable picture on the screen.

longitudinal time code: In contrast to *VITC*, a method of recording digital SMPTE/EBU time code information along the edge of a videotape, generally on an audio track.

search mode: An editing system control that switches a VCR into a shuttle mode so that tape can move forward or backward at varying speeds in order to locate and cue needed segments.

2. During the manufacture of 16mm and 35mm motion picture film, numbers are placed along the edges of the film to facilitate the logging of scenes. In 1991, bar code numbers also started being used. Many liken film edge numbers to SMPTE/EBU time code.

Recording Longitudinal Time Code Longitudinal time code can be recorded (or rerecorded) at any time. If you are recording with a single camera in the field, you may elect to add longitudinal time code as you are taping scenes or later, as you review the footage. Today, professional camcorders can automatically record time code on the tape as the video is shot.

When two or more cameras and tape machines are being used in multiple-camera field production (Chapter 17), it is essential that a common time code be simultaneously sent to all machines as the recordings are made. This is the only way that the machines can later be synchronized for editing. In addition, a specific time code number can be used to cut to any of the tapes at the same precise point in time. This eliminates the possibility of a jump in action when cutting from one tape to another.

Vertical Interval Time Code (VITC)

VITC time code overcomes most of the problems inherent in longitudinal time code. As the name suggests, with VITC the time code information is recorded in the vertical interval of the picture. (This area is normally hidden from view, but it is revealed as the black bar that separates frames when a picture on a TV set loses vertical sync and rolls.) Because VITC is recorded in the vertical interval by the video heads of a recorder, this means that whenever a picture is visible (including when the tape is stopped on a freeze-frame) the time code can be read. Because standard VITC is recorded by the VCR's video heads, it can't be erased the way longitudinal time code can—at least not without having to rerecord the video in the process. In addition to solving problems associated with generational loss and varying tape speeds, there are three other advantages to VITC time code:

- VITC provides indexing down to the individual video fields (1/60-second intervals). This level of accuracy is sometimes needed in doing precise audio and video editing.

- Since the VITC signal doesn't take up an audio track, the track can be used for a number of audio needs in production or editing. Although some formats have a special longitudinal track reserved for time code, others use one of the audio tracks for time code recording.[3]

- Finally, because of error-checking components of the VITC signal, it is highly immune to reading errors caused by tape dropouts.

Although VITC has several advantages, the longitudinal method is simpler, so some video equipment is limited to the longitudinal approach.

Some newer time code recording systems use the VITC data scheme but record the signal in a special digital track. With some of today's professional camcorders, two time code recording systems are used simultaneously. The equipment automatically switches from one to another as necessary to attain the greatest accuracy.

Recording VITC Time Code With the help of either a time code generator built into a VCR or a separate (standalone) time code generator, standard VITC time code is recorded with the original video. These time code numbers can be set to start at any point. Both numeric keypads and small thumbwheel dials are used for setting the numbers. If user bits are not imple-

---

3. Keeping audio tracks free for other purposes can be important. With formats that only provide for two audio tracks, stereo is impossible when one track is taken up with time code. Sometimes it is desirable to put music or effects on a separate audio track. Finally, an extra audio track may be needed for a *scratch track*—audio information intended only as a guide for production and editing.

FIGURE 15.6
On this simple editor the time codes for both the player (source machine) and the edit recorder (editor) are visible. The two large black knobs at either side of the edit controller are used to control variable-speed searches for the source machine and the editor.

mented, you may want to use the hours column of the time code to identify the reel numbers. Hour 01 becomes reel one etc. (This assumes, of course, that the material on the tapes is less than one hour in length.)

How Time Code Is Displayed

There are three ways of displaying time code:

- Small numerical displays are used by some simple time code editors. Although these normally consist of illuminated red or green displays, occasionally, LCD displays are used. In Figure 15.6 you will note that the time codes for both the player (source machine) and the edit recorder (editor) are visible on the edit controller.

- The second method displays the time code numbers over the video itself. In Figure 15.7 the eight-digit time code numbers can be seen at the bottom of the video for both the source machine and the editor.

- Some edit controllers use a high-resolution color monitor to display both the time codes and actual video frames of the in-points and out-points of video (Figure 15.8).

There are two approaches to displaying time code numbers over the picture itself (Figure 15.7). With *keyed-in time code* a character generator is coupled with a time code reader, and the eight-digit code is keyed over the video. In contrast to keyed-in code, which is only temporarily superimposed over the video picture, there is burned-in time code. Instead of two signals being combined as they are displayed, in *burned-in time-code* the video and the numbers are permanently merged into one signal. This is done as a copy of the original footage is made. The resulting **window dub** has a major advantage; it can be played back on any VCR and viewed on a standard TV set. Since only special tape machines are equipped to read and reproduce keyed-in time code, *window burns* (tapes with burned-in time code) represent a major advantage. When it's necessary to review footage away from a production facility, especially on a

keyed-in time code: As opposed to *burned-in time code,* SMPTE time code numbers electronically and temporarily keyed over background video.

burned-in time code: As opposed to *keyed-in time code,* SMPTE/EBU time code numbers that are a permanent part of the corresponding video.

window burn: Window dub. An off-line copy of an original videotape that contains a permanent display of SMPTE/EBU time code.

FIGURE 15.7

One method of displaying time code is to superimpose it over the video itself. Note the eight-digit time code numbers at the bottom of the monitors.

FIGURE 15.8

Some edit controllers use a high-resolution color monitor to display time codes and actual video frames of the in-points and out-points of selected video segments. Special software and hardware for this standard desktop computer turn it into a sophisticated editing system. Note the addition of a special control panel between the keyboard and the computer.

distant location, special equipment doesn't have to be shipped; any tape machine can be used.

With both keyed-in and burned-in time code you are given many options on how you want the code displayed: large numbers, small numbers, white numbers, black numbers, colored numbers, numbers with drop shadows, numbers against a solid background etc. Probably the most legible display is simply white numbers with black borders, where the numbers are just large enough to be seen from the distance you will be viewing the display.

Logging Time Codes

Searching for points on tapes without the aid of time code can be time-consuming and frustrating as you repeatedly go forward and backward looking for various segments. It can be particularly confusing if multiple takes of scenes are on a tape. Since the time code numbers associated with various scenes are (more or less) permanent, it is possible to describe needed segments by simply logging the time codes of starting and ending points (Figure 15.9). Later, you will be able to find a segment either by looking for the time code address or by entering the eight-digit codes into the edit controller and letting the machine find it for you. In the latter case the controller will simply compare the numbers you've entered with the frame currently cued on the tape and either fast-forward or rewind the tape to the desired point. When it finds the time code numbers you entered, the machine will automatically stop with the correct frame cued.

With all this as a background, we can now move to on-line and off-line editing.

ON-LINE AND OFF-LINE EDITING

In on-line editing the original footage is used to create the final edited master. In off-line editing a *copy* of the original footage is used to assemble a *work print,* which is used as a guide in creating the final on-line version. Why divide editing into two seemingly redundant phases?

FIGURE 15.9

The first step in logging time codes is to go through video footage and find the in-points and exit points of needed segments. This is simplified with editing systems that can display video segments on the screen along with time codes and scene descriptions.

Any creative process is time-consuming. Hours are often spent on just a few minutes (or sometimes just a few seconds) of a production. An important part of the editing process is trying out music and effects in a variety of ways to see what works best. Even after a production is seemingly finished, further input from a producer, sponsor or director may necessitate adding, tightening or eliminating segments. This time-consuming process of trial and error can be extremely expensive if full-time engineers and costly, high-quality equipment are involved throughout the entire process. On a per-hour basis, the on-line editing of dramatic productions typically costs more than five times as much per hour as off-line editing. Early in the history of video editing it was found that a great amount of money could be saved if editing was divided into off-line and on-line phases.

Off-Line Editing

rough cut: The initial edit intended to provide a general idea of a production. A kind of rough draft of the final edit.

The purpose of off-line editing is to create a preliminary version (a *rough cut*) of a production from a copy of the original videotape(s). This rough cut is then used as a visual representation of the final on-line production (possibly to show to a client or sponsor) and as a blueprint for creating the final, on-line production. More importantly, time codes determined during the off-line phase are compiled into an edit decision list (*EDL*) that can be used to program the automatic sequencing of on-line editing equipment.

EDL (edit decision list): A handwritten listing or computer printout of time code numbers associated with selected scenes.

In brief, off-line editing has the following advantages:

- It can save a producer a considerable amount of money.
- Since a copy of the original footage is used, there is no worry about damaging original footage.[4]
- A variety of personal computers can be used to do off-line editing.
- Since some off-line systems can print storyboards showing the beginning and ending frames of edits, including notes on accompanying dialogue and effects, a client or advertiser can have hard copy illustrations of what the final product will look like (Figure 15.10).
- Once an off-line EDL is created, it can be loaded into an on-line or off-line editor at a later date and used as a basis for revisions (without the need to re-enter all of the previous editing decisions).
- An EDL can be used with MIDI (see Chapter 6) to automatically control a complete spectrum of audio and music effects.
- The execution of a full range of paint box, electronic graphic and general video effects can be linked with specific time code numbers.
- By using an off-line window burn of a production, footage can be evaluated, and pencil-and-paper EDLs can be created using only a simple consumer VCR.

The first step in the off-line process is to make a copy of the original footage, complete with the original time code. Typically this off-line copy is made on a VHS, S-VHS, Hi8, or ¾-inch machine. The original footage is then put safely away to await the on-line phase of editing.

---

4. In the process of shuttling tapes back and forth, the tape is often stretched, and occasionally even damaged.

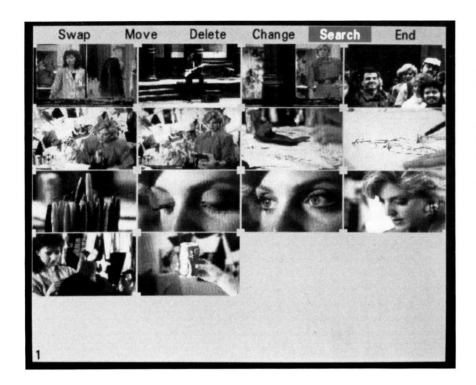

FIGURE 15.10
Many editing systems can print story-boards showing the beginning and ending frames of edits. Notes on accompanying dialogue and effects normally accompany each picture. Here, a storyboard is being assembled from an edited rough cut stored in computer memory. Before editing continues, the storyboard will be printed out on a color printer and given to a client for approval.

On-Line Editing

For short production segments that must be edited quickly or that are only going to be used once, the off-line phase of editing is generally skipped. Television news falls into this category. At their most basic levels, on-line and off-line editing procedures are identical, except that in on-line editing you are working with your original footage, and you end up with your final edited version. As we will see later in the chapter when we discuss on-line editing in more detail, productions that take full advantage of an initial off-line stage allow for much more sophisticated and technically precise editing techniques when they reach their final on-line phase. Regardless of whether you are doing an off-line edit or going directly to the on-line phase, there are a number of techniques you will need to know, starting with logging scenes.

Logging Scenes

Before you can start editing, you need to make a time code listing of your available scenes. This is done by reviewing all of the footage and listing (logging) the beginning and ending time codes on each usable segment. Figure 15.11 shows a form for logging scenes.

During the logging process, the person reviewing the tape can determine which scenes should be rejected (and not logged) because of major problems. At the same time, all acceptable scenes that can conceivably be used should be logged. This will provide the editor with a full range of editing options.

Although many tape logs are filled in by hand, computer programs are also available (see Figure 15.9). Most people who learn to use computers for logging not only feel they are able to log tapes faster, but the results don't suffer from the legibility problems associated with hastily scribbled notes.

FIGURE 15.11

VIDEOTAPE LOG

Production _____ Operator _____ Date: _____ Page __ of __

ORDER	REEL#	START CODE	END CODE	SCENE DESCRIPTION/COMMENTS

THE PAPER-AND-PENCIL EDIT

Once scenes are logged, a **paper-and-pencil edit** can be done. This simply involves reviewing the log and numbering the scenes (in the left-hand column) in the most logical order. If a computer logging system is being used, the scenes can simply be moved around on the screen and assembled in whatever sequence is desired.

Later, the editor may elect to make changes in the order suggested by this so-called pencil-and-paper edit (based on time or script restraints or whatever). Even so, this phase is important. It suggests the basic story outline intended by the reporter, and it provides initial structure to get the off-line process underway.

Figure 15.12 shows the newstape log generated by the homicide scenario covered in the last chapter. After the tape was shot and brought back to the studio, the reporter wrote down the codes and scene descriptions as she reviewed the tape.

Once the scenes are logged, the reporter or editor can do a rough pencil-and-paper edit by writing in the most logical order of the scenes. The numbers shown in the left-hand column of Figure 15.12 indicate the desired sequence for the scenes during editing. (Note that the total number of scenes has been expanded somewhat from the sample shown in Chapter 14.) Once the scenes are

NEWSTAPE LOG

FIGURE 15.12

Story: Elm Street Homicide   Date: 04/23/92   Tape: N159

Reporter: West   Camera: Myers   Page: 1 of

ORDER	START CODE	END CODE	SCENE DESCRIPTION
5	00:04:12:22	00:04:20:02	ECU knife
6	00:04:20:02	00:04:30:00	CU, police picking up knife
2	00:04:30:00	00:04:45:07	loading victim in stretcher
3	00:04:45:07	00:04:56:02	suspect being handcuffed
4	00:04:56:02	00:05:01:27	CU suspect
7	00:05:01:27	00:05:46:12	loading victim in ambulance
8	00:05:46:12	00:06:02:22	policeman questioning man
1	00:06:02:22	00:06:12:28	LS crime scene
--	00:06:12:28	00:06:15:28	pool of blood
9	00:06:15:28	00:06:21:25	WS onlookers
10	00:06:21:25	00:06:32:02	ambulance driving off
11	00:06:32:02	00:06:44:27	CU three bereaved onlookers
12	00:06:44:27	00:06:54:29	police car driving off with suspect
15	00:06:54:29	00:07:01:13	police photographer taking pictures
16	00:07:01:13	00:07:19:24	WS onlookers
14	00:07:19:24	00:07:29:01	CU woman watching
13	00:07:29:01	00:07:39:02	2-shot, two policemen looking at knife

logged and the paper-and-pencil edit is done, the off-line or on-line process can begin.

CREATING EDLs AND NEWS SCRIPTS WITH NOTEBOOK COMPUTERS

For people in news who must prepare EDLs and scripts in a hurry, the current generation of lightweight notebook-sized (or laptop) computers are ideal for this purpose. The time codes and scene descriptions can be logged while viewing the videotape on a monitor. Then the computer can be moved to another (possibly quieter) area while the script is written. If a split screen is used, one-half of the computer screen can be devoted to the word processor for writing the script. The other half of the screen contains the log of the scene descriptions and associated time codes. (A time code calculator, which can be popped up on the screen, will allow you to quickly determine the length of needed segments.)

FIGURE 15.13

EDIT DECISION LIST

Event	Roll	A/V	Play In	Play Out	Record In	Record Out
1	1	AV	01:03:33:10	01:03:46:01	01:04:00:01	01:04:12:23
2	1	AV	01:06:20:01	01:06:56:24	01:04:12:23	01:04:39:17
3	1	V	01:06:47:01	01:06:56:11	01:04:39:17	01:04:48:28
4	1	V	01:07:36:03	01:07:55:24	01:04:48:28	01:05:08:20
5	2	A	04:08:04:10	04:08:09:23	01:05:08:20	01;05:14:04
6	2	A	04:04:53:07	04:05:06:05	01:05:14:04	01:05:57:27
7	1	AV	01:05:11:11	01:05:21:19	01:05:57:27	01:06:08:06
8	1	AV	01:06:45:01	01:06:53:03	01:06:08:06	01:06:16:09
9	1	AV	01:07:06:26	01:07:16:11	01:06:16:09	01:06:26:04

Once the script is finished, you can print out both the time code log for the person doing the videotape editing and a copy of the script. After you view the edited version of the tape, you can bring up the script again on your computer, make adjustments as needed and then feed the final script from your computer directly into the newsroom computer.

PREPARING THE FINAL EDL

Once off-line editing is finished, the edit decision list (EDL) can be cleaned up by the computer to eliminate unwanted gaps and frame overlaps.[5] Then the final EDL can be saved to disk and printed in the form of a hard copy EDL. An abbreviated sample of an EDL is reproduced in Figure 15.13.

The *Event* column refers to the edit number, and the *Roll* is the videotape reel number. The *A* and *V* in the third column indicate that either audio and/or video will be used from the tape. *Play In* and *Play Out* are the time code listings for the in- and out-points for the source (playback) machine segments. *Record In* and *Record Out* time codes represent the start and stop points for the scenes on the edit recorder.

More sophisticated editing systems display EDLs with a corresponding visual display of the in-points and out-points of highlighted segments (Figure 15.14).

The EDL information stored on the computer disk can be fed to any compatible editing machine and all of the edit decisions automatically duplicated. Considering that a one-hour documentary can contain 600 or so edits (each with a reel number, in-point, out-point etc.), having this information in a form that can be read into an editor in a few seconds will save many hours of rekeying (re-entering) all the time code information.

THE EDITING PROCESS

When only straight cuts and fades to black are required, only two VTRs are needed: a source machine for raw footage and an edit recorder where the edited master will be built. A simple two-machine setup, the kind that can be used for

---

5. Some editing systems do this automatically as off-line editing progresses; some require the running of a clean-up program at the end of off-line editing.

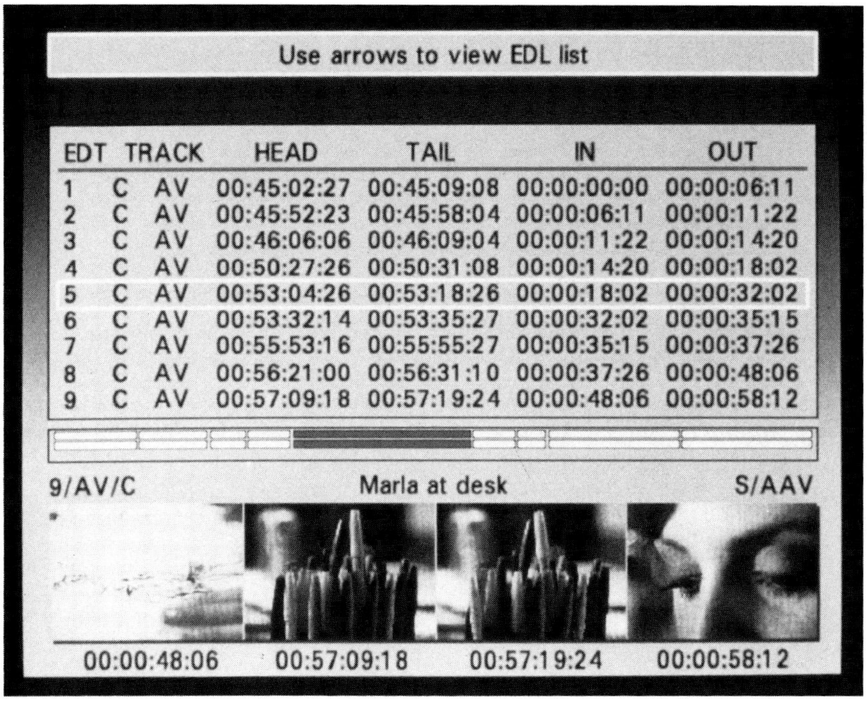

FIGURE 15.14
Before off-line editing can begin, an edit decision list (EDL) must be created. The EDL is used for the automatic sequencing of on-line editing equipment. Sophisticated editing systems display EDLs with the corresponding video for the in-points and out-points of highlighted segments.

basic news and documentary work, is shown in Figure 15.1. Simple, two-machine editing setups do not require time code. In fact, with allowances for some loss of accuracy, control track (non–time code) editing will probably prove faster for doing simple segments.

With only two machines, dissolves, wipes and many special video effects are not possible. For these you need to be able to tie in a video switcher or special-effects unit and be able to overlap multiple sources of video at the same time. It is also at this point that the use of time code becomes essential. In addition to controlling multiple video sources, sophisticated editing units can also be used to control an audio mixer and a variety of audio playback machines.

Assemble Editing

From this overview, we'll now examine the actual editing process. There are two general types of editing: assemble and insert.

In *assemble editing* the edited master is built sequentially, like links on a chain, complete with audio, video and control tracks. This "all-at-once" feature represents both an advantage and a disadvantage. The advantage is that the process is much faster than insert editing. The disadvantage is that since the all-important control track is transferred along with the audio and video, problems will quickly arise from any disruption that takes place when these control pulses are transferred from one tape to another. During playback, any control track disturbance can cause the edited master to suddenly lose color or sync, or cause the picture to roll or break up. Control track problems will also cause speed variations as the playback machine tries to regain synchronization. If music is recorded on the tape, these variations can be quite noticeable.

Because of the possibility of these instability problems under less-than-perfect technical conditions, assemble editing is generally used only when a limited number of edits is required, for example, when splicing together a few

assemble editing: Electronically editing segments onto a tape, one after another, complete with associated control tracks. This contrasts with the method of *insert editing*, where video and audio are recorded onto a tape containing a pre-existing control track.

major program segments. If an assemble edit is done during a fade to black, the chance of problems being visible (or audible) are minimized. The general success of using assemble editing will depend on how good the editing equipment is and on the quality and stability of the control track in the original video footage.

Insert Editing

insert editing: As opposed to *assembly editing,* the editing process that inserts video and audio information over an existing control track.

blanking (blacking) a tape: Recording black, sync and a control track on a videotape. Also called blacking a tape, or creating a crystal tape.

The danger of the control problems is minimized with the more widely used technique of **insert editing**. Here, a continuous, uninterrupted control track is first laid down (recorded) on the edited master even before editing starts. This is done by first recording black or color bars on a segment of the final tape — enough to cover the length (duration) of the piece being created. This process is called **blanking (blacking) a tape**. In recording black or color bars a stable signal source such as a direct feed from a sync generator must be used. On most machines this process cannot be speeded up (it takes 60 minutes to blank a 60-minute tape); tapes are often blanked during lunch breaks.[6] Of course, blanking erases whatever was previously on the tape.

During editing, video from the source machine(s) is then inserted, edit by edit, onto the tape, replacing the black or color bars. The control track is left undisturbed.

Edit controllers have INSert and ASM (assemble) buttons to let the operator select the desired editing mode. It is important not to confuse the two. If you accidentally hit assemble during a normal insert editing session, the original control track on the blanked tape will be erased.

The Pre-Roll Phase

Since multiple machines cannot instantly come up to speed and synchronize, a pre-roll phase is needed. This means that about a five-second head start is required before each edit. The pre-roll phase has definite implications for how productions are shot. If action or dialogue start immediately after the original tape is rolled, this important pre-roll interval will not be possible, which may make the segment impossible to use.

Once the editing machines start from their pre-roll point, the control track pulses or the SMPTE/EBU time code numbers are used by each machine to automatically vary its speed (from about 50 percent above and below normal playback speed) until it gets in sync.

Defining an Edit

As we've noted, in editing a simple production you typically are working with two reels: the reel containing the material you've shot and the (edited master) reel, which will eventually become your finished project. Although to many people the basic editing process seems complicated, in essence it is as easy as finding and entering the following:

- The starting point on the playback reel for the material you want to add
- The starting point for the new material on the edited master
- The stopping point on the edited master[7]

---

6. At least one machine is available that can blank a tape at twice the normal speed.

7. On many machines simply hitting *record* again at the end of the segment stops the machine and enters an end-point time code marker.

When using a control track (non–time code) editor, these edit points are entered by pushing a button at the desired points. Although editing equipment varies in its operation, often these points are entered with buttons labeled *MARK IN* and *MARK OUT*. With time code machines the desired edit points can either be noted by entering the eight-digit codes, or the controller will automatically enter the appropriate time codes when the desired position on the tape is noted. There are four types of edits:

- Audio only
- Video only
- Audio follow video (when both are kept together)
- Split edit, where the audio of a new scene leads the corresponding video by a few seconds

Although audio and video are normally transferred together, there will be many occasions when you will want to record the video separately from the audio. This is commonly done, for example, when you want to continue with the audio from an interview while substituting B-roll video segments. The "Miss New England" ENG piece that follows illustrates this.

EDITING NEWS AND DOCUMENTARY PIECES

Preparing a Typical News Package

A news package is a preproduced, ready-to-run news segment on videotape — typically introduced live by the news anchorperson. ENG pieces often start out with a *stand-up* (or *standupper*). This is where a field reporter (generally standing in front of the news scene) **intros** (introduces) and **extros** (a word coined by the profession referring to the on-camera wrap-up) the segment. Although news has gotten away from the standard 1-2-3 sequence of a (1) stand-up intro, (2) an interview and (3) a stand-up extro, this (rather timeworn) approach is still valuable in illustrating how a simple news package can be shot and assembled.

stand-up (standupper): An on-location shot of a reporter talking to the camera, often used to introduce or conclude a news piece.

In the example to follow, let's assume that after an opening stand-up there is a short sound-on-tape (SOT) interview, and at the end of the interview there is the extro where the field reporter signs off with the standard tag: "This is Mark Mirthful reporting for TV-3."

Let's assume that you were sent to do a 60-second ENG report on Miss Cindy Chimerical, who has just won the title of Miss New England. You are the on-camera reporter and Miss Chimerical has agreed to grant you an afternoon interview . . . in just enough time to edit the piece and get it on the 6 p.m. newscast.

You decide to start the report with a stand-up outside the Abstemious Finishing School, where Miss Chimerical is a student. First, you write out both an opening and a closing to the piece on 3-by-5 cards. The stand-ups, you decide, will be more interesting with some between-class activity in the background; so while you wait for classes to change, you can memorize the stand-up opening and close.

The A-Roll Footage   Once classes start to change, you will have about eight minutes to get good takes of both the intro and extro. The camcorder has been white-balanced, and the shot is framed with the Administration Building in the background. Suddenly, students start emerging from doors, and you have the camera operator roll tape. You wait about seven seconds and tag the piece with an identifying audio slate: "Miss New England intro, take one."

You then wait for a few seconds and start your introduction. If you fluff some words, someone walks in front of the camera, or a motorcycle roars by, obliterating the sound, you can start the whole thing over with the preface: "Miss New England intro, take two." It will save time if you just keep the tape rolling between takes.

When the intro is finished, you find you have time to do the extro. In most circumstances you would find it preferable to record the opening and close after doing the interview; but, since the interview is in the afternoon and the piece needs to be edited before news time, this approach will save time. If something surprising does come out of the interview, you could hurriedly re-do either the intro or the extro before leaving the campus. But you've done your research, and at this point this seems like a pretty predictable story.

Before starting the closing segment, you look over your notes as the camera operator changes the camera angle slightly, reframes, refocuses and rolls tape. Both the intro and extro are recorded on the camcorder's A-roll.

From here, you and your camera operator move the equipment into the library, where Miss Chimerical has agreed to do the interview. The library has strong exterior light coming through windows, and your camera operator decides to use it as a key and back light. A filtered 5,600° K quartz light (which matches the color temperature of the daylight coming through the window) is set up on a stand for a fill (see Figure 15.15).

After Miss Chimerical arrives, a lav mike is clipped to her blouse, and an audio check is made. The camera is white balanced, framed and focused on a close-up. Note in Figure 15.15 that each of the camera angles provides strong, over-the-shoulder shots, rather than the much weaker profile shots associated with a side angle. In the first setup position (camera position #1) the camera is focused on Miss Chimerical. Note that from this angle two shots are possible: a close-up looking almost directly into her line of the vision, and a shot over the shoulder of the interviewer. Although television is a close-up medium, and most of this (rather short) interview should consist of a close-up of Miss Chimerical, the camera operator may elect to add visual variety by zooming back to an over-the-shoulder shot. When the camera position is reversed (camera position #2), the same two shots are possible on the interviewer.

After the tape is rolled, you wait for about five seconds and start asking Miss Chimerical the questions you've prepared. You lead off with a question about her family, which you will probably not use; it's simply designed to get Miss Chimerical to relax a bit in front of the camera. All of her responses will be recorded on the A-roll. As the interview progresses you make a note of two things that can be illustrated with B-roll cutaways: she regularly plays basketball to keep in shape, and she has been working this term as a teacher's aide.

The B-Roll Footage   Once your questions are answered, the B-roll cassette is inserted into the camcorder and it is moved about 150 degrees (camera position #2) to get reverse-angle shots of you re-asking each question. This time, of course, the lav mike is on you, rather than Miss Chimerical. Your subject consents to stay in the same place, providing reverse-angle, over-the-shoulder shots. Since most guests are not familiar with the single-camera technique of re-asking each of the interview questions for the B-roll, you caution Miss Chimerical to refrain from answering your questions. If your guest didn't have the time to stay through the recording of the B-roll questions, the camera operator could just hold a close-up on you as you asked the questions. (To match up the camera shots and angles in the latter case, it would be important that the interviewer address questions to the exact space previously occupied by the guest.)

For editing purposes, it is important to leave a pause of several seconds

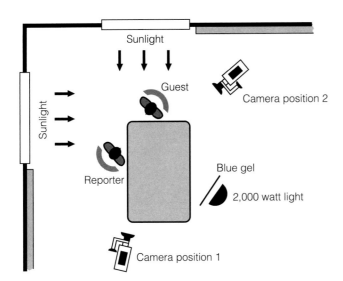

FIGURE 15.15
Since the library has strong exterior light coming through windows, you can use it for both a key and back light effect for these subjects. You will need to set up a strong 5,600° K light to fill the resulting shadows. A blue gel or dichroic filter over an incandescent light will match its color temperature to that of the exterior light. Note that the lighting arrangement will work for both camera positions.

between each question. Ideally, when the piece is edited, Miss Chimerical's answers can be assembled in such a way that the questions will be obvious and therefore unnecessary. To include them will simply slow down the interview. Just the same, you'll want to tape them. Once you start editing the piece, you may find that one or more of the questions ends up being essential to make sense out of Miss Chimerical's answers.

Although the interview is seemingly over at this point, there are still three things left to shoot on the B-roll. First, 15 or so seconds of "noddies." This is footage of you (the interviewer) just looking at Miss Chimerical (or, if she has to leave, looking at the place where she was). Depending upon the interview, you can register subtle expressions appropriate to the content—interest, concern, a humorous reaction or whatever. These reverse-angle cutaways will be important in covering edits. Next, you may elect to shoot 10 or 15 seconds of two-shot silent footage over the shoulder of Miss Chimerical as you look on and she talks (about anything at all that will result in appropriate head movements). The latter, which does not show Miss Chimerical's face, can also be used to cover an edit as she speaks. (Since this is a short interview, you probably won't need both of these.) Finally, your camera operator should record 10 to 15 seconds of *room tone* (ambient background sound that exists when no one is speaking). This is recorded simultaneously on all three (one mono and two stereo) audio tracks. We'll discuss the function of room tone later. Although you will probably only use a small portion of this after-the-interview footage during editing, there seems to be a Murphy's law that governs this whole phase: *You'll always seem to find an indispensable need for whatever footage you fail to get!*

At this point you'll need to move on to the B-roll cutaway shots. The first will be a short sequence of Miss Chimerical assisting a teacher in a classroom. Your camera operator should get at least two camera angles on this. To cover the basketball angle, you get Miss Chimerical to find one of her friends for a brief one-on-one session in the gym. On both of these segments the camera operator should use the built-in stereo mic on the camcorder to get general background sound.

This finishes up the taping at the school. Once you're back at the station, you can dig through the news cooperative footage from the night before and find the story on Miss Chimerical's coronation. At this point you have all the elements for your ENG package:

room tone: The ambient sound present in a room, recorded during original taping and used during editing to add needed intervals of "silence" between edits. It is important in maintaining the audio atmosphere existing at a location.

A-roll

A-1.   The stand-up intro to the piece

A-2.   The stand-up extro to the piece

A-3.   Miss Chimerical's answers to your questions

B-roll

B-1.   All of your questions to Miss Chimerical

B-2.   Your silent reaction shots

B-3.   An over-the-shoulder shot of Miss Chimerical

B-4.   Library room tone on both the mono and stereo tracks

B-5.   Footage of Miss Chimerical helping a teacher

B-6.   Shots in the gym of the one-on-one basketball session

C-roll

C-1.   Shots of the coronation

C-2.   Shots of Miss Chimerical walking down the ramp

Armed with these three tapes, you find a playback machine with a SMPTE/EBU time code recorder.

First you watch the A-roll footage of Miss Chimerical's answers to your questions. As you view the tapes you fill out a paper-and-pencil EDL listing a description and the starting and ending time codes of the best segments. (This is similar in form to Figure 15.12.) You then do a bit of time code math and discover that you have almost two minutes of footage. Since you've only been given one minute for the whole package, you draw a line through the interview segments that seem less important. Although it's still too long, you'll be able to condense some of Miss Chimerical's comments during editing. During this "pruning process" you are careful to keep references to your cutaway footage: the coronation, being a teaching assistant and playing basketball.

Putting in the B-roll, you find the good takes of the intro and extro. You write in the starting codes and the total times. You now have about 53 seconds. In order to keep an appropriate transition between two of Miss Chimerical's answers, you decide you will probably have to use at least one of your on-camera questions.

After logging that on the B-roll, you review the footage of Miss Chimerical helping a teacher and enter the beginning codes of two short segments. Next come the shots in the gym. Finally, you put in the C-roll and review the footage of the coronation. Since the reference to the coronation in the interview was brief, you log the codes on two short segments: the moment of the actual coronation and a few seconds of Miss Chimerical walking down the platform with a bouquet of roses.

With the codes noted on the A, B and C-rolls, it's off to the on-line editing bay. Since by this time it will probably be only a short time before the news broadcast, the videotape editor will probably be backlogged with several other pieces for the night's news. You will have to take your turn. (In small production facilities you will have to do your own editing.) When the time for your editing session comes, you can give the editor a copy of your rough paper-and-pencil EDL, and things can get underway. In outline form, here is the complete (but tentative) sequence for the ENG package:

1.   The stand-up introduction

2.   Miss Chimerical's first interview response, talking about her coronation, over which you will insert

a. video footage (with low background audio) of the coronation, and

b. video footage (with low background audio) of her walk down the runway

3. Your question on extracurricular activities

4. Miss Chimerical's answer to the extracurricular activity question, over which you will insert

a. two shots of Miss Chimerical helping a teacher, and

b. shots of the one-on-one basketball session

5. Your closing extro

In the interest of making smoother transitions, or to add visual variety to the piece, the videotape editor may decide to change some things on your paper-and-pencil edit. The amount of sprucing up that can be done will depend on how much time the editor has. Feature and soft news pieces differ from hard news in this regard. Since soft news and feature pieces can normally be done during slack hours (well ahead of the news deadlines), more editing time can be devoted to them. For this reason, these pieces often display more editing refinement and creativity. Since Miss New England was crowned the night before, and the producer wants to get the package on the evening's news, it is treated like any other news piece.

Linear Editing Procedures

Using the Miss New England piece as an example, at this point we can look at the step-by-step procedures involved in linear editing. Starting with a blanked tape containing SMPTE/EBU time code, the videotape editor first cues in the tape about 10 seconds. Tapes need to be cued in a few feet before being used because over time the first few feet undergo severe wear as they are repeatedly threaded into machines. Within a short time this area will exhibit dropouts and other problems.

The first segment on the tape will be countdown leader. This is similar to Academy Leader in film, which flashes numbers in one-second intervals from 10 to 3. In video the leader commonly ends with 2. After the 2 appears, the screen blanks out for two seconds. When the tape is played back on the preview monitor in the control room it will be possible to switch to the tape exactly two seconds after the number 2 disappears from the screen. After that, the first scene of the ENG piece should immediately appear.

Initial Procedures for Full-length Programs If the on-line editing session is designed to create a full-length program and not just a short ENG piece, two additional things will be recorded on the edited master before the countdown leader. First, it is standard practice to record 60 seconds of bars and tone (electronic test pattern, or ETP, and a 1,000 Hz audio tone recorded at zero dB).[8] (See Figure 15.16.) This allows those playing back the tape at a later

8. Audio recorded in Dolby stereo, surround-sound or other audio enhancing systems may use a slightly different approach.

FIGURE 15.16

For recording full-length programs, a basic sequence is followed at the beginning of each tape. First, it is standard practice to record from 30 to 60 seconds of bars and tone (electronic test pattern, or ETP, and a 1,000 Hz audio tone recorded at zero dB). This allows those playing back the tape at a later time to adjust equipment for the audio and video levels and the color balance represented by the tape. After the ETP, the tape goes to black and silence, and the second item, an audio and video slate, is recorded. The slate, which will generally be about 10 seconds, will visually and aurally identify the program with several types of information: the title of the program or series, the number of the program (if it has one), the director and the date of recording and the planned air date (if there is one). At this point the countdown leader starts, indicating one-second intervals from 10 to 2. After the 2, there are two seconds of black and silence. Immediately following this, the program starts.

Bars and tone	Black	Slate	Count down	Black	Start of program
60 seconds	Up to 10 sec.	About 10 sec.	10 sec.	2 sec.	

time to adjust their equipment for the audio and video levels and color balance represented by the tape.

After the ETP the tape goes to black and silence for a few seconds, the second item, an audio and video slate, is recorded. The slate will visually and aurally identify the program with several types of information: the title of the program or series, the number of the program (if it has one), the director and the date of recording and the planned air date (if there is one). Since both the ETP and slate are a normal part of the original videotape recording, they can simply be transferred over to the edited master.[9] For short news pieces, however, a slate and ETP are seldom recorded.

Continuing with our Miss New England news package, after the number 2 on the countdown leader disappears from the screen, the operator lets the tape roll in black for exactly two seconds and enters the starting point of the first insert edit. In our example this will be the start of the stand-up intro to the Miss New England piece. Using your paper-and-pencil EDL as a guide, the video editor can quickly switch back and forth between your A-roll, B-roll and C-roll tapes to find and cue needed segments. After each segment is found and checked, its in-point and out-point are entered into the edit controller. The in-point (starting point) for each new segment on the recorded master (final edited) tape must also be entered in the edit controller. The out-point on the edited master is generally not necessary, since you can just stop the machine when you see that the full segment has been recorded. Although equipment will vary, time code machines normally have *set in* and *set out* buttons to electronically record the time code start and stop points for each edit. When you are entering editing decisions "on the fly," with non–time code equipment, *mark in* and *mark out* buttons will be used. These controls apply to both the source machine(s) and the edit recorder.

A *preview button* on the edit controller will allow you to take a look (and adjust) each proposed edit prior to actually recording it on the edited master. **Trim controls** make it possible to automatically add or subtract frames from these tentative edit decisions without having to enter a new start or stop point. (At 30 frames per second, dropping 15 frames from a scene will reduce its length by one-half second; adding seven frames will add a quarter second, etc.) It is best to allow each segment on the edited master to run a bit long. It will be trimmed to the exact length needed as the next edit is made.

Let's assume that at this point we now have the countdown leader, two seconds of black and the stand-up introduction recorded on our master tape. The next thing is to record the first segment of the interview. We want to start with Miss Chimerical talking about the coronation the night before. (This will be important in setting up the piece, as well as giving everyone a chance to see the consummate moment.) Since you know that the C-roll footage runs about eight seconds, you need to hold Miss Chimerical's references to that time.

Unfortunately, the answer to your question (in which she talks about both the crowning and her walk down the ramp afterward) runs 39 seconds. That obviously presents a problem—albeit only a temporary one. It will be necessary to cut out several parts of Miss Chimerical's dialogue to bring the references to the crowning and the walk down the ramp closer together so they will later coincide with the C-roll footage. You and the editor find that you can cut out numerous peripheral comments and bring the total segment time to about eight seconds. Obviously, making these edits results in some visual jump cuts where the segments were deleted, but these will be later covered with the C-roll coronation footage. Right now you are only interested in the A-roll audio.

trim control: A control on an editor that makes it possible to add or delete a specified number of frames to an edit point.

---

9. Some postproduction facilities prefer to rerecord a new ETP instead of simply copying it from the original tape.

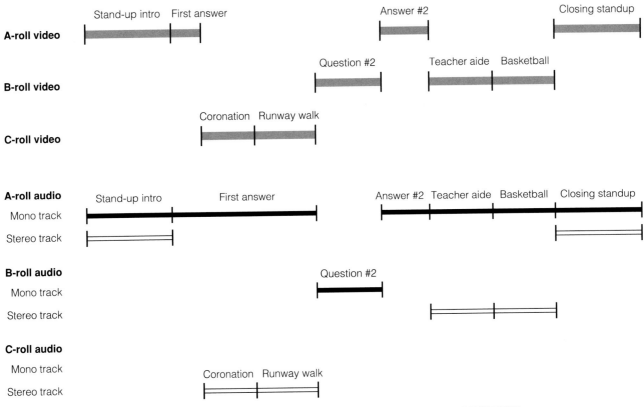

FIGURE 15.17

The sequence of the various video and audio elements in the Miss New England ENG package is illustrated here. Note that the video and the audio (including both the mono and the stereo tracks) are from three videotapes: an A-roll, B-roll and C-roll.

In making the deletions, you must be careful not only to retain the essence of Miss Chimerical's comments, but in no way distort what she said. Significantly misrepresenting what someone says through editing can result in anything from a future lack of cooperation to a lawsuit.[10]

After doing this A-roll segment, you can move onto comments about Miss Chimerical's plans for the year, including her finishing college. This brings up her life at the Abstemious Finishing School, so the A-roll on her comments on being a teacher's aide can be cued. Since there is no natural audio transition into this, the editor cues up your audio and video B-roll question to introduce it. After that, about 10 seconds of A-roll footage of Miss Chimerical's response about her work as a teacher's aide can be used. The video portion of this will later be covered by B-roll footage of her at work. Again, Miss Chimerical's comments must be condensed. The resulting jump cuts will later be covered by B-roll footage (Figure 15.17).

Room Tone

Sometimes, it is necessary to create a pause in narration. This might be appropriate for signaling a major transition, or to simply allow the B-roll video to continue without interruption. Although it would seem that pauses in narration would mean total silence in the audio, this is seldom the case. On most locations (including many "silent" TV studios) there is general, low-level background

10. A young woman in California threatened a TV station with a lawsuit when she felt that the reporter's questions and her answers were edited together in such a way as to distort the meaning of her comments.

sound called *room tone,* which only becomes obvious when it suddenly disappears. Room tone is especially important in stereo and when the general level of ambient sound on the location is high. Rather than suddenly cutting to absolute silence, most editors will splice in room tone to discretely bridge these pauses. Such refinements are even more important now that many TV sets have high-quality sound systems.

Let's assume that at this point in editing the Miss New England piece, the editor decides to depart from the expected a bit by cutting away from the interview narration for a few seconds and going directly to the basketball session, complete with background sound. After holding the audio for a few seconds, it is faded under and Miss Chimerical's voice comes in explaining that she keeps physically fit by playing basketball. During the concluding seconds of her comments the editor cuts back to a close-up of Miss Chimerical.

Now all that's left is your stand-up extro (wrap-up) to the story. That runs 10 seconds. A running check of the edited segments to this point shows about 50 seconds; thus, with the 10-second extro, things should work out just about right. (They can easily do that in textbook examples!)

If the piece runs long, you have two choices: request more time for the piece, or cut it down. If it's a heavy news day or you are close to the deadline (and everything has been tightly scheduled), it will probably be safer to just look for a segment in the package to drop. Assuming that the piece was 15 or 20 seconds over, you could package it in two versions: with the teaching aide section for the early newscast and a second version with the basketball segment for the late-night news. (In the latter case you would want to make some other changes anyway to give viewers of the later newscasts a fresh perspective.)

Assuming you now have the segment at about 50 seconds, you can edit in the stand-up extro. After this there should be about ten seconds of black. (Otherwise, if the tape is not immediately cut during the broadcast, you risk getting some inappropriate video or audio on the air.)

Adding Cutaway and Insert Shots

At this point all of the A-roll footage has been recorded (including a short question from the B-roll). Now the cutaway shots (and in some cases insert shots) from the B- and C-rolls can be added. These will primarily be video-only insert edits that will leave the existing audio narration undisturbed. However, for the sake of added realism, it will be best if at least two of the insert edits carry low background audio. This will have to be recorded on a second audio track.

Splitting Audio From Video

In making edits, you will often not want to transfer the audio and video together. For example, in many documentaries and dramatic scenes the audio from an upcoming segment precedes the video. This is referred to as a **split edit,** or an **L-cut.** To accommodate this need, editing equipment has an A/V option. If you want to record only video, you can go with the V-only option; if you want the audio and no video, you can set the edit for audio only. In the interview with Miss Chimerical, you'll be making a number of video-only edits as you insert the B-and C-roll cutaway footage over the continuing audio of the interview.

In the B-roll footage of the one-on-one basketball session and the coronation footage, you may elect to bring in very low audio under Miss Chimerical's voice (assuming it has general background sound and not narration). If this background audio was recorded in stereo, it will add an element of realism to the cutaway segments. The audio mix can be handled in two ways.

First, for the intro you can use three audio tracks on the edited master tape. One track will contain a monophonic recording of questions, answers and commentary. The second track is stereo and will consist of all background sound in the piece: the general sound behind the opening and closing narration, the background sound from the C-roll coronation footage and sound in the B-roll classroom and gym footage. When the videotape is broadcast, an audio engineer (using a well-marked script for a guide) can mix the audio from mono (voice) and stereo (background sound) tracks together.

Second, if single stereo mics were used during all the voice segments, the audio engineer can mix the basic stereo track with B-roll stereo as the piece is broadcast. (This same basic procedure would be used in monophonic audio.) Both of these approaches require that the A-roll, and the B- and C-roll, audio be recorded on different audio tracks on the edited master.

The fastest way to prepare a news piece is to leave the various audio sources unmixed on two or more tracks of the videotape and have an audio engineer mix them live as the piece is broadcast. For a piece that will only be used once, the time involved in making a more complete mix during editing may be unnecessary. But in the pressure of a live broadcast, instructions can get garbled, concentration can lapse, or technical problems can suddenly emerge. At this point pessimists (some would say realists) are quick to quote Murphy's first law of live television: *If anything* **can** *go wrong it* **will** *go wrong.* (Some authorities add at the end: *and, at the worst possible moment.*) These people prefer to remove some of element of risk by mixing down all audio tracks onto a basic stereo track before broadcast.

Adding Narration

In producing many ENG packages, voice-over narration by a reporter will be appropriate. With the help of a video monitor, this narration is sometimes read live by the reporter as the piece is aired. An audio engineer can then mix the live narration with the appropriate audio on the videotape. Doing narration live assumes nothing will go wrong and that timing will be perfect—which, as we've noted, is never a safe assumption in live television. It is much better to have the announcer record the narration on a programmable DAT or audio cart prior to the start of the editing session (Figure 15.18). During editing the audio segments

FIGURE 15.18

Rather than do narration live, it is safer to have the announcer record the narration on a programmable DAT or audio cart prior to the start of the editing session. During editing the prerecorded audio segments are "rolled" into the piece as needed. This approach also makes it possible to backtime narration so that the audio cuts end precisely at the start of sound bites — something that's very difficult when narration is done live.

are "rolled" into the piece as needed. In both cases time code numbers on the videotape can be used to trigger the prerecorded audio at precise points. In addition to being safer, this approach makes it possible to backtime sound so that the audio cuts end precisely at the start of sound bites—something that's very difficult when narration is done live. Many edit controllers can be programmed to fade audio levels in and out during playback. (The levels are determined and programmed into the editing sequence during the preview process.)

Producing the audio portion of a news package can, in many instances, be more demanding than producing the video portion. Because the narration is often the backbone of an ENG package, some news producers and videotape editors find it easier to start with a complete audio track of music and narration and then cut the video to the audio.

RANDOM-ACCESS EDITING

Although most of the pre-editing work will be the same for linear and random-access editing, there are a number of procedural differences.

If we were using random-access editing, we would prepare for the session by transferring all the time coded segments we think we might need onto the editing system's hard or recordable optical disk. These segments are entered with both time code numbers and scene descriptions. In some networked facilities this transfer can be done from playback machines outside of the editing area. When this can be done, valuable editing time (and operator expertise) will not be tied up for this routine and time-consuming process.

Once all the scenes have been transferred into the editing system, they can be called up and listed in an index on the screen. With the help of a mouse or trackball, the first step will be to "tag" several of the initial video and audio segments so they can be displayed on the screen (Figure 15.19). Many systems use a relatively low resolution freeze-frame of the opening (and sometimes closing frames) of each tagged segment. The fewer the scenes displayed, the

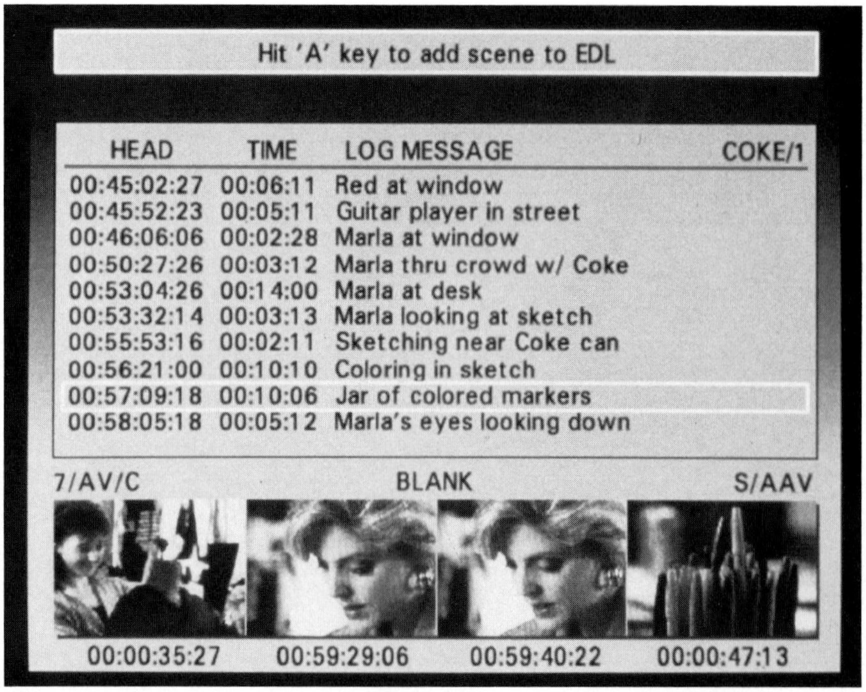

FIGURE 15.19

Once all the scenes have been transferred into a computer-based editing system, they can be listed on the screen by time-code and a short descriptive statement. With the help of mouse or track ball, the needed scenes can then be "tagged" for use and added to an edit decision list (EDL). Many editing systems can display a freeze-frame of the beginning and ending of each segment.

		Hit 'A' key to add scene to EDL	
HEAD	TIME	LOG MESSAGE	COKE/1
00:45:02:27	00:06:11	Red at window	
00:45:52:23	00:05:11	Guitar player in street	
00:46:06:06	00:02:28	Marla at window	
00:50:27:26	00:03:12	Marla thru crowd w/ Coke	
00:53:04:26	00:14:00	Marla at desk	
00:53:32:14	00:03:13	Marla looking at sketch	
00:55:53:16	00:02:11	Sketching near Coke can	
00:56:21:00	00:10:10	Coloring in sketch	
00:57:09:18	00:10:06	Jar of colored markers	
00:58:05:18	00:05:12	Marla's eyes looking down	

7/AV/C   BLANK   S/AAV

00:00:35:27   00:59:29:06   00:59:40:22   00:00:47:13

larger they can be—and the easier it will be to see details. Without the ability to see needed detail, it is possible to inadvertently do something like cut to a person when they have their eyes closed. The number and clarity of the scenes that can be displayed on the editing screen at one time (as well as the basic editing procedures) depend upon the editing system.

Once the segments are visible on the screen, you will need to go through the sequence of steps required by the software to assemble the audio and video elements in the desired order. Unlike linear editing, these decisions reside entirely in the electronic memory of the editing system. This means they can be instantly rearranged, adjusted and previewed.

With random-access (non-linear) editing, there is no need to go back later and do the insert edits or cutaways; they can all be programmed into the sequence as you go. Once you are satisfied with the result, it can be transferred from memory onto a videocassette for broadcast or distribution.

DIGITAL EDITING

Digital recording and playback, which is used in both linear and random-access editing, has many advantages. In addition to superior audio and video quality, digital machines allow for the *layering* of video effects (repeatedly adding one video effect on top of another until you achieve the desired result). Being able to layer effects without an appreciable loss in quality is important in elaborate **matting** effects, where various video sources are used to build composite pictures through repeatedly recording, manipulating and rerecording the results.

layering: Adding video effect sequences over existing video-effect footage to create more complex effects.

Since digital recorders also have the ability to play back and record simultaneously, basic editing is also possible—without using an editor. This means that electronic graphics, titles, basic effects and cutaways can be added to existing video without going through the editing process. Of course, the disadvantage is that this technique allows no margin of error. If a problem develops, it is permanently recorded, and unless you have a backup copy of the original footage (always a good idea!) there may be no way of undoing the mistake.

The same ability to repeatedly rerecord without a loss in quality also applies to digital audio. This means that you can manipulate existing audio and use the same basic layering techniques used in video. With audio, however, there is an important safety factor. Since digital recorders have multiple audio tracks, you don't need to destroy one audio track in the process of creating another. If a mistake is made, you can always move back to the previously recorded audio and try again.

Time Compression and Expansion

Digital tape machines also make it possible to speed up or compress material as it's played back. To avoid a pitch change in the audio during this process, digital equipment regularly "pulls out" minute segments of audio data. A 60-minute production can be "shrunk down" to about 48 minutes, for example—creating just enough extra time to add commercials. Beyond about a 20 percent reduction, the effects become noticeable.

Time can be expanded in the same way—up to about 20 percent without becoming noticeable.[11] Beyond that, a "slow motion" effect starts to become apparent in video, and audio starts to drag. Of course, when slow motion *is*

11. When familiar music is involved in the audio track, the percentage of change possible may be considerably less than 20 percent.

desirable, video time can be expanded or slowed down right up to the point of stopping motion with a freeze-frame.

ON-LINE CONSIDERATIONS

In the Miss New England piece we needed to get things done as quickly as possible; therefore, we skipped off-line and went directly to on-line editing. This is standard practice in news. However, as we've pointed out, in critical editing applications an off-line step offers many advantages. You will recall that the goal of the off-line session is to create three things:

- An EDL (generally on a $3\frac{1}{2}$- or $5\frac{1}{4}$-inch computer disk) in a format that can be read into the on-line system
- A hard copy printout of the EDL
- A cassette of the completed off-line production, which will serve as an aural and video blueprint for the final on-line edit

However, on-line time is expensive, and before we rush out the door to the on-line facility, we need to make sure our EDL is accurate.

Compensating for Off-Line Problems

There are a number of things that can cause problems and delays during the off-line session. First, in indicating a dissolve, wipe or special effect while using a cuts-only off-line editor, you must remember to allow enough footage on the A- and B-rolls. Let's say you want a 64-frame (slow) dissolve. First, even though the off-line linear editor (because of its limitations) may only show a cut at this point, you must remember there is a three-second overlap between the A-roll and the B-roll footage. With your off-line tape showing a cut just before footage ends or a bad camera jump occurs, you may end up with some unexpected results in the on-line dissolve. Therefore, you must check to see that there is good footage on both video sources for the duration of any video effect.

In building the off-line EDLs, time code errors inevitably creep in. These generally have to do with code gaps between segments, overlapping frames between edits, errors in logging lap dissolves and wipes, etc. Although these problems may go unnoticed on the off-line version, they will cause definite problems when carried over to on-line. Some off-line editors do not automatically correct these errors, and the EDL must be "cleaned up" with the help of a special computer program. A clean EDL will save considerable time (and expense) during the on-line phase.

In an ideal world, you should be able to take a copy of any off-line computer disk to any on-line facility and have it quickly read into the on-line editor. Unfortunately, in this not-so-ideal world there are several incompatible EDL standards in use. You should make sure that the EDL standard you are using will be compatible with the on-line system you intend to use. (Even though you should have a hard copy time code printout of your off-line decisions, having someone re-key them all into a new system standard is a time-consuming and costly process.) Fortunately, most editing systems are able to save EDLs in more than one standard.

The Trace Capability In analog editing it is important to use the original audio tapes and videotapes in the on-line session. But in finding all the original recordings for the on-line session, there can be a problem. When the audio and video used for the off-line edit has gone through several generations of time code transfers, you can lose track of the time codes on the original audio or video segments. (New codes will have replaced the original codes in subsequent versions.) Without the original time code to go by, trying to find a short segment in one of several two- or four-hour cassettes is like trying to find a needle in a haystack—not most people's idea of a good time! To help solve such problems, many editing systems have a **trace capability** that keeps internal time code records on previously used EDLs. Although these normally aren't printed out on the current EDL, they can be accessed with trace software if needed. If you need to depend upon the trace feature, you should make sure that these time code records are not lost in converting data from one editing system to another.

A final word about the off-line version of a production. In video production it is a good idea, if time allows, to put the off-line version of the production aside for a few days—and then come back and look at it again. During lengthy off-line sessions editors can become "too close" to a production. Time provides an important fresh perspective—closer to that of the audience when they see the production for the first time. This new perspective will generally suggest a number of editing changes that should be made before the production goes on to the final on-line session.

Preparing On-Line Materials

In order to mix together two audio or video signals, they must be simultaneously played back from two tapes. If these sources were originally recorded on the same tape, you have a problem. In this case you must dub (copy) part of the footage to a different cassette and create a B-roll. During the on-line phase these two sources will be rolled at the same time and mixed together. Occasionally, you may even need to have three sources mixed at one time, which will require A-, B- and C-rolls.

Taking the Off-Line EDL to the On-Line Phase

We'll assume at this point that you have done the following:

- Reached agreement on the off-line editing decisions with the key people involved

- Built an off-line, time coded version of your show that will act as an on-line reference

- Cleaned up and revised the off-line EDL so that it lists the time codes from all of the original audio and video sources

- Made a record (floppy disk) of the EDL in the format required by the on-line facility

- Made accurate time code notes on all video and audio effects that must be added during the on-line session

- Made notes on corrections that must be made: color balancing, audio sweetening, significant audio or video level changes etc.

- Put any video or audio that must be mixed together (as in a lap dissolve or an audio mix or cross-fade) on separate reels

- Gathered all of the original tapes and audio sources necessary for the final edited master of the show

With all this taken care of, it's off to the on-line session.

Since on-line time is expensive, you will want to resist making changes at this point. Many on-line production facilities will provide suggestions to improve your production—which you will want to at least seriously consider. The

FIGURE 15.20
Only by spending many hours doing editing can a person move beyond the technology of editing to the art of editing. The sought-after video editors — the ones who win Emmy awards for their work — learn the operation and capabilities of their equipment so well that they are able to totally concentrate on the creative potential of the editing process.

major creative phase of your work should be done when you turn your tapes and EDL over to the on-line facility. At this point you just may be called on to make decisions on problems you didn't foresee. As on-line editing progresses, you will want to carefully follow audio sweetening, video corrections and effects and other on-line elements to make sure they end up the way you envisioned them. If you have done your job in the off-line phase, the final on-line phase should go smoothly.

Audio Sweetening

Although you can sometimes do some simple audio mixing during the off-line editing, real audio sweetening and mixing will have to wait until the on-line phase. Here audio levels can be evened out, frequency response and presence (within limits) can be matched between segments, and sound effects can be added. Since most shows are now done in stereo, the final stereo mix will also be done during the on-line session.

When your production emerges from the on-line session, it should conform to the off-line version; in addition, it should include all special effects, titles, credits and video and audio corrections and improvements. In short, within production-time and budget constraints, it should be as good as you can make it and ready for broadcast, duplication or distribution.

Editors vs. Technicians

As you've undoubtedly begun to realize after reading these two chapters on editing, the editing phase of production can be the most important of all. Just as a ball game can be won or lost during the last inning or quarter, the success or failure of a production can be decided during this final, all-important phase.

Many technicians can efficiently operate editing equipment, but there are few skilled and creative editors. These are the men and women who, over time, have developed an almost intuitive understanding of the audio and video communication process (Figure 15.20). The sought-after video editors — the ones who win Emmy awards for their work—learn the operation and capabilities of their equipment so well that they are able to totally concentrate on the creative potential of the editing process. Only by spending many hours doing editing can a person move beyond the technology of editing to the art of editing.

SUMMARY

In basic editing two videotape machines, called a source machine and an edit recorder, are electronically controlled by an edit controller. The person doing the editing uses the edit controller to find each segment, mark the beginning and ending edit points and perform the actual edit. In the editing process, segments can be rearranged and shortened, audio can be added, and a wide range of special effects can be introduced.

Time code (SMPTE/EBU time code) is an eight-digit numerical code that can electronically and visually identify each individual frame in a video production—in some cases to an accuracy of 1/60 second. Because of its many advantages over control track editing, time code editing is widely used today in both audio and video postproduction. Drop-frame time code, which compensates for the difference between 60 Hz video standards and the NTSC color standard, is used in network productions and in any application requiring split-second accuracy. Time code can be recorded longitudinally along an audio-type track on the edge of the videotape, or it can be encoded within the video signal.

The editing process is commonly divided into on-line and off-line phases, although, to save time, news and documentary work normally skip the off-line phase. Off-line editing, which is designed to develop an edit decision list (EDL) and a small-format videotape "blueprint" for the final on-line phase, is important in doing high-quality, creative production. A variety of desktop and laptop personal computers can be programmed to do off-line editing. The EDL, which is created during the off-line session, is used to program editing equipment for the final on-line session. Although audio sweetening (fixing audio problems, adding music and effects and doing the final stereo mix-down) is sometimes done by an on-line facility, in high-end professional production, audio sweetening is left to a facility specializing in sound work.

Before insert editing occurs, the edited master must first be blanked, or blacked, by recording black on the tape. Digital editing equipment has many advantages over analog, including the ability to go through many generations of effects without adversely affecting audio or video quality. Digital machines also allow for time compression and expansion up to about 20 percent without, in most cases, any negative effects on subject matter.

Single-camera, on-location interviews are typically shot with an A-roll containing the answers to the interviewer's questions and a B-roll containing reverse-angle shots of the reporter asking the questions, plus insert shots, cutaways and room tone.

KEY TERMS

assemble editing	edit recorder
blanking (blacking) a tape	EDL (edit decision list)
burned-in time code	extro
control track	hard copy
control track editing	insert editing
drop-frame time code	intro
edit controller	jogged

keyed-in time code
layering
L-cut
longitudinal time code
matting
paper-and-pencil edit
room tone
rough cut
search mode
source machine

split edit
stand-up (standupper)
time code
time code generator
trace capability
trim control
user bits
window burn
window dub

ENG and Single-Camera, Film-Style Production

16

DEVELOPMENTS LEADING TO ENG

To understand the present status of ENG (electronic news gathering) we need to briefly trace its evolution. In the 1970s, small, portable television cameras and tape machines were being widely used in non-broadcast applications, but they were not suitable for over-the-air broadcasting. In contrast to the large studio cameras and 1,000 pound, 2-inch, quad tape machines, these small cameras and recorders could not meet the technical requirements of the Federal Communications Commission (FCC). But the development of a "little black box" changed that. The time-base corrector or TBC took the less-than-perfect signals from the small, non-broadcast-quality equipment and reprocessed them (primarily stabilizing their timing pulses) to bring them up to FCC broadcast standards. Suddenly, a whole new arena of equipment was available to broadcasters, especially broadcast journalists who needed small, lightweight and highly portable equipment. The TBC revolutionized television newsgathering and introduced ENG, or electronic news gathering.[1]

Although newsfilm had been highly developed for covering news, it had two weaknesses: it required time-consuming processing, and it did not allow for the live coverage of events. When ENG hit the scene, it was quickly realized that the audience liked both the feeling of live coverage and the realistic atmosphere of non-studio reporting. As a result, stations initially seemed to be covering things live just for the sake of being "live from the scene." Minor news stories, stories that would have been ignored with film, were highlighted just because they could be covered live.

1. Some production facilities, such as NBC, initially preferred the term *electronic journalism,* or *EJ.*

As with any new toy, the novelty soon wore off, and stations started to regain their news perspective. When things settled down, stations were covering an average of 30 percent more field stories than they had been with film, and in about the same amount of time. Some stations began scheduling two live news feeds from a field reporter within a single, 30-minute newscast. The reporter might do one live report toward the beginning of the newscast, and then the ENG crew would tear down the camera and microwave link and quickly move to another part of town. With luck, they would be able to set up the equipment at the new location, establish a good microwave path and go on live with the second story during the last part of the newscast. The fact that luck didn't always hold introduced another requirement: the need to reorganize a newscast while it was being broadcast. When a live ENG segment runs long because of unexpected developments, or when a report is canceled because the story doesn't develop as expected, the rest of the newscast must be immediately rearranged. As we noted in Chapter 13, with the help of computers, the news producer can quickly see the effect of story additions and deletions as the show progresses.

IMPLICATIONS OF THE ENG REVOLUTION

Stations quickly found that the ENG revolution had implications far beyond cameras, tape machines and TBCs. The move to electronic newsgathering also introduced many content-related problems that news directors are still grappling with.

Knowing that live television cannot be edited, politicians and others who depend on publicity started scheduling announcements and "news events" when stations could (and probably would) cover them live. Politicians saw that they could have control over what was broadcast by simply timing the remarks to start at the beginning of a live news feed and then leading their talk with what they wanted to get on the air. (Often the videotape of the comments was then edited and used on a later newscast.)

When there is the possibility of cutting to an event live, the local station's news director often ends up with a dilemma. Which is more important: the psychological advantage of a live feed (especially when your competition may be covering the story live), or broadcasting the story at a later time — after the tape is edited — in order to provide a more balanced and comprehensive version of the event?

Later, the "sound bite" approach emerged. Knowing that news directors would only use five or 10 seconds (a sound bite) of what they had to say, those who wanted to "make the 6 o'clock news" would carefully craft a short statement that would attract the attention of news directors.

The Impact of ENG Coverage on War

The impact of live ENG coverage on war became especially apparent during the 1991 war in the Persian Gulf (Figure 16.1). Events unfolded on live television for everyone around the world to witness simultaneously — from world leaders and military commanders on both sides of the conflict right down to the person on the street. The immediate psychological effect of political and military actions, as instantly and often rather graphically relayed to viewers around the world, was of prime concern to both sides in the war. As a result, both sides in the conflict put considerable effort into controlling the public perception of the war as reflected (in particular) by the television media.

FIGURE 16.1
The impact of live ENG coverage on international politics became especially apparent during the 1991 war in the Persian Gulf. Events unfolded on live television for everyone around the world to witness simultaneously. Here CNN correspondent Charles Jaco holds up a Scud missile fragment a short time after it exploded in Saudi Arabia.

Reporting News vs. Making News

A second content-related issue emerged early in the history of ENG when it was discovered that ENG crews could inadvertently create news instead of just report it. As an example, one Jacksonville, Florida, ENG reporter routinely went to the scene of a civil disturbance with an a ENG crew. Neighborhood factions, divided primarily on racial differences, had almost come to the point of open warfare. When the news crew arrived, everything was quiet. But, the presence of a news camera and a clearly-marked ENG truck (and the chance to take the issue to the general public) quickly brought people out of their homes by the dozens. The scene quickly heated up as each side struggled to get in the TV spotlight. Caught in the middle of both hostile groups, the ENG crew was saved by the arrival of a dozen police cars. Such happenings have caused many TV stations, especially in larger cities, to use unmarked ENG vans. Suffice it to say that the objective of electronic journalism is to accurately report an event without appreciably altering the character or dynamics of that event.

ENG-EFP DIFFERENCES

We've noted that ENG is a part of the larger category of non-studio production called *electronic field production (EFP)*, which includes commercials, music videos, on-location dramatic productions and various types of sports coverage. In 90 percent of news work there will be time to ensure optimum audio and video quality, which is what the news director and producer will expect. But news production differs from other types of production in that content comes first. The primary objective is to *get the story*. The most-watched and celebrated television news story in history was shot with one, low resolution black-and-white video camera. It was humankind's first steps on the moon. Although the quality of the footage was poor, no TV news editor said to NASA, "you've got some interesting footage there, NASA, but we'll have to pass; the quality just isn't up to our usual standards."

Sometimes ENG stories will have to be shot with a camera-mounted sungun while running backward in front of a moving subject. Although picture, sound and camera stability may be sadly lacking, poor video and sound on an important story are better than nothing. In one important, fast-breaking story that unfolded inside a dark building, the camera operator noted that the camera's exposure indicator "didn't register 'low light,' it registered 'no light.'" In his words, "I had to use large measures of imagination even to see something resembling an image in the viewfinder. But, it was an important story so I figured I'd better just keep shooting." When the tape was viewed in the control room, an image could barely be made out. The video white level on the wave-form monitor was only a few wrinkles above reference black. With only 30 minutes to go before air time, the tape was played back through a video monitor with the brightness and contrast controls turned up to near maximum. Then a studio camera with its gain control turned up was focused on the monitor and the image was recorded. Although the resulting grainy, noisy video image made the moon footage look good by comparison, images could be made out. The story was told, and no one complained about video quality.

TELEVISION NEWS

As we noted in an earlier chapter, for most TV stations the local newscast represents not only a major source of revenue for the station, but the primary way the station interacts with its community. Since people in most cities have access to several on-air newscasts, TV news also ends up being highly competitive. In some TV markets a single rating point is worth more than a million dollars a year in added revenue. Since ENG stories are much more interesting and involving than stories that are simply read from a script by an on-camera newsperson, many stations go so far as to limit the number of non-ENG stories in each newscast. This, of course, puts pressure on assignment editors to *get pictures* whenever possible.

ENG production has unique problems, and in this respect is not like other types of video production. Anyone who expects to be successful in ENG production must understand not only the production process, but, even more important, the basic principles of newsgathering. (Some of the thorny legal, professional and ethical issues surrounding news will be covered in Chapter 19.)

Sources of Television News

There are five primary sources of news for TV stations:

- News agencies and cooperatives, including CNN, and (for network stations) the affiliates' daily satellite news feeds
- Wire services such as the Associated Press (AP)
- Competing media outlets (newspapers, radio stations and area TV stations)
- Press releases and videotapes provided by a wide variety of institutions and special-interest groups
- The station's local news beats, such as the police station and city hall

Today, most stations have computerized newsrooms. Twenty-four hours a day, a steady stream of news from sources such as the Associated Press is electronically written to a hard disk on the newsroom's main (server) computer.

Using a computer terminal, the news editor can quickly scroll through an index of stories that have been electronically stored. Key words and phrases can be used to find stories relating to specific topics—generally issues of local concern. It is the job of the assignment editor to develop local angles of national and international stories, as well as to see that local stories are covered. A major event taking place in a foreign country may lend itself to reactions from local people of the same nationality; a shake-up in a New York company may impact employees or related businesses in the station's area; or a crime wave in an adjoining county may cause local people to react.

Reporters use computer terminals to write and edit their stories. Afterward, the stories are saved to a file in the newsroom's main computer. The stories can thereafter be selected, reviewed and edited as needed for specific newscasts. Then they can be fed directly to a studio prompter for on-camera reading. Once broadcast, the stories can be *archived* (transferred to long-term computer storage). Thereafter, they are available for doing research on future stories. In addition, background information on most any subject is also accessible via modem (a computer-to-telephone-line link) from scores of computer databases across the country. Newsroom computers are also used to schedule equipment and facilities, and to keep an inventory of supplies.

archive: Long-term electronic storage of text or images, generally on some form of disc or magnetic tape.

Balancing News and Production Elements

In planning a newscast, several areas of balance must be maintained. Depending on the orientation of the newscast and the relative importance of the stories on a particular day, a news director will attempt to balance the number of local, regional, national and international news stories. As we noted in Chapter 12, different stations have different formulas for determining this mix. An attempt is also made to have minute-to-minute (even second-to-second) visual variety. In particular—and depending upon the events of the day—this involves a balance between live feeds, ENG segments and stories that simply have supporting graphics. Finally, there is generally an attempt to achieve the desired ratio between hard and soft news stories; that is, stories that are straight, factual stories and those that are basically human-interest and feature stories.

Ten Factors in Newsworthiness

Those involved in ENG work must understand the 10 factors that constitute news value, or *newsworthiness:*

1. Timeliness
2. Proximity
3. Exceptional quality
4. Prominence
5. The number of people affected
6. Conflict
7. Consequence
8. Human interest

newsworthiness: Elements that make a news story interesting and noteworthy from the perspective of an audience.

FIGURE 16.2
One of the criteria for newsworthiness is the prominence of the people involved. Even a sightseeing stroll through the corridors of an old building is newsworthy — if it's done by the President of the United States.

9. Titillation component
10. Shock value

Timeliness: News is what's new. An afternoon raid on a underground nursery growing marijuana may warrant a live ENG report during the 6 p.m. news. However, tomorrow, unless there are major new developments, the same story will probably not be important enough to mention.

Proximity: If 15 people are killed in your home town, your local TV station will undoubtedly consider it news. But if 15 people are killed in Manzanillo, Montserrat, Moyobambaor or some other distant place you've never heard of, it will probably pass unnoted. But there are exceptions.

Exceptional quality: One exception centers on how the people died. If the people in Manzanillo were killed because of a bus accident, this would not be nearly so newsworthy as if they died because of stings from killer bees, feared insects that have invaded the United States. Exceptional quality refers to how uncommon an event is. A man getting a job as a music conductor is not news — unless the man is blind.

Possible future impact: The killer bee example illustrates another news element: possible future impact. The fact that the killer bees are now in the United States and may eventually be a threat to people watching the news, or to their relatives living in another state, makes the story much more newsworthy. A mundane burglary of an office in the Watergate Hotel in Washington, D.C., was hardly news — until two reporters named Woodward and Bernstein saw the implications and the possible future impact. Eventually, the story behind this seemingly common burglary brought down a presidency.

Prominence: The 15 deaths in Manzanillo might also go by unnoted by the local media unless someone prominent was on the bus — perhaps a movie star or a well-known politician. If a U.S. Supreme Court Justice or your local mayor gets married, it's news; if John Smith, your next-door neighbor, gets married, it probably isn't (Figure 16.2).

Conflict: Conflict in its many forms has long held the interest of observers. The conflict may be physical or emotional. It can be open, overt conflict, such as a civil uprising against police authority, or it may be ideological conflict between political candidates. The conflict could be as simple as a person standing on her principles and spending a year "fighting city hall" over a parking citation. In addition to "people against people," there can be conflict with wild animals, nature, the environment or even the frontier of space.

Human interest: Human-interest stories are generally soft news. Examples would be a baby beauty contest, a person whose pet happens to be a nine-foot boa constrictor or a man who makes a cart so that his two-legged dog can again move around. On a slow news day even a story of fire fighters getting a cat out of a tree might make a suitable story. Human-interest angles can be found in most hard news stories. A flood in Tennessee will undoubtedly have many human-interest angles: a child reunited with its parents after two days, a boy who lost his dog or families returning to their mud-filled homes.

Titillation component: This factor primarily involves sex and is commonly featured — some would say exploited — during rating periods. This category includes everything from the new fashions in men and women's swim wear to an in-depth series on legal prostitution in Nevada. (The fact that the latter story has suddenly surfaced during a rating period, even though prostitution has legally and more or less quietly existed in parts of Nevada for decades, is, of course, purely coincidental!)

Shock value: An explosion in a factory has less shock value if it was caused by a gas leak than if it was caused by a terrorist. The story of a six-year-old boy

FIGURE 16.3
Since stories tend to break when they are least expected, this means that, day or night, TV newspeople must be prepared. Here a news crew prepares to take off for the scene of a late-breaking story.

who shot his mother with a revolver found in a bedside drawer has more shock (and therefore news) value than if the same woman died in an automobile accident. Both shock value and the titillation factor are well known to the tabloid press. The lure of these two factors is also related to some stories getting inordinate attention, such as the sordid details of a politician's or evangelist's affair.

Packaging the News

With the exception of features and special in-depth reports, the newscasts in most TV markets will feature many, if not most, of the same stories. What makes one station favored over another is how the news is presented. (It's not so much what you say as how you say it.) This not only includes how professional and well liked the on-air personalities are, but also how well stories are illustrated with graphics and ENG reports.

Videographers working in news commonly receive their basic instructions from reporters or assignment editors. However, depending on the station and the reputation a particular videographer has for creativity and an understanding of news, considerable latitude may be given in selecting shots and even in pursuing specific angles of a story. First of all, since stories tend to break when they are least expected, this means that, day or night, they must always be prepared (Figures 16.3 and 16.4A and 16.4B). Not to be may mean missing the story completely.

But, as important as it may be, there is much more to covering the news than just getting to the scene with both yourself and your equipment intact. Reporters must find creative ways to effectively communicate the essential ideas of a story. Those who thoroughly understand news and the full range of audio and video techniques available will be able to go beyond simply getting technically acceptable video. Talented videographers are not only in demand by the best reporters, but they also get the most challenging and interesting assignments.

FIGURE 16.4
Video equipment must often be hastily transported great distances to the scene of a story. Not to pack it securely means that it may not be operational when it arrives. The case (A) is designed to protect a camcorder in rather severe conditions. A "rain jacket" (B) protects camcorders from rain, sleet and snow.

(a)

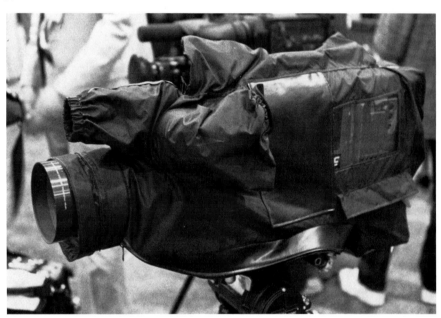

(b)

Building National Credentials

Good newstape is often picked up by a network or a news service for national distribution. This results not only in extra money, but national credits as well. Although a few people want to stay in a small market (geographical area) because of family reasons, or whatever, most talented people want to move on to larger, more prestigious (and better-paying) jobs. An impressive, up-to-date résumé reel of news segments is an important key to opening professional doors. As in most areas of production, a résumé reel in news should contain a short assortment of high-quality segments covering a wide variety of production assignments.

FIGURE 16.5
Part of the excitement of ENG work is being on the "front line" of news events. By comparison, other professions seem rather dull. Here, a CNN team hastily sets up a flyaway satellite link to broadcast live pictures from the scene of destruction during the Gulf War.

If in Doubt, Check It Out

Repeating an erroneous and damaging rumor to your friend will probably have no consequences; broadcasting the same rumor can result in multimillion dollar lawsuits and cut short a promising career. Although there is constant pressure at stations to be "first with the news," the legal and public-relations consequences of airing a story with a damaging factual error or unintentional distortions of truth can be injurious to all concerned. (We'll cover this issue in more detail in Chapter 19.) Suffice it to say that one of the most important axioms in news is *If in doubt, check it out.*

The Hazards of ENG Work

Part of the excitement of ENG work is being on the "front line" of news events (see Figure 16.5). If there is a major airline crash, ENG reporters are on the scene reporting; if a major civil disturbance breaks out in a large city, ENG reporters may find themselves reporting the story while dodging bricks and exploding canisters of tear gas. There is no doubt that by comparison, other professions seem rather dull.

Although most local ENG assignments are rather routine, during major accidents, emergencies and disasters ENG personnel may face definite hazards. Although celebrated heroes sometimes emerge in these situations, people not accustomed to extreme stress often react irrationally, irresponsibly and dangerously. Physiologists might attribute this to adrenalin interfering with the normal reasoning processes. Whatever the reason, ENG reporters quickly learn that people often go into a kind of "shock fog" and cannot be counted on to respond rationally during (and for some time after) extreme stress. Add to this the fact that an ENG crew will be working under its own broadcast-related pressures, and it becomes obvious that special precautions must be observed when major accidents and life-threatening assignments are covered. Personal precautions and safeguards are a critical part of the newsgathering process.

Once a reporter leaves the arena of local news, risks can become even greater. During 1990, nearly 50 newspeople were killed around the world, and scores of others reported missing. Most newspeople were killed in countries that have reason to fear the free flow of information. However, even in Western countries like the United States, reporters—especially investigative reporters working on sensitive stories—have been killed before they could broadcast their findings. To cite one example, in 1990, Kati Marton published "*The Polk Conspiracy*," chronicling the death of George Polk, a CBS news correspondent. Even though his death was originally blamed on Communists, Ms. Marton's investigations point to a Washington-based, right-wing conspiracy and cover-up. Although the truth may never be known, it would seem that Mr. Polk discovered information that some powerful people didn't want revealed.

A major part of ENG, especially live ENG, is the field-to-studio link. Personnel in the control room must have the ability to coordinate the work of numerous field crews and, during a fast-breaking news story, assemble a news show as it is broadcast (Figure 16.6). The reports from the field arrive via satellite, microwave, coaxial and fiber optic links. These will be discussed in Chapter 17.

ENG represents a rather elemental form of single-camera production. The single-camera technique becomes much more complex in film-style production, where multiple camera angles are shot and cut together to depict continuous action.

THE DEVELOPMENT OF FILM-STYLE PRODUCTION TECHNIQUES

Although today single-camera video makes use of basic film techniques, film and video actually started out "miles apart" in their production approaches. Film's single-camera production style was based primarily on technical limitations; but as the system evolved, it became evident that although it was time-consuming, the single-camera approach provided many important artistic advantages.

Video had quite different beginnings. For several decades after the invention of television, there was no practical way to edit scenes together from one camera to provide multiple camera shots. Being essentially a live, all-electronic process, it required multiple cameras for multiple camera angles.

The "production chasm" between video and film production has now greatly diminished. Each regularly "borrows" techniques from the other. For example, in film production *video assist* (a video camera fastened to a film camera) is often used so a director can watch a TV monitor to see what a particular camera is getting on film. In video, the single-camera, film-style approach to production is commonly used, not only in news, but for much more sophisticated and artistically demanding types of production. It was, of course, electronic editing that opened the door to single-camera production in video. Today, much of the random-access video editing software emulates film editing techniques.

It is commonly felt that film is superior to video for general production. For

FIGURE 16.6
Personnel in the control room of a news production center must have the ability to coordinate the work of numerous field crews. During a fast-breaking news story, they must be able to assemble a news show as it is broadcast.

some, "the film look" is a desirable goal in video production. As we will see, this difference is primarily artistic rather than technical. As we noted in Chapter 7, the artistic potential of lighting and editing is limited in multicamera productions—the kind we regularly see in situation comedies and studio-based daytime drama. A scene that has to be lit and shot from three or four divergent angles at the same time will inevitably be compromised in the process.

In contrast, the level of quality and sophistication that can be achieved by breaking a scene down into its major components and lighting, micing and rehearsing each segment before it is shot—and typically shot several times—is understandably superior. Each scene and camera angle setup is normally tried out and rehearsed until the director is completely satisfied. In film-style production, actors typically concentrate on only a few lines and a few moves at a time. In contrast, in many types of video dramas, actors have to memorize lines for a complete production and go through it without stopping.

Instead of having one camera angle and take to choose from, film editors can normally choose from several takes and angles. (A take is a short, discrete segment of action, or simply an attempt to photograph a usable shot. In film production many takes may be necessary before directors feel they have a single usable **shot.**)

With film, editing decisions are typically spread out over weeks or months—ample time to reflect, experiment and reconsider before final decisions are made. In contrast, editing decisions in live or live-on-tape video productions are done in real time on a second-by-second basis. There is seldom the opportunity to look back, rethink and revise.

Film-Style Production Comes to Video

Although a few major television productions throughout the 1970s and early 1980s tried to duplicate single-camera, film-style production for drama and commercial production, it was not until high-definition production got under way that video production was able to compete on virtually an equal basis with film. Today, many video productions are shot in single-camera film style. In the remainder of this chapter we will examine single-camera, film-style video production techniques. We will draw our major example from the most artistically demanding area of single-camera production: drama.

The Master Shot Perspective

cover shot: An establishing wide-angle or long shot of a set used primarily to establish the relationships between subject matter in a scene.

Probably the greatest area of similarity between film and film-style video production is in what is called the ***cover shot*** in video and the **master shot** in film — the wide shot showing the full working (acting) area. This wide shot is useful not only in showing viewers the overall disposition of the scene, but as a way of bridging jumps in continuity during editing. More specifically, the master shot is used:

- to show major changes in the scene's basic elements or center of interest;
- to cover major talent moves, including the entrance or exit of actors;
- to periodically remind viewers of a scene's geography (this is often referred to as a *reestablishing shot*);
- when necessary, during editing, to momentarily cover for a lack of a good medium shot or close-up.

In dramatic video production (as well as in film production), many directors start out by shooting a scene, beginning to end, from the master shot perspective. Once they get a good take, they make lighting and audio adjustments and break down the scene into the essential ***setups***—the important medium shots and close-ups. Generally these consist of shots of speaking parts by the principal actors. The series of setups associated with a scene is called ***coverage***.

Setups

setup: In single-camera, film-style production, a single-camera position from which one or more segments in a scene are done.

coverage: In single-camera, film-style production the videotaping of dialogue and action in a dramatic scene from the perspectives of the essential camera positions.

Once the master shot is taped, the director can reposition the camera for the setups. To accommodate the new camera distances and angles, setups often require changes in lights, microphone position and sometimes even makeup.

It is the director's responsibility to break down the script into individual shots and setups. Seldom is the most efficient shooting sequence represented by the actual script (chronological story) sequence. In order of importance, the following should be considered when planning the shooting sequence of a single-camera production:

- All shots involving specific talent/actors (starting with the highest paid) should be shot as close together in time as possible, regardless of script sequence.
- All shots at a particular location (especially when a daily or hourly fee is being paid) should be shot at the same time.
- All shots requiring specific production personnel should be shot at the same time.
- All shots requiring specialized (especially leased or rented) production equipment, such as special cameras, lenses, microphones, generators etc., should be shot at the same time.

One of the major problems in single-camera production is to keep everything visually consistent between all setups and shots, even though they may be made over a period of hours or even days. A handkerchief that is seen to mysteriously jump from one breast pocket to another when shots are cut together can be an unwelcome distraction in an ongoing scene. Although subtle adjustments will often have to be made to accommodate new setup angles, you should guard against obvious breaks in continuity. A back light or a kicker light that did not exist in the master shot may add a lot to a close-up, but the sudden change, especially as you cut back and forth between the setup and the master shot, may call attention to itself.

Shooting a Scene From a Dramatic Production

As a way of illustrating setups and the whole concept of single-camera, film-style production, a short sequence from "*The Professor and the Minx*" will be traced (Figure 16.7). Since knowing the story and visualizing the characters are essential to blocking and directing the production, here is a brief scenario of the story.

There are two principal actors in the scene, Barbi and Professor Timorous. Two years earlier Barbi was involved in psychological experiments headed by Dr. Timorous. Without notice or explanation, she abruptly dropped out of the experiments—and out of school. Over the two-year period, Barbi has experienced disturbing psychic episodes and weeks of sleepless nights, which she associates with the experiments. Meanwhile, Timorous has taken a year's sabbatical to analyze and write up his research. To keep from being disturbed, he has moved into a remote seaside chalet.

The consequences of the experiments aren't Barbi's only problems. On this particular night she has had to escape her nightclub job right after work to keep from encountering Ken. Barbi has for some time been trying to break off a relationship with him, but Ken, who has a history of violence, has demonstrated major problems in coping with her rejection.

FIGURE 16.7

The shot sequence illustrated on pages 440 and 441 is based on the two script pages reproduced here. Although there is no one "right" way to interpret the script, the series of drawings on the next two pages suggest setups that would provide an editor with a number of options. The text discussion (starting on page 440) suggests one possible sequence.

CONTINUED:

EXT. RUSTIC SEASIDE CHALET - NIGHT

Barbi pulls up to the chalet in her late-model sports car. She grabs her long-haired Persian cat from the seat beside her and jumps out of the car. Barbi quickly makes her way to the front door and knocks impatiently. As she waits, she nervously looks back at the road to see if she has been followed. Finally, the door opens.

DR. TIMOROUS
Miss Stevens?

BARBI
Barbi. And this is Tiffy.

INT. SEASIDE CHALET - NIGHT

Before Dr. Timorous invites her in, Barbi gives one more glance back and quickly moves past him into the chalet. She comes to a halt in the center of a large, rustic room. The furnishings belong in the 18th Century. Heavy hewn beams support a high cathedral ceiling. A wooden stairway leads to a large loft, now being used as an office. Small windows look out over a restless ocean. On the left of the downstairs area there is a small kitchen with an antique stove and a wooden kitchen table. A modern refrigerator betrays the atmosphere. On the right side of the central area is a bedroom, partially hidden behind a freestanding divider.

Barbi carefully puts her cat down, takes off her coat and lays it on a chair. She is still wearing her abbreviated cocktail dress. Dr. Timorous, becoming more uncomfortable by the minute, watches with obvious disapproval.

BARBI
(continuing)
Jeez, is this a museum or something?

DR. TIMOROUS
No, a quiet place where I should be able to work.

BARBI
Tiffy and I won't be much trouble.

(CONTINUED)

CONTINUED:

DR. TIMOROUS
(glaring at the cat)
You picked a pretty strange time to invite yourself over.

BARBI
(shrugs)
Didn't have much choice. Plus the mess I'm in is mostly your doing. If I had a lawyer... but that's too long a story to start on now.

While Barbi starts exploring the chalet, Timorous goes to the kitchen, pours himself a glass of milk. Barbi walks into the adjoining bedroom. In the foreground is a huge, four-poster bed. ANOTHER ANGLE shows Barbi, engulfed by fatigue, looking into the bedroom area.

BARBI
(looking around, amazed)
Right out of a 1900 Sears and Roebuck catalog!

Barbi checks the bed for firmness. Timorous is now at the doorway watching, glass of milk in hand.

BARBI
(continuing)
It's been days since I've had any sleep.
(Makes a decision; kicks off shoes) So, right now that comes first. (glances up at him.)
And I am not going to sleep in this $400 dress.
So you better close your eyes or whatever you have to do.

DR. TIMOROUS
Wait just a minute! We need to discuss....

BARBI
(interrupting)
First things first. We can talk tomorrow.
Would you mind getting the light?

Seeing that she's not going to be stopped, he quickly turns to leave, pausing for a second, without looking back, to meekly flip off the light. Timorous moves to the kitchen table and sits down. There is silence. Timorous and the cat stare menacingly at each other.

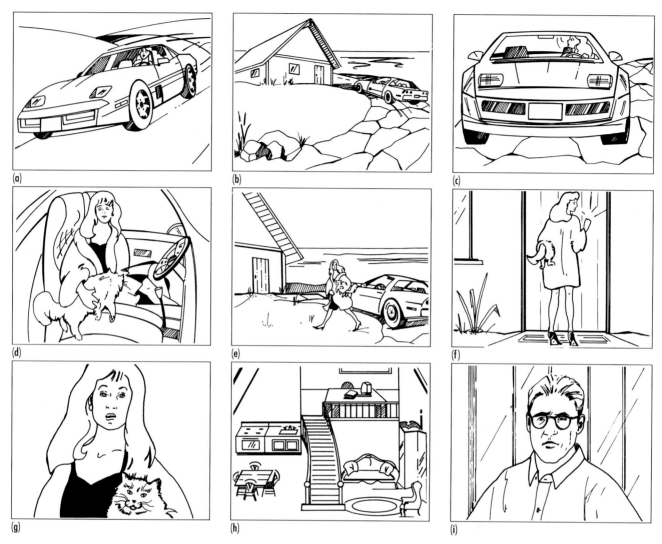

FIGURE 16.8

Barbi gets Timorous' telephone number, calls him from work at 2 a.m and tells him about the reactions to the experiments. In the course of the conversation she finds out where he is. Desperately needing a "safe port" for a while, she announces that she is on her way over. Before Dr. Timorous can object, she hangs up. Barbi rushes home to change out of her cocktail dress, but just as she gets there, Ken screeches up in front of her condo. With no time to change, she grabs her cat and flees down the back stairs.

We know that going into this scene, Barbi's demeanor is "threadbare" because of her turbulent personal problems, her lack of sleep and her ongoing reaction to the experiments. Although Barbi thinks Timorous wrote the book on "stuffed shirts," he apparently holds the key to her psychological problems. Timorous disdains Barbi's libertine lifestyle (the minx); however, on the phone she threatened a lawsuit if he didn't set things straight.

Although every director would approach these scenes differently, let's look at one method.

The first sequence is of Barbi driving up to the chalet and getting out of her car. Many directors would first shoot the entire arrival sequence from a master shot perspective (Figure 16.8B): the car driving up, parking, Barbi getting her

(i)   (k)   (l)

(m)   (n)   (o)

(p)   (q)

FIGURE 16.8, continued

cat and getting out of the car and walking up to the door. Although this wide-shot perspective would not really show any detail, it would provide the editor with footage that could be used between the closer setups.

At least two setups could be added. First is a cut to Barbi driving (Figure 16.8A) before she turns left into the driveway of the chalet (Figure 16.8B). The next shot (Figure 16.8C) would serve two purposes: it is a needed transition between the long shot and the close-up to follow, and we need to add additional information on Barbi's mental state. As the car comes to a stop, we could then cut to Figure 16.8C as Barbi turns off the ignition and quickly and nervously looks around before hastily leaving the car. To clearly establish the presence of the cat, we'll probably want a close-up of Barbi scooping up the cat from the seat (Figure 16.8D). At this point we could cut to a variation of the master shot as she gets out of the car and walks toward the front door (Figure 16.8E).

We could then cut to a medium, over-the-shoulder shot (Figure 16.8F) as she walks to the door, knocks and nervously looks over her shoulder. Then the door opens, and Timorous delivers his line.

We might make the next sequence more interesting by putting effect before cause. As Barbi enters the room, we could cut immediately to a medium close-up of her reaction. (Figure 16.8G). As the audience is wondering what caused her response, we can cut to a reverse-angle wide shot of the room (Figure 16.8H). If we wanted to put cause before effect, we could cut to a wide shot of the room from Barbi's viewpoint as she goes in and then to a close-up of her reaction. The final decision in this case can be made during editing.

Barbi has a line at this point, so we could either cut to a medium close-up of her (similar to Figure 16.8G) or simply have her deliver it over the wide shot of the room (Figure 16.8H). Although this would not underscore Barbi's reaction ("Is this a museum or something?"), it would give the audience a bit more time to study the room.

We now need a shot of Timorous at this point for three reasons. First, a question has been asked, and we expect an answer; second, we haven't seen Timorous for a while, and we need to know how he's handling things; and third, we need to see him close the door and move into the room.

We can cut to a shot of Timorous as he closes the front door, moves toward Barbi and delivers his line (Figure 16.8I). At this point we have two options. We could hold the same shot of Timorous as Barbi delivers her line: "Tiffy and I won't be much trouble." This will allow us to see the look of disapproval that comes into Timorous' eyes. Or we could cut immediately to a two-shot (Figure 16.8J) so we can see Barbi as she speaks. In either case we now need a shot to cover Barbi's action as she puts down the cat (we need to see this to explain why she will be without it in subsequent shots) and moves out of frame to explore the chalet. In a wide, reverse-angle shot similar to Figure 16.8H, we could then see Barbi starting to explore things. Holding the same wide shot at this point will do three things: emphasize the nature of the chalet, establish Barbi's explorations and show that Timorous has been left standing powerlessly as Barbi takes over the situation.

Knowing what Barbi is doing, we can now cut to a medium shot of Timorous moving toward the kitchen, opening the refrigerator and pulling out a half-gallon of milk (Figure 16.8K). As soon as we see the milk carton, we know what's going on, so we can rejoin Barbi. Although the shot is not in the script, to establish that there's only an office upstairs, we could cut to a shot of Barbi emerging at the top of stairs of the loft and looking at a large desk piled high with reports (Figure 16.8L). We then need to see her turn and start down the stairs.

A cut to the bottom of the stairs shows Timorous standing there with a glass of milk (Figure 16.8M). To further emphasize the helplessness of Timorous in the situation, there could be silence as Barbi brushes past him and moves toward the bedroom. By holding a medium shot of Timorous at this point, we can emphasize the look of dismay on his face as Barbi announces (out of the shot) that she and Tiffy are going to stay for a while.

In a reverse-angle shot we then see what Timorous sees: Barbi checking out the bed (Figure 16.8N). She then delivers her lines as she kicks off her shoes and starts to take off her dress. At the appropriate point, we can cut to a reaction shot of Timorous (Figure 16.8O) as he starts to back away while strenuously objecting to what's going on. As he starts to leave, Barbi calls out, "Would you mind getting the light," which causes him to (without looking at Barbi) to reach around and meekly flip off the light.

We can avoid a jump cut and condense the sequence of Timorous moving into the kitchen and sitting down with a brief back-lit shot of Barbi slipping under the covers (Figure 16.8P). To end the scene, we could then cut to a medium wide shot of Timorous, glass in hand, staring down at the cat in silence (Figure 16.8Q).

Of course, there is no single, "right" way to do this sequence. Each director and editor would interpret these script pages in a slightly different way. Allowance for creativity and personal interpretation is one of the strengths of dramatic production. By including more shots of Barbi, we could emphasize her whirlwind, minx personality. By staying on Timorous in more shots, the incredulity of the situation (from his perspective) would be emphasized. Whatever the approach, it should not be at odds with the basic story-line and character personalities conveyed in the script.

Maintaining Interscene Relationships

Since scenes will probably not be shot in script sequence, the director (and actors) will not be able to rely on any logical, time-based development in the characters. As an extreme example, let's assume that in a drama a couple meet, fall in love, get married, have two children and after 20 years start fighting fiercely. In an effort to patch things up, they decide to return to the hotel where they spent their first romantic night together; but, unfortunately, they start arguing, and in a final rage, one partner kills the other.

For scheduling purposes it is desirable to shoot the scenes of the vicious fighting and arguing in the same hotel room and on the same day as the scenes showing their first shy lovemaking. In the final production, of course, the two scenes will be separated by a life story—but possibly by only an hour or so when the scenes are actually shot. (This abrupt transition obviously demands a lot from the actors.) Behind-the-scenes changes will be minimal, except that new set dressing will be relied upon to appropriately age the hotel room, and make-up will be used to age the actors.

In order to ensure proper continuity between scenes, the director must analyze the script for what comes before and after the scenes being shot. The scene must create a smooth bridge between the segment that precedes it and the one that follows. Specifically, the level of energy, emotion, love or hate that precedes the scene must be established. This will be the starting point. Then the same level of emotion and motivation for the scene that follows will have to be understood. This will be the ending point for the scene.

Working With Actors and Talent

In working with actors, the director will want to find an optimum point that lies somewhere between forcing the actors to follow his or her own rigid interpretation, and granting them absolute freedom to do as they wish. This optimum point will depend upon the experience of the actors and the personality of the director.

During **read-throughs** (the informal group sessions where the actors initially read through their lines), most directors will carefully watch the character interpretation that an actor is developing. (Although we are mostly speaking of dramatic productions here, the same concerns would apply in working with many other types of productions, including commercials.) If the interpretation differs significantly from how the director has envisioned it, suggestions should be made. Directors who have limited experience in directing actors will want to tread lightly here; at least until they acquire the necessary sensitivity for the acting process and the personality of specific actors. Since working with actors takes considerable sensitivity to the dynamics of acting, directors who have had acting experience have a definite advantage.

Controlling Script Revisions

Occasionally in shooting scenes, lines are rewritten or rephrased. The level of autonomy and control delegated to the director and actors involved will determine the amount of freedom in making such changes. But many problems have inadvertently resulted from seemingly minor script changes. In one weekly, 60-minute television series, lines were changed during the shooting of an early scene in the production. Although the change seemed harmless enough at the time, later it was discovered that the exact phrasing was critical to later dialogue and events. Since it was too late to reshoot the early scene, the final production ended up making less than perfect sense. The fact that the director had not done his preproduction "homework" for this $780,000.00 production became painfully obvious.

Writers labor over script dialogue for some time, and after that, a whole string of people typically go over every line before the script is approved. Generally, there are numerous rewrites before everyone agrees on details. Suffice it to say that script lines should not be changed unless you know you are on solid ground. With this said, it should be noted that lines (and actions) are sometimes changed to accommodate actors or situations. Generally, when a script is written, the actors who will be selected for the parts are not known, so lines sometimes must be "fitted" during production to the personality, interpretation and approach of specific actors.

Inventing "Business"

business: The realistic actions of actors that take place as a scene progresses. Examples would be reading a newspaper, knitting or fixing a drink.

The basic actions and "business" of actors are decided upon by the actors and the director during rehearsals. (*Business* refers to the secondary action associated with scenes; it would include fixing a drink, lighting a cigarette or paging through a magazine.) In our preceding sample scene, one part of Dr. Timorous' business is getting and drinking a glass of milk. The script may or may not describe actor business, but it will very much influence camera shots, setups and editing.

Plans B and C

"The only thing you can really count on during an on-location production is that something will go wrong." Although this dictum may seem pessimistic, it commonly reflects the realities of on-location conditions. Unexpected technical problems, weather problems, illness etc. are just some of the complications. For this reason, directors should always have a "Plan B," and possibly even a "Plan C" for each shooting day. If exterior scenes are scheduled for a particular day and it begins to rain, Plan B, which involves interior shots, should be "ready to roll." If your lead character becomes ill, Plan C might call for all the shots for the day that involve other actors. Once facilities, equipment, talent and crew are all ready, the one thing you don't want to do is nothing!

Creative Compromises

creative compromise: Including and excluding elements in a production based primarily on budget concerns. An example would be passing over a top star in favor of enhanced special effects or an exotic production location.

Since time is money, and money is the primary limiting factor in production, a producer must weigh the relative merits of different possibilities and make the *creative compromises* necessary to achieve the most effective result for the least investment in time and resources. If shooting film-style adds $100,000 to the cost of a production, the producer may have to consider whether spending the money on a "name star" would be more attractive to viewers than the higher production values. By dropping several sophisticated special effects, possibly enough money can be saved to shoot some key scenes on location rather than simply using "back lot" simulations. Even when doing modest productions, it is important to compare resources against possibilities, and then make the creative compromises that will result in the strongest production for a given set of limitations.

Learning to Visualize

As they go through scripts, production personnel should be able to visualize scenes in their minds. Directors, in particular, need to visualize a script from various camera angles. Some directors practice breaking down episodes from real-life scenes around them—quietly "cutting them" in their minds as they develop. Above all else, the job of the director is to use camera shots and angles to direct the audience's attention toward an ongoing succession of ideas and details.

Single-Camera vs. Multiple-Camera Production

As we've indicated throughout this chapter, with productions such as serious drama, the film-style approach offers many important creative advantages. But for some types of productions, especially when time or budget limitations demand a faster and more efficient approach, the video producer can turn to multiple-camera production—which is the topic of the next chapter.

SUMMARY

The development of the time-base corrector made it possible to use portable cameras and videotape machines in over-the-air broadcasting. This development had at least three major implications: (1) film was phased out for news and documentary work, (2) the number of productions done live from the field increased, and (3) the ability to do news segments either live or without the delay associated with film significantly changed the content of news.

There are five primary sources of broadcast news for TV stations: (1) a variety of news agencies, including CNN and (for network stations) daily affiliate news feeds by satellite; (2) wire services such as the AP; (3) competing media outlets (newspapers, radio stations and other TV stations); (4) press releases and videotapes provided by a variety of institutions and special-interest groups; and (5) the station's local news beats, such as the police station and city hall.

The move to computerized newsrooms resulted not only in greater newsroom efficiency, but in the availability of electronic databanks of written and graphic information. There are 10 factors associated with newsworthiness: timeliness, proximity, exceptional quality, prominence, the number of people affected, conflict, consequence, human interest, titillation component, and shock value.

Television news, especially at the national and international levels, is one of the most exciting, demanding and challenging professions known. The history of newsgathering has also shown that it can involve personal risk, especially during times of civil unrest or when a reporter finds out information that individuals or institutions are trying to keep from the public.

In the last decade film and video have been moving closer in their production approaches; film has been borrowing many of the postproduction techniques of video, and video has been borrowing many film techniques. As an example, many of the single-camera, film-style production techniques that originated with film are now being used in on-location video production.

The basic scene-to-scene actions and business of actors are agreed upon during rehearsals. In working with actors, the director will want to find an optimum point somewhere between forcing the actors to follow his or her own rigid interpretation of a script, and granting absolute freedom of interpretation and actions.

Key production personnel should be able to visualize scenes in their minds as they go through scripts. The primary job of the director is to use camera shots and angles to direct the audience's attention toward the ongoing succession of ideas and details. Time is money, and money is the primary limiting factor in production. Therefore, a producer must weigh the relative merits of different production possibilities and make the creative compromises necessary to achieve the most effective result for the least investment in time and resources. Because things commonly go wrong with shooting schedules, directors should have a Plan B and possibly even a Plan C for each shooting day.

KEY TERMS

archived
business
conflict
cover shot
coverage
creative compromises
exceptional quality
human interest
master shot
newsworthiness

possible future impact
prominence
proximity
read-throughs
setup
shock value
shot
timeliness
titillation component

<h1>Multiple-
Camera Field
Production</h1>

17

The Super Bowl, the Academy Awards, the Rose Parade, government hearings, the Olympics — in some ways these multicamera field productions are similar to studio productions. There is one major area of difference, however. Studios are especially designed to accommodate the needs of television. In the field, productions must not only accommodate existing conditions, but they must readily adapt to such things as unpredictable weather, changing sunlight and the intrusion of bystanders. To accommodate field conditions, cameras are typically mounted on tripods or carried on the shoulder, lights are mounted on floor stands, and the control room is typically housed in a truck or van (Figure 17.1).

In this chapter we will look at the complete on-location multiple-camera production process. In particular, we'll focus on five major areas: preproduction planning, site surveys, facilities requests, directing and setups for specific events.

THE IMPORTANCE OF PREPRODUCTION PLANNING

Although **preproduction planning** may not be the most glamorous aspect of on-location production, it is the most important. More than one production has come to an untimely conclusion when it was discovered that a specific permit hadn't been obtained, or that someone had forgotten to do a preproduction check on power. Even if something as extreme as losing the entire production doesn't happen, a lack of planning can result in compromised quality and weakened production values. Since multicamera remote productions involve a wide range of production personnel, a lack of preproduction planning can also waste the most costly aspect of production: the time of talent and crew. Directors who go

FIGURE 17.1
The control center for multiple-camera productions is normally in a truck or van. This mobile production unit includes facilities equal to those found in some of the best studio control rooms.

into a production saying, "Well, I'm not sure how we're going to handle that, but I'm sure we'll figure something out once things get underway," are living dangerously — and foolishly.

Now we'll turn to an outline of the steps involved in doing a major production. These steps, of course, will have to be scaled down to meet the needs of smaller productions.

THE ON-LOCATION SURVEY

The most important step in doing an on-location production is the first one: doing an on-location survey. Although situations vary, an initial survey should include the following 11 points:

1. *A check of available power*. What will your total power needs be on the location in terms of watts or amps? Does the remote van take 120- or 220-volt power? Are there fuse boxes or breakers nearby, or will long power lines have to be installed? Is a portable generator the best solution?

2. Assuming the production is not going to be videotaped on location, *does the location provide for a clear satellite uplink or microwave path?* Will buildings or other structures block a practical satellite uplink? In the case of microwave, can a signal be sent directly to the studio or production facility, or will one or more microwave hops have to be established? (The more links, the greater the chances for problems — and, of course, the more time-consuming and costly the production becomes.) Finally, is the origination point in an area already saturated with microwave signals that could cause interference problems? (We'll discuss microwave and satellite links later in the chapter.)

3. *Will there be sound problems*? Is there a street or playground nearby that

FIGURE 17.2
Settings for period pieces are among the most difficult to create. To make them authentic-looking, considerable research must typically go into settings, wardrobe and props of the era being depicted.

is noisy during certain hours of the day? Depending on changing wind conditions, is it possible that an exterior location may end up being in the flight path of an airport? If the production will be done inside, will the existing acoustics present special problems?

4. *What are the existing lighting conditions?* If it's an interior shoot, will a large assortment of extra lights have to be set up? Will the facility's air conditioning be able to handle the heat resulting from extra lights? If the shoot is exterior, where will the sun be during the hours of the shoot? Will deep shadows caused by the position of the sun add to lighting requirements?

5. *What changes will be necessary at the location to accommodate the script, talent and production equipment?* For exterior locations this might include covering or changing signs, or altering structures to accommodate cameras and equipment. For interior locations there may be a need for renovations, repainting or redecorating. All this becomes especially important in period pieces that are set in specific eras. See Figure 17.2. (Would a room with a shag rug and stucco walls be appropriate in a story about Henry Ford?)

6. *Location availability.* Will all of the needed facilities be available during the time needed, plus a few more hours or days (depending on the production), "just in case." In most situations a contract will be drawn up (1) specifying the time in days or hours when the facility will be needed; (2) listing the compensation that will be paid to the owner; (3) outlining any changes that will be made to the property, including the interior or exterior of buildings (repainting, remodeling, redecorating etc.); (4) explaining the user's responsibility for restoring the location to its original condition (if that's deemed desirable); (5) detailing necessary insurance and bonds, and outlining financial responsibility for taking care of property damage or related liability.

7. *What are the total costs and conditions for using the location*? Included are property rental, parking and needed modifications and renovations. Are there local ordinances affecting production? Some areas (especially Southern California and New York City) have strict ordinances covering production. Often production hours and conditions are limited. Frequently, special permits, insurance and security bonds are required.

8. In the case of a scripted production, *does the location meet the needs of the script*? Is the setting fully consistent with the atmosphere suggested?

9. *Does the location offer adequate toilet facilities for cast and crew*? Are they readily available (as would normally be the case in a large athletic facility), or will portable facilities have to be rented?

10. *Will adequate security, police and first-aid services be available*? If equipment is to be left overnight, one or more security guards may have to be hired. If the production is in a densely populated area, off-duty police may have to be hired to keep onlookers from interfering with the production. Personal concerns for cast and crew (if not union contracts) will require that first-aid and emergency services be available. This is especially important for stunt work.

11. *Are there nearby restaurants, or will food (a catering service) have to be brought in*? Even a nearby restaurant may not be able to handle a large crew within a short time, which can add unexpected delays to a production schedule.

On-Location Survey Factors

Although production needs, of course, will vary widely, we'll show two types of production forms here. One (Figure 17.3) is an initial survey, designed to aid early preproduction planning. Some items may need explanation. The *location contacts* are the people responsible for the property or facilities for the event. This would include head security personnel or public relations, press or event coordinators. *Available amps* refers to the maximum amperage that will be available in a designated area (above and beyond that which may be normally required at the location). Most circuits allow for 20 or 30 amps, which conservatively translates into 2,000 or 3,000 watts. (To provide a safety factor, 100 volts are used instead of 115 to 120 volts in the formula Amps = Watts ÷ 100.) Although two or three 20- to 30-amp circuits will generally be adequate for basic video and audio equipment, lighting instruments can quickly exceed these limitations. Completely equipped mobile production vans often require more than 100 amps of power.

Although technical personnel will have the final say on a *microwave* or *satellite path*, it is helpful if the initial survey team makes notes on obstructions, possible RF (radio frequency) interference from nearby radar or microwave equipment etc. *Contractual limitations* refers to written stipulations governing the use of the property. This could include a limitation on the number of vehicles that can be parked at the site, hours when taping will not be allowed, areas that will be off limits to production personnel etc. To reduce overall costs (even with overtime expenses included), production crews often put in 10-hour days. However, in deference to local residents, a site contract may specify that no production work take place before 8 a.m.

pyrotechnics: Special effects involving explosions.

Limitations may also be placed on the use of **pyrotechnics** (special effects involving fire, explosions etc.). Inherent site limitations include possible noise or ventilation problems, a lack of restroom facilities and possible crowd-control problems. *Probable alterations required* refers to any obvious changes that will

```
┌─────────────────────────────────────────────────────────────┐
│                  REMOTE SURVEY INFORMATION                    │
│                                                               │
│                                                               │
│   PRODUCTION: _____  PRODUCTION DATE: _____ │
│   PRODUCER: _____  DIRECTOR: _____  │
│   LOCATION ADDRESS: _____  │
│   LOCATION CONTACT: _____  PHONE: ( _____ ) _____  │
│           CONTACT: _____  PHONE: ( _____ ) _____   │
│           CONTACT: _____  PHONE: ( _____ ) _____   │
│   POWER: ____ 120 V. ____ 220 V.  AVAILABLE AMPS WITHIN 700 FT. _____ │
│   MAIN POWER BOX LOCATION: _____  │
│   NEAREST TELEPHONE (S): _____   │
│   MICROWAVE/SATELLITE PATH NOTES:                             │
│                                                               │
│   _____   │
│   _____   │
│   _____   │
│                                                               │
│   CONTRACTUAL OR INHERENT LIMITATIONS:                        │
│                                                               │
│   _____   │
│   _____   │
│   _____   │
│                                                               │
│   PROBABLE ALTERATIONS REQUIRED:                              │
│                                                               │
│   _____   │
│   _____   │
│   _____   │
│                                                               │
└─────────────────────────────────────────────────────────────┘
```

FIGURE 17.3
Initial survey form.

have to be made to conform to story, script or production needs. Cleaning, painting or remodeling may need to be done, or scaffolding or platforms may have to be built to accommodate equipment, cameras or microwave dishes.

Once the information in the initial survey is obtained, reviewed and approved, the director and all related production personnel will visit the site to draw up a list of specific personnel and equipment needs.

THE FAX SHEET

Most television stations and production facilities have their own FAX sheet (facilities/equipment request form). The form illustrated in Figure 17.4 is typical. Generally, the FAX form will be supplemented with drawings of camera and mic positions, information on permits, parking, sketches of special construction needed etc. Once the initial concerns outlined in Figure 17.4 are taken care of, more specific facility and equipment needs can be assessed and requested.

If the production is to be recorded on location (as opposed to being done live or sent back to a production facility for recording), it will require special taping considerations. We'll discuss some of these in a moment. Even when

FIGURE 17.4
FAX sheet.

REMOTE FACILITIES / EQUIPMENT REQUEST

PRODUCTION:_____ PRODUCTION DATE:_____
SETUP TIME:_____ REHEARSAL TIME:_____
PRODUCTION TIME:_____ DIRECTOR:_____
LOCATION:_____

MASTER TAPES:_____
_____ VTR _____ OFF-LINE COPIES:_____
_____ COMMON SMPTE TIME CODE   START:_____ :00:00:00

_____ MICROWAVE   LINKS REQUIRED _____
_____ LIVE _____ SATELLITE   TRANSMISSION START _____ STOP _____
_____ AUTHORIZATION _____ CONFIRMATION DATE:_____
_____ SETUP NOTES:_____

CAMERAS	LOCATION	MOUNT	LENS	CABLE RUN
CAM #1				
CAM #2				
CAM #3				
CAM #4				
CAM #5				

MIC TYPE	LOCATION	CABLE RUN	MIC TYPE	LOCATION	CABLE
#1			#9		
#2			#10		
#3			#11		
#4			#12		
#5			#13		
#6			#14		
#7			#15		
#8			#16		

PRIMARY LIGHTING: _____ AVAILABLE   BASE LIGHT LEVEL _____ FC.
FILL/DIFFUSION ANTICIPATED:

LIGHTING INSTRUMENTS: _____

MAXIMUM LIGHTING WATTS: _____ SITE ELECTRICIAN: _____
OUTLETS, WATTS, LOCATIONS: _____

SPECIAL PL DROPS: _____
COMMUNICATION   TWO-WAYS: _____
IFB: _____

done live, productions are not transmitted to viewers directly from the field; instead, they must first be sent to a TV station or a production facility and then to a transmitter, or "head end," distribution point. A signal can be sent from the field in three ways:

- By fiber optics (optical fiber)
- By one or more microwave links
- By satellite

Each of these requires specific preproduction planning. Where cameras, mics and lights are to be placed must also be carefully thought out. (We'll return to some of these considerations later in the chapter.) *Setup time* refers to the time when arrangements have been made for the mobile van and equipment to be installed at the site. This obviously must be far enough in advance of the rehearsal time to keep the on-camera talent from having to wait around for the setup to be finished. And the rehearsal time must be far enough in advance of actual production to ensure that any problems that crop up during the rehearsal — a totally inevitable occurrence — can be adequately dealt with before the actual production.

If the production is to be taped, the number and type of master tapes should be specified. There are two things which should be noted here. Multiple-camera productions should be **double-recorded**. Although tape machines are highly reliable, making two master recordings ends up being cheap insurance against sudden head clog or an electronic or mechanical failure in a machine. If the length of the production goes beyond the duration of a single recording tape, one or more additional tape machines will have to be started before the first tapes run out.

The blank for the SMPTE time code information is for setting the time code generator to a specific starting point in hours. As previously noted, when multiple reels are used in editing, a unique hour number can be selected to represent a VTR cassette or reel number. (If multiple tapes are used in editing and each starts with the 00 hour number, there is a good chance that a segment on one or more reels or cassettes will have the same time code number.)

SELECTING CAMERA POSITIONS

Next on the form comes camera positions. A supplementary sketch is generally attached to the facilities request form to show the camera positions decided upon by the director. Camera mounts could include field tripods, rolling dollies, cranes, camera jibs and cherry pickers. (Cherry pickers are tall, industrial crane devices, which are normally used for changing street lamps etc. They can be rented from heavy equipment companies and often make good camera cranes for high-angle shots.)

Several things should be kept in mind when deciding on camera locations. In addition to the obvious things such as not shooting against the sun and not placing a camera in a position that would result in a reversal of action ("crossing the line"), there are some special considerations for stationary cameras. Members of the press or ENG camerapersons may also find the camera angle you've selected to be ideal. (They probably will, if it's a good one.) If people suddenly jump up in front of your camera during the most exciting play in a game and block your shot, there may be little you can do. If they don't stand directly in front of your camera, they may simply block your shot from one or more angles. And there is another problem: if people in the crowd start jumping up and down in their excitement and shaking the camera platform, the resulting video may be unusable. Suffice it to say that in selecting camera positions you need to run through a number of "what if" scenarios.

There is also another side to the camera placement issue that must be considered. In order to hold public relations problems to a minimum, you will need to check to see if the location of cameras, lights or other equipment you will be using will block the view of individuals who have paid to attend the event.

ON-LOCATION AUDIO CONCERNS

The next part of the FAX sheet covers audio needs. Here the type of mic, its location and the amount of cable required should be noted. Because of the ambient noise common to remote locations, directional microphones are almost always required. If it is not possible to wire talent with personal mics, wireless mics will be the logical choice. In the latter case, have an assistant test each of the RF mics by slowly walking through the areas where they will be used (while counting, reciting a nursery rhyme or whatever). RF reflections (multipath reception) and dead spots are unpredictable. Since mic problems are common, back-up mics that can be put into service at a moment's notice should be provided for each area. When mounting crowd mics (mics that will pick up audience or crowd reaction), make sure they cover a wide area rather than favoring a few people closest to the mic. (More than one misplaced "crowd" mic has ended up getting the colorful comments of just a few close people rather than more generalized crowd reactions.) In determining where microphone cables will be run, plan for the shortest distance, and avoid running the cables parallel to AC cords or power lines. (If 60 or 120 Hz hum or buzz is heard in an audio line, it is generally caused either by nearby power lines or by a disconnected ground wire in a mic cable.) In wet weather or when rain is possible, seal up cable connectors with black plastic tape. When installing either mic or camera cables across hallways, run the cables over the top of doorways. This not only keeps people from walking over the cables (which can break wires) but it can eliminate injury (and possibly even a lawsuit) if someone trips over a cable.

DETERMINING LIGHTING NEEDS

Next are lighting needs. For exterior productions, the director will generally want to make certain that the sun is behind the cameras. Although it is possible to use high-powered (generally HMI) lights to fill in the shadows resulting from shooting against the sun, this will only work for subject matter that is rather close to the camera (and the lights). Even when shooting with the sun, some fill light in the form of a reflector board or a 5,500° K light is desirable for close-ups.

For interior shoots, the FAX sheet asks for an estimate of the normal light level. Although this is primarily intended for productions such as athletic events that will be done under existing light, it is also helpful in situations where lights will be added and some indication of base light levels is needed. Once a lighting director visits the location, a list of needed lighting instruments and accessories can be drawn up. In order to handle any problems with power, it is important to have the name and telephone number of an electrician with a knowledge of the location. By listing the locations of outlets and their power rating, the requirements for power cables and connector boxes can be determined.

PRODUCTION COMMUNICATION

Finally, there is the important matter of production communication. For live productions or productions that are relayed back to a station or production facility, there should be at least two communication links: technical and production. Engineers at both ends of the remote link must be in contact to make video and audio level adjustments and to keep microwave or satellite signals in optimum adjustment. Production personnel at both ends of the link must be able to plan for commercial and station identification breaks (which generally originate from VTRs at the station) and for updates on program and segment times. Except for some microwave and satellite feeds, which have their own PL audio channels, engineering and production links to the station or production facility are generally handled by cellular telephones (in the case of ENG assignments) or common telephone lines (in the case of multiple-camera shoots).

As discussed in Chapter 7, interrupted feedback (IFB) lines are used to communicate with on-camera talent. During a sports telecast, for example, a director may need to notify an announcer to go to commercial, or tell a color commentator that an instant replay of a specific play is being cued for playback. During live sports broadcasts, a "spotter" can use IFB to update sports announcers on statistics and general information appropriate to their commentary. Unlike live ENG reporters who wear only a small, single IFB earpiece, announcers for sports events often prefer padded, noise-canceling earphones that cover both ears. Although the earphones can be wired in several ways, in their normal mode both earphones carry program audio. This makes it possible for commentators to hear each other over the noise of the crowd. When a brief message needs to be relayed to an announcer (preferably when he or she is not talking) the audio on just one of the earphones is interrupted.

Although some field cameras allow for plugging in more than one PL headset, extra PL "drops" (added outlets) generally have to be installed in field locations to accommodate production personnel who are not working close to a camera. Of course, maximum mobility is possible if these crew members use wireless PL systems.

Whatever the system, a reliable two-way communication link to all production personnel is essential. If communication is lost, no one will know what is going on or what is expected of them. At best, confusion will result; at worst the entire production will become paralyzed. Because of the importance of PL communication, it is highly desirable—some would say *absolutely essential*—to have a fully-functional standby PL that everyone can instantly switch to if problems develop in the primary system.

High noise situations, where the sound of a cheering crowd or loud music can quickly drown out the best PL communication system, require special considerations. If tightly-fitting, padded, double earphones are used, much of the exterior noise will be eliminated. But if the noise is being picked up in each of the PL headset microphones, this approach will only allow crew members to more clearly hear the interfering noise! Normally, the microphones on PL headsets are on all the time, but to reduce accumulated interference under high noise conditions, push-to-talk switches are used. This means that PL microphones will all be off except when a specific crew member relays information or responds to a question.

The last area of production communication mentioned on the FAX sheet is *two-ways*. These are small transceivers similar to what police or security guards carry. They make it possible for production personnel to move around a remote site while still being in constant contact with key coordinating personnel.

PERMITS, CLEARANCES, BONDS AND INSURANCE

In small towns local officials probably will not have established procedures for handling on-location productions. However, some large cities not only require production permits, but security bonds, insurance and specially-assigned police. Most of the larger cities have film commissions that can provide a wide range of help to on-location film and video production personnel.

Remember, in covering paid events, that things can radically change between the camera rehearsal and the actual production. For example, before the event, crew members may be able to move freely throughout a facility. But during a performance, ushers or gatekeepers may have instructions to bar people

FIGURE 17.5
The first method devised for conducting video signals was coaxial cable. Four of the most commonly used video connectors are (from the left): the BNC connector, the UHF connector, the RCA phono connector and the F-connector. The phono connector is the same type used in audio.

from entering certain areas unless they have special passes. Complicating this issue are the increased security measures that are common with most public events.

THE EQUIPMENT INVENTORY

Since space for production equipment is generally at a premium inside mobile trucks and vans, and since it is desirable to hold transportation costs to a minimum, only things that will be used should be transported to the scene of the remote. This does not mean that such things as extra lamps for lights, extra mics and mic cables etc. should be excluded. It is a rare remote in which some piece of equipment doesn't fail. The remote survey form and the FAX sheet should be used as guides in deciding on the list of production equipment. This list should be carefully drawn up and then double-checked as the equipment is packed. Arriving at the scene of a remote without a major connecting cable or piece of equipment may mean that everyone will have to sit around until someone can get the needed item.

DIRECTING THE REMOTE PRODUCTION

Studio directors don't automatically make good field directors. Although directing a multicamera remote production is similar to directing a studio production, the remote director must be much more innovative and able to handle a wide range of unexpected problems. In a regular studio production, crew members typically get to know the basic routines associated with programs and often don't even have to be prompted by the director. But during a field production, all crew members will depend heavily—if not completely—on the director for second-by-second cues. For one thing, multiple-camera field productions often involve material that can't be scripted. Although the director will typically have an outline of what will happen during a parade, an athletic event or an awards program, much of the content will unfold virtually on a second-by-second basis.

We've already discussed the importance of a reliable PL system, but, as we noted in Chapter 13, the most effective system will be useless without clear and effective communication from the director. Because production involves the activities of a number of crew members (the number can range from 6 to 60) and conditions at many on-location sites is far from ideal, the director's instructions must be phrased clearly and succinctly. Recall that we covered many of the attributes of effective directing in Chapter 13.

COAXIAL CABLE

The first method devised for conducting video signals from one point to another was ***coaxial cable (coax)*** (see Figure 17.5). Coaxial cable still represents the basic medium for interconnecting video equipment. Unlike fiber optics, microwave or satellite links (to be discussed below), coax does not require transduction (a fundamental alteration of the basic video signal form) before the video can be transmitted.

Coaxial Cable Problems

Coaxial cable is the ideal choice for carrying normal video signals over distances of up to a few hundred feet. Beyond this, the loss in signal strength will adversely affect quality unless the signal is reamplified. Although it is possible to repeatedly reamplify the signal for transmission over long distances, quality problems develop with analog video and audio signals. For one thing, every time a standard analog signal is amplified, at least some small amount of signal degradation takes place, and the problem is cumulative. Each stage of amplification adds (however slightly) to the overall degradation. Therefore, the fewer times the signal has to be reamplified, the better. A point-to-point transmission medium that requires much less amplification than coax is fiber optics.

FIBER OPTICS

Unlike coaxial cables, which rely on electrical energy to carry signals, the medium for conducting signals in ***fiber optic*** cables, also called **optical fiber (OF)** cables, is light. Light waves have an extremely high frequency (about 10^{-6} m) and travel at a speed of about 186,000 miles, or 2,910 cm, per second. The extremely high frequencies mean that a single OF cable can theoretically carry trillions of bits of information per second. However, because of practical limitations in most equipment, data speeds generally do not exceed about 300 Mb/s (million bits per second). The high information-carrying capacity of OF is the reason it is widely used both in computer networks and telephone links and for the transmission of standard and high-definition video signals.

Although it would seem that a conductor that is capable of carrying millions of bits of information per second would have to be very large, a basic optical fiber is about the size of a human hair (Figure 17.6). The tiny, flexible glass or plastic fiber is coated, both for protection and to enhance its characteristics as a wave guide for the light it carries. Fiber optic cables normally carry numerous OF strands within a single enclosure.

coaxial cable (coax): An electrical cable designed to carry video signals that has a metal conductor in the center surrounded by an insulator and a braided wire shield.

fiber optics: Optical fiber. A flexible, hair-like, glass or plastic conduit for light waves. The light waves can be modulated by a television signal and sent great distances without experiencing many of the disadvantages of other point-to-point links.

FIGURE 17.6
The medium for conducting signals in fiber optic cables is light. Although it would seem that a conductor that is capable of carrying millions of bits of information per second would have to be very large, an optical fiber is about the size of a human hair. Fiber optic cables used for television production normally carry several strands such as this within a single enclosure.

The Advantages of Fiber Optics

Compared to a coaxial cable, an optical fiber has the following advantages:

- Much greater capacity. The information-carrying capacity of OF is more than 100 times that of a normal copper wire.

- Low and very uniform attenuation over a wide frequency range. The loss of signal strength in coaxial cables varies with video frequencies, which greatly complicates uniform amplification of multiple signals.

- Virtual immunity to interference. Radio frequency interference of various types can interfere with coaxial cable signals.

- No problems with leakage. When coaxial cables are used to conduct video at radio frequencies, the signal can create interference by being induced into nearby electronic components.

- Insensitive to temperature variations. Unlike OF transmissions, electrical resistance and attenuation in coaxial cables are directly related to temperature.

- Extremely small size.

- Will not "short out" in bad weather or even in water.

- Low cost. The basic ingredient in the glass fiber is sand, a raw material that is considerably cheaper than copper, the central conductor used in coaxial cable. (Some optical fibers are made out of a special plastic, which costs even less than glass fibers.)

- High reliability. The fibers do not corrode or break down in moisture or salt air.

- Light weight. Since they are not based on metal conductors, OF cables are lighter and much easier to transport and install.

Converting Audio and Video to Light

As shown in Figure 17.7, the video signal is used to modulate a light source. (Recall that modulation is the process by which one form of energy is used to alter basic characteristics of another energy form.) Although this light source is generally an LED (light-emitting diode), when high light output is needed, a laser is used. (Laser stands for "light amplification by simulated emission of radiation." A laser generates an intense beam of coherent light.)

Once the modulated light signal is generated and projected ("launched") into the optical fiber, the fiber acts as a highly efficient conduit or wave guide for the light beam. Unlike a beam of light that can only go in a straight line, an optical fiber can conduct the light around corners and even in circles without

FIGURE 17.7

Optical fiber has many advantages over microwave links, coaxial cable and satellite links. Once a modulated light signal is projected ("launched") into the optical fiber, the fiber acts as a highly efficient conduit or wave guide for the light beam. Unlike a beam of light, which can only go in a straight line, an optical fiber can conduct the light around corners and even in circles without appreciable light loss.

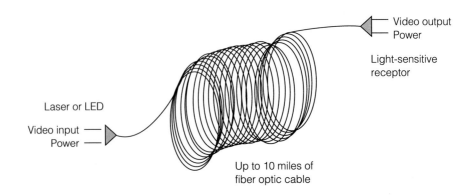

FIGURE 17.8

Remote sports broadcasts commonly use microwave links to send the signal to the production facility. Baseball games at this Malibu, California, university are often covered by Prime Ticket. From the mobile van on the playing field, the signal is microwaved back to the main production facility before being uplinked for satellite distribution.

appreciable light loss. One of the reasons the light beam within the fiber is able to continue for long distances is that it does not encounter the dust particles and other light-scattering obstructions that it does in air.

At the end of the optical fiber there is a photosensitive receptor that can respond to the modulated, ultra high frequency variations in the light beam's intensity (Figure 17.7). These variations, which correspond to the varying nature of the original video, are then changed back into a standard video signal.

The light beam can be modulated in either a digital or analog form. In addition to being used in permanent video links, such as those associated with regional TV networks, fiber optics are also widely used in video field production.

Fiber Optic Cable Applications

The traditional video cables required in doing remotes can be extremely heavy and bulky. (A good example would be a major golf tournament, which requires many thousands of feet of camera cable.) By using a single, high-capacity OF cable instead of multiple coax-based cables, both the number and weight of required cables are reduced.

As telephone companies continue to move toward optical fiber as the basic medium for communications, coast-to-coast video transmissions are becoming as simple as hooking up video equipment to a telephone circuit and dialing the right number. Once this technique becomes commonplace, some of the need for microwave and satellite links (to be discussed below) will be eliminated.

MICROWAVE LINKS

Although microwave links have been used in television for several decades, with the advent of fiber optics and satellite communications, microwave applications have significantly changed. Originally, these line-of-sight, point-to-point links were primarily used in broadcasting to provide the coast-to-coast links for the television networks and for studio-to-transmitter links. As remote broadcasting became more popular, TV stations invested in large production trucks equipped with microwave dishes for transmitting video signals back to the studio from remote locations. Athletic events (Figure 17.8), parades, major civic meetings and other multicamera productions were among the special events covered. These productions typically required at least one large truck full of equipment,

FIGURE 17.9
Short-hop microwave transmitters and receivers can be mounted on lightweight tripods. These small, highly portable transmitters make it possible to set up a link from the window of an office building, for example, and relay the signal to a central production van.

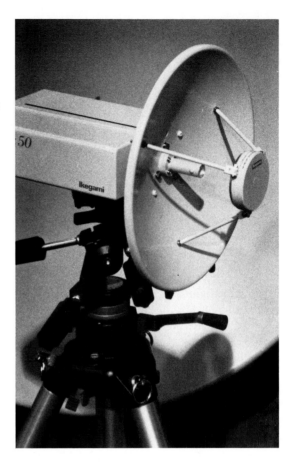

a dozen crew members, one or two engineers and about a full day of setup time. Consequently, setting up a microwave link to telecast a 40-second, live insert in a newscast—something that is commonly done today—was highly impractical.

Short-Hop Transmitters

Today, small, short-hop, solid-state microwave transmitters and receivers can be mounted on lightweight tripods. (See Figure 17.9.) These small, highly portable transmitters (sometimes referred to as "window-ledge transmitters") make it possible to set up a link from an office building, for example, and relay the signal to a central production van. At this point a more powerful microwave transmitter can be used to send the signal to one of the city's primary relay points (generally on top of a tall building). From there the signal is relayed back to the studio or production center, either by a microwave or fiber optic link. (See Figure 17.10.)

Microwave Characteristics

In setting up microwave transmitters and receivers, it is useful to think of the invisible microwave signal as acting somewhat like a focused beam of light. Microwaves will be reflected from some surfaces such as metal, but will (with some attenuation) pass through others, like wood, glass and wallboard. Microwaves can be attenuated or even obliterated by rain and snow.

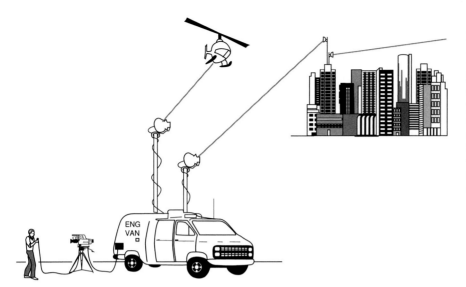

FIGURE 17.10
Microwave transmitters and receivers make it possible to link a number of video sources together in the field. A helicopter at the scene of a news story can relay aerial views of the scene to a production van while a news reporter does live commentary. From the production van, the signals can then be relayed to a more powerful microwave transmitter (often on top of a tall building). From here they are relayed back to the studio or production center.

Unlike a broadcast signal, which is designed to be basically omnidirectional, normal microwave signals are super-directional. The maximum reliable distance that can be achieved by full-power microwave links is about 75 miles. This assumes that no buildings, mountains or other obstructions are between the transmitting and receiving dishes. When obstacles exist or when distances exceed the normal microwave range, fiber optic cables or satellites are preferred.

Although the microwave energy used in television is of a different frequency than that used by microwave ovens, a direct microwave beam of a sufficient power can be harmful to the human body. However, when properly used, the power levels and frequencies associated with the point-to-point use of microwave broadcast links do not constitute a hazard for broadcast personnel.

Vans, Boats and Airplanes

The news vans used by many TV stations are often equipped with "golden-rod" antennas that can—assuming there are no obstructions—beam a microwave signal back to the station from almost anywhere in the station's coverage area. Although most microwave signals go in a straight line, occasionally it is necessary to modify the signal so that it can be received over a relatively large area. For example, if a television signal were coming from a moving car, motorcycle, boat or helicopter, it would be virtually impossible to keep the transmitter and receiver in perfect alignment (see Figure 17.11). For these applications, special omnidirectional transmitters and microwave "horns" (modified dishes) are used that can send signals over wider areas. The latest generation of mobile microwave transmitters and receivers can continually align themselves to maximize their point-to-point signals.

One of the limiting factors in using a microwave system is that permission must first be granted by the FCC. (One of the functions of the Federal Communications Commission is regulating over-the-air radio frequency transmissions of all types in an effort to eliminate interference.) In large cities where microwave signals are used by a wide range of telephone and data transmission services, getting FCC permission to use a microwave system can be a problem.

FIGURE 17.11
For microwave signals originating from moving vehicles, such as helicopters, special transmitters and receivers are used that can continually align themselves to maximize signal strength.

SATELLITE LINKS

The first live broadcast between the United States and Europe was made possible by Telstar I, a satellite that was put in orbit in July 1962. Because early satellites stood still in relation to the earth's rotation, ground stations had to track the satellites across the sky until they disappeared beyond the horizon. Because of this, transmissions were only possible for a limited number of hours. This problem was solved in mid-1965 when the first geosynchronous satellite, Intelsat I (also called "Early Bird"), was placed into orbit over the Atlantic Ocean.

Geosynchronous Satellites

geosynchronous satellite: A satellite that orbits at the same speed as the earth and, therefore, stays in the same place in the sky.

Geosynchronous satellites rotate at the same speed as the earth and are therefore stationary in relation to the earth's surface (Figure 17.12). With the tracking problem solved, satellite communications became much more attractive. Consequently, in the last few decades scores of satellites have been placed in orbits around the earth, leading to a fair amount of "heavenly congestion" and the need to aim dishes with an accuracy of at least 2 degrees in order to hit the intended satellite.

Ground Control Centers

Over time, satellites can slowly drift out of their assigned areas. Therefore, ground control centers must regularly make remote-controlled course corrections to keep them in their designated positions. Because most satellites are solar powered, electricity is not a problem; but on-board fuel for correcting variations in the satellite position is. This course-correcting fuel is the primary factor limiting the life of a satellite. Even so, satellites can have long lives. Westar II, which was launched in 1974, was still faithfully working when it was retired from service in 1987.

Satellite Transponders

transponder: A combination transmitter and receiver. Commonly used in satellite transmission and reception.

Each satellite, or "bird," is composed of a number of *transponders*—independent receive-transmit units. The number of transponders per satellite ranges from 10 to more than 20. C-band transponders normally handle a single television

FIGURE 17.12
Geosynchronous satellites rotate at the same speed as the earth and are therefore stationary in relation to terrestrial transmitting and receiving dishes. Scores of satellites have been placed in orbit around the earth, leading to a fair amount of congestion and a need to aim satellite dishes with an accuracy of at least 2 degrees.

channel. Each transponder on the higher frequency Ku-band satellites can receive and transmit two television channels. Most satellites are designed to be exclusively C-band or Ku-band (to be discussed below).

Satellite Consortiums

Although the networks and cable systems are the major users of satellite time, many news and satellite consortiums and cooperatives buy large blocks of satellite time and parcel it out to subscribers or buyers. (A year of time on a single transponder can cost more than a million dollars.) These customers include production facilities and local stations. Satellite transponder time is rented in precise intervals, which means that field productions must adhere to split-second timing. Although the basic audio and video signals can be uplinked and downlinked via satellite, there is typically no provision for two-way production communications (Figure 17.13). For PL and IFB communications, cellular phones are commonly used.

As shown in Figure 17.14, two classifications of satellites are used: those that use **C-band** frequencies (between 3.7 and 4.2 GHz, and from 5.9 and 6.4 GHz) and those that operate on the much higher **Ku-band** frequencies (between 11 and 12 GHz). (A **gigahertz**, or **GHz**, is one billion cycles per second.)

C-Band

C-band was the first satellite frequency range to be widely used in broadcasting. Compared to Ku-band, this range is more reliable under adverse conditions — primarily heavy rain and sleet. At the same time, the frequencies used are more congested and vulnerable to terrestrial interference. Because C-band frequencies

FIGURE 17.13
Today, many TV stations and news services rely on satellite uplinks to get stories from the field back to their production facility.

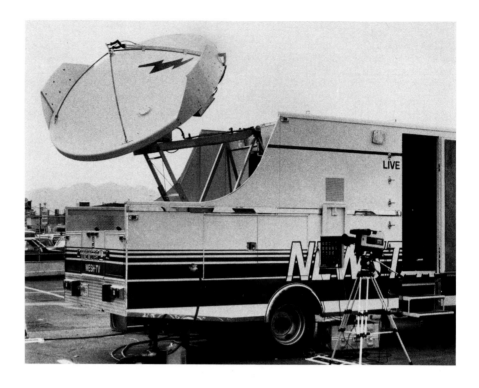

are also used in standard (ground-based) microwave transmissions, problems develop between C-band satellite receivers and nearby microwave transmitters. The C-band also requires large receiver and transmitting dishes—up to 30 feet for a full-size ground station. Although dish size may not be a major problem in permanently-mounted installations, even the scaled-down, 3- to 4-meter C-band dishes impose limitations on SNG trucks. For one thing, these vehicles encounter problems in getting to remote areas—a major consideration in covering news.

Ku-Band

Ku-band dishes are about one-third the size of those used in C-band. In SNG vehicles this greatly simplifies transportation and setup. Because Ku-band has

FIGURE 17.14
Two classifications of satellites are used in television: C-band and Ku-band. Although both types of satellites are 22,500 miles above the earth, for the sake of clarity they are shown at different levels in this drawing.

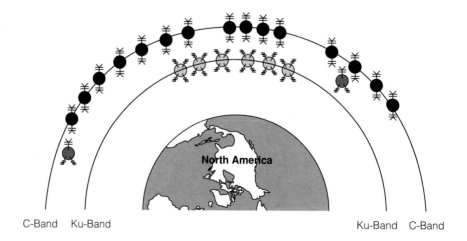

C-Band   Ku-Band   Ku-Band   C-Band

FIGURE 17.15
Ku-band dishes are about one-third the size of those used for C-band. In SNG (satellite newsgathering) vehicles, this smaller size greatly simplifies transportation and setup.

fewer technical restrictions, it means that users can set up satellite links and immediately start transmitting without waiting for FCC clearance. This "spontaneity factor" is an important advantage for Ku-band — especially in electronic newsgathering (Figure 17.15).

Satellite Distribution of Network Programming

A signal originating on the West Coast of the United States can be **uplinked** to a satellite over North America and then relayed, or **downlinked**, to a satellite ground station on the East Coast. This is typically how productions originating in the Los Angeles-Hollywood area are sent to the East Coast for network distribution. Once they arrive on the East Coast, they are recorded, scheduled into the network agenda and then beamed up to a satellite at intervals appropriate to the time zones of affiliated stations across North America. Each network affiliate has a permanently-mounted satellite receiving dish (Figure 17.16). The downlinked program can be broadcast directly from the satellite feed or, in some instances, recorded for later use. As we noted in our discussion of news in Chapter 12, when the network-to-affiliate link is not being used to relay regular programming, it is used to send short news stories, **promos** (program promotion segments) and other useful segments.

uplink: A ground-to-satellite transmitter link.

downlink: A satellite-to-ground receiver link.

FIGURE 17.16

A television production originating on the West Coast of the United States can be uplinked to a satellite over North America and then downlinked to a satellite ground station on the East Coast. Once the production arrives, it is recorded, scheduled into the network agenda and then beamed up to a satellite at intervals appropriate to the time zones of affiliated stations across North America. Each network affiliate has one or more permanently mounted satellite receiving dishes such as these.

satellite newsgathering (SNG): Electronic newsgathering that relies on a satellite uplink to get the story from the field.

flyaway unit: A portable satellite uplink commonly used in electronic newsgathering.

SNG Satellite Links

Whereas network satellite services use dedicated satellite links, SNG productions schedule satellite time on an "as needed" basis. (*SNG* stands for *satellite newsgathering,* the relaying of news stories from the field to production facility via a satellite link.) When a news story develops requiring a satellite link back to a TV station or production facility, a company that buys large blocks of satellite time will be contacted and arrangements made to schedule a specific block of satellite time.

The next problem for an SNG crew is to get a signal from the earth to the satellite. Without the aid of computer programs, it would be an almost impossible task to align a satellite dish so that its narrow beam would hit a satellite. Since satellites are about 22,500 miles above the earth and are spaced a mere 2 degrees apart in the sky (refer to Figure 17.14), precise aiming of the SNG dish is essential.

Flyaway Satellite Links

Not all satellite dishes are mounted on vehicles. In the late 1980s, portable, free-standing satellite uplinks — commonly referred to as *flyaway units* — were introduced (Figure 17.17). These units can be disassembled and transported to the scene of a news story in packing cases. Flyaway units are used in areas not accessible to SNG vehicles, including remote regions, off-shore areas and third-world countries. During the 1991 Persian Gulf war, the flyaway satellite uplink, with its ability to be set up anywhere within 30 minutes, permanently changed the nature of international electronic newsgathering (Figure 17.18).

For an on-going news story — one that would require the presence of a satellite newsgathering vehicle (SNV) for several days — portable satellite uplinks are the best choice. When the SNV is owned by the station or production agency, tying it up at one location for several days takes it out of service for covering other news stories. If the SNV must be rented, especially for several

FIGURE 17.17 (left)
In the late 1980s, portable, free-standing satellite uplinks—commonly referred to as flyaway units—were introduced. These units can be disassembled and transported to the scene of a news story in packing cases.

FIGURE 17.18 (right)
Flyaway satellite uplinks are used in areas not accessible to SNG vehicles, including remote regions, off-shore areas and third-world countries. The smallest satellite uplinks will fit into a suitcase.

days, the accumulated costs will be much greater than for using a portable satellite uplink.

Setting Up a Satellite Dish

Although most readers won't be personally involved in setting up satellite links (this should be left to an engineer experienced in the area), a knowledge of this procedure is important in making basic SNG decisions.

The first step is to park the SNG vehicle in a level area and anchor it with several stabilizing jacks. This not only provides a level starting point for calculating the dish position, but the anchoring keeps wind and movement within the vehicle from rocking the truck-mounted dish. The dish is then carefully positioned for the appropriate sector of the sky. Dishes can be aimed with the help of an automated system or by a computer-assisted approach. In the latter case the first step is to consult a topographic map for the exact geographic location of your uplink dish. These coordinates, together with data on the location of the satellite, are then fed into an engineering calculator or small, lap-top computer. A computer program will determine the dish coordinates: the elevation of the dish and it's azimuth (horizontal position). Modern SNVs (Figure 17.19) have computerized navigation systems that can determine the vehicle's location and then automatically aim the dish at a designated satellite.

Once the dish is physically aligned as closely as possible to the coordinates of the target satellite, a radio frequency (RF) **pilot signal** from the satellite is used to fine tune the coordinates and the RF signal. Engineers use a spectrum analyzer to make sure they have the right satellite and to do the final electronic "tweaking" of the signal.

FIGURE 17.19
The computerized navigation systems in today's satellite news vehicles can determine the vehicle's location and then automatically aim the dish at the desired satellite. Two satellite uplink transmitters and two receivers (on the left) are part of this SNG vehicle.

Through a technical process of polarizing signals, each satellite transponder is able to simultaneously receive and transmit more than one signal on the same frequency. An error in correctly setting the polarization of an uplinked signal may mean that it will obliterate another signal—a mistake that will make you very unpopular with at least one other producer trying to uplink a signal! An engineer with a knowledge of satellite transmissions is critical in SNG work.

Because satellite time is scheduled to the split second, major multiple-camera field productions must be extremely well planned and coordinated. It is almost never possible to get an extra few minutes, or even an extra few seconds, of satellite time to compensate for a late start or a momentary technical problem. And, since satellite time is somewhat expensive, scheduling an extra 30 minutes of time, "just in case," is hard to justify.

COVERING SNG ASSIGNMENTS

For short (30- to 60-second) news segments, the situation is a bit different. Since the "window" for the feed (the total reserved transponder time) will generally be much longer than the segment, the segment can often be repeated if there are technical problems.

Today, satellite transmissions have become routine and, for the most part, quite reliable. However, there are still occasional problems. At times it is safer to transmit a videotape from a field location instead of doing a live feed. The videotape can be done a short time before the scheduled satellite time without sacrificing timeliness. Since satellite time and the operation of SNG mobile equipment are costly, this "procedural insurance" can occasionally spell the difference between getting the segment back in the short time allotted or losing the opportunity to transmit it. Another type of "insurance" should also be considered when uplink problems are being experienced. If the field segment is double-recorded (recorded simultaneously on two machines) and a momentary problem interferes with the uplink transmission of the first tape, the second tape can be started and transmitted with a minimal loss of time.

Depending on travel time, a well-planned and coordinated SNG story can be done in less than two hours. Once the SNG truck is on location, it can take as little as 10 minutes for the coordinates to be established and the dish raised and aimed at the appropriate satellite. While this is taking place, the production crew can set up and white balance the camera(s).

B-Roll Satellite Footage

If the segment requires B-roll footage, as most will, this can be immediately taped and beamed back to the studios. After being quickly edited, this footage can be rolled into "wraparound commentary" from the reporter in the field. Typically, the latter is done live. When the station switches to the live satellite feed, the reporter first does the stand-up introduction. The prerecorded footage is then rolled in from the studio while the field reporter does VO narration (generally while looking at an off-air monitor). On-camera procedures will be covered in more detail in the next chapter.

Typical Field-Production Setups

To conclude this section, we'll show some multiple-camera setups associated with various events (Figures 17.20 through 17.27). Although the setups illustrated have been used successfully, available equipment and the specific conditions encountered at the remote site will, of course, determine the final setup.

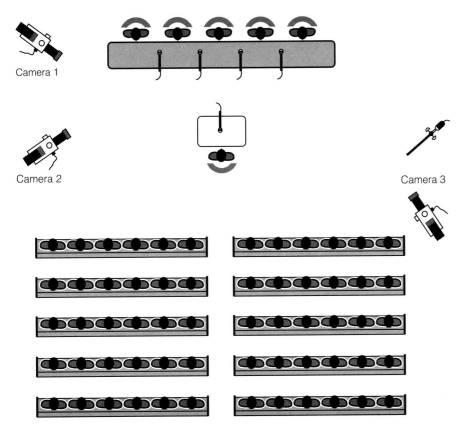

FIGURE 17.20

A major problem in doing many remotes, especially in meeting rooms, is positioning the cameras so that they do not block the view of spectators. This sometimes means cameras must be placed in less-than-ideal positions. Camera 1 can get a close-up of the person testifying at the desk, as well as occasional shots of the audience. Cameras 2 and 3 can get shots of the panel members. A shotgun mic covers the audience.

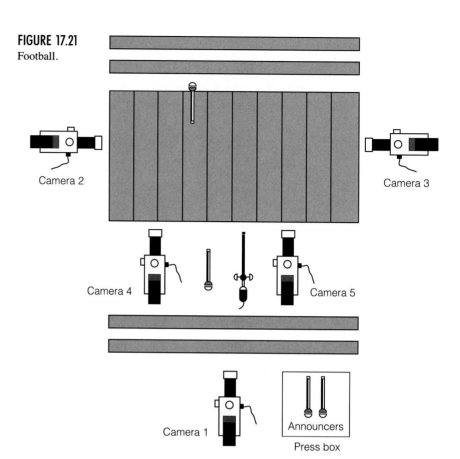

FIGURE 17.21
Football.

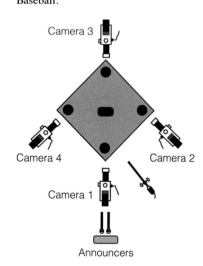

FIGURE 17.22
Baseball.

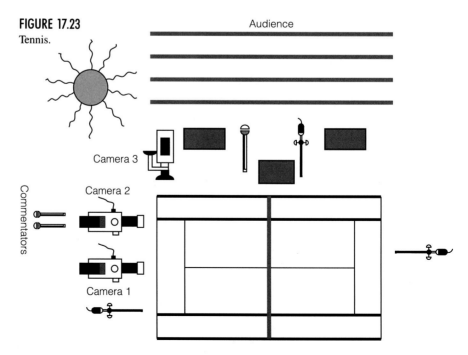

FIGURE 17.23
Tennis.

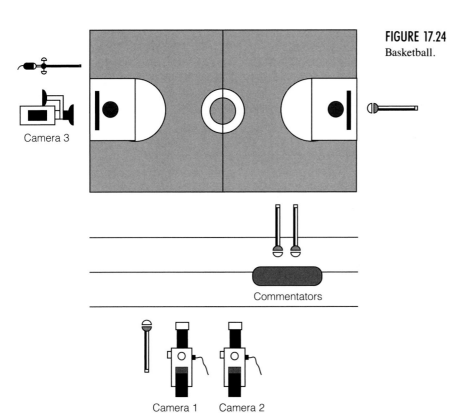

FIGURE 17.24
Basketball.

Commentators

Camera 1   Camera 2

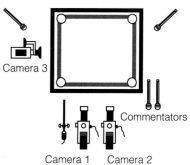

FIGURE 17.25
Boxing.

Camera 3

Commentators

Camera 1   Camera 2

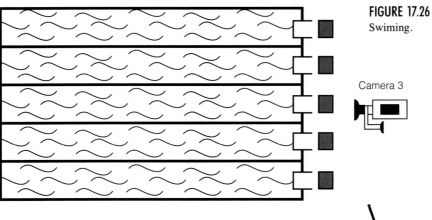

FIGURE 17.26
Swiming.

Camera 3

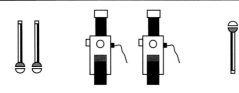

Commentators   Camera 1   Camera 2

FIGURE 17.27
Track.

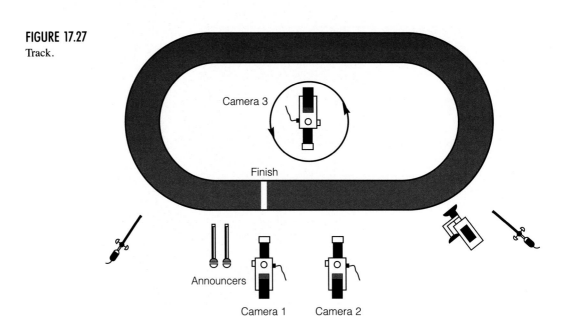

The quality of production coverage doesn't necessarily depend on the amount of production equipment. Although a Super Bowl telecast may use 20 or more cameras, football games (with extensive and imaginative preproduction planning) have been acceptably covered with only two cameras.

SUMMARY

Although preproduction planning may not be the most glamorous aspect of on-location production, it is the most important. The most critical step in doing an on-location production is the first one: the on-location survey. This survey should address the following 11 concerns: (1) available power; (2) a clear satellite uplink or microwave path; (3) the existence of environmental sound problems; (4) prevailing lighting conditions; (5) changes that might be necessary at the location to accommodate the script, talent and the production equipment; (6) location availability and restrictions; (7) total costs and conditions for using the location; (8) suitability of the location in meeting the needs of the script; (9) restroom facilities for cast and crew; (10) adequate security, police and first aid; and (11) the availability of food and refreshments. To request and reserve crew and facilities, most production facilities use a formal FAX sheet, supplemented by drawings of camera and mic positions, information on permits, parking, sketches of special construction needed etc.

A television signal can be sent from the field in three ways: by fiber optics, by one or more microwave links and by satellite. Compared to a coaxial cable, optical fiber has the following ten advantages: (1) much greater capacity; (2) low and very uniform signal attenuation over a wide frequency range; (3) virtual immunity to interference; (4) no problems with leakage; (5) insensitivity to temperature variations; (6) extremely small size; (7) superior signal conductivity in bad weather and even through water; (8) low cost; (9) high reliability; and (10) light weight.

Today, small, solid-state microwave transmitters and receivers can be mounted on window ledges and lightweight tripods. These highly portable transmitters make it possible to set up a microwave link in an office, for example, and then relay the signal to a central production van. At this point a more powerful microwave transmitter can be used to send the signal to one of the city's primary relay points (generally on top of a tall building). From here the signal can be relayed back to the studio or production center, either by a microwave or fiber optic link. Microwaves are reflected from some surfaces, such as metal, but will (with some attenuation) pass through others, like wood, glass and wallboard. Microwave signals can be attenuated or even obliterated by rain and snow.

Geosynchronous satellites rotate at the same speed as the earth and are therefore stationary in relation to the earth's surface. Two classifications of satellites are used: C-band (between 3.7 and 4.2 GHz, and from 5.9 and 6.4 GHz) and those that operate on the higher Ku-band frequencies (between 11 and 12 GHz). C-band was the first satellite frequency range to be widely used in broadcasting. Compared to Ku-band, this range is more reliable under adverse conditions; primarily in heavy rain and sleet. At the same time, the frequencies used are more congested and vulnerable to terrestrial interference. Ku-band dishes are about one-third the size of those used in C-band. In SNG vehicles this greatly simplifies transportation and setup. Because the Ku-band has fewer technical restrictions, it means that users can set up satellite links and immediately start transmitting without waiting for FCC clearance. This "spontaneity factor" is an important advantage in electronic newsgathering.

In the late 1980s, portable, free-standing satellite uplinks, commonly referred to as flyaway units, were introduced. These units can be disassembled and transported to the scene of a news story in packing cases. Flyaway units are used in areas not accessible to SNG vehicles, including remote regions, offshore areas and third-world countries.

In doing live productions or productions that are relayed back to a station or production facility, there should be at least two communication links: technical and production. Although directing a multicamera remote production is similar to directing a studio production, the remote director must be much more innovative and able to handle a wide range of unexpected problems. The quality of production coverage doesn't necessarily depend on the amount of production equipment. Although Super Bowl telecasts may use more than 20 cameras, football games (with extensive and imaginative preproduction planning) have been acceptably covered with only two cameras.

KEY TERMS

C-band
coaxial cable (coax)
double-recorded
downlink
fiber optics
flyaway units
geosynchronous satellites
gigahertz (GHz)
Ku-band

optical fiber (OF)
pilot signal
preproduction planning
promo
pyrotechnics
satellite newsgathering (SNG)
transponder
uplink

18

On-Camera Concerns

In this chapter we will look at a wide range of on-camera considerations, including the principles of announcing and presentation, studio hand signals and makeup and wardrobe.

ANNOUNCING

Although producers and directors may never deliver a line on camera (and may have absolutely no aspirations in this direction), they are still responsible for the caliber of on-camera presentations and for getting the best possible performance from talent. In particular, key production personnel need to

- be able to identify specific on-camera problems,
- help non-professionals achieve satisfactory results in their on-camera presentations,
- work with professional talent in bringing about the most effective results and
- understand the principles of presentation, so that they can make effective editing decisions.

Scripted Narration

The ability to effectively read a script is an art that is generally developed after some training and considerable experience (Figure 18.1). Several things are needed. First, an ability to quickly and accurately recognize words, including uncommon words and foreign names. A mispronounced name or a grammatical

FIGURE 18.1
The ability to effectively read a script is an art — generally developed after considerable experience. Since it is time-consuming and costly to rerecord narration after music and effects have been mixed, producers and directors must have a sharp ear for catching announcing and writing problems early in the production process.

error readily stands out to informed listeners. Although only a small percentage of audience members who catch a problem will call and complain, the result is diminished credibility. Since it is time-consuming and costly to rerecord narration after music and effects have been mixed, producers and directors must have a sharp ear for catching announcing and writing problems early in the production process.

Good broadcast announcers keep up with the news and regularly monitor newscasts to catch the names of unfamiliar people and places. Sometimes pronunciations will vary because of "Anglicizing." To cite one example, the Canadian province of Newfoundland is pronounced by the English-speaking inhabitants of that island as New-fin-LAND, with the accent on the last syllable. In the United States the name is Anglicized and pronounced NEW-finlend, with the accent on the first syllable. To confuse things further, the purists who live on that island province insist on New-found-land, with an equal emphasis on each syllable.

The preferred pronunciation of Newfoundland (or Praia, or Tegucigalpa) can be checked in a dictionary or guide to pronunciation. News services such as the AP have pronunciation guides in their style handbooks. However, new names that pop up in the news may not be listed. For these, announcers should rely on either a trusted source such as a network newscast, or the "pronouncers" included in parenthesis within wire service copy. In the latter case the dictionary-type symbols (ä, ô, ñ etc.) will not be used; instead, names will be divided into syllables and spelled out phonetically (FA-NET'-IC-LY) with accent marks on syllables that should be stressed. Some announcers prefer a combination of lowercase and capital (CAP-i-tal) letters.

As in the case of Newfoundland, you will often find regional differences in pronunciation. Miami, New Orleans, Buena Vista and Calais are just a few examples of cities that are pronounced differently — even within the United States. In doing local productions, the rule is always to use the locally accepted pronunciation.

Effective Announcing Traits

Conveying the intended meaning of a script goes far beyond just getting the words right. Meaning must be communicated through proper phrasing, appropriate pauses and the subtle and periodic stress on words and word groups. Depending upon the content and complexity of the script, it will probably take a while for the narrator to fully understand what the writer is trying to say. Hurrying announcers or forcing them to read a script that they are not totally familiar with compromises quality.

One of the most important talents announcers must develop is the ability to read ahead. This means that while they are saying one word, their eyes are several words ahead—getting the jump on difficult or unfamiliar words and looking for clues to meaning and needed emphasis. Although reading ahead takes some practice, it is the only way to master the art of broadcast announcing.

Unfortunately, when using camera prompters, it becomes impossible to read too far ahead, since only a dozen or so words can be displayed at a time. Because of this, professional announcers familiarize themselves with a script by studying a hard copy before reading prompter copy on the air.

When doing narration directly from a script, most announcers (given the time) will mark up scripts with their own symbols. Figure 18.2 shows an example. Although it may at first seem that marking a script in this way should be unnecessary for experienced announcers, remember that during a production, announcers will typically have many things on their minds: time cues, pacing themselves (speeding up or slowing down) to match video footage in a monitor and possibly even listening to the director's commands in a headset. Because their attention is divided, these symbols provide guidance at crucial points.

Note in Figure 18.2 that three heavy lines are placed at the ends of sentences. (Although there are actually supposed to be three vertical lines, when done quickly they often end up looking like a large letter *N*.) This bold symbol is used not only to provide a "look-ahead flag" for the end of a sentence, but to provide a clearly visible marker. Announcers who must periodically look up from a script—either to look at a camera or check a monitor—cannot risk the awkward pause that would result if they lost their place. By silently reading ahead to the end-of-sentence marker, announcers can then look up while they finish a sentence. When they glance back at their script, they look for the last bold marker to start the next sentence. A single vertical line dividing words indicates a pause.

An underlined word or phrase indicates stress or emphasis. Every sentence has **key words**, which should be emphasized to convey meaning. Much of the art of announcing is being able to recognize these key words. Emphasis is achieved by adding a slight pause before key words and by subtle (and sometimes not-so-subtle) stress.

A wavy line under a word or phrase signals caution; the word is unusual, it's a tongue-twister, or it can easily be mistaken for another word. Vertical lines dividing segments of a word break it down to facilitate pronunciation. Generally, accent marks are added in this process. As noted, a rewriting of a name in parenthesis above the word is referred to as a *pronouncer*.

Parentheses signal a group of words that should be read together as a single phrase. (Be careful: *typed* parentheses are sometimes used to set off production or reading instructions—words that should not be read aloud. Ideally, however, a different case or typeface or should be used to set off instructions.)

Placing numbers above groups of words indicates a sequence of items that should be read as a list. A half-arrow at the end of a line indicates that, although it may seem as if a thought is complete, the phrase continues on the next line.

STEEL FROM OVERSEAS, (AT LOW PRICES THAT U-S PRODUCERS CAN'T MATCH,) HAS BEEN ONE OF THE COMPLAINTS OF A-D-I STEEL DURING MORE THAN THREE STRAIGHT YEARS OF PRE-TAX LOSSES. NOW THE NATION'S EIGHT LARGEST STEELMAKER IS MOVING TO DO SOMETHING ABOUT IT. A-D-I STEEL SAYS IT IS DISCUSSING SALE OF A SUBSTANTIAL PORTION OF ITS ASSETS TO ETON KOKAN, JAPAN'S THIRD LARGEST STEEL PRODUCER. THE ANNOUNCEMENT FROM A-D-I HEADQUARTERS IN LOS ANGELES SAID DISCUSSIONS ARE WELL UNDERWAY BUT THAT NO FURTHER DETAILS ARE AVAILABLE AT THIS TIME. AN AGREEMENT, IF REACHED, WOULD BE SUBJECT TO THE APPROVALS OF THE GOVERNMENTS OF JAPAN, THE UNITED STATES AND THE STATE OF CALIFORNIA.

FIGURE 18.2
Sample script.

Pausing at the end of the line (for those who do not read far enough ahead) would improperly break continuity. (Poetry is often inappropriately read with pauses at the end of each line, a procedure that fragments and obscures meaning.)

Eliminating In-Studio Distractions

It is easy for a production crew to forget that effective narration takes considerable concentration. Therefore, it is important for a director to reduce or eliminate all possible distractions, especially behind-the-camera distractions, during a production. A "one-liner" (joke) by a director that causes a floor director or cameraperson to snicker may be all it takes to break the concentration of on-camera talent (who might then be wondering — as they are trying to talk — if they said something wrong).

Correcting Problems in Narration

Even the best of announcers occasionally fluff a word. If a production is being done live, the more subtle and matter-of-fact the correction, the better. Unless an announcer shows his or her frustration or embarrassment, the audience may hardly notice. If the narration is being taped, problems can be corrected by redoing segments. However, having to repeatedly stop to retape segments because of announcing problems ends up being time-consuming and costly. It also introduces problems during postproduction. Whenever a narrator stops to re-do a segment, it becomes difficult to accurately match the previous pace and energy level. This sometimes becomes obvious when it's too late — when the segments are being spliced together during postproduction. It is best to start "re-dos" from major transition points in the script — places where a change of pace might be expected. During editing, the insertion of a (room-tone) pause or even a short segment of background music will help cover a mismatch in pace or energy.

Considerations in Using Prompters

Although we covered the basics of camera prompters in Chapters 1 and 4, some additional information from the perspective of on-camera talent is now appropriate.

For live productions, on-camera people should always have a hard copy of the script with them. Things happen: a prompter will malfunction, a computer will bring up the wrong segment of a file for display, or a distracted prompter operator will get totally lost in the copy. Even when the on-camera talent is using a prompter, it is a good idea (if the production makes this possible) to have them keep their script pages in sync with the prompter. To aid this, page-turn symbols and numbers can be placed on prompter copy. Each time one becomes visible — generally at the end of a segment or story — the on-camera talent can turn a page. This assures minimum delay if the talent has to (or wants to) revert to the script. In the latter case announcers sometimes find it effective to defer to their script while stressing important quotes or complex numbers.

The second reason that talent should be provided with a script is that it allows them to glance ahead when they are not on the air to review or check upcoming segments. Having the ability to flip ahead in the script and get ready for what's coming can eliminate on-camera problems.

Before starting a production, especially a live show, an announcer should check the visibility of the prompter in all camera positions. Occasionally, a camera position will result in an overhead light being reflected in the prompter glass, or a camera shot will necessitate a camera dollying under a strong key light. In both cases the text may become obscured. Occasionally, a camera operator will position the camera at a much greater distance than expected (rehearsed). Although a zoom lens can still get the needed shot, the greater distance may make it difficult for the on-camera talent to see the prompter. With any of these problems, it will be awkward for an on-camera person to gracefully communicate the unexpected problem to a director—at least, while on the air.

If a color monitor is being used to display prompter copy, different colors should be used to represent production-related notes (*videotape: 2 minutes*) and different on-camera people (*Joe, Janice* etc.). At the risk of indulging in sexism, Joe's copy might be in black letters on a light blue background and Janice's in black letters with a pink background. (Interestingly, an announcer inadvertently reading the wrong copy during a newscast is one of the most frequent on-camera problems.) Production notes should clearly contrast with text to be read: possibly white letters on a black background. Of course, creative color coding always takes second place to legibility.

Although a prompter that is close to the talent is easy to read, their left-to-right eye movements will probably be noticeable. This problem is reduced or eliminated when the camera is pulled back; but then, of course, the prompter becomes more difficult to read. A happy medium should be worked out during a rehearsal.

Maintaining Optimum Eye Contact

Audiences prefer a balance between constant eye contact and none at all. A constant staring at a prompter (camera lens) seems unnatural to an audience, because it appears as if the performer is intently staring at them—an action that makes most people uncomfortable. This is a common mistake made by performers who are not comfortable enough with a prompter to be able to occasionally glance away, generally to look at their script. A reasonable balance in eye contact is maintained if narrators glance down at their scripts as they turn the page at the end of each story. Conversely, an on-air person whose eyes are constantly buried in a hard copy of the script (when prompters are not used) appears to be ignoring the audience. In this case it is desirable for narrators to read ahead far enough so that they can glance up at the camera for a few seconds, generally for the final words of sentences.

Recognizing Effective Voice Characteristics

When inexpensive tape recorders hit the market in the 1960s, many people were amazed (and more often rather distressed) to find out what they sounded like. Some people even refused to accept the fact that it was their voice they were hearing. ("I'm sure I couldn't sound like that; there's obviously something terribly wrong with that machine!") What we think we sound like and what we actually sound like may be quite different.

TV performers who are serious about their work make it a point to review recordings of themselves at regular intervals. These are called *air checks.* Even performers who have been successful in their profession for 10, 20 or more years do this. Among other things, this is a way to catch and eliminate the lazy habits of normal conversation that creep into on-air delivery: dropping *ing*'s, acquiring unnatural patterns of emphasis or losing (as one professional puts it) "the smile in your voice."

There are thousands of people who can read scripts without making mistakes, but only a few (the ones that often make six-figure salaries) who make

air check: A recording of an on-air segment done by or for a particular announcer to evaluate diction, voice quality and general effectiveness.

you want to keep listening. These on-air personalities typically communicate a feeling of ebullience, assurance and warmth in their voices (voice smile). Although these attributes can't be quantified, they have a definite effect upon an audience; and what affects an audience must, by necessity, be a concern of every successful TV producer and director.

Restricting Hand and Head Gestures

In ordinary speech most people make extensive use of hand gestures, head nods and facial expressions to emphasize points. On camera, these must be far more subtle, or else they will look awkward and out of place. One of the best ways to help people to get ready for on-camera presentations—if time allows—is to do a videotape and let them study it. Since most people now have VHS players at home, simply giving them a tape of an early rehearsal or run-through may be adequate to help them overcome basic problems. Most people have considerable experience in looking at good TV role models; therefore, they sometimes end up being their own best teachers—and worst critics. Deep-rooted articulation or pronunciation problems, regional accents and unnatural patterns of speech and delivery will probably require the expertise of a speech therapist.

WORKING WITH ACTORS

Often directors have a problem converting seasoned stage actors to television. Although appropriate for the stage, their gestures, facial expressions and intonations tend to be much too expansive for the close-up medium of television. Although a sensitive TV mic can easily pick up conversation at normal levels, stage actors may have had years of experience at projecting their voices so they can be heard in the last row of a theater. This comes across as unnatural and affected on television. A director may need to emphasize these differences while diplomatically suggesting that an actor's presentation may need to be "brought down a bit." Again, a preproduction videotape may be the most effective teacher.

RESEARCH ON EFFECTIVE ON-CAMERA PRESENTATION

Over the years, a considerable amount of money has been spent researching what is and what is not effective in on-camera presentation. Much of the research has been done in the area of news presentation. Apart from the more obvious things (we like to watch positive, confident and attractive people, and we don't like to watch negative, inept and unattractive people) results are sometimes hard to predict. At the same time, millions of dollars can ride on an audience's acceptance or rejection of an on-camera personality. Not unexpectedly, considerable effort has gone into testing various people, program formats and even wardrobe combinations on sample audiences.

Early in audience research it was found that audiences could not always clearly verbalize why they preferred one presenter or type of presentation over another. To complicate matters, verbal responses don't always match behavior. This is particularly evident in television programming, where people will say that a particular program is good but, given a chance, will watch something else. (This explains why programs that people say are "thought-provoking" with "quality and substance" are often quietly passed over in favor of those that are perceived as being "a bit trashy.")

Since verbal responses aren't always dependable predictors of success, producers have had to look for more reliable measures. They found that certain unconscious physiological reactions to stimuli sometimes represent more honest indicators of human response: blood pressure, galvanic skin response, breathing, (all used in lie detector tests) and even pupil dilation.

Today, physiological and psychological research regularly influences television production. To stay competitive, production personnel must go beyond production hardware and its operation and keep abreast of findings that affect production and program content.

MAKEUP

With the advent of high-definition television, the need for people skilled in the application of subtle but effective makeup procedures has increased. Although many people automatically assume that the purpose of makeup is to "make you look better," in television it's often just to make you look natural and normal. Like many behind-the-scenes aspects of television, makeup is best when it goes unnoticed.

Since television is a close-up medium, there is great emphasis on the human face and its appearance. With most subjects, the use of some amount of makeup is desirable, both to ensure that they photograph naturally and to improve their appearance by emphasizing desirable characteristics and de-emphasizing undesirable ones.

There are three classes of make-up:

- *Basic makeup* compensates for undesirable changes in appearance brought about by the television process. An application of basic makeup takes from 3 to 10 minutes for men and from 5 to 20 minutes for women.

- *Corrective makeup* enhances positive personal attributes and downplays flaws in skin, hair etc. Corrective makeup takes from 20 minutes to an hour to apply.

- *Character makeup* brings about a major change in appearance. Elaborate character makeup can take many hours.

basic makeup: Primary or elemental makeup. As opposed to corrective or character makeup, makeup intended to slightly enhance appearance as seen on TV.

corrective makeup: Makeup intended to significantly change appearance; generally to hide certain original facial features.

character makeup: Makeup (generally accompanied by hair pieces etc.) designed to change an actor's appearance into that of the character being played.

Basic Makeup

Normal skin contains a certain amount of oil at its surface that generally goes unnoticed until it appears full-frame in a carefully focused and lit television picture. This problem is intensified by the heat of studio lights and the tension that is usually associated with on-camera appearances. Unless basic makeup is used, a distracting and unnatural-looking shine results. The major problems in this respect are bald heads and shiny noses and foreheads.

There are also a number of less obvious problem areas that may require basic makeup. Normal skin color consists of subtle green and purple hues that are generally not noticeable to the eye. These hues are unnaturally intensified by some types of television cameras, especially under fluorescent lights.

The television system also intensifies shadow areas in the face. In particular, the limited brightness range of the television system can exaggerate the dark areas around the eyes, nose and chin. Probably the most significant of the dark area problems is represented by men's beards. Without makeup, dark-

FIGURE 18.3
These "before" (A), "during" (B) and "after" (C) pictures show a subject being made up for television. The text covers the basic steps in applying makeup.

(a)

(b)

(c)

complected, cleanly shaven men will still appear to be very much in need of a shave.

There is one other area in which some basic makeup may be necessary. Fair-skinned subjects who are placed on camera next to people with very dark complexions need to be "toned down" to keep from appearing abnormally light. In these cases, makeup will probably be needed to bring skin tones into a brightness range that will be perceived as normal.

Often there is no further need for makeup after this first, rather necessary phase — that of just making subjects appear relatively normal on the screen.

Corrective Makeup

In doing corrective makeup, decisions must be made on the emphasis or accentuation of desirable facial features and the de-emphasis of undesirable features. Skin blemishes and unattractive skin colorations may need to be covered with one or more layers of makeup. Although some general procedures for doing this will be outlined below, the ability to recognize the unique qualities in a face that need to be subtly emphasized or de-emphasized takes considerable experience. Figures 18.3A to 18.3C show a female subject before, during and after the application of makeup.

Character Makeup

Character makeup covers a great range: from adding or subtracting a few years to today's grisly science fiction or horror-film transformations that have replaced the Frankenstein's monster conversions of early film (see Figures 18.4A to 18.4E). Most character makeup requires less-than-spectacular changes — facial reshaping, changes in hair etc. — that are appropriate to a character being played in a dramatic production. Except for a few basic principles to be discussed below, character makeup will not be dealt with in detail. It is a specialized area that has a limited use in most day-to-day television production work. Readers who need to develop an understanding of character makeup can find materials listed in the bibliography.

Makeup Basics

Although some makeup is almost always desirable for television work, some situations make it difficult, if not impossible, to apply. An example would be people selected from a studio audience to appear immediately on camera. Sometimes, in television discussion shows, guests arrive at the studio too late to be completely made up. Even so, there may be time to apply translucent face powder to dull an objectionable shine.

Although regular "street" makeup is sometimes suitable for television, experience has shown that unpleasant surprises can be reduced and consistency increased if makeup especially manufactured for television is used. Several well-known manufacturers of cosmetics make complete lines of TV makeup suitable for any skin coloration. Once you become familiar with the color and tone designations of a particular manufacturer, you can quickly build speed and confidence in the effective use of the product line.

Applying the Base

The first step in making up an individual is to prepare the skin for the makeup **base**, or makeup **foundation**. For men, this simply means that a cleansing lotion is used to remove excess oil. In the case of women wearing street

FIGURE 18.4
Character makeup can take a young man (A) and transform him into a caricature of an old man (E). In (A) a bald cap is applied to cover up the young man's hair. Then the basic makeup is started (B). The neckbone section of prosthesis has been applied in (C). Eyebrows are added and trimmed in (D). Photo (E) shows the final result.

(a)

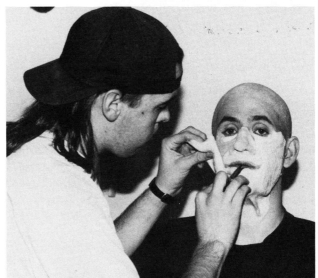

(b)

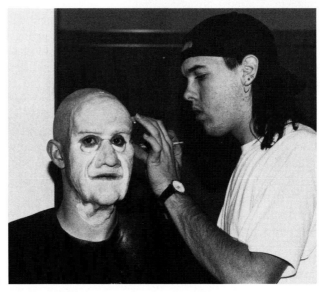

(c)

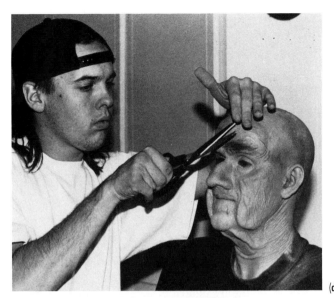

(d)

FIGURE 18.4, continued

(e)

makeup, the makeup will have to be completely removed with a cleansing cream or lotion. With both men and women, an astringent should be used after cleansing in order to tighten facial pores.

Base, or foundation, makeup is available with either an oil or water base. Water-base makeup has a couple of important advantages: it generally does not require the use of face powder, and it is easier to remove. One type of water-base foundation is supplied in stick form and is available in about 20 different shades and colors (Figure 18.5).

Two or more shades can be blended together to arrive at subtle colorations. Unless it is appropriate to darken or lighten the skin tone, a base shade should be selected (or created through blending) that most closely approximates the subject's natural skin color.

Using a foam rubber sponge, the base should be carefully applied to the face, ears and neck (Figure 18.6C). If the applicator is moistened slightly, the base will cover the skin more evenly and smoothly.

FIGURE 18.5
One type of water-base foundation is available in stick form in about 20 shades and colors. Water-base makeup has two important advantages: it generally does not require the use of face powder, and it is easier to remove.

Occasionally it is desirable to slightly lighten or darken natural skin tones. As we've noted, for a person with a very dark tan who must appear next to someone with rather light, pallid skin, it is best to bring the two subjects closer together in tonal values. The dark tan can be lightened by selecting a base shade one to two gradations lighter than the normal skin shade. Conversely, a light-skinned subject can be toned down by using a base one to two shades darker than the normal skin shade. However, exceeding two shades of correction in either direction is not recommended. The degree of control that can be provided should be more than enough to avoid the rather disturbing contrast that can result when the television system tries to cope with major differences in skin tone in the same picture. Keep in mind, however, that these differences will be expected when blacks or dark-skinned people appear in the picture. In such cases you generally only need to use a make-up base that matches their skin coloration.

Often with a deeply tanned person it is necessary to even out the coloration around the eyes or bridge of the nose by mixing the base in these areas with a touch of rouge. Other evidences of an uneven tan, such as the halter strap marks over the shoulders of a woman, can also be filled in when applying the makeup base. As previously mentioned, men's beards can be a particularly noticeable problem, even right after shaving. This can be reduced or eliminated by a subtle blending in of foundation in the beard areas.

Concealing and Emphasizing Features

Since few faces are perfect, it may be necessary to play down undesirable facial features or to emphasize stronger elements through **contouring** and **highlighting**. With makeup, there is a basic rule: Dark shading slims; light shading widens. So, if you want to make a wide nose appear narrower, you would shade the sides with a deeper shade of makeup than your foundation. High foreheads can be shortened by carefully applying makeup several shades darker than usual from the hairline to the middle of the forehead. Contouring also can help achieve that classic jaw line, which most women wish they had. Simply use a darker base shade and apply the makeup from the chin line up to the earlobe and into the hollows of the cheek. Contouring and highlighting can be done before applying the foundation or after the base has been applied. In all cases, gently but thoroughly blend the shading together to achieve the desired coloration and contour. This process has been used with a male model in Figures 18.6A to 18.6D.

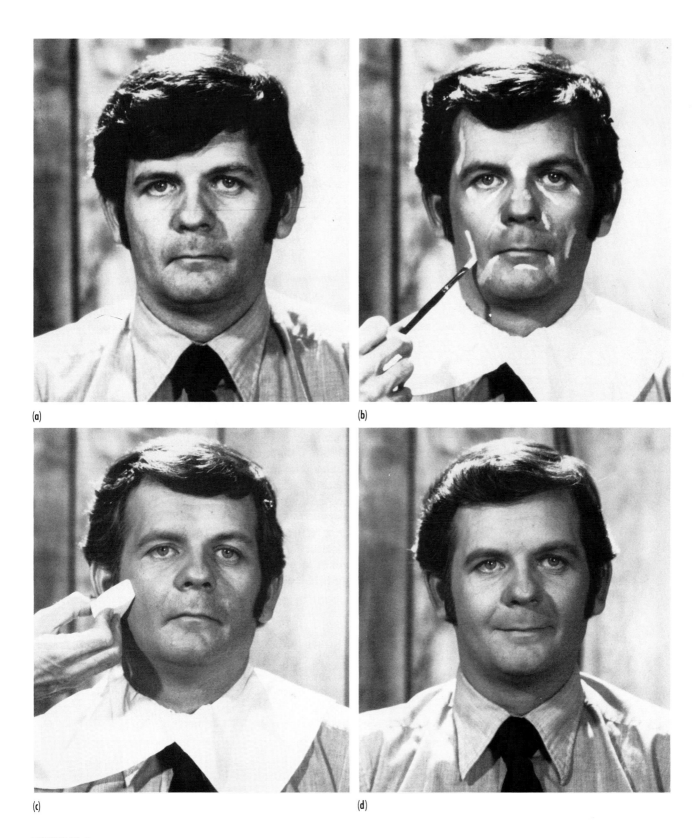

(a)

(b)

(c)

(d)

FIGURE 18.6

The television system intensifies shadow areas in the face. In particular, the limited brightness range of the television system can exaggerate the dark areas around the eyes, nose and chin (A). In (B) these areas have been highlighted to "bring them up." The highlighting is then blended into a base (C). The final result is shown in (D).

Shadowy areas under the eyes, around the nostrils and under the lower lip may need to be selectively lightened by either using base material one to three shades lighter than normal, or by using a translucent white highlighter designed especially for this purpose. Color can be added to the cheeks by mixing a very light trace of rouge with the existing base makeup. A soft sponge can be used to apply the rouge, blending the color on the cheekbones below the center of the eye up to the hairline. Rouge is appropriate for both men and women to add subtle color to the cheeks.

When the application of the base is completed, it may be necessary to use some translucent powder to dull down facial sheen. This can be done with a powder puff or soft, bristled brush. Do not try to remove all traces of facial sheen, since this will appear unnatural. This is especially true for men.

The Eyes

Eyebrows should be brushed with a clean eyebrow brush and plucked of any stray or unruly hairs. Though bushy eyebrows may be acceptable for men, women should carefully shape their brows into a gentle arch, which tapers off at the ends. Using fine delicate strokes, an eyebrow pencil of an appropriate shade should be used to fill in or reshape the eyebrows. For women, a touch of eye shadow is desirable. The dry powder, or cake form, of eye shadow is preferred over the cream type, since it both lends itself to easier and more subtle blending and holds up better under hot studio lights.

Whether a woman's eye shadow should match her eyes, clothes or neither is a fashion opinion, which can vary from season to season. Whatever the color choice, it should be subtle. A darker shade of the same color used on the eyelids (or a soft brown shade) can be lightly brushed into the lid crease to add depth and size to the eye. Women with heavy-lidded eyes should avoid this last technique since it will probably emphasize their problem. A dot of ivory or pale yellow eye shadow smoothed under the brow bone will lighten and "open" the eyes. Eyeliner can be applied close to the top lashes using either a soft, fine brush or a sharp eyebrow pencil. An eyelash curler and a light application of mascara will accent eyelashes. Excess clumps of mascara should be removed with a few upward strokes of a clean brush. False eyelashes can be used, but they should be carefully trimmed to fit the individual's eyes.

The Lips

Another aspect of particular importance to women is the proper selection of lipstick. Some types of lipstick and rouge not designed for television have a latent blue hue, which can take on a decided purple appearance when televised. A pure red lipstick that will harmonize with the skin coloration and wardrobe is best.

Before applying lipstick, lips should be outlined by using either a lipstick brush or a lip pencil (Figure 18.7). If the lips are well proportioned, this accentuates them. But lip outlining can also be used as a corrective technique. People with either overly thin or full lips can improve their lip line by first covering their lips with their base makeup and then drawing or outlining a more desired shape. A lip brush should also be used to give color to the entire lip.

After the application of lipstick, you should blot the lips with a tissue to avoid an unnatural shine. Lip gloss is generally undesirable for television. Although lipstick is not generally used on men, it is sometimes appropriate to add a touch of a natural-colored lipstick to smooth out a possible line between the lips and the beginning of the base makeup. A brown shade of lipstick applied with a brush is recommended.

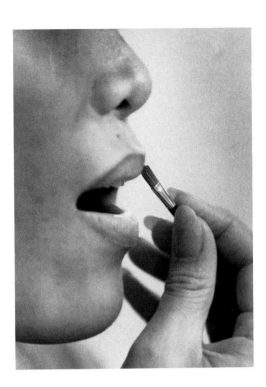

FIGURE 18.7
Before applying lipstick, lips should be outlined by using either a lipstick or a lip pencil. If the lips are well proportioned, this accentuates them. People with either overly thin or full lips can improve their lip line by first covering their lips with their base makeup and then drawing or outlining a more desired shape.

Hands, Ears and Teeth

If hands are to appear on camera, as when products are demonstrated through close-ups, special care must be taken. Use an appropriate shade of makeup base to ensure that hands match other parts of the body and to minimize wrinkles and color variations. Nails should be well manicured. Clear or colored fingernail polish can be used. The appearance of the hands should be carefully checked on a TV monitor prior to a production. Extreme close-ups will often reveal makeup flaws that are not normally visible.

Ears can be a special problem, since they are often slightly lighter and redder than adjacent skin tones. Added to this problem is the fact that back lights will often shine through ears to a degree, further raising their tonal value. To control this and bring ears back to their proper tonal perspective, they should be covered with a base makeup that is two or three shades darker than the face. The makeup base should then be covered with a translucent face powder.

Bad teeth can be minimized with an appropriate shade of tooth enamel or dentine fluid. Special coverings are available for this purpose.

Dark-Skinned People

The makeup needs of dark-skinned people are not greatly different from what has been outlined. Appropriate shades of makeup are available for most of the darker skin tones; however, it may be necessary to do slightly more in the way of blending different makeup shades to arrive at the needed tone. Generally, makeup for dark-skinned people should be applied sparingly. Black males and other males with dark skin may not need makeup at all. They often photograph quite well without it. Problems can arise, however, with very dark-skinned black males who do not exhibit a natural skin sheen, since the tonal reflectance level can drop so low that a loss of form and dimension results. It is desirable to preserve these highlights, and occasionally even accent them with baby oil or glycerine.

Children

Generally speaking, children of all skin colors will photograph well without makeup. Occasionally, it may be desirable to apply a base color sparingly and finish it off with a translucent face powder. Subtle applications of cheek color and lipstick may also be used in certain situations. However, the rule with children and makeup is *If in doubt, don't.*

Removal of Makeup

Women may prefer to leave their makeup on when they leave the studio. (Unlike stage makeup, it should be so subtle and natural-looking that there would be no need to remove it.) Men, being a bit more sensitive to such things, will probably want it removed.

All makeup should be removed by using a cleansing cream or lotion. The application of a mild astringent for women or aftershave lotion for men should leave the skin with a natural feeling.

General Makeup Considerations

As illustrated in Figures 18.3A to 18.3C, and Figures 18.6A to 18.6 D, makeup can result in definite change in appearance; however, whenever a subject appears made up, the job has been done improperly. A general rule in the application of makeup is *Better too little than too much.*

Since base makeup should be extended right to the fabric line of shirts, blouses and other wearing apparel, traces of the makeup can easily rub off on clothing. There is no practical solution to this, other than to be aware of it and frequently clean clothing. Dark-skinned subjects wearing dark makeup will find this a particular problem, since their makeup can easily be seen on light clothing.

Finally, all makeup should be checked on camera to ensure that some minor point has not been missed or that the television process is not introducing some unexpected effect. Even the experts in makeup are occasionally surprised to find an effect somewhat different than they expected.

WARDROBE AND JEWELRY

Wardrobe Considerations

In general, clothes that are stylish and that flatter the individual are acceptable on TV. There are, however, six caveats.

- Avoid white, bright yellow and tones that are above 80 percent reflectance. As noted in Chapter 4, this can cause clipping or tonal compression. (If guests show up wearing white, an engineer may be able to adjust the camera's tonal values to alleviate the problem.)
- Black clothes, especially against a dark background, can unnaturally lighten skin tones.
- Closely spaced stripes can cause an interaction with the camera's scanning, resulting in a distracting moiré pattern.
- Bold patterns can take on a distracting, facetious appearance.

- Sequinned, metallic and other shiny clothing, which may otherwise look good, can be distracting on television, especially under hard light sources.

- Finally, some fabrics generate considerable on-camera noise with movement. Although this might not ordinarily be noticeable, a mic can amplify the problem.

Jewelry

Although it can provide a needed accent to a wardrobe, jewelry can present two problems. First, if it's highly reflective, the on-camera results can vary from a simple distraction to offensive video aberrations, such as trailing streaks. Although soft lighting will alleviate the problem, in severe cases the jewelry will either have to be removed or a soluble dulling spray used.

The second problem is noise. Although an overhead, line or hand-held mic will occasionally pick up the sound of beads or metal jewelry, the major problem lies in the use of personal (clip-on) mics. A long string of beads moving back and forth over a personal mic not only creates an unpleasant noise, but can even drown out speech. Now that we've covered makeup, wardrobe and jewelry, we can turn to some on-camera concerns.

CONSIDERATIONS IN DOING LIVE STAND-UPS

One of the most potentially difficult situations for an on-camera reporter is a live stand-up. Often, the scenes of major news events are chaotic and uncontrolled—sometimes even dangerous. Being able to keep your head in such a situation and at the same time present a rational, informed and concise perspective on what's going on takes a special kind of individual. It helps to have all the technological help you can muster.

Although camera prompters are often used in the field for non-news electronic field production, they are generally not appropriate for news. As we noted in Chapter 4, news reporters working in the field typically refer to hand-held note cards or a small notebook containing names, figures and basic facts. If time allows, they can memorize their opening and closing on-camera comments. When they are off camera (i.e., when the camera pans off of them or when a tape is rolled) they can read directly from their notes.

Some on-camera people prefer large cue cards with the script written out in a bold black marker. But cue cards have three disadvantages: they are rather difficult and time-consuming to prepare; they require the aid of an extra person (a card puller); and the on-camera person must constantly look slightly off to the side of the camera to see the cards.

Some reporters have mastered the technique of fully writing out the script, recording it on an audio cassette machine and then playing it back in an earphone while simultaneously repeating the words to the camera. Although this technique demands great concentration (not to mention a lot of practice and a reliable audio playback scheme), once mastered, it can result in effective on-camera delivery.

When reporters are not on camera themselves, they need to know what is so they can provide appropriate commentary. If the report is being done within the range of a TV station's broadcast signal, a small TV receiver can be placed on the ground or next to the camera. This is used by reporters both to see when they are appearing on camera, and as a guide for doing the voice-over narration of prerecorded segments.

IFB Communication

interruptible foldback; interruptible feedback (IFB):   A wired or wireless system allowing communication with the talent while they are on the air. Normally, a small earpiece is worn by on-the-air talent that carries program sound that can be interrupted by instructions from the producer or director.

If the stand-up location is out of the range of the TV station, the reporter will have to rely on an interruptible feedback earpiece and audio cues from the news producer or director. An *interruptible feedback (IFB)* system relies on a small hearing-aid-type earphone and is part of the PL (private line or production line) communication system. Reporters will normally hear all program audio through their earpieces, including their own voices when they are speaking live, on the air. When the news producers or directors want to talk to reporters, the program audio can be interrupted, and they can speak directly to them. Obviously, IFBs must be used with discretion. It is difficult for reporters to concentrate on what they are saying and at the same time understand (and subsequently respond to) cues given through IFB communications. Most IFB messages are simple: "Go to tape," "30 seconds" or "Wrap it up."

Since broadcast program audio is a basic part of IFB, reporters can also use this communication link during a live newscast to respond to questions from studio anchorpersons. This is commonly done to impart a feeling of "live coverage." If possible, reporters should be tipped off ahead of time on what the questions will be. This serves two purposes. First, it reduces the need to have the anchorperson repeat the question. (Although everyone in the audience may have clearly heard the question, in the field, especially in high noise situations, reporters often have trouble hearing.) Second, it allows reporters to get whatever facts are necessary for an informed answer.

HAND SIGNALS

Hand signals are used both in the studio and in the field to silently communicate information—generally time cues—to on-camera people. In the studio this is normally the floor director's job, although a camera operator can take over when a floor director is not available. On-camera talent can't hear the PL conversation, of course, so they have no way of anticipating camera changes. Since addressing the wrong camera, even for a few seconds, looks rather awkward, floor directors should use hand signals to prepare talent for camera changes. As a director gives a "standby" for the camera change, the floor director should step next to the camera that is currently on the air and raise an arm (Figure 18.8A). When directors call for the camera change, floor directors should lower their arms and point to the new camera (Figure 18.8D). If hand signals are given with proper timing, the talent can smoothly shift their gaze from one camera to the next just as the camera change is made. Even if the talent happens to be looking in another direction at the time (possibly at a studio guest) they should be able to catch bold gestures such as this in their peripheral vision. When they again look up, they can immediately address the proper camera.

Hand signals should be given as close to the on-line camera lens as possible. An on-camera person doesn't need to be anxiously looking around the recesses of the studio trying to locate the person giving cues. Figures 18.8A to 18.8M illustrate commonly-used hand signals. The caption explains the meaning of each.

SUMMARY

A knowledge of the on-camera process is important in identifying and correcting presentation problems. Since a mispronounced name or a grammatical error stands out to informed listeners, and it is time-consuming and costly to rerecord

(a)   (b)   (c)

(d)   (e)   (f)

FIGURE 18.8

The stand-by cue (A) means you are only a few brief seconds away from going on the air. The hand is brought down (B) as the floor director hears the director switch up the camera. You are now on the air! A finger on the nose (C) indicates things are "on the nose"; that is, you do not need to speed up, slow down or alter the scripted sequence. When a new camera is switched on line, the floor director will swing his arm toward the camera lens (D). When it's time for a commercial (a spot) or public service announcement (PSA), the floor director points to a spot in the palm of his hand (E). A need to move closer or farther away from the camera is indicated in (F) and (G).

(g)   (h)   (i)

(j)   (k)   (l)

(m)

FIGURE 18.8, continued.

Fingers (or numbered cards) indicate minutes (H). When the talent is about to go into a taped segment, or is coming out of a taped segment, the fingers (right beside the camera lens) are used to count down the seconds. In (I) the floor director is signaling the talent to stretch out, or lengthen, the on-camera presentation. Moving the hand rapidly in a circle (J) is the signal to speed up. The arms crossed (K) signal 30 seconds. A fist (L) indicates 15 seconds. When time is completely gone, or the segment needs to immediately be cut, fingers are drawn across the throat (M).

narration after music and effects have already mixed, producers and directors need a sharp ear to catch announcing and writing problems early in the production process.

Conveying the intended meaning of a script goes far beyond just "getting the words right"; meaning must be communicated through proper phrasing, appropriate pauses and the subtle and periodic stress on words and word groups. One of the most important talents an announcer must develop is the ability to read ahead. Since effective on-camera presentations take considerable concentration, it is important for a director to reduce or eliminate all possible studio distractions during a production.

When a studio prompter is being used, an announcer should check the visibility of the prompter in all camera positions. On-camera talent, especially during live shows, should have a hard copy of the script for two reasons: they can revert to it if the prompter malfunctions, and, when they are not on the air, they will be able to look ahead and get ready for upcoming segments. Color coding a prompter display reduces presentation problems.

To be most effective in a fiercely competitive profession, key production personnel must keep up with the latest research in programming and on-camera presentation. Regular air checks on the part of on-camera talent are a way of catching and eliminating the lazy habits of normal conversation that creep into on-air delivery: dropping *ing*'s on words, acquiring unnatural patterns of emphasis, or losing "the smile in the voice." Although appropriate for the stage, the gestures, facial expressions and intonations of stage actors will, without modification, be too expansive for the close-up medium of television.

Even though many people assume that the purpose of makeup is simply to "make you look better," in television it's often intended just to make on-camera talent look natural and normal. Like many behind-the-scenes aspects of television, makeup is best when it goes unnoticed. The skillful application of makeup is especially important in high-definition television. There are three categories of makeup: basic, corrective and character.

In general, clothes that are stylish and that flatter the individual are acceptable on TV. However, performers should avoid white and tones that can cause clipping or tonal compression; dark clothes against a dark background; closely spaced stripes; bold patterns; and sequinned, metallic and other shiny fabrics.

Although jewelry can add needed accent to a wardrobe, it can present two problems. If it's highly reflective, it can cause offensive video aberrations, such as trailing streaks, and when it is used with personal mics, dangling jewelry such as beads can cause noise problems.

KEY TERMS

air check
base
basic makeup
character makeup
contouring
corrective makeup

foundation
hand signals
highlighting
interruptible feedback (IFB)
key words

19

Legal and Ethical Guidelines

Production personnel who ignore the legal and ethical aspects of production do so at their own risk, and the risk can be very great. This chapter points out some of the legal and ethical hazards in audio and video production and suggests some guidelines. At the same time, it can't be stressed too strongly that the law in these areas is enigmatic, and that legal decisions vary with time, place and specific circumstances. In this chapter, we will cover six areas:

- Invasion of privacy
- Libel and slander
- Access restrictions and rights
- Staging
- Copyright
- Talent releases

In addition, this chapter introduces some concerns that come under the heading of ethical and professional issues. While these issues are not defined by law, they have definite implications for an individual's professional credibility. We'll start our discussion with one of the most fundamental issues: privacy.

PRINCIPLES OF PRIVACY

Many formal discussions of invasion of privacy divide the subject into four categories: intrusion on seclusion, public disclosure of private facts, false light and commercial appropriation. However, since many of the examples we'll cite will have implications for more than one category at the same time, no attempt will be made here to divide these categories.

Private and Public Individuals

Before discussing some of these issues, we need to make a distinction between *private* and *public* individuals. As we will see, once individuals enter the public spotlight (either intentionally or through accidental circumstances) they are afforded much less legal protection in each of the four divisions of privacy.

Intrusion on Seclusion

Legal action can be taken against camerapersons if they wrongfully intrude on the solitude or seclusion of another person. Legally, this is a form of trespassing, and it is variously referred to as **intrusion on seclusion, invasion of privacy** or just **privacy**. The intrusion may be direct and physical, such as entering a person's home or place of business to get pictures without permission, or it may be figurative, such as when a cameraperson uses an extremely long lens or a night viewing device to videotape private scenes. The latter area could also include shooting through a skylight from a rooftop; using secret, two-way mirrors; or using a hidden recorder or wireless microphone. Most cases of intrusion stem from the inherent conflict between the desire of individuals—especially well-known individuals—to keep certain aspects of their lives from being publicized or exposed and the curiosity of viewers (and therefore newspeople) to find out everything they can about these individuals. Movie stars and popular singers are favorite targets of camerapersons, as are alleged criminals.

intrusion on seclusion: Related to *invasion of privacy;* a legal term denoting the unlawful entering into a place or state without invitation or legal right.

invasion of privacy: Intrusion on seclusion. Illegally and inappropriately prying into someone's personal business. It may be actual, such as trespassing on private property to secure a news story, or figurative, such as when a telephoto lens or an electronic eavesdropping device is used.

privacy: An individual's—especially a private citizen's—legal right to be left alone and not badgered by newspeople. Privacy includes intrusion on seclusion, the public disclosure of private facts, false light and commercial appropriation.

Conflicts in Constitutional Rights

With intrusion there are two legal areas that can come into conflict: the constitutional right of the media to be free to report the news, and the right of individuals to maintain personal privacy. The principles of freedom of speech and freedom of the press can also conflict with the right of the individual to have an impartial jury trial, free from the influence of pretrial (media) publicity.

Unlike the freedom of the press, protection against invasion of privacy is not specifically guaranteed by the U.S. Constitution. Nevertheless, over the years the right of individuals to their privacy has become an accepted part of tort and U.S. constitutional law.

The Roots of Invasion of Privacy

Ironically, the original basis for much of the reasoning behind invasion of privacy decisions can be traced back, not to laws, but to an 1890 article in the *Harvard Law Review.* Although the Constitution doesn't cover the right of privacy, the authors argued that such a right was implied and necessary. In one part of their now famous article, the authors noted that "the intensity and complexity of life" and the "refining influence of culture" make it essential that individuals be allowed solitude and privacy. They noted that modern enterprise and invention make possible an invasion of personal privacy, which can end up inflicting more mental "pain and distress" than "mere bodily injury."

The Public's Right to Know

There is also another important side to the privacy issue, a side that sometimes outweighs these personal rights. Some individuals wish to keep certain acts private because the acts are illegal, unethical or at least morally questionable. The issue then becomes one of *the public's right to know,* which gets into the area of the disclosure of private facts. For example, does the public have a right to know that a person they are considering for public office is guilty of significant illegal acts? Do they have a right to know that a popular religious leader (whom many try to emulate) widely proclaims certain moral values while personally disregarding these same values in his own life?

Our system of government and our way of life depend on an informed public. The degree to which the voting public is denied information is the degree to which it is vulnerable to the duplicity of self-serving individuals. Recognizing this fact, our courts have been quick to protect the news media's rights to gather and disseminate information. But the *degree to which* the media has a right to intrude on the private lives of people in the pursuit of this information is an issue that often must be settled in court.

In the process of examining different aspects of the intrusion issue, we'll cite the findings of several important court cases. Although they by no means provide a hard-and-fast rule on future decisions, they do at least suggest some guidelines.

Some years back, a TV station was sued for intrusion on seclusion after a cameraperson had videotaped an employee of a pharmacy through the front window. A druggist working inside had been charged with cheating the state out of Medicaid funds. When the employee refused to talk with reporters, the camera operator set up the camera outside of the front window of the store and photographed the man through the window as he talked on the telephone. Since the taping was done from the exterior of the building from a place that was deemed public, the court ruled that intrusion had not taken place because the cameraperson was showing something which the general public was free to view.

First Guideline for Intrusion

This ruling and others like it suggest a general guideline: *If what you intend to photograph can be seen by the average person on public property, intrusion on seclusion would be difficult to prove.* **Public property** includes streets and sidewalks; therefore, photographing things that take place in these areas, as well as things that can be seen from these vantage points, is generally safe. "Off-limit" areas would include the backs and sides of private dwellings that are not visible from public property and the interiors of buildings that would not normally be exposed to the general public.

Privately owned buildings are not considered public property. In one case a network news crew was sent to do an ENG story on restaurants cited for health code violations. The crew entered the restaurant—an expensive French restaurant in New York City—with "cameras rolling." The proprietor asked the crew to leave. The journalists continued to tape until they were finally escorted from the restaurant. During the commotion, some customers ducked under tables and some even fled without paying their bills. Dismissing a First Amendment defense, the court ruled against the network, saying that the First Amendment is not "a shibboleth before which all other rights must succumb." In addition to the restaurant being private property, an important issue in the case was undoubtedly the disruptive nature of the intrusion.

When the Camera Distorts the Truth

Although ENG personnel are generally free to photograph people in public places without worry, there have been some exceptions. In *Holmes v. Curtis Publishing Co.* Curtis Publishing ran a photo captioned "High Rollers at the Monte Carlo Club" as part of a story about mafia involvement in gambling. A tourist, James Holmes, just happened to be sitting at a table near the mafia men.

A photographer used a long focal length lens to photograph the scene and as a consequence compressed the distance between the people in the picture. This made it appear as if Holmes was with the mafia men. Holmes sued, charging the picture, accompanying caption, and article put him in a false light. The court agreed, and Curtis Publishing lost the case. Interestingly, if a normal or wide-angle lens had been used—probably not an option, considering the circumstances—Holmes would have been clearly set apart from the mafia subjects and there would have been no confusion.

Offensiveness and Harassment

A second exception to the guideline on photographing in public places emerges when harassment or offensiveness is at issue. In *Galella v. Onassis*—admittedly, a rather exceptional case—the court ruled that photographers, even in public places, can't be so offensive as to seriously interfere with the subject's right to be left alone. Galella, a still photographer, had for some time been pursuing Jackie Onassis (President John F. Kennedy's widow) and her children in order to get candid pictures. In its decision, the court ordered Galella not to block Ms. Onassis' movements (which could place her life or safety in jeopardy) and to stay at least twenty-five feet away from Jackie and even further away from her children.

Six Guidelines for Intrusion

In deciding on the merit of an invasion of privacy suit, several questions should be asked. (We'll discuss them in more detail later.)

- Was there either direct or implied consent to enter the property?
- Could the reporter have gotten the information from another source?
- Is the information obtained newsworthy and of legitimate concern to the public?
- Is there proof of prying on the part of the cameraperson or reporter?
- Does the alleged intrusion relate to something that is generally agreed to be of a private nature?
- Finally, would the alleged intrusion be deemed objectionable to a reasonable person?

Although such terms as *legitimate concern, prying, private,* and *objectionable,* are all subject to interpretation—often by a court—some past interpretations may help.

The phrase *legitimate concern to the public* touches upon an important point and a significant area of defense in intrusion cases. Videographers and still photographers who cross the line on intrusion often use the defense that the information they are able to photographically obtain is in the public's interest. In other words, the public has a right and possibly even a need to know the information. This "ends justify the means" defense has been used successfully in defending many charges of intrusion. Although the public interest can constitute a valid defense, the burden of proof in these cases is on the defendant. Clear evidence must be presented that the information gathered was of legitimate concern to the public and that no other way of obtaining the information was available. At the same time it should be emphasized that courts have rather consistently recognized the obligation of reporters and photographers to show respect for the "dignity, privacy and well-being" of subjects.

Prying connotes something beyond basic curiosity and moves into the area of offensive and inappropriate snooping. The disclosure of private facts is generally interpreted as relating to information about a person's private life that is not a legitimate concern to the public, the disclosure of which would be highly offensive (objectionable) to a reasonable person.

FREE AND RESTRICTED ACCESS

These issues move us into one of the most troublesome areas for producers and ENG crews: access. It is important to note that access is rooted in state laws regarding trespassing, and therefore differs somewhat in every state.

access: In the context of newsgathering, the legal right of a news reporter to go onto private property to obtain information or videotape footage.

Legally, *access* implies a number of things, but here we'll look at the area where news personnel and public safety officials (primarily police) are most likely to clash. One of the grayest areas of access law—and one that, unfortunately, is most often encountered by working photojournalists—is access to public locations that are under the control of public safety officials. Crime scenes, public demonstrations and disasters fall in this category. ENG crews covering breaking news stories seldom have time to consult lawyers; therefore, the better their understanding of legal precedents in this area, the less likely they are to encounter problems.

Although, admittedly, the press and ENG crews are frequently (even routinely) given special access privileges to cover news, when "push comes to shove" (and barring state laws to the contrary), court decisions have generally held that the press has no privileges beyond those granted to the general public. With this in mind, it then becomes a matter of knowing local trespass laws. In general, trespass restricts access to areas posted as private or to property where the owner or the owner's agent has refused you permission. (In the latter case, however, you will be allowed to broadcast any footage taken before you were asked to leave.)

Official Invitation

The only exception to the private property injunction is if you are invited onto the property by an authorized public safety officer. In *Florida Publishing Co. v. Fletcher* a newspaper photographer was invited into a badly burned house by the Fire Marshal and asked to photograph a silhouette left on the floor by the body of 17-year-old girl, who died in the fire. The girl's mother, who first learned the facts of her daughter's death from the newspaper article and its accompanying photographs, sued for invasion of privacy. Since the owner of the property was not present at the time, and the photographer was invited to enter, the trial judge ruled in favor of the newspaper, saying "It is my view that entry in this case was by implied consent. . . . there was not only no objection to the entry, but there was an invitation to enter by the officers investigating the fire."

Press Passes

The issuance of official press IDs acknowledges that to some degree the media has some special privileges, even though courts have been reluctant to recognize this fact. Most law-enforcement officials try to work with the media by recognizing that press cards and press passes identify working members of the media, and as a result, they give special access privileges.

Even so, there are two sides to the access issue. Overzealous reporters have often impeded the work of officials, disturbed evidence and added to the confusion already present at a news scene. (There is no shortage of dramatic films and TV programs that make use of this hackneyed theme.) At the same time, officials have been known to bar, remove and even arrest reporters when the story they were trying to cover was either embarrassing to their superiors or would have documented improper police conduct. Although arrests sometimes ensue, officials seldom let subsequent interference and disorderly conduct charges go to trial; the cases are usually dropped. Even so, the arrest or removal of ENG crews may accomplish their intended purpose—to keep newsgathering people from getting the story. In at least one case it was determined that an ENG crew was fully within their rights in covering an event; at the same time, however, they were found guilty of illegally disregarding an officer's requests to leave. For reporters this is one definition of a quandary!

Civil Disobedience

Some photojournalists have been prepared to break the law to get an important story. However, as with any type of civil disobedience, the reporter must be prepared to pay the penalty. And when you come right down to it, reporters have little chance against armed police officers bent on stopping them. Even so, five guidelines have been suggested for the legitimacy of civil disobedience:

- Exhaustion of all legal avenues
- True belief that the restraining action is unjust
- Nonviolence
- Belief that the importance of the story to the public outweighs legal obligations
- Willingness to face the consequences

SHIELD LAWS

Another area where reporters have had to face the legal consequences of their actions is when they try to protect the confidentiality of their sources of information. Although about half the states have **shield laws** designed to keep courts from forcing newspeople to reveal their sources, these laws vary all the way from being essentially meaningless to, in the case of Nevada, fully protecting news source confidentiality. Without the assurance that newspeople will protect their confidentiality, few people are willing to risk their own welfare and "name names" in revealing inside information about crime and corruption. Some reporters have chosen to serve time in jail on contempt of court charges rather than break a promise to keep a source's name confidential. (One investigative reporter who has broken numerous stories about corruption and wrongdoing in high places wryly notes that without an ability to keep names confidential, he would instantly lose all his inside sources and end up writing gardening articles or a "*Dear Abby*" column.)

shield law: A law that exists in various forms and degrees in many states that keeps a news reporter from having to identify the source of confidential information.

Confidentiality and the My Lai Massacre

One of the more famous examples of information released only on the guarantee of confidentiality related to the infamous My Lai Massacre in South Vietnam, where more than a hundred civilians, mostly women and children, were killed— ostensibly because they were a threat to U.S. forces. The story of this massacre leaked out (and the U.S. Army Lieutenant responsible was eventually court-martialed) only after Army personnel who knew what had happened were promised confidentiality by the media.

The Two Sides of Shield Laws

Of course, there are two sides to the shield law issue. The Constitution says that citizens have a right to "face their accuser," which is difficult if the identity of that person or persons is kept secret. At the same time, no responsible news medium would run a major accusatory story based on a single confidential source. Some news organizations, in fact, require that stories of this type be verified by three independent sources. The original source, therefore, only serves to launch an investigation.

MISREPRESENTATION

TV stations and production agencies have guidelines that forbid using any kind of *deceit* or *misrepresentation* in doing a production or getting a news story. A number of years ago reporters for a national magazine went to the home of a plumber who was suspected of practicing medicine without a license. In order to gain admittance a reporter posed as someone in need of medical assistance. Photos were taken with a hidden camera, and the reporter used a concealed microphone to tape the conversation. The audio recordings (which were turned over to the government) were important to the subsequent case against the plumber. However, after the article was published, the plumber sued for invasion of privacy and was able to win damages. The court said, "We have little difficulty in concluding that clandestine photography of the plaintiff in his den and recordation and transmission of his conversation without his consent resulting in his emotional distress warrants recovery for invasion of privacy in California." The clear misrepresentation that was involved undoubtedly influenced the court's decision.

COMMERCIAL APPROPRIATION

commercial appropriation: A legal aspect of invasion of privacy relating to the unauthorized use of the name or likeness of a well-known individual for the personal or economic gain of a third party.

Commercial appropriation also relates to privacy and intrusion because it involves an unauthorized use of an individual's or organization's prominence in order to influence a listening or viewing audience. A suggestion of endorsement of a product or establishment by a known personality, without the consent of that person, is seen as exploiting their prominence. The courts have recognized that well-known people acquire an identity that is of value, and these people deserve to be protected from someone "cashing in" on that value without their consent.

The Boundaries of Commercial Appropriation

Let's look at an example. If you were televising a public event and wanted to show general shots of the audience in attendance, there would be no problem—even if one or more of the members of the audience were well known. Individuals in this case are considered "background," much the same as a rock or a tree would be in another type of production. But if one of the people in the audience was a well-known, easily recognizable person and by your choice of camera shots you appeared to go out of your way to bring this fact to the attention of the audience, you could be guilty of trying to "cash in on" the person's prominence. As in many areas of the law, the distinction could end up being rather subjective. But in the first case the notable person is "just one of many" in the audience; in the second case the choice of the camera shot or shots very deliberately brings the person's presence to the attention of the viewing audience.

There is an exception here. If the public figure is actively taking part in an event being covered, he or she can be considered a part of the event. In such cases, the camera shots may dwell on the person as much as they wish.

DEFAMATION, LIBEL AND SLANDER

Ancient Roman law held that if any person slandered another "by words or defamatory verses" and thereby harmed his reputation, that person should be beaten by a stick. Since judgments in defamation suits have in some cases run into the tens of millions of dollars, some television people might prefer ancient Roman law to present U.S. laws.

Defamation

Defamation is the communication to a third party of false and injurious ideas that tend to lower the community's estimation of a person, expose a person to contempt or ridicule or injure a person in his or her personal or professional life. *Libel* is defamation by written or printed word and is generally considered more serious than *slander,* which is defamation by spoken words or gestures. As in all cases of defamation, the injured person must be apparent to the audience (although not necessarily *specifically* named), and negligence on the part of the defendant (journalist) must be established.

Since the cost of defending a libel or slander suit averaged about $250,000 in 1991, many stations and production agencies have insurance against libel and slander. But insurance is expensive, and it is a poor substitute for a basic knowledge of the law.

Depending upon the state, a false statement that is broadcast may be viewed as either libel or slander. The reasoning in some states is that when a statement is presented from a written script, it implies more forethought than an ad-lib comment and should be considered libel—just as a defamatory statement in a newspaper or magazine is considered libel. In some states, courts have felt that defamatory ad-lib statements are more spontaneous and "less considered" and should therefore be treated as slander. A few states have removed all distinctions between libel and slander. Ultimately, of course, the decision rests with the particular court.

libel: A legal term relating to an inaccurate published (or sometimes broadcast) statement that subjects someone to public ridicule or contempt or injures the person's reputation.

slander: Uttering false statements deemed harmful to another person's character or reputation.

Per Se and *Per Quod* Defamation

Defamation can be of two types: *per se* and *per quod*. When a statement is defamatory "on its face" without the need of additional information or knowledge, it is **defamation** *per se*. Erroneously stating that a certain person is a Communist would be defamation *per se*. All the erroneous and damaging facts are conveyed by the statement. The "statement" could be either written or visual. In the latter case it could be a picture of Sam Smith with the words "Member, Communist Party" keyed over the picture.

In **defamation** *per quod* additional facts are needed. To erroneously state that Mrs. Sally Smith lives at 101 Park Street would not constitute defamation— until the additional fact that this address is a known house of prostitution is

defamation **per se:** A legal term relating to the utterance of slanderous words, especially false and malicious words, that injure a person's reputation. As opposed to *defamation per quod,* statements that are deemed slanderous or libelous "on their face," that is, without the need for other information.

defamation **per quod:** As opposed to *defamation per se,* statements that are deemed slanderous or libelous only when supplemental (generally, widely known information) is considered along with the statement in question.

taken into consideration. In this case the quite respectable Mrs. Sally Smith might be justified in initiating a defamation (*per quod*) case. In general, injury is presumed by the court in a *per se* offense, and it is not necessary for the injured person to prove actual damage.[1] However, in *per quod* cases the plaintiff typically must prove actual damage.

Guarding Against Trade Libel

trade libel: A false or grossly misleading statement that damages a business or product.

actual malice: Broadcasting or publishing something that is either known to be false or is disseminated with reckless disregard for its truth or accuracy.

Companies, corporations or groups can be damaged just as badly as individuals. Untrue statements that are broadcast about products—"All X-brand cars are lemons"—can cost the manufacturers thousands of dollars in sales and result in **trade libel** suits. In addition to being almost impossible to prove, such statements carry connotations of actual malice. (**Actual malice,** which is an extremely important consideration in defamation cases, is seen as disregard for a statement's lack of truth and known falsity.) Instead of using a capricious word like *lemon,* a carefully verified statement like, "In Tazewell County 350 of the 400 X-brand cars that were sold in 1992 were returned to the dealer for transmission repairs within 10 days of purchase" could be used. Not only is the latter statement much more responsible, but it conveys essential information on the nature of the problem.

There are three possible defenses in a defamation suit: truth, consent and privilege.

Legal Defenses Against Defamation Suits

Truth A defense of truth—proving that the statement in question is actually true—may not be as simple as it appears. Sometimes courts have required that the defense prove every minute detail of a statement—a task that can be difficult. There is one unusual case on record where an Indiana man sued for libel because he was accused of stealing 10 sheep. The defense of truth fell through, and the plaintiff was awarded libel damages when it was proven that, in fact, 14 sheep had been stolen. Generally, however, courts require that the defendant only needs to establish that the statement in question is true in substance.[2]

Many people assume that if video producers or broadcasters accurately attribute a defamatory statement to the person who said it, they can escape legal action. Not so. A policeman at the scene of an accident in which three people were killed may say, "The accident was caused by John Smith, who was drunk." Even if it seems clear that John Smith was inebriated at the time of the accident, the fact may not be able to be substantiated legally (because of a technicality, or whatever). Without substantiation, Smith may choose to sue a broadcaster who quoted the policeman.

Consent The second defense against libel is consent. If a defendant can prove that the statement was broadcast with some type of consent on the part of the plaintiff, the libel or slander suit will fail. There have been cases where someone revealed something personal or incriminating about themselves to a reporter, and after the fact was revealed in a broadcast (and reaction was negative), they decided to deny the statement and try to save face by suing for

---

1. Recent decisions have focused somewhat more on the presence or absence of *malice* in *per quod* cases.

2. In some cases, rather than the media having to prove *truth*, the plaintiff may be asked to prove *falsity*. This obviously simplifies the media's case.

libel. If the reporter can prove that the subject volunteered the statement as part of the interview, the defamation case will collapse. (Having the complete interview on audio or videotape is good insurance here.)

Privilege   The last defense against libel is privilege. Privilege is generally limited to statements by public officers and statements made during legislative and judicial proceedings. For example, members of the U.S. Congress have a constitutional guarantee against libel or slander in statements made on the floor of either house, regardless of the question of malice. When a privileged proceeding is broadcast or videotaped, the broadcaster is protected against libel — assuming that the presentation is not edited or altered to reflect malice on the part of the broadcaster.

Under another form of privilege, producers and broadcasters can air opinions on matters of public interest. This was established early in libel law when a performing group sued a newspaper for publishing a highly derogatory review of their stage performance. The performers lost the case. The court decided that people who go on stage can be freely criticized, as long as no malice or "evil purposes" can be proven. It was at this point that an important legal distinction between public and private individuals was established. After finding themselves in the public spotlight (either by design or accident), people forfeit much of the legal protection they previously had against public criticism and invasion of privacy.

FALSE LIGHT

The charge of presenting someone in a "false light" is perhaps the most difficult to judge. Again, using the example of Mrs. Smith, let's assume you are doing a documentary on prostitution. During the course of the documentary, you tape night scenes in the area of 101 Park Street, which the announcer states is where most of the prostitutes in the city solicit. Let's also assume that by chance Mrs. Smith (who has been visiting her aunt at the time of your taping) is clearly visible in one of your scenes. Although you did not identify Mrs. Smith as a prostitute, in the context of the documentary the audience might make that inference. The result of this inference on the part of the audience could constitute a case of *false light* and could precipitate a law suit.

false light: Impression created by distorting the truth of a situation through such things as wrongful association, or unduly emphasizing negative attributes.

Another example happened a number of years ago when a cameraman and a reporter did an ENG piece on a New York ghetto. Slum residents welcomed them after the crew informed them that they were doing a series that might help clean up the ghetto. Footage of rat-infested alleys and overflowing garbage cans was included, and several residents eagerly provided vivid descriptions of the undesirable conditions. After the story was broadcast, residents from a single housing unit brought the reporter and cameraman to court. They said that the coverage sensationalized the living conditions (putting them in a false light) and violated their right of privacy. Regardless of the outcome of such cases, the broadcaster or producer must invest considerable time, effort and money in a legal defense.

LEGAL PITFALLS IN DOING DOCUDRAMAS

With the popularity of the **docudrama** (a drama based on a true story) has come another problem in false light: fictionalization. In writing a script for a docudrama, time is condensed, the chronology of events is often altered, and "dra-

docudrama: A dramatic production based on factual events or on an actual situation.

matic license" is commonly used to make the production more dramatic and interesting. In the process many authors and producers have been sued for putting people or even institutions in a false light. Although some courts have stated that actual malice must be proven in these cases, the docudrama remains a highly controversial type of production, which requires expert legal advice.

HONEST MISTAKES

To err may be human, but honest mistakes still cause damage, and the courts have held that false statements arising from accident, error or carelessness may still be subject to settlement. However, once again, the severity of the offense is seen as being much greater if some type of malice can be proven, and if the individual is not a public figure. In the previous example in which it was erroneously stated that Sally Smith lived at 101 Park Street (a known house of prostitution), the writer could say that it was "an honest mistake" caused by a typing error and that no actual malice was present. But Mrs. Smith (who lives at 9101 Park Street) might still be justified in launching a defamation suit if damage in the form of public ridicule and humiliation resulted from this "honest mistake."

CONFRONTING LAWSUITS

With this discussion as a background, it should be obvious that the best defense is no offense, and that producers must carefully check any questionable material before broadcast or distribution. At one TV station the writer-producer subjects her work to a series of credibility checks. A questionable segment is viewed by the executive producer, the news director and by the station's attorneys before broadcast. But what if after due care you are still served a subpoena?

Handling Subpoenas

First, don't volunteer to appear as a witness in your own case. If the plaintiff's attorney asks you for background on the broadcast, be cautious. By agreeing, you could weaken your rights under an existing shield law. Second, if a subpoena is issued, your lawyer and a superior should be notified at once.

Any action to suppress a subpoena must be taken immediately to be most effective. Third, never agree to hand over a tape or transcript of the segment in question unless ordered to by the court.

Producers should also be aware that they should never make a comment regarding the truth of the challenged statement to anyone except their lawyers. If an error is broadcast and a producer says, "I'm really sorry, I was in a hurry and I just didn't take the time to check my facts," this could constitute an admission of guilt—even a "reckless disregard for the truth," which could constitute malice. Many cases have been lost after such admissions.

Issuing Corrective Statements

If a definite error in fact is discovered after it has been telecast, you should immediately air a full corrective statement with an apology. This may not eliminate a lawsuit, but it frequently has served to reduce the damages awarded.

STAGING

Staging applies to news and documentary work, and in its negative sense it involves the alteration or misrepresentation of a situation. The motivation for doing this can range from a blatant effort to alter the truth to a subtle attempt to enhance the look of a scene. If staged footage is broadcast and it represents a conscious effort to alter the truth in a news story, it can result in fines by the Federal Communications Commission. Simply enhancing a scene, on the other hand, is more of an ethical issue. Let's look at some examples.

Unacceptable Staging

First, let's say you are taping an interview with a bereaved father of a boy who was shot by a policeman. During a shoot-out the unarmed boy was mistaken for a criminal. Let's also assume there has been a public outcry over the incident and that the family has gotten a number of letters of sympathy. You arrange to videotape a short interview with the father sitting at his desk, and you want to emphasize the public response to the incident. Since the few letters he has received seem "lost" on his big desk, you decide that it would make the picture much more dramatic if you borrowed a few dozen letters from your office and piled them on his desk.

Although the story is, indeed, more dramatic as a result of your actions, you have changed the truth, and you are guilty of misrepresenting the facts. If the deceit becomes known, both you and your news department face a loss of credibility and possible disciplinary action. A pattern of misrepresentation of this type could threaten the station's broadcast license.

Questionable Staging

As another example, let's assume that you are doing the same interview but instead of misrepresenting the mail response, you simply ask the man to bring a framed 8-by-10 photo of the dead boy with him to the interview. You then place the photo on the desk so that it will assume a dominant position in the visual frame. Here we have a ethical issue — one that some people would say would be an example of acceptable staging. Although the large photo sitting on the desk would, indeed, embellish the dramatic statement surrounding the father's loss, you have "creatively altered" the situation, suggesting that the photo normally assumes a dominant position on the man's desk. Some videographers and reporters see nothing wrong with "minor staging" of this nature; others feel that "tampering with the truth" in any way violates their own code of professional and personal ethics.

To some degree, altering a scene for the benefit of composition, lighting, sound or visual clarity is a normal and expected part of videography. For example, you might have to bring extra lights to the interview. Strictly speaking, in the process you are altering the reality of the situation. Or you might note before the interview that some polished brass bookends on a desk are highly distracting and ask if they can be removed during the interview. Again, you have altered the situation. But a professional and ethical distinction can be made between removing distractions for the sake of video technical quality, and altering or distorting the essential elements of a story.

Acceptable Staging

Let's say that you are doing an ENG story on the passing of the gavel from an outgoing president of a civic organization to the new president. You might find that the actual event was awkwardly done, the lighting was bad, or that your camera's view was blocked by a member of the audience. It would be reasonable (and probably even expected) for you and other members of the press to ask for a re-enactment of the event. In fact, since such occasions are often intended as "media events" anyway, the authenticity of such moments is almost never an issue.

When Authenticity Is an Issue

Sometimes, however, the authenticity of an actual event is important. Trying to restage the moment when an athlete cleared the pole to set a world high-jump record would be an entirely different matter than the passing of the gavel to a new president of a civic organization. Another example of unacceptable staging would be if you "arranged" an event for a news or documentary piece. Let's say you are doing a documentary on an inner-city gang, and as part of the program you want to show a controversial initiation procedure. Let's assume that you contact the leader of the gang, who decides to cooperate. But you find that the initiation of the last gang member took place a month earlier and another initiation is not planned. At this point you suggest that the gang restage the last initiation ceremony for the benefit of your camera. After discussing your camera and sound needs and suggesting the gang members you would like in the segment, they agree. Is there a problem here?

Most definitely—at least if you later represent the initiation as being the original initiation. For one thing, you created this initiation ceremony solely for the sake of the documentary; otherwise it wouldn't have taken place. Since the ceremony was staged solely to accommodate the needs of the documentary, there is the question of just how "authentic" it would end up being, and how much it would be altered—both by you and by the gang members—in the interest of the documentary. If the ceremony were quite important to your documentary and you didn't mind a certain loss of authenticity, keying the word *re-enactment* over the staged scene might solve the problem.

Using "Comparable Footage"

Although it's not "staging" per se, a related issue that frequently comes up is the use of "comparable footage" in editing news and documentary pieces. As a videotape editor in a highly competitive news market, you might be tempted to cover today's lack of good footage of a forest fire with some dramatic scenes from a similar fire that happened last year, or you might be tempted to cut in some unused scenes from yesterday's fire in today's story on the same forest fire. All professional and ethical issues aside, you should be aware that the FCC has taken a very dim view of such "substitutions," unless the fact was made quite clear to the viewing audience. Simply keying the phrase *file footage* or an earlier date over the footage will suffice.

DRAMATIC LICENSE

Quite in contrast to the guidelines covering news and documentary production is the **dramatic license**, which can be used in dramatic production. For example, feature films on Vietnam have frequently been done in the Philippines because it is safer and more economical, and the landscape is similar. If the scene of the gang initiation were a part of a dramatic feature film, staging would not only be acceptable, but given the nature of feature film production, essential. In dramatic productions, the audience does not expect to be told what is and is not authentic, but news and documentary production is an entirely different matter.

COPYRIGHTED MATERIALS

Music, illustrations and published passages are almost always copyrighted and cannot be used in productions without clearance or permission from the copyright holder. Occasionally, this permission is granted without charge and with only on-screen credit. More often a fee must be paid to the copyright holder.

Background Music

Music is a normal and even an expected part of dramatic productions. Even documentaries frequently use music for transitions, to establish moods etc. But almost all musical recordings are covered by copyright laws that will not allow them to be used in radio, video productions or multimedia presentations without prior *clearance,* which includes the payment of *royalty fees*. Works not copyrighted—and there aren't too many—are said to be in the *public domain* and may be used royalty-free.

clearance: The process of getting permission from a copyright holder to use copyrighted material.

royalty fees: Copyright fees paid to artists for the use of their work.

public domain (PD): A work is in the public domain when it can be used without concern for copyright, either because it is not copyrighted or because the copyright has expired.

Public Domain Music

In the United States, a musical work can be copyrighted for the lifetime of the composer plus 50 years.[3] A work that falls outside of this time span is said to be in the public domain. The original version of a public domain work may be used without paying royalty fees; but watch out for more recent recordings of these original pieces. Not only is a musical performance itself subject to legal clearance, but changes in the original music may again bring it under copyright restrictions.

ASCAP and BMI Music Licenses

It is important to note that the standard ASCAP (American Society of Composers, Authors and Publishers) and BMI (Broadcast Music Incorporated) **performing rights license,** which broadcast stations must have to play musical selections on the air, does not cover the use of music in commercials, public service announcements and productions. These licenses only cover the standard on-air broadcast of recordings, such as you would find featured on most music radio stations.

Securing Rights to Use Music

Obtaining clearance is a three-step process:

- First, you need to request a **synchronization license** from the music copyright owner that grants you permission to use the music for the interval needed.

---

3. The law differs somewhat in the protection of materials published before and after January, 1978—the point at which a new copyright act took effect.

- Next, you must negotiate with the record company for **dubbing rights** to obtain permission to use the recording produced by the specific record firm.
- Finally, you must obtain **artist permission** from any vocal or instrumental artist featured in the recording.

Since this three-step process can be cumbersome and time-consuming, video producers commonly use the services of agencies that specialize in securing music clearance. These agencies can rather quickly find the owner of a copyright, negotiate a fee and obtain written permission to use the music.

Music Libraries

Music production libraries, which exist in many cities to serve the needs of producers, contain cleared versions of all types of pop and classical music. In this case payment is made to the library only once, and the production may feature the music indefinitely, or for the time specified. If the terms of usage change (the production is redone or substantially changed, for example) this must be reported to the library.

Many production facilities purchase DATs or CDs of a vast array of music and sound effect recordings designed specifically for production use. Along with the purchase come the rights to use the collection as needed. The musical selections in these libraries are easier to cut and edit than most popular songs because they have been written with the needs of the video and film producer in mind. In the case of sound effects, complete libraries of recordings are routinely transferred onto a hard disk, to be instantly called up during the computerized editing process.

Advantages of Original Music

Many producers prefer to use original music. Not only does this solve clearance problems, but since the music is tailored to the production, it can meet the pace, mood and time requirements of the scenes. There is another important advantage of using original music. Many compositions, especially recent popular songs, have emotional baggage associated with them. The music may bring to mind a scene in a movie or a specific situation in a music video. Although this might seem desirable, since people react to films and videos in different ways, it can also be unpredictable. For this reason it is often better to start off with a "clean psychological slate."

If original music involves numerous musicians or an orchestra that must abide by the requirements of a union contract, producing original music can be costly. However, if the background music is relatively simple (i.e., a guitar, flute or organ) and it is performed by the composer, original music can be done rather inexpensively.

Synthesized Music

Today, music synthesizers and MIDI samplers create music for the majority of dramatic TV productions (Figure 19.1). In the hands of an expert, a synthesizer and sampler can duplicate anything from a single instrument to a full orchestra. Since synthesizers and MIDI samplers can also be used to create almost any needed sound effect, this equipment is also now being used with editing workstations to create and synchronize sound effects with video. Synthesizers have mitigated many of the cost and copyright problems previously associated with the use of music and effects.

FIGURE 19.1
Today, music synthesizers and MIDI samplers create music for the majority of dramatic TV productions. In the hands of an expert, a synthesizer and sampler can duplicate anything from a single instrument to a full orchestra.

Other Types of Published Works

Music, of course, is not the only thing that is copyrighted. Text from books, magazines and newspapers, drawings, photos, videotapes and voice recordings are almost always copyrighted. Except in news, where in most cases a limited portion of a work may be used if it directly ties in with a story,[4] copyrighted materials, cannot be included in a production without the permission of the copyright holder. With most published materials clearance is a two-step process: getting permission from the publisher or producer and getting permission from the author or talent involved. Sometimes permission will be given with only a request for a credit at the end of the production; other times the copyright holder will request a fee or royalty. In the latter case the producer will have to decide if the use of the copyrighted material warrants the fee requested.

Whatever the case, since verbal agreements are difficult to later substantiate, it is important to get the agreement in writing. Such agreements should clearly outline usage terms, including the fee paid, a description of the copyrighted material, the name of the production and the broadcast or syndication time frame.

As we've noted, there are depositories of audio and video materials that exist solely to serve the needs of film and video producers. These libraries contain a range of films, videotapes, photos and drawings on almost every subject. Anything from drawings of World War I battles to video of the most recent Playboy playmate of the year is available. The fee charged, which gives the user the right to use the material under agreed-upon conditions, is based on such things as acquisition costs, talent fees and duplication expenses.

---

4. There is an exception here. If the "essence" of the material is broadcast, thereby substantially damaging the copyright holder's material gains from the work, the court may rule against "fair use."

ELECTRONICALLY ALTERED VIDEO AND AUDIO MATERIALS

Digitized Images

Recently, digitized video scanners have made it possible for video artists to use a copyrighted photo or drawing as the basis for their own electronically embellished "creations." Although the final result (after it is resized, recolored, solarized or whatever) may bear little resemblance to the original material, there is still a copyright issue — if the original artist, photographer or publisher recognizes the material and chooses to pursue a case of copyright infringement.

Sampling Audio Recordings

The use of audio samplers can create a similar problem. If electronically sampled music or effects used in the building of music or effects are recognizable by the original artists, a copyright infringement lawsuit can be launched. Admittedly, however, this is an area that is fraught with problems and has sparked very little litigation to date. Even so, as in most litigation of this type, the legal costs involved in a defense can be substantial — regardless of the final result.

TALENT RELEASES

talent release: A form signed by a person appearing in a videotape that grants legal permission to a production agency to broadcast the segment under specified terms.

Talent releases grant a videographer or producer permission to "publish" (broadcast or distribute) a "person's likeness" (a picture), with or without compensation, under the conditions specified in the release. When it comes to talent releases, news is treated differently from other types of production. In news and ENG work the courts have recognized that it is highly impractical to require subjects to sign releases prior to the broadcast of footage. However, in producing segments that do not come under the heading of "news," the rules change. Except for subjects in public places who are unrecognizable and appear as "background" to your scenes, it is wise to always have releases signed. This would be especially important if the person's appearance contributed to some sort of direct "commercial compensation" that you might receive, or if the person appeared in scenes that were shot on private property.

Most producers make it a habit to have releases signed before taping starts. This can save problems when, after a production is shot (and production expenses incurred), the people involved decide to "hold out" for more favorable terms. Having a witness sign the release helps ensure that "after-the-fact" objections don't arise.

The sample talent release shown in Figure 19.2 is a rather brief and all-encompassing release (some legal authorities would say it is too brief and too all-encompassing to meet demanding needs). Whenever possible, a talent release should go beyond this and specify usage, including the specific production, broadcast or distribution conditions, specific fees paid (if any) and any other conditions and terms.

Having a signed talent release doesn't automatically protect you from all possible suits. (A lawyer may try to prove compulsion, misrepresentation or that you exceeded the conditions of the release.) However, once they have signed, most subjects rightly feel that a suit will be on tenuous legal ground.

In some instances, releases are necessary for shooting images of property. Facilities where admission is charged, including some popular theme parks, are an example. If in doubt, check.

TALENT RELEASE FORM

Talent Name: _____

Project Title: _____

I hereby consent for value received and without further consideration or compensation to the use (full or in part) of all photographs, videotapes or film, taken of me and/or recordings made of my voice and/or written extraction, in whole or in part, of such recordings or musical performance

at _____ on _____ 19_____
　　　　(Recording Location)　　　　　　　(Month)　　(Day)　　　　(Year)

by _____ for _____
　　　(Producer)　　　　　　　　　　　(Producing Organization)

for the purposes of illustration, broadcast, distribution, or publication in any manner.

Talent's Signature_____

Address _____ City _____

　　　　　　　State _____ Zip Code _____

　　　　　　　　　　　　　　　　　　　Date: ____/____/____

_____

If the subject is a minor under the laws of the state where modeling, acting or performing is done:

Legal guardian _____ Guardian _____
　　　　　　　　(Signature)　　　　　　　　　　　(Please Print)

Address _____ City _____

　　　　　　　State _____ Zip Code _____

　　　　　　　　　　　　　　　　　　　Date: ____/____/____

_____

Note: No talent release form, including this very basic version, provides absolute protection against possible legal action.

FIGURE 19.2
Talent release form.

SUMMARY

Although a number of general legal guidelines have been presented in this chapter, it should be emphasized that court decisions affecting the shooting and use of videotape have varied with time, place and circumstances. Even court cases that were decided one way at a state or regional level have often been reversed when appealed to a higher court.

In this chapter we have covered invasion of privacy, libel and slander, false light, access restrictions and rights, shield laws, staging, copyright and talent releases. In addition, we've looked at some ethical and professional issues.

Although the privacy of the individual is important, the public's right to know sometimes outweighs this personal right. Decisions on invasion of privacy suggest that if what you intend to photograph can be seen by the average person on public property, intrusion becomes difficult to prove. There are three exceptions: the intentional or unintentional distortion of depicted events or situations, the harassment of subjects or—especially for a private citizen—a reasonable expectation of privacy.

There are several guidelines for intrusion:

- Was there either direct or implied consent to enter the property?
- Could the reporter have gotten the information from another source?
- Is the information obtained newsworthy?
- Is the information obtained of legitimate concern to the public?
- Is there proof of prying on the part of the cameraperson or reporter?
- Does the incident of intrusion relate to something that is generally agreed to be of a private nature?
- Would the intrusion be deemed objectionable by a reasonable person?

One of the grayest areas of access law—and one that is most often encountered by working photojournalists—is access to public locations that are under the control of public safety officials: typically, crime scenes, public demonstrations and various types of disasters. In general, news personnel may not trespass upon private property without permission of the owner or tenant. An exception exists in the case of invitations or requests extended by an authorized public safety officer. The issuance of official press IDs acknowledges that to some degree the media has special privileges; at the same time, however, courts have been reluctant to recognize this fact. Courts have held that TV stations or production agencies cannot use any kind of deceit or misrepresentation in getting a news story.

Commercial appropriation involves exploiting an individual's or organization's prominence without permission in order to influence a listening or viewing audience. A suggestion of endorsement of a product or establishment by a known personality, without the consent of that person, is seen as illegally exploiting his or her prominence.

Defamation is the communication to a third party of false and injurious ideas that tend to lower the community's estimation of the person, expose the person to contempt or ridicule or injure a person in his or her personal or professional life. Libel is defamation by written or printed word and is generally considered more serious than slander, which is defamation by spoken words or gestures. Defamation can be of two types: *per se* and *per quod*.

In judging invasion of privacy cases and libel cases, courts have made a distinction between public and private individuals. Once in the public spotlight, people give up much of the legal protection they had against public criticism and invasion of privacy.

"Honest mistakes" on the part of newspeople or producers can cause damage and personal harm, and the courts have held that false statements arising from accident, error or carelessness may still be subject to settlement. If a definite error in fact is discovered after it has been broadcast, the broadcaster should immediately air a full corrective statement with an apology. This may not eliminate a lawsuit, but it frequently has served to reduce the damages awarded.

Staging applies to news and documentary work. In its negative sense it involves the alteration or misrepresentation of a situation. If staged footage is broadcast and it represents a conscious effort to alter the truth in a news story, it can result in fines by the Federal Communications Commission. A professional and ethical distinction can be made between altering or distorting the essential elements of a story and removing distractions and optimizing technical quality. Quite in contrast to the guidelines covering news and documentary production is the dramatic license, which can be used in doing dramatic productions where the audience does not expect to be told what is and is not authentic.

Except in news, where a limited portion of a work that ties in with a current story may be used, copyrighted materials cannot be included in a production without the permission of the copyright holder. Music, illustrations and published passages are almost always copyrighted and cannot be used in non-news productions without clearance or permission from the copyright holder. The standard ASCAP and BMI performing rights license, which entitles most broadcast stations to play musical selections, does not cover the use of music in commercials, public service announcements and productions.

To use copyrighted music, you must get clearance, a three-step process. First, you need to request a synchronization license from the music copyright owner; next, you must negotiate with the record company for dubbing rights to obtain permission to use the recording produced by the specific record firm; finally, you must obtain artist permission from any vocal or instrumental artist featured in the recording. Fortunately, there are many services available to producers that specialize in obtaining clearance on copyrighted materials.

Many production facilities purchase music or sound effect DAT or CD recordings designed specifically for production use. Along with their purchase come the rights to use the selections as needed. Producers often prefer to use original music because it solves clearance problems and allows music to be tailored to the production. Since music synthesizers and MIDI samplers create music and sound effects for the majority of dramatic TV productions today, many of the previous clearance problems have been eliminated.

Talent releases grant a videographer or producer permission to broadcast or distribute a "person's likeness" (a picture), with or without compensation, under the conditions specified in the release. Except for subjects in public places who are unrecognizable and appear as "background" to your scenes, it is wise to have releases signed. This would be especially important if the person's appearance contributed to some sort of direct commercial compensation, or if the person appeared in scenes that were shot on private property. In news and ENG work the courts have recognized that it is highly impractical to require subjects to sign releases prior to the broadcast of footage. In some instances, releases are necessary for shooting images of property. Facilities where admission is charged, including some popular theme parks, are an example.

KEY TERMS

access
actual malice
artist permission
clearance
commercial appropriation
defamation
defamation *per quod*
defamation *per se*
docudrama
dramatic license
dubbing rights
false light
intrusion on seclusion

invasion of privacy
libel
music production libraries
performing rights license
privacy
public domain
public property
royalty fees
shield law
slander
synchronization license
talent release
trade libel

20

Institutional and Private Video

When most people think of television they think of broadcasting. Although broadcast television is, of course, the most visible and prominent part of the television business, this visibility is deceptive. In terms of personnel and equipment, the *largest* segment of television is actually associated with *non-broadcast* production. In this chapter we'll look at the two major divisions of non-broadcast video: institutional video and *private video* (the use of video equipment for personal and avocational pursuits).

THE SCOPE OF INSTITUTIONAL VIDEO

Included in the category of institutional video are corporate, religious, educational, medical and governmental applications. This general non-broadcast area is variously referred to as *corporate video, non-broadcast television, institutional video, professional video* and *private television*. In this chapter we'll refer to all of these under the general heading of *institutional video*.

Although the field of institutional video may not be as visible or glamorous as over-the-air broadcasting, for the aspiring television professional it holds a number of important advantages. In addition to being larger in terms of personnel and equipment, salaries are often higher, job security is better, working hours and conditions are much more predictable, and there are typically more perks.

The primary goal of institutional video, of course, is to serve the needs of a specific institution or organization. These needs can lie in a wide variety of areas, including education and training, internal or external public relations, maintaining basic news and information networks or serving as a marketing tool for new products and services (Figure 20.1).

FIGURE 20.1
The primary goal of institutional video is to serve the needs of a specific organization. These needs can lie in a wide variety of areas, including education and training, internal or external public relations, maintaining basic news and information networks or serving as a marketing tool for new products and services.

THE SCOPE OF PRIVATE VIDEO

For some time, the fastest-growing segment of video recording has been private video. As a result of this growth, a large percentage of U.S. families own a camcorder today. As in the case of institutional video, there is no well-defined terminology in this area. In this discussion we include the range that extends from "home videos" to various types of personal avocational videography.[1] The latter includes video work intended to directly or indirectly generate revenue.

To start our discussion of institutional and private video, we'll look at a type of video production that spans both broadcast television and institutional video: religious programming.

RELIGIOUS PROGRAMMING

Although the popularity of religious programming declined somewhat in the late 1980s,[2] religious production and programming still represents a very large and viable component of television production today. The broadcast aspect is represented by the country's many religious broadcast stations and by programming produced for satellite and cable distribution. Religious programming can have a wide range of goals, including

- Programming intended to inform an audience about an acute human need, such as hunger in a third-world country
- Programming intended to stir an audience to act on a social problem, such as gangs, drug abuse or teen-age pregnancy
- Programming designed for instructional and inspirational use, such as talks by a spiritual leader

1. Some people use the term *private television* or *private video* in referring to institutional video.

2. This may be temporary. Although causes are difficult to delineate, the impact of the sex-related scandals of two top TV evangelists in the late 1980s undoubtedly was responsible for much of this loss.

- Programming intended to provide basic information, such as a production documenting the work of a particular denomination's missionaries
- Closed-circuit programming, which can range from regular educational productions delivered by satellite (such as those used by Catholic schools across the country) to simply putting TV cameras in an overcrowded church sanctuary so that an overflow crowd can see the service on TV monitors in other locations

We'll discuss other types of institutional production later in the chapter.

THE HISTORY OF INSTITUTIONAL VIDEO

Since the early 1960s, the field of institutional video has experienced a steady (but often uneven) growth. Early in its history, institutional television got off to a flawed start when it was "sold" (primarily by equipment suppliers) as the ideal answer to many problems. In particular, it was touted as the solution to the problems of large classrooms and inadequate teaching staffs. Millions of dollars were invested in video equipment. Caught up in the euphoria of the new technology, some people even went so far as to predict the demise of the classroom teacher.

It quickly became evident that much of the wearisome television programming that was (rather hastily) produced was worse than dull and unengaging classroom teachers. When video didn't live up to these initial, inflated expectations, disappointment set in.

As time passed, those in the field were able to more objectively evaluate the strengths and weaknesses of video. With these in mind, new production approaches were instituted. It was soon demonstrated that video could play an important — even vital — role in educational and corporate settings.

INSTITUTIONAL VIDEO APPLICATIONS

Institutional video has proven itself in many areas:

- As *a tool for supervisors or management* to reach employees with information on policies, progress or problems, or just to relay holiday greetings. Without an effective management-to-employee link, morale can suffer, and rumors are prone to fill the information vacuum. Institutional video can be particularly valuable if the institution has branches in diverse areas.
- *Instructional video.* In an era of ever-accelerating change, the ability to keep employees up on the latest techniques and developments is crucial. Video, especially *interactive video,* which can vary a presentation according to user input, has become a powerful tool. Among its many advantages is its ability to use on-camera specialists to provide consistent training. More about this later.
- *Public relations.* Many institutions regularly create videos to announce products, research developments or major institutional changes. These tapes, which are considered a kind of high-tech press release, are sent to the news directors of area TV stations in hopes of getting them on the air (Figure 20.2). If the news director uses the piece, or even some portions of it — which often happens on a slow news day — the resulting publicity can be well worth the production expenses.

instructional video: A video production primarily designed to communicate specific information, especially within an educational or institutional setting.

interactive video: The video presentation in which the user's actions, choices and decisions affect the course of the presentation.

FIGURE 20.2
Many institutions regularly create videos to announce products, research-developments or major institutional changes. These videotapes, which are considered a kind of high-tech press release, are sent to the news directors of area TV stations in hopes of getting them on the air.

- *Marketing.* New products and services are of little value unless potential consumers know about them. "Point-of-sale" videos highlighting a new product or service are common in many retail stores. These are often seen in the home improvement, makeup and hardware departments.

Even more important for marketing are the many products and services designed for a specialized audience (Figure 20.3). While the mass media may

FIGURE 20.3
An important phase of institutional video is in marketing the many products and services designed for specialized audiences. If a large manufacturer of boats introduces a new model, video ends up being an ideal way to demonstrate and explain new features to the relatively small number of dealers and boating enthusiasts across the country.

be a cost-effective way of reaching a general audience, it is not a cost-effective way of informing a limited number of people about specialized products and services. For example, if a large manufacturer of farm equipment introduces a self-propelled combine with many new features, a way is needed to demonstrate and detail these features to the relatively small number of farmers across the country (and possibly around the world) who might be interested. By producing a video of this new combine and distributing it to dealers, not only will the dealers be informed about the new equipment, but farmers who are interested will probably also want to view the tape.

videoconferencing (teleconferencing): Closed-circuit television productions that link two or more locations and are designed to facilitate discussions and interaction between professionals.

- **Videoconferencing.** While the cost of travel has been going up, the cost of high-quality video equipment has been decreasing. This, together with the time and hassle generally associated with business travel, has provided a perfect opportunity for videoconferencing. *Videoconferencing* (also referred to as **teleconferencing**)[3] is a kind of live, conference-room-to-conference-room, "party-line" telecast that can pull together institutional groups located in two or more geographic areas. While it lacks most of the embellishments of a sophisticated video production, it can be highly effective in bringing together groups scattered over different geographical areas. We'll discuss this in more detail later.

INSTITUTIONAL VIDEO TODAY

Workers in the field of institutional video are of two basic types: those who work full-time for an institution that has a television production division, and those who work for the many independent production facilities that routinely take on institutional projects under contract. Even if productions are contracted out to an independent production facility, media personnel within an institution must have a knowledge of video production techniques and be able to effectively coordinate the work of these outside professionals.

Typical Organizational Approaches

Today, the organization of institutional production can take four forms:

- A fully staffed and equipped in-house department that produces all its own productions. Figure 20.4 illustrates the typical structure of a large institutional television division.

- A fully staffed and equipped in-house department that not only produces videos for its own organization, but brings in additional revenue through outside sources. This can be through producing programming for other organizations or renting out facilities to other agencies whenever they are not tied up with their own work.

- The maintenance of a basic full-time staff to handle routine in-house work, while contracting out major productions that require more specialized facilities, equipment and personnel (including professional on-camera talent). For example, by drawing upon scores of free-lance producers, some of the large U.S. corporations are able to turn out more than 150 productions a year.

---

3. Some people make the following distinction between videoconferencing and teleconferencing: videoconferencing uses two-way video and audio, while teleconferencing uses either one-way video and two-way audio, or simply two-way audio and no video.

FIGURE 20.4

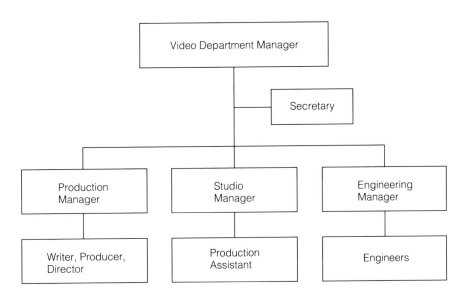

- The maintenance of a partially staffed in-house facility that uses outside contractors (also called *outside vendors*) to do all basic production work. In these cases the in-house staff is used to initiate, guide and coordinate work that has been contracted to independent production facilities. This provides several advantages. First, it reduces the pay and benefits associated with maintaining a large staff of full-time employees; second, it enables the organization to shop around for the best talent and prices for each project; lastly, it can readily be expanded or reduced, as needed, to keep pace with the varying (often seasonal) production needs of the organization.

outside vendors: Outside production agencies hired to do production work. Typically an in-house staff is used to initiate, guide and possibly supplement the work.

Whatever the approach, production work often requires the help of equipment-rental houses that can supplement the in-house equipment—equipment that would not be cost-effective to purchase for occasional in-house use.

The Field of Institutional Video

In the early 1990s, it was estimated that there were more than 35,000 nonbroadcast businesses in the United States producing regular television programming. Since many are not listed in production directories, the number may actually be larger. The institutions represented range all the way from high schools and colleges with simple facilities designed to develop instructional videos to the large corporations. In the latter case the facilities are often more elaborate and impressive than those of most TV stations in the country.

Several organizations are associated with institutional video. One of the most well known is the International Television Association (ITVA). Other organizations, such as the International Association of Business Communication, the International Teleproduction Society and the Society of Motion Picture and Television Engineers (SMPTE) have strong institutional video components.

Areas of Proven Effectiveness

Institutional video has been found to be particularly effective in seven areas:

- Where immediate feedback is necessary to analyze behavioral skills

FIGURE 20.5
After this instructor started individually videotaping the performance of equestrian students, he found a dramatic improvement in performance. Jim Wiley, who heads the Equestrian Education program at Pepperdine University in Malibu, California, has used video to teach hundreds of students to ride, including Olympic contestants and a number of Hollywood stars.

- Where close-ups are required to convey important information
- Where subject matter can best be seen and understood by altering its speed
- Where special effects such as animation can best convey information
- When it is necessary to interrelate a wide variety of diverse elements
- Where it is difficult to transport specific personnel to needed locations
- When the same basic information must be repeated to numerous audiences over time

Some of these require elaboration.

The Power of Immediate Feedback

Sometimes video feedback can be much more effective than even personal feedback from a teacher. We'll cite just one example.

The Equestrian Education program at Pepperdine Univesity (Malibu, California) has been in existence for many years. Over the years, Mr. Jim Wiley, who heads the program, has taught hundreds of students to ride, including Olympic contestants and some well-known Hollywood stars. Classes have intentionally been kept small, allowing Wiley to give students personal feedback on riding problems and techniques. Results of this personal instruction were always positive, but slow. Wiley often had to repeat the same information numerous times before a student would be sufficiently motivated to incorporate the suggestions into actual performances.

When television came along, Wiley started individually videotaping the performance of students (Figure 20.5). Afterward, he would review the tapes—often in slow motion—and use one of the audio tracks on the videotape to record a personal critique. By studying the tapes, the students could clearly see what they were doing while the specific problems were being pointed out.

Since Wiley kept careful statistical records of student progress over the

FIGURE 20.6
A frame-by-frame video study of a golf swing, a tennis return or a triple somersault can reveal information on athletic performances that can be an invaluable aid to coaches and performers.

years, it was easy to chart the rate of improvement before and after television. After he started using television as an instructional tool, the average rate of student progress accelerated dramatically.[4]

With the advent of high-speed shutters on CCD cameras that can slice time into clear, 1/10,000-second intervals, it has become much easier to study slow-motion playbacks of a wide range of athletic performances. A frame-by-frame study of a golf swing, a tennis return or a triple somersault can reveal information on athletic performances that can be an invaluable aid to both coaches and performers (Figure 20.6).

The Power of Close-Ups

Video is also the best route when information must be shown through close-ups, especially extreme close-ups (Figure 20.7). The video camera can also photograph objects or events that are humanly impossible to witness first-hand. With high-quality video cameras not much bigger than your thumb, it is also possible to get pictures in hazardous and small, hard-to-reach places. This has been especially important in medical television.

Medical Applications

Cameras can now be incorporated into small fiber optic probes that can examine the condition and functioning of living organisms. Prior to the development of what is called ***endoscopic television,*** problems could only be clearly seen during an autopsy — after it was a bit late to do anything about them.

4. Actually, video is integrated into the equestrian program in numerous ways, but a full explanation would go far beyond what can be covered here.

endoscopic television: Obtaining television images inside a living body, generally by inserting fiber optic probes.

FIGURE 20.7
When information must be shown through close-ups, video can be quite valuable. This photo shows how sound modulates the microscopic grooves in a phonograph record.

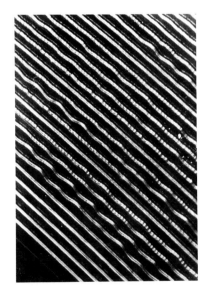

A camera over an operating table can document noteworthy medical procedures, either for a closed-circuit audience or, through videotape, for later review by physicians and medical students. Although remote-controlled video cameras are typically mounted above the operating table, cameras and lights strapped to the headbands of surgeons are also frequently used. The close-ups that are possible are far superior to what students, residents and interns can see from a traditional operating-room observation theater.

Today, most of the large medical facilities have production centers. Both NTSC and high-definition video systems are used. Many medical production facilities are now interconnected by video networks so that productions can be shared.

Pharmaceutical and medical supply companies are major sources of medical productions. These productions are not only designed for hospitals, clinics and educational facilities, but for viewing by the general public via special health-related cable and satellite channels. Many physicians also routinely use videotapes in their offices to explain surgical techniques to patients.

Interrelating Diverse Elements

Video and film have the unique ability to interrelate elements. For example, if we wanted to instill an understanding of the artistic dimension of good video lighting, we could start by bringing together a collection of artistic masterpieces illustrating how form and texture have traditionally been emphasized by lighting. From here we could move to samples of well-lit scenes from classic films. After instilling an artistic perspective, we could then move to video and look at the effect of various lighting approaches in television. The resulting perspective would be much different than if we initially approached lighting from the perspective of typical lighting instruments and optimum light levels as revealed by a waveform monitor.

As we noted in the first chapter on editing, the interrelationship of visual elements in a production generates its own meaning and emotional response. With the video medium, this can be done much more powerfully and convincingly than with words, alone. A primary factor here is television's ability to engage the viewer with sight, sound and motion all at once. This opens the door to affecting the emotions, and once these are tapped, a message becomes more compelling.

As an example, we might be assigned to do an environmental piece demonstrating the effects in Canada of acid rain from the United States. Since a link between pollution and environmental destruction needs to be established (and the two can be separated by hundreds of miles), we might decide to intercut shots of blameworthy factories belching smoke with the negative environmental effects on Canadian trees and wildlife. We would assume that seeing dead trees, fish and wildlife would cause a negative emotional response in viewers.

Here is another example, one that shows how corporate television can be used to benefit both the corporation and its employees. A study within a large corporation found a strong correlation between smoking and health-related job absenteeism. From a purely economic standpoint, it was decided that if a documentary could convince only 14 percent of employees to stop smoking, the total cost of the production could be recouped within three years.

Since the most harmful effects of smoking aren't immediately apparent, again you would need to bring the cause and effect together. The point could be made rather dramatically by showing long-time smokers with severe emphysema, including some who are forced to roll around oxygen bottles in a cart in order to breathe. A cross-section of a blackened lung from an autopsy of a four-pack-a-day-smoker might also dramatically make a point. But there can also be a problem with such dramatic approaches.

Problems in Overstatement

Admittedly, attempts to change behavior or beliefs are more associated with institutional video than with standard broadcast productions. However, in attempting to persuade an audience — especially a well-educated audience — we must be careful not to overstate points. To do so can result in a wholesale rejection of our ideas. This can happen if our points are exaggerated or overly dramatized. In extreme circumstances a *boomerang effect* sets in, and a reversal of the intended effect can take place. Early drug films, for example, were so emotionally overstated as to be ludicrous. This resulted in a wholesale rejection of *all* the arguments presented, and it was assumed that *everything* said in the productions was fallacious — even perfectly valid points.

Today's audiences are rather wary of being manipulated, especially by those they perceive as having their own vested interests. This issue is a particular problem in corporate video, where the interests of companies and employees are sometimes perceived as not coinciding. While accurately representing the goals of an employer, the corporate television producer must approach productions from the perspective of the needs and interests of the target audience. The ability to span these two factions often ends up being a producer's most difficult task.

Altering Time

The next major advantage of video, especially in the institutional setting, lies in its ability to alter events in ways which make information more accessible and understandable. Although we may witness a key football play in real time, it may not be until we see the slow-motion playback that we are able to fully understand what took place.

A number of years ago a large Canadian paper mill put a high-speed, pulp-to-paper machine into operation — the kind that produces the huge rolls of newsprint used by newspapers. At low speeds the machine worked fine, but each time the machine reached full speed the paper would tear, and the facility would be transformed into a confetti factory. The difficulty was that at full speed the machine simply moved too fast to see where the problem developed.

After repeated failures (and many hours of cleaning up the resulting messes), the corporation called upon a production company with high-speed photographic equipment. Bright lights were set up to illuminate every recess of the machine. The start-up process was repeated once more.

When the footage was played back, seconds were transformed into minutes. As the machine reached full speed, a tear started to appear in a span of paper between two high-speed rollers. As soon as the tear was complete (within a fraction of a second in real time) the supply of paper suddenly had nowhere to go. Instantly, it flew throughout the room and entered parts of the machine and was chewed up. It then became evident that some of the moving parts were out of balance, and at high speed the rollers shifted enough to tear the already taut paper. Once the problem was seen, it could be fixed.

At the other end of the scale are the ***time-motion studies*** intended to speed up actions. Most of us nonchalantly accept seeing a period of many hours represented in just a few seconds every night on our local television station. Satellite weather photos taken at regular intervals and displayed in succession

time-motion study: Similar to *time-lapse photography,* except that the condensation of time is designed to allow researchers to analyze (generally human) actions over a period of time in an effort to minimize wasted or inefficient movement.

time-lapse photography: Significantly slowing down the frame rate of motion photography so that events, which may take minutes, hours, or even days, can be shown and observed within seconds.

create a ***time-lapse*** photographic record of cloud (and often storm) movements over many hours.

In the corporate arena, an hour's work of a secretary sitting in an office, for example, can be compressed into ten or fifteen seconds. In this way the full pattern of actions over a period of time can be studied. Awkward, repeated movements become obvious. For example, it might become evident that although a telephone seems nicely positioned on the desk, a secretary, who spends much of her time at the computer keyboard, must regularly reposition herself to answer the phone. And, although having a filing cabinet on either side of the desk might be aesthetically pleasing, a time-and-motion study might make it clear that considerable time and energy were wasted over the course of eight hours in simply moving from one cabinet to another. Photographic studies of assembly-line workers have also revealed awkward motions that not only resulted in fatigue, but have contributed to assembly-line errors.

Although film was originally the only medium that could be used to alter time, today, special video equipment can both compress and expand time. With this powerful tool at their disposal, video personnel should be familiar with the basics of altering time. Let's look at two examples.

Let's asume that a company wants to study the effects of a new industrial solvent that takes 30 minutes to work. Let's further assume that the department involved would like to include a demonstration of the solvent in an institutional production intended to introduce the new product to corporate executives and sales personnel. Watching a solvent slowly attack a surface for 30 minutes would not only take up all the production time (and set a new record for boring television), but the effects of the solvent would be lost to viewers over this lengthy time span. However, by compressing the 30 minutes into 20 seconds, the process would become clear. The question then becomes now to convert 30 minutes to 20 seconds.

Since the production is intended to be played back on standard VCRs (running at a standard NTSC rate of 30 frames per second), the only practical solution is to alter the frame-recording rate of the camera. As a standard rule, we need to know that if we shoot fewer than 30 frames per second, we will (upon playback) speed up time; if we shoot more than 30 frames per second we'll slow down time. The trick is to know just how much to speed up or slow down the camera's recording rate.

Our solvent example, where we need to condense 30 minutes into 20 seconds, can be diagramed this way:

$$30 \text{ frames per second for 20 seconds } = 600 \text{ frames}$$
$$600 \text{ frames divided by 30 minutes } = 20 \text{ frames per minute}$$
$$20 \text{ frames per minute } = \text{ one frame every 3 seconds}$$

Thus, by recording (or editing) one frame every 3 seconds, 30 minutes can be shown in 20 seconds. The same basic approach of dividing the total number of frames needed by the actual time of an event will work for other time-compression problems as well. Here's another problem: If a rose takes 24 hours to bloom, how can the process be shown in about 5 seconds?[5] (Answer: by capturing one video frame every 10 minutes.)

Now let's reverse things and expand time. Let's say that the industrial solvent was found to be too slow. Another department discovers that a high-powered laser beam will do the job in just 1 second. In order to make necessary adjustments in the laser, they need to study the progressive effects of the high-powered

5. For those of you who insist on complete accuracy, the figure is 4.8 seconds.

beam over a period of at least 6 seconds. How many frames per second are necessary to slow down the action?

$$30 \text{ (frames per second)} \times 6 \text{ seconds} = 180 \text{ frames per second}^6$$

By increasing the camera recording speed by a factor of 6, an event that takes 1 second can be stretched out over a 6-second period.

Animation

One of video's real strengths is in representing and explaining concepts through animation and visual effects. Although the time-lapse photography we previously mentioned falls into this category, here we're primarily talking about artificially generated illustrations designed to show complex ideas in a simplified fashion. Although computer-generated drawings can be effective in illustrating concepts, the real strength of video lies in adding illustrative movement—in animating sequences. **Animation** can be defined as the presentation of a succession of still images in such a way as to give an illusion of continuous movement. As we've already noted, early in the history of motion pictures it was discovered that if still images were presented at a rate of 16 to 18 per second, the human faculties of persistence of vision and the phi phenomena would act to blend the images together and create an illusion of motion. When sound motion pictures arrived, the frame rate was increased to 24 per second. And, of course, NTSC video uses a frame rate of 30 per second, and the rate for most PAL and SECAM systems is 25 per second. As we will see, these specific frame rates are important in creating animation.

Figure 20.8 shows how a succession of still images of a bird flying can be combined to create continuous movement. Note that each frame represents a discrete step in the movement sequence. By repeating the sequence over and over, we can make the bird appear to be in continuous flight.

Although creating the picture-by-picture and frame-by-frame animation process is quite time-consuming (and therefore costly) the effectiveness of the results often justifies the expense. In recent years computer-based technology has significantly reduced the cost of animation. Today, electronic paint (graphic) programs can simplify the animation process by using basic instructions to extrapolate an animated sequence. In the case of the bird in Figure 20.8 an electronic artist can program the beginning frame and the ending frame and the computer can electronically create the intermediate steps (frames) of movement. As computing power has expanded, and the cost of animation has come down, animation has become a much more attractive production option.

Portable Expertise

The next major advantage for video in institutional settings is the ability to videotape recognized experts and have this expertise readily accessible over time to many people in many places (Figure 20.9). Although this advantage is taken for granted today, in the beginning of institutional video being able to disseminate important information of this type was a major step forward. "Transporting expertise" in this way can be done in two ways. First, by creating a well-designed television production using the full complement of postproduction resources and then sending tapes to the people and locations where they can be best used. The second method is by videoconferencing.

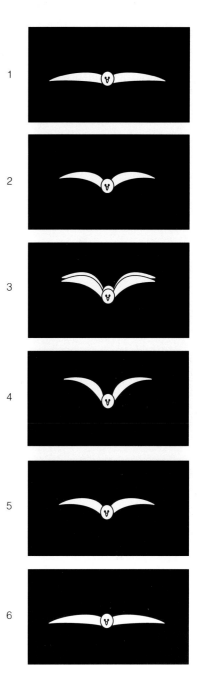

FIGURE 20.8

The figures show how a succession of still images of a bird flying can be combined to create continuous movement. Note that each frame represents a discrete step in the movement sequence. By repeating the sequence over and over, we can make the bird appear to be in continuous flight.

---

6. By changing the basic NTSC rate of 30 frames per second to 25, solutions will be valid for most PAL and SECAM systems; by shifting it to 24, answers will be applicable to film.

FIGURE 20.9
A major advantage for video in institutional settings is the ability to videotape recognized experts and have this expertise readily accessible over time to many people in many places.

Videoconferencing

Videoconferencing is commonly used by a corporate headquarters to do three things:

- To make general news and product announcements to branch offices
- To allow groups working out of several geographic regions within an organization to regularly "meet" and discuss problems, options and progress
- To reduce the need for business travel by "bringing together" representatives of various companies to discuss professional issues.

Leased satellite and high-quality, two-way digital telephone lines are a common way of carrying programming, but these are expensive. In recent years the popularity of videoconferencing has greatly expanded with the introduction of optical fiber phone lines and video compression techniques that can make use of comparatively inexpensive two- to four-wire phone lines.[7]

Although a videotape segment can be "rolled in" if needed, typically, "production" is limited to keeping a camera on the person speaking at a given moment. The latter can be a formidable task with a group of 10 or 12 people and a limited number of cameras (often only one). In videoconferencing, seeing and clearly hearing the person speaking are objectives that overshadow production embellishments.

Audio has always been a problem in videoconferencing. To meet the special needs represented, microphones have been developed with an ability to *gate* sound. These **gated mics** can suppress (or even eliminate) background sound while allowing a dominant sound (generally the person speaking at the time) to come through. This can become quite important when more than two conference sites are on-line at the same time, and the noise from each is added to the other.

gated mics: Mics commonly used in teleconferencing that are designed to pick up a predominant sound source (generally, a speaker) while minimizing the input (and ambient noise) from all other mics.

---

7. By digitizing the video and audio signals and eliminating all but the most essential video information, signals are commonly shrunk (compressed) by a factor of between 1,000 to 2,000 to one.

Gated mics also reduce the "bottom of the barrel" echo effect that results from using several omnidirectional mics at the same time. Finally, since videoconferencing involves both open mics and audio speakers at each location, sound gating reduces the possibility of audio feedback. Gated mics are not without their problems, however. Sometimes they are slow in responding to a sound, or they cut out during momentary pauses in speech.

Even though good-quality mics are used, the acoustics of the rooms used for videoconferencing are still a primary consideration in audio intelligibility. Carpeted floors, acoustic tile ceilings and walls that break up sound reflections are highly desirable.

Many institutions have a permanent videoconference facility consisting of a large, well-lit conference room with two or more cameras and a simple switching capability. A large-screen video projector, a slide chain and VCR playback are sometimes added. To serve the smaller institutions that don't use videoconferencing on a regular basis, there are numerous companies that can come in, set up equipment and establish networking capabilities as needed.

Replicative Advantages

The last major advantage of institutional video production lies in cost savings derived from repeating presentations at minimal cost. Although there may be a substantial cost involved in doing such productions, once done, many of them can be used for months or even years.

Let's assume that a corporation spends $10,000 on a simple, 60-minute production designed to indoctrinate new employees. (The content would typically include a basic explanation of benefits, insurance options, retirement, sick leave, vacation options, and explanation of the many forms that have to be periodically filled out.) Let's also assume that when the various branches of the corporation are added together, the company hires about 600 employees per year. Finally, let's assume that the basic subject matter of the production can last five years without a major revision.[8] This means that the audience for the production will total about 3,000 persons. In terms of cost-per-viewing this comes down to about $3.00 per person.

In determining the cost-effectiveness of this production, three things should be considered: first, the session would take about an hour, and the personnel representative and the new employees would both be making more than this in hourly wages; second, the new-employee sessions would have to be scheduled around the responsibilities of everyone involved; and, finally, having to repeat the same basic information over and over again for each new employee would not be the most effective use of a personnel person's time. When all these things are taken into consideration, a video production becomes a cost-effective and desirable option.

A second example illustrates another aspect of this issue. A number of years ago the architectural department of a large university wanted to include the ideas of a well-known and highly creative architect in their curriculum. However, the man, who was semiretired in Europe, had no interest in traveling to the United States. Arrangements were made to send a production crew to his home (where he had many photographs and models of his work). A highly informative interview was conducted, and the many photos and models were used as B-roll to illustrate the discussion. Because of this production, the university had much more than a "once-only" personal appearance; they had a clearly illustrated and

---

8. Minor revisions involving insert edits of new video material and a redubbing of sections of the sound track are common and comparatively inexpensive to do.

highly informative production that could be used for many years. By offering this interview to other universities for a standard rental fee, they could also, over time, recoup a good percentage of their production expenses.

Today, *education* represents the largest segment of institutional video. There are hundreds of companies that specialize in producing informational, educational and instructional productions for schools. One of the most well-known sources of daily informational programming for grade schools is the Channel One service. Although this news and information service was at first quite controversial because of its commercial content, by 1992, more than 10,000 U.S. schools were using the programming on a regular basis.

BASIC PROGRAM FORMATS

Although most institutional productions incorporate more than one content format, it may be helpful to isolate the various formats for the sake of discussion.

- First is the **lecture format**. In terms of holding audience interest over time, this is by far the most difficult to sustain. Without an array of attention-holding audio and video embellishments, the success of this format rests entirely upon the skill of on-camera talent.

  Probably the worst version of the lecture format is the so-called chalk talk, where speakers stand at a podium and occasionally write notes on a chalk board (while, of course, turning their backs on the camera.) The presentation can be slightly improved by using an overhead projector. But unless the light intensity on the screen is carefully balanced with the light on the speaker, major brightness problems develop. The advantage of the lecture format, of course, is that it's easy, fast and inexpensive.

- In the **interview format** a host interviews a guest (generally an expert or high-ranking official) on specific topics. The interview is the mainstay of documentary programming, although most producers wisely strive to reduce the "talking heads" component to a minimum by adding as much B-roll footage as possible. Unless this is done—and especially if a truly skillful interviewer can't be found—the interview ends up being only a small step above the lecture approach in its ability to hold an audience.

  Often corporate executives will suggest interviews to communicate basic information. While many executives are quite effective in their jobs, they may be poor performers on camera. Since these people are typically above—sometimes far above—video production personnel on the corporate ladder, working with them to produce the best possible on-camera presentation can require real diplomacy. Although suggestions can be made, production personnel can only go so far in dictating production elements and approaches.

- The **documentary format** uses broadcast newsgathering techniques to cover material centering around a single, cohesive theme. While broadcast documentaries typically try to document both sides of an issue, in institutional video a distinct point of view is more typical. Also, unlike broadcast television, institutional documentaries are typically shown to many audiences over time. The documentary approach is almost always single-camera, film-style.

- Finally, there are the **semidramatic** and **dramatic formats**. Although drama is typically the most engaging way of presenting information, it is also the most demanding. While it is difficult for those working in institutional video to compete with the dramatic programming seen on broadcast television, it is regularly done, sometimes even rather effectively. Production centers located near large cities—primarily Los Angeles (Hollywood), New York,

Chicago and Miami—can draw upon the scores of struggling actors waiting for their chance to "be on the screen"—any screen. Some will even work for no pay—just for the chance to gain professional credits by getting a speaking part in a production. Even more experienced actors who are between jobs will often work for *scale*, the minimum pay set by **SAG (Screen Actors' Guild)**.

In doing dramatic productions, it is best to try to find a director with experience in dramatic television. Often this will be a free-lance director. Since directors vary greatly in both their experience and their actual involvement in productions, it is important to request a résumé of previous work. You should then take the extra step of checking with people who have worked with the director during these productions. Questions such as how the director related to personnel and whether the production was brought in on time and within the budget should be among your primary concerns.

HOLDING VIEWER ATTENTION

Some say that the primary thing "sold" by commercial television is "viewers delivered" and that the real goal of commercial television is to sustain viewer interest through the commercials. While this might be debated, the goal of institutional video goes far beyond just holding an audience's attention; information must be imparted in such a way as to be understood and retained by viewers.

Many studies have been done on what makes effective television programming. One of the things that consistently emerges is the need for constant variation. There must be variety in sound, variety in visual information and variety in presentation style. While these have been covered in earlier chapters, the importance of varying presentation style in maintaining viewer interest is critically important in institutional video. Interestingly, in commercial television commercial breaks serve to add variety and give viewers a needed intermission from program content.

It is estimated that, no matter how effectively it is presented, most viewers can't absorb more than 10 minutes of straight information at a time. At this point the ability to follow and absorb the information falls off, and you may lose much of your audience to several minutes of drifting attention—*unless* you regularly alter the presentation in some way. In a lecture or interview this can be done by interjecting a story or cutting to a preproduced supplementary segment that explains or illustrates the matter being discussed. Short, prerecorded dramatic skits can be used to emphasize points in a humorous way (Figure 20.10). Bad acting is often easier to overlook when it isn't supposed to be taken seriously. Just varying the rate at which content is presented will provide some variety. Whatever method is used, make sure you break or at least momentarily alter the presentation at least every 10 minutes. Ideally, this should be done in a way that supplements (rather than diverts attention away from) the central subject matter.

THE FUTURE OF INSTITUTIONAL VIDEO

We are approaching a time when a broadcast-quality video camcorder will be within the reach of most families and everyone with a personal computer will be able to do audio and video editing. Even now S-VHS and Hi8 camcorders exceed broadcast norms for picture resolution and sound quality. In addition, each generation of equipment becomes even easier to operate. As people become

FIGURE 20.10
To vary pace and capture interest in institutional productions, short, humorous segments can be used to emphasize points.

even more comfortable with camcorders, they will see more and more applications for video in their professions or workplaces.

Even though reliable, high-quality technology will be within the reach of most people, this does not mean that the content or effectiveness of productions will automatically improve. Good pictures do not ensure good content. As audiences for broadcast television are exposed to ever-more-sophisticated television production techniques, their expectations for corporate video will also rise. With basic worries about equipment operation diminishing, the emphasis will increasingly shift to effective new ways of using this sophisticated equipment to meet personal and institutional goals. Those who best understand the principles underlying these electronic tools will be in a position to push the limits of technology into creative new areas.

Today, institutional video is using a wide variety of techniques for measuring the effectiveness of productions. Since this type of *accountability* will certainly continue to be emphasized, there will undoubtedly be an ever-increasing effort to measure and compare the effectiveness of productions. Even though many positive results can't be quantified, it is only by attempting to measure effectiveness that those working in the field can justify large expenditures of time and resources.

PRIVATE TELEVISION

When the technical quality of simple, inexpensive camcorders became acceptable for over-the-air broadcasting, private television production rapidly began to change. Numerous shows, such as ABC's "*America's Funniest Home Videos,*" took advantage of the new capabilities of video equipment and encouraged the production of home videos for more than just catching nostalgic family moments. In addition to the over-the-air programming mentioned, numerous special-interest cable channels exhibit personal videos of everything from personal travelogues to ribald bedroom encounters. With the prospect of almost everyone stealing a bit of the aura of a television star, video has the ability to authenticate personal experiences by putting them on television. As the number of families that own a camcorder approaches 25 percent, the personal and avocational use of video is going far beyond recording birthday parties, trips to Disneyland and that new arrival in the family. Here are some examples:

- A woman in Los Angeles uses the video camera as a kind of personal therapist. By videotaping herself as if talking to a trusted friend, she is able to more fully articulate fears and yearnings. After a period of time, when the tape is played back, she is able to somewhat objectively view herself almost as if watching and listening to another person. (Are not most of us much better at recognizing and solving the problems of *other* people?)

- A citizen concerned about a dangerous intersection spends days videotaping near misses. Afterward, he edits the tape and shows it to the city council. A stop light in installed.

- In an effort to preserve family history, a dying woman is videotaped while she discusses the life and times of family members who have passed on.

- An animal rights group uses video to record evidence of the inhumane treatment of cattle. The tape ends up in a network documentary.

- A family member coldly records the embarrassing antics of another family member who is regularly under the influence of alcohol. The resulting tape has a profoundly sobering effect.

- A psychiatrist uses a camcorder to treat anorexia. In an effort to break the physical illusion they hold about themselves, he tries to get patients to see themselves as others (the camera) see them.

- A young woman who could never get her grandmother to write down her strudel recipe makes a video documenting each step, including the "pinch of this" and the "handful of that."

- Actors Demi Moore and Bruce Willis document the birth of their first child on video.

- A dying man records a complete will on videotape, talking personally to each person named.

- For insurance purposes, a homeowner carefully videotapes the contents of each room of his house.

- During the Persian Gulf war of 1991, 450 camcorders, 350 TV sets, 370 VCRs and 250,000 blank videocassettes are sent to soldiers in Saudi Arabia as part of the "Better Than a Letter" campaign to stay in touch with friends and relatives back home.

- In the same war, in an effort to get footage of conditions within the country during the Iraqi occupation, the networks hand out camcorders to citizens as they cross the border to Kuwait.

- A Tampa, Florida man focuses a video camera on a hot tub in his neighbor's back yard. The resulting footage reportedly documents "lewd and lascivious behavior" taking place between the neighbor and his girlfriend.[9]

As many people become adept at handling a camcorder, they often move onto avocational and even vocational applications. Here are just a few examples:

9. People using the camcorder to record evidence of this type have been referred to as *video vigilantes.*

FIGURE 20.11
There are numerous ways to make money with video equipment. A college student with an interest in sports videotaped segments from athletic events and sold them to local TV stations. Hundreds of people across the country who have a high-quality camcorder, videotape area news events and sell the tapes to local TV stations and news organizations such as CNN.

- A camp counselor videotapes the daily experiences of a group of scouts and sells the videotapes to parents.
- After doing a creative job of videotaping his sister's wedding, an enterprising young man starts his own business producing videotapes of weddings.
- A law student earns money by taking video depositions for law firms.
- A young woman makes money by producing videotapes of college graduations and selling them to parents.
- Another woman produces videotapes of various types of athletic competition and sells them to contestants.
- A college student with an interest in sports videotapes segments from athletic events and sells them to a local TV station (Figure 20.11).
- Another college students becomes a *stringer* (a free-lance agent) for area TV stations, selling them Hi8 footage of local news events.
- A husband-and-wife team travel the world recording its people and places. The footage is edited and sold to video libraries around the United States to be used as stock footage in productions (Figure 20.12).

These are just a few examples of the burgeoning possibilities in private video production. With the advent of comparatively inexpensive camcorders, including PC-based video editing and special-effects equipment, video production is no longer reserved for those who can invest hundreds of thousands of dollars in production equipment. We seem to be "democratizing video." Anyone with sufficient motivation to get an idea across can commit it to video and go in search of an audience.

FIGURE 20.12
Some videographers travel the world recording its people and places. They then sell their footage to video libraries around the United States to be used as stock footage in productions.

SUMMARY

Institutional video goes under various names, including corporate video, non-broadcast television, institutional video, professional video and private television. Educational and instructional video and religious television are also included in institutional video. Compared to broadcast television, institutional video holds several advantages for aspiring professionals: it is a larger field in terms of personnel and equipment, salaries are typically higher, job security is better, there are more perks, and working hours and conditions are more predictable.

The primary goal of institutional video is to serve the needs of a specific institution or organization. These needs lie in a wide variety of areas, including education and training, internal or external public relations, maintaining basic news and information networks and serving as a marketing tool for new products and services.

Institutional video has proven itself in many areas, including being used as a tool for supervisors or management, for instructional purposes, for public relations, for marketing new products and services and for videoconferencing.

Institutional video has been found to be particularly effective in seven areas: (1) where immediate feedback is necessary, (2) where close-ups are required to convey important information, (3) where subject matter can be better seen and understood by altering its speed, (4) where animation and visual effects will best convey information, (5) when it is necessary to interrelate a wide variety of diverse elements, (6) where it is difficult to transport specific personnel to needed locations and (7) and when the same basic information must be repeated to numerous audiences over time.

There are four basic program formats used in institutional video: the lecture format, the interview format, the documentary format and the semidramatic and dramatic formats. Institutional video must go further than commercial television; it must not only hold the attention of an audience, but it must be able to create a measurable effect on its audience.

For some time, the fastest-growing segment of video production has been private video. When the technical quality of simple, inexpensive camcorders became acceptable for over-the-air broadcasting, numerous cable and over-the-air TV shows spurred an interest in producing videos of more than just nostalgic family moments. Today, private video extends from home videos to various types of personal avocational videography. The latter includes video work intended to directly or indirectly generate revenue.

With each new generation of video equipment, the basic worries about the technical aspects surrounding the operation of equipment diminish. This means that the emphasis in institutional and personal video will increasingly shift to effective new ways of using this equipment to meet personal and institutional goals. Those who best understand the principles underlying these electronic tools will be in a position to push the limits of technology into creative new areas.

KEY TERMS

animation
documentary format
dramatic format
endoscopic television
gated mics
instructional video
interactive video
interview format

lecture format
outside vendors
SAG (Screen Actors' Guild)
semidramatic format
teleconferencing
time-lapse photography
time-motion study
videoconferencing

GLOSSARY

Note: Some terms are listed by their abbreviations. For example, *personal computer* is listed under *PC,* and *American Standard Code for Information Interchange* is listed under its more common designation of *ASCII.*

A and B Rolls; A-B Rolls: Refers to the use of two videotapes in recording a single-camera segment. During editing, the audio and/or video from the B-roll (generally consisting of cutaways and insert shots) is inserted over the primary A-roll footage.

Aberration: Any optical or electronic distortion of an image.

Above-the-Line: Budgetary division focusing on non-technical, creative expenses. Included are the producer, director, writer and the on-camera talent.

AC: Alternating current. Standard 120-volt, 60-Hz (cycle) household electricity. Also called line voltage.

AC Adapter: Converts power from a standard AC electrical outlet to low-voltage direct current (DC) for use with battery-operated audio or video equipment.

Acceleration Editing: Condensing or expanding time through editing. In a dramatic production, several hours of activity can be condensed into a few short scenes. Conversely, some directors will "drag out" an event beyond its actual time in order to heighten dramatic impact.

Access: In the context of newsgathering, the legal right of a news reporter to go onto private property to obtain information or videotape footage.

Access Time: Delay between the time information or action is requested from equipment and the desired response.

Acoustics: Characteristics added to basic sound resulting from reflective interactions within a room or studio.

Acquisition Format: Typically, footage shot on S-VHS or Hi8 intended to be transferred to a higher quality format in order to retain better quality during subsequent editing and copying.

Action Cutting: Using editing to cut from one shot and camera angle to another during an action scene, giving the impression that multiple cameras are being used. During single-camera production, action is repeated for a single camera positioned at different angles and distances, and footage is cut together in editing to give the impression that there is uninterrupted action covered from a variety of camera angles.

Action Still: A still-frame captured during a production by an electronic still-store device. Sometimes used at the end of a production to key credits over.

Active Lines: The total number of visible scanning lines in a video frame, or the total number of lines minus the lines devoted to vertical blanking.

Active Matrix Display: A flat CCD color display in which an image is created directly from glowing red, blue and green pixel points. This type of CCD display is capable of creating a brighter, sharper picture than a *passive matrix display.*

Actual Malice: Broadcasting or publishing something that is either known to be false or is disseminated with reckless disregard for its truth or accuracy.

Actuality: Tape or film of a non-studio event done as it is happening.

Acutance: The measure of sharpness of a clearly defined object in a scene as reproduced by a lens.

AD: Associate or assistant director. Individual who performs numerous functions assigned by the director, including scheduling, supervising crews, conducting rehearsals etc.

Adaptation: A film or video script written from a book, play or story.

Adapter Shell: A holder for the VHC-C and Compact-8 formats that allows their cassettes to fit into standard VHS and 8mm players.

ADC: Analog-to-digital converter. Circuit designed to convert analog video or audio to a digital signal.

Additive Color: Process used in color television in which colored light is combined in various proportions to create a full spectrum of colors. See *additive primaries.*

Additive Primaries: Red, blue and green. Colors added together in different combinations to create white and all other colors.

Address Code: SMPTE/EBU time code. Digitized eight-digit coded information recorded on a videotape that identifies each video field or frame.

Address Track: An approach to recording SMPTE/EBU time code within the basic video signal.

Affiliate: A broadcast station with a contract with one or more networks to carry their programming.

AFM: American Federation of Musicians. Musicians' union.

AFT: Automatic fine tuning. An electronic circuit in a receiver that "locks onto" a station and (within limits) doesn't allow the receiver to drift off frequency.

AFTRA: American Federation of Television and Radio Artists. The union to which broadcast artists belong.

AGC: Automatic gain control. Circuit that automatically maintains a preset audio or video level. Although convenient, the use of AGC circuits does not achieve the best results in some situations.

Air Check: A recording of an on-air segment done by or for a particular announcer to evaluate diction, voice quality and general effectiveness.

Air Date: Day on which a specific program is to be broadcast.

Air Quality: Program material that meets technical (generally FCC) standards for quality.

ALC: Automatic level control. See *AGC.*

Aliasing: Distortions occurring in the analog-to-digital conversion resulting from the creation of false signal components during the sampling process. Typically results in sawtooth edges around curved or diagonal lines. Can be eliminated with filters.

Alignment Tape: An audio or videotape containing picture and sound reference signals. Used for aligning a tape machine.

Alpha Wrap: Tape-wrap configuration around the video and audio heads associated with one type of helical scan videotape machine.

Alphanumeric: Referring to both numbers and letters.

Ambient Sound: Prevailing background sound at a specific location.

Amplifier: Circuit that increases the amplitude or level of an electronic signal.

Amplitude: The strength of a video or audio signal.

Analog: As opposed to a *digital* signal, a signal that varies smoothly between certain ranges. An analog signal bears an exact, continuous relationship to the original information.

Analog-to-Digital Conversion (ADC): The process of converting an analog signal to digital data.

Angle of Acceptance: Vertical and horizontal angle of view of a lens.

Angle of View: See *angle of acceptance*.

Angle On: Script direction indicating another camera angle is to be taken of specific shot.

Animation: Process of taking a series of still frames of slightly different drawings or objects that, when presented at normal speed, give the illusion of motion. Typically, two or three frames of the drawing or object are exposed before changes are made and the next frames are exposed.

Animation Stand: Adjustable structure that holds and controls camera and drawings (or objects) for creating animation.

ANNCR: Script abbreviation for "announcer."

Announce Booth: A small, soundproofed room or enclosure with a microphone where voice recordings or on-air announcements are made.

Antenna: Device that either receives or radiates a radio frequency signal.

Anthology: A collection of short segments or stories assembled into a single production.

Anti-Aliasing: Smoothing a sawtooth, jagged effect around curved and diagonal lines in electronic graphics through the use of filters.

Aperture (Aperture Setting): F-stop. Lens opening based on a ratio between focal length and the diameter of the lens opening that determines how much light will pass through the lens.

Approximate Color Consistency: The human ability to visually correct for changes in color temperature. For example, a white piece of paper will appear white under both daylight and incandescent light even though the actual color will vary more than 2,000° K.

Arc: The movement of a camera on its dolly along a curved path.

Arc Light: Intense light produced by electricity passing between (arcing across) two electrodes.

Archive: Long-term electronic storage of text or images, generally on some form of disk or magnetic tape.

Art Director: Person in charge of designing and developing production elements that relate to graphics and sets.

Artifacts: Any type of visible or aural defect resulting from aberrations in the television process.

Artist Permission: Authorization from a recording artist to use copyrighted works in a production.

ASCAP: American Society of Composers, Authors and Publishers. A trade guild that protects the publication and performance rights of composers, authors and publishers.

ASCII: American Standard Code for Information Interchange (pronounced "ask-key"). Refers to a computer code that provides compatibility between computers and programs.

Aspect Ratio: The numerical ratio of picture width to height. The standard broadcast aspect ratio is 4 × 3.

Assemble Editing: In contrast to *insert editing*, an editing process whereby a new video or audio sequence is consecutively added to a previously edited scene, complete with the associated control track.

Assignment Editor: The individual in a broadcast newsroom who has the responsibility of assigning news and ENG stories to specific reporters.

Assistant Cameraman: Person who aids the camera operator or director of photography by doing such things as setting up the camera, loading tape and shifting focus as needed during taping.

Associate Director: An individual who assists the director during a production with such things as keeping track of time, seeing that camera shots and tape and film inserts are ready when needed etc.

Associate Producer: An individual delegated certain producing responsibilities by the producer or executive producer.

Asynchronous Sound: Sound that is part of and is appropriate to a scene, but is not necessarily synchronized with visible action. It is commonly added in postproduction to add atmosphere and feeling. The sound of waves at a beach, birds in a forest, or crickets in a night scene are examples.

ATF: Automatic track finding. An electro-mechanical process that eliminates the need for a manual tracking adjustment on a VCR. Also referred to as AST, or automatic scan tracking.

Atmosphere: Aspects added to scene to enhance mood or feeling. Rain, lightning or asynchronous sounds commonly add a dimension of realism to a scene.

Atmosphere Introduction: Beginning a video segment with a scene or series of scenes intended to establish the conditions, habitat environment, spirit or climate of the central subject matter.

Attenuate: To decrease the level or loudness of a signal.

Audio Board (Audio Console): A basic desktop control center used to switch, mix and control audio levels for a variety of audio sources.

Audio Booth: An area (often a separate room) in a production facility where audio signals are controlled and mixed.

Audio Channel: A single audio circuit, generally consisting of an amplifier and one or more audio controls.

Audio Compressor: Audio-processing circuit that reduces dynamic range by simultaneously raising low audio levels and lowering high levels so that a higher average level is achieved.

Audio Console: See *audio board*.

Audio Dub: Making a copy of an audio tape. In television, the recording of sound only, without disturbing the picture.

Audio Expander: An electrical circuit that increases the dynamic range of an audio signal.

Audio Limiter: An electronic device intended to restrict the maximum amplitude of a signal.

Audio Mix: Audio track created by combining multiple sound sources.

Audio Mixer: A device that allows the simultaneous combining and blending of several sound inputs into one or two outputs.

Audio Monitor: An audio amplifier and speaker system used to check and listen to audio during a production.

Audio Slate: Voice-track information recorded at the start of a tape identifying the production. This might include the series title and episode number, the director, the production date and the planned air date. Generally a video slate is also included with essentially the same information.

Audio Speaker: An electro-mechanical device for reproducing audio that changes electrical energy into sound.

Audio Sweetening: A postproduction process designed to correct problems in audio as well as to enhance and supplement audio tracks.

Audio Technician: A person who is in charge of some phase of audio. Generally, a person who operates an audio board.

Audio Track: The portion of the videotape that records sound.

Audio-Follow-Video: A switcher that automatically switches audio with its corresponding video.

Audition Channel: An audio monitor system enabling a technician to listen to, preview and cue audio sources before sending them through the audio console.

Auto-Assemble: Automatic editing of videotape to conform to a previously generated edit decision list (EDL).

Auto-Iris: System that automatically adjusts a lens aperture to compensate for the brightness of a scene. (See *automatic exposure control*.)

Auto-Focus Lens: Lens that works by any one of several electro-mechanical methods allowing it to be automatically focused.

Auto-Key Tracking: Chroma key tracking. Ability of a video-effects system to retain the appropriate size of a keyed-in image when the camera supplying the background video is zoomed in or out.

Automatic Exposure Control: System that responds to varying light conditions by adjusting a camera's iris in an effort to automatically attain optimum overall exposure.

Automatic Gain Control: See *AGC*.

Available Light: The naturally existing light that illuminates a scene.

Avant Garde: A new, experimental or strikingly different production approach.

Azimuth: The angle of a recording head in relation to the tape. When this angle varies from an optimum setting, sound quality suffers. Azimuth angles of multiple recording and playback heads are often intentionally offset to reduce adjacent channel interference.

Back Focus: Adjusting the distance between the back of a lens set at infinity and the camera target to attain the sharpest image possible of an object at infinity. Back focus adjustment determines whether a zoom lens will stay in focus when moved through its focal length range.

Back Light: Light directed from behind and above the subject; used to separate and add dimension to a scene. Slightly stronger than front light.

Background Light: Light intended to illuminate a background. Generally about two-thirds the intensity of the key light.

Background Music: Sound track music intended to enhance drama or visual elements during a production.

Background Projection: See *rear projection*.

Backlight Compensator (BLC): A camera control that opens up the lens aperture two to three f-stops. Used to compensate for the error made by automatic iris circuits when shooting into light or against a bright background.

Backlight Switch: Camera control that overrides the auto-iris system and opens the iris two or three f-stops. Commonly used in backlit situations where auto-iris would result in dark skin tones and underexposure.

Backtime: Calculating time for a show backward from the end to determine when segments should start in order to bring the show out on time.

Backup Schedule: A "plan B" schedule of shots or scenes that can be substituted for the planned shooting schedule in case of illness of a principal actor, bad weather, mechanical or technical problems etc.

Balanced Audio Input: An audio input into a device that consists of two conductors surrounded by a grounded shield.

Balanced Line (Balanced Mic): Typically, a two-conductor audio cable enclosed in a metal shield, which as a result is relatively immune to hum and other electronic interference. Unbalanced lines have only two conductors.

Bandwidth: The difference in Hz (hertz) between the highest and lowest frequency com-

ponents of a radio frequency (RF) signal. The total radio frequency range used by a signal.

Bar Chart: A graphic consisting of bars of varying length that show the relative difference between selected variables.

Barn Door: Side and/or top flaps that attach to front of light and shape the light beam. Commonly used with a Fresnel light.

Barney: A cover for a video or film camera designed to protect it from dirt, rain, snow, sand etc.

Bars and Tone: A carefully controlled audio and video signal generally recorded at the beginning of a videotape and later used to properly set up playback equipment. *Bars* consist of a test pattern of color bars; *tone* consists of an audio signal of a certain frequency at zero dB.

Base Light: Even lighting used over a set or production area. Often a set is initially lit with basic (base light) illumination, and then the key and back lights are added.

Base Station: Central digital control system used for adjusting levels, color balance etc. of several studio cameras.

Basic Makeup: Primary or elemental makeup. As opposed to *corrective* or *character makeup*, makeup intended to slightly enhance appearance as seen on TV.

Bass: Audio tones of low frequency, typically below 300 Hz.

Battery Light: A battery-operated, portable light commonly used for ENG work. Often mounted on top of a camera.

Baud Rate: The speed at which computer data is transmitted in terms of bits per second. Modems typically operate at 2,400 and 9,600 baud.

Bayonet Mount: A camera mount that locks a lens securely into place with only a partial turn. This contrasts with the C-mount that requires numerous turns to secure.

BBS: Electronic bulletin board system. An electronic source of text, images and computer programs available over telephone lines by computer modem hookups.

Beam Projector (Beam Spot Projector): A spotlight that projects a focused, hard and generally narrow beam of light. Often used to simulate sunlight coming through a window.

Beam Splitter: A prism or dichroic mirror device used behind a color TV camera lens to divide the light into the three primary colors.

Beat: An assigned area covered by a reporter on a regular basis.

Beauty Shot: Identifying close-up shot of an advertised product.

Below-the-Line: Production costs associated with technical rather than creative services. Technical services include editing, general labor, makeup, special effects, costumes, scenery, transportation, among others.

Betacam: A broadcast-quality format developed by Sony and used in several types of camcorders.

Betamax: A consumer-quality ½-inch vid-

eocassette format developed by Sony, which eventually was supplanted by VHS.

Bias Light: A dim light inside a camera directed toward the front surface of the CCDs or pickup tubes and intended to increase camera sensitivity while controlling video noise.

Bicycling: Routing a videotape from station to station instead of sending individual tapes to each.

Bidirectional: A microphone pickup pattern with two primary areas of sensitivity, typically in a figure-8 pattern.

Binary System: A number system with a base of two. Each digit has only two possible states 0 and 1, or on and off. Binary numbers are the basis for computer languages.

BIOS: Basic input/output system. Computer device that manages communications between the basic computer and peripherals, such as the keyboard and monitor.

Bird: A satellite. Sometimes used as a verb to indicate the transmission of a video program or segment.

Bit: A binary digit, 0 or 1. The smallest amount of information a computer can handle.

Bit Speed: Speed at which units of digital information can be transmitted from one point to another.

Bite: Sound bite. A short interview segment with associated audio intended as part of a production.

Black Balancing: Electronically setting the black level of a camera to correspond to TV black.

Black Clipping: A circuit used to limit the black level of video so that it does not intrude into the sync.

Black Level: The darkest portion of the video picture. Reference black.

Blanked Tape: A videotape intended for insert editing onto which black (or color bars) and a control track have been recorded. Also called a crystal tape.

Blanking (Blacking) a Tape: Recording black, sync and a control track on a videotape. The process of creating a blanked tape.

Blanking Interval: The retrace interval of 10.5 microseconds in which the effect of the electron beam is extinguished so that it can return from the right to the left side of the screen. Also the 1.3 millisecond interval in which the effect of the electronic beam is extinguished so that it can move from the bottom of one field to start scanning the top of the next field.

Blanking Pulse: Video signal that blacks out a video image between successive scanning lines, fields and frames. See *blanking interval*.

Blocking: To establish camera angles and positions and the movements and positions of actors before a production rehearsal.

Bloom, Blooming: A dark halo that surrounds bright areas in a scene, caused by aberrations in the video process. Generally associated with tube-type cameras.

Blooper: An error in speech made by on-camera talent.

Blue Pages: Revised pages (of any color) that are substituted for existing script pages.

Blue-Pencil: To edit or censor a script.

Blue-Screen Process: Process of photographing action in front of a blue screen to make a matte special effect possible.

Body Brace: A type of camera mount that attains some measure of stability by resting on the shoulder and attaching to the chest or belt area.

Body Wash: Body makeup used by actors.

Boom: Cantilevered camera mount allowing adjustment of camera height. Also balanced pole device used to suspend microphone.

Boom Up; Boom Down: To raise or lower the height of a camera mounted on a boom or pedestal.

Border Merger: A composition problem in which subject matter is awkwardly and inappropriately cut off at one edge of the video frame.

Bounce Light: An even, diffused light over an area that results from light being reflected off of the ceiling or wall in a room.

Breakaway: A prop used during action sequences that looks real but is constructed so that it will break easily without harm to performers.

Breakdown: Analysis of script segments for the purpose of determining the best sequence for shooting scenes and setups. Also referred to as *breakdown sheets.* Term also refers to analyzing a script for a cost analysis.

Breakup: A brief interruption of video caused by a technical problem.

Bridge: Short visual or audio sequence designed as a transition between two program elements.

Bridging Shot: A shot inserted between two scenes to indicate a break in time or continuity.

Brightness Range: Range in reflectance from the darkest to the lightest subject matter in a scene as measured by a reflected light meter.

Broad: A broad-beam floodlight with a rectangular reflector used to light backgrounds and to throw light over a wide set area.

Broad-Beamed Lamp: A lighting instrument within a rectangular reflector that creates a broad, somewhat diffused light.

Budget Tracking: A process whereby the actual expenses in a production are regularly compared to originally projected expenses.

Budgeting: Process of determining costs for a production.

Build Up: Creating tension in a dramatic production by arranging scenes and selecting music that build to a crisis or climax.

Bulk Erase: To completely erase an audio or videotape by the use of a strong electromagnet.

Bump Up: To copy segments from one vid-

eotape format to a larger or higher quality format.

Bump-Down: Copying video information from higher quality VTR format to a lower quality one.

Burn (Burn In): An undesirable after-image of a (generally bright) subject that remains on a camera tube target.

Burned In: SMPTE/EBU time code numbers that are a permanent part of the corresponding video.

Burned-in Time Code: As opposed to *keyed-in time code,* SMPTE/EBU time code numbers which are a permanent part of the corresponding video.

Bus (Buss): A single row of buttons on a video switcher.

Business: The realistic actions of actors that take place as a scene progresses. Examples would be reading a newspaper, knitting or fixing a drink.

Bust Shot: Camera shot of an actor from the waist up.

Busy: A scene that contains an inordinate amount of activity or distracting background elements.

Butterfly Diffuser: A large net diffusion screen used between direct sunlight and a subject to soften the harshness of the sun.

Byte: Eight bits; computer-language information used to define an alphabetic character.

Cable Television: Non-broadcast, point-to-point transmission of television programming by coaxial or fiber optic cable. Used for programming intended for a more limited audience than over-the-air broadcast television.

CAD: Computer-aided design; computer-assisted design.

Cam Head: A type of pan head for a camera mount. Commonly associated with studio cameras. Pan and tilt actions are controlled by variable drag adjustments.

Camcorder: An all-in-one *cam*era and re*corder.*

Cameo Background: A totally black background.

Cameo Lighting: The use of special lighting with a dark background so that subjects appear as if they are being photographed against a totally black background.

Camera Blocking: Working out camera and talent positions and movements prior to the taping of a show.

Camera Car: A car or truck with a camera mount, used for the taping of scenes while the vehicle is in motion.

Camera Cards: Graphic cards designed to be picked up by a camera.

Camera Chain: A complete camera system: camera, cables, video controls and power supply.

Camera Control Unit (CCU): A device containing electronics and controls used for setting up and adjusting the video (e.g., color

correction, luminance) from one or more cameras. CCUs for studio cameras are generally found in the video control room.

Camera Cue Light: Tally light. A red light on the camera that indicates when it is on-the-air or being recorded.

Camera Head: The actual television camera, which is at the "head" of a chain of camera-related electronics.

Camera Jib: Remotely operated, cranelike camera mount that can typically move a camera from floor or ground level to a height of 10 or more feet.

Camera Left and Right: Directions given from the camera's point of view. The reverse of *stage left* and *stage right,* used in theater.

Camera Light: A light normally mounted on the top of a camera to provide added illumination.

Camera of Record: Videotaping an event as it happens, generally without effects or production embellishments. Intended only as a "raw record" of the event.

Camera Operator: Person who is responsible for operating a camera, generally under the command of a director.

Camera Prompter: An electrical device for displaying a script that can be read by talent during a production. Also called Tele-prompter.

Camera Rehearsal: Rehearsal using cameras, designed to make final checks before a production.

Camera Tube: The primary light-sensitive device in a tube-based video camera that converts the light image from the camera lens into an electrical signal.

Canon Connector: A shielded, three-pin audio connector. Generally used with professional microphones. More commonly called an XLR connector.

Canted Camera (Canted Shot): Camera angle achieved by turning the camera slightly to one side, causing the subject matter to run up or down hill. Result is also referred to as *Dutch angle.*

Canvas Drop: A canvas background that can be lowered into place from the studio grid.

Cap Up: To cover the lens of a camera.

Capacitor: Electronic device that can store an electric charge. A central part of a condenser microphone.

Capstan: A motor-driver roller and rotating shaft in the VTR that pulls the tape over the heads.

Cardioid Pattern: A microphone with a heart-shaped pattern of sensitivity.

Carrier Wave: An electromagnetic wave modulated with audio or video information used to broadcast radio and television signals.

Cart (Cartridge): A plastic container with audio or videotape that threads automatically when inserted into a recorder or playback machine. In contrast to a cassette, the tape is commonly in a continuous loop.

Cascading: The flow of a signal through a sequence of electronic stages, each stage adding an additional effect.

Cassette: A plastic container with a supply and take-up reel of audio or videotape that threads automatically when placed in a record or playback machine. Unlike the cartridge, the tape is not in a continuous loop and must be rewound.

Catadiatropic Lens (Cat Lens): A telescopic lens that uses an internal mirror to reduce the physical length of the lens.

Catchlight: A small, concentrated reflection from a major light source that appears in a subject's eyes.

Cathode Ray Tube (CRT): Any video screen employing an electron gun; used for displaying information. TV sets, computer monitors and vectorscopes all have CRTs.

CATV: See *community antenna television.*

Causality: The arrangement of scenes in editing to suggest cause-and-effect relationships.

C-Band: The original and most widely-used band of frequencies used by satellite transponders. Compared to the Ku-band, the C-band has both advantages and disadvantages.

CCD (Charge-Coupled Device): A solid-state camera imaging device that has a number of advantages over camera tubes.

C-Clamp: A screw-down clamp used to mount lights to studio grid pipes and lighting stands.

CCTV: See *closed-circuit television.*

CCU: See *camera control unit.*

CD (Compact Disk): An audio recording and playback medium that uses digitally encoded information on a laser disk. The sound is decoded by optical laser for high-quality audio playback.

CD-ROM: Compact disk-read only memory. A computer information storage system centering on compact disks.

Cel: A transparent sheet for use in animation, on which individual drawings appear. Multiple cels (cel sandwiches) may be overlaid to build scenes and to eliminate the need to redraw areas.

Cel Animation: Animating portions of an image through the use of multiple layers (cels) of transparent acetate sheets. Specific types of content are confined to specific cel layers.

Center Spot Filter: A diffusion filter with a clear central area. Gives a clear central area and slightly diffuses surrounding areas.

CGA: Color graphics adapter. A relatively low resolution color display system for PC-type computers.

Channel: A band or frequency assigned to a broadcast station.

Character Generator (CG): A device that electrically creates letters and symbols for TV titles and other graphic displays.

Character Makeup: Makeup (generally accompanied by hair pieces etc.) designed to change an actor's appearance into that of the character being played.

Charge-Coupled Device: See *CCD.*

Charger: An electrical, AC-to-DC device that replenishes (recharges) battery power.

Cheat: To arrange talent or props so that an optimum camera angle is achieved, often without regard to how realistic it may be for actors.

Chip Camera: A camera that uses one or more CCDs. See *CCD.*

Chip Chart: A test chart consisting of shades of gray, from TV white to TV black, used for setting up cameras.

Chroma: Color.

Chroma Channels: The separate light-sensitive pickup devices or color circuits in a TV camera. Typically there are three channels: red, blue and green.

Chroma Crawl: An undesirable moving color artifact or pattern in an NTSC picture. Generally caused by a television set decoding color information as high-detailed luminance information.

Chroma Key: An electronic matting effect that keys out or removes a portion of video of a specific color. Another video source is then substituted for the removed area. Generally, a deep, saturated blue is used as a keying color.

Chroma Key Blue: A deep shade of blue commonly used in backgrounds that is intended to be keyed out and replaced with other video. See *chroma key.*

Chroma Processor: A computer program associated with desktop editing programs that can subtly or drastically alter colors and color balance in sources of video.

Chroma Resolution: As distinct from luminance detail, the amount of detail in color channels.

Chromatic Aberration: Color fringing or other color abnormalities caused by imperfections in a camera lens.

Chrominance: Color. TV camera color channel.

Cinemascope: The first modern wide-screen movie format. It achieved a 2.35 × 1 aspect ratio by using a 2-to-1 anamorphic lens.

Clean Edit: An edit with no accompanying electronic noise, distortion or other disruption.

Clearance: The process of getting permission from a copyright holder to use copyrighted material.

Clip: To cut off video levels above a certain point in order to stay within a set contrast ratio. This problem commonly results in "chalky whites."

Clip-on Mic: A small personal microphone that can be attached to clothing.

Clipper Gain Knob: A knob on a video effects unit used to set the threshold level for color or luminance keying.

Clipping: Cutting of the peaks of a signal. In video this generally affects the white level.

Clock Speed: The speed in MHz (megahertz) at which the computer's central processing unit operates.

Clone: A computer that simulates the functions of a more expensive make and model.

Closed Set: A television studio that is closed to all but specific crew and talent involved in the scene.

Closed-Captioned: Printed words and dialogue intended for hearing-impaired viewers broadcast along with a TV signal. The term *closed* means that a special electronic device must be used to decode and display the information.

Closed-Circuit Television: Non-broadcast programming. Television that goes to an audience by a direct, point-to-point distribution system.

C-Mount: A common type of camera lens mount used on 16mm motion picture cameras and on some video cameras.

Coated Lens: A lens with elements having a magnesium-fluoride coating designed to reduce light reflections.

Coaxial Cable (Coax): An electrical cable designed to carry video signals. It has a metal conductor in the center surrounded by an insulator and a braided wire shield.

Co-Channel Interference: Interference caused by two or more stations using the same channel (frequency).

Coherence: A descriptive dimension of light that characterizes its hardness or softness. The harder a light source is, the more coherent it is said to have. Professional photographers refer to coherence as light *quality.*

Color Balance: To adjust the chroma channels in a video camera so that whites in a scene will be reproduced as true white.

Color Bars: A series of colored bars of established properties used as an electronic standard for adjusting brightness, contrast, color intensity and color balance.

Color Burst: The color timing information contained in the TV signal. A 3.58 MHz subcarrier frequency timed to a quarter-millionth of a second is used to synchronize color information to the luminance signal.

Color Compatibility: The ability of different color subject matter to translate into a black-and-white picture and maintain adequate tonal contrast and separation.

Color Conversion Filter: A camera filter used to convert light from indoor to outdoor color temperature.

Color Correction: Adjustments that alter and correct the color qualities of video.

Color LCD: A flat, liquid-quartz-type display that can reproduce a full-color image.

Color Media: See *gel.*

Color Phase: As shown on a vectorscope, the electronic phase difference in degrees between the color standard and specific colors reproduced by video equipment.

Color Resolution: The degree to which the color channels in a video system can reproduce fine details.

Color Standard: A color criterion or reference used to set up color video equipment.

Color Temperature: The dominant color of a light source, measured in degrees Kelvin.

Color Temperature Meter: A measuring device that indicates dominant color temperature in degrees Kelvin.

Color Under: Heterodyne-type color process used in most videocassette recorders. To facilitate recording (with some loss of quality) the basic 3.58 MHz color frequency is converted to a lower frequency.

Colored Filter: A glass or plastic material placed either in back or in front of a camera lens to subtract certain colors of light. Used to alter the colors in a scene.

Colorimetry: Characteristics of color reproduction. In TV, the range of colors that a system can reproduce.

Colorization: Adding or modifying the color in a video image.

Colorizer: An electronic circuit that generates color, which is added to or made to modify an image.

Colorizing Control: A knob that can move through the entire range of colors. Used to select colors for electronic effects.

Color-Subcarrier: A subchannel of a broadcast signal designed to add color information to a basic black-and-white video signal.

Comet Tail: A smear or black-trailing image in video cameras used under certain conditions. Associated with subject movement.

Commercial Appropriation: A legal aspect of invasion of privacy relating to the unauthorized use of the name or likeness of a well-known individual for the personal or economic gain of a third party.

Community Antenna Television (CATV): The use of a master antenna to pick up on-air stations for distribution to homes via coaxial or fiber optic cable. Although originally used to solve reception problems in fringe TV areas, now CATV systems include their own free and pay programming.

Compact-8: A version of the 8mm and Hi8 video formats, which uses a smaller cassette.

Compatibility: The ability of the elements in a color television picture to be reproduced on a black-and-white receiver with adequate tonal contrast and subject matter separation.

Compilation Editing: Commonly used editing style in documentaries. Continuity can jump around and not adhere to any logical or time-based sequence. In compilation editing, continuity is usually provided by narration.

Complementary Colors: Colors that are opposite each other on the color wheel.

Complexity Editing: Assembling shots with a primary regard to building story or dramatic effect rather than following a logical or temporal sequence.

Component: Refers to the use of independent, individually controlled audio or video elements in a single television or audio system. A TV system having a separate monitor, tuner and audio system would be an example.

Component Recording: Videotape recording in which the color information is recorded separately from the luminance and synchronization information.

Component Signals: In contrast to a *composite signal,* non-encoded video signals. Typically, refers to separate luminance and chromanance signals.

Component Television: Home television systems that consist of a separate video monitor, tuner, audio amplifier and speakers.

Composite Master: Final product of an editing session, including all program elements and special effects.

Composite Signal: A video signal that contains all of the necessary synchronizing pulses. A video signal in which the luminance and chrominance information have been combined using a standard such as NTSC, PAL or SECAM. The composite video format is also used for consumer video recording systems.

Compositing: The process of combining multiple layers of special digital video effects to achieve complex special effects.

Composition: The controlled ordering of elements in a scene, designed to provide the strongest artistic arrangement and the most effective communication of a central idea. See also *dynamic composition* and *static composition.*

Compression: The reduction of the amplitude of a video or audio signal to keep it within specific limits.

Computer Graphics: The creation of still and animated video through the use of computer-based equipment.

Computer Network: Two or more computers linked together with the ability to interact and exchange data.

Computer Platform: A basic desktop computer. Many editing and special-effects hardware and software products use a computer as the basis of their systems.

Condenser Microphone: A microphone that detects sound by amplifying changes in electrical capacitance between two closely spaced plates.

Confidence Heads: VCR audio and video playback heads that immediately play back signals after they are recorded. In this way signals can be monitored for quality as recordings are being made.

Conflict: A basic psychological ingredient in news and dramatic productions that has the power to capture and hold audience attention.

Consortium: A partnership of a number of TV stations or production facilities that exchange programming or services. They are generally linked by satellites.

Consumer Equipment: Relatively inexpensive audio and video equipment intended for home or non-professional use.

Contact: A person who knows about an event and its location and can assist the production team during a telecast.

Content: In the context of the text discussion in Chapter 12, the goals and visions of a production, including the production's emotional attributes.

Contingency Fund: A percentage added to the cost of a production budget to take care of delays and production problems.

Continuity: The process of monitoring and ensuring consistency in production details from shot to shot. Production details include consistency in prop positions, lighting, clothes and makeup.

Continuity Editing (Continuity Cutting): An editing approach based on either a temporal or logical sequence that centers on maintaining a smooth flow of events.

Contouring: One of the initial steps in the application of makeup, designed to emphasize or de-emphasize certain facial features and dimensions.

Contrast: Ratio of light and dark in a scene.

Contrast Filter: One of seven possible types of optical filters designed to reduce image contrast, generally to bring it into optimum range for video.

Contrast Range (Contrast Ratio): The maximum range of brightness from white to black in a scene.

Control Room: A room associated with a production studio in which a director, technical director, audio engineer and others work to coordinate and control various sources of audio and video during a production.

Control Track: The portion of a videotape signal consisting of timing pulses associated with video fields and frames. Used in editing and maintaining playback synchronization.

Control Track Editing: Method of editing based on an electronic count of control track pulses for cuing and editing functions rather than SMPTE/EBU time code numbers.

Convergence: The adjustment of the three electronic guns in a TV receiver so that the colors will reproduce accurately, without blur or fringing.

Conversion Filter: A lens attachment designed to convert the color temperature of outdoor light to indoor color temperature or vice versa.

Converter (Standards Converter): An electronic device that changes one international broadcast television standard to another.

Convertible Camera: A video camera that can be quickly switched between use in the studio and in the field.

Cookie: A small metal pattern placed in front of or inside a focusing light to project a patterned shadow on a background.

Cool: A television picture that has a slightly blue or green cast.

Cooperatives: Groups of broadcast stations and production facilities that exchange programming, typically news segments.

Copy Protection Device: A system designed to foil attempts to make illegal copies of copyrighted audio or video recordings.

Copy Stand: Device for holding flat artwork

and a camera. Used for photographing artwork under controlled conditions.

Coring Out: The process of removing video noise by converting the analog signal into a digital signal and then back again.

Corner Insert: A square or rectangular key insert into a segment of a background picture. Generally used in news to show graphics behind a newscaster.

Corrective Makeup: Makeup intended to significantly change appearance; generally used to hide certain original facial features.

Cost Per Measured Results: Comparing the costs of a production with the intended results. In commercial television this could consist of comparing increased sales revenue with the costs of doing a commercial.

Cost Per Minute: Production costs divided by total production time.

Cost Per Viewer: Production costs divided by the number of viewers.

Costing-Out: The process of figuring out the costs of a production.

Countdown: Visual cues to talent, usually from 10 seconds, giving the time remaining until the start or the end of a production or segment.

Countdown Leader: Similar to academy leader in film; a visual (and sometimes aural) second-by-second countdown from 10 to 3 seconds. Used to cue the beginning of segments for playback.

Cover Shot: An establishing wide-angle or long shot of a set, used primarily to establish the relationships between subject matter in a scene.

Coverage: In single-camera, film-style production, the videotaping of dialogue and action in a dramatic scene from the perspectives of the essential camera positions.

CPM: Cost per thousand. Dividing the cost of a production by the number of people (in thousands) who see it.

CPU: Central processing unit. The heart of a computer that processes information according to the instructions received from software.

Crab Dolly (Crab): A camera mount with steering controls that can move the camera in any direction.

Crabbing: Moving a camera sideways or in arc on a crab dolly. Also referred to as *trucking*.

Cradle Head: A heavy, cradle-shaped camera pan head consisting of two half-circle elements.

Crane (Camera Crane): A camera mount capable of booming to a high vantage point.

Crash Edit: An assemble edit made by manually switching the VTR into record. The resulting edit may not be frame-locked and may leave a slight glitch or distortion at the edit point.

Crawl: The movement of credits or other graphic material across the screen.

Creative Compromise: Including and excluding elements in a production based primarily on budget concerns. An example would be deciding against a top star in favor of enhanced special effects or an exotic production location.

Credits: An on-screen listing of all key people involved in a production.

Cross Back Lights: Using two back lights a few feet apart in such a way that when viewed from the camera position, the light very slightly wraps around the sides of the subject.

Cross Light: The use of two keys on opposite sides of a subject; often at a 180-degree spacing.

Cross-Cut: To cut back and forth from one scene to another, often to follow action happening at the same time in two different places.

Cross-Fade: The process of bringing down one audio or video source while simultaneously bringing up another.

Crossing the Line: A 180-degree or more shift in camera position, resulting in a reversal of on-screen action or audience perspective. *The line* is also referred to as the *imaginary line* and the *action axis*.

Crosstalk: The inadvertent induction of a second, interfering signal into a primary signal.

CRT: See *cathode ray tube*.

CU: A close-up shot.

Cube Flip (Cube Spin): A special effect in which pictures appear to be glued to the sides of a cube.

Cucalorus (Cookie): (kukaloris; kookie) A pattern used in a focusing spotlight to create a pattern or silhouette on a background.

Cue: A signal to start a production event; also, to find a desired spot on an audio or a videotape.

Cue Cards: Large white cards used by on-camera talent to help them remember dialogue. Black markers are normally used to write material in large letters.

Cue Channel: See *audition channel*.

Cue Track: A videotape audio track that can be used in several ways: to record SMPTE/EBU time code, to record the PL conversation or in-house identification or cues, or for a second audio track.

Cursor: A marker such as a line or rectangle that indicates specific positions on a computer screen.

Cut: The instantaneous changing from one shot to another. The term also refers to the removal of scenes in a script or production.

Cutaway: A shot that is not part of the basic scene but is relevant to it and occurring at the same time. In an interview a cutaway is commonly used to show the interviewer's reaction to what is being said.

Cut-in Shot: The use of a close-up shot of something within a scene in order to show added detail.

Cutting in the Camera: Shooting scenes in the desired sequence so that little or no editing is required. Often used in covering news stories where there will not be enough time for editing.

Cutting on the Beat: Editing shots in time with music. Generally cuts begin at the start of a measure of music or on any beat within a measure.

Cyan: Blue-green. A secondary color in the television additive process; a primary color in the subtractive printing process.

Cyc (Cyclorama): A large, curved, seamless background, generally white or light gray.

Cyclic Redundancy Check Code (CRCC): A mathematically derived number encoded with a digital signal intended as a check on possible data errors. The method of error detection employed in the CD format.

DAT: See *digital audio tape*.

Data Compression: A technique for shrinking or reducing digital data without significantly altering the basic information represented. By applying mathematical algorithms to shrink the space needed for computer data, the data can be stored in a fraction of the original space, or transmitted within a fraction of the amount of time required by non-compressed data.

dB: See *decibel*.

dB Meter: A device that measures sound levels in decibels (dB).

dB/SPL: A unit of sound intensity based on sound-pressure differences in air.

dBm: An electrical unit of audio level used with standard VU meters, which is based on a milliwatt reference level.

DBS: Direct broadcast satellite. Transmission of signals directly from satellites to homes.

DC: Direct current. Electrical current that maintains a steady voltage and electrical polarity.

DCC (Digital Compact Cassette): An audio recording system that records a digitized audio signal on an audio cassette using non-rotating heads.

Decibel: A unit of measurement for the loudness of sounds. Equal to about the smallest difference of loudness normally detectable to the human ear.

Decibel (dB): Unit of sound amplitude or loudness. One decibel is 1/10 of a bell. The designation dBm is used as an electrical measure of sound amplitude when a power of 1 milliwatt is the reference level.

Decoding: The process of recovering the original information in a previously coded signal.

Dedicated Equipment: Electronic equipment designed for a specific purpose, as opposed to software computer-based equipment that represents one of many possible computer applications.

Defamation: A legal term relating to the utterance of slanderous words, especially false and malicious words, that injure a person's reputation.

Defamation *Per Quod:* As opposed to *defamation per se,* statements that are deemed slanderous or libelous only when supplemental (generally, widely known) information is considered along with the statement in question.

Defamation *Per Se:* A legal term relating to the utterance of slanderous words, especially false and malicious words, that injure a person's reputation. As opposed to *defamation per quod,* statements that are deemed slanderous or libelous "on their face," that is, without the need for other information.

Definition: The clarity and sharpness of an image; amount of detail in the reproduction of a television picture.

Defocus Transition: A cross-fade between scenes that includes going out of focus on one scene and coming into focus on another.

Degauss: To completely erase an audio or videotape. Bulk erase.

Delegation Control: Switcher control that can assign different functions to the buses.

Demographics: Audience characteristics such as age, sex, marital status, income etc.

Depth of Field: The range of distance in sharp focus along the lens axis.

Depth Staging: Arrangement of objects on a set so that foreground, middleground and background are each clearly defined on a TV screen.

Desktop Video (DTV): Video effects and postproduction using desktop computers; generally involves low-cost video equipment.

Dew Light: A warning light that protects a VCR by indicating moisture or condensation present inside the unit.

DGA: Directors' Guild of America. A union for directors and stage managers.

Diaphragm: A lens aperture or iris made of overlapping metal leaves that controls the amount of light passing through the lens.

Diascope: A type of internal test pattern built into a zoom lens that can be flipped into position to register and align pickup tubes.

Dichroic Filter: An optical device that passes or reflects only certain wavelengths of light. Normally used in three-CCD color cameras to separate red, blue and green.

Dichroic Mirror: A mirror/filter that reflects only certain wavelengths or colors and allows others to pass. See also *dichroic filter.*

Diffused Light: Soft light. Light that casts an indistinct, soft shadow.

Diffuser: An attachment that fits over the front of a light and softens its quality.

Diffusion Filter: Filter that decreases image sharpness of a lens. Used for smoothing out skin blemishes and for dreamlike effects. Filter consists of polished glass with one side smooth and the other slightly rippled that causes light passing through it to be deflected slightly to decrease image sharpness.

Digital: In contrast to the analog process,

the encoding of electronic information in the form of discrete "on" or "off" pulses.

Digital Audio Tape (DAT, R-DAT): A high-quality audio recording format that uses rotating heads and a tape cartridge containing 3.81 mm metal particle tape. Standard DAT contains a copy protection scheme; R-DAT is a professional format that allows for copying.

Digital Compact Cassette (DCC): An audio recording format that uses a standard compact cassette to record data-compressed audio signals. Unlike the *DAT* system, non-rotating heads are used.

Digital Recording: Method of recording that makes use of a sequence of pulses or on-off signals rather than a continuously variable or analog signal.

Digital Video: Video information translated into a sequence of discrete binary numbers.

Digitize: To convert an audio or video signal from its analog form into a digital form.

Digitizer: An electronic device that converts a video image into a digitized computer graphic.

Dimensional Merger: A composition problem often caused by lighting or tonal contrast problems, where objects at different distances in a scene merge together and cannot be adequately distinguished.

Dimmer: An adjustable electrical circuit that lowers the voltage on a light, thereby reducing its intensity and color temperature.

Directional Microphone: A microphone that is sensitive along a particular (generally narrow) angle of acceptance. Commonly used to attenuate unwanted off-axis sound.

Director: Person in charge of coordinating production elements before and during a production. Typically, the director calls the shots during a production.

Discharge-Type Lamp: Any one of several types of lights that does not rely on a tungsten filament for illumination. Typically, a lamp that creates illumination through the interaction of a high voltage with gas.

Discrepancy Report: A written account of any technical or operational problems or errors that affect broadcast programming.

Disk Drive: A sealed computer storage device that utilizes a magnetic disk; or, the actual mechanism that turns the disk to read and write digital information to the computer disk.

Display Size: The actual screen area of a monitor. Generally, the diagonal distance across the screen.

Dissolve: A cross-fade between two video sources. As one source fades out, the other simultaneously fades in. Often used to signify a change in time or place.

Distortion: An optical aberration commonly associated with an unnatural change in the shape or character of an object.

Distribution Amplifier: An audio or video device that accepts one signal and transmits multiple signals with the same characteristics.

Commonly used to send one signal to multiple destinations.

Dither: A computer-aided process of adding digital data to a computer graphic in order to smooth the appearance of an image.

Dithering: Using a computer-graphic or image-processing program to blur the transition from one color to another in a computer picture.

Diversity Antennas: A radio-frequency (RF) mic system using two or more receiving antennas in an attempt to eliminate or reduce multipath interference.

Docudrama: A dramatic production based on factual events or an actual situation.

Documentary: An informative, nonfictional depiction of occurrences.

Documentary Format: A script format associated with news and documentary work.

Dolby System: A noise-reduction method for audio that, in its most basic form, manipulates the recording and playback frequency responses. There are several Dolby approaches with different levels of sophistication.

Dolly: To move the camera on its mount in a straight line directly toward or away from a subject. A wheel-based camera mount.

Dolly Shot: A shot made with a moving dolly.

D-1, D-2, D-3, D-4 and D-5 Formats: Videotape systems that record signals in terms of digital information, each providing a number of advantages over analog videotape systems.

DOS (Disk Operating System): Initially loaded software program that makes it possible for the computer to accept and interpret commands.

Dot Pitch: The distance between the phosphor dots in a color CRT. Directly related to resolution.

Double: A person who looks like the star and who substitutes for him or her, often during dangerous sequences.

Double Fog Effect Filter: A combination filter that uses soft fog with a heavy, low-contrast filter. Allows for clearer detail than the standard fog filter, while maintaining a dense fog appearance.

Double Headset: Earphones that carry the PL (production line) audio in one ear and program audio in the another.

Double Re-entry: A switcher that permits the output of one mix/effects bus to be re-entered into another mix/effects bus for further video manipulation

Double System: Instead of the sound and picture both being recorded on a single tape (single system), they are recorded on separate audio and video machines; generally used when the number of tracks available on a VCR is inadequate for recording needs.

Double-Recorded: Making two recordings of a production in case one experiences a technical problem.

Downlink: A satellite-to-ground receiver link.

Downstream Keyer: A device that allows titles to be keyed over a line-out signal.

dpi: Dots per inch. The number of image-producing dots to a linear inch. The unit is used to describe the resolution of computer printers.

Drag: Amount of friction in the camera head that restricts panning and tilting movements.

Dramatic Format: A script format associated with film and teleplays.

Dramatic License: Generally refers to embellishing a true story with elements designed to simplify its structure or increase its dramatic impact.

Dress Rehearsal: A camera rehearsal. Final rehearsal with final facilities, sets and wardrobe. Often videotaped.

Drop: Backgrounds of scenery painted on canvas.

Drop Shadow: Shadows, generally electronically produced, that are added around letters.

Drop-Frame Time Code: A system that electronically skips frames at regular intervals to compensate for the timing difference that exists between black-and-white and color signals.

Dropout: A momentary loss of a picture signal during tape playback.

Dropout Compensator: An electronic device that can, on a limited basis, restore momentary losses of video information due to videotape *dropouts*.

Dry Rehearsal: Rehearsal without production facilities, generally done outside the studio, right after the camera *blocking* phase.

Dry Run: A rehearsal of actors without equipment; generally intended to establish blocking.

Dual-Redundancy: The use of two identical condenser microphones on a subject, one intended as a backup in case the primary mic goes out.

Dub: To duplicate an audio tape or videotape; also, to re-record dialogue with lip synchronization after a production is finished.

Dubbing Rights: Legal rights, generally obtained after copyright fees are paid, making it possible to use copyrighted works for production purposes.

Dulling Spray: A wax-based aerosol spray used on shiny surfaces to reduce reflections.

Dutch Angle: A canted shot. A shot in which the subject matter appears tilted (normally running up or down hill) on the screen.

DVE (Digital Video Effects): A device for electronically creating video effects. Often a component of a video switcher.

Dynamic Composition: Elements of composition related to the moving image and to the interrelationship between scenes.

Dynamic Editing: Editing with primary regard to building an effect rather than presenting scenes in a logical, linear fashion.

Dynamic Limiter: An audio circuit that restricts the dynamic range of audio.

Dynamic Microphone: A rugged type of microphone with a diaphragm attached to a moving coil suspended in a magnetic field. It responds to changes in air pressure.

Dynamic Range: The range between the weakest and loudest sounds that a particular piece of equipment can effectively reproduce.

EBR (Electron Beam Recording): A videotape-to-film transfer process using direct stimulation of film emulsion by an electron beam, in which the three primary colors of a color picture are electronically scanned onto a color film (or onto three black-and-white films).

EC Camera: Electronic cinematography camera. A high-quality video camera designed to closely resemble a film camera, both in operation and technical quality. Associated with single-camera video production.

ECU: Extreme close-up; generally a head shot.

ED-Beta: Extended definition Betamax. A high-quality consumer/professional videocassette format developed by Sony.

Edit: The recording of one or more videotaped sources onto a second tape. Also, any point on a videotape where the audio or video content has been modified through editing. See also *editing*.

Edit Controller: The master control panel and associated electronics that control the VTRs etc. during the editing process.

Edit Recorder: The destination VTR that records the source tapes onto the edited master during the editing session.

Edited Master: The final tape created during the editing process.

Editing: The process of arranging in a predetermined sequence various segments from one or more master tapes.

Editing Block: A metal editing device that holds two pieces of audio tape in place for cutting and splicing.

Editing Pace: The number of edits per unit of time.

Editing Workstation: A complete computer-controlled desktop system used to edit audio and/or video productions.

Editor: The term refers both to the individual responsible for editing and to a device by which videotape editing is done.

Editorial Assistant: Typically a videotape editor's assistant.

EDL (Edit Decision List): A handwritten listing or computer printout of time code numbers associated with selected scenes.

Effects Bank: A group of buttons on a video switcher that can be used for fades, wipes or special effects.

Effects Monitor: A video monitor where video effects are set up and checked before use.

EFP: Electronic field production. The use of portable video equipment for taping on location.

EGA: Enhanced graphics adapter. A relatively high-resolution computer color graphics adapter for PCs.

EIA: Electronic Industries Association. An organization that determines audio and video standards.

8mm Video: A consumer video format using videotape that is 8mm wide. Hi8 is a higher quality version that is often used as an *acquisition format*. Compact-8 is a version of the original 8mm videotape format that uses a smaller cassette.

Electret Mic: A microphone that uses a condenser-type sound-sensing element.

Electronic Beam Recording: See *EBR*.

Electronic Cinematography: Videography. Using video cameras to do production, especially single-camera production.

Electronic Cinematography Camera: See *EC camera*.

Electronic Clapper: An electronic slate. A device shown at the beginning of a production or shot providing such information as production title, director, air date etc.

Electronic Graphics: Titles, credits, drawings etc. that are produced electronically.

Electronic Palette: Peripheral device used to input commands into a computer. An *electronic pencil* is commonly used with the palette to draw shapes and select drawing and paint functions.

Electronic Pencil: Pencil-like, hand-to-computer device used to input commands and make drawings. Commonly used with an *electronic palette*.

Electronic Still Store (ESS): An electronic device that can capture a full frame of video and store it in digital form.

Electronic Test Pattern (ETP): An electronically generated pattern used for setting up video systems. Includes, among other things, the primary and secondary colors.

Electronic Viewfinder: A small picture tube (CRT) or liquid crystal display (LCD) built into a video camera that enables the operator to see what the camera is photographing.

Electrostatic Microphone: A type of microphone that uses a sound-sensing element similar in principle to that of a condenser microphone.

Ellipsoidal Spotlight: A spotlight producing a focused, sharply defined beam of light.

ELS: Script designation for "extreme long shot."

Endoscopic Television: Obtaining television images inside a living body, generally by inserting fiber optic probes.

ENG: Electronic news gathering. The use of portable cameras and videotape machines or microwave links to cover on-location television news stories.

ENG Coordinator: The individual under the assignment editor and news producer responsible for integrating the resources of the technical and news personnel in a TV news room.

Enhancer (Image Enhancer): An electronic circuit that sharpens the detail of a video image.

Equalization: A signal-modifying technique that selectively increases or decreases the amplitude of specific frequencies.

Erase: Electronically wiping clean or degaussing a video or audio tape.

Erase Head: A degaussing magnetic field produced by a special head in a video or audio recorder to eliminate previously recorded material on the tape.

Essential Area: See *safe action area; safe title area.*

Establishing Shot: A wide shot meant to orient the audience to an overall locale and the relationship between scene elements.

ETP: See *electronic test pattern.*

Exceptional Quality: An element of newsworthiness that distinguishes a story or plot from the commonplace and captures and holds viewer attention.

Executive Producer: The individual primarily in charge of the financial aspects of a production and who may also make major creative decisions.

Existing Light: The normal, prevailing light at a location.

Expander: An audio device that increases the dynamic range of an audio signal.

EXT: Script designation for exterior. Exterior and interior (INT) designations are used to describe scenes in film-style scripts.

Exteriors: Shots in an outside location.

External Key: As opposed to an internal key, a key that depends on three video sources: background video, a video source to determine the shape of the area to be keyed out of the background video and a video source to be placed in the keyed out area.

External Sync: As opposed to internal sync, video synchronizing pulses from an external source, such as a sync generator. Used to synchronize multiple pieces of equipment.

Extra: An actor who plays a minor role in a production; often just seen in the background.

Extro: A concocted term that, as opposed to *intro,* refers to the final on-camera wrap-up in an EFP segment.

Eye Light: A small light used in close-ups to illuminate the upper facial area.

Eyeline: The direction in which an actor is looking. To maintain continuity during the intercutting of single-camera, film-style scenes, shots of people talking to each other need to have consistent eyelines.

Fade In (Fade Up): To increase audio or video from no signal to maximum signal. Often follows a fade-out to indicate major divisions within a production.

Fade Out: To decrease audio or video from maximum signal to zero. Often indicates the end of a segment.

Fader: A volume control or potentiometer used to control the amplitude of an electrical signal.

Fader Bars: A pair of levers on the switcher that allow for gradual changes video levels. They can be used to produce superimpositions, dissolves, fades, keys or wipes at different speeds.

False Light: Impression created by distorting the truth of a situation through such things as wrongful association, or unduly emphasizing negative attributes.

Fantasy Set: A television setting that is abstract or bears only limited resemblance to a realistic setting.

Fast Lens: A lens that transmits a great amount of light. Can be used in low lighting conditions.

FAX Sheet: Facilities request form. A form listing all technical facilities needed for a production.

FCC: Federal Communications Commission. The primary federal governing body over broadcast television. Sets technical standards for audio and video quality.

Feed: Signal transmission from a specific source. Examples would be a network feed and a remote feed.

Feedback: Sound regeneration caused by a microphone picking up the output from its own speakers. Commonly results in a ringing sound or a high-pitched squeal.

Feeders: Microwave trucks that relay ENG or EFP signals from the field back to the station.

Fiber Optics: Optical fiber. A flexible, hair-like, glass or plastic conduit for light waves. The light waves can be modulated by a television signal and sent great distances without experiencing many of the disadvantages of other point-to-point links.

Field: One-half of a complete television picture or frame. One complete vertical scan of a video image. See *field frequency.*

Field Frequency: The number of video fields per second. NTSC field frequency is 60 per second; PAL frequency is 50 per second.

Figure-8 Response: See *bidirectional.*

File: A categorical collection of information stored on a computer disk.

Fill Light: A soft light used to partially fill in the shadows caused by the key light. Typically, one-half the intensity of the key light.

Fill Pattern: Solid color or design used to fill in or give texture and pattern to elements of a chart or a drawing.

Film Chain: A cluster of film and slide projectors directed into a single TV camera by a multiplexer. Film projector system; camera, cables, monitor, controls and power supply. Used to transfer films and slides to video.

Film-Style Video Production: Single-camera video production. Video shot out of sequence with one camera and then assembled into a complete show in postproduction. Typically, multiple takes are made of each scene.

This contrasts with switch-feed video productions, where multiple cameras are used, and the production is edited on a video switcher as it is shot.

Filter: A plastic or glass material placed in front of or behind a camera lens to alter the light in some way. Primarily used to change color temperature. Also, a device that allows certain parts of an electronic signal to pass while stopping others.

Filter Frame: Holder used on the front of a light or a camera that holds colored gels, filters, diffusers etc.

Filter Wheel: A holder containing multiple filters that can be rotated into place behind the camera lens.

Final Cut: An editor's last version of an edited piece.

First Generation: Either the first print from a film original or a magnetic tape original. (There is occasional disagreement on whether the original or the first copy constitutes the first generation.)

Fish-Eye Lens: An extreme wide-angle lens.

Fishpole: A hand-held microphone suspension pole or device.

Fixed-Focal-Length Lens: A prime lens. A lens of a set focal length.

Flag: An opaque piece of material placed in front of a light used to block a portion of the beam.

Flagging: A videotape problem associated with certain formats. The problem is related to an improper skew adjustment on the playback machine.

Flare: Light reflections from shiny objects.

Flash EPROM: A non-volatile computer memory chip that can retain information after power is shut off.

Flat: A single unit of scenery. See also *softwall flat* and *hardwall flat.*

Flat Lighting: Soft, even lighting that produces minimal shadows and minimizes the depth or dimension in subject matter.

Flat Response: The ability of a microphone or piece of audio gear to reproduce sound equally well over the entire frequency range.

Flip Stand: Device holding camera cards that can be flipped so rapidly that the change is not apparent.

Floor Manager: Person in charge of the studio during production.

Floor Plan: A preproduction drawing, generally to scale, that indicates all set pieces, walls and often lights and camera positions.

Fluid Head: The pan head of choice for EFP cameras because its internal parts move through a heavy liquid, making very smooth pans and tilts possible.

Fluorescent Light Filter: Color correction filters that attempt to give natural color renditions under fluorescent lighting.

Flutter: Undesirable, rapid change in frequency of an audio or video signal due to variations in tape or disc speed.

Flyaway Unit: A portable satellite uplink commonly used in electronic newsgathering.

Flying Erase Head: A moving video erase head, mounted just ahead of the video record head in a video recorder that erases previously recorded video. As opposed to stationary erase heads, they make possible stable insert edits.

FM: Frequency modulation. As opposed to *AM* (amplitude modulation) the form of RF modulation used for television sound transmission. Also used in satellite video transmission and for videotape recording.

Focal Length: The distance from the optical center of the lens to the focal plane when a lens is focused at infinity.

Focal Plane: The point behind and perpendicular to a camera lens where a sharp image will appear. This is the target point of a camera CCD where the image is formed.

Focusing Knob: A control that adjusts the focus of a lens.

Fog Filter: An optical filter that fits over a camera lens and creates the illusion of fog.

Foldback Speaker: PA-type speaker intended to be heard only by talent. Often used in music concerts so performers can hear accompaniment from surrounding instruments.

Follow Focus: Shifting camera focus to accommodate subject movement.

Follow Shot: A moving camera shot that keeps a moving subject within the frame.

Follow Spot: A large, high-powered, stand-mounted spotlight. Typically operated by hand and used to follow action on a stage.

Following Source: The use of lights in a lighting design that are consistent with the apparent sources of light within the room or setting. If a table lamp in a scene is visible and supposedly turned on, subjects near the lamp should be keyed so that the lamp appears to be supplying their illumination.

Font: Particular set of letters and symbols of one size and typeface.

Foot Candle: The measure of light intensity used in non-metric countries. The number of lumens per square foot.

Footprint: The ground reception area covered by a satellite. Technically, the ground area that is able to receive a satellite signal of a predetermined strength.

Form: The basic design, genre and logical construction of a script, such as lecture, panel discussion, drama, variety show, news program, demonstration or animated sequence.

Format: In videotape, the size of the tape, the way it is spooled or housed and the way in which the video and audio information is recorded on the tape. Betacam, M-2, S-VHS and Hi8 are popular tape formats.

Foundation: A makeup base over which additional makeup is applied.

Four-Way Barn Doors: Flaps attached by hinges to the four sides of a spotlight, intended to mask off and shape the beam.

Frame: A complete TV picture of (in NTSC) 525 horizontal lines. In the NTSC system, frames are composed of two scanned fields of 262.5 lines each.

Frame Animation: Animation procedure in which images are drawn frame-by-frame and then recorded one-by-one on frames of film or video.

Frame Grabber: A computer expansion board that has the ability to digitize and store a single video frame.

Frame Rate: The speed at which the video frames are scanned; 30 per second in NTSC video.

Framestore: An electronic device that captures and stores complete video pictures.

Framestore Synchronizer: Device that can hold a complete video frame in electronic memory. Commonly used to synchronize signals from two or more video sources.

Freeze-Frame: A still image captured from action on a videotape or film.

Frequency: Sound wave repetition rate in Hz or cycles per second. In electronics, the number of times a signal changes from positive to negative (or vice versa) per second.

Frequency Interleaving: The process by which color and brightness signals are combined into one NTSC signal.

Frequency Response: The sound range from high to low (in Hz), which a piece of equipment can effectively reproduce.

Fresnel Spotlight: A spotlight with steplike concentric rings, commonly used as a key light. Named after the inventor of its lens.

Friction Head: Camera mounting head that locks its movement through the action of adjustable friction between moving parts. Sometimes counterbalanced by a strong spring.

Front-Screen Projection: As opposed to *rear-screen projection,* an image projected on the camera side of a light-reflecting screen.

f-Stop: Lens aperture. The number attained by dividing the focal length of a lens by its aperture. Indicates the amount of light passing through the lens and, consequently, exposure.

Full Focus Lens: An auto-focus lens that can continually (and often automatically) focus from infinity to the macro (extreme close-up) mode.

Full Value Visual: Television visual that contains a full range of tones from black to white.

Full-Motion Video: Video sequences that consist of enough images (generally, 30 frames per second) to result in smooth motion.

Full-Track: An audiotape recorder, or recording, that uses the full width of the tape for making recordings.

Fully Scripted Show: A script for a production in which all dialogue is fully written out.

F/X: Special audio or video effects.

Gaffer: The chief electrician responsible for lighting.

Gaffer Grip: A clamp used to attach small lighting instruments to scenery, furniture, doors and other set pieces.

Gain: Audio or video amplification. The strength of an audio or video signal.

Gain Control: A volume-controlling device manipulated by either a sliding fader or a rotating knob.

Gamma: The contrast ratio between the input and output of the camera. The contrast gradient.

Gamma Correction: A CCU control that can alter the progression of the black-to-white tonal range. Often used to open up shadow areas in a low-key picture or to hold picture detail in bright video areas.

Gated Mics: Mics commonly used in teleconferencing that are designed to pick up a predominant sound source (generally, a speaker) while minimizing the input (and ambient noise) from all other mics.

GB (Gigabyte): A computer term for one billion units of data. More accurately, 1,073,741,824 bytes.

Gear Head: A camera pan head in which gears are used to achieve smooth, controlled pans and tilts. Primarily used in motion picture and single-camera HDTV work.

Gel (Gelatin): A piece of optically pure-colored, translucent material used to filter the light coming into a camera lens.

Generated Graphics: Graphic material that is generated and/or manipulated by a computer.

Generation: Refers to the number of times a tape is copied. A copy of a copy is a second generation tape; a copy of that copy becomes the third generation etc. See also *first generation.*

Genlock: A device or procedure used to synchronize multiple video sources.

Geometric Distortion: The warping or alteration of the true proportions of an image, often just in specific areas.

Geosynchronous Satellite: A satellite that orbits at the same speed as the earth's rotation and therefore stays in the same place in the sky.

Ghosting: The momentary overlapping or superimposition of video images; generally associated with standards conversion.

Gigabyte: See *GB.*

Gigahertz (GHz): One billion cycles per second.

Giraffe: A medium-sized microphone boom that extends about 15 feet and is mounted on a rolling tripod base.

Glitch: Any brief electrical disturbance in a picture.

Goal: In scriptwriting, the goal relates to what the writer wants the audience to experience, feel or gain.

Gobo: In video a scenic piece through which the camera shoots and that will become a part of the scene's foreground. For example, by shooting through a gobo of a keyhole-shaped piece of black cardboard, the impression is given that the camera is peering through a keyhole.

Graininess: Video noise. An image corrupted by minute, moving particles.

Graphic Equalizer: A series of adjustable frequency filters designed to vary the amplitude of successive parts of the audio spectrum.

Graphics: All two-dimensional visuals prepared for a television camera, such as title cards, charts and graphs.

Gray Card: A medium gray card that reflects 17.5 percent of the light falling on it. Used as a standard for medium or average reflectance.

Gray Scale: A card or test chart containing a range of gray patches from white to black used in setting up gamma or the gray-scale response of cameras.

Gray-Scale Compression: A distortion of successive shades of gray when subject matter is reproduced by video. Typically the brightness values at the darker end of the scale are pushed together so that they merge. This results in most tones, especially skin tones, appearing much darker than they should be.

Grid: A criss-cross arrangement of pipes near the ceiling of a studio, used primarily to hang lights.

Grip: An on-location person who helps carry and set up equipment.

Ground Row: Row of lights at the bottom of a cyc (generally hidden from cameras) that provide even illumination across the front surface of the cyc.

Guardband: Safety area separating two different segments of a broadcast signal.

Gyro Head: A tripod mount containing a gyroscope mechanism designed to minimize camera movement.

Half-Track: An audio tape recorder or recording that uses one-half the width of the tape for recording an audio signal. The tape can then be reversed and the other half of the tape used during a reverse pass.

Hand Props: Any object on a set that is used or handled by the talent. Also called a *property*.

Hand Signals: Production information communicated silently by the hands to on-camera talent by a floor director.

Hard Copy: As opposed to soft copy, a copy of text or data printed out on paper. See *soft copy prompter*.

Hard Copy Prompter: A camera prompting device that incorporates a moving paper script. See also *soft copy prompter*.

Hard Disk: A high-capacity computer storage disk.

Hard Disk Recording: Digitally recording audio or video on a computer-type disk drive system.

Hard Light: A sharp, focused light that casts harsh shadows.

Hard News: As opposed to *soft news*, news stories that center on straight facts and do not emphasize the human-interest angles.

Hard Wired: An electronic piece of equipment that is more or less permanently wired to other equipment.

Hardwall Flats: A set piece used for the background of a set, generally composed of a wooden frame covered with a rigid material, such as plywood. See also *softwall flats*.

Hardware: The physical components of a computer and its associated equipment.

Harmonics: Acoustical or electrical frequencies that are multiples of the basic frequency or musical tone.

Haze Filter: A filter that removes ultraviolet light and diminishes haze in a scene.

HDTV (HD; High-Definition Television): Any one of several systems of television that use more than 1,000 scanning lines and an aspect ratio of about 16×9.

Head: Device that records and plays back video or audio on a magnetic tape.

Head Clog: A loss of video signal resulting from dirt in the microscopic gap of a video head.

Head Drum: A cylinder, set at an angle in a helical videotape machine, around which videotape is wound. The recording *heads* are mounted within the head drum.

Head End: Initial portion of cable television distribution system where signals are collected and initially amplified.

Headroom: The area between the top of an actor's head and the top of the picture frame.

Helical Scan: A video signal recorded at a slight angle along the horizontal dimension of a videotape. In contrast to segmented recording, one complete video field or frame is recorded with each pass of a video head.

Hi8: An 8mm videotape format developed by Sony that is of higher quality than the standard 8mm format. Often used as an *acquisition format*.

High Density: Videotape or computer disks that pack more magnetic particles per square inch and thus allow a greater concentration of data.

High-Definition Television: See *HDTV*.

High-Key Lighting: Lighting characterized by minimal shadows and a low key-to-fill ratio.

Highlighting: A makeup technique designed to emphasize selected facial features, generally by the subtle application and blending of makeup that is slightly lighter in tonal value than surrounding skin tones.

Highlights: The brightest parts of a video image.

High-Z: High impedance. See also *impedance*.

Hiss: Audio noise.

HMI Light: A high-efficiency, discharge-type light source that has the same color temperature as sunlight.

Hook: An attention-getting incident in a pro-

duction designed to capture an audience's attention.

Horizontal Blanking: The period in the scanning of the TV picture when the electron beam is momentarily extinguished as it moves from right to left. During this period the beam can return unseen to scan another line.

Horizontal Resolution: The ability of horizontal scanning lines of a video system to reproduce picture detail. This is based primarily on how quickly the system can appropriately respond to changes in image intensity.

Horizontal Scan Rate: The speed at which the electronic beam scans across the screen of a CRT. Horizontal scanning rates are typically between 15 KHz and 40 KHz.

Hot: A wire carrying an electrical current; an instrument that is turned on; for example, a "hot camera" or "a hot microphone."

Hot Spot: Undesirable concentration of light on a set or subject.

Hue: Color. Refers to specific color only, without the dimensions of brightness or saturation.

Hum: An intrusive steady sound or tone caused by electrical problems. Often a 60- or 120-cycle hum is heard in audio from AC power.

Human Interest: In contrast to *hard news*, stories in which news value is secondary to an appeal to feelings, emotions or sensations.

Hypercardioid: A highly directional mic pickup pattern.

Hz (Hertz): Cycles per second. A unit of frequency measurement for sound and electromagnetic waves named after Heinrich Hertz.

IATSE: International Alliance of Theatrical and Stage Employees. A trade union for various behind-the-scenes workers.

IBEW: International Brotherhood of Electrical Workers. A trade union of electrical workers.

IC (Integrated Circuit): A very small electronic component consisting of scores of transistors, resistors, capacitors and diodes all in one sealed housing.

Icon: Symbolic images in software displays that users can select to carry out desired tasks.

IEC Subcode Format: A time code system that makes it possible to automatically cue and control DATs with split-second accuracy. The system also ensures that tapes recorded on one DAT machine can be played back without problems on any other machine using the time code format. Since the time code format has been designed to be universal, it can be used with any of the world's video standards.

IEEE: Institute of Electrical and Electronics Engineers. An organization responsible for creating a number of technical standards in television.

IFB (Interrupted Feedback System): A small earpiece worn by talent that carries program sound or (when interrupted) instructions from a director.

Image Enhancer: An electronic circuit that sharpens detail in video pictures. Image enhancers commonly improve edge sharpness, reduce color edge fringing, correct color displacement and reduce snow and noise.

Image Intensifier: An electronic attachment to a lens system that amplifies incoming light. Also called a *night viewing device.*

Image Stabilizer: A device that is part of a camera lens or camera mount that reduces or cancels vibration or moderate movement. Often used when a camera is hand-held or mounted in a moving vehicle.

Impedance: A unit of electrical resistance. Generally expressed as high impedance (hi-Z) or low impedance (low-Z). The impedance of various pieces of interconnected video and audio equipment must match, or else various types of distortion and inefficiency will result.

In-Camera Editing: Videotaping shots in the order you want them to appear in the final production. Also called *editing in the camera.*

Incident Light Meter: As opposed to a *reflected light meter,* a photoelectric meter that measures the intensity of light falling on an object.

Independent (Station): A broadcast station that is not affiliated with a network.

Industrial Video Equipment: A quality classification for audio and video equipment that lies between high-end professional (broadcast-quality) equipment and consumer equipment; associated with institutional television.

Input Selector Switch: A multiposition switch found on many audio control boards that connects any one of several sources to a specific audio channel.

Insert Editing: As opposed to *assembly editing,* an editing process that inserts video and audio information over an existing control track.

Insert Mode: A video editing approach that uses a tape containing only a control track onto which segments from one or more other tapes are recorded. Not transferring a control track with each edit (as in the case of assembly editing) results in a more stable picture.

Insert Shot: A close-up shot of something within the basic scene that is used to show features or details.

Instant Replay: Immediately repeating a segment of a televised event for viewers to see again, usually in slow motion.

Institutional Video (Institutional Television): Television production not intended for a mass audience or for general broadcast. Includes most corporate, educational and medical productions.

Instructional Video: A video production primarily designed to communicate specific information, especially within an educational or institutional setting.

INT: A script designation for an interior scene.

Intensity: The brightness of a light source as measured in foot candles or lux.

Interactive Video: A video presentation in which the user's actions, choices and decisions affect the course of the presentation.

Intercom: See *PL.*

Intercutting: Cutting back and forth between scenes to show action occurring at the same time in different places.

Interface: The connection between two devices, such as a computer and a peripheral.

Interlaced: The scanning process that combines the odd and even fields to produce a full video frame.

Internal Focus: A lens design in which focusing takes place within the lens structure, thus eliminating the need to vary lens-to-target distance or rotate the lens barrel (and lens attachments).

Internal Key: As opposed to *external key,* with internal key the cutout portion of a background video source is filled with a signal from the switcher.

Interpolation: The process of replacing missing digital data when the loss goes beyond the system's basic error-correction capability. Computations are performed on the previous and subsequent valid data values to replace the missing information. The last valid data value is normally held and repeated until a new valid data value is available.

Interruptible Foldback (Interruptible Feedback; IFB): A communication system allowing communication with talent while they are on the air. A small earpiece worn by the talent which normally carries program sound, but this can be interrupted by instructions from the director.

Interview Format: Using a basic interview as the basis of a production or program segment.

Intro: Introduction. The beginning or introductory portion of a production or production segment.

Intrusion on Seclusion: Related to *invasion of privacy*; a legal term denoting unlawful entry into a place or state without invitation, right or welcome.

Invasion of Privacy: *Intrusion on seclusion.* Illegally and inappropriately prying into someone's personal business. It may be actual, such as trespassing on private property to secure a news story, or figurative, such as when a telephoto lens or electronic eavesdropping device is used.

I/O Board: Input/output board. An electronic board that can transfer information from a computer to related devices.

ips: Inches per second. Generally refers to tape speed or tape writing speed.

IRE Unit: A unit of amplitude originally standardized by the Institute of Radio Engineers.

Iris: An adjustable diaphragm that controls the amount of light passing through a lens.

Isolated Camera (Isod Camera): A camera that is both routed through the switcher and has its own separate VTR. The recorded signal from an isod camera is typically used for instant replays.

Jack: A female electrical connection; typically a phone-plug receptacle. Also, a brace for scenery.

Jog: The slow, frame-by-frame viewing of a videotape, generally to make edit decisions.

Joystick: A hand-operated control that can be moved in any of four directions (sometimes even vertically) to control various computer operations.

Judder: A motion artifact consisting of dim multiple images; generally associated with standards conversion.

Jump Cut: Generally, an inappropriate edit between two scenes that, for any number of reasons, keeps the segments from flowing together smoothly and unobtrusively.

KB: Kilobyte. A computer term for a unit of data. Although commonly translated as 1,000 bytes, it is actually 1,024 bytes.

Kelvin Scale: Unit of measurement used in TV lighting that indicates the color temperature of a light source.

Key: An electronic effect in which a video source is electronically inserted into background video.

Key Card: A camera card with white lettering on a black background commonly used to add (key in) titles and other written material over a background scene.

Key Clip: A control on a video effects unit used to set the threshold level for color or luminance keying.

Key Light: The brightest frontal light on a scene. A light that establishes the form, dimension and overall appearance of a subject.

Key Source: A video source keyed into background video.

Key Words: The more important words within sentences that, when emphasized, more effectively convey essential meaning.

Keyboard: The primary input device for a computer; contains alphanumeric and other keys that activate specific computer functions.

Keyed-in Time Code: As opposed to *burned-in time code,* SMPTE time code numbers electronically and temporarily keyed over background video.

Keystoning: Optical distortion of a picture, especially apparent in parallel lines, due to shooting subject matter at an angle not perpendicular to lens axis.

Kicker (Kicker Light): A light typically placed between the back light and the fill lights. Sometimes used to simulate the light from a window behind a subject.

Kilobyte: See *KB*.

Kilohertz (kHz): A unit of frequency equal to 1,000 Hz.

Kinescope Recording: Recording a video production by making a motion picture from the screen of a television monitor.

Ku-Band: A bank of frequencies, higher than the C-band, used by some satellite transponders.

Lag: A cometlike trail that follows a moving image, primarily associated with vidicon camera tubes at low light levels.

Lap Dissolve: Fading one video or audio source out while simultaneously fading up on (going to) another source. Midway through a lap dissolve, both signals will be present in equal proportions.

Lapel Microphone: A personal microphone attached to a lapel.

Laser Disk: The reflective optical videodisc system used to record and play back audio and video.

Laser Printer: A fast computer printer capable of producing high-resolution images.

Lavaliere, Lav Mic: A small, personal microphone clipped to clothing or suspended from a cord around the neck.

Layering: Adding video effect sequences over existing video effect footage to create more complex effects.

LCD (Liquid Crystal Display): A technology used in flat panel displays to show alphanumeric data or graphics.

L-Cut: An intentional videotape edit where audio comes before the associated video or the video comes before its corresponding audio. Also called a *split edit*.

Leader Numbers: Visible numbers that appear on countdown leader used to cue up a videotape. Normally, numbers from 10 to 3 (or 2) flash at 1-second intervals. The numbers are generally accompanied by short audio beeps.

Lead-in: The announcer's introduction to an ENG/EFP segment.

Leading Blacks: A term used to describe a technical picture aberration in which the edge preceding a black object appears white.

Leading Lines: In composition the use of either visible or implied lines within a scene to direct the eye to a specific location, generally, to the scene's center of interest.

Leading the Subject: See *looking space*.

Lecture Format: An approach to doing a production or program segment that features an individual communicating information directly to a camera, in somewhat the same manner as a teacher addresses a class.

LED (Light-Emitting Diode): A light-emitting pixel point used in instrument read-outs and some flat television screens.

Lens Aperture: See *f-stop*.

Lens Coating: See *coated lens*.

Lens Extender: An optical lens unit to in-crease the effective focal length of a zoom or fixed-focal-length lens. Some lens extenders are electrically flipped into position within the lens housing; others are manually placed in front of or behind the lens.

Lens Flare: A bright spot in an image caused by a bright light hitting the elements of a lens.

Lens Shade: Lens hood. A round or rectangular black hood that fits over the end of a camera lens to shield the lens from strong sidelight or inclement weather.

Lens Speed: The f-stop that transmits the maximum amount of light for a specific lens. The smallest f-stop number.

Letterbox: Term used for one method of adapting a 16 × 9 aspect ratio to a 4 × 3 ratio, which results in a black or patterned bar at the top and bottom of the 4-to-3 image. Since this technique does not involve altering original images or scenes in any way, it is considered the "most honest" form of conversion.

Level: The strength or amplitude of an audio or video signal.

Libel: A legal term relating to an inaccurate published (or sometimes broadcast) statement that subjects someone to public ridicule or contempt or injures the person's reputation.

Light Level: The intensity of light measured in foot candles or lux.

Light Meter: A device that measures the amount of light that is either reflected from or is falling on a subject. See *reflected* and *incident light meters*.

Light Pen: A hand-held device allowing the user to write or draw on the screen of a cathode ray tube. Highly sensitive light pens are used to read the surface of the screen and to input information.

Lighting Board: A centralized control system for studio lights. Most lighting boards allow for the dimming of lights and include provisions for controlling each AC outlet in a studio *lighting grid*.

Lighting Director: An individual responsible for the planning, design and setup of lights for a production.

Lighting Grid: A criss-cross arrangement of pipes suspended below the studio ceiling and used to hold lights.

Lighting Plot: A detailed drawing, generally to scale, showing the placement of each light in relation to talent positions and scenic elements.

Lighting Ratio: The relationship between the key and fill lights. Typically 2-to-1 for color and 3-to-1 for black-and-white television.

Lighting Tent: A white fabric enclosure that totally covers a subject. Lighting tents are illuminated by two or more soft light sources to produce an extremely flat lighting effect that can be useful in photographing bright, shiny objects.

Limbo Background: A background of any color or brightness that has no discernible detail.

Line Mic: A highly directional, hand-held mike, generally mounted within a reinforced foam rubber enclosure and normally used in video field production just out of camera range.

Line Out Monitor: A video monitor displaying the final video output intended for broadcast, recording or distribution.

Line Transformer: An electrical device generally used to change or match the impedance of audio sources. Line transformers are also used to electrically isolate sources of audio.

Linear Editing: As opposed to *random-access editing*, an editing approach that requires edits to be entered and done in the sequence required for the final edited version. Each segment has to be found, cued and then recorded in sequence, which necessitates the stopping of both tapes as each segment is located and cued.

Linear Fader: As opposed to a *rotary fader*, a volume control that is moved along a straight line.

Linearity: The ability of a video camera or TV set to accurately reproduce a test pattern with geometric accuracy.

Line-Level: In contrast to a mic-level input, a high-level audio input associated with pre-amplified sources of audio.

Lineup: A listing of the basic elements in a production in the order in which they will appear.

Lip Flap: When an individual's lips are seen moving before accompanying audio is heard. The problem is generally associated with film edits.

Lip Sync: Having on-camera performers mouth words to a prerecorded soundtrack to make it appear as if they are actually singing during a production.

Live: Refers to the process of transmitting a program to viewers while it is taking place.

Live Copy: Copy read by an announcer at the time it is aired.

Live-on-Tape: A production that is recorded, but treated as if were being done live. During the production process, there is normally no stopping. The approach is designed to lower production costs.

Location: (also, *on location*) Any out-of-studio setting.

Location Manager: Individual in charge of arrangements and production issues related to a specific production location.

Location Sketch: A rough drawing of a setting for a remote telecast.

Location Survey: Written appraisal of production requirements required for a field production.

Lockup Time: The time required by a tape machine to stabilize after it has been rolled.

Log: An operational document for broadcast operations, generally issued daily, that includes information such as program source or origin, scheduled program time, program title and other program-related information.

Logging a Tape: The listing of time code numbers of video and audio segments prior to editing.

Logical Sequence: An editing approach in which segments are assembled in a natural, time-based progression.

Logo: Identifying symbol, generally associated with a product brand name or trademark.

Long Lens: A telephoto or long-focal-length lens.

Long Shot: A shot from a great distance.

Longitudinal Time Code: In contrast to *VITC*, a method of recording digital SMPTE/EBU time code information along the edge of a videotape, generally on an audio track.

Looking Space: In composition, the blank space left in front of a subject looking off screen. Also referred to as *leading the subject*.

Looping: The process of rerecording dialogue in postproduction to correspond with dialogue that was originally part of a scene. Often sound is looped to improve quality and to eliminate distracting sounds in the original recording.

Loudness: The perceived strength or intensity of a sound.

Loudness Meter: A volume units meter that responds to the loudness of sounds as humanly perceived, as opposed to the milliwatt dB reference used by most VU meters.

Loudness Monitor: See *loudness meter*.

Low Band: Video recording system that uses relatively low FM carrier frequencies. Often used in non-professional videocassette systems.

Low-Contrast Filter: An optical camera filter that lowers contrast of subject matter and mutes colors. Often used to bring the brightness ratio of a scene within video range and allow more detail in dense shadow areas.

Low-Pass Filter: An electrical filter that passes frequencies below a specified frequency and attenuates those above. Required in digital audio to prevent sampling of signals above one-half the sampling frequency.

Low Frequency Roll-Off: An audio circuit associated with microphones and amplifiers that attenuates undesirable low frequencies.

Low-Key Lighting: Lighting characterized by a high key-to-fill ratio which results in predominant shadow areas. Typically used for night scenes in dramatic productions.

Low-Power TV (LPTV): A classification for TV stations designed to serve small communities through the use of transmitters with very limited power.

LS: In scripts, an abbreviation for *long shot*.

Lumen: Measurement of light quantity. Lumens per square foot equal foot candles.

Luminance: The black-and-white aspect of a television signal; also called the *Y signal*. When part of a composite color signal, the luminance signal consists of 0.30 percent red, 0.59 percent green and 0.11 percent blue.

Luminance Channel: The black-and-white circuitry associated with a color video signal. See *luminance*.

Luminance Key: An electronic key effect controlled by the brightness of one video source.

Lux: Unit of light intensity used in metric countries. One foot candle is equal to 10.74 lux.

Macro (Macro Setting): A zoom lens setting that allows for extreme close-ups.

Magenta: A purplish-red secondary TV color.

Make-Good: To rebroadcast a commercial or program segment because of a technical problem that interfered with the original broadcast.

Makeup Person: Individual in charge of the makeup (and sometimes hair) for the talent associated with a particular production.

Malice: Untrue statements, often motivated by ill-will or an attempt to harm another. When used in the legal sense, malice can refer to a published or broadcast statement that results from a careless disregard for the truth.

Master: The original or primary recording.

Master Black Control: An adjustment on a camera base station that controls the blanking, pedestal or black level in one or more video cameras.

Master Control: An audio and video control center that is the final switching point before signals are sent to the television transmitter.

Master Control Switcher: Video switcher with limited video effect capabilities designed to serve the specific needs of a master control area. Most such switchers control video and audio simultaneously.

Master Scene: A wide shot intended to orient an audience to the relative positions of actors and objects in a scene.

Master Shot: A wide, all-inclusive shot of a scene that establishes major elements. Often in single-camera, film-style production, action and dialogue are taped from the master shot perspective before the closer insert shots are done.

Master-Scene Style: An approach to scriptwriting where only the basic scenes are described. Decisions on the various shots within the scenes are not outlined in the script and are left to the discretion of the director.

Match Dissolve: A dissolve between two scenes that have similar content.

Matched Action: A technique in which a single camera is used to photograph a repeated sequence of action. When the various takes are edited together, it appears that the scene was simultaneously photographed from various angles.

Matched Cut: An edit in single-camera, film-style production during which the camera position and angle are switched during action.

The action smoothly continues from one shot to the other.

Matching Transformer: An impedance-changing device used to make different pieces of equipment electronically compatible. Often used to alter the output of high-impedance mics so they can be used with low-impedance equipment inputs.

Matte: Electronic keying process in which one source of video acts as a pattern to define the area for visual material from another source. This combination is then inserted into a background picture.

Matte Box: An adjustable square box, typically constructed with bellows, that goes on the front of a camera and acts as a lens shade and filter and matte holder.

Matte Key: Commonly refers to keying letters or symbols from one video source into background video. In the process, the letters or symbols can be electronically filled in with any desired color.

Matting: A video effect in which a source of video is substituted in a background picture throughout an area corresponding to a specific (matte) pattern. See also *matte*.

MB (Megabyte): Unit of computer data equal to 1,048,576 bytes (but commonly rounded off to 1,000,000 bytes).

MCU: Script designation for medium close-up.

M/E: See *mix/effects bank*.

Medium Shot (MS): Object seen from a medium distance. Normally covers framing between long shot and close-up.

Megabyte: See *MB*.

Menu: In computer terms, an on-screen index of possible choices.

Metal Evaporated Tape: A high-quality audio and videotape that can record higher frequencies with a high *signal-to-noise* ratio.

MHz (Megahertz): Millions of cycles per second.

Mic-Level: As opposed to *line-level*, an unamplified or low-level signal directly from a microphone.

Microphone (Mic): A sound-detecting device that converts sound waves to electrical energy.

Microphone Boom: A device for suspending, directing and moving a mic over a production area.

Microprocessor: A single computer chip that is capable of processing information according to programmed instructions. Microprocessors are used in digital cameras, for example, to set up and maintain a camera's optimal performance.

Microwave: A directional, point-to-point transmission, generally of an audio and video signal using high-frequency RF energy. Typically used to get a TV signal from the field to the studio or from the studio to the transmitter.

Microwave Relay: A point-to-point, line-of-sight transmission method that relies on high-frequency RF energy as a medium.

Often a number of microwave relays are spaced 50 or so miles apart to send signals over great distances.

MIDI (Musical Instrument Digital Interface): A standardization system allowing various pieces of digital audio equipment, including computers, to work together.

Mid-Side (M-S) Micing: A stereo micing technique commonly used in broadcast television. Important, centered sounds are sharper and more stable than those produced by the X-Y method.

Mike: See *microphone (mic)*.

Mini Disk (MD): A very small, CD-type audio recording-playback format.

Minicam: A small, lightweight television camera.

Minus Lens: A supplementary lens that increases the effective focal length of a basic lens to produce telephoto effects.

Mix: To combine two or more sources of audio or video.

Mix-Down: The process by which numerous audio tracks are appropriately combined into the final one or two audio tracks needed for program distribution.

Mixed Sources: Two or more light sources with significantly different color temperatures. Commonly, sunlight and incandescent light.

Mix/Effects Bank: A double row of buttons on a switcher that can be used in the creation of video effects.

Mix/Effects Monitors: Video monitor dedicated to setting up and viewing video effects from one or more *mix/effects banks*.

Mixer: A device that blends two or more audio or video sources.

MLS: Script designation for medium long shot.

Mobile Unit: A mobile television control center used to cover events in the field. Signals are commonly sent back to the studio by microwave or satellite.

Modeling Effect: Effectively using light to create depth and dimension in subject matter.

Modem: Acronym for modulator-demodulator. A device that converts digital information from a computer to analog sound signals that can be transmitted over telephone lines. At the receiving end, the modem converts the sound back into digital information.

Modular Camera: A video camera that can be configured in various ways in terms of the attachment of different viewfinders, recorders etc.

Modulation: The superimposition of audio and video signals on a radio-frequency carrier wave so that the signals may be broadcast.

Moiré Effect: Color reverberations that occur in video when narrow, contrasting stripes of a design interfere with the scanning lines.

Moiré Pattern: A unintended wavy, moving pattern in a picture often caused when an interaction occurs between striped wardrobe patterns and the TV scanning system.

Monitor: A TV set, normally without an RF tuner or audio circuitry, used to check color, composition etc. during a production.

Monochrome: Although it means "one color," it generally denotes a black-and-white television picture.

Monopod: A one-legged camera support.

Montage: An edited sequence in which a juxtaposition of seemingly unrelated shots is designed to create a mood or basic theme.

Montage Editing: Although the term as used in early film work had a different meaning, today *montage editing* refers to a rapid, impressionistic sequence of disconnected scenes linked by a variety of transition devices that are designed to communicate feelings or experiences. A montage does not tell a story by developing an idea in a logical sequence.

Mood Music: Background music intended to evoke a particular feeling.

Morphing: A visual (generally, computer-generated) effect in which a person or object is progressively transformed into another person or object.

MOS (Metal Oxide Semiconductor): A solid-state electronic imaging device used in some video cameras.

Mosaic: Visual effect in which an image is broken down into a moving pattern of squares.

Motion Artifacts: Picture defects that appear only when there is motion in the scene. This often occurs when international broadcast standards are converted.

Moving-Coil Mic: See *dynamic microphone*.

MS: Script designation for *medium shot*.

MTS (Multichannel TV Sound): Commonly designates a broadcast stereo TV system.

Multicamera: Simultaneous use of more than one camera in a production.

Multi-Image Lens: Multifaceted, polished optical-glass lens that produces multiple images of a subject in a single picture.

Multipath Reception: Interference with a primary radio or TV signal resulting from reflections from objects between the transmitter and receiver. Multipath interference results in "ghosts" in TV reception.

Multiplex: To combine and transmit more than one signal on a single electronic signal or carrier wave.

Multiplexer: A mirror device that is part of a film island that selectively directs the light from multiple projectors into a single television camera.

Multitasking: A computer system that can do more than one task at the same time.

Music Production Libraries: Collections of music covering a wide variety of moods and needs, which have been especially designed for productions.

NAB: National Association of Broadcasters. The primary trade organization representing the interests of commercial broadcasting.

NABET: National Association of Broadcast Employees and Technicians. Union for technical personnel.

Nanosecond: One-billionth of a second.

NCTA: National Cable Television Association.

Needle Drop: The single use of a transcribed musical piece, generally for a fee.

Neutral Density Filter (ND Filter): A filter that reduces the light coming into a camera lens without altering its color.

Netural (Indeterminate) Set: A production set that does not suggest a specific setting or locale.

Neutral Shot: A head-on shot of a subject commonly used between two successive shots taken from opposite sides of the action axis so that screen direction can be reversed.

News Cooperative: A broadcast station association in which news stories are exchanged between members.

News Director: The person responsible for the content, production and presentation of a newscast. Exact responsibilities depend on the news organization.

News Producer: Although responsibilities vary widely, producers are generally under the news director and in charge of specific newscasts. Producers often write basic transitional news copy.

Newsworthiness: Elements that make a news story interesting and noteworthy from the perspective of an audience.

Night Viewing Device: An optical light amplifier that makes possible the taping of scenes under virtually no light.

No Fax: A rehearsal without cameras, sets or lights.

Noddies: Cutaway shots of an interviewer's visual responses (nodding, smiling etc.). Noddies are useful as transition devices during editing.

Noise: Any background interference in video or audio signals. Typically manifested as hiss or hum on sound tracks, and as snow or graininess in video.

Non-Composite Video Signal: Video signal containing picture and blanking information but no sync signals.

Non-Directional Microphone: A microphone with a circular polar pattern of response, equally sensitive to sound from all directions.

Non-Diversity Antenna: Use of a single receiving antenna for an *RF mic* system. See also *diversity antenna*.

Non-Drop Frame: SMPTE time code that runs in continuously ascending numbers. These times will not perfectly match actual elapsed time when the NTSC color system is used. See also *drop-frame time code*.

Non-Segmented: A video recording process in which a complete (as opposed to a partial) video frame is recorded or played back with each pass of a video head.

Non-Volatile Memory: Computer memory that is not lost when electrical power is shut off.

Normal Lens: A camera lens that gives a normal image perspective and has a focal length approximately equal to the diagonal of the focal plane.

NTSC: National Television Standards Committee. A professional group that sets television standards. The TV color system defined by the National Television Standards Committee is used in the United States.

NTSC Standard: Normally refers to the 525-line, 60-field system of broadcast television that combines chroma with luminance information into one composite signal.

O-and-O: A broadcast station owned and operated by a network.

Objective Camera: A sustained camera angle that approximates the viewpoint of a human observer.

Off-Line Editing: Editing or making editing decisions from a copy (work print) of an original videotape. Once off-line editing decisions are made, they are used in *on-line editing* to create the final edited master from the original videotape footage.

Omega Wrap: The tape path used in some helical videotape machines that resembles the Greek letter omega (Ω).

Omnidirectional Mic: A microphone with a sensitivity pattern in which sounds are picked up (more or less) equally from all directions.

On-Air Director: The technical director. Primarily responsible for video switching during a production.

On-Line Editing: Using the original videotapes to make the final edited master.

On-Lining: Editing process that produces the final edited master.

Open Architecture: A computer design that allows for the easy addition of circuit boards produced by a variety of manufacturers.

Operating System: Software that manages a computer's basic capabilities, including command interpretation. A common example is the *DOS* system.

Optical Disk: A recording medium for audio and/or video where a laser beam is used to record and play back digitally coded information.

Optical Fiber (OF): A glass strand designed to conduct light waves modulated with audio or video information. (See also *fiber optic*.)

Opticals: Film special effects associated with optical printing.

Option: Money paid to a writer by a producer for exclusive rights to a script. A specific time is specified during which the producer tries to put together funding to put the project into production.

OS Shot: A shot taken over the shoulder of one person, focusing on the face of a second person.

OSV: A script designation for an off-screen voice.

Outside Vendors: Outside production agencies hired to do production work. Typically an in-house staff is used to initiate, guide and possibly supplement the work.

Out-Takes: Shots deleted or not used in the final edit.

Overexposure: Excessive amounts of light from the lens transmitted to the camera's target, resulting in loss of video quality. The problem is solved by using a smaller iris opening.

Overhead Expenses: Basic on-going costs related to maintaining a production facility, not directly related to a specific production.

Overscanning: A loss of some information around the outer edges of a picture, typically, as a result of the broadcast and reception process.

Overtone: Acoustical or electrical frequencies that are multiples of the fundamental frequency or sound. Overtones add richness and uniqueness to sound.

PA: See *production assistant*.

PA System: Public address (loudspeaker) system. Often used as part of a studio talkback system.

Package (News Package): A completed news segment containing all needed audio and video components, ready for insertion (rolling into) a news production.

Packing the Tape: Completely fast-forwarding a videotape to the end and then rewinding it. It is recommended that this be done to equalize tension, dislodge loose tape oxide and reduce recording problems before videotapes are used for the first time.

Paint Pots: Controls that adjust video color.

Paint Program: A computer program designed to create and modify graphics.

PAL (Phase Alternate Line): The TV color standard used in most of western Europe and other parts of the world, including Australia, India, China, Argentina, Brazil and most of Africa.

Palette: The total number of colors a computer graphic system is capable of creating.

Pan (Panning): Moving the camera left or right on the pan head.

Pan Handle: The handle attached to the pan head of a camera that enables the cameraperson to pan or tilt the camera.

Pan Head: Device connecting the camera to the camera mount that allows the camera head to be tilted vertically and to be panned horizontally.

Pan Pot: An attenuator-based device that can "place" a sound to varying degrees in a left or right stereo channel by raising or lowering the volume of the sound.

Pan Stick: A grease-based foundation makeup commonly used to cover a beard or skin blemishes.

Panaglide: A brand-name for a body camera mount that uses a system of counterbalanced springs to keep a camera reasonably steady, even when the camera operator is walking or running.

Pan-and-Scan: A type of aspect ratio conversion where the smaller area of a new display is electronically moved left and right across the original source's wider area in order to follow action occurring at the sides of the original picture.

Pancake: A type of makeup base. Pancake makeup is usually water-based and applied with a sponge.

Panning: Moving the camera left or right on the pan head.

Pantograph: Expandable device for hanging lighting instruments and TV monitors from a studio lighting grid.

Paper-and-Pencil Editing: Logging time codes by hand on an editing log as opposed to entering the decisions directly in a videotape editing system.

Parabolic Microphone: A highly directional microphone that uses a reflector in the shape of a parabola to focus sound into a microphone.

Parallel Action: Action taking place at the same time but in different places edited together in a single dramatic production. See *parallel cutting*.

Parallel Cutting: The alternate intercutting of two stories so that each is regularly updated and both reach a conclusion at about the same time. The stories are generally related in some way.

Parallel Port: Typically, a computer interface (connection) that sends and receives information eight bits at a time.

Parallel Stories: See *parallel cutting*.

Parity: A simple form of data error detection based on adding an extra bit to each digital word. This extra bit is derived by a counting of the zeros or ones in a word. Data losses during transmission can thereby be detected.

Passive Matrix Display: A flat CCD color display in which pixel points respond to a color TV signal by either passing or blocking light from a background source of illumination. Color is created by the interaction of red, blue and green polarizing filters.

Patch: Using cables to connect video and audio equipment through a central panel.

Patch Bay: See *patch panel*.

Patch Cord: The cord on a patch panel used to complete a connection between various audio or video sources and desired pieces of equipment. See *patch panel*.

Patch Panel (Patch Bay): Traditionally, a master controlling device in which patch cords were used to route various audio and video sources to appropriate pieces of production equipment. Today, patch panels rely on solid-state or computer-based switching.

Path: The trail along which a computer-graphics object travels.

Pattern Projector: An ellipsoidal spotlight

that includes a cucalorus insert. Used to create a wide variety of designs on a background.

PC: Personal computer. Normally refers to a computer using the IBM operating standard.

Peak Program Meter (PPM): A meter that monitors audio levels and, unlike a normal VU meter, is able to accurately respond to rapid transient peaks (changes) in volume.

Ped Down: To lower the height of a camera through the action of the camera pedestal.

Ped Up: To use the camera pedestal to raise the camera or move it vertically.

Pedestal: An adjustable camera dolly or support with wheels. Pedding the camera up or down refers to raising or lowing the camera on the pedestal. Also, the black level of a television picture as shown on a waveform monitor.

Pels: Picture elements. The smallest dots that can be transmitted for any given bandwidth and scanning system.

Perambulator Boom: Large mic boom extending 30 or so feet, normally mounted on a dolly, that permits rapid and quiet relocation of a mic anywhere on a set.

Performance Continuity: See *continuity*.

Performer: On-camera talent. A person who appears on camera in non-dramatic productions.

Performing Rights License: General permission, normally by ASCAP (American Society of Composers, Authors and Publishers) and BMI (Broadcast Music Incorporated), to play copyrighted music. Such licenses only cover general music-centered programming and not commercials, public service announcements and productions.

Periaktos: A triangular piece of scenery.

Period Piece: A dramatic production that takes place during a specific historic time period.

Peripherals: Accessories and auxiliary computer attachments that expand a computer's capabilities.

Persistence of Vision: Tendency of human vision to retain images for a fraction of a second. Discrete images presented at a rate of about 16 or more per second—even when change takes place between them—blend together, creating the illusion of motion in TV and film.

Personal Mic: A small, individual microphone, generally attached to clothing with a clip.

Perspective: Visual phenomena in which parallel lines appear to converge as camera-to-subject distance increases.

Phase: Timing relationship between two signals.

Phase Cancellation: Interference resulting in reduced audio levels, caused by a sound source being picked by two microphones.

Phase Distortion: Changes in desired picture color caused by shifts in chroma phase.

Phi Phenomenon: A physiological effect that, along with persistence of vision, creates the illusion of motion when consecutive images are presented in a rapid sequence.

Phosphor: Material at the front of a CRT that glows when struck by the electron beam.

Phosphor Aging: Reduction in the amount of light emitted by CRT phosphors due to extended use.

Photoemission: The process of converting light—generally, as focused on a camera target—into electrical energy.

Photoflood Lamp: A lamp that resembles a normal light bulb except that it produces a much higher light output. Photoflood lamps normally last only about six hours.

Pickup Pattern: Area of sound sensitivity surrounding a microphone.

Pickup Shots: Scenes that are shot after the main taping and that will later be edited into the production.

Pie Chart: A method of presenting data where categories resemble pieces of a whole pie.

Pilot Signal: A signal from a satellite transponder used by ground stations to align uplink dishes.

Pinning: Narrowing down and concentrating a light beam from an adjustable spotlight.

Pirate: To illegally copy or broadcast a copyrighted production without permission.

Pitch: The highness or lowness (frequency) of a sound.

Pixel: Acronym for picture element. The smallest part of a picture element that a computer can address or recognize.

Pixillation: A technique consisting of jerky, speeded-up animation resulting in an exaggerated "silent movie" effect. To achieve this effect, video frames are omitted at regular intervals throughout the sequence.

PL (Private Line; Phone Line; Production Line): Wired or wireless headset intercommunication link between production personnel.

Playback Head: The device on an audio or videotape machine responsible for detecting prerecorded material.

Plot: The basic story line of a dramatic production.

Plumbicon: A trade name for a high-quality television camera tube that uses a lead oxide target.

Polar Pattern: The range of sensitivity surrounding a microphone as plotted in a two- or three-dimensional drawing.

Polarity: The positive or negative characteristics of an image or electrical signal.

Polarity Reversal: In video, the reversal of the gray-scale tones (white becomes black etc.) or colors (colors turn into their complements). In audio, a reversal of wires resulting in a positive charge becoming negative, and the negative becoming positive.

Polarizing Filter: A filter (often adjustable) that reduces or eliminates reflections from glass, water and shiny surfaces. Also used to dramatically intensify contrast between the sky and clouds.

Pole Cat: A pole with spring-loaded, telescoping sections placed between the floor and grid pipes and used to attach scenery and set pieces.

Pool-Hall Lighting: Lighting from a single source, usually hanging in the middle of the set and visible in the scene.

Pop Filter: A screen placed over a microphone that reduces the effect of speech plosives and wind.

Ports: Openings in a microphone case designed to achieve a specific pickup pattern and frequency response. Also, connections on a computer used for plugging in accessories.

Positioner: A video effects control that can move an inserted key source to any position in background video.

Possible Future Impact: A measure of *newsworthiness* relating to the possible consequences to an audience of events outlined in a story.

Post: Short for *postproduction*.

Postproduction: Any production work done after all the main taping has been completed. The term typically refers to *editing*.

Postproduction Switcher: A video switcher that is capable of interfacing with two or more videotape machines and is designed to meet the specific needs of editing.

Postrecording: Any audio work done after the main taping has been completed.

Pot: A potentiometer. A control that uses a variable resistance to alter the intensity of audio and video signals.

POV: Point of view. A shot from an angle that approximates what a designated actor is seeing at a particular moment.

Power Zoom: A lens with a servo motor that makes possible electrically controlled zooms.

Practical: A prop that will actually be used in a scene, as opposed to those that are meant to be seen only. For example, a light that can be switched on or off by an actor.

Pre-Amp: Preamplifier. The initial electronic device used to increase the strength of signals from microphones and other audio equipment.

Pre-Roll: The time needed between the start of a videotape and the point at which it stabilizes.

Preproduction (Preproduction Planning): The planning stage of a production.

Preproduction Planning: All planning and preparations for a production that take place before it is videotaped or broadcast.

Presence: The subjective feeling of spacial "closeness" a listener has to a performer, typically as achieved through a specific balance of frequencies within a reproduced audio signal.

Preset Monitor (PST): Preview monitor. A video display allowing sources to be previewed and adjusted before use.

Pressure Zone Microphone (PZM): Microphone mounted on a reflecting surface. Sound waves build up a pressure zone within the mic housing before being transferred to the microphone. Often used for group discussions around a table.

Preview Bus: A row of buttons on a switcher, generally connected to a preview monitor, used for setting up and checking video sources before use.

Preview Monitor: A video monitor that can be used to check any camera or video effect before use.

Prime Lens: A fixed-focal-length lens.

Principal Photography: Scenes that include the major actors.

Print-Through: The undesirable transfer of an audio or video signal from one layer of tape to another on a tape reel.

Prism Block: See *beam splitter*.

Prism Lens: A special-effects device that attaches to the front of the camera lens and breaks up the primary image into multiple images.

Privacy: An individual's—especially a private citizen's—legal right to be left alone and not badgered by newspeople. Privacy includes intrusion on seclusion, the public disclosure of private facts, false light and commercial appropriation.

Private Television: Institutional television. Non-commercial television that includes corporate, educational, medical and religious television production.

Privilege; Privileged: A legal term relating to a degree of freedom that certain types of communication have from libel or slander actions. Certain political and legislative communication can be broadcast without being actionable under slander or libel.

Proc Amp: Processing amplifier. Electronic device designed to correct levels of a video signal, and to replace or reshape sync pulses with new pulses.

Producer: The creator and organizer of television shows, usually in charge of financial matters.

Production Assistant: An assistant to a producer or director; can be assigned responsibilities for a wide variety of production details, including script changes, personnel issues, talent coordination, logistical arrangements etc.

Production Breakdown: The division of the script into individual scenes and shots so that an efficient shooting schedule can be planned.

Production Line: See *PL*.

Production Manager: The individual under the producer and director who supervises and coordinates all of the business and technical aspects of production.

Production Outline: A preproduction outline of the basic elements or steps involved in doing a specific production.

Production Schedule: A daily agenda showing time periods of various activities during a production day.

Production Switcher: As opposed to an editing switcher or a *master control switcher*, a switcher designed to work in conjunction with productions originating from a control or remote van.

Professional Video Equipment: A term that covers industrial and broadcast-quality equipment.

Program: Specific computer software. A sequence of instructions given to the computer to perform specific functions or tasks.

Program Audio: Final audio mix intended for recording, broadcast or distribution.

Program Bus: The master bus on a video switcher that determines the output signal of the switcher.

Program Proposal: A treatment. An outline of the basic elements of a proposed production. Often used to interest investors or talent in the production.

Progressive Scanning: Sequential scanning; non-interlaced video scanning. A television scanning system in which each scanning line follows its predecessor in a progressive fashion, rather than skipping intermediate lines to be filled in by the next field. In a progressive scanning system, the field rate and the frame rate are identical, and there are no interlace artifacts.

Projection Television: An optical and electronic system for creating a large-screen video display.

Prominence: A measure of *newsworthiness* relating to how important or well-known the people, places or things in the story are to an audience.

Promo: Short for *promotion*. A brief (15, 30 or 60 second) piece promoting a TV program.

Prompter: Teleprompter. An electrical device for displaying a script that can be read by talent during a production.

Prop (Property): Something that is handled or used within a set by talent during a production.

Prosumer Video Equipment: A combination term denoting equipment that lies between professional and consumer-quality video equipment.

Protection: A backup copy of a recording made in case the primary recording has problems.

Proximity: An aspect of *newsworthiness* related to how close geographically a news event is to the viewing audience.

Proximity Effect: The exaggeration of low-frequency response associated with most microphones when they are used at very close distances. Some microphones have built-in adjustments that can compensate for proximity effect.

PSA: Public service announcement. A non-commercial announcement broadcast by a television station.

Pseudo 3-D System: A computer-based vector graphics system used to do drawings that, rather than appearing flat, seem to have three dimensions.

Public Access Programming: Cable channels or CATV programs designed to serve the interests of the community.

Public Domain (PD): A work is in the public domain when it can be used without charge because it is not copyrighted or because the copyright has expired.

Public Property: Property, generally owned by a government, that does not have the legal access limitations inherent in private property. Property that can be freely used by news reporters and photographers.

Pulse Code Modification: A method of sampling an analog signal. The process uses a reduction in the number of required pulses, resulting in lower bandwidth requirements.

Pulse Count System: A system of editing in which the machine counts the control track pulses on a videotape to establish edit points and pre-roll times. Accuracy problems result with very slow or very fast shuttle speeds.

Pure Metal Tape: A recording tape capable of a high signal-to-noise ratio, high-frequency response and excellent record-playback efficiency.

Push-Off Wipe: An electronic video effect in which one image replaces another by appearing to push it off the screen.

Pylon: Triangular set piece resembling a pillar.

Pyrotechnics: Special effects involving explosions.

Quad (Quadruplex): The original system of tape recording in which four rotating video heads record and play back the image. The tracks on the tape are nearly vertical as opposed to those in longitudinal recording.

Quad Machine: The first widely used system of video recording. Four video heads were used with 2-inch videotape. Each frame was broken into four segments.

Quad Mic: A four-element microphone designed to detect quadrants of sound around a full 360-degrees. See *quadraphonic sound*.

Quadraphonic Sound: A system of sound reproduction that goes beyond stereo and attempts to record and play back a 360-degree sound perspective. See *quad mic*.

Quality: A dimension of light relating to its hardness or softness. See *coherence*.

Quality Control Form: See *discrepancy report*.

Quantization: Related to the process of converting an analog signal to a digital signal. The accuracy resolution is dependent on the total number of bits in the final digital word.

Quantization Error: The difference between the actual value of the analog signal when it is sampled and the resulting digital word value.

Quarter-Inch Tape: A standard width of audio tape used in some reel-to-reel audio recorders and audio cart machines.

Quarter-Track: An audio tape recording system that divides the tape into two sets of stereo tracks. Two tracks are recorded as the tape moves in one direction, and two tracks are recorded as the tape moves in the opposite direction.

Quartz Lamp: Tungsten-halogen lamp. An incandescent lamp with a number of internal improvements over standard lamps, including a consistent color temperature and uniform light output over its life.

Rack Focus: Shifting camera focus from one part of a scene to another, thereby forcing a shift in audience attention.

Radio Frequency (RF): Electromagnetic radiation within a certain frequency range. Radio and television transmitters both utilize RF energy to broadcast their signals.

Rails: Tracks for camera mounts laid on the ground (resembling small railroad tracks), which allow for smooth follow shots for cameras.

Rainbow Filter: Special-effect optical filter that creates multicolor streaks of light around spectral highlights and lights.

RAM: Random-access memory. A computer's basic working memory, which holds information only as long as the computer is turned on.

Ramping: Related to the tendency of zoom lenses to have reduced light transmission capabilities as the lens is zoomed in. Good zoom lenses compensate for this effect and automatically open up the iris as the lens is zoomed in and close it down as the lens is zoomed out.

Random Interlace: Scanning associated with industrial (non-broadcast) sync. Video scanning method in which the horizontal and vertical scan controls run independently of each other and have a somewhat random relationship.

Random-Access Editing: The ability of an editing playback system to find and cue successive, non-sequential segments in an editing session before they are needed. This makes it possible for a sequence of edits to be previewed in real time.

Range Extender: An optical attachment to a lens that increases focal length.

Raster: The illuminated part of a CRT (TV) display, normally in a 4 × 3 or 16 × 9 ratio.

Rating: Percentage of television households with their sets tuned to a specific station compared to the total number of homes in the area with television sets.

Reaction Shot: A cut to performer's face that registers a response. Generally a close-up of someone reacting to the central dialogue or action.

Read-Throughs: The somewhat informal sessions attended by the director and actors in which scripts are initially reviewed and re-

hearsed to decide on dramatic and production emphasis.

Realistic Set: A production setting that appears (from the camera's viewpoint) to be authentic.

Rear-Screen Projection (RP): Screen used for video effects onto which images are projected from the rear. When actors are photographed from the front, it appears as if they are part of the projected scene.

Receiver: A radio or TV set. An electronic device for detecting RF transmissions and demodulating them so they can be seen and/or heard.

Record Head: The electromagnetic device that places an audio or video signal onto a recording medium for later playback.

Record VTR: The videotape recorder that produces the final edited master by recording the edits from one or more source machines.

Reel-to-Reel: In contrast to a cartridge or cassette tape format, a tape format that depends on two separate reels—a supply reel and a take-up reel.

Re-establishing shot: A wide shot intended to re-orient an audience to the basic elements of a scene and their relative positions.

Reference Black: The darkest portion of the video picture, generally with a reflectance value of 3 percent.

Reference White: The whitest portion of the video picture, generally with a reflectance value of 60 percent or above.

Reflected Light Meter: A photoelectric device that measures the amount of light reflected from a subject. In determining exposure, reflected light meters assume 17.5 percent reflectance.

Reflector Board: A silver or bright white surface used to reflect light onto a subject. Generally used outside to soften and fill in the light from the sun.

Registration: Adjusting the chroma channels in a tube-type TV camera so that the video from the three primary colors perfectly overlaps (registers).

Rehearsal Hall: Any area in which a *dry rehearsal* takes place.

Relational Editing: In relational editing, scenes that by themselves seem not to be related take on an interrelated significance when spliced together.

Relay Lens: An internal optical device used in some cameras that transports (relays) the image from the lens over an extended path before it reaches the camera's target.

Release Print (Release Tape): The final film or videotape intended for distribution or broadcast.

Remote: Any multiple-camera telecast from outside the studio.

Remote Survey: An evaluation of a field location by key production and engineering personnel so production needs can be ascertained.

Remote Truck: A vehicle containing basic field-production gear.

Replica Set: A production setting that is a copy of and is designed to look exactly like a well-known site.

Representational-Supportive Set: A production setting, such as a news or weather set, designed solely to support the function of the production.

Resolution: The ability of the camera system to distinguish and reproduce fine detail.

Resolution Chart: A test pattern used to set up and check a camera that shows camera sharpness and the condition of the camera system.

Resolving Power: The ability of a lens to optically reproduce fine detail.

Reveal: To dolly or zoom back a camera to show additional material.

Reverb: Reverberation. Subtle echo effect accompanying a sound.

Reverberation Unit: A mechanical or an electronic device that creates controlled sound reverberation or echo. Used for special effects and in postproduction sweetening to balance location presence between different sources of audio.

Reverse Video: Polarity reversal. Negative image. Changing from dark characters on a light background to light characters on a dark background, for example.

Reverse-Angle Shot: Used in dialogue scenes where a shot of someone speaking is followed by a shot of a person who is listening. Normally taken from over the shoulder at an angle of about 140 degrees.

RF (Radio Frequency): A specific portion of the electromagnetic spectrum used by carrier waves in broadcasting.

RF Carrier Wave: Radio frequency energy that carries a video and/or audio signal in broadcasting.

RF Interference: An unwanted radio frequency signal that interferes with an audio or video signal.

RF Mics: Wireless mic; radio frequency mic. A combination microphone and miniature broadcast transmitter that eliminates the need for mic cables.

RF Modulator: An electronic circuit that converts the audio and video into a single radio frequency TV signal. When included as part of a videotape machine, the resulting signal can be viewed on a standard TV set, generally on either channel 3 or 4.

RGB: Red, green and blue. The primary colors of light used to create a color TV image.

RGB Encoder: Device that converts composite video into RGB video.

RGB Monitor: A type of color monitor with separate inputs for red, green and blue. Normally associated with high-resolution display systems.

RGB Video: A video (generally computer) viewing system that uses discrete red, green and blue signals in separate wires.

Ribbon Mic: A type of microphone that

makes use of a metal ribbon suspended in a magnetic field. When sound waves strike the ribbon, the resulting vibratory movement of the ribbon creates a minute voltage.

Ride Focus: See *follow focus*.

Ride Gain: To manually keep the audio or video levels within acceptable limits.

Rim Lighting: Placing a lamp behind a subject, often with little or no front light, to give a glowing edge or outline of light around the subject.

Ringing: A common filter artifact in video that appears as ghostlike images with sharp edges.

Riser: A small platform.

Robotic Camera: Any one of several types of remotely controlled, automated camera positioning systems. Most allow for camera pans, tilts, dollies and trucks.

Roll: A lack of vertical synchronization that causes a complete TV picture to appear to rotate upward or downward.

Roll-Off: Preset attenuation in electronic equipment of a predetermined range of lower frequencies. Used by microphone manufacturers to reduce the proximity effect.

Room Tone: The ambient sound present in a room recorded during original taping and used during editing to add needed intervals of "silence" between edits. It is important in maintaining the audio atmosphere existing at a location.

Rotary Fader: As opposed to a *linear fader*, a volume control regulated by rotation.

Rough Cut: The initial edit, intended to provide a general idea of a production. A kind of rough draft of the final edit.

Roundy-Round: See *reverse-angle shot*.

Routing Switcher: A device used to select and direct various sources to specific pieces of audio or video equipment.

Royalty Fees: Copyright fees paid to artists for the use of their work.

Rule of Thirds: A composition guideline that suggests putting the center of interest near one of four points. These areas are at the cross-points of two vertical and two horizontal lines that divide the frame into equal segments.

Runaway Production: A production done outside of California or outside the United States, generally with the intent of saving money.

Runout Signal: A few seconds of black at the end of a videotape recording intended to keep the screen in black and the sync stable while other programming is switched up.

Safe Action Area: Also called *essential area*. The inner 90 percent of the video frame. Since the outer 10 percent of a broadcast picture is typically cut off by overscanning, this area is considered safe for most subject matter. See also *safe title area*.

Safe Area: See *safe action area* and *safe title area*.

Safe Title Area: The inner 80 percent of the video raster or frame. Since the outer 20 percent of a broadcast picture is cut off by some home receivers, this is considered safe for essential subject matter such as titles and text. See also *safe action area*.

Safety Chain: A metal chain (sometimes a cable) attached to both a light and a lighting grid, designed to keep a light from falling if its clamp comes loose.

SAG (Screen Actors Guild): Trade union for motion picture and television actors.

Sample: Digitized version of a unit of sound as processed by a *sampler*.

Sampler: Device that converts analog sound into digital information, which thereafter can be fully manipulated by a computer or MIDI device.

Sampling: Digital representation of an analog sound or video signal made at precise intervals of time. Also, digitally recording sounds or short musical segments from live or prerecorded sources. Once a sound is sampled, it can be endlessly modified. Sampling is used in MIDI-based sound creation systems.

Sampling Rate: The measure of how often the values of an analog signal are translated into digital equivalents.

Satellite: An orbiting space station designed to receive and retransmit audio and video signals from a wide area (*footprint*) of the earth.

Satellite News Vehicle (SNV): A field production used to uplink ENG signals to a satellite. Often contain VTRs and basic editing facilities.

Satellite Newsgathering: See *SNG*.

Saticon: A type of camera pickup tube. An improved variation of the vidicon tube.

Saturated Color: A pure color, one that does not have significant amounts of white or black.

Saturation: The purity of a color; its freedom from black or white.

Scale: The minimum fees prescribed by unions for television talent.

Scan Rate: The speed at which an electron beam traces the TV raster. Computer displays operate on different scan rates than standard NTSC video.

Scanner: A device that translates hard copy images into digital data that can be stored, processed and retrieved by a computer.

Scanning: Process of moving an electron beam horizontally and vertically to reproduce television pictures. Also, the process of moving a video head across a videotape to record or play back.

Scanning Area: Full picture area scanned by a camera. This area is reduced somewhat during subsequent stages of signal processing and transmission.

Scene: A script-designated locale in single-camera production that typically constitutes a basic setting for a series of shots.

Scenery: Backgrounds and related set pieces within a setting.

Scenic Designer: An individual who carefully studies the script of a production and then works with the producer and possibly the director in devising appropriate sets.

Scheduling: Breaking down scenes and shots into a convenient and cost-efficient sequence to create a production timetable.

Scoop: A floodlight, often used as a fill light, that has a deep, diffuse and generally elliptical reflector.

Scouting (Scouting Locations): Searching for a suitable location for doing one or more on-location scenes in a production.

Scramble: To encode an electronic signal so that it cannot be received by normal audio and video equipment. Commonly used for cable television and satellite systems to prevent subscribers from receiving specific channels without paying a subscription fee.

Scratch Track: An audio track containing production cues or information. Used only as a guideline or reference during production or editing.

Screen Direction: General direction of movement within a scene or a visual frame. To avoid viewer confusion, screen direction must remain consistent from shot to shot.

Screenplay: A film-style script for a production.

Scrim: A spun-glass material placed over the front of a light to reduce intensity.

Script: The written blueprint for a production.

Search: An *editor* mode used to locate a specific video frame. In interactive video systems, the process of requesting a specific frame from any point in a disk or tape and having the system access it.

Search Mode: An editing system control that switches a VCR into a shuttle mode so that tape can move forward or backward at varying speeds and needed segments can be located and cued.

SECAM: *System electronique couleur avec memoire*. A broadcast standard for broadcast used in France and the Soviet Union.

Second Unit: A video or film production team responsible for doing supplementary scenes.

SEG: See *special-effects generator*.

Segment Producer: A producer who takes charge of a specific production segment, generally a segment of a newscast.

Segment Rundown: A listing of the basic elements in a production in the order in which they will appear.

Segmented Video: A videotape format in which each complete video frame is recorded through the action of two or more video heads.

Segue: To smoothly go directly from one audio element to another.

Selective Focus: Using limited depth of field to make only one plane of focus in a scene sharp, thereby forcing an audience to concentrate on that area.

Semidramatic Format: A production containing dramatic scenes with actors.

Semiscripted Show: In contrast to a *fully scripted show*, which contains all the elements and written dialogue of a show, a semiscripted show contains only the beginning, the end and a basic outline of the show.

Sequencer: Computer software for controlling MIDI sound devices. Somewhat like word processors, sophisticated sequencers make possible unlimited control over digitally recorded sounds, including copying, deleting, moving sections around and the elaborate layering of sounds.

Sequential Scanning: Progressive scanning. Scanning lines are transmitted or reproduced in a straight numerical sequence, rather than in interlaced, odd- or even-numbered fields.

Servo Zoom (Servo-Controlled Zoom): A lens that uses a motor-driven mechanism to alter focal length.

Servo-Controlled: An electronically controlled mechanical device, generally within a tape machine, that uses electronic feedback to maintain a desired and accurately controlled speed.

Set Designer: An individual who handles the initial phases of creating a production setting.

Set Props: Objects on a set that are handled or used by talent.

Sets: Scenery and properties supporting the suggested locale, idea and mood of a production.

Setup: In single-camera, film-style production, a single camera position from which one or more segments in a scene are done.

SFX: Special audio or video effects.

Shader: The video engineer responsible for maintaining the luminance and color quality of a camera.

Shading: To adjust the chroma and video levels on a video camera; generally, an ongoing process that takes place throughout the broadcast or taping of a production.

Shadow Mask: A perforated metal plate within a color TV picture tube that controls which colored dots or stripes the electron beams will activate. The shadow mask keeps the specific electron beams from hitting the phosphors of the wrong color.

Share: Percentage of television sets tuned to a specific station compared to the total sets turned on at that time.

Sharpness: Apparent image resolution or clarity.

SHF: Super high frequency. The frequencies ranging from 3 GHz to 30 GHz. These include communications satellite signals and most microwave transmissions.

Shield Law: A law that exists in various forms and degrees in many states that keeps a news reporter from having to identify the source of confidential information.

Shift Register: An electronic memory bank associated with CCDs that holds a charge before being read out by the system's scanning process.

Shock Mount: A rubber or spring-based mic holder that reduces or eliminates the transfer of sound or vibration to the mic.

Shock Value: An element in news value based on the amount of amazement, surprise, horror or scandal represented by a story.

Shoot and Protect: A term that relates to keeping the left and right sides of the HDTV 16 × 9 aspect ratio free of extraneous subject matter, even if it is reproduced in a 4 × 3 ratio. Action should be confined to the 4-by-3 area (the shoot range), but the 16-by-9 area (the protect range) must be free of microphone booms, lights and other distracting elements.

Shooting Ratio: The amount of tape recorded relative to the amount of tape actually used.

Shot: Individual production setup. A video segment that will later be combined with other shots in a meaningful sequence.

Shot Box: A control that can electronically present various zoom speeds and focal lengths for a zoom lens. Preset positions are activated by push buttons.

Shot-by-Shot Style: As opposed to the *master-scene style*, which outlines only general scenes, the shot-by-shot style lists each individual shot.

Shotgun Mic: A highly directional microphone capable of picking up sound over a great distance.

Shoulder Brace (Shoulder Mount; Shoulder Pod): A support for a video camera that rests on both the shoulder and the body.

Showscan: A film process using 70mm film (65mm in the camera) shot and projected at 60 frames per second (rather than 24). The process incorporates an expanded audio range and results in much greater realism than traditional motion picture methods.

Shuttle Speed: How quickly a tape recorder can move a tape forward and backward.

Sibilance: A splattering, hissing vocal sound commonly caused by the combination of "s" sounds and poor audio equipment.

Signal-to-Noise Ratio (S/N): The degree to which a desired signal stands out from background noise or interference. The higher the signal-to-noise ratio, the better the quality of the resulting sound or picture.

Simultaneous Contrast: The effect of a surrounding tone or color on a specific color or tonal value. Certain color combinations or brightness values, when placed in proximity, interact and affect each other.

Single System: As opposed to *double system,* the process of recording both sound and video on the same videotape.

Single-Frame Recorder: A VCR capable of recording one video frame at a time.

Skew Control: A playback control on a videotape machine that adjusts videotape tension and the length of the video tracks read from the videotape. Improper skew adjustment results in various picture aberrations.

Slander: Uttering false statements deemed harmful to another person's character or reputation.

Slant Track: A *helical scan* videotape recorder.

Slate: A small blackboard-type visual photographed at the beginning of a scene that identifies the scene in terms of basic production information such as the date, scene, take, director etc.

Slide Fader: See *linear fader.*

Slip-Cuing: Method of cuing record that involves moving the record forward and backward until the precise starting point of a selection is found. Allows for the instantaneous start of a selection as needed.

Slo-Mo: A video record-playback machine capable of playing back in slow motion.

Slung Mic: A microphone that is suspended above performers by wire, cord or rope.

Smear: A trailing image associated with motion caused by any one of several video problems. Normally associated with vidicon, tube-type cameras when used under low light levels.

SMPTE: Society of Motion Picture and Television Engineers. A professional engineering society responsible for establishing technical standards in film and television. The SMPTE is the largest such society in the world.

SMPTE/EBU Time Code: A digital electronic signal recorded on a video or audio tape that provides a precise time-based numbering system together with other information. Also called *address track.* The name designates a standard agreed upon by the Society of Motion Picture and Television Engineers and the European Broadcast Union.

Snap Zoom: A very rapid zoom from a wide angle into a close-up of some person or object, intended to achieve a dramatic effect.

SNG: Satellite newsgathering. Electronic newsgathering that relies on a satellite uplink to get the story from the field.

Snoot: Metal cone used to restrict the light beam from a lighting instrument.

Snow: A rapidly moving grainy effect in video caused by little or no picture information.

SOF: Sound-on-film. Film that includes a soundtrack.

Soft Copy Prompter: A camera prompting device that uses a video display, as opposed to a *hard copy prompter* that uses paper.

Soft News: As opposed to *hard news,* stories that emphasize human-interest events and appeals.

Soft Wipe: A video wipe in which the demarcation line between the two sources blends into a soft line.

Soft-Contrast Filter: A filter that reduces

the contrast ratio of a scene, typically used to bring it within the desired 30-1 video ratio.

Softlight: A floodlight producing an extremely soft and virtually shadowless light.

Softwall Flats: Set pieces consisting of wooden frames covered with canvas or burlap.

Software: Programs or coded instructions that, when loaded into a computer, make it perform certain tasks.

Solarization: Visual effects produced by a partial reversal of colors or tonal values. Sometimes caused by extreme overexposure.

SOT: Sound-on-tape. Videotape that includes a sound track.

Sound Bite: Videotape segment where the corresponding audio remains intact and in lip-sync with the video.

Sound Effects: Studio-created sounds to give the illusion of real-life sounds.

Source Machine(s): In videotape editing, the machine(s) that contain the original footage that will be edited onto the edited master.

Special Effects: Video effects. A wide range of electronic video transitions and methods of combining video sources including wipes, keys, mattes and inserts.

Special-Effects Generator (SEG): A video-mixing device that allows switching between several cameras and a variety of video effects, such as dissolves, fades, inserts and wipes.

Spectral Highlights: Bright reflections from shiny subject matter that often cause spikes on a waveform monitor and video brightness range problems.

Spectrum Analyzer: A receiver capable of receiving, monitoring and analyzing specific RF frequencies. Often used in *SNG* work.

Split Edit: See *L-cut*.

Split Screen: TV screen electronically divided to show two or more pictures at once.

Split-Field Lens; Split Focus Lens: A "bi-focal-type" lens that fits over the front of the standard camera lens and makes it possible to divide the scene and bring near and far objects into focus at the same time.

Spot Meter: A reflected light meter with an extremely narrow angle of acceptance (often about 5 degrees) designed for accurate light readings at a distance.

Spotlight: Lighting instrument that produces a focused, relatively undiffused light.

Spotlight Effect: Video effect resulting in a circular section of the screen appearing brighter in order to highlight a particular element.

Stacked Bar Chart: A graphic consisting of overlapping bars designed to show and compare data values.

Stagehand: An assistant who can be assigned a wide variety of studio responsibilities including setting up and moving sets, props and equipment.

Staging: The re-enactment of an event for the purposes of video production. In doing news, staging refers to the sometimes questionable re-enactment of a happening for the

purposes of a news story. Also, a temporary structure used for a production setting.

Standards Converter: A device for converting signals from one standard to another.

Stand-in: An individual who resembles the main talent and can substitute for them during specific phases of production. Often used during lighting setups.

Stand-up (Standupper): An on-location shot of a reporter talking to the camera, often used to introduce or conclude a news piece.

Star Filter: An optical filter with finely etched criss-crossing lines on the surface that creates fingers of light around bright lights and spectral reflections.

Static Composition: Elements and guidelines of composition related to still images. See also *dynamic composition*.

Status Indicators: The collection of various lights, patterns and alphanumeric characters visible in and around a video camera viewfinder that show the operating condition of the camera, recorder and battery.

Steadicam: A brand name for a body camera mount that uses a system of counterbalanced springs to keep a camera reasonably steady, even when the camera operator is walking or running.

Stereo Mic: A microphone containing two sound-sensitive elements designed and arranged in such a way as to reproduce a stereo sound perspective.

Stereo Separation: The degree to which left and right stereo channel information is perceived as being distinct and separate.

Stereo Synthesizer: An electronic circuit that modifies a monophonic audio signal to simulate stereo.

Sticks: A slang term for a camera tripod.

Still Frame: A graphic of any kind presented as a single, static video image.

Still Video Camera: A camera that allows still video frames to be stored on small computer-type magnetic disks or removable solid-state devices.

Still-Frame Storage Unit: A digital device that stores individual video frames, which can be instantly recalled by entering an address number. Eliminates the need for slides and camera cards.

Stock Footage: Scenes from a film or tape library that show common, generally exterior scenes, which can be used for a fee in a production. This eliminates the time and expense involved in reshooting or recreating the footage.

Storyboard: A series of rough drawings of the basic shots or scenes in a planned production. They normally include a brief written description of the associated action and audio.

Streaking: Smearing effect around objects in a picture caused by aberrations in the video system.

Strike: To take down and remove scenery after a production.

Striped Filter: Microscopic vertical stripes

on the surface of a color CCD imaging device designed to break up the picture into two basic color components. Serves the same basic function as dichroic mirrors in three-CCD or three-tube cameras.

Studio Floor Plan: A scale drawing of a studio area showing where scenery and props (and sometimes lights and cameras) are to be placed.

Subcarrier: An extra information carrier added to the main RF carrier wave.

Subjective Shot: A camera shot that appears to take the viewpoint of a person.

Submaster: A volume control that enables an operator to group a number of different audio or lighting sources together and then to control them with one fader.

Subtractive Colors: Typically, magenta, cyan and yellow. Any three colors, which when mixed together, filter each other out and produce black. Basically the opposite of the *additive color process*.

Subtractive Primaries: Magenta, cyan and yellow. Used in color printing, paints and pigments. When mixed, they act as filters for a white light source, subtracting specific colors and leaving a dominant color.

Success d'Estime: A production that is well received by critics but that does not achieve popular or financial success.

Successive Contrast: The tendency of certain complementary colors or tones to exaggerate each other when viewed in temporal proximity. For example, the green color of grass will be exaggerated if a scene with large areas of intense red, magenta or blue precedes it.

Sungun: A small, battery-powered light mounted on a film or video camera. Sometimes called a headlight.

Super: Superimposition. A double-exposure effect. The simultaneous showing of two pictures on a video screen.

Supercardioid: A moderately directional microphone response pattern.

Superconductors: A general classification of experimental conductors that exhibit zero or near-zero resistance to the passage of an electrical current.

Superimposition: A type of "double exposure" video effect in which one video image is laid over another so that both appear simultaneously.

Supplementary Lenses: An optical attachment used with a video camera lens that alters its optical characteristics. Three general categories are used: those that enable a camera lens to focus on objects at very close distances, those that increase the effective focal length of the lens (creating a telephoto effect) and those that decrease effective focal length (providing a wide-angle effect).

Surround-Sound: A system of sound recording and reproduction that goes beyond stereo in its dimensional perspective and approximates quadraphonic sound.

Sustaining Program: Program not supported by advertising. Commonly, public service programming.

S-VGA: Super video graphics array. A high-resolution video display for computers.

S-VHS: Super VHS. A videotape format superior to standard VHS with a potential horizontal resolution of more than 400 lines. Allows component recording and playback without cross-luminance or cross-color artifacts.

Sweep Reversal: The reversal of electronic video scanning that results in the left-to-right and/or top-to-bottom reversal of a television picture.

Sweetening: The postproduction addition of sound effects, laughter, music etc. to a production sound track. Various problems in audio are also corrected during sweetening.

Switchback: A camera shot that returns to the central action after a cutaway.

Switcher: The main production video control device, capable of handling and manipulating numerous sources of video and selecting which video source is recorded or goes on the air.

Symbolic Set: A non-realistic set intended to suggest an environment or setting, often somewhat abstractly.

Sync: Synchronization. The basic synchronizing pulse in video. The crucial timing signal that keeps various pieces of video equipment electronically coordinated.

Sync Buzz: An undesirable noise in TV audio often related to the transmission of electronic graphics that exceed NTSC broadcast capabilities.

Sync Generator: An electronic device that generates the variety of timing pulses needed to keep the video equipment synchronized.

Sync Roll: The momentary or continuous vertical rolling of a television picture due to loss of sync.

Synchronization License: One of the documents involved in obtaining clearance to use a copyrighted work that grants a producer permission to use the music for a specific period.

Synthesized Music: Music created entirely by electronic means without the use of traditional musical instruments.

Synthesized Stereo: An approach to creating a simulated stereo effect from one or more monophonic audio signals.

Synthesizer: An electronic device with associated software, used to create sound effects.

Take: A single shot. In single-camera production, a specific shot often requires several takes before it meets the approval of the director.

Talent: Individuals who perform in front of a camera.

Talent Release: A form signed by a person appearing in a videotape that grants legal permission to a production agency to broadcast the segment under specified terms.

Talking Head: Slang for the typical on-camera interview shot.

Tally Light: The red light on a video camera that indicates the camera is on the air or that videotape is rolling.

Tape Format: Any of several tape widths and recording methods, such as Betacam, S-VHS and Hi8, used in video recording systems.

Tapeless Recording: Audio and/or video recorded on a non-tape medium such as a hard disk.

Tapeless Workstation: An audio or video editing console or *workstation* that typically uses computer disks as a recording medium.

Target: The light-sensitive front surface of a television camera imaging device. It coincides with the focal plane of the lens.

Target Audience: The intended audience for a production.

TBC: Time-base corrector. Electronic device that corrects time inconsistencies in a camera or videotape recorder's signal, stabilizing the scanning and timing pulses. Typically used to stabilize video from small field cameras and recorders and to make it meet broadcast-quality technical specifications.

TD (Technical Director): The individual who operates the control room switcher and is in charge of various technical aspects of a production.

Tearing: A video scanning aberration that makes the edges of an object appear rough and jagged.

Tease: A short, initial, often provocative segment of a production intended to grab and hold attention.

Technical Continuity Problem: Any one of several types of unintentional changes in video or audio quality. Examples are unintended changes in color balance or changes in audio levels during the course of consecutive shots.

Telecine: An area of a production facility with equipment for converting film and slides to video.

Teleconferencing: See *videoconferencing*.

Telephoto Lens: A lens that seemingly brings subject matter closer to the camera. A prime lens with a focal length of more than twice the camera's normal focal length.

Teleplay: A script for a video production.

Teleprompter: Camera prompter. A device used by on-air talent that rolls an image of a script across a screen near the camera lens. Originally a brand name for a prompter system.

Television Production: The process of creating television programming.

Tempo Mapping: Using a computer screen representation of a musical segment, complete with discernible music measures, to create electronic music and effects for a production.

Temporal Resolution: The smallest elements of time that can be perceived in a system. The higher the temporal resolution, the clearer the system will reproduce moving objects.

Termination: The resistance or load that marks the end of coaxial video conductors; usually 75 ohms. A lack of termination generally causes video problems.

Test Pattern: Any number of standardized electronic patterns or camera charts intended to evaluate specific video qualities such as linearity and resolution.

Test Tone: A zero-decibel tone used as a reference standard.

Thematic Editing: See *montage editing*.

3-D Animation: Building a 3-D computer model of an object on a video screen and thereafter being able to rotate the object in several directions.

Threefold Set: A free-standing, three-section set, hinged in two places.

Three-Shot: A video picture containing three individuals.

Throw Focus: Rack focus. Shifting the lens focus from one subject to another within a scene. Also called pull focus.

TIFF: Tagged-image file format. A data format standard associated with one type of computer graphics.

Tighten Up: To zoom in or dolly in on a subject.

Tilt: A camera move from the pan head involving moving the lens up and down along the camera's vertical Y-axis.

Titling: The process of creating the opening and closing credits of a production. Sometimes refers to the process of creating subtitles for dialogue.

Timbre: Sound characteristics, including overtones, that differentiate musical instruments.

Time Code: SMPTE/EBU time code. A series of eight numbers identifying the hours, minutes, seconds and frames related to a specific video frame on a tape.

Time Code Generator: A device that supplies an electronic SMPTE/EBU time code signal to recording equipment.

Time Compressor: Electronic signal processing system allowing a recorded videotape to be replayed somewhat faster or slower than normal without noticeable effects.

Time-Base: The timing component of a video signal, particularly the horizontal and vertical sync pulses.

Time-Base Corrector: See *TBC*.

Time-Lapse Photography: Significantly slowing down the frame rate of motion photography so that events that may take minutes, hours or even days, can be shown and observed within seconds.

Timeliness: A measure of *newsworthiness* relating to how recent or new the developments in a story are.

Time-Motion Study: Similar to *time-lapse photography*, except that the condensation of time is designed to allow researchers to analyze (generally human) actions over a period of time in an effort to minimize wasted or inefficient movement.

Timing: How long a total production is, including time allotted to the individual scenes and program components.

Titillation Component: A measure of *newsworthiness* relating to the sexual or sensual components of a story.

Toe: In television the bottom portion of a gray-scale gamma curve representing the reference black and the darker portions of the gray scale.

Tonal Compression: Commonly, a darkening of skin tones associated with either underexposure, or exceeding the optimum contrast ratio of a video system. The inability of a video system to differentiate between different gray-scale reflectance values.

Tonal Merger: An undesirable visual blending of different objects in such a way that they cannot be clearly distinguished.

Tongue: To move a camera boom to the left or right.

Touch-Screen System: Computer function selection approach where you can use a finger to touch options on a computer screen to initiate actions.

Trace Capability: The ability of some editing systems to retain and display the original time code references on footage after the codes have been changed during later stages of editing. This capacity can be important in going back to original footage and locating needed segments.

Track: The path of a reordered signal on a videotape or disc.

Tracking: An adjustment to the playback heads of a videotape machine to make them match the phase of recording heads. Sometimes the adjustment is necessary because the tape was recorded on another machine. Tracking problems cause video breakup and aberrations at the top or bottom of the picture.

Tracking Shot: A dolly shot that follows a moving subject or moves with respect to a stationary subject.

Trade Libel: A false or grossly misleading statement that damages a business or product.

Trades: Publications intended to serve the special interests of specific segments of the television and film community.

Transmission Standard: The broadcast standard used for transmitting signals to the home.

Transmitter: In television, an electronic device that modulates the audio and video signals onto a carrier wave for broadcast.

Transponder: A combination transmitter and receiver. Commonly used in satellite transmission and reception.

Traveling Shot: A moving camera shot.

Treatment: A summary of a film or video script that includes a description of the char-

acters and the story plot. Often samples of action or dialogue are included.

Treble: Sounds representing the higher audio frequencies, generally from about 4,000 Hz up.

Triad: Three-color phosphor dots or stripes on the faceplate of a tri-color CRT.

Triangular Lighting: Formula lighting. The commonly used triangular arrangement of key, back and fill lights for lighting a subject.

Triax: A coax-type video cable with three conductors.

Trim Control: A control on an editor that makes it possible to add or delete a specified number of frames to an edit point.

Triple Re-entry: A video switcher system in which the results of one mix-effects bank can be directed through another, and then the results of that can, in turn, be directed through a third mix-effects bank, thus combining three layers of video effects.

Tripod: Three-legged camera mount. Sometimes wheels are attached to facilitate camera movement.

Tripod Head: See *pan head*.

Truck: A left or right movement of the camera along with its mount.

Truth: A legal defense against libel or slander. If the truth of a statement can be proven, it cannot be considered slanderous or libelous.

t-Stop: As opposed to relying on the simple mathematical ratio used for f-stops, an iris setting that designates the actual amount of light going through a lens. T-stops are more accurate than f-stops, which do not take into consideration light losses within the lens.

Tungsten-Halogen Light: Quartz lights. The most-used type of studio and on-location light. They get their name from the tungsten element that is encased within a quartz globe or envelope filled with halogen gas.

Turnkey: A system or installation that is complete and ready to run without need of further additions or modifications.

TV Black: The blackest part of a TV picture; generally 3 percent reflectance.

TV Receiver: TV set. Video display device that has the capability of tuning in video channels, demodulating them and reproducing audio and video.

TV White: The whitest part of a TV picture; generally 60 percent or more reflectance.

Tweak: To accurately align electronic equipment.

Twofold Set: A free-standing, two-section set, hinged at the midpoint.

Two-Shot: A picture showing two individuals.

Two-Way Barn Doors: Flaps attached by hinges to two sides of a spotlight, intended to mask off and shape the beam.

Type-B Videotape Machine: An approach to 1-inch videotape recording used in Europe. It uses multiple rotating heads and records each complete video picture in segments.

Type-C Videotape Machine: An approach

to 1-inch videotape recording used in NTSC countries. A complete television picture is recorded with each helical scan of the tape heads.

UHF: Ultra high frequency. Television Channels 14 to 83.

Ultradirectional: A mic with a highly directional response pattern.

Ultraviolet Filter (UV Filter): Transparent filter that absorbs UV wavelengths. Used to help penetrate haze and give clearer video of distant views. Also used over a lens simply to protect the surface of the lens.

U-matic: Trade name for the 3/4-inch tape format invented by Sony.

Umbrella Reflector: A white or silver umbrella with a bright light placed near the center used for creating soft light.

Unbalanced Line: Audio sources associated with non-professional equipment that rely on two-conductor cables. Unbalanced lines tend to be susceptible to hum and electronic interference. See also *balanced line*.

Underexposure: An inadequate amount of light from the lens being transmitted to the camera's target, resulting in a dark picture; specifically, a loss of shadow detail and a compressed gray scale.

Underscan: Video display scanning technique in which the entire video signal, including black borders, is displayed on the CRT.

Unicam: Camcorder. A combination all-in-one camera and recorder.

Unidirectional Mic: A microphone with a cardioid pattern of sensitivity that is primarily responsive to sound coming from one specific direction.

Unipod: A camera support consisting of a single, adjustable leg. Also called a monopod.

Up-Cut: Switching to a videotape late, resulting in momentary loss of video or audio at the start.

Uplink: A ground-to-satellite transmitter link.

User Bits: Additional digital information that can be recorded within the SMPTE/EBU time code. A limited number of user bit letters or numbers can be entered to register reel number, date of scene, take etc.

Variable-Focal-Length Lens: See *zoom lens*.

VCR: Videocassette recorder.

Vector Graphics System: A computer-based drawing system in which the appearance of three dimensions is created by being able to rotate or move the subject matter. The moving perspectives (vectors) are automatically calculated and created by the software involved.

Vectorscope: A CRT instrument that displays the phase and saturation of the primary and secondary video colors. Use to align cameras and equipment.

Velocity Mic: See *ribbon mic*.

Vertical Blanking Interval: A period in which the electron beam in display is blanked out while it travels from the bottom of the screen to the top.

Vertical Fader: See *linear fader*.

Vertical Interval: Vertical blanking. Period when the electron beam is extinguished between fields and frames.

Vertical Resolution: The amount of video detail that can be perceived in the vertical direction.

Vertical Sync: Pulses that define the end of one television field and the start of the next at a rate of 59.94 Hz for NTSC color and 60 Hz for black-and-white and some HDTV standards.

VGA: Video graphic array. A high-resolution computer video display standard.

VHF: Very high frequency. Commonly, television Channels 2 through 13.

VHS: Video home system. A consumer-oriented videotape format using 1/2-inch tape housed in a cassette.

Video Cassette: A plastic videotape housing containing both a supply and takeup reel.

Video Digital Effects (VDE): Electronic special effects that make it possible to alter video in a variety of ways, such as compressing, flipping and reversing polarity.

Video 8 (8mm Video): Videocassette format that uses 8mm tape in a cassette.

Video Engineer: An individual who operates the video controls of a CCU to attain the best video quality.

Video Field Production: Non-studio video production.

Video Gain Switch: A selector switch on a camera or CCU that increases gain or amplitude of a video signal—generally at the expense of some video quality. Used to compensate for the lack of light.

Video Head: The small signal-to-tape transfer device responsible for recording the video signal in a VTR. Video heads are mounted on a head wheel that rotates at a high rate of speed in relation to the videotape.

Video Leader: Countdown leader. A visual and audio countdown at the beginning of a videotape. Generally starts 10 seconds before the beginning of the show and counts down to 2 seconds.

Video Level: The strength or amplitude of a video signal.

Video Monitor: A high-quality television display device, generally without a tuner or audio circuitry.

Video Noise: See *noise*.

Video Switcher: See *switcher*.

Videoconferencing (Teleconferencing): The use of a two-way video system to communicate with groups at distant locations, partly so that they can participate in meetings at the same time.

Videodisc: Video storage medium that uses thin circular plates and translucent plastic, on which video, audio and various control signals are encoded along a spiral track. Optical disk systems use a laser beam to read the surface of the disk.

Videospace: All visual elements in a production that interact to create the experience of reality.

Vidicon: A once-popular type of camera tube known for its reliability and long life.

Viewfinder: A viewing screen built into a video camera enabling the operator to monitor the images being recorded. Most electronic viewfinders also allow the playback and review of recorded material.

Vision: How the tools of the trade are used to translate the goal of a production into an audio and visual experience for the viewer. The vision component of production should be unique in that it springs from the dictates of personal perspective and viewpoints.

Visual Effects: Special effects. A wide range of electronic video transitions and methods of combining video sources. Included are wipes, keys, mattes and inserts.

VITC: Vertical interval time code. A system of recording NTSC/EBU time code in the vertical interval of the video signal.

VL Bayonet Mount: A standardized lens mount system used on many video camcorders.

VLS: A script designation for a very long shot.

Voice Recognition Module: A computer system that can recognize certain voice commands and respond appropriately.

Voice-Over (VO): Speech heard over related video, without the person talking being seen on the screen.

Volatile Memory: Digitized information stored in a computer or microprocessor that remains only as long as there is electrical power.

VTR: Videotape recorder.

VU: Volume unit. Unit of measure for audio level or signal strength.

VU Meter: An instrument (meter) that measures the loudness of sound in terms of decibels and percentage of modulation.

Walk-Through: A rough rehearsal in which no cameras are used. Generally the actors walk from place to place and check their actions without speaking any dialogue.

Wardrobe Person: Individual responsible for selecting and supplying clothes and accessories for talent.

Warm: A color picture that contains too much red or yellow.

Wattage: A unit of electrical power equal to the voltage times the amperage.

Waveform Monitor: A type of oscilloscope or CRT that displays the amplitude of a video signal along with such things as sync, blanking and color burst.

Wedge Mount: Mounting device enabling cameras to be rapidly mounted and dismounted from camera pedestals or tripods.

Whip-Pan: A very rapid camera panning action where subject matter is deliberately blurred. An early in-camera special effect used to link shots or sequences. Also known as a *swish pan*.

White Balancing: Electronically adjusting a camera's chroma channels for a light source so that white will be reproduced as true white. Most professional video cameras can automatically white balance when the operator fills the screen with a white card and pushes a white balance button.

Wide Angle: A lens or a scene that represents an angle of view significantly wider than normal. A wide-angle lens or shot is either a prime lens with a focal length significantly less (at least 25 percent less) than a normal lens, or a zoom lens used at a focal length significantly less than normal.

Wild Sound (Wild Track): Sound, generally background sound, recorded independently of the video and added during post-production. Does not need to be synchronized with the video.

Window Burn: *Window dub*. An off-line copy of an original videotape that contains a permanent display of SMPTE/EBU time code.

Window Dub: A copy of a production that contains permanent, visible time code numbers.

Windscreen: A small fabric or foam rubber cover for the top of a microphone that reduces or eliminates the sound of moving air or wind.

Wipe: Visual effect where a moving line or pattern acts as a border as one video signal gradually replaces another. As one picture disappears, another is revealed.

Wireless Microphone: A microphone that has a built-in, low-power transmitter or is connected to a transmitter. Wireless mics are used when a mic cord would create a problem.

Workprint: A copy of the original footage in a production. Used in off-line editing.

WORM: Write once read many (times). A videodisc system that permanently writes information onto a disc.

Wowing: The audible, undesirable result of starting a record before the turntable has reached full speed.

Writer: In television and film the individual responsible for creating the production script.

WS: Script designation for *wide shot*.

WYSIWYG: An acronym (pronounced "wizzywig") for what-you-see-is-what-you-get. Refers to a computer screen representation of text or graphics being the same as the subsequent hard copy printout.

X-Axis: The horizontal line (axis) of a graph or chart.

XCU: Script designation for extreme close-up.

XLR Connector: A standard, three-prong professional audio connector. Also called a Canon connector.

XLS: A script designation for extra long shot.

X-Y Pickup: A mic configuration used in stereo recording in which two directional mics are mounted next to each other; one directed 45 degrees to the right and one 45 degrees to the left.

X-Y Micing: A stereo micing technique using two directional microphones aimed in a Y-pattern.

Y; Y Signal: The symbol for the luminance or brightness part of a video signal.

Y-Axis: The vertical line on a graph or chart, usually containing the values for data points.

Y/C: Refers to the separate processing of the luminance (Y) and chrominance (C) video signals. Separate Y/C signals offer a number of advantages over a single composite signal.

Yo-Yo Shots: Repeated zooming in and out on subjects. An annoying effect associated with amateur productions.

Z-Axis: The front-to-back dimension of a data chart. Usually contains values for data points.

Zebra Stripes: Black lines superimposed over specific areas of an image in the viewfinders of some cameras and used as an aid in making video level adjustments.

Zoom Control: A mechanical crank or variable electronic control that changes the focus of a *zoom lens*.

Zoom Lens: A lens with a continuously variable *focal length* and *angle of acceptance*.

Zoom Ratio: Numbers indicating zoom range for a lens. The mathematical ratio for a zoom lens is derived by dividing its shortest focal length into its longest focal length.

Zooming: The process of varying the focal length and, therefore, the angle of view of a zoom lens.

References

Advertising

Baldwin, Huntley. *How to Create Effective TV Commercials.* 2d ed. Lincolnwood, IL: NTC Business Books, 1989.

Batra, Rajeev, and Rashi Glazer, eds. *Cable TV Advertising: In Search of the Right Formula.* Westport, CT: Quorum/Greenwood, 1989.

Broadbent, Simon. *The Advertiser's Handbook for Budget Determination.* Lexington, MA: Lexington Books, 1988.

Fueroghne, Dean Keith. *"But the People in Legal Said . . .": A Guide to Current Legal Issues in Advertising.* Homewood, IL: Dow Jones-Irwin, 1989.

Hagerman, William L. *Broadcast Advertising Copywriting.* Boston: Focal Press, 1990.

Hecker, Sidney, and David W. Stewart, eds. *Nonverbal Communication in Advertising.* Lexington, MA: Lexington Books, 1988.

Heighton, Elizabeth J., and Don R. Cunningham. *Advertising in the Broadcast and Cable Media.* 2d ed. Belmont, CA: Wadsworth, 1984.

Jones, Kensinger, et al. *Cable Advertising: New Ways to New Business.* Englewood Cliffs, NJ: Prentice Hall, 1986.

Stewart, David W., and David H. Furse. *Effective Television Advertising: A Study of 1,000 Commercials.* Lexington, MA: Lexington Books, 1986.

Ulanoff, Stanley M. *Advertising in America: An Introduction to Persuasive Communication.* New York: Hastings House, 1977.

White, Hooper. *How to Produce Effective TV Commercials.* 2d ed. Chicago: National Textbook Co., 1986.

Zeigler, Sherilyn K., and Herbert H. Howard. *Broadcast Advertising.* 2d ed. Ames: Iowa State Univ. Press, 1984.

Announcing

Dudek, Lee J. *Professional Broadcast Announcing.* Boston: Allyn & Bacon, 1982.

Ehrlich, Eugene, and Raymond Hand, Jr. *NBC Handbook of Pronunciation.* 4th ed. New York: Harper & Row, 1984.

Hyde, Stuart W. *Television and Radio Announcing.* 5th ed. Boston: Houghton Mifflin, 1987.

Keith, Michael C. *Broadcast Voice Performance.* Boston: Focal Press, 1989.

O'Donnell, Lewis B., et al. *Announcing: Broadcast Communicating Today.* Belmont, CA: Wadsworth, 1987.

Audio

Alkin, Glyn. *Sound Techniques for Video and TV.* 2d ed. Boston: Focal Press, 1989.

Atlen, Stanley R. *Audio in Media.* 2d ed. Belmont, CA: Wadsworth, 1986.

Clifford, Martin. *Microphones.* 3d ed. Blue Ridge Summit, PA: TAB Books, 1986.

Hubatka, Milton C., et al. *Audio Sweetening for Film and TV.* Blue Ridge Summit, PA: TAB Books, 1985.

Huber, David Miles. *Audio Production Techniques for Video.* Indianapolis: Howard W. Sams, 1987.

Huber, David Miles. *Microphone Manual: Design and Application.* Indianapolis: Howard W. Sams, 1988.

Multichannel TV Sound: How Audio Came to Video. Washington, DC: Television Digest, 1985.

Nisbett, Alec. *The Technique of the Sound Studio: For Radio, Recording Studio, Television and Film*. 4th ed. London: Focal Press, 1979.

Nisbett, Alec. *The Use of Microphones*. 2d ed. London and Boston: Focal Press, 1983.

Oringel, Robert S. *Audio Control Handbook: For Radio and Television Broadcasting*. 6th ed. Boston: Focal Press, 1989.

Pohlmann, Ken C. *Principles of Digital Audio*. 2d ed. Indianapolis: Howard W. Sams, 1989.

Prentiss, Stan. *AM Stereo and TV Stereo: New Sound Dimensions*. Blue Ridge Summit, PA: TAB Books, 1985.

Rumsey, Francis. *Stereo Sound for Television*. London and Boston: Focal Press, 1989.

Sweeney, Daniel. *Demystifying Compact Discs: A Guide to Digital Audio*. Blue Ridge Summit, PA: TAB Books, 1986.

Thom, Randy. *Audio Craft: An Introduction to the Tools and Techniques of Audio Production*. 2d ed. Washington, DC: National Federation of Community Broadcasters, 1989.

Watkinson, John. *The Art of Digital Audio*. London and Boston: Focal Press, 1988.

Careers in Television

Allman, Paul. *Exploring Careers in Video*. Rev. ed. New York: Rosen Publishing Group, 1989.

Blanksteen, Jane, and Avi Odeni. *TV: Careers Behind the Screen*. New York: John Wiley, 1987.

Bone, Jan. *Opportunities in Cable Television*. Lincolnwood, IL: National Textbook Co., 1984.

Costello, Marjorie, and Cynthia Katz. *Breaking Into Video*. New York: Simon & Schuster, 1985.

Ellis, Elmo I. *Opportunities in Broadcasting Careers*. 3d ed. Lincolnwood, IL.: National Textbook Co., 1986.

Horwin, Michael. *Careers in Film and Video Production*. Boston: Focal Press, 1990.

Norona, Shonan F. R. *Opportunities in Television and Video Careers*. Lincolnwood, IL: National Textbook Co., 1988.

Pearlman, Donn. *Breaking Into Broadcasting: Getting a Good Job in Radio or TV—Out Front or Behind the Scenes*. Chicago: Bonus Books, 1986.

Reed, Maxine K., and Robert M. Reed. *Career Opportunities in Television, Cable, and Video*. 2d ed. New York: Facts on File, 1986.

Ulmer, Shirley, and C. R. Sevilla. *The Role of Script Supervision in Film and Television: A Career Guide*. New York: Hastings House, 1986.

White, Ray. *TV News: Building a Career in Broadcast Journalism*. Boston: Focal Press, 1990.

Electronic Field Production

Bernard, Robert. *Practical Videography: Field Systems and Troubleshooting*. Boston: Focal Press, 1990.

Compesi, Ronald J., and Ronald E. Sherriffs. *Small Format Television Production: The Technique of Single-Camera Television Field Production*. Boston: Allyn & Bacon, 1985.

Glasser, Jeffrey, et al. *Progressive Video Programming: A Strategy for Making Informational Video On Location*. Los Angeles: Videowaves Publishing, 1984.

Medoff, Norman J., and Tom Tanquary. *Portable Video ENG and EFP*. White Plains, NY: Knowledge Industry Publications, 1986.

Quinn, Gerald V. *The Camcorder Handbook*. Blue Ridge Summit, PA: TAB Books, 1987.

Schihl, Robert J. *Single-Camera Video: From Concept to Edited Master*. Boston: Focal Press, 1989.

Whittaker, Ron. *Video Field Production*. Mountain View, CA: Mayfield, 1989.

Engineering/Technical

Alkin, Glyn. *Sound Recording and Reproduction*. London and Woburn, MA: Focal Press, 1981.

Amos, S. W. *Dictionary of Electronics.* 2d ed. London and Boston: Butterworth, 1987.

Ballou, Glen, ed. *Handbook for Sound Engineers: The New Audio Cyclopedia.* Indianapolis: Howard W. Sams, 1987.

Bartlett, Bruce. *Introduction to Professional Recording Techniques.* Indianapolis: Howard W. Sams, 1987.

Baylin, Frank, and Brent Gale. *KU-Band Satellite TV: Theory, Installation and Repair.* Boulder, CO: Baylin/Gale Productions, 1986.

Benson, K. Blair. *Television Engineering Handbook.* New York: McGraw-Hill, 1986.

Camras, Marvin. *Magnetic Recording Handbook.* New York: Van Nostrand Reinhold, 1988.

Crutchfield, E. B., ed. *National Association of Broadcasters Engineering Handbook.* 7th ed. Washington, DC: NAB, 1985.

Ennes, Harold E. *Television Broadcasting: Systems Maintenance.* 2d ed. Indianapolis: Howard W. Sams, 1978.

Ennes, Harold E. *Television Broadcasting: Equipment, Systems and Operating Fundamentals.* 2d ed. Indianapolis: Howard W. Sams, 1979.

Friedman, Jeffrey, ed. *Better Video Images.* White Plains, NY: Society of Motion Picture and Television Engineers, 1989.

Hartings, Robert L. *Basic TV Technology.* Boston: Focal Press, 1990.

Jorgensen, Finn. *The Complete Handbook of Magnetic Recording.* 3d ed. Blue Ridge Summit, PA: TAB Books, 1988.

Lambert, Steve, and Jane Sallis, eds. *CD-1 and Interactive Videodisc Technology.* Indianapolis: Howard W. Sams, 1986.

Mathias, Harry, and Richard Patterson. *Electronic Cinematography: Achieving Photographic Control Over the Video Image.* Belmont, CA: Wadsworth, 1985.

McWhorter, Gene (Eugene W.). *Understanding Digital Electronics.* 2d ed. Dallas: Texas Instruments, 1984.

Medoff, Norman J., and Tom Tanquary. *Portable Video ENG and EFP.* White Plains, NY: Knowledge Industry Publications, 1986.

Noll, A. Michael. *Television Technology: Fundamentals and Future Prospects.* Norwood, MA: Artech House, 1988.

Noll, A. Michael. *Introduction to Telecommunications Electronics.* Norwood, MA: Artech House, 1988.

Noll, Edward M. *Broadcast Radio and Television Handbook.* 6th ed. Indianapolis: Howard W. Sams, 1983.

Pensinger, Glen, ed. *4:2:2 Digital Video: Background and Implementation.* White Plains, NY: Society of Motion Picture and Television Engineers, 1989.

Prentiss, Stan. *Television From Analog to Digital.* Blue Ridge Summit, PA: TAB Books, 1985.

Prentiss, Stan. *HDTV: High-Definition Television.* Blue Ridge Summit, PA: TAB Books, 1990.

Robinson, J. F., and P. H. Beards. *Using Videotape.* 2d ed. London and Woburn, MA: Focal Press, 1981.

Runstein, Robert E., and David Miles Huber. *Modern Recording Techniques.* 2d ed. Indianapolis: Howard W. Sams, 1986.

Rzeszewski, Ted, et al., eds. *Color Television.* New York: Institute of Electrical and Electronics Engineers, 1983.

Rzeszewski, Theodore S., ed. *Television Technology Today.* New York: Institute of Electrical and Electronics Engineers, 1985.

Souter, Gerald A. *The Disconnection: How to Interface Computers and Video.* White Plains, NY: Knowledge Industry Publications, 1988.

Spottiswoode, Raymond, ed. *The Focal Encyclopedia of Film & Television Techniques.* New York: Hastings House, 1969.

Tomorrow's Television. Scarsdale, NY: Society of Motion Picture and Television Engineers, 1982.

General Readings in Television

Bittner, John R. *Broadcasting and Telecommunication: An Introduction.* 2d ed. Englewood Cliffs, NJ: Prentice Hall, 1985.

Foster, Eugene S. *Understanding Broadcasting*. 2d ed. Reading, MA: Addison-Wesley, 1982.

Gross, Lynne Schafer. *The Internship Experience*. Belmont, CA: Wadsworth, 1981.

Gross, Lynne Schafer. *The New Television Technologies*. 3d ed. Dubuque, IA: Wm. C. Brown, 1990.

Hanson, Jarice. *Understanding Video: Applications, Impact, and Theory*. Newbury Park, CA: Sage, 1987.

Head, Sydney W., and Christopher H. Sterling. *Broadcasting in America: A Survey of Electronic Media*. 6th ed. Boston: Houghton Mifflin, 1990.

Hilsman, Hoyt R. *The New Electronic Media: Innovations in Video Technologies*. Boston: Focal Press, 1989.

Keirstead, Phillip O., and Sonia-Kay Keirstead. *The World of Telecommunication: Introduction to Broadcasting, Cable, and New Technologies*. Boston: Focal Press, 1990.

McDonald, James R. *The Broadcaster's Dictionary*. Rev. ed. Broomfield, CO: Wind Rivers Books, 1987.

Paiva, Bob. *The Program Director's Handbook*. Blue Ridge Summit, PA: TAB Books, 1983.

Pelligrino, Ronald. *The Electronic Arts of Sound and Light*. New York: Van Nostrand Reinhold, 1983.

Sherman, Barry L. *Telecommunications Management: The Broadcast and Cable Industries*. New York: McGraw-Hill, 1987.

Sterling, Christopher H. *Electronic Media: A Guide to Trends in Broadcasting and Newer Technologies, 1920–1983*. New York: Praeger, 1984.

Van Duesen, Richard E. *Practical AV/Video Budgeting*. White Plains, NY: Knowledge Industry Publications, 1984.

Weinstein, Stephen B. *Getting the Picture: A Guide to CATV and the New Electronic Media*. New York: Institute of Electrical and Electronics Engineers, 1986.

Wiese, Michael. *Film & Video Budgets*. Boston: Focal Press, 1984.

Winship, Michael. *Television*. New York: Random House, 1988.

The World Radio TV Handbook. New York: Watson-Guptill Publications, 1990.

Issues in Television Production

Christians, Clifford G., et al. *Media Ethics: Cases and Moral Reasoning*. 2d ed. New York: Longman, 1987.

Fore, William F. *Television and Religion: The Shaping of Faith, Values and Culture*. Minneapolis: Augsburg Publishing House, 1987.

Frankl, Razelle. *Televangelism: The Marketing of Popular Religion*. Carbondale: Southern Illinois Univ. Press, 1987.

Hoover, Stewart M. *Mass Media Religion: The Social Sources of the Electronic Church*. Newbury Park, CA: Sage, 1988.

Orlik, Peter B. *Critiquing Television and Radio Content*. Boston: Allyn & Bacon, 1988.

Rivers, William L. *Ethics for the Media*. Englewood Cliffs, NJ: Prentice Hall, 1988.

Rosen, Phillip T., ed. *International Handbook of Broadcasting Systems*. Westport, CT: Greenwood Press, 1988.

Broadcast Law

Barber, Susanna. *News Camera in the Courtroom: A Free Press/Fair Trial Debate*. Norwood, NJ: Ablex Publishing Corp., 1987.

Benko, Robert P. *Protecting Intellectual Property Rights*. Washington, DC: American Enterprise Institute, 1987.

Bensman, Marvin R. *Broadcast Regulation: Selected Cases and Decisions*. 2d ed. Lanham, MD: University Press of America, 1985.

Bezanson, Randall P., et al. *Libel Law and the Press: Myth and Reality*. New York: Free Press, 1987.

Bittner, John R. *Broadcast Law and Regulation*. Englewood Cliffs, NJ: Prentice Hall, 1981.

Braverman, Burt A., and Frances J. Chetwynd. *Information Law: Freedom of Information, Privacy, Open Meetings, Other Access Laws*. 2 vols. New York: Practicing Law Institute, 1985.

Brenner, Daniel L., and William L. Rivers. *Free but Regulated: Conflicting Traditions in Media Law.* Ames: Iowa State Univ. Press, 1982.

Carter, T. Barton, et al. *The First Amendment and the Fifth Estate: Regulation of Electronic Mass Media.* 2d ed. Westbury, NY: Foundation Press, 1989.

Dannay, Richard. *How to Handle Basic Copywright and Trademark Problems.* New York: Practicing Law Institute, 1990.

Dennis, Everette E., et al., eds. *Media Freedom and Accountability.* New York: Greenwood Press, 1989.

Ferris, Charles D., et al. *Cable Television Law: A Video Communications Practice Guide.* 3 vols. Albany, NY: Matthew Bender & Co., 1983.

Francois, William E. *Mass Media Law and Regulation.* 4th ed. New York: Wiley, 1986.

Franklin, Marc A. *Cases and Materials on Mass Media Law.* 3d ed. Mineola, NY: Foundation Press, 1987.

Gilmor, Donald M., and Jerome A. Barron. *Mass Communication Law: Cases and Comment.* 4th ed. St. Paul, MN: West, 1984.

Ginsburg, Douglas H. *Regulation of Broadcasting: Law and Policy Towards Radio, Television and Cable Communications.* St. Paul, MN: West, 1979. 1983 Supplement, 1983.

Henn, Harry G. *Copyright Law: A Practioner's Guide.* 2d ed. New York: Practicing Law Institute, 1988.

Ingelhart, Louis Edward. *Press Freedoms.* Westport, CT: Greenwood Press, 1987.

Introduction to Copyright and Trademark Law, 1987. New York: Practicing Law Institute, 1987.

Kane, Peter E. *Murder, Courts and the Press: Issues in Free Press/Fair Trial.* Carbondale: Southern Illinois Univ. Press, 1986.

Krasnow, Erwin G., et al. *The Politics of Broadcast Regulation.* 3d ed. New York: St. Martin's Press, 1982.

Krasnow, Erwin G., and Jill MacNiece. *101 Ways to Cut Legal Fees & Manage Your Lawyer: A Practical Guide for Broadcasters and Cable Operators.* Washington, DC: Broadcasting Book Division, 1985.

Labunski, Richard. *Libel and the First Amendment: Legal History and Practice in Print and Broadcasting.* New Brunswick, NJ: Transaction Books, 1987.

Lawrence, John Shelton, and Bernard Timberg, eds. *Fair Use and Free Inquiry: Copyright Law and the News Media.* 2d ed. Norwood, NJ: Ablex Publishing, 1989.

Leibowitz, Matthew L., and Sanford H. Bohrer. *Broadcasting and the Law News Handbook.* Miami: Broadcasting and the Law, 1988.

Leibowitz, Matthew L., and John M. Spencer. *Broadcasting and the Law Political Handbook.* Miami: Broadcasting and the Law, 1988.

Meeske, Milan D., and R. C. Norris. *Copyright for the Electronic Media: A Practical Guide.* Belmont, CA: Wadsworth, 1987.

Nelson, Harold L., et al. *Law of Mass Communications: Freedom and Control of Print and Broadcast Media.* 6th ed. Westbury, NY: Foundation Press, 1989.

Pember, Don R. *Mass Media Law.* 4th ed. Dubuque, IA: Wm. C. Brown, 1987.

Powe, Lucas A., Jr. *American Broadcasting and the First Amendment.* Berkeley: Univ. of California Press, 1987.

Robertson, Geoffrey, and Andrew G. L. Nicol. *Media Law: The Rights of Journalists, Broadcasters and Publishers.* London, Beverly Hills: Sage, 1984.

Zuckman, Harvey L., et al. *Mass Communications Law in a Nutshell.* 3d ed. St. Paul, MN: West, 1988.

Lighting

Carlson, Verne, and Sylvia Carlson. *Professional Lighting Handbook.* Boston: Focal Press: 1985.

LeTorneau, Tom. *Lighting Techniques for Video Production: The Art of Casting Shadows.* White Plains, NY: Knowledge Industry Publications, 1986.

Millerson, Gerald. *The Technique of Lighting for Television and Motion Pictures.* 2d ed. Boston: Focal Press, 1982.

Millerson, Gerald. *TV Lighting Methods.* 2d ed. Boston: Focal Press, 1982.

Sweet, Harvey. *Handbook of Scenery, Properties and Lighting.* Vol. 1. *Scenery and Props.* Boston: Allyn & Bacon, 1990.

News/Electronic Journalism

Altschull, J. Herbert. *Agents of Power: The Role of the News Media in Human Affairs.* New York: Longman, 1984.

Atkins, Gary, and William Rivers. *Reporting With Understanding.* Ames: Iowa State Univ. Press, 1987.

Becker, Lee B., et al. *The Training and Hiring of Journalists.* Norwood, NJ: Ablex Publishing, 1987.

Biagi, Shirley. *Interviews That Work: A Practical Guide for Journalists.* Belmont, CA: Wadsworth, 1986.

Biagi, Shirley. *Newstalk 2: State-of-the-Art Conversations With Today's Broadcast Journalists.* Belmont, CA: Wadsworth, 1987.

Bliss, Edward, Jr., and John M. Patterson. *Writing News for Broadcast.* 2d ed. New York: Columbia Univ. Press, 1978.

Block, Mervin. *Writing Broadcast News—Shorter, Sharper, Stronger: A Professional Handbook.* Chicago: Bonus Books, 1987.

Bohrer, Sanford L., et al. *News Handbook.* Miami: Broadcasting and the Law, 1988.

Burkett, Warren. *News Reporting: Science, Medicine, and High Technology.* Ames, IA: Iowa State Univ. Press, 1986.

Cohen, Akiba A. *The Television News Interview.* Newbury Park, CA: Sage, 1987.

Cohler, David Keith. *Broadcast Journalism: A Guide for the Presentation of Radio and Television News.* Englewood Cliffs, NJ: Prentice Hall, 1985.

Cohler, David Keith. *Broadcast Newswriting.* Englewood Cliffs, NJ: Prentice Hall, 1990.

Designing for Television: News Graphics. Harlingen, TX: Broadcast Designers' Association, 1981.

Denniston, Lyle W. *The Reporter and the Law: Techniques of Covering the Courts.* New York: Hastings House, 1980.

Fang, Irving E. *Television News, Radio News.* 4th ed. St. Paul, MN: Rada Press, 1985.

Fensch, Thomas. *Sportswriting Handbook.* Hillsdale, NJ: Lawrence Erlbaum Associates, 1988.

Fink, Conrad C. *Media Ethics: In the Newsroom and Beyond.* New York: McGraw-Hill, 1988.

Garrison, Bruce, and Mark Sabljak. *Sports Reporting.* Ames, IA: Iowa State Univ. Press, 1985.

Garvey, Daniel E., and William L. Rivers. *Newswriting for the Electronic Media: Principles, Examples, Applications.* Belmont, CA: Wadsworth, 1982.

Goedkoop, Richard J. *Inside Local Television News.* Salem, WI: Sheffield Publishing, 1988.

Goodwin, H. Eugene. *Groping for Ethics in Journalism.* 2d ed. Ames, IA: Iowa State Univ. Press, 1987.

Hall, Mark W. *Broadcast Journalism: An Introduction to News Writing.* 3d ed. New York: Hastings House, 1986.

Hewitt, John. *Air Words: Writing for Broadcast News.* Mountain View, CA: Mayfield, 1988.

Hood, James R., and Brad Kalbfeld, comps. and eds. *The Associated Press Broadcast News Handbook: Incorporating the AP Libel Manual.* New York: Associated Press Broadcast Services, 1982.

Hosley, David H., and Gayle K. Yamada. *Hard News: Women in Broadcasting Journalism.* Westport, CT: Greenwood Press, 1987.

Hough, George A. *News Writing.* 4th ed. Boston: Houghton Mifflin, 1988.

Irvine, Robert B. *When You Are the Headline: Managing a Major News Story.* Homewood, IL: Dow Jones-Irwin, 1987.

Kessler, Lauren, and Duncan McDonald. *When Worlds Collide: A Journalist's Guide to Grammar and Style.* 2d ed. Belmont, CA: Wadsworth, 1988.

Klaidman, Stephen, and Tom L. Beauchamp. *The Virtuous Journalist.* New York: Oxford Univ. Press, 1987.

Lewis, Carolyn Diana. *Reporting for Television.* New York: Columbia Univ. Press, 1984.

MacDonald, R. H. *A Broadcast News Manual of Style.* New York: Longman, 1987.

Mencher, Melvin. *Basic News Writing.* 3d ed. Dubuque, IA: Wm. C. Brown, 1989.

Metzler, Ken. *Newsgathering.* 2d ed. Englewood Cliffs, NJ: Prentice Hall, 1986.

Olen, Jeffrey. *Ethics in Journalism.* Englewood Cliffs, NJ: Prentice Hall, 1988.

Paisner, Daniel. *The Imperfect Mirror: Inside Stories of Television Newswomen*. New York: Morrow, 1989.

Papper, Robert A. *A Broadcast News Writing Stylebook*. Delaware, OH: Ohio Wesleyan Univ., 1987.

Pollock, John Crothers. *The Politics of Crisis Reporting: Learning to Be a Foreign Correspondent*. New York: Praeger, 1981.

Richstad, Jim, and Michael H. Anderson, eds. *Critics in International News: Policies and Prospects*. New York: Columbia Univ. Press, 1981.

Shook, Frederick. *Television Field Production and Reporting*. New York: Longman, 1989.

Smeyak, G. Paul. *Broadcast News Writing*. 2d ed. Columbus, OH: Grid, 1983.

Stephens, Mitchell. *Broadcast News*. 2d ed. New York: Holt, Rinehart and Winston, 1986.

Stepp, Carl Sessions. *Editing for Today's Newsroom: New Perspectives for a Changing Profession*. Hillsdale, NJ: Lawrence Erlbaum Associates, 1989.

Stewart, Charles J., and William B. Cash, Jr. *Interviewing Principles and Practices*. 5th ed. Dubuque, IA: Wm. C. Brown, 1988.

Strentz, Herbert. *News Reporters and News Sources: Accomplices in Shaping and Misshaping the News*. 2d ed. Ames, IA: Iowa State Univ. Press, 1989.

Ullman, John, and Steven Honeyman. *The Reporter's Handbook: An Investigator's Guide to Documents and Techniques*. New York: St. Martin's Press, 1983.

The UPI Broadcast Style: A Handbook for Writing and Preparing Broadcast News. New York, Chicago: United Press International, 1979.

Vahl, Rod. *Exploring Careers in Broadcast Journalism*. New York: Rosen Publishing Group, 1983.

Walters, Roger L. *Broadcast Writing: Principles and Practice*. New York: Random House, 1988.

White, Ted, et al. *Broadcast News Writing, Reporting and Production*. New York: Macmillan, 1984.

Wulfemeyer, K. Tim. *Broadcast Newswriting: A Workbook*. Ames, IA: Iowa State Univ. Press, 1983.

Wulfemeyer, K. Tim. *Beginning Broadcast Newswriting: A Self-Instructional Learning Experience*. 2d ed. Ames, IA: Iowa State Univ. Press, 1984.

Yoakam, Richard D. *ENG: Television News and the New Technology*. Carbondale: Southern Illinois Univ. Press, 1985.

Yorke, Ivor. *The Technique of Television News*. 2d ed. Boston: Focal Press, 1987.

Zousmer, Steven. *TV News Off-Camera: An Insider's Guide to Newswriting and Newspeople*. Ann Arbor: Univ. of Michigan Press, 1987.

Postproduction

Anderson, Gary H. *Electronic Post-Production: The Film-to-Video Guide*. White Plains, NY: Knowledge Industry Publications, 1986.

Anderson, Gary H. *Video Editing and Post-Production: A Professional Guide*. 2d ed. White Plains, NY: Knowledge Industry Publications, 1988.

Browne, Steven E. *Videotape Editing: A Postproduction Primer*. Boston: Focal Press, 1989.

The Complete Guide to Videotape Editing. Level One: VTV Productions. Los Angeles: Sony Institute of Applied Video Technology, 1988.

Kerner, Marvin M. *The Art of the Sound Effects Editor*. Boston: Focal Press, 1989.

Mott, Robert L. *Sound Effects: Radio, TV and Film*. Boston, Focal Press, 1990.

Schneider, Arthur. *Electronic Postproduction and Videotape Editing*. Boston: Focal Press, 1989.

The Video Post-Production Survival Kit, The Producers Group. Los Angeles: Sony Institute of Applied Video Technology, 1988.

Weynard, Diana. *Computerized Videotape Editing*. Woodland Hills, CA: Weynard Associates, 1983.

Weynard, Diana, ed. *The Post-Production Process*. Woodland Hills, CA: Weynard Associates, 1985.

Satellites, Cable and Fiber Optics

Baldwin, Thomas F., and D. Stevens McVoy. *Cable Communication*. 2d ed. Englewood Cliffs, NJ: Prentice Hall, 1988.

Baughcum, Alan, and Gerald Faulhaber, eds. *Telecommunications Access and Public Policy: Proceedings of the Workshop on Local Access*. Norwood, NJ: Ablex Publishing, 1984.

Baylin, Frank, and Brent Gale. *Satellite and Cable TV Scrambling and Descrambling*. Boulder, CO: Baylin/Gale Productions, 1986.

Binkowski, Edward S. *Satellite Information Systems*. Boston: G. K. Hall, 1988.

Cunningham, John E. *Cable Television*. 2d ed. Indianapolis: Howard W. Sams, 1980.

Dalgleish, D. I. *An Introduction to Satellite Communications*. London: Institute of Electrical Engineers, 1989.

Eastman, Susan Tyler, et al. *Broadcast/Cable Programming: Strategies and Practices*. 3d ed. Belmont, CA: Wadsworth, 1989.

Easton, Anthony T. *The Satellite TV Handbook*. Indianapolis: Howard W. Sams, 1983.

Elbert, Bruce R. *Introduction to Satellite Communication*. Norwood, MA: Artech House, 1987.

Fthenakis, Emanuel. *Manual of Satellite Communications*. New York: McGraw-Hill, 1984.

Garay, Ronald. *Cable Television: A Reference Guide to Information*. Westport, CT: Greenwood Press, 1988.

Goodale, James C. *All About Cable: Legal and Business Aspects of Cable and Pay Television*. Rev. ed. New York: Law Journal Seminars Press, 1981–1989.

Hecht, Jeff. *Understanding Fiber Optics*. Indianapolis: Howard W. Sams, 1989.

Jansky, Donald M. *World Atlas of Satellites*. Dedham, MA: Artech House, 1987.

Jansky, Donald M., and Michel C. Jeruchim. *Communication Satellites in the Geostationary Orbit*. Norwood, MA: Artech House, 1987.

Kantor, L. Ya, ed. *Handbook of Satellite Telecommunication and Broadcasting*. Norwood, MA: Artech House, 1987.

Killen, Harold B. *Digital Communications With Fiber Optics and Satellite Applications*. Englewood Cliffs, NJ: Prentice Hall, 1988.

Long, Mark, comp. *World Satellite Almanac*. 2d ed. Indianapolis: Howard W. Sams, 1987.

Maral, G., and M. Bousquet. *Satellite Communications Systems*. New York: Wiley, 1986.

Martinez, Larry. *Communications Satellites: Power Politics in Space*. Dedham, MA: Artech House, 1985.

Mobilizing the Future: The Evolution of Mobile Satellite Services. Washington, DC: Television Digest, 1988.

Negrine, Ralph., ed. *Cable Television and the Future of Broadcasting*. New York: St. Martin's Press, 1985.

Prentiss, Stan. *Satellite Communications*. 2d ed. Blue Ridge Summit, PA: TAB Books, 1987.

The World Satellite Directory. Potomac, MD: Phillips Publishing, 1990.

Video Production, General

Aldridge, Henry B., and Lucy A. Liggett. *Audio/Video Production: Theory and Practice*. Englewood Cliffs, NJ: Prentice Hall, 1990.

Armer, Alan A. *Directing Television and Film*. Belmont, CA: Wadsworth, 1986.

Blum, Richard A. *Working Actors: The Craft of Television, Film and Stage Performance*. Boston: Focal Press, 1989.

Blumenthal, Howard J. *Television Producing and Directing*. New York: Barnes & Noble, 1987.

Breyer, Richard, and Peter Moller. *Making Television Programs: A Professional Approach*. New York: Longman, 1984.

Broughton, Irv, ed. *Producers on Producing: The Making of Film and Television*. Jefferson, NC: McFarland, 1986.

Burrows, Thomas D., et al. *Television Production: Disciplines and Techniques*. 4th ed. Dubuque, IA: Wm. C. Brown, 1989.

Carlson, Verne, and Sylvia Carlson. *Professional Cameraman's Handbook*. Boston: Focal Press: 1981.

Cartwright, Steve R. *Training With Video*. White Plains, NY: Knowledge Industry Publications, 1986.

Designing for Television: The New Tools. Harlingen, TX: Broadcast Designers' Association, 1983.

DiZazzo, Raymond. *Corporate Television: A Producer's Handbook*. Boston: Focal Press, 1990.

Fielding, Ken. *Introduction to Television Production*. New York: Longman, 1990.

Hayward, Stan. *Computers for Animation*. London and Boston: Focal Press, 1984.

Hindman, James, et al. *TV Acting: A Manual for Camera Performance*. New York: Hastings House, 1979.

Iezzi, Frank. *Understanding Television Production*. Englewood Cliffs, NJ: Prentice Hall, 1984.

Kehoe, Vincent J. R. *The Technique of the Professional Make-up Artist for Film, Television, and Stage*. Boston: Focal Press, 1985.

Kuney, Jack. *Take One: Television Directors on Directing*. Westport, CT: Greenwood/Praeger, 1990.

LeBaron, John. *Making Television: A Video Production Guide for Teachers*. New York: Teachers College Press, 1982.

McQuillin, Lon. *The Video Production Guide*. Indianapolis: Howard W. Sams, 1983.

Merritt, Douglas. *Television Graphics—From Pencil to Pixel*. New York: Van Nostrand Reinhold, 1987.

Millerson, Gerald. *Basic TV Staging*. 2d ed. London and Woburn, MA: Focal Press, 1982.

Millerson, Gerald. *Effective TV Production*. 2d ed. London and Boston: Focal Press, 1983.

Millerson, Gerald. *Video Camera Techniques*. London and Boston: Focal Press, 1983.

Millerson, Gerald. *The Technique of Television Production*. 11th ed. London: Focal Press, 1985.

Millerson, Gerald. *Video Production Handbook*. Boston: Focal Press, 1987.

Millerson, Gerald. *TV Scenic Design Handbook*. Boston: Focal Press, 1989.

Oringel, Robert. *Television Operations Handbook*. Boston: Focal Press, 1984.

Rabiger, Michael. *Directing the Documentary*. Boston: Focal Press, 1987.

Rosen, Frederic W. *Shooting Video*. Boston: Focal Press, 1983.

Rowlands, Avril. *The Production Assistant in TV and Video*. Boston: Focal Press, 1987.

Rowlands, Avril. *Continuity in Film and Video*. 2d ed. Boston: Focal Press, 1989.

Stokes, Judith Tereno. *Microcomputers in TV Studios*. White Plains, NY: Knowledge Industry Publications, 1986.

Stokes, Judith Tereno. *The Business of Nonbroadcast Television: Corporate and Institutional Video Budgets, Facilities and Applications*. White Plains, NY: Knowledge Industry Publications, 1988.

Utz, Peter. *Today's Video: Equipment, Setup and Production*. Englewood Cliffs, NJ: Prentice Hall, 1987.

Verna, Tony. *Live TV: An Inside Look at Directing and Producing*. Boston: Focal Press, 1987.

Weise, Marcus. *Videotape Operations*. Woodland Hills, CA: Weynard Associates, 1984.

Wershing, Stephen, and Paul Singer. *Computer Graphics and Animation for Corporate Video*. White Plains, NY: Knowledge Industry Publications, 1988.

White, Gordon. *Video Techniques*. London: Newnes, 1982.

Wiegand, Ingrid. *Professional Video Production*. White Plains, NY: Knowledge Industry Publications, 1985.

Wiese, Michael. *The Independent Film & Videomakers Guide*. Rev ed. Boston: Focal Press, 1984.

Wiese, Michael. *Home Video: Producing for the Home Market*. Boston: Focal Press, 1986.

Wilkie, Bernard. *The Technique of Special Effects in Television*. 2d ed. Boston: Focal Press, 1989.

Wurtzel, Alan, and Stephen R. Acker. *Television Production*. 3d ed. New York: McGraw-Hill, 1989.

Zettl, Herbert. *Sight-Sound-Motion: Applied Media Aesthetics*. 2d ed. Belmont, CA: Wadsworth, 1990.

Zettl, Herbert. *Television Production Handbook*. 5th ed. Belmont, CA: Wadsworth, 1992.

Writing, General

Armer, Alan A. *Writing the Screenplay: TV and Film*. Belmont, CA: Wadsworth, 1988.

Berman, Robert A. *Fade In: The Screenwriting Process*. Stoneham, MA: Focal Press, 1988.

Blum, Richard A. *Television Writing: From Concept to Contract*. Rev. ed. Boston: Focal Press, 1984.

Coe, Michelle E. *How to Write for Television*. New York: Crown Publishers, 1980.

Fensch, Thomas. *Writing Solutions: Beginnings, Middles & Endings*. Hillsdale, NJ: Lawrence Erlbaum Associates, 1989.

Garvey, Daniel E., and William L. Rivers. *Broadcast Writing*. New York: Longman, 1982.

Hilliard, Robert L. *Writing for Television and Radio*. 4th ed. Belmont, CA: Wadsworth, 1984.

Kessler, Lauren, and Duncan McDonald. *Mastering the Message: Media Writing With Substance and Style*. Belmont, CA: Wadsworth, 1989.

Kilpatrick, James J. *The Writer's Art*. Kansas City, MO: Andrews and McMeel, 1984.

Lee, Robert, and Robert Misiorowski. *Script Models: A Handbook for the Media Writer*. New York: Hastings House, 1978.

Maloney, Martin, and Paul Max Rubenstein. *Writing for the Media: Film, Television, Video and Radio*. 2d ed. Englewood Cliffs, NJ: Prentice Hall, 1988.

Mayeux, Peter E. *Writing for the Broadcast Media*. Boston: Allyn & Bacon, 1985.

Miller, William. *Screenwriting for Narrative Film and Television*. New York: Hastings House, 1980.

Nash, Constance. *The Television Writer's Handbook: What to Write, How to Write it, Where to Sell it*. New York: Harper & Row, 1978.

Newsom, Doug, and James A. Wollert. *Media Writing: Preparing Information for the Mass Media*. 2d ed. Belmont, CA: Wadsworth, 1988.

Orlik, Peter B. *Broadcast Copyrighting*. 4th ed. Boston: Allyn & Bacon, 1990.

Rubenstein, Paul Max, and Martin Maloney. *Writing for the Media: Film, Television, Video and Radio*. 2d ed. Englewood Cliffs, NJ: Prentice Hall, 1988.

Stovall, James Glen. *Writing for the Mass Media*. 2d ed. Englewood Cliffs, NJ: Prentice Hall, 1990.

Swain, Dwight V. *Film Scriptwriting: A Practical Manual*. 2d ed. Boston: Focal Press, 1988.

Van Nostran, William. *The Scriptwriter's Handbook*. White Plains, NY: Knowledge Industry Publications, 1989.

Wolff, Jurgen. *Successful Sitcom Writing*. New York: St. Martin's Press, 1988.

INDEX

ABC Network, 359, 532

Accountability, 532

Acoustics, 163, 182, 382, 449, 529

Acquisition formats, 263, 511

Acting
actor, 3, 30, 149, 245–247, 289, 301, 324–326, 333, 335, 339, 349, 352–353, 373, 377–379, 382, 385–386, 437–439, 443–444, 480, 495, 531, 534

Actual malice, 504, 506

Advertiser, 96, 109, 321, 323

Advertising, 3, 342, 346, 349, 362

Affiliates, 359

AGC (automatic gain control), 68, 165–167, 208

Agent, 208, 390–391, 500, 534

Air check, 479, 495

Amega computer, 251

Ampex Corp., 257, 259, 282, 364

Amplifier, 77, 159, 163, 169, 176, 204, 207

Amps, 156, 448, 450

Animation, 109, 250, 272, 309, 311–314, 316, 522, 527, 535
cels, 312

Announce, 173, 179, 190, 192, 200, 202, 246, 295–296, 308, 323, 329, 349, 353, 372, 376, 428, 440, 442, 455, 475–476, 478–479, 494–495, 505, 509, 515, 518, 528

Antenna, 28, 30, 180–181, 461
diversity, 181

Antialiasing, 311

AP (Associated Press), 34, 43–45, 48, 64, 94, 181, 187, 190, 213, 217–218, 225, 259, 305, 316, 349–350, 364–365, 377, 413, 436, 455, 466, 475, 480, 499

Apple computers, 106, 229, 250–252, 364

Approximate color consistency, 96, 112

Arabia, 534

Archival storage, 271

Art director, 284, 315

Artifacts, 64

ASCAP, 509, 515

Aspect ratio, 20–21, 30, 61, 73, 302–303, 306, 316

Associate director, 3, 360

Associate producer, 358, 360–361

Atmosphere introduction, 213, 222

Attenuator, 199–200

Audio
audition channel, 202
board, 10–11, 13, 165, 199–203
booth, 11, 173, 382

cancellation, 184

channel, 191, 200, 202, 273, 454

compressor, 165, 167, 208

console, 10, 13, 199–204, 209, 232
cue channel, 202
expander, 167, 208
limiter, 165, 208
looping, 382
loudness meter, 160, 167–168, 199, 208
monitor, 171, 201
monophonic, 159, 177, 189–190, 192, 194, 201, 261, 418–419
MTS, 159
pitch, 23, 64, 118, 161–162, 206, 421
speaker, 169, 201, 203, 207, 529
sweetening, 6, 172, 207, 326, 423–425
technician, 5, 13

Audio tape, digital, 24, 196

Audition, 202

Auditions, 324

Automated, 87, 254, 393, 397, 467

Automation, 86–87

Azimuth, 467

Backgrounds, 68, 96, 114, 120, 127, 129, 138, 141, 143, 183, 226, 245–246, 287–290, 295, 310, 315, 383
cameo, 285–287, 315

Backtiming, 383

Balanced line, 177

Bandwidth, 29, 63, 258, 262, 267, 271

Barcelona Olympics, 273

Batteries, 87, 153, 175

Battery, 22, 58, 65, 73, 77, 124, 180, 204, 266

BBC, 259

BBS system, 253

Binary numbers, 22–24, 30

Bit speed, 23

Blanking pulses, 26–27, 30, 410

Bloom, 526

BMI, 509, 515

Body brace, 79

Boom, 8, 114, 132, 141, 143, 183–184, 187, 209, 212, 248, 286, 525

Broadcasting, 2, 17, 19, 22, 28, 30, 63, 257, 259–260, 276, 396, 427–428, 435, 459, 463, 516, 532, 536

Budgets, 3, 278, 317, 320, 324, 342, 346, 360, 363, 424, 445, 531

Bump up, 267

Cable, 2, 28, 65, 77–78, 81, 86–88, 177, 180, 191, 254, 261, 266, 304, 358, 454, 456–459, 461, 463, 517, 524, 533, 536

coax, 436, 457–459
triax, 65

California, 253, 257, 277, 450, 502, 522

Cam head, 84–85

Camcorder, 37, 43, 68, 73, 77–79, 101, 133, 153, 176–177, 180, 250, 266–267, 274, 400, 411–413, 517, 531–534, 536

Camera
backlight switch, 68
base station, 9, 13, 65, 70, 77, 91
blocking, 5
cam head, 84–85
cards, 305–306, 308, 316
CCD, 41, 53–54, 57–62, 64, 68, 87, 91, 100–101, 104, 108, 112, 148, 154–155, 218, 278, 307, 346, 523
CCU, 8–9, 13, 45, 64–65, 67, 70, 73, 77, 91
convertible, 57, 77, 91
eyepieces, 74
fluid head, 84
friction, 85
gear head, 85
jib, 84, 91, 297, 315, 453
pan head, 7, 12, 80, 84–85, 91, 247, 353
pedestal, 80–81, 87
prompters, 7, 12, 88–91, 431, 476, 478–479, 491, 495
shoulder mount, 79, 91
tally light, 7, 12, 75, 353
viewfinder, 7, 12, 29, 57, 62, 68, 73–77, 79, 87, 91, 95, 104, 109, 140, 167, 279–280, 430

Camera mounts
crane, 82–84, 91, 453
jib, 84, 91, 297, 315, 453
pedestal, 80–81, 87

Camera of record, 2

Canada, 17, 524

Canadian, 475, 524–525

Canted shot, 333

Canvas drop, 295

Capitalization, 334–335

Carrier wave, 11, 27–28, 30

Casting, 113, 324

CATV, 28

CBS Network, 359, 364, 436

CCD (charged coupled device), 41, 53–54, 57–62, 64, 68, 87, 91, 100–101, 104, 108, 112, 148, 154–155, 218, 278, 307, 346, 523
shift register, 58

CDs, 192, 194–196, 198, 209, 510

CG (character generator), 243–244

Chip chart, 70–71, 91

Chroma, 9, 100–101, 138, 141, 244–249, 251, 256, 272, 287

Chroma channels, 100–101

Chrominance, 30, 102, 261–262, 268, 272

Clandestine videography, 502

CMX Corp., 364

CNN, 87, 430

Color
  additive, 93, 97, 99, 107, 112, 290
  approximate color consistency, 96, 112
  burst, 106
  compatibility, 73, 109, 112, 289
  complementary, 96, 98–99, 112
  standard, 94, 96, 118
  subtractive, 93, 97, 99, 112, 290
  subcarrier, 27

Colorized, 244

Colorizer, 243

Comedies, 2, 5, 148, 288, 386, 437

Commentary, 419, 455, 491

Commentator, 179, 245, 455

Commercial, 2, 5, 7, 12, 96, 126, 140, 164–165, 196–197, 215, 249, 254, 258, 300, 316, 319, 321, 349, 353, 356, 362, 384, 389, 437, 455, 496, 502, 512, 514–515, 530–531, 535

Commercial appropriation, 502, 514

Composers, 329, 509

Composite signal, 261, 272

Composition
  dimensional merger, 227–228
  dynamic, 165, 173–175, 177–180, 183, 214, 218, 225, 230
  leading lines, 214, 224–225, 231
  rule of thirds, 220, 231
  static, 214, 218, 229–230
  tonal mergers, 46, 48, 52, 121, 211, 213–214, 216–220, 223–231, 291–293, 356, 384, 507, 510

Compression, 63, 66–67, 196, 198, 421, 425, 490, 495, 526, 528

Computer
  BBS systems, 253
  mouse, 200, 251, 254, 313–314, 316, 420
  open architecture, 251
  platform, 251, 310

Computer network, 253, 457

Constitution, U.S., 497, 502, 505

Consumer equipment, 261, 268

Control room, 8, 11, 13, 29–30, 75, 86, 88, 109, 201, 237, 254, 256, 352, 356, 362, 415, 430, 436, 447

Control track, 274, 281, 364, 393–394, 409–411, 425

Convergence, 40

Copy stand, 308

Copyright, 196, 326, 496, 509–513, 515

Corner insert, 248–249, 305

Cost per measured results, 349

Cost per minute, 349, 362

Cost per viewer, 349, 362

Costumes, 5, 216, 324, 341

Countdown, 415–416

Cover shot, 300–301, 332, 438

Coverage, 28, 30, 190, 278, 359, 427–429, 438, 461, 492, 505

CPM (Cost per thousand), 349

Crab, 82–83, 91

Crab dolly, 82–83

Crawl, 310

Creative compromise, 444–445

Credits, 21, 30, 234, 238, 248, 250, 255, 277, 305, 333, 353, 424, 434, 531

Cropped, cropping, 228, 302–304, 306, 333

Cue card, 5, 88, 491

Cues, 5, 7, 87, 179, 353, 362, 397, 415, 417, 456, 476, 492

Cuing, 193, 202, 249, 281

Curtains, 126, 155, 284, 287

Cutaway, 34, 213, 230, 371, 379, 385, 389–392, 412–414, 418, 421, 425

Cuts, 19, 194, 213, 298, 332–333, 339, 377–379, 382, 384–386, 392, 408, 416–418, 420, 422

Cutting, 30, 54, 194, 213, 215, 329, 332, 353, 364, 368–369, 371, 377, 379, 381–385, 388–389, 392, 400, 418, 428, 445, 531

Cyc, 8, 13, 18, 27, 123–124, 127, 161, 175, 259, 285–286, 288, 290, 315, 463

DAT (digital audio tape), 22–23, 63, 194–198, 203, 207–209, 215, 253, 271, 280, 315, 394–395, 397, 400, 419, 421, 423, 431, 461, 467, 515

Database, 431

Db, 10, 13, 160–162, 165, 199–203, 208, 415

Dbm, 160–161, 208

DCC (digital compact cassette), 192, 198, 207–209

Dedicated equipment, 250

Defamation, 503–506, 514
  per quod, 503–504, 514
  per se, 16–19, 23, 27–28, 30, 161, 193, 198, 215, 258, 274, 313, 341, 364, 393, 398–399, 416, 457, 463, 503–504, 508, 514, 526–527

Defamatory, 503–504

Defendant, 499, 503–504

Desktop video, 109, 250, 254, 256

Dibie, George, 148

Dichroic mirrors, 100, 112

Diffuser, 116, 129, 134

Diffusion, 54, 56

Directing, 212–213, 218, 230–231, 245, 341, 350–351, 353, 356, 362, 439, 443, 447, 456–457

Discrepancy report, 362–363

Dissolve, 9, 208, 236, 238, 240, 247, 339, 364, 376, 384, 409, 422–423

Docudrama, 505–506

Documentaries, 2, 276, 320, 418, 509, 530

Documentary, 42, 60, 78–79, 158, 191, 214, 222, 231, 265, 267–268, 283, 320, 325, 327, 339, 386, 389, 408–409, 411, 425, 505, 507–509, 514, 524, 530, 535

Documentary format, 535

Dolly, 7, 12, 36, 39, 80, 82–83, 87, 230, 288, 333, 361, 379, 442, 479

Drama, 2, 8, 13, 137, 288, 291, 319–320, 333–334, 369, 379, 386, 437–438, 443, 445, 505, 530

Dramatic format, 530, 535

Dramatic license, 508, 514

Drop shadow, 244, 310, 403

Dropout compensator, 280

Dropouts, 271, 279–280, 282, 400, 415

Dubbing rights, 510, 515

Dutch angle, 230, 333

DVE (digital video effects), 9, 232, 255

Dynamic range, 161, 167, 208

Earphone, 88, 167, 171, 179, 182, 186, 455, 491–492

EC (Electronic Cinematography), 77, 91, 182, 185, 203, 206, 529

Echo, 182, 185, 203, 206, 529

Editing, 6, 102, 119, 159, 166, 172, 186, 193–194, 202, 206–208, 212–214, 216, 232, 251–252, 254, 258, 263–264, 267, 270–271, 274–276, 279, 281, 314, 320, 326, 341–342, 346, 356, 362, 364–365, 368–371, 373, 376–377, 379, 382–389, 391–394, 398–400, 403–406, 408–425, 436–438, 444, 453, 474, 478, 508, 510, 524, 526, 531, 534
  assemble, 6, 156, 299, 329, 373, 392, 403, 406, 409–411, 413, 436
  continuity, 119, 157, 352–353, 368–369, 371, 378, 382–383, 392, 438–439, 443, 478
  control track, 274, 281, 364, 393–394, 409–411, 425
  EDL, 326, 404, 407–408, 414, 416, 422–425
  insert, 248–249, 305, 409–410, 414–416, 425
  master, 326, 394, 403, 408–411, 415–416, 418–419, 423, 425
  montage, 216, 329, 334, 376–377, 388
  off-line, 326, 404, 422–424
  on-line, 403–404, 414–415, 422–424, 492
  pace, 377, 388
  random access, 253, 270–271, 364, 391, 415, 421, 436
  recorder, 393, 408, 416, 425
  relational, 373, 392
  thematic, 376–377, 392

Editors, 5, 22, 211, 214, 266, 361, 364, 368–373, 376, 379, 385, 388, 401, 418, 420, 422–424, 430, 433, 437

EFP (electronic field production), 7, 12, 79, 116, 153, 167, 173, 276, 379, 429

Electronic palette, 314

Electronic pencil, 251, 313–316

Electronic test pattern (ETP), 107

Endoscopic television, 523

ENG (electronic newsgathering), 5, 7–8, 10–13, 42, 64, 68, 70, 74–75, 114, 134, 151, 153–154, 157–158, 167, 173–174, 184, 186–187, 222, 229–230, 249, 276, 278, 280, 285, 293, 319–321, 324, 328–329, 342, 356, 358–359, 361, 364, 369–370, 372–373, 379, 388–389, 411, 414–415, 419–420, 427–433, 435–436, 453–455, 467–468, 490, 498, 500–501, 505, 508, 512, 515, 524, 530

Engineer, 5, 8, 10–11, 13, 74–75, 114, 184, 186–187, 278, 280, 342, 364, 419, 454, 467–468, 490
Engineers, 10, 25, 72, 168, 250, 364, 383, 396, 404, 460, 467, 521
Engineering, 8, 75, 114, 342, 454, 467
EPROM, 275–276
Equestrian education, 522
Establishing shot, 189, 217, 284, 332, 369, 386
Ethical/ethics, 369–370, 430, 496, 507–508, 513–514
Executive producer, 1, 3, 361, 506
Exposure, 9, 32, 45, 54, 56, 58–60, 62, 64–65, 68, 120, 133, 140–141, 153–154, 218, 278, 306
External sync, 261
Eyeline, 382, 488

Fader, 189, 199–202, 204, 236–242, 247–248, 255
    bars, 236–242, 247–248, 255
    rotary, 199
    slide, 199
Fades, 9, 200, 238, 240, 247, 408
Fading, 181, 240
False light, 370, 496, 499, 505–506, 513
Fashion, 28, 82, 102, 104, 215, 219, 231, 327–328, 432, 488, 527
FAX sheet, 351, 451, 453–455
FCC, 181, 260, 427, 461, 465, 508
Feedback, 203, 326, 455, 492, 522, 529, 535
Fiber optics, 64, 452, 457–459
Fictionalization, 505
Film, 3, 10, 15–16, 18, 20–21, 30, 34, 40–41, 55, 64, 70, 77, 113–114, 126–127, 147–148, 157, 212, 214–218, 222–224, 232, 234, 244, 257, 261, 266, 276–279, 283, 306–308, 311–312, 319–320, 324–326, 332–334, 339, 350, 364–365, 368, 370–374, 376–377, 382, 384, 386, 390–391, 399, 415, 427–428, 436–439, 444–445, 455, 483, 509–511, 524, 526, 530
    chain, 10, 234
Filmmakers, 148
Filtered, 134, 206, 412
Filtering, 6, 186, 312
Filters, 53–56, 98, 100–101, 104, 112, 125, 151, 178, 218, 312
    colored, 53, 56
    dichroic, 100, 112
    diffusion, 54, 56
    fog, 47, 54, 56, 72–73, 330, 435
    neutral density, 53–54, 56, 218
    polarizing, 54–56, 104, 468
    soft contrast, 54
    star, 54, 56
    ultraviolet, 53, 125
Fishpole, 183–184
Flags, 128, 157, 218
Flash EPROMs, 275–276
Flashbacks, 328
Floor manager, 5
Florida, 429, 500, 534
Flyaway satellite uplinks, 466

FM, 27, 161, 180–181, 270
Foldback speaker, 203
Follow focus, 51
Following source, 147–149, 157
Fonts, 250, 304, 310
Football, 35, 245, 265, 525
Formats, 20, 90, 260, 263–269, 271, 277, 281, 317, 326, 334, 339, 399–400, 480, 530, 535
Framestore synchronizer, 248
France, 18
Fuse, 156, 158
FX, 334

Gain control, 64, 68, 165, 199, 202, 204, 430
Galella vs. Onassis, 499
Gamma correction, 67, 278
Gatekeepers, 455
Geometric distortion, 39, 58, 74
Germany, 124, 258
Gestures, 385, 480, 492, 495, 503, 514
Ghosting, 19
Gobo, 288, 290
Graphic equalizer, 163, 172, 382
Graphics, 9, 233–234, 247, 250, 253, 272, 284, 287, 301–305, 310, 313–316, 325, 341, 360, 362, 421, 431, 433
Griffolyn screen, 133
Guardband, 27

Hand signals, 474, 492
Hard copy, 88–89, 91, 395, 404, 408, 422, 476, 478–479, 495
Hard wired, 199
HARPICON, 62
HDTV, 19–21, 30, 34, 47–48, 51, 56, 62–63, 73, 77, 85, 91, 108, 114, 126, 264, 276–277, 320, 398
Headsets, 75, 77, 86, 315
Hollywood, 127, 278, 522
Hue, 15, 94, 96, 106–108, 243–244, 481, 488

IBM, 250–251, 313, 364
Iconoscope, 61
IFB, 455, 463, 492
Indiana, 504
Input selector switch, 200
Insert shot, 213, 230, 333, 371, 379, 389–392, 418, 425
Institutional video, 2, 12, 516–518, 520–521, 525, 527, 529–532, 535
Instructional video, 327, 518, 521, 535
Intelligibility, 10, 182, 189, 529
Intelsat satellite, 462
Interactive video, 518
Interview format, 530, 535
Intros, 411
Intrusion on seclusion, 496–498
Invasion of privacy, 496–497, 499–500, 502, 505, 513–514
Iraq, 534
IRE, 25, 68

Japan, 17, 20, 265
Jewelry, 115, 177, 490–491, 495
Journalism, 306, 429

Journalist, 427, 498
Judder, 18
Jump cut, 374, 377, 379, 381, 384–385, 392, 416–417, 442
JVC, 266

Kelvin scale, 94, 102, 112, 119
Key
    clip, 243
    luminance, 241, 243–244, 255
    matte, 243–244, 255
    source, 241, 243–244
Key words, 329, 431, 476
Kinescope, 18, 257, 276
Korea, 297
Kubrick, Stanley, 15
Kuwait, 534

Lap dissolve, 364, 423
Laptop computers, 425
Laser, 195, 271, 458, 527
Lashline, 293–294, 315
Lawsuit, 417, 435, 440, 506, 512, 514
Layering, 311–312, 421
LCD displays, 104, 112, 401
Lecture format, 530, 535
Legibility, 90, 243–244, 304–305, 479
Lens, 7, 16, 21, 32–34, 36–57, 59, 64, 70, 75–77, 86, 89–90, 95, 98, 100, 127–128, 137, 217, 219, 225–226, 289, 301, 479, 492, 497, 499
    aberration, 64, 491, 495
    anamorphic, 21
    angle of view, 34, 40–42, 55
    aperture, 43–45, 48, 64, 217–218
    auto-focus, 52
    back focus, 52, 56, 61
    bayonet mount, 43, 56
    depth of field, 32, 47–51, 53, 56, 217
    diascope, 108
    extender, 42, 45
    focal length, 32–34, 36, 39–42, 44–45, 47, 49–50, 55–56, 76–77, 217, 225, 301, 499
    focusing, 7, 12, 34, 48, 50, 52, 56, 73, 84, 118, 129, 195, 217–218, 284, 305
    hood, 52–53, 55–56
    iris, 32, 43–45, 47–50, 56, 64–65, 68, 70, 91, 133, 218
    macro, 50–51, 56, 314, 316
    prime, 33–34, 40–41, 43, 45, 50–51
    range extender, 42, 45
    shade, 52–53, 97, 105–106, 244, 246, 301, 485–486, 488–489
    speed, 45
    stabilizer, 42, 56, 79–80
    supplementary, 41–42, 45, 379, 389–390, 531
    zoom, 7, 12, 32–43, 45, 49–52, 55–56, 75–77, 84, 86–87, 90, 101, 108, 217, 225–226, 230, 246–247, 249, 280, 288, 305, 333–334, 353, 361, 379, 381, 412, 442, 479
Letterbox, 21, 30
Libel, 496, 503–505, 513–514

Light meter, 120–121, 140–141, 157
  reflected, 120
Lighting, 4–5, 53, 67, 94, 112–116, 119–121,
    125, 127, 129–132, 134, 136–141,
    143–149, 151, 154–158, 213, 218, 227,
    231, 246, 284, 289, 301, 320, 352, 376,
    437–438, 444, 449–450, 454, 524
  back light, 137–138, 143, 228, 246, 489
  backlight, 68, 133, 136–137, 140–141,
    145–147, 152, 155–157, 412, 439
  barn doors, 128, 141, 145, 151, 157, 218,
    287
  base light, 146–147
  board, 149, 151, 157
  bounced, 116, 135, 151–153, 157
  bulbs, 126
  catchlight, 50, 131, 134, 147, 154
  coherence, 113–114, 131, 140, 157
  color temperature, 93–94, 96, 112, 114,
    118–119, 122–126, 141, 154, 156–157,
    290, 376, 412
  cookie, 129, 290, 315
  cross back lights, 156
  ground row, 286
  dimmers, 122–123, 141, 149, 157, 290
  dimming, 124, 149
  existing, 90, 154, 158, 449, 454
  eye light, 154
  fill, 16, 39, 51, 62, 66, 74, 107, 124–125,
    130, 133–134, 136, 138–141, 143–147,
    149, 151, 153, 155–157, 241,
    243–244, 280, 282, 286–287, 291,
    294, 304, 310–311, 320, 362–363,
    389, 405, 412, 414, 454, 486, 488,
    518, 529
  flat, 113, 116, 140, 148
  flood, 121, 128, 146, 151, 157, 432
  fluorescent, 54, 94, 114, 125–126, 147,
    152, 154, 157
  Fresnel, 127–129, 136, 138, 146, 154, 157,
    290
  grid, 87, 143–144, 151, 155, 157, 183, 187,
    203, 294–296, 300
  high-key, 147
  HMI, 124, 134, 157, 454
  incandescent, 94–96, 101, 112, 118,
    122–127, 154, 157
  key light, 131–136, 139–141, 146–147, 151,
    156, 216, 479
  kicker, 149, 439
  low key, 147, 216, 376
  moonlight, 119, 127
  pattern projector, 129, 290
  quartz, 94, 104, 123–124, 126, 134
  ratio, 121, 139–140, 143, 146–147, 149,
    244
  safety chain, 143
  scoop, 129, 134, 138, 157, 441
  scrims, 121, 124, 129, 151, 157
  tent, 118, 226, 323, 398, 414
  tungsten-halogen, 123–124, 129, 151, 153
  umbrella reflector, 116, 151, 157
Line out monitor, 10, 13, 235–237
Linear editing, 364, 415, 421
Lip sync, 203, 382
Litigation, 512

LPTV, 28
Lux, 64, 80, 119–120, 223

Macros (computer), 314, 316
Magnetophon, 258
Makeup
  beards, 481, 486
  contouring, 486
  corrective, 481, 483, 488, 495, 506, 514
  cosmetics, 483
  eyebrows, 488
  eyelash, 488
  eyeliner, 488
  glycerine, 489
  lipstick, 488, 490
  mascara, 488
  powder, 364, 483, 485, 488–490
  rouge, 486, 488
  teeth, 488–489
  eyelids, 488
  wrinkles, 4, 490
Master black control, 70
Master control, 11, 13, 254–256
Master control switcher, 254–256
Matching transformer, 176
Matsushita, 269
Matte box, 55–56
Metal evaporated tape, 274
Miami, 475, 531
Microphone, 5, 8, 10, 12–13, 37, 114, 159,
    162, 166, 169–184, 194, 199, 203,
    207–208, 217, 352, 382, 438, 453, 455,
    497, 502, 528
  bidirectional, 189
  booms, 8, 141, 143,184
  condenser, 173–177, 180, 183–184, 187,
    208
  dynamic, 165, 173–175, 177–180, 183,
    214, 218, 225, 230
  electret, 175
  gated, 529
  lav, 177, 412
  line, 171, 184–185
  moving-coil, 5, 8, 10, 12–13, 37, 114, 159,
    162, 166
  omnidirectional, 118, 169–170, 175, 182,
    461, 529
  parabolic, 170–171
  personal, 8, 12, 177–180, 209, 454, 491,
    495
  polar pattern, 171, 175, 189
  quadraphonic, 177, 190–191
  RF, 180–182, 454
  ribbon, 173, 175, 177, 183, 208, 216, 391
  shock mount, 183
  shotgun, 171, 184, 208, 330, 360
  stereo, 187, 190, 413, 419
  transduction, 457
  velocity, 173
  wireless, 87–88, 177, 180–181, 208,
    454–455, 497
Microphonics, 58
Microprocessor, 65
Microwave, 276, 428, 436, 448, 450–452,
    454, 457, 459–461, 464
MIDI, 159, 204–206, 404, 421, 510, 515

Mid-side (M-S) micing, 188
Mini disk, 196
Misrepresentation, 502, 507, 512, 514
Mixer, 176, 189, 204, 409
Modulation, 27–28, 161, 180, 274, 458
Monitors, effects, 10, 13, 237, 242–243
Morale, 518
Multiplexed, 261–262
Music
  composers, 329, 509
  production libraries, 510
  synthesized, 185, 204, 510
Musicians, 203–205, 510
Muslin, 8, 13, 285, 291

Narrator, 3, 203, 305, 328–329, 376, 476,
    478–479
NBC network, 87, 270, 359
Negligence, 503
Networks, 7, 253, 358–359, 457, 459, 463,
    516, 524, 534–535
  affiliates, 359
Nevada, 432, 501
News, 2, 5, 7–8, 12, 42, 52–53, 60, 64,
    78–79, 87–88, 126, 145, 147, 153–154,
    158, 191, 222, 231, 247–250, 261, 265,
    267–268, 276, 278, 283, 287, 298,
    304–308, 310, 319–320, 325, 327–328,
    330–331, 339, 356–363, 369–371, 373,
    389–390, 398, 407–409, 411–416,
    418–420, 422, 425, 427–436, 460–461,
    463–466, 468, 475, 479–480, 491–492,
    497–498, 500–502, 506–509, 511–512,
    514–516, 518, 528, 530, 534–535
  anchoring, 155, 295, 467
  anchorperson, 361, 411, 492
  assignment editor, 358–359, 362, 430–431
  consortium, 359, 463
  cooperatives, 430, 463
  correspondent, 436
  hard, 327, 360, 415, 432
  human interest, 360, 431–432, 433
  newscasters, 360–361
  newsgathering, 320, 356, 427, 430, 466,
    501, 530
  packages, 151, 358–359, 419
  possible future impact, 432
  reporter, 3, 88, 174, 180, 358–361, 406,
    411, 419, 425, 428–433, 435–436,
    455, 491–492, 498–502, 504–505,
    507, 514
  shock value, 332, 432–433
  SNG, 464, 466–468
  soft, 43, 46, 54, 88–91, 116, 118, 128,
    133–135, 140–141, 151–153, 157, 160,
    162, 167, 178, 202–203, 247, 278,
    298, 327–328, 360, 415, 431–432,
    488, 491
  timeliness, 431–432, 468
  titillation component, 432–433
Newscasts, 3, 7, 356, 358–359, 362–363,
    389, 418, 430–431, 433, 475
Newspaper, 108, 284, 331, 349, 358–359,
    430, 500, 503, 505, 511, 525
Newsphoto, 305–306
Newsworthiness, 358–359, 431

Nichols, Mike, 15, 40
Noddies, 379, 413
NTSC, 17–21, 27, 30, 47–48, 62–63, 77, 85, 101–102, 109, 247, 250, 258, 302–304, 307, 332, 398–399, 425, 524, 526–527

Olympics, 273, 447, 522
Optical fiber, 457–459, 528
Orthicon, 61
Outside vendors, 521
Overscanning, 29, 303
Overstate, 525

Packing the tape, 282
Paint program, 251, 309
PAL, 17–21, 30, 48, 63, 106, 253, 302, 313–314, 486, 488, 527
Pan heads
  cam, 37, 84–85, 87
  fluid, 84, 384, 489
  friction, 84–85
  geared, 84–85, 281
Pan pot, 187, 189–190, 209
Panaglide, 79
Panasonic, 268
Parallel cutting, 369, 392
Parallel stories, 328, 369, 388
Patch cord, 149, 200
Patch panel, 149, 200, 254
PC (personal computer), 274, 534
PCM (pulse-code modulation), 274
Performing rights license, 509, 515
Periakta, 296–297
Period piece, 322, 449
Persian, 428, 466, 534
Persistence of vision, 16, 30, 527
Phase cancellation, 184
Phi phenomenon, 16, 30
Philippines, 508
Phone, cellular, 463
Phosphors, 100, 105
Photoconductor, 58
Photoemission, 57, 91
Photojournalists, 500–501, 514
Pillars, 296
Pilot signal, 467
Pitch, 23, 64, 118, 161–162, 206, 421
Pixel, 58, 104, 307, 313
PL (private line), 12, 75, 77, 353, 455
Plumbicon, 61
Plywood, 246, 298
Pop filter, 178–179
Postproduction, 364, 383, 395
POV, 333
Preproduction planning, 350
Preroll, 391
Preset monitor, 237
Preview bus, 237
Preview monitor, 10, 13, 237, 415
Prism block, 100
Privacy, 496–497, 499–500, 502, 505, 513–514
Privilege, 500, 504–505, 514
Producer, 1, 3–4, 6, 12, 20–21, 72, 112, 151, 165, 214, 262, 267–268, 278–279, 284,

301, 315, 319, 321–322, 324, 326, 341–342, 349, 351, 356, 358–362, 364, 370–371, 404, 415, 420, 428–429, 444–445, 468, 474–475, 480–481, 492, 494, 500, 504–506, 510–512, 514–515, 520, 525, 530
Production assistant, 3
Production outline, 322, 328
Production schedule, 323
Production switcher, 232, 234, 236, 247, 254–255
Professional video equipment, 279
Program bus, 234–237, 239, 255
Program proposal, 317, 322
Prominence, 359, 431–432, 502–503, 514
Promos, 465
Prompter, 7, 12, 88–91, 431, 476, 478–479, 491, 495
Prompting, 7, 12, 57, 88, 90–91
Pronunciation, 330, 475–476, 480
  Anglicizing, 475
Props, 5, 213, 246, 284, 287, 289, 300–301, 315–316, 341–342, 346, 352, 362
Proximity effect, 171–172, 178
PSA, 349
Public domain, 509
Public property, 498, 513
Pudovkin, 364, 373
Pylons, 296–297
Pyrotechnics, 450

Quadraphonic sound, 190
Quality control form, 362–363
Quantization, 24

Rack focus, 219, 231
Rails, 83
RAM, 253, 275–276, 364, 414, 416
Rating, ratings, 326, 360, 430, 432, 454
RCA, 259, 268–269
Reaction shot, 353, 379, 389, 391, 414, 442–443
Records, 16, 192, 194–195, 202, 250, 276, 382, 423, 522, 534
Reference black, 25, 66, 430
Reference white, 26
Reflector board, 134–135, 454
Registration, 58, 64, 108
Rehearsal, 3, 5, 146, 324, 326, 351, 455
  dress, 5, 96, 146, 177, 228, 324, 326, 374, 440, 442–443
  dry, 5
  hall, 5
Remote, 5, 7, 45, 77, 84, 86–87, 157, 284, 315, 439, 447–448, 453–456, 459, 462, 464, 466, 524
Rental, 265, 324, 346–347, 450, 521, 530
Resolution, 24, 47–48, 57, 62–63, 73, 77, 91, 108–109, 232, 267, 304, 306, 312, 332, 401, 531
  chart, 62
  horizontal, 62–63, 91, 267
  vertical, 62, 91
Reverberation, 171, 182, 186, 199, 382
Reverse-angle shot, 412
RF interference, 181

Riding gain, 167
Robotic camera, 7, 76, 86–88, 91
Room tone, 413–414, 417–418, 425
Rough cut, 404
Royalty, 326, 509, 511
Russian, 364, 373

Safe area, 29–30, 73, 302–303, 316
Safe title area, 29–30, 303
SAG (Screen Actors Guild), 531
Sampling, 23–24, 58, 205, 512
Satellite, 9–10, 13, 18, 28, 63, 159, 167, 234, 245, 254, 257, 304, 310, 325, 358–360, 362, 398, 436, 448, 450, 452, 454, 457, 459, 461–468, 518, 525, 528
  downlink, 463, 465
  geosynchronous, 462
  uplink, 276, 448, 463, 465–468
  transponder, 462–463, 468
  newsgathering, 466
Saticon, 61
Saturation, 107, 243
Sawtooth effect, 311
Scenery, 5, 246, 284, 300, 315
Scenic designer, 5, 284, 315
Scheduling, 258, 320, 339, 358, 428, 443, 468
Screenplay, 332
Scripting, 314, 320, 328, 339
Scripts
  fully scripted shows, 5, 326–327, 339
Scriptwriting, 317, 330, 332–333, 339
Search mode, 399
SECAM, 17–21, 30, 48, 63, 302, 527
Seclusion, 496–498
Second unit, 325–326
Segment rundown, 360
Semi-scripted show, 326
Set designer, 4, 112, 284, 295, 300, 315, 323–324
Set props, 284, 315
Setpieces, 316
Sets, 5–6, 8, 15, 28, 81, 83, 104–105, 109, 128, 182–183, 188, 194, 201, 213, 216, 242, 244, 246, 266–267, 284–285, 287–289, 291, 295–298, 300–301, 315–316, 324, 352, 418, 525, 534
  fantasy, 246, 285, 289, 300, 315, 371
  flats, 291–295, 297, 315
  hardwall, 291, 293–294, 297, 315
  limbo, 285, 287, 289–290, 315
  neutral, 285
  realistic, 288
  replica, 87, 250, 288–289, 293, 300, 394, 529
  striking, 6, 40, 140, 211, 352
  symbolic, 216, 285, 288, 315, 388
  threefold, 294
  twofold, 294
Settings, 8, 13, 32, 34, 39, 44–45, 50–52, 54, 56, 58, 64–65, 70, 74–76, 79, 87, 90, 107, 127, 134, 144, 147, 151, 154–157, 215–216, 237, 245–247, 249, 264, 266, 278, 280, 288–290, 293–294, 296, 315, 320, 324, 339, 352, 372, 374, 391, 400, 416, 450, 460, 467–468, 483, 518, 525, 527

Setups, 113, 144, 203, 438–439, 444, 447
Sex, 215, 223, 319–321, 328, 432, 443, 479
Sexism, 479
SFX, 334
Shadow mask, 102
Shadows, 113–116, 124, 131–134, 141, 147, 151, 153–155, 157, 183, 244, 246, 286–288, 290, 310, 315, 403, 449, 454
Shooting ratio, 370
Sideband, 27
Signal-to-noise ratio, 270
Silhouette, 66, 137, 286, 290, 374, 500
Simultaneous contrast, 96–97, 112, 488
Single system, 191
Skew control, 280
Skylight, 94, 119, 497
Slander, 496, 503–505, 513–514
Slides, 10, 66, 129, 303, 305–306, 308, 312, 316
SMPTE, 186, 198, 206, 281, 394, 396–399, 410, 414–415, 453
Snap zoom, 38, 381
SNV, 466–467
Solarized, 512
Sound recording
 double system, 191, 395
 single system, 191
Special effects, 6, 9, 22–23, 53, 55, 75, 263, 270, 274–275, 279, 326, 334, 364, 409, 424–425, 444, 522, 534
Spectral highlights, 62, 68
Sports, 5, 8, 145, 171, 179, 190, 287, 298, 360, 429, 455, 534
Spotlight effect, 249
Standards converter, 18–19
Status indicators, 73, 91, 281
Steadicam, 79
Stereo separation, 187
Stock footage, 325, 341, 383, 534
Studio floor plan, 300–301
Subcarrier, 27
Subjective shot, 333
Subpoena, 506
Sunlight, 43, 49, 53, 66, 94–97, 102, 115, 118–120, 124, 126–127, 133–134, 447
Switcher, 22, 232–234, 238–241, 243, 247–249, 254–256, 303
 colorizing control, 243
 clipper gain knob, 243
 downstream, 242–243
 master control, 254–256
 production, 232, 234, 236, 247, 254–255
 routing, 254–256
Sync, 26–27, 261, 395, 400, 410
Sync generator, 27, 261, 410
Synchronization license, 509, 515
Syndication, 511
Synthesized stereo, 185
Synthesizer, 159, 169, 204, 510

Talent, 3–5, 8, 12–13, 51, 87–90, 124, 131–132, 141, 144–147, 171, 177,

181–183, 208, 214, 247, 277, 284, 287, 298, 305, 324, 333, 342, 350–351, 362, 379, 438, 443–444, 447, 449, 474, 478–479, 492, 495–496, 511–513, 515, 521
Talent release, 351, 496, 512–513, 515
Tapeless workstation, 207
Target audience, 5, 223, 231, 317, 321, 525
Technical continuity problem, 119, 157, 382
Technical director, 4, 8–10
Teleconferencing, 520
Telstar Satellite, 462
Tempo mapping, 206
Test pattern, 62, 74, 107–108, 415
Texture, 115, 131, 139–140, 153, 162, 216, 292–293, 524
Time code, 186, 197–198, 206–207, 261, 267, 281, 329, 383, 394–401, 403–405, 407–411, 414–416, 420, 422–423, 425, 453
 burned-in, 403
 drop frame, 397–398, 425
 generator, 399, 453
 keyed-in, 401, 403
 logging, 399, 403, 405–406, 414, 422
 longitudinal, 270, 274, 399–400, 425
Time-base corrector, 260, 281, 427
Titles, 21, 29, 170, 198, 233–234, 238, 251–252, 255, 305, 310, 320, 333, 364, 421, 424
Tonal compression, 66–67, 490, 495
Tort, 497
Trace capability, 422–423
Trade libel, 504
Transmitter, 1, 11, 13, 28, 30, 87, 180–181, 254, 256, 460–461, 464
Trim control, 416
Tripod, 42, 51, 79–81, 85, 91, 184, 325, 447, 453
Tungsten, 123–125, 129, 151, 153
TV black, 26, 66, 70, 72–73, 91
TV receiver, 17, 28, 30, 102, 112, 163, 491
TV white, 26, 66, 68, 70, 72, 91, 244

UHF, 11, 28, 181
Unbalanced line, 176–177
Underexposure, 68, 120, 133
Unethical, 497
Universities, 359, 530
User bits, 397, 400

VTR/VCR, 204, 207, 258–260, 261, 264, 269–270, 274, 279–280, 282–283, 310, 325, 333, 342, 364, 400
 Beta, 265–270, 399
 Betacam, 268–270, 399
 Betamax, 265, 268
 color under, 262–263, 265
 confidence heads, 274, 279
 erase head, 194, 274
 head clog, 207–208, 279, 453
 helical, 259, 265, 274, 282, 364, 391

playback head, 194, 207–208, 283
 quad, 59, 177, 190–191, 259–260, 263, 265, 282, 364, 391, 427
 tracking, 249, 281, 462
 type-C, 261
Vectorscope, 93, 107–108
Vertical fader, 199
VHS, 250, 263, 265–268, 404, 480, 531
Video
 effects, 9, 30, 232–233, 250–252, 254–255, 271–272, 276, 364, 393, 404, 409, 421
 engineer, 5, 8, 13, 278
 fields, 66, 80, 124, 184, 259, 269–270, 274, 276, 280, 400, 459
 levels, 8, 13, 24, 57, 64–65, 68, 70–71, 77, 238, 280, 383, 416
 monitor, 9–10, 13, 28, 63, 74, 84, 163, 184, 245, 257, 281, 290, 419, 430
 switcher, 4, 9, 232, 234, 247, 250–251, 254–255, 261, 409
Videoconferencing, 520, 527–529, 535
Videographer, 36, 39, 41, 51–52, 54, 68, 116, 126, 156, 211, 217–218, 223–224, 228, 268, 358, 379, 381, 433, 499, 507, 512, 515, 536
Vidicon, 61
Voice recognition module, 315
Volatile memory, 275–276, 314, 394
Voltage, 23, 104, 122–124, 156, 175, 199, 260, 275
VU meter, 10, 13, 24, 160–162, 164, 167–169, 201, 204, 208, 382

Wardrobe, 5, 96, 112, 216, 244, 289, 315, 342, 346, 352, 360, 362, 474, 480, 488, 490–491, 495
Wardrobe person, 5, 112
Watt, 11, 28, 94, 123, 128–129, 151, 156, 158, 290, 448, 450
Waveform monitor, 16, 24–27, 30, 45, 54, 66, 68, 70–72, 91, 106, 114, 430, 524
Weather, 8–9, 145, 175, 245, 287, 310, 360, 444, 447, 454, 458, 525
Wedge mount, 81
Westar satellite, 462
White balancing, 101–102
Window burn, 401, 404
Workstations, 159, 198, 206–207, 254, 384, 510
Writer, 3, 5, 12, 206, 212, 214–215, 223, 317, 319, 321–322, 324, 329–330, 333–335, 342, 360–362, 376, 391, 444, 476, 506

XLR connector, 177
X-Y micing, 187

Zebra stripes, 68
Zoom ratio, 34–35, 41
Zworykin, 61